W9-BAH-149

Fodor's

NORTHERN CALIFORNIA

2nd Edition

Where to Stay and Eat for All Budgets

Must-See Sights and Local Secrets

Ratings You Can Trust

Excerpted from *Fodor's California*
Fodor's Travel Publications   New York, Toronto, London, Sydney, Auckland
www.fodors.com

FODOR'S NORTHERN CALIFORNIA

Editor: William Travis

Editorial Production: Bethany Cassin Beckerlegge

Editorial Contributors: Cheryl Crabtree, Lisa M. Hamilton, Satu Hummasti, Constance Jones, Andy Moore, Reed Parsell, Sharon Silva, John A. Vlahides, Christine Vovakes, Sharron Wood

Maps: David Lindroth, *cartographer*; Rebecca Baer and Bob Blake, *map editors*

Design: Fabrizio La Rocca, *creative director*; Guido Caroti, *art director*; Moon Sun Kim, *cover designer*; Melanie Marin, *senior picture editor*

Production/Manufacturing: Colleen Ziemba

Cover Photo: Thinkstock/Creatas

ISBN: 1–4000–1602–9

ISBN-13: 978–1–4000–1602–0

ISSN: 1543–1045

SPECIAL SALES

This book is available for special discounts for bulk purchases for sales promotions or premiums. Special editions, including personalized covers, excerpts of existing books, and corporate imprints, can be created in large quantities for special needs. For more information, write to Special Markets/Premium Sales, 1745 Broadway, MD 6-2, New York, New York 10019, or e-mail specialmarkets@randomhouse.com.

AN IMPORTANT TIP & AN INVITATION

Although all prices, opening times, and other details in this book are based on information supplied to us at time of writing, changes occur all the time in the travel world, and Fodor's cannot accept responsibility for facts that become outdated or for inadvertent errors or omissions. So **always confirm information when it matters,** especially if you're making a detour to visit a specific place. Your experiences—positive and negative—matter to us. If we have missed or misstated something, **please write to us.** We follow up on all suggestions. Contact the Northern California editor at editors@fodors.com or c/o Fodor's at 1745 Broadway, New York, NY 10019.

PRINTED IN THE UNITED STATES OF AMERICA

10 9 8 7 6 5 4 3 2 1

Be a Fodor's Correspondent

Your opinion matters. It matters to us. It matters to your fellow Fodor's travelers, too. And we'd like to hear it. In fact, we *need* to hear it.

When you share your experiences and opinions, you become an active member of the Fodor's community. That means we'll not only use your feedback to make our books better, but we'll publish your names and comments whenever possible. Throughout our guides, look for "Word of Mouth," excerpts of your unvarnished feedback.

Here's how you can help improve Fodor's for all of us.

Tell us when we're right. We rely on local writers to give you an insider's perspective. But our writers and staff editors—who are the best in the business—depend on you. Your positive feedback is a vote to renew our recommendations for the next edition.

Tell us when we're wrong. We're proud that we update most of our guides every year. But we're not perfect. Things change. Hotels cut services. Museums change hours. Charming cafés lose charm. If our writer didn't quite capture the essence of a place, tell us how you'd do it differently. If any of our descriptions are inaccurate or inadequate, we'll incorporate your changes in the next edition and correct factual errors at fodors.com *immediately.*

Tell us what to include. You probably have had fantastic travel experiences that aren't yet in Fodor's. Why not share them with a community of like-minded travelers? Maybe you chanced upon a beach or bistro or B&B that you don't want to keep to yourself. Tell us why we should include it. And share your discoveries and experiences with everyone directly at fodors.com. Your input may lead us to add a new listing or highlight a place we cover with a "Highly Recommended" star or with our highest rating, "Fodor's Choice."

Give us your opinion instantly at our feedback center at www.fodors.com/feedback. You may also e-mail editors@fodors.com with the subject line "Northern California Editor." Or send your nominations, comments, and complaints by mail to Northern California Editor, Fodor's, 1745 Broadway, New York, NY 10019.

You and travelers like you are the heart of the Fodor's community. Make our community richer by sharing your experiences. Be a Fodor's correspondent.

Happy traveling!

Tim Jarrell, Publisher

CONTENTS

CLOSEUPS

MAPS

ABOUT THIS BOOK

Our Ratings

Sometimes you find terrific travel experiences, and sometimes they just find you. But usually the burden is on you to select the right combination of experiences. That's where our ratings come in.

As travelers we've all discovered a place so wonderful that its worthiness is obvious. And sometimes that place is so unique that superlatives don't do it justice: you just have to be there to know. These sights, properties, and experiences get our highest rating, Fodor's Choice, indicated by orange stars throughout this book.

Black stars highlight sights and properties we deem **Highly Recommended**, places that our writers, editors, and readers praise again and again for consistency and excellence.

By default, there's another category: any place we include in this book is by definition worth your time, unless we say otherwise. And we will.

Disagree with any of our choices? Care to nominate a place or suggest that we rate one more highly? Visit our feedback center at www. fodors.com/feedback.

Budget Well

Hotel and restaurant price categories from ¢ to $$$$

are defined in the opening pages of each chapter. For attractions, we always give standard adult admission fees; reductions are usually available for children, students, and senior citizens. Want to pay with plastic? **AE, D, DC, MC, V** following restaurant and hotel listings indicate whether American Express, Discover, Diners Club, MasterCard, and Visa are accepted.

Restaurants

Unless we state otherwise, restaurants are open for lunch and dinner daily. We mention dress only when there's a specific requirement and reservations only when they're essential or not accepted—it's always best to book ahead.

Hotels

Hotels have private bath, phone, TV, and air-conditioning and operate on the European Plan (aka EP, meaning without meals), unless we specify that they use the Continental Plan (CP, with a Continental breakfast), Breakfast Plan (BP, with a full breakfast), or Modified American Plan (MAP, with breakfast and dinner) or are all-inclusive (including all meals and most activities). We always list facilities but not whether you'll be charged an extra

fee to use them, so when pricing accommodations, find out what's included.

Many Listings
★ Fodor's Choice
★ Highly recommended
⊠ Physical address
✛ Directions
🕮 Mailing address
☎ Telephone
🖷 Fax
⊕ On the Web
🖉 E-mail
🖄 Admission fee
🕓 Open/closed times
► Start of walk/itinerary
Ⓜ Metro stations
🚌 Credit cards

Hotels & Restaurants
🏨 Hotel
🛏 Number of rooms
🛆 Facilities
🍴 Meal plans
✕ Restaurant
🖎 Reservations
🏛 Dress code
🚬 Smoking
🍷 BYOB
✕🏨 Hotel with restaurant that warrants a visit

Outdoors
⛳ Golf
🏕 Camping

Other
🕓 Family-friendly
🎯 Contact information
⇨ See also
🖂 Branch address
☞ Take note

WHAT'S WHERE

SAN FRANCISCO 	It's possible that no city in America outnumbers San Francisco in recognizable landmarks: the Golden Gate Bridge, Fisherman's Wharf, cable cars, Alcatraz, Chinatown—the list goes on and on. But if you look beyond all that, you'll see something even better: the real San Francisco. Dump the car, hop on the great public transport, and use your feet to get out into the diverse neighborhoods, from exclusive Pacific Heights to the Hispanic Mission to the gay Castro. That's where the city's personality—an amalgam of gold-rush history, immigrant traditions, counterculture proclivities, and millennial materialism—looms large in a population only around the size of Indianapolis. This character also manifests itself in spirited dining, arts, and shopping scenes packed into San Francisco's small and very manageable footprint. Remember to carry a thick wallet and dress in layers for the weird and changeable weather.
THE WINE COUNTRY 	No longer the state's only wine-producing region, Napa and Sonoma counties nonetheless retain their title as *the* California wine country famed around the country and the world. Along Highway 29 in the Napa Valley and Highway 12 in the Sonoma Valley the wineries stand cheek by jowl, as do the cars and buses in high season. Come when the crowds have thinned, though, and avoid the dumbed-down category of tasting rooms with tiny plastic cups, and you will find your reward. An orgy of impossible-to-find-elsewhere bottles awaits you, as well as restaurants that stand among Northern California's best, indulgent spas, and extravagant inns and hotels. Throw in the velvety green hills and the gentle climate, and you can almost forgive the steep tasting fees.
THE NORTH COAST 	The 400 northernmost miles of California's coastline unfurl gradually as you drive winding, two-lane Highway 1 from the Golden Gate Bridge to the Oregon state line. Indeed, slowly is the best way to experience natural knockouts such as Point Reyes National Seashore, Salt Point State Park, and Redwood National and State Parks. Even when rain or fog turns the land lonesome, nature's beauty is the main attraction, with shopping and nightlife a novelty and inspired cuisine a rarity. A few pockets of civilization—sophisticated southern Marin, unassuming Gualala, Yankee-ish Mendocino, gingerbready Eureka—serve as oases, as do several noteworthy lodgings in isolated spots. But if your heart doesn't race at

WHAT'S WHERE

the sight of whales migrating past craggy bluffs or of mist filtering through the boughs of colossal redwoods, you'll miss the point of the North Coast.

THE PENINSULA & SOUTH BAY 	South of San Francisco, Silicon Valley occupies the eastern shore of the peninsula that sequesters the bay from the Pacific Ocean. In this prosperous land of corporate parks, technology eclipses tourism, though the twain do meet in places such as Stanford University and San Jose's Tech Museum of Innovation. The bump and hustle of dot-com business, which can make for heavy traffic along the many freeways, imparts an energetic buzz to the restaurants and bars of downtown Palo Alto and San Jose. A world away across a mountain range, nature still reigns on the often foggy coastal peninsula. Highway 1 threads up rugged shoreline past the elephant seal rookery at Año Nuevo State Reserve and beach getaways such as Half Moon Bay.
MONTEREY BAY 	Monterey well deserves its popularity as a vacation destination. The city has carefully preserved history, an outstanding aquarium, souvenir and gift shops galore, and a setting on a broad bay. Herds of tour buses stampede daily in season, but to the south, on either end of 17-Mile Drive, Victorian-flavored Pacific Grove and the exclusive mission town of Carmel are generally quieter. On the northern edge of the bay Santa Cruz feels less ready for prime time, with its old-school beach boardwalk and its downtown cafés geared to self-consciously alternative college students. All around Monterey Bay you can spend a lot to dine very well or badly, and you'll probably pay dearly for your room.
THE CENTRAL VALLEY 	On the arid plain between the Sierra Nevada and the Coast Ranges, the incredibly fertile land works. Mile after mile of irrigated fields, vineyards, and pastureland produce fruits, vegetables, and livestock. Farm equipment often lifts a haze of soil and agricultural chemicals into the brutal summer heat; dense tule fog shuts out the sun for much of the winter. Built for function rather than form, the valley's towns and cities are less destinations than stopovers off I–5, the fastest route between Los Angeles and the San Francisco Bay Area. Fresno serves as the major gateway to the Southern Sierra, and about 40 wineries operate around Lodi.

YOSEMITE & SIERRA 	People from around the world travel to Northern California to see Yosemite National Park's towering granite monoliths, verdant glacial valleys, and lofty waterfalls. The park's natural attributes do live up to the hype, but if you come May through September, you're likely to see more visitors than vistas. The same holds true for neighboring Sequoia and Kings Canyon national parks, which share Yosemite's jaw-dropping Sierra Nevada backdrop, thick with giant sequoias. If you can take the road less traveled by the motor coaches, miles of hiking trails await in all three parks. In winter the Sierra's magically powdery snow drifts high, bestowing the state's best skiing on the resorts around Mammoth Lakes.
THE GOLD COUNTRY 	Like some mammoth historical theme park that's been dynamited and blown across several counties, the Gold Country freezes time, circa 1848–98, on the western face of the Sierra Nevada. The delirious 1849 gold rush that built San Francisco and Sacramento started here, and the former mining camps strung out along 185 mi of Highway 49 replay their past to the hilt. In family-oriented towns such as Sutter Creek and Nevada City small museums, galleries, and cafés occupy Victorian buildings on Old West main streets; most of Coloma falls within Marshall Gold Discovery State Historic Park. It seems appropriate that gold-rush history saturates Sacramento, the state capital, otherwise an unremarkable place. You'll catch unmistakable whiffs of cheesiness along the Gold Country trail, as well another, much lovelier, scent: the Sierra Foothills wine country is booming, especially in the Shenandoah Valley north of Amador City.
LAKE TAHOE 	When you first visit Lake Tahoe, especially if you arrive on a sunny day, you will be awed by the sight of miles of crystalline, intensely blue water against the peaks of the High Sierra. A perfect setting for outdoor activities from hiking to golf in summer and from skiing to snowmobiling in winter, the lake also has another side—the Nevada side. Casinos in all their tacky splendor butt up to the state line bordering South Lake Tahoe at one end of the lake and delimiting Nevada's Incline Village at the other. Whether for the sightseeing, the exercise, the gambling, or all three, the throngs overrun Tahoe in summer.

WHAT'S
WHERE

THE FAR NORTH	
	California's far northeast corner has a backwoods character that appeals to hard-core outdoorsy types. Hiking in thermally active Lassen Volcanic National Park, mountaineering on Mt. Shasta, and rock climbing in Castle Crags State Park number among the ways you can enjoy the cool air and the alpine scenery. All summer, anglers fish the Far North's trout-rich lakes and streams while houseboats and Jet Skis buzz around Lake Shasta. Many of the humble—and humbly priced—visitor services shut down in winter, though not those near Mt. Shasta's ski resort.

WHEN TO GO

°F SAN FRANCISCO °C

The climate varies amazingly in Northern California, sometimes within an hour's drive. A foggy, cool August day in San Francisco makes you grateful for a sweater, but head north 50 mi to the Napa Valley, and you'll probably need no more than short sleeves. Similarly, nighttime temperatures may differ greatly from daytime temperatures.

Because the weather is so varied throughout the state, it's hard to generalize much about it. Rain comes in the winter, with snow at elevations above 3,000 feet. Summers are dry everywhere, except for the rare summer thunderstorm in the mountains. As a rule, compared with the coastal areas, which are cool year-round, inland regions are hot in summer and cool in winter. As you climb into the mountains, the climate changes more distinctly with the seasons: winter brings snow, autumn is crisp, spring can go either way, and summer is sunny and warm, with only an occasional thundershower.

🔢 Forecasts **National Weather Service** ⊕ www.wrh.noaa.gov. **Weather Channel** ⊕ www.weather.com.

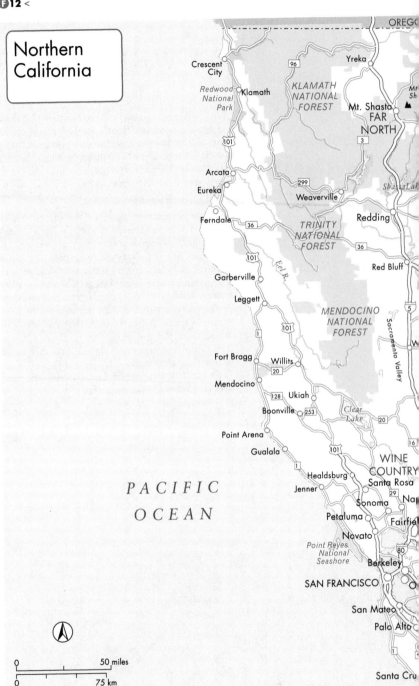

Northern California

OREGO

Crescent City
Redwood National Park
Klamath
KLAMATH NATIONAL FOREST
Yreka
Mt. Shasta
Mt Sh
FAR NORTH
96
101
3

Arcata
Eureka
299
Weaverville
ShastaLak
Ferndale
36
TRINITY NATIONAL FOREST
Redding
Red Bluff
101
36
36
5
Garberville
Eel R.
Leggett
MENDOCINO NATIONAL FOREST
Sacramento Valley
101
1
Fort Bragg
Willits
W
20
Mendocino
128
Ukiah
Boonville
253
Clear Lake
20
Point Arena
16
Gualala
101
WINE COUNTRY
Healdsburg
Santa Rosa
Jenner
29
Na
Sonoma
Petaluma
Fairfie
Novato
Point Reyes National Seashore
Berkeley
80
SAN FRANCISCO
San Mateo
Palo Alto
1
Santa Cru

PACIFIC OCEAN

0   50 miles
0   75 km

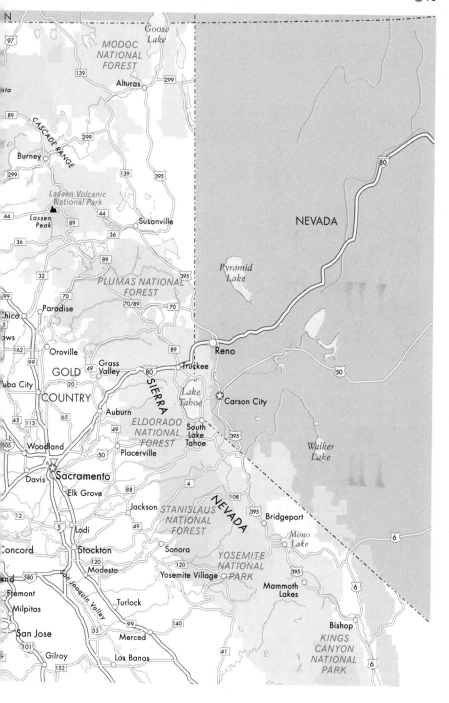

QUINTESSENTIAL NORTHERN CALIFORNIA

The Wine

If California were a country, it would rank as the world's fourth-largest wine producer, after Italy, France, and Spain. In those countries, wine represents delicious nourishment to be shared with friends and family, a national art form of infinite variety, a source of prosperity. A modern, Americanized version of that mentality integrates wine into daily life in Northern California, and a visit to Wine Country can give you a glimpse of this world. Beyond the Napa and Sonoma valleys, Mendocino County and the Sierra Foothills are respected appellations where numerous wineries offer tours and tastings. Simply driving through mile after mile of vineyard-blanketed countryside lets you catch the Wine Country mood. Better restaurants and wineshops anywhere in the region will do the same if you take the time to ask their friendly experts which Northern California bottles you might like.

The Outdoors

One of the great attractions of living in Northern California—the wondrous natural beauty of most of the region—inspires the people here to spend as much time outdoors as they can. They have tremendous enthusiasm for every conceivable outdoor sport and wilderness activity, and nearly everyone owns at least one pair of hiking boots. You can join Northern Californians in their native habitat any time of year: Ski the deep powder of the Sierra Nevada and the Cascade Range; bicycle on back roads and mountain trails; surf the breaks north and south of San Francisco; paddle pristine rivers, lakes, and coastal coves. Everywhere, hiking trails crisscross public lands. You don't have to backpack the Pacific Coast Trail—a quiet walk along a rocky beach or through a redwood grove will fill you with the spirit of Northern California.

Northern Californians live so large that they seem sometimes to forget about the rest of the country. They have a distinctive culture all their own, which you can delve into by doing as the natives do.

The Automobile

If America has a love affair with the car, Northern California (with the possible exception of San Francisco) has an out-and-out obsession. Even when gasoline prices go through the roof and freeway traffic slows to a crawl, this passion burns as hot as ever. Drive through the heart of Yosemite and over California's highest automobile pass on Tioga Road/Big Oak Flat Road; follow 17-Mile Drive along the precipitous edge of the Monterey Peninsula; circle the largest alpine lake in America on the ring road around Lake Tahoe. Gorgeous for almost every mile, the Pacific Coast Highway runs from Monterey Bay over the Golden Gate Bridge and up the North Coast to Leggett. Wherever you go on the road, you'll see Northern California the way many locals prefer: from inside a car.

The Alternative

Ever since the 1950s, when Jack Kerouac and other luminaries of the Beat Generation made San Francisco their headquarters, alternative ways of thinking and living have flourished in Northern California. The hippies of Haight-Ashbury and the student activists of Berkeley, among others, brought progressive attitudes into the mainstream in Northern California as they became the region's leaders. New Age spiritualism, liberal politics, non-Western healing practices, and environmentalism flower here as nowhere else in America. You'll find organic produce and vegetarian dishes on the menu at restaurants and mom-and-pop cafés alike. Independent bookstores still sell the works of the Beats, plus all manner of broad-minded literature. Stroll the rainbow-flagged streets of the Castro, or take a side-trip to xenophobic Bolinas in Marin County, and you'll feel the alternative vibe. Don't forget to recycle your road maps.

IF YOU LIKE

Food

Little wonder that some of the world's best chefs prefer to work in Northern California, which grows more, and more varieties of, fruits and vegetables than any other state. The organic foods movement got its start here, sparking an appreciation for seasonal ingredients.

Many of Northern California's chefs take inspiration from the region's dynamic immigrant communities, bringing flavors and techniques from China, the Philippines, Korea, Vietnam, India, Mexico, and elsewhere into their kitchens. You'll find the finest restaurants and the greatest abundance of high-quality dining in and around San Francisco and in the Napa and Sonoma Wine Country. A meal at one of these culinary shrines can be the high point of your trip to Northern California.

- **Cafe Beaujolais,** Mendocino. In a Victorian cottage surrounded by gardens, the exquisite Cal-French menu highlights the freshest organic and local ingredients.

- **Erna's Elderberry House,** Oakhurst. The cute name belies the formal elegance of this Yosemite-area favorite, where the staff serves the six-course dinner with perfect choreography.

- **Jardinière,** San Francisco. The superb contemporary cooking of chef-owner Traci Des Jardins packs Opera House patrons into one of the city's sexiest restaurants.

- **Mustard's Grill,** Yountville. Not an ounce of pretension weighs down the solid service or hearty, updated American fare here.

Nature

Fog-shrouded redwood groves and sun-baked golden hills, sheltered coastal coves and snowy mountain ranges: Northern California's geographical diversity is staggering. You can easily get up close and personal with this amazingly varied landscape and explore tide pools, chaparral, lava beds, forests, and just about any other kind of ecological zone. Even if your idea of an ideal nature experience is sitting on a rock outdoors, you don't have to miss out: from almost any beach or bluff you can glimpse migrating whales in season.

Northern California has five national parks, four national monuments, two national recreation areas, and one national seashore. The state park system extends your reach to wildlife reserves, long stretches of coastline, and other environmentally sensitive habitats. An exceptional encounter with nature awaits you at each of these locations.

- **Emerald Bay State Park,** Lake Tahoe. Massive glaciers carved this fjordlike bay millions of years ago.

- **Monterey Bay Aquarium,** Monterey. Commune with creatures native to California's shores: sardines in a circular tank swim around your head; otters backstroke at eye level.

- **Point Reyes National Seashore,** Marin County. Elephant seals, tule elk, and 225 bird species thrive along this ragged stretch of shoreline.

- **Yosemite Falls,** Yosemite National Park. The highest waterfall in North America will leave you awestruck.

History

In 1770 Franciscan Father Junipero Serra established a mission at Monterey, moving it to Carmel a year later. Monterey became the capitol of Spain's California colony in 1776, the year Captain Juan Bautista de Anza brought in Northern California's first European settlers. From its origins as a Mexican outpost, the region grew into a kind of perpetual promised land that has represented many things to many people.

Northern California has given American history some of its most recognizable characters: indigenous peoples victimized by Euro-American hubris, forty-niners who rushed here in search of gold, Chinese workers who helped build the West's railroads, Haight-Ashbury hippies, Silicon Valley dotcommers. Their human drama echoes at museums and historic sites throughout the region.

- **Bodie Ghost Town,** Bodie State Historic Park. Preserved in a state of "arrested decay," this remote place in the eastern Sierra was once a wild mining town.

- **California State Railroad Museum,** Sacramento. Trains opened the American West, and they get their due at this display of 21 antique locomotives and railroad cars.

- **Columbia State Historic Park,** Columbia. Pan for gold in a restored gold-rush town where history lives in shops, forges, and newspaper offices.

- **Palace of Fine Arts,** San Francisco. This rococo palace, a San Francisco landmark, was built for the 1915 Panama-Pacific International Exposition.

Distinctive Lodgings

Hoteliers throughout Northern California have done their utmost to create accommodations that match the glories of the region's landscape. Whether in downtown San Francisco or the High Sierra, in Napa–Sonoma Wine Country or on the jagged coast, exceptional lodgings abound.

Treat yourself to a night, or several, in some of Northern California's distinctive inns and hotels and you will experience rooms of character and comfort. Often, the throughly up-to-date amenities come in a rustic or historical package: a triple-sheeted bed in a woodland cabin, plasma TVs in a former rail baron's castle. Always, guest service shines. For some first-rate pampering, it's worth splurging at these properties.

- **Carneros Inn,** Napa. The spa and the infinity pool overlook vineyards, and private gardens, heated bathroom floors, and outdoor showers make each tin-roofed cottage a sanctuary.

- **Hotel Rex** San Francisco. Richly retro colors and textures in the guest rooms and literary soirées in the book-lined lobby evoke the spirit of salon society in the 1920s.

- **MacCallum House,** Mendocino. Rose bushes surround a Victorian mansion and cottages in the heart of the blufftop village, and the lush rooms brim with modern extras.

- **Stonepine Estate Resort,** Carmel Valley. Hike, bike, or ride horseback on the château's 330-acre grounds before retiring to your suite or cottage for a massage or afternoon tea.

GREAT ITINERARY

SIERRA RICHES
YOSEMITE, GOLD COUNTRY, AND TAHOE

Day 1: Arrival/San Francisco

Straight from the airport, drop your bags at the lighthearted Hotel Monaco near Union Square and request a goldfish for your room. Chinatown, chock-full of dim sum shops, storefront temples, and open-air markets, promises unfamiliar tastes for lunch. Catch a Powell Street cable car to the end of the line and get off to see the bay views and the antique arcade games at Musée Mécanique, the hidden gem of otherwise mindless Fisherman's Wharf. No need to go any farther than cosmopolitan North Beach for cocktail hour, dinner, and live music.

Day 2: San Francisco

A Union Square stroll packs a wallop of people-watching, window-shopping, and architecture-viewing. In Golden Gate Park, linger amid the flora of the conservatory and the arboretum, soak up some art at the de Young Museum, and find serene refreshment in the Japanese Tea Garden. The Pacific surf pounds the cliffs below the Legion of Honor art museum, which has an exquisite view of the Golden Gate Bridge—when the fog stays away. Sunset cocktails at circa-1909 Cliff House include a prospect over Seal Rock (actually occupied by sea lions). Eat dinner elsewhere: Pacific Heights, the Mission, and SoMa teem with excellent restaurants.

Day 3: Into the High Sierra

First thing in the morning, pick up your rental car and head for the hills. A five-hour drive due east brings you to Yosemite National Park, where Bridalveil Fall and El Capitan, the 350-story granite monolith, greet you on your way to Yosemite Village. Ditch the car and pick up information and refreshment before hopping on the year-round shuttle to explore. Justly famous sights cram Yosemite Valley: massive Half Dome and Sentinel dome, thundering Yosemite Falls, and wispy Ribbon Fall and Nevada Fall. Invigorating short hikes off the shuttle route lead to numerous vantage points. Celebrate your arrival in one of the world's most sublime spots with dinner in the dramatic Ahwahnee Hotel Dining Room.

Day 4: Yosemite National Park

Ardent hikers consider John Muir Trail a must-do, tackling the rigorous 12-hour round-trip to the top of Half Dome in search of life-changing vistas. The merely mortal hike downhill from Glacier Point on Four-Mile Trail or Panorama Trail, the latter an all-day trek past waterfalls. Less demanding still is a drive to Wawona for a stroll in the Mariposa Grove of Big Trees and lunch at the 19th-century Wawona Hotel. In foul weather, take shelter in the Ansel Adams Gallery and Yosemite Museum; in fair, drive up to Glacier Point for a breathtaking sunset view.

Day 5: Gold Country South

Highway 49 traces the mother lode that yielded many fortunes in gold in the 1850s and 1860s. Step into a living gold-rush town at Columbia State Historic Park, where you can ride a stage coach and pan for riches. Sutter Creek's well-preserved downtown bursts with shopping opportunities, but the vintage goods displayed at J. Monteverde General Store are not for sale. A different sort of vintage powers the present-day bo-

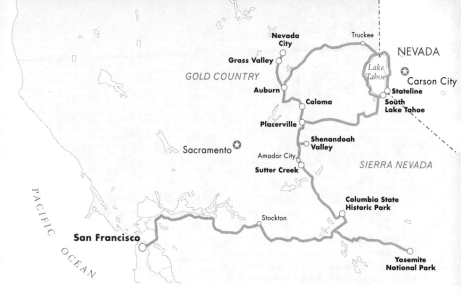

nanza in the Shenandoah Valley, heart of the Sierra Foothills wine country. Taste your way through Zinfandels and Syrahs at boutique wineries such as Domaine de la Terre Rouge, Renwood, and Sobon Estate. Amador City's 1879 Imperial Hotel places you firmly in the past for the night.

Day 6: Gold Country North

In Placerville, a mine shaft invites investigation at Hangtown's Gold Bug Mine, while Marshall Gold Discovery State Historic Park encompasses most of Coloma and preserves the spot where James Marshall's 1849 find set off the California Gold Rush. Old Town Auburn, with its museums and courthouse, makes a good lunch stop, but if you hold out until you reach Grass Valley you can try authentic miners' pasties. A tour of Empire Mine State Historic Park takes you into a mine, and a few miles away horse-drawn carriages ply the narrow, shop-lined streets of downtown Nevada City. Backtrack to Auburn or Placerville to overnight in historic or modern lodgings.

Day 7: To the Lake

Jewel-like Lake Tahoe lies a straight shot east of Placerville on Highway 50; stop for picnic provisions in commercial South Lake Tahoe. A stroll past the three mag-

TIPS

① Try to time your trip for late spring or early fall to avoid the worst of the crowds and the road-closing snowfalls in Yosemite and around Lake Tahoe. Yosemite's falls peak in spring and early summer, while fall brings the grape harvest in the Sierra Nevada foothills.

② Parking in San Francisco is expensive and scarce. When you fly in, take a shuttle or taxi from the airport to the city, then use the excellent public transport to get around. Car rental from downtown locations costs no more than at the airport.

③ For a visit in any season, reserve your hotel or campground accommodations in Yosemite as far in advance as possible—up to a year ahead. Staying in the park itself will cost extra, but it will also save you precious time and miles of driving from the gateway communities.

④ If you can stay longer, extend your Tahoe-area stay with a day in the Nevada mining boom towns around Virginia City and a night amid the bright lights of Reno.

GREAT ITINERARY

nificent estates in Pope-Baldwin Recreation area hints at the sumptuous lakefront summers once enjoyed by the elite. High above a glittering cove, Emerald Bay State Park offers one of the best lake views as well as a steep hike down to (and back up from) Vikingsholm, a replica 9th century Scandinavian castle. Another fine, old mansion—plus a nature preserve and many hiking trails—lies in Sugar Pine Point State Park. Tahoe City offers more history and ample dining and lodging choices.

Day 8: Lake Tahoe

With advance reservations, you can tour the ultra-luxe 1936 Thunderbird Lodge and its grounds. The picture-perfect beaches and bays of Lake Tahoe-Nevada State Park line the Nevada shoreline, a great place to bask in the sun or go mountain biking. For a different perspective of the lake, get out on the azure water aboard the stern-wheeler MS *Dixie II* from Zephyr Cove. In South Lake Tahoe, another view unfurls as the Heavenly Gondola travels 2.5 mi up a mountain. Keep your adrenaline pumping into the evening with some action at the massive casinos clustered in Stateline, Nevada.

Day 9: Back to the City

After a morning of driving, return your rental car in San Francisco and soak up some more urban excitement. Your options include lunch at the Ferry Building followed by a visit to the San Francisco Museum of Modern Art, or lunch in Japantown followed by shopping in Pacific Heights. People-watching excels in the late afternoon bustle of the Castro and the Haight. Say goodbye to Northern California at one of the plush lounges or trendy bars in the downtown hotels.

Day 10: Departure/San Francisco

Check the weather before you start out for the airport: Fog sometimes causes delays at SFO. On a clear day, your flight path might give you one last fabulous glimpse of the City by the Bay.

ON THE CALENDAR

Hundreds of festivals and events are held annually in Northern California. Here are a few of the favorites. If you plan to visit during a big festival, book your accommodations and event tickets well in advance.

WINTER December	Over the first two weekends in December the Miners' Christmas Celebration in Columbia is an extravaganza of costumed carolers and children's piñatas. Related events include a Victorian Christmas feast at the City Hotel, lamplight tours, an equestrian parade, and Las Posados Nativity Procession. The internationally acclaimed El Teatro Campesino annually stages one of two nativity plays, *La Virgen del Tepeyac* or *La Pastorela*, in the Mission San Juan Bautista.
February	The legendary AT&T Pebble Beach National Pro-Am golf tournament begins in late January and ends in early February. San Francisco's Chinatown is the scene of parades and noisy fireworks, all part of a several-day Chinese New Year celebration. From early February through March, the Napa Valley Mustard Festival highlights the art, culture, cooking, and—of course—the wines of Napa.
SPRING March	The North Tahoe Snow Festival celebrates the region's winter sports, with everything from slope-side parties to kids' events at venues all around North Tahoe. The Mendocino/Fort Bragg Whale Festival includes whale-watching excursions, marine art exhibits, wine and beer tastings, crafts displays, and a chowder contest.
April	The Cherry Blossom Festival, an elaborate presentation of Japanese culture and customs, winds up with a colorful parade through San Francisco's Japantown.
May	Inspired by Mark Twain's story "The Notorious Jumping Frog of Calaveras County," the Jumping Frog Jubilee, in Angels Camp, is for frogs and trainers who take their competition seriously. Sacramento is host to the four-day Sacramento Jazz Jubilee; the late-May event is the world's largest Dixieland festival, with 125 bands from around the world.

ON THE CALENDAR

SUMMER	
June	The San Francisco Lesbian, Gay, Bisexual, and Transgender Pride Celebration culminates on the last Sunday in June, with a giant parade and festival, one of the largest of its kind in the world.
	The Napa Valley Wine Auction, in St. Helena, is accompanied by open houses and a wine tasting.
July	During the three weeks of the Carmel Bach Festival, the works of Johann Sebastian Bach and 18th-century contemporaries are performed; events include concerts, recitals, and seminars.
	During the last full weekend in July, Gilroy, self-styled "garlic capital of the world," celebrates its smelly but delicious product with the Gilroy Garlic Festival, featuring such unusual concoctions as garlic ice cream.
August	The late-August Cabrillo Festival of Contemporary Music, in Santa Cruz, is one of the longest-running contemporary orchestral festivals.
	The California State Fair showcases the state's agricultural side, with a rodeo, horse racing, a carnival, and big-name entertainment. It runs 18 days from August to early September in Sacramento.
FALL	
September	The San Francisco Blues Festival is held at Fort Mason in late September.
October	The Grand National Rodeo, Horse, and Stock Show, at San Francisco's Cow Palace, is a 10-day competition straddling the end of October and the beginning of November.
	The Tor House Fall Festival honors the late poet Robinson Jeffers, an area resident for many years.

SMART TRAVEL TIPS

Finding out about your destination before you leave home means you won't spend time organizing everyday minutiae once you've arrived. You'll be more streetwise when you hit the ground as well, better prepared to explore the aspects of Northern California that drew you here in the first place. The organizations in this section can provide information to supplement this guide; contact them for up-to-the-minute details, and consult the A to Z sections that end each chapter for facts on the various topics as they relate to the Northern California's many regions. Happy landings!

AIR TRAVEL

BOOKING

When you book, look for nonstop flights and remember that "direct" flights stop at least once. Try to avoid connecting flights, which require a change of plane. Two airlines may operate a connecting flight jointly, so ask whether your airline operates every segment of the trip; you may find that the carrier you prefer flies you only part of the way. To find more booking tips and to check prices and make online flight reservations, log on to www. fodors.com.

CARRIERS

United, with a hub in San Francisco, has the greatest number of flights into and within Northern California. But most national and many international airlines fly here.

🛪 Major Airlines **Air Canada** ☎ 888/247-2262 ⊕ www.aircanada.com. **Alaska** ☎ 800/426-0333 ⊕ www.alaskaair.com. **America West** ☎ 800/235-9292 ⊕ www.americawest.com. **American** ☎ 800/433-7300 ⊕ www.aa.com. **British Airways** ☎ 800/247-9297 ⊕ www.britishairways.com. **Cathay Pacific** ☎ 800/233-2742 ⊕ www.cathaypacific.com. **Continental** ☎ 800/525-0280 ⊕ www.continental.com. **Delta** ☎ 800/221-1212 ⊕ www.delta.com. **Japan Air Lines** ☎ 800/525-3663 ⊕ www.japanair.com. **Northwest/KLM** ☎ 800/225-2525 ⊕ www.nwa.com. **Qantas** ☎ 800/227-4500 ⊕ www.qantas.com. **Southwest** ☎ 800/435-9792 ⊕ www.southwest.com. **United** ☎ 800/241-6522 ⊕ www.united.com. **US Airways** ☎ 800/428-4322 ⊕ www.usairways.com.

⚃ Smaller Airlines American Trans Air ☎ 800/435-9282 ⊕ www.ata.com. **Horizon** ☎ 800/547-9308 ⊕ www.horizonair.com. **JetBlue** ☎ 800/538-2583 ⊕ www.jetblue.com. **Midwest Airlines** ☎ 800/452-2022 ⊕ www.midwestairlines.com.
⚃ From the U.K. American ☎ 0845/778-9789. **British Airways** ☎ 0870/850-9850. **Delta** ☎ 0800/414-767. **United** ☎ 0845/8444-777. **Virgin Atlantic** ☎ 0870/380-2007.

CHECK-IN & BOARDING

Always **find out your carrier's check-in policy.** Plan to arrive at the airport about two hours before your scheduled departure time for domestic flights and 2½ to 3 hours before international flights. You may need to arrive earlier if you're flying from one of the busier airports or during peak air-traffic times. To avoid delays at airport-security checkpoints, try not to wear any metal. Jewelry, belt and other buckles, steel-toe shoes, barrettes, and underwire bras are among the items that can set off detectors.

Assuming that not everyone with a ticket will show up, airlines routinely overbook planes. When everyone does, airlines ask for volunteers to give up their seats. In return, these volunteers usually get a several-hundred-dollar flight voucher, which can be used toward the purchase of another ticket, and are rebooked on the next available flight out. If there are not enough volunteers, the airline must choose who will be denied boarding. The first to get bumped are passengers who checked in late and those flying on discounted tickets, so get to the gate and check in as early as possible, especially during peak periods.

Always **bring a government-issued photo ID** to the airport; even when it's not required, a passport is best.

CUTTING COSTS

The least expensive airfares to Northern California are priced for round-trip travel and must usually be purchased in advance, generally 21 or 14 days before departure. Airlines generally allow you to change your return date for a fee; most low-fare tickets, however, are nonrefundable. It's smart to call a number of airlines and check the Internet; when you are quoted a good price, book it on the spot—the same fare may not be available the next day, or even the next hour. Always check different routings and look into using alternate airports. Also, price off-peak flights and red-eye, which may be significantly less expensive than others. Travel agents, especially low-fare specialists (⇨ Discounts & Deals), are helpful.

Consolidators are another good source. They buy tickets for scheduled flights at reduced rates from the airlines, then sell them at prices that beat the best fare available directly from the airlines. (Many also offer reduced car-rental and hotel rates.) Sometimes you can even get your money back if you need to return the ticket. Carefully read the fine print detailing penalties for changes and cancellations, purchase the ticket with a credit card, and confirm your consolidator reservation with the airline.

ENJOYING THE FLIGHT

State your seat preference when purchasing your ticket, and then repeat it when you confirm and when you check in. For more legroom, you can request one of the few emergency-aisle seats at check-in, if you're capable of moving obstacles comparable in weight to an airplane exit door (usually between 35 pounds and 60 pounds)—a Federal Aviation Administration requirement of passengers in these seats. Seats behind a bulkhead also offer more legroom, but they don't have under-seat storage. Don't sit in the row in front of the emergency aisle or in front of a bulkhead, where seats may not recline. SeatGuru.com has more information about specific seat configurations, which vary by aircraft.

Ask the airline whether a snack or meal is served on the flight. If you have dietary concerns, request special meals when booking. These can be vegetarian, low-cholesterol, or kosher, for example. It's a good idea to pack some healthful snacks and a small (plastic) bottle of water in your carry-on bag. On long flights, try to maintain a normal routine, to help fight jet lag. At night, get some sleep. By day, eat light meals, drink water (not alcohol), and **move around the cabin** to stretch your legs. For additional jet-lag tips consult *Fodor's FYI: Travel Fit & Healthy* (available at bookstores everywhere).

Smoking policies vary from carrier to carrier. Many airlines prohibit smoking on all of their flights; others allow smoking only on certain routes or certain departures. Ask your carrier about its policy.

FLYING TIMES

Flying time to Northern California is roughly six hours from New York and four hours from Chicago. Travel from London to San Francisco takes about 10 hours and from Sydney approximately 14. Flying between San Francisco and Los Angeles takes one hour.

HOW TO COMPLAIN

If your baggage goes astray or your flight goes awry, complain right away. Most carriers require that you **file a claim immediately.** The Aviation Consumer Protection Division of the Department of Transportation publishes *Fly-Rights,* which discusses airlines and consumer issues and is available online. You can also find articles and information on mytravelrights.com, the Web site of the nonprofit Consumer Travel Rights Center.

▮ Airline Complaints **Aviation Consumer Protection Division** ⊠ U.S. Department of Transportation, Office of Aviation Enforcement and Proceedings, C-75, Room 4107, 400 7th St. SW, Washington, DC 20590 ☏ 202/366-2220 ⊕ airconsumer.ost.dot.gov. **Federal Aviation Administration Consumer Hotline** ⊠ for inquiries: FAA, 800 Independence Ave. SW, Washington, DC 20591 ☏ 800/322-7873 ⊕ www.faa.gov.

RECONFIRMING

Check the status of your flight before you leave for the airport. You can do this on your carrier's Web site, by linking to a flight-status checker (many Web booking services offer these), or by calling your carrier or travel agent.

AIRPORTS

The major gateways to Northern California are San Francisco International Airport (SFO) and San Jose International Airport (SJC).

▮ Airport Information **San Francisco International Airport** ☏ 650/761-0800 ⊕ www.flysfo.com. **San Jose International Airport** ☏ 408/277-4759 ⊕ www.sjc.org.

BIKE TRAVEL

There are beautiful places to bike throughout Northern California. For each part of the state, please see the specific chapter on that area for biking ideas.

BIKES IN FLIGHT

Most airlines accommodate bikes as luggage, provided they are dismantled and boxed; check with individual airlines about packing requirements. Some airlines sell bike boxes, which are often free at bike shops, for about $20 (bike bags can be considerably more expensive). International travelers often can substitute a bike for a piece of checked luggage at no charge; otherwise, the cost is about $100. Most U.S. and Canadian airlines charge $40–$80 each way.

BUS TRAVEL

Because of the state's size, traveling by bus in Northern California can be slow. But if you don't want to rent a car and wish to go where the train does not, a bus may be your only option. Greyhound is the major carrier for intermediate and long distances. If you've taken the bus in the past, however, don't assume it still serves your destination. In 2005, service was discontinued in many small Northern California cities and towns, so be sure and call ahead. Regional bus service is available in metropolitan areas. Check the specific chapters for the regions you plan to visit. Smoking is prohibited on all buses in California.

▮ Bus Information **Greyhound** ☏ 800/231-2222 ⊕ www.greyhound.com.

BUSINESS HOURS

Banks in Northern California are typically open from 9 to 4 and are closed most holidays (⇨ Holidays). Smaller shops usually operate from 10 to 6, with larger stores remaining open until 8 or later. Hours vary for museums and historical sites, and many are closed one or more days a week. It's a good idea to check before you visit a tourist site.

CAMERAS & PHOTOGRAPHY

The pounding surf, majestic mountains, sprawling deserts, towering trees, and sparkling beaches—not to mention the cities and towns in between—make Northern California a photographer's dream destination. Bring lots of film (or plenty of digital memory) to capture the special moments of your trip.

The *Kodak Guide to Shooting Great Travel Pictures* (available at bookstores everywhere) is loaded with tips.

⚑ Photo Help **Kodak Information Center** ☎ 800/242-2424 ⊕ www.kodak.com.

EQUIPMENT PRECAUTIONS

Don't pack film or equipment in checked luggage, where it is much more susceptible to damage. X-ray machines used to view checked luggage are extremely powerful and therefore are likely to ruin your film. Try to ask for hand inspection of film, which becomes clouded after repeated exposure to airport X-ray machines, and keep videotapes and computer disks away from metal detectors. Always keep film, tape, and computer disks out of the sun. Carry an extra supply of batteries, and be prepared to turn on your camera, camcorder, or laptop to prove to airport security personnel that the device is real.

CAR RENTAL

A car is essential in most parts of Northern California, though in compact San Francisco it's better to use public transportation to avoid parking headaches.

Rates in San Francisco begin at around $35 a day and $175 a week. This does not include tax on car rentals, which is 8½% in San Francisco. The tax is an additional 7¾%. If you pick up at an airport, there may also be a facility charge of as much as $12 per rental.

⚑ Major Agencies **Alamo** ☎ 800/327-9633 ⊕ www.alamo.com. **Avis** ☎ 800/331-1212, 800/879-2847 or 800/272-5871 in Canada, 0870/606-0100 in the U.K., 02/9353-9000 in Australia, 09/526-2847 in New Zealand ⊕ www.avis.com. **Budget** ☎ 800/527-0700 ⊕ www.budget.com. **Dollar** ☎ 800/800-4000, 0800/085-4578 in the U.K. ⊕ www.dollar.com. **Hertz** ☎ 800/654-3131, 800/263-0600 in Canada, 0870/844-8844 in the U.K.,

02/9669-2444 in Australia, 09/256-8690 in New Zealand ⊕ www.hertz.com. **National Car Rental** ☎ 800/227-7368 ⊕ www.nationalcar.com.

CONVERTIBLES & SUVS

If you dream of driving down the coast with the top down, or you want to explore the mountain landscape not visible from the road, consider renting a specialty vehicle. Agencies that specialize in convertibles and sport-utility vehicles will often arrange airport delivery in larger cities.

⚑ Specialty Car Agencies In San Francisco, **Specialty Rentals** ☎ 800/400-8412 ⊕ www.specialtyrentals.com; in Los Angeles, **Budget of Beverly Hills** ☎ 800/729-7350 ⊕ www.budgetbeverlyhills.com; in San Diego, **Rent-a-Vette** ☎ 800/627-0808 ⊕ http://sandiegosportscar-rental.com.

CUTTING COSTS

For a good deal, book through a travel agent who will shop around. Also, price local car-rental companies—whose prices may be lower still, although their service and maintenance may not be as good as those of major rental agencies—and research rates on the Internet. Consolidators that specialize in air travel can offer good rates on cars as well (⇨ Air Travel). Remember to ask about required deposits, cancellation penalties, and drop-off charges if you're planning to pick up the car in one city and leave it in another. If you're traveling during a holiday period, also make sure that a confirmed reservation guarantees you a car.

INSURANCE

When driving a rented car you are generally responsible for any damage to or loss of the vehicle. You also may be liable for any property damage or personal injury that you may cause while driving. Before you rent, see what coverage you already have under the terms of your personal auto-insurance policy and credit cards.

For about $9 to $25 a day, rental companies sell protection, known as a collision- or loss-damage waiver (CDW or LDW), that eliminates your liability for damage to the car; it's always optional and should never be automatically added to your bill. In most states you don't need a CDW if you have personal auto insurance or other liability insurance. Some states, including California, have capped the price of the CDW and LDW, but the cap has a floating value, depending on the cost of the vehicle; for those valued at more than $35,000, there is no maximum. Verify the cost of the CDW/LDW at the time you book. Make sure you have enough coverage to pay for the car. If you do not have auto insurance or an umbrella policy that covers damage to third parties, purchasing liability insurance and a CDW or LDW is highly recommended.

Some credit-card companies cover the cost of CDW/LDW if you pay using that card. Check with the credit-card company to determine if you are eligible for these coverages. Credit cards do not provide liability insurance, only CDW/LDW.

Rental agencies in California aren't required to include liability insurance in the price of the rental. If you cause an accident, you may expose your assets to litigation. When in doubt about your own policy's coverage, take the liability coverage that the agency offers. If you plan to take the car out of California, ask if the policy is valid in other states or countries. Most car-rental companies won't insure a loss or damage that occurs outside of their coverage area—particularly in Mexico.

REQUIREMENTS & RESTRICTIONS

In California, you must be 21 to rent a car, and rates may be higher if you're under 25. Some agencies will not rent to those under 25; check when you book. You'll pay extra for child seats (about $5–$10 per day), which are compulsory for children up to age six and weighing up to 60 pounds. There is no extra charge for an additional driver who meets the agency's age requirements. Non-U.S. residents must have a license whose text is in the Roman alphabet. Though it need not be entirely written in English, it must have English letters that clearly identify it as a driver's license. An international license is recommended but not required.

SURCHARGES

Before you pick up a car in one city and leave it in another, ask about drop-off charges or one-way service fees, which can be substantial. Also inquire about early-return policies; some rental agencies charge extra if you return the car before the time specified in your contract while others give you a refund for the days not used. Most agencies note the tank's fuel level on your contract; to avoid a hefty refueling fee, return the car with the same tank level. If the tank was full, refill it just before you turn in the car, but be aware that gas stations near the rental outlet may overcharge. It's almost never a deal to buy a tank of gas with the car when you rent it; the understanding is that you'll return it empty, but some fuel usually remains.

CAR TRAVEL

Three major highways—Interstate 5 (I-5), U.S. 101, and Highway 1—run north–south through Northern California. The main routes into the region from the east is I-80.

EMERGENCY SERVICES

Dial 911 to report accidents on the road and to reach police, the California Highway Patrol (CHP), or the fire department. On some rural highways and on most interstates, look for emergency phones on the side of the road.

GASOLINE

Gasoline prices in Northern California vary widely, depending on location, oil company, and whether you buy it at a full-serve or self-serve pump. At this writing regular unleaded gasoline costs about $3 a gallon. It is less expensive to buy fuel in the southern part of the state than in the north. If you are planning to travel near Nevada, you can save a lot by purchasing gas over the border.

Gas stations are plentiful throughout the state. Most stay open late (24 hours along major highways and in big cities), except in rural areas, where Sunday hours are limited and where you may drive long stretches without a chance to refuel.

ROAD CONDITIONS

Rainy weather can make driving along the coast or in the mountains treacherous. Some of the smaller routes over the mountain ranges are prone to flash flooding. When the rains are severe, coastal Highway 1 can quickly become a slippery nightmare, buffeted by strong winds and obstructed by falling debris from the cliffs above. When the weather is particularly bad, Highway 1 may be closed due to mudslides. Drivers should check road and weather conditions before heading out.

Many smaller roads over the Sierra Nevada are closed in winter, and if it is snowing, tire chains may be required on routes that are open, most notably those to Yosemite and Lake Tahoe. From October through April, if it is raining along the coast, it is usually snowing at higher elevations. Do not wait until the highway patrol's chain-control checkpoint to look for chains; you'll be unable to turn around, and will get stuck and have to wait out the storm. Rent a four-wheel-drive vehicle or purchase chains before you get to the mountains. (Chains or cables generally cost $30–$45, depending on tire size; cables are easier to apply than chains, but chains are more durable.) If you delay and purchase them in the vicinity of the chain-control area, the cost may double. Be aware that most rental-car companies prohibit chain installation on their vehicles. If you choose to risk it and do not tighten them properly, they may snap; insurance will not cover the damage that could result. Uniformed chain installers on I–80 and U.S. 50 will apply them at the checkpoint for $20 or take them off for $10. On smaller roads you are on your own. Always carry extra clothing, blankets, and food when driving to the mountains in the winter, and keep your gas tank full to prevent the fuel line from freezing.

In larger cities the biggest driving hazards are traffic jams. Avoid major urban highways, especially at rush hour.

🚗 **Road Conditions Statewide hotline** 📞 800/GAS–ROAD or 916/445-1534 ⊕ www.dot.ca.gov/hq/roadinfo.

🚗 Weather Conditions **National Weather Service** 📞 707/443-6484 (northernmost California), 831/656-1725 (San Francisco Bay Area and central California), 775/673-8100 (Reno, Lake Tahoe, and the northern Sierra) ⊕ www.weather.gov.

ROAD MAPS

You can buy detailed maps in bookstores and gas stations and at some grocery stores and drugstores.

RULES OF THE ROAD

Always strap children under age six or weighing 60 pounds or less into approved child-safety seats; also children up to age six and weighing up to 60 pounds must be placed in booster seats designed to reduce seat belt injuries. Seat belts are required at all times; tickets can be given for failing to comply. Children must wear seat belts regardless of where they're seated (studies show that children are safest in the rear seats).

Unless otherwise indicated, right turns are allowed at red lights after you've come to a full stop. Left turns between two one-way streets are allowed at red lights after you've come to a full stop. Drivers with a blood-alcohol level higher than 0.08 who are stopped by police are subject to arrest, and police officers can detain those with a level of 0.05 if they appear impaired. California's drunk-driving laws are extremely tough. The licenses of violators may immediately be suspended, and offenders may have to spend the night in jail and pay hefty fines.

The speed limit on many rural highways is 70 mph. In cities, freeway speed limits are between 55 mph and 65 mph. Many city routes have commuter lanes during rush hour, but the rules vary from city to city: in San Francisco, you need three people in a car to use these lanes. Read the signs. Failure to comply with the rules could cost you nearly $300 in fines.

CHILDREN IN CALIFORNIA

Northern California is made to order for traveling with children: youngsters love the Monterey Bay Aquarium; San Francisco cable cars; the gold mine in Placerville; Forestiere Underground Gardens in Fresno; and the caverns near Lake Shasta. *Fodor's Around San Francisco with Kids* (available in bookstores everywhere) can help you plan your days together.

If you are renting a car, don't forget to arrange for a car seat when you reserve. For general advice about traveling with children, consult *Fodor's FYI: Travel with Your Baby* (available in bookstores everywhere).

FLYING

If your children are two or older, ask about children's airfares. As a general rule, infants under two not occupying a seat fly at greatly reduced fares or even for free. But if you want to guarantee a seat for an infant, you have to pay full fare. Consider flying during off-peak days and times; most airlines will grant an infant a seat without a ticket if there are available seats.

Experts agree that it's a good idea to use safety seats aloft for children weighing less than 40 pounds. Airlines set their own policies: if you use a safety seat, U.S. carriers usually require that the child be ticketed, even if he or she is young enough to ride free, because the seats must be strapped into regular seats. And even if you pay the full adult fare for the seat, it may be worth it, especially on longer trips. Do **check your airline's policy about using safety seats during takeoff and landing.** Safety seats are not allowed everywhere in the plane, so get your seat assignments as early as possible.

When reserving, request children's meals or a freestanding bassinet (not available at all airlines) if you need them. But note that bulkhead seats, where you must sit to use the bassinet, may lack an overhead bin or storage space on the floor.

LODGING

Most hotels in Northern California allow children under a certain age to stay in their parents' room at no extra charge, but others charge for them as extra adults; be sure to find out the cutoff age for children's discounts.

SIGHTS & ATTRACTIONS

Places that are especially appealing to children are indicated by a rubber-duckie icon (🦆) in the margin.

CONSUMER PROTECTION

Whether you're shopping for gifts or purchasing travel services, **pay with a major credit card** whenever possible, so you can cancel payment or get reimbursed if there's

a problem (and you can provide documentation). If you're doing business with a particular company for the first time, contact your local Better Business Bureau and the attorney general's offices in your state and (for U.S. businesses) the company's home state as well. Have any complaints been filed? Finally, if you're buying a package or tour, always consider travel insurance that includes default coverage (⇨ Insurance).

🔏 BBBs **Council of Better Business Bureaus** ✉ 4200 Wilson Blvd., Suite 800, Arlington, VA 22203 ☎ 703/276-0100 🖨 703/525-8277 ⊕ www. bbb.org.

CUSTOMS & DUTIES

When shopping abroad, keep receipts for all purchases. Upon reentering the country, be ready to show customs officials what you've bought. Pack purchases together in an easily accessible place. If you think a duty is incorrect, appeal the assessment. If you object to the way your clearance was handled, note the inspector's badge number. In either case, first ask to see a supervisor. If the problem isn't resolved, write to the appropriate authorities, beginning with the port director at your point of entry.

IN AUSTRALIA

Australian residents who are 18 or older may bring home A$900 worth of souvenirs and gifts (including jewelry), 250 cigarettes or 250 grams of cigars or other tobacco products, and 2.25 liters of alcohol (including wine, beer, and spirits). Residents under 18 may bring back A$450 worth of goods. If any of these individual allowances are exceeded, you must pay duty for the entire amount (of the group of products in which the allowance was exceeded). Members of the same family traveling together may pool their allowances. Prohibited items include meat products. Seeds, plants, and fruits need to be declared upon arrival.

🔏 **Australian Customs Service** 🏛 Customs House, 10 Cooks River Dr., Sydney International Airport, Sydney, NSW 2020 ☎ 02/6275-6666 or 1300/363263, 02/ 8334-7444 or 1800/020-504 quarantine-inquiry line 🖨 02/8339-6714 ⊕ www.customs.gov.au.

IN CANADA

Canadian residents who have been out of Canada for at least seven days may bring in C$750 worth of goods duty-free. If you've been away fewer than seven days but more than 48 hours, the duty-free allowance drops to C$200. If your trip lasts 24 to 48 hours, the allowance is C$50; if the goods are worth more than C$50, you must pay full duty on all of the goods. You may not pool allowances with family members. Goods claimed under the C$750 exemption may follow you by mail; those claimed under the lesser exemptions must accompany you. Alcohol and tobacco products may be included in the seven-day and 48-hour exemptions but not in the 24-hour exemption. If you meet the age requirements of the province or territory through which you reenter Canada, you may bring in, duty-free, 1.5 liters of wine *or* 1.14 liters (40 imperial ounces) of liquor *or* 24 12-ounce cans or bottles of beer or ale. Also, if you meet the local age requirement for tobacco products, you may bring in, duty-free, 200 cigarettes, 50 cigars or cigarillos, and 200 grams of tobacco. You may have to pay a minimum duty on tobacco products, regardless of whether or not you exceed your personal exemption. Check ahead of time with the Canada Border Services Agency or the Department of Agriculture for policies regarding meat products, seeds, plants, and fruits.

You may send an unlimited number of gifts (only one gift per recipient, however) worth up to C$60 each duty-free to Canada. Label the package UNSOLICITED GIFT—VALUE UNDER $60. Alcohol and tobacco are excluded.

🗋 **Canada Border Services Agency** ⌗ Customs Information Services, 191 Laurier Ave. W, 15th floor, Ottawa, Ontario K1A 0L5 ☎ 800/461-9999 in Canada, 204/983-3500, 506/636-5064 ⊕ www.cbsa.gc.ca.

IN NEW ZEALAND

All homeward-bound residents may bring back NZ$700 worth of souvenirs and gifts; passengers may not pool their allowances, and children can claim only the concession on goods intended for their own use. For those 17 or older, the duty-free allowance also includes 4.5 liters of wine or beer; one 1,125-ml bottle of spirits; and either 200 cigarettes, 250 grams of tobacco, 50 cigars, *or* a combination of the three up to 250 grams. Meat products, seeds, plants, and fruits must be declared upon arrival to the Agricultural Services Department.

🗋 **New Zealand Customs** ⌗ Head office: The Customhouse, 17–21 Whitmore St., Box 2218, Wellington ☎ 09/300-5399 or 0800/428-786 ⊕ www.customs.govt.nz.

IN THE U.K.

From countries outside the European Union, including United States, you may bring home, duty-free, 200 cigarettes, 50 cigars, 100 cigarillos, or 250 grams of tobacco; 1 liter of spirits or 2 liters of fortified or sparkling wine or liqueurs; 2 liters of still table wine; 60 ml of perfume; 250 ml of toilet water; plus £145 worth of other goods, including gifts and souvenirs. Prohibited items include meat and dairy products, seeds, plants, and fruits.

🗋 **HM Customs and Excise** ⌗ Portcullis House, 21 Cowbridge Rd. E, Cardiff CF11 9SS ☎ 0845/010-9000 or 0208/929-0152 advice service, 0208/929-6731 or 0208/910-3602 complaints ⊕ www.hmce.gov.uk.

DISABILITIES & ACCESSIBILITY

California is a national leader in making attractions and facilities accessible to people with disabilities.

LODGING

Despite the Americans with Disabilities Act, the definition of accessibility seems to differ from hotel to hotel. Some properties may be accessible by ADA standards for people with mobility problems but not for people with hearing or vision impairments, for example.

If you have mobility problems, ask for the lowest floor on which accessible services are offered. If you have a hearing impairment, check whether the hotel has devices to alert you visually to the ring of the telephone, a knock at the door, and a fire/emergency alarm. Some hotels provide these devices without charge. Discuss your needs with hotel personnel if this equipment isn't available, so that a staff member can personally alert you in the event of an emergency.

If you're bringing a guide dog, get authorization ahead of time and write down the name of the person with whom you spoke.

RESERVATIONS

When discussing accessibility with an operator or reservations agent, ask hard questions. Are there any stairs, inside *or* out? Are there grab bars next to the toilet *and* in the shower/tub? How wide is the doorway to the room? To the bathroom? For the most extensive facilities meeting the latest legal specifications, opt for newer accommodations. If you reserve through a toll-free number, consider also calling the hotel's local number to confirm the information from the central reservations office. Get confirmation in writing when you can.

TRANSPORTATION

Hertz and Avis (⇨ Car Rental) are able to supply cars modified for those with disabilities, but they require one to two days' advance notice. Discounts are available for travelers with disabilities on Amtrak (⇨ Train Travel). On Greyhound (⇨ Bus Travel), your companion can ride free.

🛂 Complaints **Aviation Consumer Protection Division** (⇨ Air Travel) for airline-related problems; ⊕ airconsumer.ost.dot.gov/publications/horizons. htm for airline travel advice and rights. **Departmental Office of Civil Rights** ⊠ for general inquiries, U.S. Department of Transportation, S-30, 400 7th St. SW, Room 10215, Washington, DC 20590 ☎ 202/366-4648, 202/366-8538 TTY 🖷 202/366-9371 ⊕ www.dotcr.ost.dot.gov. **Disability Rights Section** ⊠ NYAV, U.S. Department of Justice, Civil Rights Division, 950 Pennsylvania Ave. NW, Washington, DC 20530 ☎ ADA information line 202/514-0301, 800/514-0301, 202/514-0383 TTY, 800/514-0383 TTY ⊕ www.ada.gov. **U.S. Department of Transportation Hotline** ☎ for disability-related air-travel problems, 800/778-4838 or 800/455-9880 TTY.

TRAVEL AGENCIES

In the United States, the Americans with Disabilities Act requires that travel firms serve the needs of all travelers. Some agencies specialize in working with people with disabilities.

🛂 Travelers with Mobility Problems **Access Adventures/B. Roberts Travel** ⊠ 1876 East Ave., Rochester, NY 14610 ☎ 800/444-6540 ⊕ www. brobertstravel.com, run by a former physical-rehabilitation counselor. **Accessible Vans of America** ⊠ 37 Daniel Rd. W, Fairfield, NJ 07004 ☎ 877/282-8267, 888/282-8267, 973/808-9709 reservations 🖷 973/808-9713 ⊕ www.accessiblevans.com. **Care-Vacations** ⊠ No. 5, 5110-50 Ave., Leduc, Alberta, Canada, T9E 6V4 ☎ 780/986-6404 or 877/478-7827 🖷 780/986-8332 ⊕ www.carevacations.com, for group tours and cruise vacations. **Flying Wheels Travel** ⊠ 143 W. Bridge St., Box 382, Owatonna, MN 55060 ☎ 507/451-5005 🖷 507/451-1685 ⊕ www. flyingwheelstravel.com.

🛂 Travelers with Developmental Disabilities **New Directions** ⊠ 5276 Hollister Ave., Suite 207, Santa Barbara, CA 93111 ☎ 805/967-2841 or 888/967-2841 🖷 805/964-7344 ⊕ www.newdirectionstravel.com. **Sprout** ⊠ 893 Amsterdam Ave., New York, NY 10025 ☎ 212/222-9575 or 888/222-9575 🖷 212/222-9768 ⊕ www.gosprout.org.

DISCOUNTS & DEALS

Be a smart shopper and compare all your options before making decisions. A plane ticket bought with a promotional coupon from travel clubs, coupon books, and direct-mail offers or purchased on the Internet may not be cheaper than the least expensive fare from a discount ticket agency. And always keep in mind that what you get is just as important as what you save.

You can find discounts on sights and attractions by contacting local visitor bureaus. The major cities print trip-planning guides that are chock-full of coupons for everything from museum admissions to ferryboat trips. Smaller cities and towns often have brochure racks in their offices, where you can browse for coupons and get advice on saving money. For addresses and phone numbers of visitor centers, see the A to Z sections at the end of each chapter.

DISCOUNT RESERVATIONS

To save money, look into discount reservations services with Web sites and toll-free numbers, which use their buying power to get a better price on hotels, airline tickets (⇨ Air Travel), even car rentals. When booking a room, always

call the hotel's local toll-free number (if one is available) rather than the central reservations number—you'll often get a better price. Always ask about special packages or corporate rates.

🏨 Hotel Rooms **Accommodations Express** ☎ 800/444-7666 or 800/277-1064. **Central Reservation Service (CRS)** ☎ 800/555-7555 or 800/548-3311 ⊕ www.crshotels.com. **Hotels.com** ☎ 800/246-8357 ⊕ www.hotels.com. **Quikbook** ☎ 800/789-9887 ⊕ www.quikbook.com. **Steigenberger Reservation Service** ☎ 800/223-5652 ⊕ www.srs-worldhotels.com. **Turbotrip.com** ☎ 800/473-7829 ⊕ w3.turbotrip.com.

PACKAGE DEALS

Don't confuse packages and guided tours. When you buy a package, you travel on your own, just as though you had planned the trip yourself. Fly/drive packages, which combine airfare and car rental, are often a good deal. In cities, ask the local visitor's bureau about hotel and local transportation packages that include tickets to major museum exhibits or other special events.

DIVERS' ALERT

Do not fly within 24 hours of scuba diving.

EATING & DRINKING

California has led the pack in bringing natural and organic foods to the forefront of American cooking. Though rooted in European cuisine, California cooking sometimes has strong Asian and Latin influences. Wherever you go, you're likely to find that dishes are made with fresh produce and other local ingredients.

The restaurants we list are the cream of the crop in each price category. Properties indicated by a ✕🏠 are lodging establishments whose restaurant warrants a special trip.

CUTTING COSTS

If you're on a budget, take advantage of the "small plates" craze sweeping California by ordering several appetizer-size portions and having a glass of wine at the bar, rather than having a full meal. Also, better grocery and specialty-food stores have grab-and-go sections, with prepared foods on par with restaurant cooking, perfect for picnicking (remember, it rarely rains between May and October). At resort areas in the off-season (such as Lake Tahoe in October and May), you can often find two-for-one dinner specials at upper-end restaurants; check local papers or with visitor bureaus.

MEALTIMES

Unless otherwise noted, the restaurants listed in this guide are open daily for lunch and dinner. Lunch is typically served 11:30–2:30, and dinner service in most restaurants begins at 5:30 and ends at 10. Some restaurants in larger cities stay open until midnight or later, but in smaller towns evening service may end as early as 8.

RESERVATIONS & DRESS

Reservations are always a good idea; we mention them only when they're essential or not accepted. Book as far ahead as you can, and reconfirm as soon as you arrive. (Large parties should always call ahead to check the reservations policy.) We mention dress only when men are required to wear a jacket or a jacket and tie.

WINE, BEER & SPIRITS

If you like wine, your trip to Northern California won't be complete unless you try a few of the local vintages. Throughout the state, most famously in the Napa and Sonoma valleys, you can visit wineries, most of which have tasting rooms and many of which offer tours. The legal drinking age is 21.

ECOTOURISM

When traveling in wilderness areas and parks, remember to tread lightly. Do not drive an SUV through sensitive habitats, and pack out what you pack in. Many remote camping areas do not provide waste disposal. It's a good idea to bring plastic bags to store refuse until you can dispose of it properly. Recycling programs are abundant in California, and trash at many state and national parks is sorted. Look for appropriately labeled garbage containers. Numerous ecotours are available in the state (⇨ Tours & Packages).

GAY & LESBIAN TRAVEL

San Francisco is among the California cities with the most visible lesbian and gay communities. Though it is usually safe to be visibly "out" in many areas, you should always use common sense when in unfamiliar places. Gay bashings still occur in both urban and rural areas. For details about the gay and lesbian scene, consult *Fodor's Gay Guide to the USA* (available in bookstores everywhere).

LOCAL INFORMATION

Many Northern California cities large and small have lesbian and gay publications available in sidewalk racks and at bars, bookstores, and other social spaces; most have extensive events and information listings.

🔳 Community Centers **Billy DeFrank Lesbian & Gay Community Center** ✉ 938 The Alameda, San Jose 95126 ☎ 408/293-2429 ⊕ www.defrank.org. **L.A. Gay and Lesbian Center** ✉ 1625 N. Schrader Blvd., Los Angeles 90028 ☎ 323/993-7400 ⊕ www.laglc.org. **Lambda Community Center** ✉ 1927 L St., Sacramento 95814 ☎ 916/442-0185 ⊕ www.lambdasac.org. **Lavender Youth Recreation & Information Center** ✉ 127 Collingwood St., San Francisco 94114 ☎ 415/703-6150 ⊕ www.lyric.org. **Lesbian and Gay Men's Community Center** ✉ 3909 Centre St., San Diego 92103 ☎ 619/692-2077 ⊕ www.thecentersd.org. **Pacific Center for Human Growth** ✉ 2712 Telegraph Ave., Berkeley 94705 ☎ 510/548-8283 ⊕ www.pacificcenter.org. **The Center (San Francisco Lesbian, Gay, Bisexual, Transgender Community Center)** ✉ 1800 Market St. ☎ 415/865-5555 ⊕ www.sfgaycenter.org.

🔳 Local Publications **Bay Area Reporter** ☎ 415/861-5019 ⊕ www.ebar.com. **Bottom Line** ☎ 760/323-0552 ⊕ www.psbottomline.com. **Frontiers** ☎ 323/848-2222 ⊕ www.frontiersnewsmagazine.com. **Mom Guess What!** ☎ 916/441-6397 ⊕ www.mgwnews.com. **Update** ☎ 619/299-0500 ⊕ www.sandiegogaynews.com.

🔳 Gay- & Lesbian-Friendly Travel Agencies **Different Roads Travel** ✉ 1017 N. LaCienega Blvd., Suite 308, West Hollywood, CA 90069 ☎ 310/289-6000 or 800/429-8747 (Ext. 14 for both) 🖷 310/855-0323 ✉ lgernert@tzell.com. **Kennedy Travel** ✉ 130 W. 42nd St., Suite 401, New York, NY 10036 ☎ 800/237-7433 or 212/840-8659 🖷 212/730-2269 ⊕ www.kennedytravel.com. **Now, Voyager** ✉ 4406 18th St., San Francisco, CA 94114 ☎ 415/626-1169 or 800/255-6951 🖷 415/626-8626 ⊕ www.nowvoyager.com. **Skylink Travel and Tour/Flying Dutchmen Travel** ✉ 1455 N. Dutton Ave., Suite A,

Santa Rosa, CA 95401 ☎ 707/546-9888 or 800/225-5759 🖷 707/636-0951; serving lesbian travelers.

HOLIDAYS

Many traditional businesses are closed the following days, but tourist attractions, as well as some shops and restaurants, are usually open except on Thanksgiving, Christmas, and New Year's Day.

Major national holidays are New Year's Day (Jan. 1); Martin Luther King Day (3rd Mon. in Jan.); Presidents' Day (3rd Mon. in Feb.); Memorial Day (last Mon. in May); Independence Day (July 4); Labor Day (1st Mon. in Sept.); Columbus Day (2nd Mon. in Oct.); Thanksgiving Day (4th Thurs. in Nov.); Christmas Eve and Christmas Day (Dec. 24 and 25); and New Year's Eve (Dec. 31).

INSURANCE

The most useful travel-insurance plan is a comprehensive policy that includes coverage for trip cancellation and interruption, default, trip delay, and medical expenses (with a waiver for preexisting conditions).

Without insurance you'll lose all or most of your money if you cancel your trip, regardless of the reason. Default insurance covers you if your tour operator, airline, or cruise line goes out of business—the chances of which have been increasing. Trip-delay covers expenses that arise because of bad weather or mechanical delays. Study the fine print when comparing policies.

U.K. residents can buy a travel-insurance policy valid for most vacations taken during the year in which it's purchased (but check preexisting-condition coverage).

Always **buy travel policies directly from the insurance company**; if you buy them from a cruise line, airline, or tour operator that goes out of business you probably won't be covered for the agency or operator's default, a major risk. Before making any purchase, review your existing health and home-owner's policies to find what they cover away from home.

🔳 Travel Insurers In the U.S.: **Access America** ✉ 2805 N. Parham Rd., Richmond, VA 23294 ☎ 800/284-8300 🖷 804/673-1469 or 800/346-9265 ⊕ www.accessamerica.com. **Travel Guard In-**

ternational ✉ 1145 Clark St., Stevens Point, WI 54481 ☎ 800/826-1300 or 715/345-1041 🖷 800/955-8785 or 715/345-1990 🌐 www.travelguard.com.

FOR INTERNATIONAL TRAVELERS

For information on customs restrictions, *see* Customs & Duties.

CAR RENTAL

When picking up a rental car, non-U.S. residents need a reservation voucher for any prepaid reservations that were made in the traveler's home country, a passport, a driver's license, and a travel policy that covers each driver.

CAR TRAVEL

Highways are well paved. Interstate highways—limited-access, multilane highways whose numbers are prefixed by "I–"—are the fastest routes. Interstates with three-digit numbers encircle urban areas, which may have other limited-access expressways, freeways, and parkways as well. Tolls may be levied at bridge crossings. So-called U.S. highways and state highways are not necessarily limited-access but may have several lanes.

Along larger highways, roadside stops with restrooms, fast-food restaurants, and sundries stores are well spaced. State police and tow trucks patrol major highways and lend assistance. If your car breaks down on an interstate, pull onto the shoulder and wait for help, or have your passengers wait while you walk to an emergency phone. If you carry a cell phone, dial 911, noting your location on the small green roadside mileage markers.

Motorists drive on the right side of the road in the United States. Do obey speed limits posted along roads and highways. Watch for lower limits in small towns and on back roads. California requires front-seat passengers to wear seat belts. On weekdays between 6 and 10 AM and again between 3 and 7 PM expect heavy traffic in urban and suburban areas. To encourage carpooling, some freeways have special lanes for so-called high-occupancy vehicles (HOV)—cars carrying more than one or two passengers, depending on where you are. The pavement is marked with a white diamond. If you do not meet the criteria for travel in these lanes and you get stopped by the police, you can get fined upward of $300 and receive a point on your license.

In California you may turn right at a red light after stopping if there is no oncoming traffic, unless a sign forbids you to do so. You may also turn left on red between two one-way streets. But when in doubt, wait for the green. Be alert for one-way streets, "no left turn" intersections, and blocks closed to car traffic. Bookstores, gas stations, convenience stores, and rest stops sell maps (about $3) and multiregion road atlases (about $10). For more information on driving in California, *see* Car Travel, *above.*

CONSULATES & EMBASSIES

🇦🇺 **Australia** ✉ Century Plaza Towers, 2049 Century Park E, 19th fl., Los Angeles 90067 ☎ 310/229-4800 🖷 310/277-5620 🌐 www.austemb.org ✉ 625 Market St., Suite 200, San Francisco 94105 ☎ 415/536-1970.

🇨🇦 **Canada** ✉ 550 S. Hope St., 9th fl., Los Angeles 90071-2627 ☎ 213/346-2700 🌐 www.dfait-maeci.gc.ca ✉ 555 Montgomery St., Suite 1288 ☎ 415/834-3180.

🇳🇿 **New Zealand** ✉ 2425 Olympic Blvd., Suite 600 E, Santa Monica 90404 ☎ 310/566-6555 🌐 www.mfat.govt.nz ✉ 1 Maritime Plaza, Suite 400, San Francisco 94111 ☎ 415/399-1255.

🇬🇧 **United Kingdom** ✉ 11766 Wilshire Blvd., Suite 1200, Los Angeles 90025 ☎ 310/481-0031 🌐 www.britainusa.com ✉ 1 Sansome St., Suite 850, San Francisco 94104 ☎ 415/617-1300.

CURRENCY

The dollar is the basic unit of U.S. currency. It has 100 cents. Coins are the copper penny (1¢); the silvery nickel (5¢), dime (10¢), quarter (25¢), and half-dollar (50¢); and the golden $1 coin, replacing a now-rare silver dollar. Bills are denominated $1, $5, $10, $20, $50, and $100, all mostly green and identical in size; designs and background tints vary. In addition, you may come across a $2 bill, but the chances are slim.

ELECTRICITY

The U.S. standard is AC, 110 volts/60 cycles. Plugs have two flat pins set parallel to each other.

EMERGENCIES

For police, fire, or ambulance, **dial 911** (0 in rural areas).

INSURANCE

Britons and Australians need extra medical coverage when traveling overseas.

🔢 Insurance Information In the U.K.: **Association of British Insurers** ✉ 51 Gresham St., London EC2V 7HQ ☎ 020/7600-3333 🖷 020/7696-8999 ⊕ www.abi.org.uk. In Australia: **Insurance Council of Australia** ✉ Level 3, 56 Pitt St. Sydney, NSW 2000 ☎ 02/9253-5100 🖷 02/9253-5111 ⊕ www.ica.com.au. In Canada: **RBC Insurance** ✉ 6880 Financial Dr., Mississauga, Ontario L5N 7Y5 ☎ 800/387-4357 or 905/816-2559 🖷 888/298-6458 ⊕ www.rbcinsurance.com. In New Zealand: **Insurance Council of New Zealand** ✉ Level 7, 111-115 Customhouse Quay, Box 474, Wellington ☎ 04/472-5230 🖷 04/473-3011 ⊕ www.icnz.org.nz.

MAIL & SHIPPING

You can buy stamps and aerograms and send letters and parcels in post offices. Stamp-dispensing machines can occasionally be found in airports, bus and train stations, office buildings, drugstores, and the like. You can also deposit mail in the stout, dark blue, steel bins at strategic locations everywhere and in the mail chutes of large buildings; pickup schedules are posted. You can deposit packages at public collection boxes as long as the parcels are affixed with proper postage and weigh less than one pound. Packages weighing one or more pounds must be taken to a post office or handed to a postal carrier.

For mail sent within the United States, you need a 37¢ stamp for first-class letters weighing up to 1 ounce (23¢ for each additional ounce) and 23¢ for postcards. You pay 80¢ for 1-ounce airmail letters and 70¢ for airmail postcards to most other countries; to Canada and Mexico, you need a 60¢ stamp for a 1-ounce letter and 50¢ for a postcard. An aerogram—a single sheet of lightweight blue paper that folds into its own envelope, stamped for overseas airmail—costs 70¢.

To receive mail on the road, have it sent c/o General Delivery at your destination's main post office (use the correct five-digit ZIP code). You must pick up mail in person within 30 days and show a driver's license or passport.

PASSPORTS & VISAS

When traveling internationally, carry your passport even if you don't need one (it's always the best form of ID) and **make two photocopies of the data page** (one for someone at home and another for you, carried separately from your passport). If you lose your passport, promptly call the nearest embassy or consulate and the local police.

Visitor visas aren't necessary for Canadian or European Union citizens, or for citizens of Australia who are staying fewer than 90 days.

🔢 Australian Citizens **Passports Australia** ☎ 131-232 ⊕ www.passports.gov.au. **United States Consulate General** ✉ MLC Centre, Level 59, 19-29 Martin Pl., Sydney, NSW 2000 ☎ 02/9373-9200, 1902/941-641 fee-based visa-inquiry line ⊕ usembassy-australia.state.gov/sydney.

🔢 Canadian Citizens **Passport Office** ✉ to mail in applications: 70 Cremazie St., Gatineau, Québec J8Y 3P2 ☎ 800/567-6868, 866/255-7655 TTY ⊕ www.ppt.gc.ca.

🔢 New Zealand Citizens **New Zealand Passports Office** ✉ For applications and information, Level 3, Boulcott House, 47 Boulcott St., Wellington ☎ 0800/22-5050 or 04/474-8100 ⊕ www.passports.govt.nz. **Embassy of the United States** ✉ 29 Fitzherbert Terr., Thorndon, Wellington ☎ 04/462-6000 ⊕ usembassy.org.nz. **U.S. Consulate General** ✉ Citibank Bldg., 3rd floor, 23 Customs St. E, Auckland ☎ 09/303-2724 ⊕ usembassy.org.nz.

🔢 U.K. Citizens **U.K. Passport Service** ☎ 0870/521-0410 ⊕ www.passport.gov.uk. **American Consulate General** ✉ Danesfort House, 223 Stranmillis Rd., Belfast, Northern Ireland BT9 5GR ☎ 028/9038-6100 🖷 028/9068-1301 ⊕ www.usembassy.org.uk. **American Embassy** ✉ for visa and immigration information or to submit a visa application via mail (enclose an SASE), Consular Information Unit, 24 Grosvenor Sq., London W1A 2LQ ☎ 090/5544-4546 or 090/6820-0290 for visa information (per-minute charges), 0207/499-9000 main switchboard ⊕ www.usembassy.org.uk.

TELEPHONES

All U.S. telephone numbers consist of a three-digit area code and a seven-digit local number. Within many local calling areas, you dial only the seven-digit number. Within some area codes, you must dial "1" first for calls outside the local area. To call between area-code regions, dial "1" then all 10 digits; the same goes for calls to numbers prefixed by "800," "888," "866," and "877"—all toll free. For calls to numbers preceded by "900" you must pay—usually dearly.

For international calls, dial "011" followed by the country code and the local number. For help, dial "0" and ask for an overseas operator. The country code is 61 for Australia, 64 for New Zealand, 44 for the United Kingdom. Calling Canada is the same as calling within the United States, although you might not be able to get through on some toll free numbers. Most local phone books list country codes and U.S. area codes. The country code for the United States is 1.

For operator assistance, dial "0." To obtain someone's phone number, call directory assistance at 555–1212 or occasionally 411 (free at many public phones). To have the person you're calling foot the bill, phone collect; dial "0" instead of "1" before the 10-digit number.

At pay phones, instructions often are posted. Usually you insert coins in a slot (usually 25¢–50¢ for local calls) and wait for a steady tone before dialing. When you call long-distance, the operator tells you how much to insert; prepaid phone cards, widely available in various denominations, are easier. Call the number on the back, punch in the card's personal identification number when prompted, then dial your number.

🔢 Long-Distance Carriers **AT&T** ☎ 800/225-5288. **MCI** ☎ 800/888-8000. **Sprint** ☎ 800/366-2255.

LODGING

The lodgings we list are the cream of the crop in each price category. We always list the facilities that are available, but we don't specify whether they cost extra; when pricing accommodations, always ask what's included and what costs extra. Properties marked ✕▦ are lodging establishments whose restaurants warrant a special trip.

Assume that hotels operate on the European Plan (EP, with no meals) unless we specify that they use the Continental Plan (CP, with a Continental breakfast), Breakfast Plan (BP, with a full breakfast), Modified American Plan (MAP, with breakfast and dinner), or the Full American Plan (FAP, with all meals).

PRICES

Properties are assigned price categories based on the range from their least-expensive standard double room at high season (excluding holidays) to the most expensive.

APARTMENT & HOUSE RENTALS

If you want a home base that's roomy enough for a family and comes with cooking facilities, consider a furnished rental. These can save you money, especially if you're traveling with a group. Home-exchange directories sometimes list rentals as well as exchanges.

🔢 International Agents **Hideaways International** ✉ 767 Islington St., Portsmouth, NH 03801 ☎ 603/430-4433 or 800/843-4433 🖷 603/430-4444 ⊕ www.hideaways.com, annual membership $185. **Vacation Home Rentals Worldwide** ✉ 235 Kensington Ave., Norwood, NJ 07648 ☎ 201/767-9393 or 800/633-3284 🖷 201/767-5510 ⊕ www.vhrww.com.

CAMPING

Northern California offers numerous camping options, from family campgrounds with all the amenities to secluded hike-in campsites with no facilities. Some are operated by the state, others are on federal land, and still others are private. Rules vary for each. The most important rule is to always learn and obey local fire regulations; many of Northern California's infamous firestorms are sparked by illegal or improperly extinguished campfires.

You can camp anywhere in a national forest, but in a national park, you must use only specific sites. Whenever possible, book well in advance, especially if your trip will be in summer or on a weekend. Contact the National Parks Reservation Service to reserve a campsite in a national park. ReserveUSA handles reservations for campgrounds administered by the U.S. Forest Service and the Army Corps of Engineers; ReserveAmerica handles reservations for many of the campgrounds in California state parks. On their Web sites you can search for locations, view campground maps, check availability, learn rules and regulations, and find driving directions.

📌 Reservations **National Parks Reservation Service** ☎ 800/436-7275 or 800/365-2267 ⊕ reservations.nps.gov. **ReserveAmerica** ☎ 877/444-6777 or 800/444-7275 ⊕ www.reserveamerica.com. **ReserveUSA** ☎ 877/444-6777 ⊕ www.reserveusa.com.

HOME EXCHANGES

If you would like to exchange your home for someone else's, join a home-exchange organization, which will send you its updated listings of available exchanges for a year and will include your own listing in at least one of them. It's up to you to make specific arrangements.

📌 Exchange Clubs **HomeLink USA** ✉ 2937 NW 9th Terrace, Wilton Manors, FL 33311 ☎ 954/566-2687 or 800/638-3841 🖷 954/566-2783 ⊕ www. homelink.org; $75 yearly for a listing and online access; $45 additional to receive directories. **Intervac U.S.** ✉ 30 Corte San Fernando, Tiburon, CA 94920 ☎ 800/756-4663 🖷 415/435-7440 ⊕ www. intervacus.com; $128 yearly for a listing, online access, and a catalog; $68 without catalog.

HOSTELS

No matter what your age, you can save on lodging costs by staying at hostels. In some 4,500 locations in more than 70 countries around the world, Hostelling International (HI), the umbrella group for a number of national youth-hostel associations, offers single-sex, dorm-style beds and, at many hostels, rooms for couples or families. Membership in any HI national hostel association, open to travelers of all ages, allows you to stay in HI-affiliated hostels at member rates; one-year membership is about $28 for adults (C$35 for a two-year minimum membership in Canada, £15 in the U.K., A$52 in Australia, and NZ$40 in New Zealand); hostels charge about $10–$30 per night. Members have priority if the hostel is full; they're also eligible for discounts around the world, even on rail and bus travel in some countries.

📌 Organizations **Hostelling International–USA** ✉ 8401 Colesville Rd., Suite 600, Silver Spring, MD 20910 ☎ 301/495-1240 🖷 301/495-6697 ⊕ www.

hiusa.org. **Hostelling International–Canada** ✉ 205 Catherine St., Suite 400, Ottawa, Ontario K2P 1C3 ☎ 613/237-7884 or 800/663-5777 🖷 613/237-7868 ⊕ www.hihostels.ca. **YHA England and Wales** ✉ Trevelyan House, Dimple Rd., Matlock, Derbyshire DE4 3YH, U.K. ☎ 0870/870-8808, 0870/770-8868, 0162/959-2600 🖷 0870/770-6127 ⊕ www.yha.org.uk. **YHA Australia** ✉ 422 Kent St., Sydney, NSW 2001 ☎ 02/9261-1111 🖷 02/9261-1969 ⊕ www.yha.com.au. **YHA New Zealand** ✉ Level 1, Moorhouse City, 166 Moorhouse Ave., Box 436, Christchurch ☎ 03/379-9970 or 0800/278-299 🖷 03/365-4476 ⊕ www.yha.org.nz.

HOTELS

All hotels listed have private bath unless otherwise noted.

Most major hotel chains are represented in Northern California. Make any special needs known when you book your reservation. Guarantee your room with a credit card, or many hotels will automatically cancel your reservations if you don't show up by 4 PM. Always inquire about cancellation policies when you book, and get a confirmation number or the name of the agent with whom you spoke; if you cancel, request a cancellation number. Many hotels, like airlines, overbook. It is best to **reconfirm your reservation directly with the hotel on the morning of your arrival date.**

📌 Toll-Free Numbers **Best Western** ☎ 800/528-1234 ⊕ www.bestwestern.com. **Choice** ☎ 800/424-6423 ⊕ www.choicehotels.com. **Clarion** ☎ 800/424-6423 ⊕ www.choicehotels.com. **Comfort Inn** ☎ 800/424-6423 ⊕ www.choicehotels.com. **Days Inn** ☎ 800/325-2525 ⊕ www.daysinn.com. **Doubletree Hotels** ☎ 800/222-8733 ⊕ www.doubletree.com. **Embassy Suites** ☎ 800/362-2779 ⊕ www.embassysuites.com. **Fairfield Inn** ☎ 800/228-2800 ⊕ www.marriott.com. **Four Seasons** ☎ 800/332-3442 ⊕ www.fourseasons.com. **Hilton** ☎ 800/445-8667 ⊕ www.hilton.com. **Holiday Inn** ☎ 800/465-4329 ⊕ www.ichotelsgroup.com. **Howard Johnson** ☎ 800/446-4656 ⊕ www.hojo.com. **Hyatt Hotels & Resorts** ☎ 800/233-1234 ⊕ www.hyatt.com. **Inter-Continental** ☎ 800/327-0200 ⊕ www.ichotelsgroup.com. **La Quinta** ☎ 800/531-5900 ⊕ www.lq.com. **Marriott** ☎ 800/228-9290 ⊕ www.marriott.com. **Nikko Hotels International** ☎ 800/645-5687 ⊕ www.nikkohotels.com. **Omni** ☎ 800/843-6664 ⊕ www.omnihotels.com. **Quality Inn** ☎ 800/424-6423 ⊕ www.

choicehotels.com. **Radisson** ☏ 800/333-3333 ⊕ www.radisson.com. **Ramada** ☏ 800/228-2828, 800/854-7854 international reservations ⊕ www. ramada.com or www.ramadahotels.com. **Red Lion and WestCoast Hotels and Inns** ☏ 800/733-5466 ⊕ www.redlion.com. **Renaissance Hotels & Resorts** ☏ 800/468-3571 ⊕ www.renaissancehotels. com/. **Ritz-Carlton** ☏ 800/241-3333 ⊕ www. ritzcarlton.com. **Sheraton** ☏ 800/325-3535 ⊕ www.starwood.com/sheraton. **Sleep Inn** ☏ 800/ 424-6423 ⊕ www.choicehotels.com. **Westin Hotels & Resorts** ☏ 800/228-3000 ⊕ www.starwood. com/westin. **Wyndham Hotels & Resorts** ☏ 800/ 822-4200 ⊕ www.wyndham.com.

MEDIA

NEWSPAPERS & MAGAZINES

Northern California's major daily newspaper, the *San Francisco Chronicle,* maintains up-to-the-minute Web sites. The region's weekly newspapers are usually the best source of arts and entertainment information, from what shows are on the boards to who's playing the clubs. Visit the Web sites of the *San Francisco Bay Guardian,* the *San Jose Metro* (MetroActive), and *SF Weekly* for the latest information on events in your destination.

🔁 Web Sites **MetroActive** ⊕ www.metroactive. com **San Francisco Bay Guardian** ⊕ www. sfbayguardian.com. **San Francisco Chronicle** ⊕ www.sfgate.com. **SF Weekly** ⊕ www. sfweekly.com.

MONEY MATTERS

San Francisco tends to be an expensive city to visit, and rates at coastal and desert resorts are almost as high. A day's admission to a major theme park can run upward of $45 a head, hotel rates average $150–$250 a night (though you can find cheaper places), and dinners at even moderately priced restaurants often cost $20–$40 per person. Costs in the Gold Country and the Far North are considerably less—many fine Gold Country bed-and-breakfasts charge around $100 a night, and some motels in the Far North charge $50–$70.

Prices throughout this guide are given for adults. Substantially reduced fees are almost always available for children, stu-

dents, and senior citizens. For information on taxes, *see* Taxes.

ATMS

ATMs are readily available throughout Northern California. If you withdraw cash from a bank other than your own, expect to pay a fee of up to $2.50, plus a fee to your own bank. If you're going to very remote areas of the mountains or deserts, take some extra cash with you or find out ahead of time if you can pay with credit cards.

CREDIT CARDS

Throughout this guide, the following abbreviations are used: **AE,** American Express; **D,** Discover; **DC,** Diners Club; **MC,** MasterCard; and **V,** Visa.

🔁 Reporting Lost Cards **American Express** ☏ 800/992-3404. **Diners Club** ☏ 800/234-6377. **Discover** ☏ 800/347-2683. **MasterCard** ☏ 800/ 622-7747. **Visa** ☏ 800/ 847-2911.

NATIONAL PARKS

Look into discount passes to save money on park entrance fees. For $50, the National Parks Pass admits you (and any passengers in your private vehicle) to all national parks, monuments, and recreation areas, as well as other sites run by the National Park Service, for a year. (In parks that charge per person, the pass admits you, your spouse and children, and your parents, when you arrive together.) Camping and parking are extra. The $15 Golden Eagle Pass, a hologram you affix to your National Parks Pass, functions as an upgrade, granting entry to all sites run by the NPS, the U.S. Fish and Wildlife Service, the U.S. Forest Service, and the Bureau of Land Management. The upgrade, which expires with the parks pass, is sold by most national-park, Fish-and-Wildlife, and BLM fee stations. A major percentage of the proceeds from pass sales funds National Parks projects.

Both the Golden Age Passport ($10), for U.S. citizens or permanent residents who are 62 and older, and the Golden Access Passport (free), for persons with disabilities, entitle holders (and any passengers in their private vehicles) to lifetime free entry to all national parks, plus 50% off fees for the use of many park facilities and services. (The discount doesn't always apply to companions.) To obtain them, you must show proof of age and of U.S. citizenship or permanent residency—such as a U.S. passport, driver's license, or birth certificate—and, if requesting Golden Access, proof of disability. The Golden Age and Golden Access passes are available only at NPS-run sites that charge an entrance fee. The National Parks Pass is also available by mail and phone and via the Internet.

🏞 **National Park Foundation** ✉ 11 Dupont Circle NW, Suite 600, Washington, DC 20036 ☎ 202/238-4200 ⊕ www.nationalparks.org. **National Park Service** ✉ National Park Service/Department of Interior, 1849 C St. NW, Washington, DC 20240 ☎ 202/208-6843 ⊕ www.nps.gov. **National Parks Conservation Association** ✉ 1300 19th St. NW, Suite 300, Washington, DC 20036 ☎ 202/223-6722 or 800/628-7275 ⊕ www.npca.org.

🏞 **Passes by Mail & Online National Park Foundation** ⊕ www.nationalparks.org. **National Parks Pass** National Park Foundation ✆ Box 34108, Washington, DC 20043 ☎ 888/467-2757 ⊕ www.nationalparks.org; include a check or money order payable to the National Park Service, plus $3.95 for shipping and handling (allow 8 to 13 business days from date of receipt for pass delivery), or call for passes.

PACKING

When packing for a Northern California vacation, prepare for changes in the weather. Take along sweaters, jackets, and clothes for layering as your best insurance for coping with variations in temperature. Bring along a daypack so you can shed layers midday. Know that San Francisco and other coastal towns can be chilly at any time of the year, especially in summer, when the fog descends in the afternoon. Even when it's chilly, though, it's smart to bring a bathing suit; many lodgings have heated pools, spas, and saunas. Casual dressing is a hallmark of the California lifestyle, but in the evening men will need a jacket and tie at more formal restaurants, and women will be most comfortable in something dressier than sightseeing garb.

In your carry-on luggage, pack an extra pair of eyeglasses or contact lenses and enough of any medication you take to last a few days longer than the entire trip. You may also ask your doctor to write a spare prescription using the drug's generic name, as brand names may vary from country to country. In luggage to be checked, **never pack prescription drugs, valuables, or undeveloped film.** And don't forget to carry with you the addresses of offices that handle refunds of lost traveler's checks. Check *Fodor's How to Pack* (available at online retailers and bookstores everywhere) for more tips.

To avoid customs and security delays, carry medications in their original packaging. Don't pack any sharp objects in your carry-on luggage, including knives of any size or material, scissors, nail clippers, and corkscrews, or anything else that might arouse suspicion.

To avoid having your checked luggage chosen for hand inspection, don't cram bags full. The U.S. Transportation Security Administration suggests packing shoes on top and placing personal items you don't want touched in clear plastic bags.

CHECKING LUGGAGE

You're allowed to carry aboard one bag and one personal article, such as a purse or a laptop computer. Make sure what you carry on fits under your seat or in the overhead bin. Get to the gate early, so you can board as soon as possible, before the overhead bins fill up.

Baggage allowances vary by carrier, destination, and ticket class. On international flights, you're usually allowed to check two bags weighing up to 70 pounds (32 kilograms) each, although a few airlines allow checked bags of up to 88 pounds (40 kilograms) in first class. Some international carriers don't allow more than 66 pounds (30 kilograms) per bag in business class and 44 pounds (20 kilograms) in economy. If you're flying to or through the United Kingdom, your luggage cannot exceed 70 pounds (32 kilograms) per bag. On domestic flights, the limit is usually 50 to 70 pounds (23 to 32 kilograms) per bag. In general, carry-on bags shouldn't exceed 40 pounds (18 kilograms). Most airlines won't accept bags that weigh more than 100 pounds (45 kilograms) on domestic or international flights. Expect to pay a fee for baggage that exceeds weight limits. Check baggage restrictions with your carrier before you pack.

Airline liability for baggage is limited to $2,500 per person on flights within the United States. On international flights it amounts to $9.07 per pound or $20 per kilogram for checked baggage (roughly $640 per 70-pound bag), with a maximum of $634.90 per piece, and $400 per passenger for unchecked baggage. You can buy additional coverage at check-in for about $10 per $1,000 of coverage, but it often excludes a rather extensive list of items, shown on your airline ticket.

Before departure, itemize your bags' contents and their worth, and label the bags with your name, address, and phone number. (If you use your home address, cover it so potential thieves can't see it readily.) Include a label inside each bag and **pack a copy of your itinerary.** At check-in, make sure each bag is correctly tagged with the destination airport's three-letter code. Because some checked bags will be opened for hand inspection, the U.S. Transportation Security Administration recommends that you leave luggage unlocked or use the plastic locks offered at check-in. TSA screeners place an inspection notice inside searched bags, which are re-sealed with a special lock.

If your bag has been searched and contents are missing or damaged, file a claim with the TSA Consumer Response Center as soon as possible. If your bags arrive damaged or fail to arrive at all, file a written report with the airline before leaving the airport.

🔲 Complaints **U.S. Transportation Security Administration Contact Center** ☎ 866/289–9673 ⊕ www.tsa.gov.

SENIOR TRAVEL

To qualify for age-related discounts, mention your senior-citizen status up front when booking hotel reservations (not when checking out) and before you're seated in restaurants (not when paying the bill). Be sure to have identification on hand. When renting a car, ask about promotional car-rental discounts, which can be cheaper than senior-citizen rates.

🔲 Educational Programs **Elderhostel** ⊠ 11 Ave. de Lafayette, Boston, MA 02111 ☎ 877/426–8056, 978/323–4141 international callers, 877/426–2167 TTY 🖷 877/426–2166 ⊕ www.elderhostel.org. **Interhostel** ⊠ University of New Hampshire, 6 Garrison Ave., Durham, NH 03824 ☎ 603/862–1147 or 800/733–9753 🖷 603/862–1113 ⊕ www.learn.unh.edu.

SMOKING

Smoking is illegal in all California bars and restaurants, except on outdoor patios or in smoking rooms. This law is typically not well enforced and some restaurants and bars do not comply, so take your cues from the locals. Hotels and motels are also decreasing their inventory of smoking rooms; inquire at the time you book your reservation if any are available. In addition, a tax is added to cigarettes sold in California, and prices can be as high as $6 per pack. You might want to bring a carton from home.

SPORTS & OUTDOORS

In Northern California you can scale high peaks, hike through sequoia groves or beneath towering redwoods, fish, bike, sail, dive, ski, or golf. Whatever sport you love, you can do it in Northern California.

FISHING

You'll need a license to fish in California. State residents pay $33.35, but nonresidents are charged $89.50 for a one-year license or $33.35 for a 10-day license. Both residents and nonresidents can purchase a two-day license for $16.80. You can purchase them at outlets, such as sporting-goods stores and bait-and-tackle shops, throughout the state, or from DFG field offices (call for locations). The Web site of the California Department of Fish and Game provides information on fishing zones, licenses, and schedules.

🔲 **Department of Fish and Game; Licensing Dept.** ⊠ 3211 S St., Sacramento 95816 ☎ 916/227–2245 ⊕ www.dfg.ca.gov/licensing/fishing/sportfishing.html.

STATE PARKS

California's state parks range from lush coastside recreation areas to ghost towns in the high-mountain deserts of the eastern Sierra Nevada. The extremely useful State Park Web site has a comprehensive list of all them, including facilities lists and campground information.

🔢 **California State Park System** 🕫 Dept. of Parks and Recreation, Box 942896, Sacramento 94296 ☎ 800/777-0369 or 916/653-6995 ⊕ www.parks. ca.gov.

STUDENTS IN NORTHERN CALIFORNIA

🔢 IDs & Services **STA Travel** ✉ 10 Downing St., New York, NY 10014 ☎ 212/627-3111, 800/777-0112 24-hr service center 🖷 212/627-3387 ⊕ www.sta. com. **Travel Cuts** ✉ 187 College St., Toronto, Ontario M5T 1P7, Canada ☎ 800/592-2887 in the U.S., 416/979-2406 or 866/246-9762 in Canada 🖷 416/ 979-8167 ⊕ www.travelcuts.com.

TAXES

Sales tax in Northern California varies from about 7¼% to 8½% and applies to all purchases except for prepackaged food; restaurant food is taxed. Airlines include departure taxes and surcharges in the price of the ticket.

TELEPHONES

Pay phones cost 25¢–50¢ in Northern California.

TIME

California is in the Pacific time zone. Pacific daylight time (PDT) is in effect from early April through late October; the rest of the year the clock is set to Pacific standard time (PST). Clocks are set ahead one hour when daylight saving time begins, back one hour when it ends.

TIPPING

At restaurants, a 15% tip is standard for waitstaff; up to 20% may be expected at more expensive establishments. The same goes for taxi drivers, bartenders, and hairdressers. Coat-check operators usually expect $1; bellhops and porters should get $1–$2 per bag; hotel maids in upscale hotels should get about $2 per day of your stay. A concierge typically receives a tip of $5–$10, with an additional gratuity for special services or favors.

On package tours, conductors and drivers usually get $1 per person from the group as a whole; check whether this has already been figured into your cost. For local sightseeing tours, you may individually tip the driver-guide 10%–15% if he or she has been helpful or informative. Ushers in theaters do not expect tips.

TOURS & PACKAGES

Because everything is prearranged on a prepackaged tour or independent vacation, you spend less time planning—and often get it all at a good price.

BOOKING WITH AN AGENT

Travel agents are excellent resources. But it's a good idea to collect brochures from several agencies, as some agents' suggestions may be influenced by relationships with tour and package firms that reward them for volume sales. If you have a special interest, find an agent with expertise in that area. The American Society of Travel Agents (ASTA) has a database of specialists worldwide; you can log on to the group's Web site to find one near you.

Make sure your travel agent knows the accommodations and other services of the place being recommended. Ask about the hotel's location, room size, beds, and whether it has a pool, room service, or programs for children, if you care about these. Has your agent been there in person or sent others whom you can contact?

Do some homework on your own, too: local tourism boards can provide information about lesser-known and small-niche operators, some of which may sell only direct.

BUYER BEWARE

Each year consumers are stranded or lose their money when tour operators—even large ones with excellent reputations—go out of business. So check out the operator. Ask several travel agents about its reputation, and try to **book with a company that has a consumer-protection program.** (Look for information in the company's brochure.) In the United States, members of the United States Tour Operators Association are required to set aside funds (up to $1 million) to help eligible customers cover payments and travel arrangements in the event that the company defaults. It's also a good idea to choose a company that participates in the American Society of Travel Agents' Tour Operator Program; ASTA will act as mediator in any disputes between you and your tour operator.

Remember that the more your package or tour includes, the better you can predict the ultimate cost of your vacation. Make sure you know exactly what is covered, and beware of hidden costs. Are taxes, tips, and transfers included? Entertainment and excursions? These can add up.

🚩 Tour-Operator Recommendations **American Society of Travel Agents** (⇨ Travel Agencies). **CrossSphere–The Global Association for Packaged Travel** ✉ 546 E. Main St., Lexington, KY 40508 ☎ 859/226-4444 or 800/682-8886 🖷 859/226-4414 ⊕ www.CrossSphere.com. **United States Tour Operators Association** (USTOA) ✉ 275 Madison Ave., Suite 2014, New York, NY 10016 ☎ 212/599-6599 🖷 212/599-6744 ⊕ www.ustoa.com.

TRAIN TRAVEL

Amtrak's *California Zephyr* train from Chicago via Denver terminates in Oakland. The *Coast Starlight* train travels between Los Angeles and Seattle.

🚩 Train Information **Amtrak** ☎ 800/872-7245 ⊕ www.amtrak.com.

TRAVEL AGENCIES

A good travel agent puts your needs first. Look for an agency that has been in business at least five years, emphasizes customer service, and has someone on staff who specializes in your destination. In addition, **make sure the agency belongs to a professional trade organization.** The American Society of Travel Agents (ASTA) has more than 10,000 members in some 140 countries, enforces a strict code of ethics, and will step in to mediate agent-client disputes involving ASTA members. ASTA also maintains a directory of agents on its Web site; ASTA's TravelSense.org, a trip planning and travel advice site, can also help to locate a travel agent who caters to your needs. (If a travel agency is also acting as your tour operator, *see* Buyer Beware *in* Tours & Packages.)

🚩 Local Agent Referrals **American Society of Travel Agents** (ASTA) ✉ 1101 King St., Suite 200, Alexandria, VA 22314 ☎ 703/739-2782 or 800/965-

2782 24-hr hotline 🖷 703/684-8319 ⊕ www.astanet.com and www.travelsense.org. **Association of British Travel Agents** ✉ 68-71 Newman St., London W1T 3AH ☎ 020/7637-2444 🖷 020/7637-0713 ⊕ www.abta.com. **Association of Canadian Travel Agencies** ✉ 130 Albert St., Suite 1705, Ottawa, Ontario K1P 5G4 ☎ 613/237-3657 🖷 613/237-7052 ⊕ www.acta.ca. **Australian Federation of Travel Agents** ✉ Level 3, 309 Pitt St., Sydney, NSW 2000 ☎ 02/9264-3299 or 1300/363-416 🖷 02/9264-1085 ⊕ www.afta.com.au. **Travel Agents' Association of New Zealand** ✉ Level 5, Tourism and Travel House, 79 Boulcott St., Box 1888, Wellington 6001 ☎ 04/499-0104 🖷 04/499-0786 ⊕ www.taanz.org.nz.

VISITOR INFORMATION

Learn more about foreign destinations by checking government-issued travel advisories and country information. For a broader picture, consider information from more than one country.

For general information about Northern California, contact the California Travel and Tourism Commission. The commission's Web site has travel tips, events calendars, and other resources, and the site will link you—via the Regions icon—to the Web sites of city and regional tourism offices and attractions. For the numbers of regional and city visitor bureaus and chambers of commerce *see* the A to Z section at the end of each chapter.

If you are coming to Northern California from overseas, you can check with your home government for official travel advisories and destination information. For a broader picture, consider information from more than one country.

🚩 Tourist Information **California Travel and Tourism Commission** ✉ 980 9th St., Suite 480, Sacramento 95814 ☎ 916/444-4429 (information) or 800/862-2543 (brochures) 🖷 916/444-0410 ⊕ www.gocalif.ca.gov.

🚩 Government Advisories **Australian Department of Foreign Affairs and Trade** ☎ 300/139-281 travel advisories, 02/6261-1299 Consular Travel Advice ⊕ www.smartraveller.gov.au or www.dfat.gov.au. **Consular Affairs Bureau of Canada** ☎ 800/267-6788 or 613/944-6788 ⊕ www.voyage.gc.ca. **New Zealand Ministry of Foreign Affairs and Trade** ☎ 04/439-8000 ⊕ www.mft.govt.nz. **U.K. Foreign and Commonwealth Office** ✉ Travel Advice Unit,

Consular Directorate, Old Admiralty Building, London SW1A 2PA ☎ 0870/606-0290 or 020/7008-1500 ⊕ www.fco.gov.uk/travel.

WEB SITES

Do check out the World Wide Web when planning your trip. You'll find everything from weather forecasts to virtual tours of famous cities. Be sure to visit Fodors.com (⊕ www.fodors.com), a complete travel-planning site. You can research prices and book plane tickets, hotel rooms, rental cars, vacation packages, and more. In addition, you can post your pressing questions in the Travel Talk section. Other planning tools include a currency converter and weather reports, and there are loads of links to travel resources.

The California Parks Department site has the lowdown on state-run parks and other recreational areas. A must-visit for outdoors and adventure travel enthusiasts, the Great Outdoor Recreation Page is arranged into easily navigated categories. The site of the Wine Institute, which is based in San Francisco, provides events listings and detailed information about the California wine industry and has links to the home pages of regional wine associations. And if you're fascinated by earthquakes, the U.S. Geological Survey is a must-visit.

🗗 Web Sites **California Parks Department** ⊕ www.parks.ca.gov. **Great Outdoor Recreation Page** ⊕ www.gorp.com. **USGS Earthquake Survey** ⊕ http://earthquake.usgs.gov. **Wine Institute** ⊕ www.wineinstitute.org.

San Francisco
With Sausalito & Berkeley

WORD OF MOUTH

"A walk across the Golden Gate Bridge is an unforgettable experience. I live here and am thrilled every time I drive across. The views are unsurpassed."

—philip bewley

"Quince is absolutely amazing! The service is astounding (ask for a Suzanne table) and the food is show-stopping. You really should order from each 'course' so you can experience them all. The pastas are incredible."

—dutchbunny

IN ITS FIRST LIFE San Francisco was little more than a small, well-situated settlement. Founded by Spaniards in 1776, it was prized for its natural harbor, so commodious that "all the navies of the world might fit inside it," as one visitor wrote. Around 1849 the discovery of gold at John Sutter's sawmill in the nearby Sierra foothills transformed the sleepy little settlement into a city of 30,000. Millions of dollars' worth of gold was panned and blasted out of the hills, the impetus for the development of a western Wall Street. Fueled by the 1859 discovery of a fabulously rich vein of silver in Virginia City, Nevada, San Francisco became the West Coast's cultural fulcrum and major transportation hub, and its population soared to 342,000. In 1869 the transcontinental railway was completed, linking the once-isolated western capital to the East. San Francisco had become a major city of the United States.

Loose, tolerant, and even *licentious* are words used to describe San Francisco. Bohemian communities thrive here. As early as the 1860s the Barbary Coast—a collection of taverns, whorehouses, and gambling joints along Pacific Avenue close to the waterfront—was famous, or infamous. North Beach, the city's Little Italy, became the home of the Beat movement in the 1950s (Herb Caen, the city's best-known columnist, coined the term *beatnik*). Lawrence Ferlinghetti's City Lights, a bookstore and publishing house that still stands on Columbus Avenue, brought out, among other titles, Allen Ginsberg's *Howl* and *Kaddish.* In the 1960s the Free Speech movement began at the University of California at Berkeley, and Stanford's David Harris, who went to prison for defying the draft, numbered among the nation's most famous student leaders. The Haight-Ashbury district became synonymous with hippiedom, giving rise to such legendary bands as Jefferson Airplane and the Grateful Dead. Southwest of the Haight is the onetime Irish neighborhood known as the Castro, which during the 1970s became identified with gay and lesbian liberation.

Technically speaking, it's only California's fourth-largest city, behind Los Angeles, San Diego, and nearby San Jose. But that statistic is misleading: the Bay Area, extending from the bedroom communities north of Oakland and Berkeley south through the peninsula and the San Jose area, is really one continuous megacity, with San Francisco as its heart.

EXPLORING SAN FRANCISCO

Updated by
Andy Moore

YOU COULD LIVE IN SAN FRANCISCO a month and ask no greater entertainment than walking through it," wrote Inez Hayes Irwin, author of *The Californiacs,* an effusive 1921 homage to the state of California and the City by the Bay. Her claim remains true today: as in the 1920s, touring on foot is the best way to experience this diverse metropolis.

San Francisco is a relatively small city. About 800,000 residents live on a 46½-square-mi tip of land between San Francisco Bay and the Pacific Ocean. San Franciscans cherish the city's colorful past; many older buildings have been spared from demolition and nostalgically converted

GREAT ITINERARIES

Numbers in the text correspond to numbers in the margin and on the Far North map.

IF YOU HAVE 3 DAYS. Spend your first morning checking out Fisherman's Wharf and Pier 39. Jump a cable car (the Powell–Hyde line is the most dramatic) at the wharf and take in sweeping views of the bay as you rattle your way to Union Square. Charming Maiden Lane is worth a look. On the second day, begin with a walk on the Golden Gate Bridge, then explore North Beach, the Italian quarter, filled with tempting food, Beat-era landmarks, and reminders of the city's bawdy past. Move on to labyrinthine Chinatown. Begin your third day by taking a ferry from Pier 41 to the infamous Alcatraz prison. Spend the rest of the day in whichever neighborhood most appeals to you: the Haight, the epicenter of 1960s counterculture, whose streets are lined with excellent music and bookshops and cool vintage-clothing stores; colorful, gay-friendly Castro, brimming with shops and cafés; or the mural-filled Mission District, a neighborhood of twentysomething

hipsters and working-class Latino families. Simple Mission Dolores, built in 1776, is San Francisco's oldest standing structure.

IF YOU HAVE 5 DAYS. Follow the three-day itinerary above, and on the morning of your fourth day walk up Telegraph Hill to Coit Tower; you'll be rewarded with breathtaking views of the bay and the city's tightly stacked homes. Head for the Marina neighborhood, and if you love chocolate, stop at Ghirardelli Square, which includes a shopping center and the tempting Ghirardelli Chocolate Factory. Make a beeline for the end of the Marina and the stunning Palace of Fine Arts. Don't miss the Palace's hands-on science museum, the Exploratorium. In the afternoon join in-line skaters, joggers, and walkers in picnic-perfect Golden Gate Park—more than 1,000 acres of greenery stretching from the Haight to the Pacific. On Day 5, explore one of the neighborhoods you missed on Day 3, and in the afternoon take the ferry to Sausalito or head to the East Bay to explore formerly radical, still-offbeat Berkeley.

into modern offices and shops, and longtime locals rue the sites that got away. The neighborhoods of San Francisco retain strong cultural, political, and ethnic identities. Locals know this pluralism is the real life of the city. Experiencing San Francisco means visiting the neighborhoods: the colorful Mission District, the gay Castro, countercultural Haight Street, swank Pacific Heights, lively Chinatown, ever bohemian North Beach, and arts- and news media–oriented SoMa, among others.

Exploring by car involves navigating a maze of one-way streets and restricted parking zones. San Francisco's famed 40-plus hills can also be a problem for drivers who are new to the terrain. Cable cars, buses, and trolleys are better options and can take you to or near many attractions.

Numbers in the text correspond to numbers in the margin and on the neighborhood maps.

Union Square Area

Much of San Francisco may feel like a collection of small towns strung together, but the Union Square area bristles with big-city bravado. The city's finest department stores (including Bloomingdale's, as of fall 2006) do business here, along with such exclusive emporiums as Tiffany & Co., Prada, and Coach, and such big-name franchises as Niketown, the Original Levi's Store, Apple Store, and Virgin Megastore. There are several dozen hotels within a three-block walk of the square, and the downtown theater district and many fine arts galleries are nearby.

A GOOD WALK

Begin three blocks south of Union Square at the **San Francisco Visitor Information Center ❶** ↱, on the lower level of Hallidie Plaza at Powell and Market streets. Up the escalators on the east side of the plaza, where Powell dead-ends into Market, lies the **cable-car terminus ❷** for two of the city's three lines. Head north on Powell from the terminus to Geary Street, make a left, and walk west 1½ blocks into the theater district for a peek at the **Geary Theater ❸**. Backtrack on the north side of Geary Street, where the sturdy and stately **Westin St. Francis Hotel ❹** dominates Powell between Geary and Post streets. **Union Square ❺** is across Powell from the hotel's main entrance.

Maiden Lane ❻ is a two-block alley directly across Stockton Street from Union Square that runs east parallel to Geary. When the lane ends at Kearny Street, turn left, walk 1½ blocks to Sutter Street, make a right, and walk a half block to the **Hallidie Building ❼**. After viewing this historic building, reverse direction and head west 1½ blocks up Sutter to the fanciful Beaux-Arts–style **Hammersmith Building ❽**, on the southwest corner of Sutter Street and Grant Avenue. In the middle of the next block, at 450 Sutter, stands a glorious 1928 art deco skyscraper, a masterpiece of terra-cotta and other detailing; handsome Maya-inspired designs adorn its exterior and interior surfaces. From here, backtrack a half block east to Stockton Street and take a right. In front of the Grand Hyatt hotel sits **Ruth Asawa's Fantasy Fountain ❾**. Union Square is a half block south on Stockton.

TIMING   Allow two hours to see everything around Union Square. If you're a shopper, give yourself extra time.

What to See

☞ **❷ Cable-car terminus.** San Francisco's signature red cable cars were declared National Landmarks—the only ones that move—in 1964. Two of the three operating lines begin and end their runs at Powell and Market streets. The more dramatic Powell–Mason line climbs up Nob Hill, then winds through North Beach to Fisherman's Wharf. The Powell–Hyde line also crosses Nob Hill but then continues up Russian Hill and down Hyde Street to Victorian Park, across from the Buena Vista Café and near Ghirardelli Square. Buy your ticket ($3 one-way) on board or at the police/information booth near the turnaround. If it's just the experience of riding a cable car you're after, board the less-busy California line at Van Ness Avenue and ride it down to the Hyatt Regency hotel. ✉ *Powell and Market Sts., Union Sq.*

PLEASURES & PASTIMES

THE BAY. The bay provides a stunning backdrop to a visit here. San Franciscans often gravitate toward spaces with views of the water, especially the shoreline promenades of the Embarcadero and Marina, lounges such as the Top of the Mark, and parks that cling precariously to the hillsides. On a sunny day, simply hopping the ferry to Oakland or Sausalito and enjoying a beer among commuters is an inexpensive but exquisite pleasure.

THE HILLS. Driving the hills in San Francisco is like riding a roller coaster, as you creep up on the crest of a hill where you can't see the street coming up to greet your front tires until the very last second. If the gradient of streets on Russian Hill, Nob Hill, and Potrero Hill intimidates you, a cab ride down California Street or a cable-car ride down Hyde Street can be just as hair-raising, and you'll be free to enjoy those dazzling bay views to boot.

HIDDEN LANES & STAIRWAYS. San Francisco is full of hidden garden lanes and alleyways, as well as stairways that trace the hills between rows of homes. Macondray Lane, on Russian Hill, is a gem, worth seeking out for its lovely gardens. Also on Russian Hill, the Vallejo Steps stretch two taxing blocks from Jones Street to Mason Street. In the middle cascades Ina Coolbrith Park, whose manicured grounds and wide-open views make this one of the most popular stairway walks in the city.

GREEN SPACES. San Francisco is an outdoor-person's dream. Golden Gate Park, with more than 1,000 acres of trails and fields, is especially popular with cyclists and in-line skaters. Less famous but equally accessible is the Presidio, with almost 1,500 acres of hilly, wooded trails and breathtaking views of the bay and the Pacific. This former military base at the foot of the Golden Gate Bridge is the city's secret forest, the easiest place in San Francisco to forget you're in a big city.

CAFÉS. To experience life in San Francisco the way the locals do, while away a few hours in its cafés. The city has hundreds, each a microcosm of its neighborhood. And there's more on tap than caffeine—here you can sample some of the city's famous gastronomic fare on the (relative) cheap, without having to make a reservation weeks in advance.

❸ **Geary Theater.** The American Conservatory Theater (ACT), one of North America's leading repertory companies, uses the 1,035-seat Geary as its main venue. Built in 1910, the theater has a serious neoclassic design lightened by colorful carved terra-cotta columns depicting a cornucopia of fruits. Damaged heavily in the 1989 earthquake, the Geary has been completely restored to gilded splendor. ⊠ *415 Geary St., box office at 405 Geary St., Union Sq.* ☎ *415/749–2228.*

❼ **Hallidie Building.** Named for cable-car inventor Andrew S. Hallidie, this 1918 structure is best viewed from across the street. Willis Polk's revolutionary glass-curtain wall—believed to be the world's first such facade—hangs a foot beyond the reinforced concrete of the frame. The reflecting glass, decorative exterior fire escapes that appear to be metal

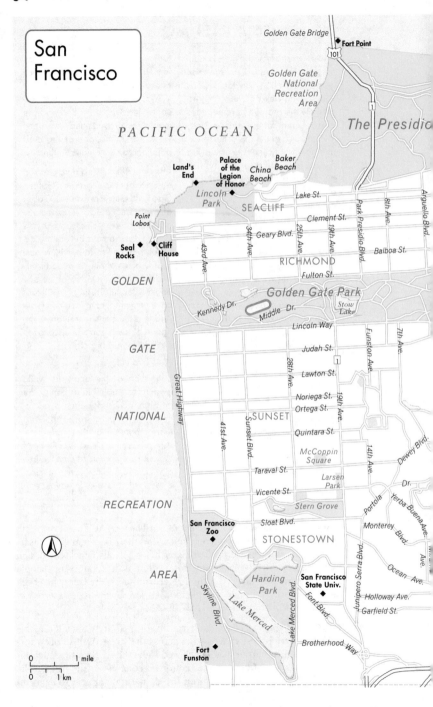

San
Francisco

PACIFIC OCEAN

Golden Gate Bridge
Fort Point
101

Golden Gate
National
Recreation
Area

The Presidio

Land's
End

Palace
of the
Legion
of Honor

China
Beach

Baker
Beach

Lincoln
Park

Lake St.

SEACLIFF

Clement St.

Point
Lobos

34th Ave.

25th Ave.

19th Ave.

Park Presidio Blvd.

8th Ave.

Arguello Blvd.

Geary Blvd.

Seal
Rocks

Cliff
House

43rd Ave.

RICHMOND

Balboa St.

Fulton St.

GOLDEN

Kennedy Dr.

Golden Gate Park

Middle Dr.

Stow
Lake

Lincoln Way

GATE

Judah St.

Funston Ave.

7th Ave.

28th Ave.

Lawton St.

19th Ave.

NATIONAL

Great Highway

41st Ave.

Sunset Blvd.

SUNSET

Noriega St.

Ortega St.

Quintara St.

McCoppin
Square

14th Ave.

Dewey Blvd.

Taraval St.

Larsen
Park

Dr.

Vicente St.

Stern Grove

Portola

Yerba Buena Ave.

RECREATION

Sloat Blvd.

Monterey Blvd.

San Francisco
Zoo

STONESTOWN

Ave.

AREA

Harding
Park

San Francisco
State Univ.

Juniper Serra Blvd.

Ocean Ave.

Skyline Blvd.

Lake Merced

Lake Merced Blvd.

Font Blvd.

Holloway Ave.

Garfield St.

Fort
Funston

Brotherhood Way

0   1 mile

0   1 km

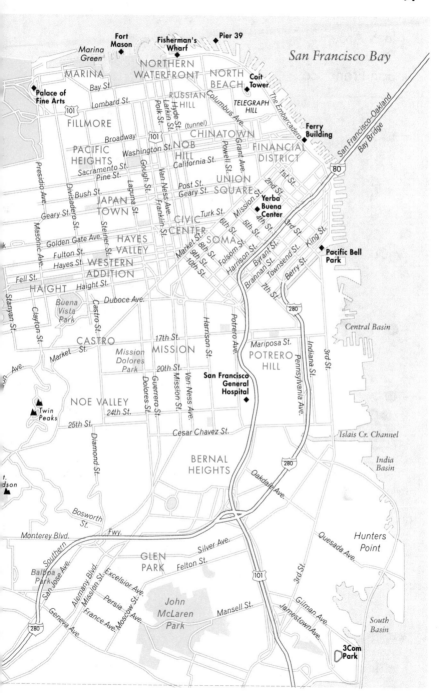

In & Around Downtown San Francisco

Chestnut St.
Lombard St.
46
47
Tattoo Art Museum ◆
Chestnut St.
Lombard St.
Greenwich St.
35
Filbert St.

Polk St.
Larkin St.
Hyde St.
Leavenworth St.
Jones St.
Powell-Mason Cable Car
Columbus Ave.

← Wedding Houses

Franklin St.
Van Ness Ave.
Gough St.
Octavia St.

RUSSIAN HILL

44 **45**
43
NORTH BEACH
34 Valf
33

Powell-Hyde Cable Car

Broadway
Broadway Tunnel
Pacific Ave.
Taylor St.
Powell St.
Stockton St.

49
48 **50**
←
51

Jackson St.
42
30
29 **28**
Wav Pl.

Lafayette Park

Washington St.
Clay St.
Sacramento St.
NOB HILL
Jones St.
31 **32**
CHINATOWN
38 **39** **40**

52
California St.
41
California Street Cable Car
Pine St.
Chinatown Gate **25**

← **53**
Octavia St.
Gough St.
Franklin St.
Van Ness Ave.
Polk St.
Larkin St.
Hyde St.

Bush St.
UNION SQUARE
9 **8**

Sutter St.
Post St.
Leavenworth St.
4 **5**
Union Square
6 Maide. Ln.

← **54**
← **55** **56**
St. Mary's Cathedral ◆

Geary Blvd.
O'Farrell St.
TENDERLOIN

Geary St.
O'Farrell St.
3
Market St.
Yer Bue Gard

Jefferson Square

Ellis St.
Eddy St.
Visitor Information Center **1**
2
Yerba Buena Lane
12

ba Powell St. BART

HAYES VALLEY

McAllister St.
Golden Gate Ave.
CIVIC CENTER
58
Fulton St.
Turk St.
Mission St.
6th St.
5th St.

60
59 City Hall
Civic Center BART
57
United Nations Plaza
ba
Howard St.
SOUTH OF MARKET (SOMA)

Grove St.
Hayes St.
8th St.
7th St.

KEY
ba BART stop
► Start of walk

0 _____ 1/2 mile
0 _____ 500 meters

balconies, and Venetian Gothic cornice are worth noting. ⊠ *130 Sutter St., between Kearny and Montgomery Sts., Union Sq.*

8 Hammersmith Building. Glass walls and a colorful design distinguish this four-story Beaux-Arts–style structure, built in 1907. The Foundation for Architectural Heritage once described the building as a "commercial jewel box." Appropriately, it was designed for use as a jewelry store. ⊠ *301 Sutter St., at Grant Ave., Union Sq.*

6 Maiden Lane. Known as Morton Street in the raffish Barbary Coast era, this former red-light district reported at least one murder a week during the late 19th century. After the 1906 fire destroyed the brothels, the street emerged as Maiden Lane, and it has since become a chic pedestrian mall stretching two blocks, between Stockton and Kearny streets.

With its circular interior ramp and skylights, the handsome brick 1948 structure at **140 Maiden Lane,** the only Frank Lloyd Wright building in San Francisco, is said to have been his model for the Guggenheim Museum in New York. **Xanadu Tribal Arts** (☎ 415/392–9999), a gallery showcasing Baltic, Latin-American, and African folk art, occupies space at 140 Maiden Lane. ⊠ *Between Stockton and Kearny Sts., Union Sq.*

9 Ruth Asawa's Fantasy Fountain. Local artist Ruth Asawa's sculpture, a wonderland of real and mythical creatures, honors the city's hills, bridges, and architecture. Children and friends helped Asawa shape the hundreds of tiny figures from baker's clay; these were assembled on 41 large panels from which molds were made for the bronze casting. ⊠ *In front of Grand Hyatt at 345 Stockton St., Union Sq.*

▶ **1 San Francisco Visitor Information Center.** A multilingual staff operates this facility below the cable-car terminus. Staffers answer questions and provide maps and pamphlets. You can also pick up discount coupons and hotel brochures here. ⊠ *Hallidie Plaza, lower level, Powell and Market Sts., Union Sq.* ☎ *415/391–2000 or 415/283–0177* ⊕ *www.sfvisitor. org* ☉ *Weekdays 9–5, Sat. 9–3; also Sun. 9–3 June–Oct.*

5 Union Square. The heart of San Francisco's downtown since 1850, the 2½-acre square takes its name from the violent pro-union demonstrations staged here before the Civil War. At center stage, the *Victory Monument,* by Robert Ingersoll Aitken, commemorates Commodore George Dewey's victory over the Spanish fleet at Manila in 1898. The 97-foot Corinthian column, topped by a bronze figure symbolizing naval conquest, was dedicated by Theodore Roosevelt in 1903 and withstood the 1906 earthquake. An open-air stage and central plaza, a café, gardens, and a visitor information booth draw strollers to the square. Four sculptures by the artist R. M. Fischer preside over the space. ⊠ *Bordered by Powell, Stockton, Post, and Geary Sts., Union Sq.*

4 Westin St. Francis Hotel. The second-oldest hotel in the city, established in 1904, was conceived by railroad baron and financier Charles Crocker and his associates as a hostelry for their millionaire friends. After the hotel was ravaged by the 1906 fire, a larger, more luxurious Italian Renaissance–style residence was opened in 1907. The hotel's checkered past includes the ill-fated 1921 bash in the suite of the silent-film comedian

Fatty Arbuckle, at which a woman became ill and later died. In 1975 Sara Jane Moore, standing among a crowd outside the hotel, attempted to shoot then-president Gerald Ford. ⊠ *335 Powell St., at Geary St., Union Sq.* ☎ *415/397–7000* ⊕ *www.westinstfrancis.com.*

SoMa & the Embarcadero

SoMa (South of Market) was once known as South of the Slot, in reference to the cable-car slot that ran up Market Street. Industry took over most of the area when the 1906 earthquake collapsed most of the homes into their quicksand bases. Huge sections of the then-industrial neighborhood were razed in the 1960s to make way for an ambitious multi-use redevelopment project, but squabbling over zoning and other issues delayed construction well into the 1970s. In the meantime, alternative artists and the gay leather crowd set up shop. Although many artists moved farther southwest within SoMa or to the Mission District when urban renewal began in earnest, they still show their work at the Center for the Arts at Yerba Buena Gardens and other galleries. Today the gentrified South Park area, not long ago the buzzing epicenter of new-media activity, has lost much of its new-economy luster. But despite the dot-com meltdown, the construction of pricey live-work lofts and major commercial ventures continues apace, causing many to scratch their heads in wonder. Glitzy projects coexist uneasily with still-gritty stretches of Mission and Market streets, creating a friction that keeps the neighborhood interesting.

A GOOD WALK

The **San Francisco Museum of Modern Art** ⑩ ► dominates a half block of 3rd Street between Howard and Mission streets. Use the crosswalk near SFMOMA's entrance to head across 3rd Street into Yerba Buena Gardens. To your right after you've walked a few steps, a sidewalk leads to the main entrance of the **Yerba Buena Center for the Arts** ⑪. Straight ahead is the East Garden of Yerba Buena Gardens and beyond that, on the 4th Street side of the block, is the **Metreon** ⑫ entertainment, retail, and restaurant complex. A second-level walkway in the southern portion of the East Garden, above the Martin Luther King Jr. waterfall, arches over Howard Street, leading to the main (south) entrance to Moscone Convention Center and the **Rooftop@Yerba Buena Gardens** ⑬ facilities.

Exit the rooftop, head north up 4th Street to Mission Street, and walk east on Mission (toward SFMOMA) past the monolithic San Francisco Marriott, also known as the "jukebox" Marriott because of its exterior design. Just before St. Patrick's Catholic Church, turn left onto the pedestrian walkway Yerba Buena Lane past a water course, shops, and restaurants to the plaza on Market Street at the foot of Grant Avenue. The Mexican Museum and the Contemporary Jewish Museum were to open on this block in 2005, but problems with funding are delaying the projects. Head east on Market Street past Lotta's Fountain, and then walk south on 3rd Street to Mission Street; a half block east on Mission is the headquarters of the **California Historical Society** ⑭. Across the street and a few steps farther east is the **Cartoon Art Museum** ⑮.

Continue east on Mission Street, turn left onto New Montgomery Street, and continue to Market Street and the **Palace Hotel** ⑯. Enter via the Market Street entrance, checking out the Pied Piper Bar, Garden Court restaurant, and main lobby. Exit via the lobby onto New Montgomery Street and make a left, which will bring you back to Market Street. Turn right and head toward the waterfront. Toward the end of Market a three-tier pedestrian mall connects the five buildings of the **Embarcadero Center** ⑰ office-retail complex. Across the busy Embarcadero roadway from the plaza stands the port's trademark, the **Ferry Building** ⑱.

The ground floor of the ornate 1889 Audiffred Building, on the southwest corner of the Embarcadero and Mission Street, houses Boulevard restaurant. Head west on Mission Street along the side of Boulevard and cross Steuart Street. In the middle of the block is the entrance to the historic sections of **Rincon Center** ⑲, worth seeing for the famous murals and the old Rincon Annex Post Office. Continue south within the center to its newer portions and make a left as you exit through the doors near Chalkers Billiards. Across Steuart Street is the Jewish Community Federation Building, which is housing the **Contemporary Jewish Museum** ⑳ for now.

TIMING   The walk above takes a good two hours, more if you visit the museums and galleries. SFMOMA merits about two hours each; the Center for the Arts and the Cartoon Art Museum, 45 minutes each.

What to See

⑭ **California Historical Society.** The society, founded in 1871, administers a vast repository of Californiana—500,000 photographs, 150,000 manuscripts, thousands of books, periodicals, and paintings, as well as gold-rush paraphernalia. ✉ *678 Mission St., SoMa* ☎ *415/357–1848* ⊕ *www. californiahistoricalsociety.org* ✉ *$3, free 1st Tues. of month* ☽ *Wed.–Sat. noon–4:30; galleries close between exhibitions.*

⑮ **Cartoon Art Museum.** Krazy Kat, Zippy the Pinhead, Batman, and other colorful cartoon icons greet you at the Cartoon Art Museum. In addition to a 12,000-piece permanent collection (only a small selection of which is on display), a 3,000-volume library, and a CD-ROM gallery, changing exhibits examine everything from the influence of underground comics to the output of women and African-American cartoonists. ✉ *655 Mission St., SoMa* ☎ *415/227–8666* ⊕ *www.cartoonart. org* ✉ *$6, pay what you wish 1st Tues. of month* ☽ *Tues.–Sun. 11–5.*

⑳ **Contemporary Jewish Museum.** Exhibits at this small museum (previously known as the Jewish Museum San Francisco) survey Jewish art, history, and culture. Call ahead before visiting; it sometimes closes between exhibits. In 2007 the museum plans to move into state-of-the-art, Daniel Libeskind–designed quarters south of Market, on Mission Street between 3rd and 4th streets. ✉ *121 Steuart St., Embarcadero* ☎ *415/591–8800* ⊕ *www.jmsf.org* ✉ *$5, free 3rd Mon. of month* ☽ *Sun.–Thurs. noon–6.*

⑰ **Embarcadero Center.** John Portman designed this five-block complex built during the 1970s and early 1980s. Shops and restaurants abound on the first three levels; there's ample office space on the floors above. Louise Nevelson's 54-foot-tall black-steel sculpture, *Sky Tree,* stands guard over Building 3 and is among 20-plus artworks throughout the center.

✉ *Clay St., between Battery St. and Embarcadero, Embarcadero* ☎ *415/ 772–0734* ⊕ *www.embarcaderocenter.com.*

★ ⓲ **Ferry Building.** The beacon of the port area, erected in 1896, has a 230-foot clock tower modeled after the campanile of the cathedral in Seville, Spain. On the morning of April 18, 1906, the four great clock faces on the tower, powered by the swinging of a 14-foot pendulum, stopped at 5:17—the moment the great earthquake struck—and stayed still for 12 months. Today the building houses local favorites such as Acme Bread, Scharffen Berger Chocolate, Cowgirl Creamery, and Slanted Door (San Francisco's beloved Vietnamese restaurant), which share space with the street-level gourmet Market Hall. The waterfront promenade extends from the piers on the north side of the building south to the Bay Bridge, and ferries behind the building sail to Sausalito, Larkspur, Tiburon, and the East Bay. ✉ *Embarcadero at foot of Market St., Embarcadero.*

☾ ⑫ **Metreon.** Child's play meets the 21st century at this Sony entertainment center. An interactive play area is based on Maurice Sendak's *Where the Wild Things Are.* Portal 1, a high-tech interactive arcade, includes an Extreme Sports Adventure Room. A 15-screen multiplex, an IMAX theater, retail shops, and outposts of some of the city's favorite restaurants are all part of the complex. ✉ *101 4th St., between Mission and Howard Sts., SoMa* ☎ *800/638–7366* ⊕ *www.metreon.com.*

⓰ **Palace Hotel.** The city's oldest hotel, a Sheraton property, opened in 1875. Fire destroyed the original Palace after the 1906 earthquake, despite the hotel's 28,000-gallon reservoir fed by four artesian wells; the current building dates from 1909. President Warren Harding died at the Palace while still in office in 1923, and the body of King Kalakaua of Hawaii spent a night here after he died in San Francisco in 1891. The managers play up this ghoulish past with talk of a haunted guest room. ✉ *2 New Montgomery St., SoMa* ☎ *415/512–1111* ⊕ *www.sfpalace.com.*

⓳ **Rincon Center.** A sheer five-story column of water resembling a mini-rain-storm is the centerpiece of the indoor arcade at this mostly modern of-fice-retail complex. The lobby of the streamline moderne–style former post office on the Mission Street side contains a Works Project Administration mural by Anton Refregier. The 27 panels depict California life from the days when Native Americans were the state's sole inhabitants, through World War I. A permanent exhibit below the murals contains photographs and artifacts of life in the Rincon area in the 1800s. ✉ *Bordered by Steuart, Spear, Mission, and Howard Sts., SoMa.*

☾ ⓭ **Rooftop@Yerba Buena Gardens.** Fun is the order of the day among these brightly colored concrete and corrugated-metal buildings atop Moscone Convention Center South. The historic **Looff carousel** ($2 for two rides) twirls daily 11–6. South of the carousel is **Zeum** (☎ 415/777–2800 ⊕ www.zeum.org), a high-tech, interactive arts-and-technology center ($7) geared toward children ages eight and over. Kids can make Clay-mation videos, work in a computer lab, and view exhibits and performances. Zeum is open 11–5 Tuesday through Sunday in summer and Wednesday through Sunday in winter. Also part of the rooftop complex are gardens, an ice-skating rink, and a bowling alley. ✉ *4th St. between Howard and Folsom Sts., SoMa.*

▶ ⑩ **San Francisco Museum of Modern Art** (SFMOMA). Mario Botta designed
Fodor'sChoice the striking SFMOMA facility, completed in early 1995, which consists
★ of a sienna brick facade and a central tower of alternating bands of black and white stone. Inside, natural light from the tower floods the central atrium and some of the museum's galleries. Works by Henri Matisse, Pablo Picasso, Georgia O'Keeffe, Frida Kahlo, Jackson Pollock, and Andy Warhol form the heart of the diverse permanent collection. The photography holdings are also strong. ✉ *151 3rd St., SoMa* ☎ *415/357-4000* ⊕ *www.sfmoma.org* ✑ *$10, free 1st Tues. of month, ½ price Thurs. 6–9* ☉ *Late May–early Sept., Fri.–Tues. 11–6, Thurs. 11–9; early Sept.–late May, Fri.–Tues. 11–6, Thurs. 11–9; call for hrs for special exhibits.*

⑪ **Yerba Buena Center for the Arts.** The dance, music, theater, visual arts, films, and videos presented at this facility in Yerba Buena Gardens range from the community based to the international and lean toward the cutting edge. ✉ *701 Mission St., SoMa* ☎ *415/978-2787* ⊕ *www.ybca.org* ✑ *Galleries $6, free 1st Tues. of month* ☉ *Galleries Thurs.–Sat. noon–8; Sun., Tues., and Wed. noon–5; box office Tues.–Sun. 11–6.*

Heart of the Barbary Coast

It was on Montgomery Street, in the Financial District, that Sam Brannan proclaimed the historic gold discovery that took place at Sutter's Mill on January 24, 1848. The gold rush brought streams of people from across America and Europe, transforming the onetime frontier town into a cosmopolitan city almost overnight. Other fortune seekers, including saloon keepers, gamblers, and prostitutes, all flocked to the so-called Barbary Coast (now Jackson Square and the Financial District). Since then the red-light establishments have edged upward to the Broadway strip of North Beach, and Jackson Square evolved into a sedate district of refurbished brick buildings decades ago.

| A GOOD WALK | Bronze sidewalk plaques mark the street corners along the 50-sight, approximately 3¾-mi Barbary Coast Trail. The trail begins at the Old Mint, at 5th and Mission streets, and runs north through downtown, Chinatown, Jackson Square, North Beach, and Fisherman's Wharf, ending at Aquatic Park. For information about the sites on the trail, pick up a brochure at the San Francisco Visitor Information Center (⇨ Union Square Area). |

To catch the highlights of the Barbary Coast Trail and a glimpse of a few important Financial District structures, start on Montgomery Street, between California and Sacramento streets, at the **Wells Fargo Bank History Museum** ㉑ ▶.

Two blocks north on Montgomery from the Wells Fargo museum stands the **Transamerica Pyramid** ㉒, between Clay and Washington streets. Walk through the tranquil redwood grove on the pyramid's east side, and you'll exit on Washington Street, across which you can see Hotaling Place to your left. Walk west (left) to the corner, cross Washington Street, and walk back to Hotaling. This historic alley is your entrance to **Jackson Square** ㉓, the heart of the Barbary Coast. Of particular note here are the former A. P. Hotaling whiskey distillery, on the corner of Hotaling Place, and the 1850s structures around the corner in the 700 block of Montgomery Street. To see these buildings, walk west on Jackson from the distillery and make a left on Montgomery. Then head south on Montgomery to Washington Street, make a right, and cross Columbus Avenue. Head north (to the right) up Columbus to the **San Francisco Brewing Company** ㉔, the last standing saloon of the Barbary Coast era and a place overflowing with freshly brewed beers and history.

TIMING Two hours should be enough time to see everything on this tour. The Wells Fargo museum (open only on weekdays) deserves a half hour.

What to See

㉓ **Jackson Square.** Here was the heart of the Barbary Coast of the Gay '90s. Although most of the red-light district was destroyed in the 1906 fire, old redbrick buildings and narrow alleys recall the romance and rowdiness of the early days. Some of the city's earliest business buildings, survivors of the 1906 quake, still stand in Jackson Square, between Montgomery and Sansome streets. Restored 19th-century brick buildings line Hotaling Place, which connects Washington and Jackson streets. The lane is named for the head of the **A. P. Hotaling Company whiskey distillery** (⊠ 451 Jackson St., at Hotaling Pl.), which was the largest liquor repository on the West Coast in its day. The Italianate Hotaling building reveals little of its infamous past, but a plaque on the side of the structure repeats a famous query about its surviving the quake: IF, AS THEY SAY, GOD SPANKED THE TOWN FOR BEING OVER FRISKY, WHY DID HE BURN THE CHURCHES DOWN AND SAVE HOTALING'S WHISKEY?

In the 700 block of **Montgomery Street**, Bret Harte wrote his novel *The Luck of Roaring Camp* at No. 730. He toiled as a typesetter for the spunky *golden-era* newspaper, which occupied No. 732 (now part of the building at No. 744). ⊠ *Jackson Sq. district bordered by Broadway and Washington, Kearny, and Sansome Sts., Financial District.*

㉔ **San Francisco Brewing Company.** Built in 1907, this pub looks like a museum piece from the Barbary Coast days. An old upright piano sits in the corner under the original stained-glass windows. Take a seat at the mahogany bar, where you can look down at the white-tile spittoon. An adjacent room holds the handmade copper brewing kettle used to produce a dozen beers by means of old-fashioned gravity-flow methods. ⊠ *155 Columbus Ave., North Beach* ☎ *415/434–3344* ⊕ *www.sfbrewing.com* ☾ *Mon.–Sat. 11:30–1 AM, Sun. noon–1 AM.*

㉒ **Transamerica Pyramid.** The city's most photographed high-rise is this 853-foot-tall structure. Designed by William Pereira and Associates in 1972, the initially controversial icon has become more acceptable to most locals over time. A fragrant redwood grove along the east side of the building, replete with benches and a cheerful fountain, is a placid patch in which to unwind. ⊠ *600 Montgomery St., Financial District* ⊕ *www.tapyramid.com.*

㉑ Wells Fargo Bank History Museum. There were no formal banks in San Francisco during the early years of the gold rush, and miners often entrusted their gold dust to saloon keepers. In 1852 Wells Fargo opened its first bank in the city, and the company soon established banking offices in the mother-lode camps throughout California. Stagecoaches and pony-express riders connected points around the burgeoning state. The museum displays samples of nuggets and gold dust from mines, a mural-size map of the Mother Lode, original art by Western artists Charles M. Russell and Maynard Dixon, mementos of the poet bandit Black Bart, and an old telegraph machine on which you can practice sending codes. The showpiece is the red Concord stagecoach, the likes of which carried passengers from St. Joseph, Missouri, to San Francisco in three weeks during the 1850s. ✉ *420 Montgomery St., Financial District* ☎ *415/396–2619* ▣ *Free* ☉ *Weekdays 9–5.*

Chinatown

Prepare to have your senses assaulted in Chinatown, bordered roughly by Bush, Kearny, and Powell streets and Broadway. Pungent smells waft out of restaurants, fish markets, and produce stands. Good-luck banners of crimson and gold hang beside dragon-entwined lampposts, pagoda roofs, and street signs with Chinese calligraphy. Honking cars chime in with shoppers bargaining loudly in Cantonese or Mandarin. Add to this the sight of millions of Chinese-theme goods spilling out of the shops along Grant Avenue, and you get an idea of what Chinatown is all about.

**▌A GOOD
WALK**

While wandering through Chinatown's streets and alleys, don't forget to look up. Above street level, many older structures—mostly brick buildings that replaced rickety wooden ones destroyed during the 1906 earthquake—have ornate balconies and cornices. The architecture on the 900 block of Grant Avenue (at Washington Street) and Waverly Place (west of and parallel to Grant Avenue between Sacramento and Washington streets) is particularly noteworthy.

Enter Chinatown through the green-tile **Chinatown Gate** ㉕ ▶, on Grant Avenue at Bush Street. Shops selling souvenirs, jewelry, and home furnishings line Grant north past the gate. Continue on Grant to Clay Street and turn right. A half block down on your left is **Portsmouth Square** ㉖. A walkway on the eastern edge of the park leads over Kearny Street to the 3rd floor of the Holiday Inn, where you find the **Chinese Culture Center** ㉗.

Backtrack on the walkway to Portsmouth Square and head west up Washington Street a half block to the **Old Chinese Telephone Exchange** ㉘ (now the Bank of Canton), and then continue west on Washington Street. Cross Grant Avenue and look for Waverly Place a half block up on the left. One of the best examples of this alley's traditional architecture is the **Tin How Temple** ㉙. After visiting Waverly Place and Tin How, walk back to Washington Street. Several herb shops do business in this area. Two worth checking out are Superior Trading Company, at No. 839, and the Great China Herb Co., at No. 857.

Across Washington Street from Superior is Ross Alley. Head north on Ross toward Jackson Street, stopping along the way to watch the bakers at the **Golden Gate Fortune Cookies Co.** ③⓪ Turn right on Jackson. When you get to Grant Avenue, don't cross it. For some of Chinatown's best pastries, turn left and stop by No. 1029, the Golden Gate Bakery. The markets in the 1100 block of Grant Avenue carry intriguing delicacies, such as braised pig noses and ears, eels, and all manner of live game birds and fish.

Head west on Pacific Avenue to Stockton Street, turn left, and walk south past Stockton Street's markets. At Clay Street make a right and head halfway up the hill to the **Chinese Historical Society of America Museum & Learning Center** ③①. Return to Stockton Street and make a right; a few doors down is the **Kong Chow Temple** ③②, and next door is the elaborate Chinese Six Companies building.

TIMING   Allow at least two hours to see Chinatown. Brief stops will suffice at the cultural center and temples.

What to See

▶ ㉕ **Chinatown Gate.** Stone lions flank the base of the pagoda-topped gate, the official entrance to Chinatown. The lions and the glazed clay dragons atop the largest of the gate's three pagodas symbolize, among other things, wealth and prosperity. The fish whose mouths wrap tightly around the crest of this pagoda also symbolize prosperity. The four Chinese characters immediately beneath the pagoda represent the philosophy of Sun Yat-sen (1866–1925), the leader who unified China in the early 20th century. The vertical characters under the left pagoda read "peace" and "trust," the ones under the right pagoda "respect" and "love." ⊠ *Grant Ave. at Bush St., Chinatown.*

㉛ **Chinese Historical Society of America Museum & Learning Center.** This airy, light-filled gallery has displays about the Chinese-American experience from 19th-century agriculture to 21st-century food and fashion trends. A separate room holds rotating exhibits by contemporary Chinese-American artists; another describes the building's time as the Chinatown YWCA, which served as a meeting place and residence for Chinese women in need of social services. ⊠ *965 Clay St., Chinatown* 🕾 *415/ 391–1188* ⊕ *www.chsa.org* ✉ *$3, free 1st Thurs. of month* ⊙ *Tues.–Fri. noon–5, weekends noon–4.*

㉗ **Chinese Culture Center.** The San Francisco Redevelopment Commission agreed to let **Holiday Inn** build in Chinatown if the chain provided room for a Chinese culture center. Inside the center are the works of Chinese and Chinese-American artists as well as traveling exhibits relating to Chinese culture. Walking tours ($12; make reservations a week ahead) of historic points in Chinatown begin here most days at 10 AM. ⊠ *Holiday Inn, 750 Kearny St., 3rd fl., Chinatown* 🕾 *415/986–1822* ⊕ *www. c-c-c.org* ✉ *Free* ⊙ *Tues.–Sat. 10–4.*

☙ ㉚ **Golden Gate Fortune Cookies Co.** Walk down Ross Alley and you'll likely be invited into this small cookie factory. The workers sit at circular motorized griddles and wait for dollops of batter to drop onto a tiny metal plate, which rotates into an oven. A few moments later out comes a cookie that's pliable and ready for folding. A bagful of cookies costs $2 or $3; personalized fortunes are also available. ⊠ *56 Ross Alley, west of and parallel to Grant Ave. between Washington and Jackson Sts., Chinatown* ☎ *415/781–3956* ◻ *Free* ⊙ *Daily 9–8.*

32 Kong Chow Temple. The god to whom the members of this temple pray represents honesty and trust. Take the elevator up to the 4th floor, where incense fills the air. Amid the statuary, flowers, and richly colored altars, a couple of plaques announce that MRS. HARRY S. TRUMAN CAME TO THIS TEMPLE IN JUNE 1948 FOR A PREDICTION ON THE OUTCOME OF THE ELECTION . . . THIS FORTUNE CAME TRUE. The temple's balcony has a good view of Chinatown. ⊠ *855 Stockton St., Chinatown* ☎ *No phone* ◻ *Free* ⊙ *Mon.–Sat. 9–4.*

28 Old Chinese Telephone Exchange. Most of Chinatown burned down after the 1906 earthquake, and this building—today the Bank of Canton—set the style for the new Chinatown. The intricate three-tier pagoda was built in 1909. The exchange's operators were renowned for their prodigious memories, about which the San Francisco Chamber of Commerce boasted in 1914: "These girls respond all day with hardly a mistake to calls that are given (in English or one of five Chinese dialects) by the name of the subscriber instead of by his number—a mental feat that would be practically impossible to most high-schooled American misses." ⊠ *Bank of Canton, 743 Washington St., Chinatown.*

26 Portsmouth Square. Captain John B. Montgomery raised the American flag here in 1846, claiming the area from Mexico. The square—a former potato patch—was the plaza for Yerba Buena, the Mexican settlement that was renamed San Francisco. Robert Louis Stevenson, the author of *Treasure Island,* lived on the edge of Chinatown in the late 19th century and often visited the square. Bruce Porter designed the bronze galleon that sits atop a 9-foot-tall granite shaft in the square's northwestern corner in honor of the writer. With its pagoda-shape structures, Portsmouth Square is a favorite spot for morning tai chi and afternoon Chinese chess. ⊠ *Bordered by Walter Lum Pl. and Kearny, Washington, and Clay Sts., Chinatown.*

★ **29 Tin How Temple.** Day Ju, one of the first three Chinese to arrive in San Francisco, dedicated this temple to the Queen of the Heavens and the Goddess of the Seven Seas in 1852. In the temple's entryway, elderly ladies can often be seen preparing "money" to be burned as offerings to various Buddhist gods or as funds for ancestors to use in the afterlife. Red-and-gold lanterns adorn the ceiling, and the smell of incense is usually thick. The gold-leaf wood carving suspended from the ceiling depicts the north and east sides of the sea, which Tin How and other gods protect. A statue of Tin How sits in the middle back of the temple. ⊠ *125 Waverly Pl., Chinatown* ☎ *No phone* ◻ *Free (donations accepted)* ⊙ *Daily 9–4.*

North Beach & Telegraph Hill

Novelist and resident Herbert Gold calls North Beach "the longest-running, most glorious American bohemian operetta outside Greenwich Village." Indeed, to anyone who's spent some time in its eccentric old bars and cafés or wandered the neighborhood, North Beach evokes everything from the Barbary Coast days to the no-less-rowdy beatnik era. Italian bakeries appear frozen in time, homages to Jack Kerouac and Allen Ginsberg pop up everywhere, and the modern equivalent of the Barbary Coast's "houses of ill repute," strip joints, do business on Broadway. North Beach is the most densely populated district in the city—and among the most cosmopolitan.

A GOOD WALK

City Lights Bookstore ③③ ▶, on Columbus Avenue, is a must-see landmark in North Beach. To the south, the triangular Sentinel Building, where Kearny Street and Columbus Avenue meet at an angle, grabs the eye with its unusual shape and mellow green patina. To the north of Broadway and Columbus is the heart of Italian North Beach.

Walk southeast across Columbus to City Lights Bookstore. Three of the most atmospheric bars in San Francisco are near here: Vesuvio, Specs, and Tosca. For joltingly caffeinated espresso drinks, also to the tune of opera, head north on Columbus a block and a half on the same side of the avenue as City Lights to Caffe Puccini, at No. 411.

Head up the east side of Columbus Avenue past Grant Avenue. On the northeast corner of Columbus and Vallejo Street is the Victorian-era **St. Francis of Assisi Church** ③④. Go east on Vallejo Street to Grant Avenue and make another left. Check out the eclectic shops and old-time bars and cafés between Vallejo and Union streets.

Turn left at Union Street and head west to Washington Square, an oasis of green amid the tightly packed streets of North Beach. On the north side of the park, on Filbert, stands the double-turreted **Saints Peter and Paul Catholic Church** ③⑤.

After you've had your fill of North Beach, head up **Telegraph Hill** ③⑥ from Washington Square. Atop the hill is **Coit Tower** ③⑦. Head east up Filbert Street at the park; turn left at Grant Avenue and go one block north, then right at Greenwich Street, and ascend the steps on your right. Cross the street at the top of the first set of stairs and continue up the curving stone steps to Coit Tower. The tower can also be reached by car (though parking is very tight) or public transportation.

TIMING   It takes a little more than an hour to walk the tour, but the point in both North Beach and in Telegraph Hill is to linger—set aside at least a few hours.

What to See

▶ ★ ③③ **City Lights Bookstore.** Designated a city landmark, the hangout of Beat-era writers—Allen Ginsberg and Lawrence Ferlinghetti among them—remains a vital part of San Francisco's literary scene. Still leftist at heart, the store has a reproduction of a revolutionary mural destroyed in Chiapas, Mexico, by military forces. ⊠ *261 Columbus Ave., North Beach* ☎ *415/362–8193* ⊕ *www.citylights.com* ☼ *Daily 10 AM–midnight.*

③ Coit Tower. Among San Francisco's most distinctive skyline sights, this

Fodor'sChoice 210-foot tower stands as a monument to the city's volunteer firefight-
★ ers. During the early days of the gold rush, Lillie Hitchcock Coit was said to have deserted a wedding party and chased down the street after her favorite engine, Knickerbocker No. 5, while clad in her bridesmaid finery. She was soon made an honorary member of the Knickerbocker Company. Lillie died in 1929 at the age of 86, leaving the city $125,000 to "expend in an appropriate manner . . . to the beauty of San Francisco." Inside the tower, 19 Depression-era murals depict economic and political life in California. ⊠ *Telegraph Hill Blvd. at Greenwich St. or Lombard St., North Beach* ☎ *415/362–0808* ⌖ *Free; elevator to top $3.75* ☉ *Daily 10–6.*

③ St. Francis of Assisi Church. The 1860 building stands on the site of the frame parish church that served the Catholic community during the gold rush. Its solid terra-cotta facade complements the many brightly colored restaurants and cafés nearby. ⊠ *610 Vallejo St., North Beach* ☎ *415/ 983–0405* ⊕ *www.shrinesf.org* ☉ *Daily 11–5.*

③ Saints Peter and Paul Catholic Church. Camera-toting visitors focus their lenses on the Romanesque splendor of what's often called the Italian Cathedral. Completed in 1924, the church has Disneyesque stone-white towers that are local landmarks. ⊠ *666 Filbert St., at Washington Sq., North Beach* ☎ *415/421–0809* ⊕ *www.stspeterpaul. san-francisco.ca.us.*

③ Telegraph Hill. The name came from one of the hill's earliest functions—in 1853 it became the location of the first Morse code signal station. Hill residents have some of the best views in the city, as well as the most difficult ascents to their aeries. The hill rises from the east end of Lombard Street to a height of 284 feet and is capped by Coit Tower. ⊠ *Bordered by Lombard, Filbert, Kearny, and Sansome Sts., North Beach.*

Nob Hill & Russian Hill

Once called the Hill of Golden Promise, Nob Hill was officially dubbed during the 1870s when "the Big Four"—Charles Crocker, Leland Stanford, Mark Hopkins, and Collis Huntington, who were involved in the construction of the transcontinental railroad—built their hilltop estates. The hill itself was called Snob Hill, a term that survives to this day. The 1906 earthquake and fire destroyed all the palatial mansions, except for portions of the Flood brownstone. The old San Francisco families of Russian Hill, a few blocks north of Nob Hill, were joined during the 1890s by bohemian artists and writers that included Charles Norris, George Sterling, and Maynard Dixon. Today, simple studios, spiffy pieds-à-terre, Victorian flats, Edwardian cottages, and boxlike condos rub elbows on the hill. The bay views here are some of the city's best.

A GOOD WALK

Begin on California and Taylor streets at the majestic **Grace Cathedral** ㉟ ▶. From the cathedral walk east (toward Mason Street and downtown) on California Street to the **Pacific Union Club** ㉟. Across Mason Street from the club is the lush **Fairmont San Francisco** ㊿, with its quirky Tonga Room tiki bar. Directly across California Street is the hotel **InterContinental Mark**

Hopkins ㊶, famed for panoramic views from its Top of the Mark lounge. Walk north on Mason Street to the **Cable Car Museum ㊷**.

From the Cable Car Museum continue four blocks north on Mason Street to Vallejo Street, turn west, and start climbing the steps that lead to the multilevel **Ina Coolbrith Park ㊸**. The Flag House, one of several brown-shingle prequake buildings in this area, is to your left at Taylor Street. Cross Taylor Street and ascend the Vallejo steps; the view east takes in downtown and the Bay Bridge. Continue west from the top of the Vallejo steps to two secluded Russian Hill alleys. Down and to your left is Florence Place, an enclave of 1920s stucco homes, and down a bit farther on your right is Russian Hill Place, with a row of 1915 Mediterranean town houses designed by Willis Polk. After reemerging on Vallejo Street from the alleys, walk north (right) on Jones Street one short block to Green Street. Head west (left) halfway down the block to the octagonal **Feusier House ㊹**. Backtrack to Jones Street, and head north to **Macondray Lane ㊺**. Walk west (to the left) on Macondray and follow it to Leavenworth Street. Head north (to the right) on Leavenworth to the bottom of **Lombard Street ㊻**, the "Crookedest Street in the World." Continue north one block on Leavenworth and then east one block on Chestnut Street to the **San Francisco Art Institute ㊼**.

TIMING   The tour covers a lot of ground, much of it steep. If you're in reasonably good shape, you can complete this walk in 3½ to 4 hours, including 30-minute stops at Grace Cathedral and the Cable Car Museum. Add time for gazing at the bay from Ina Coolbrith Park or enjoying tea or a cocktail at one of Nob Hill's grand hotels.

What to See

★ ☺ ㊷ **Cable Car Museum.** San Francisco once had more than a dozen cable-car barns and powerhouses. The only survivor, this 1907 redbrick structure, has photographs, old cable cars, signposts, ticketing machines, and other memorabilia dating from 1873. The massive powerhouse wheels that move the entire cable-car system steal the show; the design is so simple it seems almost unreal. You can also go downstairs to the sheave room and check out the innards of the system. A 15-minute video describes how it all works, or you can opt to read the detailed placards. ✉ *1201 Mason St., at Washington St., Nob Hill* ☎ *415/474–1887* ⊕ *www.cablecarmuseum.com* ✐ *Free* ☉ *Oct.–Mar., daily 10–5; Apr.–Sept., daily 10–6.*

㊵ **Fairmont San Francisco.** The hotel's dazzling opening was delayed a year by the 1906 quake, but since then the marble palace has been host to presidents, royalty, and movie stars. Things have changed since its early days, however: on the eve of World War I you could get a room for as low as $2.50 per night, meals included. Nowadays, prices go as high as $8,000, which buys a night in the eight-room, Persian art–filled penthouse suite that was showcased regularly in the 1980s TV series *Hotel*. ✉ *950 Mason St., Nob Hill* ☎ *415/772–5000* ⊕ *www.fairmont.com.*

㊹ **Feusier House.** Octagonal houses were once thought to make the best use of space and enhance the physical and mental well-being of their occupants. A brief mid-19th-century craze inspired the construction of several in San Francisco. Only the Feusier House, built in 1857 and now a private residence amid lush gardens, and the Octagon House remain standing. ⊠ *1067 Green St., Russian Hill.*

38 **Grace Cathedral.** The seat of the Episcopal Church in San Francisco, this soaring Gothic structure took 53 years to build. The gilded bronze doors at the east entrance were taken from casts of Lorenzo Ghiberti's Gates of Paradise, which are on the baptistery in Florence, Italy. A black-and-bronze stone sculpture of St. Francis by Beniamino Bufano greets you as you enter. The 35-foot-wide labyrinth, a large, purplish rug, is a reproduction of the 13th-century stone maze on the floor of the Chartres cathedral. ⊠ *1100 California St., at Taylor St., Nob Hill* ☎ *415/749–6300* ⊕ *www.gracecathedral.org* ☉ *Weekdays 7–6, Sat. 8–5:30, Sun. 7–7.*

43 **Ina Coolbrith Park.** Beloved for its spectacular bay views and manicured gardens, this spot is unusual because it's vertical—that is, rather than being one open space, it's composed of a series of terraces up a very steep hill. California poet laureate, Oakland librarian, and niece of Mormon prophet Joseph Smith, Ina Coolbrith (1842–1928) introduced Jack London and Isadora Duncan to the world of books. For years she entertained literary greats in her Macondray Lane home near the park. ⊠ *Vallejo St. between Mason and Taylor Sts., Russian Hill.*

46 **Lombard Street.** The block-long "Crookedest Street in the World" makes

Fodor'sChoice eight switchbacks down the east face of Russian Hill between Hyde and ★ Leavenworth streets. Residents bemoan the traffic jam outside their front doors, and occasionally the city attempts to discourage drivers by posting a traffic cop near the top of the hill. If no one is standing guard, join the line of cars waiting to drive down the steep hill, or avoid the whole morass and walk down the steps on either side of Lombard. ⊠ *Lombard St. between Hyde and Leavenworth Sts., Russian Hill.*

45 **Macondray Lane.** Enter this "secret garden" under a lovely wooden trellis and proceed down a quiet cobbled pedestrian street lined with Edwardian cottages and flowering plants and trees. A flight of steep wooden stairs at the end of the lane leads to Taylor Street—on the way down you can't miss the bay views. If you've read any of Armistead Maupin's *Tales of the City* or sequels, you may find the lane vaguely familiar. It's the thinly disguised setting for part of the series' action. ⊠ *Jones St. between Union and Green Sts., Russian Hill.*

41 **InterContinental Mark Hopkins.** Built on the ashes of railroad tycoon Mark Hopkins's grand estate, this 19-story hotel went up in 1926. A combination of French château and Spanish Renaissance architecture, with noteworthy terra-cotta detailing, it has played host to statesmen, royalty, and Hollywood celebrities. The 11-room penthouse was turned into a glass-walled cocktail lounge in 1939: the **Top of the Mark** is remembered fondly by thousands of World War II veterans who jammed the lounge before leaving for overseas duty. With its 360-degree views, the lounge is a wonderful spot for a nighttime drink. ⊠ *999 California St., at Mason St., Nob Hill* ☎ *415/392–3434* ⊕ *www.markhopkins.net.*

39 Pacific Union Club. The former home of silver baron James Flood cost a whopping $1.5 million in 1886, when even a stylish Victorian like the Haas-Lilienthal House cost less than $20,000. All that cash did buy some structural stability. The Flood residence was the only Nob Hill mansion to survive the 1906 earthquake and fire. The Pacific Union Club, a bastion of the wealthy and powerful, purchased the house in 1907 and commissioned Willis Polk to redesign it; the architect added the semicircular wings and 3rd floor. ⊠ *1000 California St., Nob Hill.*

47 San Francisco Art Institute. A Moorish-tile fountain in a tree-shaded courtyard draws the eye as soon as you enter the institute. The highlight of a visit is Mexican master Diego Rivera's *Making of a Fresco Showing the Building of a City* (1931), in the student gallery to your immediate left inside the entrance. Rivera himself is in the fresco—his back is to the viewer—and he's surrounded by his assistants. The older portions of the Art Institute were erected in 1926. Ansel Adams created the school's fine-arts photography department in 1946, and school directors established the country's first fine-arts film program. The **Walter & McBean Galleries** (☎ 415/749–4563 ☼ Tues.–Sat. 11–6) exhibit the often provocative works of established artists. ⊠ *800 Chestnut St., North Beach* ☎ *415/771–7020* ⊕ *www.sanfranciscoart.edu* ⊠ *Galleries free* ☼ *Student gallery daily 8:30–8:30.*

Pacific Heights & Japantown

Pacific Heights defines San Francisco's most expensive and dramatic real estate. Grand Victorians line the streets, mansions and town houses are often priced in the millions, and there are magnificent views from almost any point in the neighborhood. Japantown, or Nihonmachi, is centered on the southern slope of Pacific Heights, north of Geary Boulevard between Fillmore and Laguna streets. Around 1860 a wave of Japanese immigrants arrived in San Francisco, which they called Soko. By the 1930s they had opened shops, markets, meeting halls, and restaurants and established Shinto and Buddhist temples. Japantown is a relatively safe area, but the Western Addition, south of Geary Boulevard, can be dangerous at night; after dark also avoid straying too far west of Fillmore Street just north of Geary.

▍ A GOOD WALK   Pacific Heights lies on an east–west ridge along the city's northern flank from Van Ness Avenue to the Presidio and from California Street to the Marina. Begin your tour by taking in the views from **Alta Plaza Park** 48 ▶, at the intersection of Steiner and Jackson streets. Walk east on Jackson Street several blocks to the **Whittier Mansion** 49, on the corner of Jackson and Laguna streets. Make a right on Laguna and a left at the next block, Washington Street. The patch of green that spreads southeast from here is Lafayette Park. Walk on Washington along the edge of Lafayette Park past the formal French **Spreckels Mansion** 50, at the corner of Octavia Street, and continue east two more blocks to Franklin Street. Turn left (north); halfway down the block stands the handsome **Haas-Lilienthal House** 51. Head back south on Franklin Street, stopping to view several **Franklin Street buildings** 52. At California Street, turn right (west) to see more **noteworthy Victorians** 53 on that street and Laguna Street.

Continue west on California Street to begin the Japantown segment of your tour. When you reach Buchanan Street, turn left (south). The open-air **Japan Center Mall** ⑭ is a short block of shoji-screened buildings on Buchanan Street between Post and Sutter streets. Cross Post Street and enter the three-block **Japan Center** ⑮. A second-level bridge spans Webster Street, connecting the Kinokuniya and Kintetsu buildings. Make a right after you cross the bridge and then a left. There are usually several fine ikebana arrangements in the windows of the headquarters of the Ikenobo Ikebana Society of America. **Kabuki Springs & Spa** ⑯ is on the northeast corner of Geary and Fillmore.

TIMING   Set aside about two hours to see the sights mentioned here, not including the tours of the Haas-Lilienthal House. Although most of the attractions are walk-bys, you are covering a good bit of pavement. The Japantown tour, on the other hand, is very compact. Not including a visit to the Kabuki Springs, an hour will probably suffice.

What to See

⑱ **Alta Plaza Park.** Landscape architect John McLaren, who also created Golden Gate Park, designed Alta Plaza in 1910, modeling its terracing on the Grand Casino in Monte Carlo, Monaco. From the top you can see Marin to the north, downtown to the east, Twin Peaks to the south, and Golden Gate Park to the west. ⊠ *Bordered by Clay, Steiner, Jackson, and Scott Sts., Pacific Heights.*

㉒ **Franklin Street buildings.** What at first looks like a stone facade on the **Golden Gate Church** (⊠ 1901 Franklin St., Pacific Heights) is actually redwood painted white. A Georgian-style residence built in the early 1900s for a coffee merchant sits at 1735 Franklin. On the northeast corner of Franklin and California streets is a **Christian Science church**; built in the Tuscan-revival style, it's noteworthy for its terra-cotta detailing. The **Coleman House** (⊠ 1701 Franklin St., Pacific Heights) is an impressive twin-turreted Queen Anne mansion that was built for a gold-rush mining and lumber baron. Don't miss the large, brilliant-purple stained-glass window on the house's north side. ⊠ *Franklin St. between Washington and California Sts., Pacific Heights.*

㉑ **Haas-Lilienthal House.** A small display of photographs on the bottom floor of this elaborate 1886 Queen Anne house, which cost a mere $18,500 to build, makes clear that it was modest compared with some of the giants that fell victim to the 1906 earthquake and fire. The Foundation for San Francisco's Architectural Heritage operates the home, whose carefully kept rooms provide an intriguing glimpse into late-19th-century life. Volunteers conduct one-hour house tours three days a week and informative two-hour walking tours ($8) of the Civic Center, Broadway, and Union Street areas on Saturday afternoons, and of the eastern portion of Pacific Heights on Sunday afternoons. ⊠ *2007 Franklin St., between Washington and Jackson Sts., Pacific Heights* ☎ *415/441–3004* ⊕ *www.sfheritage.org* ⊡ *Entry $8* ⊙ *1-hr tour Wed. and Sat. noon–3, last tour at 2, Sun. 11–4, last tour at 3; 2-hr tour Sun. at 12:30.*

▶ ㉕ **Japan Center.** The noted American architect Minoru Yamasaki created this 5-acre complex, which opened in 1968. The development includes a hotel, a public garage with discounted validated parking; shops selling Japanese furnishings, clothing, cameras, music, porcelain, pearls, and paintings; an excellent spa, and a multiplex cinema. Between the Miyako Mall and Kintetsu Building are the five-tier, 100-foot-tall **Peace Pagoda** and the Peace Plaza. ⊠ *Bordered by Geary Blvd. and Fillmore, Post, and Laguna Sts., Japantown* ☎ *415/922–6776.*

54 Japan Center Mall. The buildings lining this open-air mall are of the shoji school of architecture. Seating in this area can be found on local artist Ruth Asawa's twin origami-style fountains, which sit in the middle of the mall; they're squat circular structures made of fieldstone, with three levels for sitting and a brick floor. ⊠ *Buchanan St. between Post and Sutter Sts., Japantown* ☎ *No phone.*

★ 56 Kabuki Springs & Spa. Japantown's house of tranquility offers a treatment regimen that includes facials, salt scrubs, and mud and seaweed wraps. You can take your massage in a private room with a bath or in a curtained-off area. The communal baths ($16 before 5 PM, $20 after 5 and all weekend) contain hot and cold tubs, a large Japanese-style bath, a sauna, a steam room, and showers. ⊠ *1750 Geary Blvd., Japantown* ☎ *415/922–6000* ⊕ *www.kabukisprings.com* ☉ *Daily 10–10.*

53 Noteworthy Victorians. Two **Italianate Victorians** (⊠ 1818 and 1834 California St., Pacific Heights) stand out on the 1800 block of California. A block farther is the Victorian-era **Atherton House** (⊠ 1990 California St., Pacific Heights), whose mildly daffy design incorporates Queen Anne, Stick-Eastlake, and other architectural elements. The oft-photographed **Laguna Street Victorians,** on the west side of the 1800 block of Laguna Street, cost between $2,000 and $2,600 when they were built in the 1870s. ⊠ *California St. between Franklin and Octavia Sts., and Laguna St. between Pine and Bush Sts., Pacific Heights.*

50 Spreckels Mansion. The estate was built for sugar heir Adolph Spreckels and his wife, Alma. Mrs. Spreckels was so pleased with her house that she commissioned George Applegarth to design another building in a similar vein: the Legion of Honor. One of the city's great iconoclasts, Alma Spreckels was the model for the bronze figure atop the Victory Monument in Union Square. ⊠ *2080 Washington St., at Octavia St., Pacific Heights.*

49 Whittier Mansion. With a Spanish-tile roof and scrolled bay windows on all four sides, this was one of the most elegant 19th-century houses in the state. An anomaly in a town that lost most of its grand mansions to the 1906 quake, the Whittier Mansion was built so solidly that only a chimney toppled over during the disaster. ⊠ *2090 Jackson St., Pacific Heights.*

Civic Center

The Civic Center—the Beaux-Arts complex between McAllister and Grove streets and Franklin and Hyde streets that includes City Hall, the War Memorial Opera House, the Veterans Building, and the old public library, now home of the Asian Art Museum and Cultural Center—is a product of the "City Beautiful" movement of the early 20th century. City Hall, completed in 1915 and renovated in 1999, is the centerpiece.

A GOOD WALK

Start at **United Nations Plaza** ⑤ ▶, set on an angle between Hyde and Market streets. Walk west across the plaza toward Fulton Street, which dead-ends at Hyde Street, and cross Hyde. Towering over the block of Fulton between Hyde and Larkin streets is the Pioneers Monument. The new main branch of the San Francisco Public Library is south of the monument. North of it is the **Asian Art Museum** ⑤, in the old library building. The patch of green west of the museum is Civic Center Plaza, and beyond that is **City Hall** ⑤. If City Hall is open, walk through it, exiting on Van Ness Avenue and turning right. If the building's closed, walk around it to the north—to the right as you're facing it—and make a left at McAllister. Either way you end up at McAllister Street and Van Ness Avenue. Looking south (to the left) across the street on Van Ness, you see three grand edifices, each of which takes up most of its block. On the southwestern corner of McAllister and Van Ness Avenue is the Veterans Building. A horseshoe-shaped carriage entrance on its south side separates the building from the **War Memorial Opera House** ⑥. In the next block of Van Ness Avenue, across Grove Street from the opera house, is Louise M. Davies Symphony Hall. From Davies, head west (to the right) on Grove Street to Franklin Street, turn left (south), walk one block to Hayes Street, and turn right (west). This takes you to Hayes Valley and the hip strip of galleries, shops, and restaurants between Franklin and Laguna streets. Like Japantown, the Civic Center borders the Western Addition; it's best not to stray west of Laguna at night.

TIMING   Walking around the Civic Center should take about 45 minutes. The Asian Art Museum merits an hour; another half hour or more can be spent browsing in the shops along Hayes Street.

What to See

★ ⑤ **Asian Art Museum.** One of the largest collections of Asian art in the world is housed within this museum's monumental, imposing exterior. More than 15,000 sculptures, paintings, and ceramics from 40 countries, illustrating major periods of Asian art, are stored here, with about 2,500 pieces on display. Highlights of Buddhism in Southeast Asia and early China include a large, jewel-encrusted, 19th-century Burmese Buddha seated on a throne and exquisitely painted and clothed rod puppets from Java. ⌧ *200 Larkin St., between McAllister and Fulton Sts., Civic Center* ☎ *415/581–3500* ⊕ *www.asianart.org* ⌲ *$10, free 1st Tues. of month; tea ceremony $17 includes museum admission* ◷ *Tues., Wed., and Fri.–Sun. 10–5; Thurs. 10–9.*

⑤ **City Hall.** This masterpiece of granite and marble was modeled after St. Peter's cathedral in Rome. City Hall's bronze and gold-leaf dome dominates the area. The classical influences of Paris-trained architect Arthur Brown Jr., who also designed Coit Tower and the War Memorial Opera House, can be seen throughout the structure. The palatial interior, full of grand arches and with a sweeping central staircase, is impressive. Some noteworthy events that have taken place here include the hosing—down the central staircase—of civil-rights and freedom-of-speech protesters

(1960) and the murders of Mayor George Moscone and openly gay supervisor Harvey Milk (1978). In spring 2004 thousands of gay and lesbian couples responded to Mayor Gavin Newsom's decision to issue marriage licenses to same-sex partners, turning City Hall into the site of raucous celebration and joyful nuptials for a month before the state Supreme Court ordered the practice stopped. Inside City Hall you can view pieces from the currently homeless **Museum of the City of San Francisco** (⊕ www.sfmuseum.org), including historical items, maps, photographs, and the enormous head of the *Goddess of Progress* statue, which crowned the original City Hall building when it crumbled during the 1906 earthquake. ⊠ *Bordered by Van Ness Ave. and Polk, Grove, and McAllister Sts., Civic Center* ☎ *415/554–6023* ⊕ *www.ci. sf.ca.us/cityhall* ⊠ *Free* ☉ *Weekdays 8–8, Sat. noon–4.*

▶ ⑤⑦ **United Nations Plaza.** Brick pillars listing various nations and the dates of their admittance into the United Nations line the plaza, and its floor is inscribed with the goals and philosophy of the United Nations charter. ⊠ *Fulton St. between Hyde and Market Sts., Civic Center.*

⑥⓪ **War Memorial Opera House.** All the old opera houses were destroyed in the 1906 quake, but lusty support for opera continued. The San Francisco Opera didn't have a permanent home until the War Memorial Opera House was inaugurated in 1932 with a performance of *Tosca.* Modeled after its European counterparts, the building has a vaulted and coffered ceiling, marble foyer, two balconies, and a huge silver art deco chandelier that resembles a sunburst. ⊠ *301 Van Ness Ave., Civic Center* ☎ *415/621–6600* ⊕ *www.sfwmpac.org.*

The Northern Waterfront

For the sights, sounds, and smells of the sea, hop the Powell–Hyde cable car from Union Square and take it to the end of the line. The views as you descend Hyde Street toward the bay are breathtaking—tiny sailboats bob in the whitecaps, Alcatraz hovers ominously in the distance, and the Marin Headlands form a rugged backdrop to the Golden Gate Bridge. Once you reach sea level at the cable-car turnaround, Aquatic Park and the National Maritime Museum are immediately to the west, and the commercial attractions of the Fisherman's Wharf area are to the east. Bring good walking shoes and a jacket or sweater for midafternoon breezes or foggy mists.

A GOOD WALK

Begin at Polk and Beach streets at the **National Maritime Museum** ⑥① ▶. Across Beach from the museum is Ghirardelli Square, a complex of shops, cafés, and galleries in an old chocolate factory. Continue east on Beach to Hyde Street and make a left. At the end of Hyde is the **Hyde Street Pier** ⑥②. South on Hyde a block and a half is the former Del Monte **Cannery** ⑥③, which holds more shops, cafés, and restaurants. Walk east from the Cannery on Jefferson Street to **Fisherman's Wharf** ⑥④. A few blocks farther east is **Pier 39** ⑥⑤.

TIMING   For the entire Northern Waterfront circuit, set aside a couple of hours, not including boat tours, which take from one to three hours or more. All attractions here are open daily.

What to See

★ **Alcatraz Island.** The boat ride to the island is brief (15 minutes) but affords beautiful views of the city, Marin County, and the East Bay. The audio tour, highly recommended, includes observations of guards and prisoners about life in one of America's most notorious penal colonies. A separate ranger-led tour surveys the island's ecology. Plan your schedule to allow at least three hours for the visit and boat rides combined. Reservations, even in the off-season, are recommended. ⊠ *Pier 41, Fisherman's Wharf* ☎ *415/773–1188 boat schedules and information, 415/705–5555, 800/426–8687 credit-card ticket orders, 415/705–1042 park information* ☞ *$11.50; $16 with audio tour; $23.50 evening tour, including audio* ☉ *Ferry departures every 30–45 min Sept.–late May, daily 9:30–2:15, 4:20 for evening tour Thurs.–Mon. only; late May–Aug., daily 9:30–4:15, 6:30 and 7:30 for evening tour* ⊕ *www.nps.gov/alca/index.htm.*

➏➌ **The Cannery at Del Monte Square.** The three-story structure was built in 1894 to house what became the Del Monte Fruit and Vegetable Cannery. Today it contains shops, art galleries, a comedy club (the Green Room), and some unusual restaurants. ⊠ *2801 Leavenworth St., Fisherman's Wharf* ☎ *415/771–3112* ⊕ *www.delmontesquare.com.*

☾ ➏➍ **Fisherman's Wharf.** Ships creak at their moorings; seagulls cry out for a handout. By midafternoon the fishing fleet is back to port. The chaotic streets of the wharf have numerous seafood restaurants, among them sidewalk stands where shrimp and crab cocktails are sold in disposable containers. T-shirts and sweats, gold chains galore, redwood furniture, acres of artwork, and generally amusing street artists also beckon to visitors.

Most of the entertainment at the wharf is schlocky and overpriced, with one notable exception: the splendid **Musée Mécanique** (☎ 415/346–2000 ☉ Memorial Day–Labor Day, daily 10–8; rest of yr, weekdays 11–7, weekends 10–8), a time-warped arcade with antique mechanical contrivances, including peep shows and nickelodeons. Some favorites are the giant and rather creepy "Laughing Sal," an arm-wrestling machine, and mechanical fortune-telling figures that speak from their curtained boxes. Admission is free, but you may want to bring change to play the games.

The **USS** *Pampanito* (⊠ Pier 45, Fisherman's Wharf ☎ 415/775–1943 ☉ Oct.–Memorial Day, Sun.–Thurs. 9–6, Fri. and Sat. 9–8; rest of yr, Thurs.–Tues. 9–8, Wed. 9–6) provides an intriguing if mildly claustrophobic glimpse into life on a submarine during World War II. Admission is $7. ⊠ *Jefferson St. between Leavenworth St. and Pier 39, Fisherman's Wharf.*

➏➋ **Hyde Street Pier.** One of the wharf area's best bargains, the pier always crackles with activity. Depending on the time of day, you might see boatbuilders at work or children manning a ship as though it were still the early 1900s. A highlight is the collection of historic vessels, all of which can be boarded. ⊠ *Hyde and Jefferson Sts., Fisherman's Wharf* ☎ *415/561–7100* ⊕ *www.maritime.org and www.nps.gov/safr* ☞ *Ships $5* ☉ *Daily 9:30–5.*

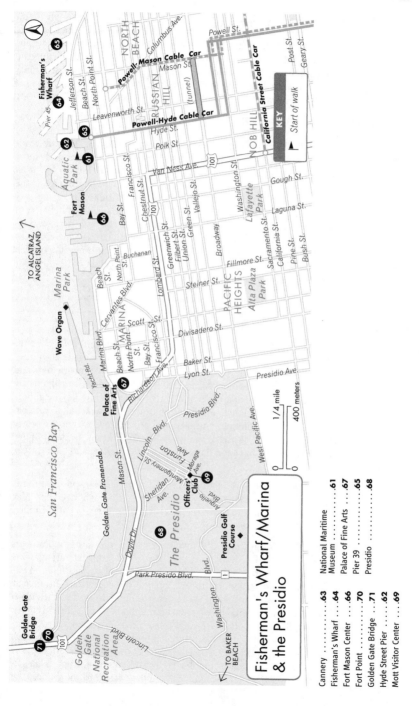

TO ALCATRAZ,
ANGEL ISLAND

San Francisco Bay

NORTH BEACH

RUSSIAN HILL

NOB HILL

PACIFIC HEIGHTS

MARINA

The Presidio

Golden Gate National Recreation Area

TO BAKER BEACH

Powell-Mason Cable Car

Powell-Hyde Cable Car

California Street Cable Car

KEY
▲ Start of walk

Wave Organ ◆

Palace of Fine Arts

Golden Gate Promenade

Presidio Golf Course ◆

Officers' Club ◆

1/4 mile
400 meters

Fisherman's Wharf/Marina
& the Presidio

▶ ⑥ **National Maritime Museum.** You'll feel as if you're out to sea when you step inside this sturdy, rounded structure. Part of the **San Francisco Maritime National Historical Park,** which includes Hyde Street Pier, the museum exhibits ship models, maps, and other artifacts chronicling the development of San Francisco and the West Coast through maritime history. ⊠ *Aquatic Park at the foot of Polk St., Fisherman's Wharf* ☎ *415/561–7100* ⊕ *www.nps.gov/safr* ⊠ *Donation suggested* ⊙ *Daily 10–5.*

🐚 ⑥ **Pier 39.** The most popular—and commercial—of San Francisco's waterfront attractions, the pier draws millions of visitors each year to browse through its dozens of shops. Ongoing free entertainment, accessible validated parking, and nearby public transportation ensure crowds most days. Brilliant colors enliven the double-decker **San Francisco Carousel** (⊠ $2 per ride), decorated with images of such city landmarks as the Golden Gate Bridge and Lombard Street. At **Aquarium of the Bay** (☎ 415/623–5300 or 888/732–3483 ⊕ www.aquariumofthebay.com ⊠ $12.95), moving walkways transport you through a space surrounded on three sides by water filled with indigenous San Francisco Bay marine life, from fish and plankton to sharks. The aquarium is open June through September daily 9–8, otherwise weekdays 10–6, weekends 10–7.

⊠ *Beach St. at Embarcadero, Fisherman's Wharf* ⊕ *www.pier39.com.*

The Marina & the Presidio

The Marina district was a coveted place to live until the 1989 earthquake, when the area's homes suffered the worst damage in the city—largely because the Marina is built on landfill. Many homeowners and renters fled in search of more-solid ground, but young professionals quickly replaced them, changing the tenor of this formerly low-key neighborhood. The number of upscale coffee emporiums skyrocketed, a bank became a Williams-Sonoma, and the local grocer gave way to a Pottery Barn. West of the Marina is the sprawling Presidio, a former military base. The Presidio has superb views and the best hiking and biking areas in San Francisco.

A GOOD DRIVE

Though you can visit the sights below using public transportation, this is the place to use your car if you have one. You might even consider renting one for a day to cover the area, as well as Lincoln Park, Golden Gate Park, and the western shoreline.

Start at **Fort Mason Center** ⑥ ▶, whose entrance for automobiles is off Marina Boulevard at Buchanan Street. If you're coming by bus, take Bus 30–Stockton heading north (and later west); get off at Chestnut and Laguna streets and walk north three blocks to the pedestrian entrance at Marina Boulevard and Laguna. To get from Fort Mason to the **Palace of Fine Arts** ⑥ by car, make a right on Marina Boulevard. The road curves past a small marina and the Marina Green. Turn left at Divisadero Street, right on North Point Street, left on Baker Street, and right on Bay Street, which passes the palace's lagoon and dead-ends at the Lyon Street parking lot. Part of the palace complex is the **Exploratorium,** a hands-on science museum. (If you're walking from Fort Mason to the palace, the directions are easier: Follow Marina Boulevard to Scott Street. Cross to the south side of the street—away from the water—and continue past Divisadero Street to Baker Street; turn left; the palace lagoon is on your right. To take Muni, walk back to Chestnut and Laguna streets and take Bus 30–Stockton continuing west; get off at North Point and Broderick streets and walk west on North Point.)

The least confusing way to drive to the **Presidio** ⑥ from the palace is to exit from the south end of the Lyon Street parking lot and head east (left) on Bay Street. Turn right (south) onto Baker Street, and right (west) on Francisco Street, taking it across Richardson Avenue to Lyon Street. Turn south (left) on Lyon and right (west) on Lombard Street, and go through the main gate to Presidio Boulevard. Turn right on Lincoln Boulevard and left on Funston Avenue to Moraga Avenue and the Presidio's **Mott Visitor Center** ⑥ at the Officers' Club. (To take the bus to the Presidio, walk north from the palace to Lombard Street and catch Bus 28 heading west; it stops on Lincoln near the visitor center.)

From the visitor center head back up Funston Avenue and turn left on Lincoln Boulevard. Lincoln winds through the Presidio past a large cemetery and some vista points. After a couple of miles is a parking lot marked FORT POINT on the right. Park and follow the signs leading to **Fort Point** ⑦, walking downhill through a lightly wooded area. To walk the short distance to the **Golden Gate Bridge** ⑦, follow the signs from the Fort Point parking lot; to drive across the bridge, continue on Lincoln Boulevard a bit and watch for the turnoff on the right. Bus 28 serves stops fairly near these last two attractions; ask the driver to call them out.

TIMING The time it takes to see this area varies greatly, depending on whether you take public transportation or drive. If you drive, plan to spend at least three hours, not including a walk across the Golden Gate Bridge or hikes along the shoreline—each of which takes a few hours. With or without kids, you could easily pass two hours at the Exploratorium.

What to See

★ ☺ **Exploratorium.** The curious of all ages flock to this fascinating "museum of science, art, and human perception." The more than 650 exhibits focus on sea and insect life, computers, electricity, patterns and light, language, the weather, and much more. Reservations are required to crawl through the pitch-black, touchy-feely Tactile Dome, a 15-minute adventure. ✉ 3601 Lyon St., at Marina Blvd., Marina ☎ 415/561–0360 general information, 415/561–0362 Tactile Dome reservations ⊕ www.exploratorium.edu ✇ $12, free 1st Wed. of month; Tactile Dome $3 extra ✆ Tues.–Sun. 10–5.

▶ ⑥ **Fort Mason Center.** Originally a depot for the shipment of supplies to the Pacific during World War II, the fort was converted into a cultural center in 1977. Here you'll find the vegetarian restaurant Greens and shops, galleries, and performance spaces, most of which are closed Monday. There's also plentiful free parking—a rarity in the city.

The **Museo Italo-Americano** (✉ Bldg. C ☎ 415/673–2200 ✆ Wed.–Sun. noon–4; noon–7 1st Wed. of month) mounts impressive exhibits of Italian and Italian-American paintings, sculpture, etchings, and photographs. Admission is $3; free on the first Wednesday of the month. Exhibits in the **Mexican Museum** (⊠ Bldg. D ☎ 415/202–9700 ⊙ Wed.–Sat. 11–5) display more than 12,000 objects dating from the preconquest era to modern times, and include contemporary Chicano art as well. Admission is $3.

The **San Francisco Craft and Folk Art Museum** (⊠ Bldg. A ☎ 415/775–0990) is an airy space with exhibits of American folk art, tribal art, and contemporary crafts. Its shop is a sure bet for whimsical gifts from around the world. The museum is open Tuesday through Friday and Sunday 11–5, Saturday 10–5. Admission is $4. At the free **SFMOMA Artists Gallery** (⊠ Bldg. A ☎ 415/441–4777) you can rent or buy what you see. It's open Tuesday through Saturday 11:30–5:30. ⊠ *Buchanan St. and Marina Blvd., Marina* ☎ *415/979–3010 event information* ⊕ *www. fortmason.org.*

🔄 ⑦⓪ **Fort Point.** Designed to mount 126 cannons with a range of up to 2 mi, the fort was constructed between 1853 and 1861 to protect San Francisco from sea attack during the Civil War—but it was never used for that purpose. It was, however, used as a coastal-defense-fortification post during World War II, when soldiers stood watch here. This National Historic Site is a museum filled with military memorabilia. On days when Fort Point is staffed, guided group tours and cannon drills take place. ⊠ *Marine Dr. off Lincoln Blvd., Presidio* ☎ *415/556–1693* ⊕ *www. nps.gov/fopo* ☎ *Free* ⊙ *Fri.–Sun. 10–5.*

★ ⑦① **Golden Gate Bridge.** The suspension bridge that connects San Francisco with Marin County has long wowed sightseers with its simple but powerful art deco design. Completed in 1937 after four years of construction, the 2-mi span and its 750-foot towers were built to withstand winds of more than 100 mph. The east walkway yields a glimpse of the San Francisco skyline and the bay islands, and the view west takes in the wild hills of the Marin Headlands, the curving coast south to Land's End, and the majestic Pacific Ocean. A vista point on the Marin side affords a spectacular city panorama. ⊠ *Lincoln Blvd. near Doyle Dr. and Fort Point, Presidio* ☎ *415/921–5858* ⊕ *www.goldengatebridge. org* ⊙ *Pedestrians: Apr.–Oct. daily 5 AM–9 PM, Nov.–May daily 6–6; bicyclists: daily 24 hrs.*

⑥⑨ **Mott Visitor Center.** Tucked away in the Presidio's Mission-style Officers' Club, the William P. Mott Jr. Visitor Center dispenses maps, brochures, and schedules for guided walking and bicycle tours, along with information about the Presidio's past, present, and future. History boards tell the story of the Presidio, from military outpost to self-sustaining park. ⊠ *50 Moraga Ave., Presidio* ☎ *415/561–4323* ⊙ *Daily 9–5.*

⑥⑦ **Palace of Fine Arts.** The rosy rococo palace is the sole survivor of the many tinted-plaster structures built for the 1915 Panama-Pacific International Exposition, the world's fair that celebrated San Francisco's recovery from the 1906 earthquake and fire. Bernard Maybeck designed this faux Roman Classic beauty, which was reconstructed in concrete and reopened in 1967. The massive columns, great rotunda (dedicated

FodorsChoice ★

to the glory of Greek culture), and swan-filled lagoon have been used in countless fashion layouts and films. ⊠ *Baker and Beach Sts., Marina* ☎ *415/561–0364 palace tours* ⊕ *www.exploratorium.edu/palace* 🎟 *Free* ⊙ *Daily 24 hrs.*

68 **Presidio.** Part of the **Golden Gate National Recreation Area,** the Presidio was a military post for more than 200 years. Don Juan Bautista de Anza and a band of Spanish settlers first claimed the area in 1776. It became a Mexican garrison in 1822 when Mexico gained its independence from Spain; U.S. troops forcibly occupied the Presidio in 1846. The U.S. Sixth Army was stationed here until October 1994, when the coveted space was transferred into civilian hands. Today, after much controversy, the area is being transformed into a self-sustaining national park with a combination of public, commercial, and residential projects. The more than 1,400 acres of hills, majestic woods, and redbrick army barracks include two beaches, a golf course, a visitor center, and picnic sites. ⊠ *Between Marina and Lincoln Park, Presidio* ⊕ *www.nps.gov/prsf.*

Golden Gate Park

William Hammond Hall conceived one of the nation's great city parks and began in 1870 to put into action his plan for a natural reserve with no reminders of urban life. John McLaren finished Hall's work during his tenure as park superintendent, from 1890 to 1943, to complete the transformation of 1,000 desolate brush- and sand-covered acres into a rolling, landscaped oasis. Urban reality now encroaches on all sides, but the park remains a great getaway. The fog can sweep into the park with amazing speed; always bring a sweatshirt or jacket.

Because the park is so large, a car comes in handy if you're going to tour it from one end to the other—though you'll still do a fair amount of walking. Muni serves the park. Buses 5–Fulton and 21–Hayes stop along its northern edge, and the N–Judah light-rail car stops a block south of the park between Stanyan Street and 9th Avenue, then two blocks south and the rest of the way west.

A GOOD WALK

The **Conservatory of Flowers** 72 ▶ is the first stop on this walk. Less than a block away at the intersection of Middle and Bowling Green drives is a sign for the National AIDS Memorial Grove. Before you enter the grove, follow the curve of Bowling Green Drive to the left, past the Bowling Green to the Children's Playground. If you have kids in tow, you'll probably be spending time here. If not, still take a peek at the vintage Herschell-Spillman Carousel.

Reverse direction on Bowling Green Drive and enter the **National AIDS Memorial Grove** 73, a sunken meadow that stretches west along Middle Drive East. At the end of the wheelchair-access ramp make a left to view the Circle of Friends; then continue west along the graded paths (ignore the staircase on the right halfway through the grove) to another circle with a poem by Thom Gunn. Exit north from this circle. As you're standing in the circle looking at the poem, the staircase to take is on your left. At the top of the staircase make a left and continue west on Middle Drive East. This brings you to the back entrance of the California

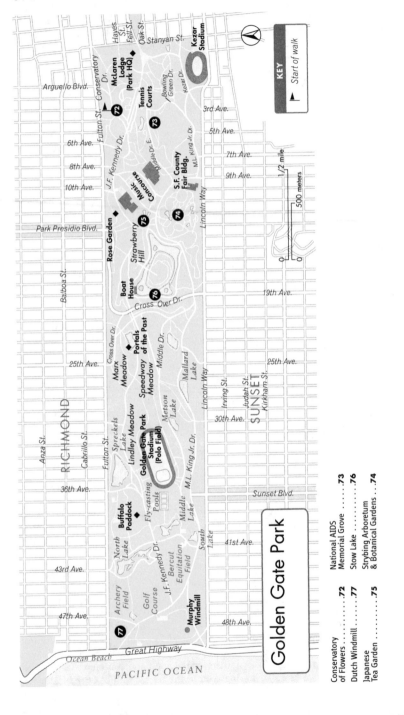

Stanyan St.

Hayes St.
Fair St.
Oak St.

Kezar Stadium ◆

Arguello Blvd.

Conservatory Dr.

McLaren Lodge (Park HQ) ◆

▲ **72**

Tennis Courts

Fulton St.

Bowling Green Dr.

3rd Ave.

73

Kezar Dr.

5th Ave.

6th Ave.

J.F. Kennedy Dr.

Middle Dr. E.

7th Ave.

S.F. County Fair Bldg.

8th Ave.

9th Ave.

10th Ave.

Music Concourse

M.L. King Jr. Dr.

Lincoln Way

74

Park Presidio Blvd.

Rose Garden ◆

75

Strawberry Hill

Balboa St.

Boat House ◆

19th Ave.

76

Cross Over Dr.

RICHMOND

Cross Over Dr.

Portals of the Past ◆

Middle Dr.

25th Ave.

Marx Meadow

Speedway Meadow

Mallard Lake

25th Ave.

Metson Lake

Lincoln Way

Anza St.

Spreckels Lake

Irving St.

Judah St.

SUNSET

Kirkham St.

Cabrillo St.

Fulton St.

Lindley Meadow

Golden Gate Park Stadium (Polo Field)

M.L. King Jr. Dr.

30th Ave.

36th Ave.

Fly-casting Pools

Middle Lake

Sunset Blvd.

Buffalo Paddock ◆

North Lake

J.F. Kennedy Dr.

Bercut Equitation Field

South Lake

41st Ave.

43rd Ave.

Archery Field

Golf Course

Murphy Windmill ●

47th Ave.

48th Ave.

77

Great Highway

Ocean Beach

PACIFIC OCEAN

◉ **N**

1/2 mile

0

500 meters

0

Golden Gate Park

Academy of Sciences, which is closed for renovations until 2008. (The temporary SoMa location is at 875 Howard Street in the ⇨ Union Square Area.)

A hundred feet shy of the 9th Avenue and Lincoln Way entrance to Golden Gate Park is the main entrance to **Strybing Arboretum & Botanical Gardens** ⑳. Take the first right after the bookstore. Follow the path as it winds north and west. Take the second right and look for signs for the Fragrance and Biblical gardens.

Backtrack from the gardens to the path you started on and make a right. As the path continues to wind north and west, you see a large fountain to the left. Just before you get to the fountain, make a right and head toward the duck pond. A wooden footbridge on the pond's left side crosses the water. Signs on the other side identify the fowl in the pond. Stay to the right on the path, heading toward the exit gate. Just before the gate, continue to the right to the Primitive Garden. Take the looped boardwalk past ferns, gingko, cycads, conifers, moss, and other plants. At the end of the loop, make a left and then a right, exiting via the Eugene L. Friend gate. Go straight ahead on the crosswalk to the blacktop path on the other side. Make a right, walk about 100 feet, and make a left on Tea Garden Drive. A few hundred feet east of here is the entrance to the **Japanese Tea Garden** ㉕.

Tour the garden, exiting near the gate you entered. Make a left and continue past the former Asian Art Museum and the M. H. de Young Memorial Museum; both buildings are closed for construction. A crosswalk leads south to the Music Concourse, with its gnarled trees, century-old fountains and sculptures, and the Golden Gate Bandshell. Turn left at the closest of the fountains and head east toward the bronze sculpture of Francis Scott Key.

Turn left at the statue and proceed north through two underpasses. At the end of the second underpass, you'll have traveled about 2 mi. If you're ready to leave the park, take the short staircase to the left of the blue-and-green playground equipment. At the top of the staircase is the 10th Avenue and Fulton Street stop for Bus 5–Fulton heading back downtown. If you're game for walking ½ mi more, make an immediate left as you exit the second underpass, cross 10th Avenue, and make a right on John F. Kennedy Drive. After approximately ¼ mi the Rose Garden is on your right. Continue west to the first stop sign. To the left is a sign for **Stow Lake** ㉖. Follow the road past the log cabin to the boathouse.

From Stow Lake it's the equivalent of 30 long blocks on John F. Kennedy Drive to the western end of the park and the ocean. If you walk, you pass meadows, the Portals of the Past, the buffalo paddock, and a 9-hole golf course. You can skip most of this walk by proceeding west on John F. Kennedy Drive from the stop sign mentioned above, making the first right after you walk underneath Cross-Over Drive, and following the road as it winds left toward 25th Avenue and Fulton. On the northwest corner of Fulton Street and 25th Avenue, catch Bus 5–Fulton heading west, get off at 46th Avenue, walk one block west to 47th Avenue, and make a left. Make a right on John F. Kennedy Drive.

By foot or vehicle, your goal is the **Dutch Windmill** 🔟 and adjoining garden.

TIMING You can easily spend an entire day in Golden Gate Park, especially if you walk the whole distance. Even if you plan to explore just the eastern end of the park (up to Stow Lake), allot at least two hours.

What to See

▶ 🔟 **Conservatory of Flowers.** Built in the late 1870s, the oldest building in the park is the last remaining wood-frame Victorian conservatory in the country. It's also a copy of the conservatory in the Royal Botanical Gardens in Kew, England, with a spectacular, 14-ton glass dome atop its perch. The gardens in front of the conservatory are planted seasonally, with the flowers often fashioned like billboards depicting the Golden Gate Bridge or other city sights. ✉ *John F. Kennedy Dr. at Conservatory Dr., Golden Gate Park* ☎ *415/666–7001* 💲 *$5* 🕐 *Tues.–Sun. 9–4:30* 🌐 *www.conservatoryofflowers.org.*

🔟 **Dutch Windmill.** Two windmills anchor the western end of Golden Gate Park. The restored 1902 Dutch Windmill once pumped 20,000 gallons of well water per hour to the reservoir on Strawberry Hill. With its heavy concrete bottom and wood-shingle arms and upper section, the windmill cuts quite the sturdy figure. ✉ *John F. Kennedy Dr. between 47th Ave. and the Great Hwy., Golden Gate Park.*

★ 🔟 **Japanese Tea Garden.** A peaceful 4-acre landscape of small ponds, streams, waterfalls, stone bridges, Japanese sculptures, *mumsai* (bonsai) trees, perfect miniature pagodas, and some nearly vertical wooden "humpback" bridges, the tea garden was created for the 1894 Mid-Winter Exposition. Go in the spring if you can (March is particularly beautiful), when the cherry blossoms are in bloom. ✉ *Tea Garden Dr. off John F. Kennedy Dr., Golden Gate Park* ☎ *415/752–4227* 💲 *$3.50* 🕐 *Mar.–Sept., daily 9–6; Oct.–Feb., daily 9–5.*

🔟 **National AIDS Memorial Grove.** San Francisco has lost many residents, gay and straight, to AIDS. This 15-acre grove, started in the early 1990s by people with AIDS and their families and friends, was conceived as a living memorial to those the disease has claimed. Coast live oaks, Monterey pines, coast redwoods, and other trees flank the grove, which is anchored at its east end by the stone Circle of Friends. ✉ *Middle Dr. E, west of tennis courts, Golden Gate Park* 🌐 *www.aidsmemorial.org.*

🔟 **Stow Lake.** One of the most photogenic spots in Golden Gate Park, this placid body of water surrounds Strawberry Hill. A couple of bridges allow you to cross over and ascend the hill, where a waterfall cascades from the top. Panoramic views make it worth the short hike up here. Just to the left of the waterfall sits the elaborate Chinese Pavilion, a gift from the city of Taipei. ✉ *Off John F. Kennedy Dr., ½ mi west of 10th Ave., Golden Gate Park* ☎ *415/752–0347* 🕐 *Boat rentals daily 10–4, surrey and bicycle rentals weekdays 9–dusk, weekends 10–dusk.*

🔟 **Strybing Arboretum & Botanical Gardens.** The 55-acre arboretum specializes in plants from areas with climates similar to that of the Bay Area, such as the west coast of Australia, South Africa, and the Mediterranean; more than 8,000 plant and tree varieties bloom in gardens throughout the grounds. Maps are available at the main and Eugene L. Friend entrances. ⊠ *9th Ave. at Lincoln Way, Golden Gate Park* ☎ *415/661–1316* ⊕ *www.strybing.org* ⊠ *Free* ⊙ *Weekdays 8–4:30, weekends 10–5* ☞ *Tours from bookstore weekdays at 1:30, weekends at 10:20 and 1:30; tours from Friend Gate Wed., Fri., and Sun. at 2.*

The Western Shoreline Including Lincoln Park

From Land's End in Lincoln Park you have some of the best views of the Golden Gate (the name was given to the opening of San Francisco Bay long before the bridge was built) and the Marin Headlands. From the historic Cliff House south to the sprawling San Francisco Zoo, the Great Highway and Ocean Beach run along the western edge of the city. The wind is often strong along the shoreline, summer fog can blanket the ocean beaches, and the water is cold and usually too rough for swimming. Carry a jacket and bring binoculars.

A GOOD DRIVE

A car is useful out here. There are plenty of hiking trails, and buses travel to all the sights mentioned, but the sights are far apart. Start at **Lincoln Park** ㉘ ▶. The park entrance is at 34th Avenue and Clement Street. Those without a car can take Bus 38–Geary—get off at 33rd Avenue and walk north (to the right) one block on 34th Avenue to the entrance. At the end of 34th Avenue (labeled on some maps as Legion of Honor Drive within Lincoln Park) is the **California Palace of the Legion of Honor** ㉙, a splendid art museum. From the museum, head back out to Clement Street and follow it west. At 45th Avenue, Clement turns into Seal Rock Drive. When Seal Rock dead-ends at 48th Avenue, turn left on El Camino del Mar and right on Point Lobos Avenue. After a few hundred yards, you see parking lots for **Sutro Heights Park** ㉚ and the **Cliff House** ㉛. (To get from the Legion of Honor to Point Lobos Avenue by public transit, take Bus 18 from the Legion of Honor parking lot west to the corner of 48th and Point Lobos avenues.) Two large concrete lions near the southeast corner of 48th and Point Lobos guard the entrance to Sutro Heights Park. After taking a quick spin through the park, exit past the lions, cross Point Lobos, make a left, and walk down to the Cliff House. From the Cliff House it's a short walk farther downhill to Ocean Beach.

The **San Francisco Zoo** ㉜ is a couple of miles south, at the intersection of the Great Highway and Sloat Boulevard. If you're driving, follow the Great Highway (heading south from the Cliff House, Point Lobos Avenue becomes the Great Highway), turn left on Sloat Boulevard, and park in the zoo's lot on Sloat. The hike along Ocean Beach from the Cliff House to the zoo is a flat but scenic 3 mi. To take public transportation from the Cliff House, reboard Bus 18, which continues south to the zoo.

TIMING Set aside at least three hours for this tour—more if you don't have a car. You can easily spend an hour in the Legion of Honor and 1½ hours at the zoo.

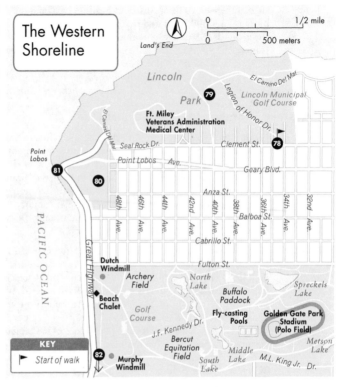

The Western Shoreline

What to See

★ **79** **Legion of Honor.** Spectacularly situated on cliffs overlooking the ocean, the Golden Gate Bridge, and the Marin Headlands, this landmark building is a fine repository of European art. A pyramidal glass skylight in the entrance court illuminates the lower-level galleries, which exhibit prints and drawings, English and European porcelain, and ancient Assyrian, Greek, Roman, and Egyptian art. The 20-plus galleries on the upper level display the permanent collection of European art (paintings, sculpture, decorative arts, tapestries) from the 14th century to the present day. The noteworthy Auguste Rodin collection includes two galleries devoted to the master and a third with works by Rodin and other 19th-century sculptors. ⊠ *34th Ave. at Clement St., Lincoln Park* ☎ *415/863–3330* ⊕ *www.thinker.org* ⊡ *$10, $2 off with Muni transfer, free 3rd Tues. of month* ☉ *Tues.–Sun. 9:30–5:15.*

81 **Cliff House.** Three buildings have occupied this site since 1863, and the current incarnation includes two restaurants and a gift shop. The upstairs Bistro is more casual, whereas downstairs is the fancier and pricier Sutro's. The vistas from both restaurants, which can be 30 mi or more on a clear day or less than a mile on foggy days, include offshore Seal Rock (the barking marine mammals there are actually sea lions). Both places appropriately emphasize seafood dishes, and though they're both fairly expensive, the grand views are priceless. To the north of the Cliff House are the ruins of the glass-roof **Sutro Baths,** which you can explore on your own. Six enormous baths (some freshwater and some seawater), more than 500 dressing rooms, and several restaurants once covered 3 acres north of the Cliff House and accommodated 25,000 bathers. ⊠ *1090 Point Lobos Ave., Lincoln Park* ☎ *415/386–3330* ⊕ *www.cliffhouse.com* 🎫 *Free* ☉ *Weekdays 9 AM–9:30 PM, weekends 9 AM–10 PM.*

▶ **78** **Lincoln Park.** Large Monterey cypresses line the fairways at Lincoln Park's 18-hole golf course, and there are scenic walks throughout the 275-acre park. The trail out to **Land's End** starts outside the Legion of Honor, at the end of El Camino del Mar. ⊠ *Lincoln Park, entrance at 34th Ave. at Clement St.*

🌱 **82** **San Francisco Zoo.** More than 1,000 birds and animals—252 species altogether—reside here. Among the more than 130 endangered species are the snow leopard, Sumatran tiger, jaguar, and grizzly bear. African Kikuyu grass carpets the circular outer area of **Gorilla World,** one of the largest and most natural gorilla habitats of any zoo in the world. Trees and shrubs create communal play areas. Ten species of rare monkeys—including colobus monkeys, white ruffed lemurs, and macaques—live and play at the two-tier **Primate Discovery Center,** which contains 23 interactive learning exhibits on the ground level. The **Feline Conservation Center,** a natural setting for rare cats, plays a key role in the zoo's efforts to encourage breeding among endangered felines. ⊠ *Sloat Blvd. and 47th Ave., Sunset, Muni L–Taraval streetcar from downtown* ☎ *415/753–7080* ⊕ *www.sfzoo.org* 🎫 *$10, $1 off with Muni transfer, free 1st Wed. of month* ☉ *Daily 10–5. Children's zoo Memorial Day–Labor Day, daily 10:30–4:30; rest of yr, weekdays 11–4, weekends 10:30–4:30.*

80 **Sutro Heights Park.** Monterey cypresses and Canary Island palms dot this cliff-top park, and photos on placards depict what you would have seen before eccentric mining engineer and former San Francisco mayor Adolph Sutro's house burned down in 1896. All that remains of the main house is its foundation. San Francisco City Guides (☎ 415/557–4266) runs a free Saturday tour of the park that starts at 2 (meet at the lion statue at 48th and Point Lobos avenues). ⊠ *Point Lobos and 48th Aves., Lincoln Park.*

Mission District

The sunny Mission District wins out in San Francisco's system of microclimates—it's always the last to succumb to fog. Italian and Irish in the early 20th century, the Mission became heavily Latino in the late 1960s, when immigrants from Mexico and Central America began arriving. In the late 1990s gentrification led to skyrocketing rents, causing clashes between the longtime residents forced out and the wealthy yuppies moving in. With the collapse of the dot-com economy, the district is yet again in transition, as rents stabilize and the landlord-tenant wars fade into memory. Still a bit scruffy in patches, the Mission lacks some of the glamour of other neighborhoods, but a walk through it provides the opportunity to mix with a heady cross section of San Franciscans.

⌐ A GOOD
WALK
The spiritual heart of the old Mission lies within the thick, white adobe walls of **Mission Dolores** ㊳ ⌐, where Dolores Street intersects with 16th Street. From the Mission, cross Dolores Street and head east on 16th Street. Tattooed and pierced hipsters abound a block from Mission Dolores, but the eclectic area still has room for a place such as Creativity Explored, where people with developmental disabilities work on art and other projects. At the intersection of 16th and Valencia streets, head south (to the right) and make a left on 24th Street. The atmosphere becomes distinctly Latin-American. A half block east of Folsom Street, mural-lined Balmy Alley runs south from 24th Street to 25th Street. A few steps farther east on 24th Street is the **Precita Eyes Mural Arts and Visitors Center** ㊴. From the center continue east past St. Peter's Church, where Isías Mata's mural *500 Years of Resistance,* on the exterior of the rectory, reflects on the struggles and survival of Latin-American cultures. At 24th and Bryant streets is the **Galería de la Raza/Studio 24** ㊵ art space.

Diagonally across from the Galería, on Bryant at the northeast corner near 24th Street, you can catch Bus 27–Bryant to downtown.

TIMING The above walk takes about two hours, including brief stops at the various sights listed. If you plan to go on a mural walk with Precita Eyes or if you're a browser who tends to linger, add at least another hour.

What to See

㊵ **Galería de la Raza/Studio 24.** San Francisco's premier showcase for Latino art, the gallery exhibits the works of local and international artists. Next door is the nonprofit Studio 24, which sells prints and paintings by Chicano artists as well as folk art, mainly from Mexico. ⊠ *2857 24th St., at Bryant St., Mission* ☎ *415/826–8009* ⊕ *www.galeriadelaraza. org* ⊙ *Gallery Wed.–Sat. noon–6, Studio 24 daily noon–6.*

★ ⌐ ㊳ **Mission Dolores.** Two churches stand side by side at this mission, including the small adobe **Mission San Francisco de Asís,** the oldest standing structure in San Francisco. Completed in 1791, it's the sixth of the 21 California missions founded by Father Junípero Serra in the 18th and early 19th centuries. Its ceiling depicts original Ohlone Indian basket designs, executed in vegetable dyes. The tiny chapel includes frescoes and a hand-painted wooden altar; some artifacts were brought from Mexico by mule in the late 18th century. ⊠ *Dolores and 16th Sts., Mission* ☎ *415/621–8203* ⊕ *www.sfmuseum.org/hist5/misdolor.html* ▣ *$3, audio tour $7* ⊙ *Daily 9–4.*

㊴ **Precita Eyes Mural Arts and Visitors Center.** The nonprofit arts organization sponsors guided walks of the Mission District's murals. Most tours start with a 45-minute slide presentation. The bike and walking trips, which take between one and three hours, pass several dozen murals. May is Mural Awareness Month, with visits to murals-in-progress and presentations by artists. You can pick up a map of 24th Street's murals at the center. ⊠ *2981 24th St., Mission* ☎ *415/285–2287* ⊕ *www.precitaeyes. org* ▣ *Center free, tours $10–$12* ⊙ *Center weekdays 10–5, Sat. 10–4, Sun. noon–4; walks weekends at 11 and 1:30 or by appointment.*

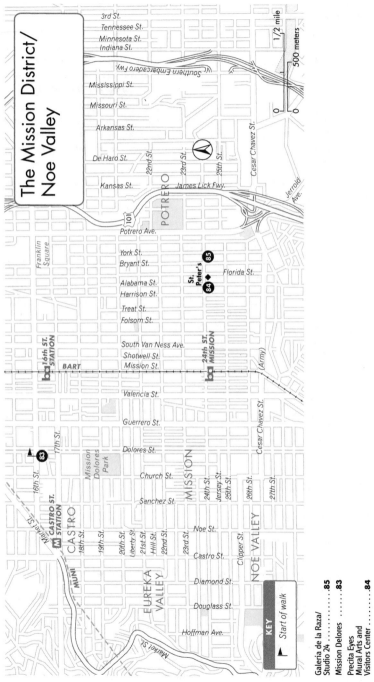

The Mission District/
Noe Valley

The Castro & the Haight

The Castro district—the social, cultural, and political center of the gay and lesbian community in San Francisco—is one of the liveliest and most welcoming neighborhoods in the city, especially on weekends. On Saturday and Sunday, the streets teem with folks out shopping, pushing political causes, heading to art films, and lingering in bars and cafés.

Young people looking for an affordable spot in which they could live according to new precepts began moving into the big old Victorians in the Haight in the late 1950s and early 1960s. By 1966 the Haight had become a hot spot for rock bands, including the Grateful Dead and Jefferson Airplane.

A GOOD WALK

Begin at **Harvey Milk Plaza** ⑧⑥ ⊳ on the southwest corner of 17th and Market streets; it's outside the south entrance to the Castro Street Muni station (K, L, and M streetcars stop here). Across Castro Street from the plaza is the neighborhood's landmark, the **Castro Theatre** ⑧⑦. Many shops line Castro Street between 17th and 19th streets, 18th between Sanchez and Eureka streets, and Market Street heading east toward downtown. After exploring the shops, get ready for a strenuous walk. For an unforgettable vista, continue north on Castro Street two blocks to 16th Street, turn left, and head up the steep hill to Flint Street. Turn right on Flint and follow the trail on the left (just past the tennis courts) up the hill. The beige buildings on the left contain the **Randall Museum** ⑧⑧ for children. Turn right up the dirt path, which soon loops back up Corona Heights. At the top you're treated to an all-encompassing view of the city.

Now continue north to walk the Haight Street tour. Follow the trail down the other side of Corona Heights to a grassy field. The gate to the field is at the intersection of Roosevelt Way and Museum Way. Turn right on Roosevelt (head down the hill) and cross Roosevelt at Park Hill Terrace. Walk up Park Hill to Buena Vista Avenue, turn left, and follow the road as it loops west and south around Buena Vista Park to Central Avenue. Head down Central two blocks to Haight Street and make a left.

Continue west to the fabled **Haight-Ashbury intersection** ⑧⑨. A motley contingent of folks attired in retro fashions and often sporting hippie-long hair hangs here. One block south of Haight and Ashbury (at 710 Ashbury) is the Grateful Dead house, the pad that Jerry Garcia and band inhabited in the 1960s. The stores along Haight Street up to Shrader Street are worth checking out.

TIMING   Allot 60 to 90 minutes to visit the Castro district. Set aside an extra hour to hike Corona Heights and visit the Randall Museum. The distance covered here is only several blocks, and although there are shops aplenty and other amusements, an hour or so should be enough.

What to See

★ ⑧⑦ **Castro Theatre.** The neon marquee is the neighborhood's great landmark, and the 1,500-seat art deco theater, which opened in 1922, is the grandest of San Francisco's few remaining movie palaces. Janet Gaynor, who

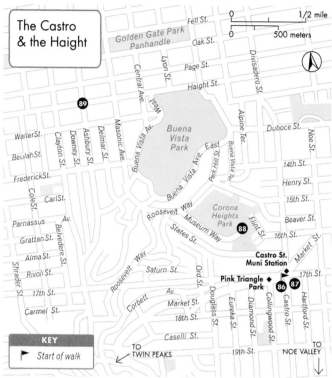

in 1927 won the first Oscar for best actress, worked as an usher here. The Castro's elaborate Spanish baroque interior is fairly well preserved. The crowd can be enthusiastic and vocal, talking back to the screen as loudly as it talks to them. ⊠ *429 Castro St., Castro* ☎ *415/621–6120.*

89 **Haight-Ashbury intersection.** Despite the Gap that today holds court on one of its quadrants, this famed corner was once the center of 1960s counterculture. Among the folks who hung out in or near the Haight during the late 1960s were writers Richard Brautigan, Allen Ginsberg, Ken Kesey, and Gary Snyder; anarchist Abbie Hoffman; rock performers Marty Balin, Jerry Garcia, Janis Joplin, and Grace Slick; LSD champion Timothy Leary; and filmmaker Kenneth Anger.

▶ **86** **Harvey Milk Plaza.** An 18-foot-long rainbow flag, a gay icon, flies above this plaza named for the man who electrified the city in 1977 by being elected to its Board of Supervisors as an openly gay candidate. The liberal Milk hadn't served a full year of his term before he and Mayor George Moscone, also a liberal, were shot in November 1978 at City Hall by Dan White, a conservative ex-supervisor. Milk's assassination shocked the gay community, which became infuriated when the infamous "Twinkie defense"—that junk food had led to diminished mental capacity—resulted in a manslaughter verdict for White. During the so-called White

Night Riot of May 21, 1979, gays and their sympathizers stormed City Hall, torching its lobby and several police cars. ⊠ *Southwest corner of Castro and Market Sts., Castro.*

🐾 **88** **Randall Museum.** In addition to a greenhouse, woodworking and ceramics studios, and a theater, the museum has an educational animal room with birds, lizards, snakes, spiders, and other creatures that cannot be released to the wild because of injury or other problems. Spread over 16 acres of public land, the museum sits beneath a hill variously known as Red Rock, Museum Hill, and, correctly, Corona Heights. ⊠ *199 Museum Way, off Roosevelt Way, Castro* ☎ *415/554–9600* ⊕ *www. randallmuseum.org* ⊠ *Free* ☉ *Tues.–Sat. 10–5.*

WHERE TO EAT

Updated by Sharon Silva

Since the city's earliest days, food lovers have flocked to San Francisco—a place where diversity rules and trends are set. Nearly every ethnic cuisine is represented—from Afghan to Indian to Vietnamese. And although locals have long headed to the Mission District for Latin food, to Chinatown and the Richmond District for Asian food, and to North Beach for Italian food, they also know that every part of the city offers dining experiences beyond the neighborhood tradition.

WHAT IT COSTS				
$$$$	$$$	$$	$	¢
AT DINNER	over $30	$23–$30	$15–$22	$10–$14	under $10

Prices are per person for a main course. The final tab will include tax of 8.5%.

Union Square

Contemporary

$$$–$$$$ ✕ **Postrio.** There's always a chance of seeing a celebrity here, including the owner of this legendary eatery, superchef Wolfgang Puck, who periodically commutes here from Los Angeles. A stunning three-level bar and dining area is connected by copper handrails and accented with museum-quality contemporary paintings. The seasonal dinner menus are Californian with Mediterranean and Asian overtones, and the restaurant's signature dish is house-smoked salmon with blini. ⊠ *545 Post St., Union Sq.* ☎ *415/776–7825* ⚠ *Reservations essential* ⊟ *AE, D, DC, MC, V.*

French

★ $$$$ ✕ **Fleur de Lys.** The creative cooking of French chef–part owner Hubert Keller has brought every conceivable culinary award to this romantic spot. The interior's distinctive feature is its tented ceiling, 900 yards of draped and swathed fabric. The three-, four-, and five-course prix-fixe menus include dishes such as roasted squab breast stuffed with truffles and foie gras, prawns with Thai red curry, and Moroccan-spiced scallops. ⊠ *777 Sutter St., Union Sq.* ☎ *415/673–7779* ⚠ *Reservations essential* 🔒 *Jacket required* ⊟ *AE, D, DC, MC, V* ☉ *Closed Sun. No lunch.*

Mediterranean

★ ¢–$$ ╳ **Cortez.** The restaurant in the theater district's Hotel Adagio serves beautifully presented small plates in a setting outfitted with Calder-inspired mobile lights in bright red, yellow, blue, and green. A young, fashionable crowd comes here for tapas-size dishes that range from raw tuna on shaved fennel and lavender-honey-glazed duck breast to date-and-mint-seasoned lamb chops and foie gras terrine. ⊠ *Hotel Adagio, 550 Geary St., Union Sq.* ☎ *415/292–6360* ▤ *AE, MC, V* ☯ *No lunch.*

Seafood

$$$$ ╳ **Farallon.** Outfitted with sculpted jellyfish lamps, kelp-covered columns, **Fodor'sChoice** and sea-urchin chandeliers, this swanky Pat Kuleto–designed restaurant ★ is loaded with style *and* customers. Chef Mark Franz cooks up impeccable seafood that draws serious diners from coast to coast. The menu changes daily, but pan-roasted mussels with pommes frites, local petrale sole with artichokes and couscous, and skate wing with trumpet mushrooms circulate in and out regularly. ⊠ *450 Post St., Union Sq.* ☎ *415/956–6969* ▤ *AE, D, DC, MC, V* ☯ *No lunch Sun. or Mon.*

Vietnamese

$$–$$$$ ╳ **Le Colonial.** The stamped tin ceiling, period photographs, slow-moving fans, and tropical plants re-create a 1920s French-colonial setting for the upscale Vietnamese food. Local blue bloods come for the ginger-glazed duck breast with rice noodles, stir-fried spot prawns with long beans and roasted tomatoes, and wok-seared beef tenderloin. ⊠*20 Cosmo Pl., Union Sq.* ☎ *415/931–3600* ⌘ *Reservations essential* ▤ *AE, MC, V* ☯ *No lunch.*

SoMa & the Embarcadero

American

$$–$$$ ╳ **Town Hall.** Chefs Mitchell and Steven Rosenthal, who have long headed up the kitchen at Wolfgang Puck's popular Postrio, have also opened their own, more casual place. The fare is new American: warm frisée salad with Smithfield ham, poached egg, and cider vinegar; slow-roasted duck with gingersnap gravy; San Francisco–inspired cioppino; cedar-planked salmon; butterscotch-and-chocolate *pot de créme*. The wines, many by the glass, complement the food. The space, with dark-wood floors, exposed brick walls, white wainscoting, contemporary art, and an outdoor patio, comfortably blends old with new. ⊠ *342 Howard St., SoMa* ☎ *415/908–3900* ▤ *AE, MC, V* ☯ *No lunch weekends.*

Contemporary

★ $$$$ ╳ **Boulevard.** Two of San Francisco's top restaurant talents—chef Nancy Oakes and designer Pat Kuleto—are responsible for this high-profile, high-priced eatery in the magnificent 1889 Audiffred Building, a Parisian look-alike that was one of the few downtown structures to survive the 1906 earthquake. Oakes's menu, with its nod to the French kitchen, is seasonally in flux, but you can count on her signature juxtapositioning of classy fare—such as pork tenderloin stuffed with chanterelles and truffles—with comfort food, such as wood-oven-roasted rack of lamb. Portions are generous; save room (and calories) for one of the dynamite

Where to Eat In & Around Downtown San Francisco

desserts. ⊠ *1 Mission St., Embarcadero* ☎ *415/543–6084* ⌖ *Reservations essential* ⊟ *AE, D, DC, MC, V* ⊘ *No lunch weekends.*

$$$–$$$$ ✕ **Bacar.** An understated brick-and-glass exterior hides one of the city's most wine-savvy restaurants. The by-the-glass list runs pages; wines by the bottle require a hefty book. In other words, serious wine drinkers feel at home in this stylish place. The food menu is far smaller—and nicely unfussy—with a long list of raw bar options and appetizers, such as house-smoked bay scallops, wok-roasted mussels, rabbit rillettes, and wood-fired pork belly with hedgehog mushrooms. ⊠ *448 Brannan St., SoMa* ☎ *415/904–4100* ⊟ *AE, DC, MC, V* ⊘ *No lunch.*

$$$–$$$$ ✕ **Fifth Floor.** Chef Melissa Perello is the latest chef to oversee the kitchen of this sophisticated dining room known for its stunning plates and well-heeled diners. Tucked away in the Palomar Hotel, the 75-seat room, all dark wood and zebra-stripe carpeting, is where exquisite dishes such as skate wing with potato confit, pan-roasted rabbit loin with salsify and apples, and scallops with truffles are served from a daily-changing menu. ⊠ *Palomar Hotel, 12 4th St., SoMa* ☎ *415/348–1555* ⌖ *Reservations essential* ⊟ *AE, DC, MC, V* ⊘ *Closed Sun. No lunch.*

★ **$$$–$$$$** ✕ **Hawthorne Lane.** The big, handsome restaurant draws a crowd to a quiet alley not far from the Yerba Buena Center. The place is divided into two rooms: the first, with a beautiful oval cherrywood bar, comfy upholstered booths, and well-spaced tables, has a lively ambience, and the second is a more formal, light-flooded dining room. Quail with corn-and-wild-rice risotto, duck breast with fig bread pudding, and Meyer lemon cheesecake are among the typical offerings on the menu, which is seasonal. The bread basket, full of house-made delights such as biscuits, bread sticks, and rolls, is the best in town. ⊠ *22 Hawthorne St., SoMa* ☎ *415/777–9779* ⊟ *D, DC, MC, V* ⊘ *No lunch weekends.*

$$–$$$$ ✕ **One Market.** A giant among American chefs, Bradley Ogden gained fame at Campton Place and later at his Lark Creek Inn in Marin County. This huge, bustling brasserie across from the Ferry Building is his popular San Francisco outpost. The two-tier dining room, done in mustard tones, seats 170 and serves a seasonal—and surprisingly homey—menu that might include scallops wrapped in pancetta, braised beef cheeks with celery-root purée, and pumpkin pie with ginger ice cream. The service is polished. The wine list includes the best California labels, and there's even a local boutique brandy to sip at meal's end. ⊠ *1 Market St., Embarcadero* ☎ *415/777–5577* ⌖ *Reservations essential* ⊟ *AE, DC, MC, V* ⊘ *Closed Sun. No lunch Sat.*

French

★ **$$–$$$** ✕ **Bizou.** Chef Loretta Keller serves a distinctive French country menu, with some Italian touches, at this comfortable corner bistro, the name of which translates as "kiss." Fans of her rustic cooking cite the thin and crisp pizzas, olive-stuffed pork loin with polenta, cassoulet with duck confit and lamb sausage, duck-liver terrine, and braised beef cheeks with mustard and watercress as evidence of her talents. The space itself is small and unpretentious, with old-fashioned hanging lamps, warm-rust-colored walls, plain banquettes, and butcher-paper-covered tables. ⊠ *598 4th St., SoMa* ☎ *415/543–2222* ⊟ *AE, MC, V* ⊘ *Closed Sun. No lunch Sat.*

Indian

★ ☺ ¢–$ ✕ **Chaat Café.** Indian snacks—*chaat*—are the specialty at this no-frills establishment (part of a small chain) adorned with big, bright-colored paintings of Indian women. Thin, chewy naan (flat bread) accompanies curries—fish, lamb, chicken, and veggie versions—and is used for wraps, including one filled with tasty tandoori lamb, onions, and cilantro. Small, hollow bread puffs into which you spoon seasoned potatoes and chickpeas—a dish called *pani puri* here—and chicken and fish *pakora* (fritters) are also good choices. ⊠ *320 3rd St., SoMa* ☎ *415/979–9946* ⌖ *Reservations not accepted* ⊟ *MC, V.*

Mediterranean

★ $$–$$$ ✕ **LuLu.** The food is satisfyingly uncomplicated and delectable. Beneath a high, barrel-vaulted ceiling, you can feast on fritto misto of artichokes, fennel, and lemon slices; mussels roasted in an iron skillet; wood-oven-roasted poultry, meats, and shellfish; and a small selection of pizzas and pastas. There is a well-supplied raw bar, and main-course specials include a rotisserie-prepared main course that changes daily. ⊠ *816 Folsom St., SoMa* ☎ *415/495–5775* ⊟ *AE, D, DC, MC, V.*

Vietnamese

★ $$–$$$ ✕ **Slanted Door.** In 2004 chef-owner Charles Phan, who has gained national fame with his upmarket, Western-accented Vietnamese fare, moved the Slanted Door into the busy Ferry Building, where it occupies a large space outfitted with sleek wooden tables and chairs, white marble floors, a cocktail lounge and bar, and a big bay view. Phan's popular dishes—Vietnamese crepe with pork and shrimp, jicama-and-grapefruit salad with candied pecans, shaking beef (tender beef cubes with garlic and onion), green papaya salad—made the move, too, to the cheers of his faithful customers. Alas, the crush of fame has also brought some ragged service. ⊠ *Ferry Building, Embarcadero at Market St., Embarcadero* ☎ *415/861–8032* ⊟ *AE, MC, V.*

Financial District

Chinese

☺ ¢–$ ✕ **Yank Sing.** The city's oldest teahouse, Yank Sing began in Chinatown in the late 1950s but moved to the Financial District in the 1980s, opening this moderate-size, handsomely decorated location on quiet Stevenson Street (it later opened a big, brassy branch in the Rincon Center). This is a welcome refuge for neighborhood office workers who want to fuel up on steamed buns and parchment chicken at lunchtime and for families on weekends. ⊠ *49 Stevenson St., Financial District* ☎ *415/541–4949* ⊟ *AE, DC, MC, V* ☾ *No dinner.*

French

★ $$–$$$$ ✕ **Jeanty at Jack's.** Chef Philippe Jeanty, who made a name for himself in the wine country (first at Domaine Chandon and then at his Bistro Jeanty and Pere Jeanty), oversees this brass-and-wood, three-story brasserie in the former Jack's restaurant, a San Francisco institution since 1864. The food is as French as the chef, with cassoulet, steak frites, rabbit terrine, steak tartare, and coq au vin among the traditional offerings. ⊠ *615 Sacramento St., Financial District* ☎ *415/693–0941* ⊟ *AE, MC, V* ⊗ *Closed Sat. No lunch Sun.*

Japanese

$$–$$$$ ✕ **Kyo-ya.** With extraordinary authenticity, this showplace in the Palace Hotel replicates the refined experience—rarely found outside Japan—of dining in a first-class Japanese restaurant. In Japan a *kyo-ya* is a non-specialized restaurant that serves a wide range of food. Here, the range is spectacular, encompassing tempuras, one-pot dishes, deep-fried and grilled meats, and two dozen sushi selections. ⊠ *Palace Hotel, 2 New Montgomery St., at Market St., Financial District* ☎*415/546–5000* ⊟*AE, D, DC, MC, V* ⊗ *Closed Sun. and Mon. No lunch Sat.*

Seafood

★ **$$$$** ✕ **Aqua.** Quietly elegant, ultrafashionable, heavily mirrored, and populated by a society crowd, this spot is among the city's most lauded seafood restaurants—and among the most expensive. The kitchen, known for using exquisite ingredients and classic techniques, assembles beautiful preparations that are refined but not overly fussy: tuna tartare with Moroccan spices and lemon confit, wild king salmon with morels, petrale sole with gratin of artichokes. ⊠ *252 California St., Financial District* ☎ *415/956–9662* ⌔ *Reservations essential* 𝄞 *Jacket and tie* ⊟ *AE, D, DC, MC, V* ⊗ *No lunch weekends.*

$$–$$$ ✕ **Tadich Grill.** Owners and locations have changed many times since this old-timer opened during the gold-rush era, but the 19th-century atmosphere remains. Simple sautés are the best choices, or cioppino during crab season (October to May), Pacific halibut in season (January to May), and old-fashioned house-made tartar sauce anytime. ⊠ *240 California St., Financial District* ☎ *415/391–2373* ⌔ *Reservations not accepted* ⊟ *MC, V* ⊗ *Closed Sun.*

Spanish

★ **$$–$$$** ✕ **B44.** The cluster of wonderful European eateries on Belden Place includes this spare, modern Spanish restaurant, which draws locals with its menu of Catalan tapas and paellas. The open kitchen sends out small plates such as white anchovies with pears and Idiazábal cheese, sherry-scented fish cheeks, warm octopus with tiny potatoes, and blood sausage with white beans. The paellas, each serving presented in an iron skillet, bring together inviting combinations such as chicken, rabbit, and mushrooms. ⊠ *44 Belden Pl., Financial District* ☎ *415/986–6287* ⊟ *AE, MC, V* ⊗ *Closed Sun. No lunch Sat.*

Chinatown

Chinese

↺ **¢–$$$** ✕ **Great Eastern.** Cantonese chefs are known for their expertise with seafood, and the kitchen here continues that venerable tradition. Tanks filled with Dungeness crabs, black bass, catfish, shrimp, and other creatures of fresh and salt water occupy a corner of the main dining room, a handsome space with jade-green wainscoting and dark-wood accents. ⊠ *649 Jackson St., Chinatown* ☎ *415/986–2550* ⊟ *AE, MC, V.*

☾ ¢–$$$ ✕ **R&G Lounge.** The name conjures up an image of a dark bar with a cigarette-smoking piano player, but the restaurant is actually as bright as a new penny. The classy upstairs space (entrance on Commercial Street) is a favorite stop for Chinese businessmen on expense accounts. The street-level space on Kearny is a comfortable spot to wait for a table to open. A menu with photographs helps you pick from the many wonderful, sometimes pricey, always authentic dishes—such as salt-and-pepper Dungeness crab. ⊠ *631 Kearny St., Chinatown* ☏ *415/982–7877 or 415/982–3811* ▭ *AE, D, DC, MC, V.*

North Beach

Afghan

★ $–$$ ✕ **Helmand.** Don't be put off by Helmand's location on a rather scruffy block of Broadway; inside, authentic Afghan cooking is served at amazingly low prices in elegant surroundings, amid white table linens and Afghan carpets. Highlights include *aushak* (leek-filled ravioli served with yogurt and ground beef), pumpkin with yogurt-and-garlic sauce, and any of the lamb dishes, in particular the kebab strewn with yellow split peas and served on Afghan flat bread. ⊠ *430 Broadway, North Beach* ☏ *415/362–0641* ▭ *AE, MC, V* ☾ *No lunch weekends.*

Contemporary

★ $$–$$$$ ✕ **Moose's.** Ed Moose and his wife, Mary Etta, are well known in San Francisco and beyond, so local and national politicians and media types typically turn up at their restaurant. The regularly changing menu, the work of chef Morgen Jacobson, is sophisticated without being fancy, with dishes such as roasted squid with sweet peppers, crackly skinned pork belly with parsnip purée, and rack of lamb with oven-dried tomatoes and eggplant. The surroundings are classic and comfortable, with views of Washington Square. ⊠ *1652 Stockton St., North Beach* ☏ *415/989–7800* ⌂ *Reservations essential* ▭ *AE, D, DC, MC, V* ☾ *No lunch Mon.–Wed.*

Italian

$–$$ ✕ **L'Osteria del Forno.** An Italian-speaking staff, a small and unpretentious dining area, and irresistible aromas drifting from the open kitchen make customers who pass through the door of this modest storefront operation feel as if they've stumbled into Italy. The kitchen produces small plates of simply cooked vegetables, a few baked pastas, a roast of the day, creamy polenta, and thin-crust pizzas—including a memorable "white" pie topped with porcini mushrooms and mozzarella. ⊠ *519 Columbus Ave., North Beach* ☏ *415/982–1124* ⌂ *Reservations not accepted* ▭ *No credit cards* ☾ *Closed Tues.*

Fodor's Choice ★

★ ☾ $–$$ ✕ **Tommaso's.** The place can claim San Francisco's first wood-fire pizza oven, installed in the 1930s when the restaurant opened. The oven is still here, and the restaurant, with boothlike dining nooks and a communal table running the length of the basement dining room, has changed little since those early days. The pizzas' delightfully chewy crusts, creamy mozzarella, and full-bodied house-made sauce have kept legions of happy customers returning for years. ⊠ *1042 Kearny St.* ☏ *415/398–9696* ▭ *AE, D, DC, MC, V* ☾ *Closed Mon. No lunch.*

Nob Hill & Russian Hill

French

$$$$ ✕ **Masa's.** Although the toque has been passed to several chefs since
FodorśChoice the death of founding chef Masa Kobayashi, the two-decade-old restau-
★ rant, with its chocolate-brown walls, white fabric ceiling, and red-silk-
shaded lanterns, is still one of the country's most celebrated food
temples. Chef Gregory Short, who worked alongside Thomas Keller at
the famed French Laundry for seven years, is at the helm these days,
and his tasting menus of three, six, and nine courses are pleasing diners and critics alike. All menus are laced with fancy ingredients—truffles, foie gras, caviar—and priced accordingly ($79–$120). ⊠ *Hotel
Vintage Court, 648 Bush St., Nob Hill* ☎ *415/989-7154* ⌲ *Reservations essential* ⌂ *Jacket required* ▤ *AE, D, DC, MC, V* ☉ *Closed Sun.
and Mon. No lunch.*

Italian

★ **$–$$** ✕ **Antica Trattoria.** With pale walls, dark-wood floors, cloth-draped ta-
bles, and a partial view of the kitchen, the dining room exudes a strong
sense of restraint. The same no-nonsense quality characterizes the food.
A small, regularly shifting menu delivers archetypal Italian dishes such
as fennel with blood oranges and red onions, *pappardelle* (wide flat noodles) with wild boar, pork tenderloin with Gorgonzola cheese, and *bis-
tecca* (steak) to rival what you find in Florence. The genial service by
the largely Italian staff is polished but not stiff. ⊠ *2400 Polk St., Russian Hill* ☎ *415/928-5797* ⌲ *Reservations essential* ▤ *DC, MC, V*
☉ *Closed Mon. No lunch.*

Van Ness/Polk

Italian

$$$$ ✕ **Acquerello.** Pale yellow walls, a lofty beamed ceiling, white linens, and
fresh flowers set a genteel scene at this longtime favorite. Both the service and the food are exemplary, and the regularly changing menu covers the full range of Italian cuisine: lobster *panzerotti* (ravioli-like stuffed
pasta); pappardelle with rabbit ragù; sea bass with artichokes, Gaeta
olives, and arugula; peppered pork loin with polenta and Gorgonzola.
⊠ *1722 Sacramento St., Van Ness/Polk* ☎ *415/567-5432* ▤ *AE, D,
MC, V* ☉ *Closed Sun. and Mon. No lunch.*

Seafood

¢–$ ✕ **Swan Oyster Depot.** Half fish market and half diner, this small, slim
FodorśChoice seafood operation, open since 1912, has no tables, only a narrow mar-
★ ble counter with about a dozen and a half stools. Most people come
in to buy perfectly fresh salmon, halibut, crabs, and the like to take
home. Everyone else hops onto one of the rickety stools to enjoy a bowl
of clam chowder—the only hot food served—a dozen oysters, half a
cracked crab, a big shrimp salad, or a smaller shrimp cocktail. ⊠ *1517
Polk St., Van Ness/Polk* ☎ *415/673-1101* ▤ *No credit cards* ☉ *Closed
Sun. No dinner.*

Lower Pacific Heights & Japantown

Contemporary

$$–$$$ ✕ **Quince.** Photographs of quinces line the walls of this small, elegant
Fodor'sChoice eatery in one of San Francisco's most fashionable neighborhoods. The
★ address draws a crowd that's mostly well heeled but not stuffy. Michael
Tusk, who has cooked at the legendary Chez Panisse and Oliveto, over-
sees the kitchen. The menu, which changes daily and marries French,
Italian, and American traditions, includes such inviting dishes as grilled
fresh sardines in a salad, pasta with wild mushrooms, duck with parsnips
and quince, pork braised in milk, and more. ⊠ *1701 Octavia St., Lower
Pacific Heights* ☎ *415/775–8500* ⌨ *Reservations essential* ▤ *AE, MC,
V* ⊙ *No lunch.*

★ **¢–$** ✕ **Chez Nous.** The concept here is Spanish tapas, although the small
dishes—duck-leg confit, baked goat cheese with oven-roasted tomatoes,
french fries and aioli spiked with *harissa* sauce—cross borders into
other cuisines. Grilled asparagus sprinkled with lemon zest, lamb rib
chops seasoned with lavender sea salt, and sautéed spinach tossed with
raisins and pine nuts are among the other choices. The stylish yet casual and noisy dining room has wood floors, zinc-topped tables, and
blue walls. ⊠ *1911 Fillmore St., Lower Pacific Heights* ☎ *415/441–
8044* ⌨ *Reservations not accepted* ▤ *MC, V.*

Italian

$$–$$$ ✕ **Vivande Porta Via.** Tucked in among the boutiques on upper Fillmore
Street, this longtime Italian delicatessen-restaurant, operated by well-known
chef and cookbook author Carlo Middione, draws a crowd at lunch and
dinner for both its take-out and sit-down fare. Glass cases holding dozens
of prepared delicacies span one wall. The regularly changing menu includes prosciutto with marsala-soaked figs, *risotto ai funghi* (mushroom
risotto), and pork chops with *mostarda di frutta* (slightly spicy preserved
fruits in simple syrup and mustard oil). ⊠ *2125 Fillmore St., Lower Pacific Heights* ☎ *415/346–4430* ▤ *AE, D, DC, MC, V.*

Japanese

$–$$$ ✕ **Maki.** *Wappa-meshi,* rice topped with meat or fish—chicken, eel,
salmon, and salmon eggs, among other items—and steamed in a bam-
boo basket, is the specialty at this small, lovely restaurant with blond-
wood tables and white walls. The sashimi; braised yams, daikon, and
pork; sukiyaki; and freshwater eel on rice in a lacquer box are also rec-
ommended. Everything is served on beautiful tableware, from the small-
est *sunomono* (salad) to a big assortment of sushi. Maki stocks an
impressive assortment of sakes. ⊠ *Japan Center, Kinokuniya Bldg.,
1825 Post St., Japantown* ☎ *415/921–5215* ▤ *MC, V* ⊙ *Closed Mon.*

☺ $–$$ ✕ **Mifune.** Thin brown soba and thick white udon are the specialties at
this North American outpost of an Osaka-based noodle empire. A line
often snakes out the door, but the house-made noodles, served both hot
and cold and with more than a score of toppings, are worth the wait.
Seating is at wooden tables, where diners can be heard slurping down
big bowls of such traditional Japanese combinations as fish cake–crowned
udon, *nabeyaki udon* (wheat noodles topped with tempura, chicken, and
fish cake), and *tenzaru* (cold noodles and hot tempura with gingery dip-

ping sauce) served on lacquered trays. ☒ *Japan Center, Kintetsu Bldg., 1737 Post St., Japantown* ☎ *415/922–0337* ⌂ *Reservations not accepted* ☐ *AE, D, DC, MC, V.*

Civic Center/Hayes Valley

Contemporary

$$$–$$$$
Fodor'sChoice
★

✕ **Jardinière.** Jardinière is *the* place to dine before a performance at the nearby Opera House—or any time you have something to celebrate. The restaurant takes its name from that of chef-owner Traci Des Jardins, and the sophisticated interior, with its eye-catching oval atrium and curving staircase, is the work of designer Pat Kuleto. From a memorable duck confit salad to exquisite chocolate and fruit desserts, the menu is a match for the decor. ☒ *300 Grove St., Hayes Valley* ☎ *415/861–5555* ⌂ *Reservations essential* ☐ *AE, DC, MC, V* ⊗ *No lunch.*

German

¢–$$

✕ **Suppenküche.** Bratwurst and braised red cabbage and a long list of German beers rule at this lively, hip outpost of simple German cooking in the trendy Hayes Valley corridor. Strangers sit down together at unfinished pine tables when the room gets crowded, which it regularly does. The food—potato pancakes with house-made applesauce, meat loaf, cheese spaetzle, schnitzel, apple strudel—is tasty and easy on the pocketbook, and the brews are first-rate. ☒ *601 Hayes St., Hayes Valley* ☎ *415/252–9289* ☐ *AE, MC, V* ⊗ *No lunch.*

Mediterranean

$$–$$$
Fodor'sChoice
★

✕ **Zuni Café.** The southern French–Italian menu, created by nationally known chef Judy Rodgers, packs in an eclectic crowd every night. A rabbit warren of rooms on the second level includes a balcony overlooking the main dining room. At the long copper bar a first-rate oyster selection is dispensed along with cocktails and wine. The menu changes daily, but the superb whole roast chicken and Tuscan bread salad for two are always there. ☒ *1658 Market St., Hayes Valley* ☎ *415/552–2522* ⌂ *Reservations essential* ☐ *AE, MC, V* ⊗ *Closed Mon.*

Fisherman's Wharf

French

$$$$
Fodor'sChoice
★

✕ **Gary Danko.** Chef Gary Danko's daily-changing menu of highly sophisticated plates has kept fans returning again and again. The cost of a meal ($59–$79) is pegged to the number of courses, from three to five. Plates may include risotto with lobster, rock shrimp, and winter vegetables; Moroccan squab with orange-cumin carrots; and venison with caramelized endive. The wine list is the size of a small-town phone book, and the banquette-lined room is as high class as the food. ☒ *800 N. Point St., Fisherman's Wharf* ☎ *415/749–2060* ⌂ *Reservations essential* ☐ *D, DC, MC, V* ⊗ *No lunch.*

Seafood

⟳ **$–$$$$**

✕ **McCormick & Kuleto's.** Located in historic Ghirardelli Square, this seafood emporium, part of a nationwide chain, is a visitor's dream come true: a fabulous view of the bay from every seat in the house, an

Old San Francisco atmosphere, and dozens of varieties of fish and shellfish prepared in scores of international ways. The food has its ups and downs—stick with the simplest preparations, such as oysters on the half shell and grilled fish. ⊠ *Ghirardelli Sq. at Beach and Larkin Sts., Fisherman's Wharf* ☎ *415/929–1730* ▭ *AE, D, DC, MC, V.*

Cow Hollow/Marina

French

¢–$$ ✕ **Isa.** Young, talented chef Luke Sung and his wife, Kitty, run this tiny storefront restaurant, which has a heated, candlelit back patio. The menu is divided into small and large plates, all of them French-inspired tapas meant to be shared. The menu changes seasonally but might offer such exquisite dishes as sea bass wrapped in paper-thin potato slices or baked goat cheese with pine nuts. Service is sometimes slow. The wine list is smartly crafted and complements the food. ⊠ *3324 Steiner St., Marina* ☎ *415/567–9588* ▭ *MC, V* ☉ *Closed Sun. No lunch.*

Italian

★ ¢–$$ ✕ **A-16.** Named for the autostrada that winds through Italy's south, this lively Marina spot serves the food of Naples and surrounding Campania. Among the kitchen's celebrated offerings are house-cured meats and crisp-crusted pizzas, including an excellent Margherita (mozzarella, tomato, and basil) and a *pizza bianca* with mozzarella, *grana padano* (a hard, crumbly cheese), and arugula. Braised pork breast with peppers and a combo of lamb riblets and lamb sausage are also popular. ⊠ *2355 Chestnut St., Marina* ☎ *415/771–2216* ⌂ *Reservations essential* ▭ *AE, MC, V* ☉ *No lunch Sat.–Tues.*

Mediterranean

$$–$$$$ ✕ **PlumpJack Café.** The clubby dining room, with its smartly attired clientele of bankers and brokers, socialites and society scions, takes its name from an opera composed by oil tycoon and music lover Gordon Getty, whose son is a partner here. The seasonal menu, the creation of chef James Ormsby, spans the Mediterranean and includes such tempting bits as a trio of duck preparations—crisp confit, flavorful sausage, seared breast—on a single plate and Dungeness crab cakes with an avocado-lemon sauce. ⊠ *3127 Fillmore St., Cow Hollow* ☎ *415/463–4755* ▭ *AE, DC, MC, V* ☉ *No lunch weekends.*

The Mission

Contemporary

$$–$$$ ✕ **Foreign Cinema.** The Bay Area is home to many of the country's most respected independent filmmakers, so it's no surprise that this innovative spot is a hit. In the hip, loftlike space you can not only sit down to oysters on the half shell, grilled squid with roasted peppers, and pork tenderloin with shell beans, but also watch film classics such as Zhang Yimou's *Raise the Red Lantern* projected on the wall in the large inner courtyard. ⊠ *2534 Mission St., Mission* ☎ *415/648–7600* ▭ *AE, MC, V* ☉ *No lunch.*

¢–$ ✕ **Andalu.** The menu includes some two-dozen globe-circling small plates, from duck confit dumplings with sweet chili sauce and tuna-tartare-filled miniature tacos to curly polenta fries and rib eye with *chimichurri* sauce (an Argentine blend of garlic, parsley, and olive oil) and fries. The wine list is equally global. The bilevel North Mission dining room has a sky-blue ceiling and tables outfitted in aquamarine and black. Don't overlook the dessert of doughnut holes and thick hot cocoa topped with whipped cream. ✉ *3198 16th St., Mission* ☎ *415/621–2211* ▤ *AE, MC, V* ⊘ *No lunch.*

French

★ **$$–$$$** ✕ **Chez Papa.** The small, simply outfitted corner restaurant has brought France to Potrero Hill. Small plates include mussels in wine, grilled lamb with rosemary salt on ratatouille, and deep-fried whiting fillets with lemon; lamb daube, pan-roasted halibut, and shellfish stew are among the big plates. Typically Parisian desserts include crème brûlée, chocolate-caramel soufflé, and cherry clafouti. ✉ *1401 18th St., Potrero Hill* ☎ *415/824–8210* ⚐ *Reservations essential* ▤ *AE, MC, V* ⊘ *No lunch Sun.*

Italian

$$ ✕ **Delfina.** The loyal clientele keeps coming for Craig Stoll's simple yet
Fodor'sChoice exquisite Italian fare at this hopping spot. The interior is simple, with
★ hardwood floors, aluminum-top tables, a tile bar, and a casual but sophisticated ambience. The menu changes daily, but among the usual offerings are salt cod *mantecato* (whipped with olive oil) with fennel flat bread, grilled squid on tiny white beans; pasta with cauliflower, olives, and toasted bread crumbs; and roast chicken with trumpet mushrooms and Yukon Gold potatoes. ✉ *3621 18th St., Mission* ☎ *415/552–4055* ⚐ *Reservations essential* ▤ *MC, V* ⊘ *No lunch.*

Latin

$$ ✕ **Alma.** Chef Johnny Alamilla creates a mix of Nuevo Latino flavors in this small, comfortably urban space of blue walls and wood floors. Nopales cactus accompanies mako shark; big white Peruvian beans are paired with lamb sirloin; and the ceviches are flavored with such Latin kitchen classics as chili, lime, and pumpkin seeds. The theme continues with sides of yucca fries and corn *arepas* (small pancakes filled with cheese, corn, and onions), and *dulce de leche pot de créme* (a sort of deluxe caramel pudding) on the dessert menu. Even the wine list carries a Latin stamp, with wines from Argentina, Chile, and Uruguay. ✉ *1101 Valencia St., Mission* ☎ *415/401–8959* ▤ *MC, V* ⊘ *Closed Sun. and Mon. No lunch.*

The Castro & the Haight

American-Casual

☾ **¢–$$** ✕ **Chow.** Wildly popular and unpretentious, this spot serves honest
Fodor'sChoice fare—pizzas from the wood-fired oven, thick burgers of grass-fed beef,
★ spaghetti with meatballs, roast chicken and mashed potatoes, soup-and-sandwich specials—made with the best local ingredients and priced for diners watching their wallets. The savvy try to leave room for an order of the superb cannoli, made according to a family recipe of chef-owner Tony Gulisano. ✉ *215 Church St., Castro* ☎ *415/552–2469* ⚐ *Reservations not accepted* ▤ *MC, V.*

Contemporary

$–$$$ ✕ **2223 Restaurant.** An instant success from its mid-1990s opening, the smart, sophisticated 2223 continues to attract a loyal clientele. Unfortunately, the restaurant's popularity makes conversation difficult. Thin-crust pizzas, big salads, crisp sweetbreads, grilled pork chops, and a luscious bread pudding are among the high-scoring dishes. The popular Sunday brunch delivers old favorites with contemporary style. ⊠ *2223 Market St., Castro* ☏ *415/431–0692* ☷ *AE, DC, MC, V* ☺ *No lunch Mon.–Sat.*

Indian

¢–$$ ✕ **Indian Oven.** One of the Lower Haight's most popular restaurants, this cozy Victorian storefront with dining on two floors never lacks for customers. Many come for the tandoori specialties—chicken, lamb, breads—but *saag paneer* (spinach with Indian cheese) and *bengan bartha* (roasted eggplant with onions and spices) are also excellent. ⊠ *233 Fillmore St., Lower Haight* ☏ *415/626–1628* ☷ *AE, D, DC, MC, V* ☺ *No lunch.*

Thai

★ **¢–$$** ✕ **Thep Phanom.** The fine fare and the lovely Thai art–cluttered interior at this Lower Haight institution keep local food critics and restaurant goers singing Thep Phanom's praises. Duck is deliciously prepared in several ways—atop a mound of spinach, in a fragrant curry, minced for salad. Seafood (in various guises) is another specialty, along with stuffed chicken wings, spicy beef salad, fried quail, and addictive Thai curries. ⊠ *400 Waller St., Lower Haight* ☏ *415/431–2526* ☷ *AE, D, DC, MC, V* ☺ *No lunch.*

Richmond District

Chinese

¢–$$$ ✕ **Parc Hong Kong Restaurant.** This tablecloth Cantonese restaurant has long been known as a place to enjoy such classy plates as smoked black cod and Peking duck. The kitchen is especially celebrated for its seafood, which is plucked straight from tanks and can be a costly indulgence; in the cool months, though, crab and lobster, prepared in half a dozen ways, are usually priced to sell. Chefs here keep up with whatever is hot in Hong Kong eateries, so check on what's new with the generally genial waiters. ⊠ *5322 Geary Blvd., Richmond* ☏ *415/668–8998* ☷ *AE, D, DC, MC, V.*

Japanese

★ **¢–$$** ✕ **Kabuto A&S.** Master chef Sachio Kojima flashes his knives before an admiring crowd, which can't get enough of his buttery yellowfin tuna or golden sea urchin on pads of pearly rice. In addition to serving fine sushi and sashimi, the restaurant also offers small, cooked plates in its cozy, 20-seat dining room and at the dozen-seat sushi bar. Don't overlook the excellent selection of sakes, each one rated for dryness and labeled with its place of origin. ⊠ *5121 Geary Blvd., Richmond* ☏ *415/752–5652* ☷ *MC, V* ☺ *Closed Wed.*

Vietnamese

¢–$$ ✕ **Le Soleil.** The kitchen at this light-filled, pastel restaurant in the heart of the Inner Richmond prepares traditional Vietnamese dishes from every part of the country. Try the excellent raw-beef salad; shaking beef (tender beef cubes in a vinegary sauce); a simple stir-fry of chicken and fresh basil leaves; or large prawns simmered in a clay pot. A large aquarium of tropical fish adds to the tranquil mood. ⊠ *133 Clement St., Inner Richmond* ☎ *415/668–4848* ⊟ *MC, V.*

Sunset District

American-Casual

$$–$$$ ✕ **Beach Chalet.** In a historic colonnaded building with handsome Works Project Administration–produced murals depicting San Francisco in the mid-1930s, the Beach Chalet is the place to watch the waves break on the shore and the sun set over the Pacific Ocean. The fine microbrewery beers run the gamut from a light pilsner to a pale ale, but the menu—barbecued baby back ribs, grilled salmon, fried calamari—won't wow sophisticated palates. ⊠ *1000 Great Hwy., Sunset* ☎ *415/386–8439* ⊟ *MC, V.*

WHERE TO STAY

By Andy Moore

Few U.S. cities can rival San Francisco's variety in lodging. Its plush hotels rank among the world's finest; its renovated buildings house small hostelries with European flair; its grand Victorian-era homes serve as bed-and-breakfasts; and its private residences rent rooms, apartments, and cottages. You can even find accommodations in boats bobbing on the bay, but the popular chain hotels and motels found in most American cities are here, too. The city's hilly topography and diversity of neighborhoods contribute to each property's unique sense of place, and you may feel like a kid in a candy store as you go about choosing which of the approximately 32,000 rooms here will be your home-away-from-home.

WHAT IT COSTS				
$$$$	**$$$**	**$$**	**$**	**¢**
FOR 2 PEOPLE over $250	$200–$250	$150–$199	$90–$149	under $90

Prices are for two people in a standard double room in high season, excluding 14% tax.

Union Square/Downtown

★ **$$$$** ▦ **Campton Place.** Highly attentive service is the hallmark of this small, top-tier hotel behind a simple brownstone facade. Many rooms are smallish, but all are elegant in a contemporary Italian style, with light earth tones and handsome pearwood paneling and cabinetry. Bathrooms have deep soaking tubs, and double-paned windows keep city noises out. ⊠ *340 Stockton St., Union Sq., 94108* ☎ *415/781–5555 or 800/235–4300* ⊟ *415/955–5536* ⊕ *www.camptonplace.com* ⇥ *101 rooms, 9 suites* ⟂ *Restaurant, room service, in-room safes, minibars, cable TV with movies and video games, in-room data ports, exercise equipment, gym, bar, lobby lounge, dry cleaning, laundry service, concierge, business services, meeting room, parking (fee), some pets allowed (fee), no-smoking floors; no kids under 17* ⊟ *AE, DC, MC, V.*

$$$$ ⊞ **Clift.** Behind a stately, beige brick facade lies this "hotel as art" showplace, as conceived by entrepreneur Ian Schrager and artist-designer Philippe Starck. The cavernous lobby contains groupings of whimsical art objects meant to encourage a surreal mood. Spacious rooms with high ceilings, in shades of ivory, gray, and lavender, have blond-wood and see-through orange acrylic furniture, plus two huge mirrors on otherwise empty walls. ⊠ *495 Geary St., Union Sq., 94102* ☎ *415/775–4700 or 800/652–5438* 🖷 *415/441–4621* ⊕ *www.clifthotel.com* 🛏 *337 rooms, 26 suites* ⚥ *Restaurant, room service, in-room safes, minibars, cable TV with movies, in-room VCRs, in-room data ports, gym, bar, lobby lounge, babysitting, dry cleaning, laundry service, concierge, Internet room, business services, meeting rooms, parking (fee), some pets allowed (fee), no-smoking floors* ▭ *AE, D, DC, MC, V.*

$$$–$$$$ ⊞ **Hotel Monaco.** A cheery 1910 Beaux Arts facade and snappily dressed
Fodor's Choice doormen welcome you into the plush lobby, with its French inglenook
★ fireplace and vaulted ceiling with murals of World War I–era planes and hot-air balloons. Rooms are full of flair, with vivid stripes and colors, Chinese-inspired armoires, canopy beds, and high-back upholstered chairs. Outer rooms have bay-window seats overlooking the bustling theater district. If you didn't bring a pet, request a "companion goldfish." ⊠ *501 Geary St., Union Sq., 94102* ☎ *415/292–0100* 🖷 *415/292–0111* ⊕ *www.monaco-sf.com* 🛏 *181 rooms, 20 suites* ⚥ *Restaurant, café, room service, in-room fax, in-room safes, some in-room hot tubs, minibars, cable TV with movies and video games, some in-room VCRs, in-room data ports, gym, hot tub, massage, sauna, spa, steam room, bar, babysitting, dry cleaning, laundry service, concierge, Internet room, business services, convention center, meeting rooms, parking (fee), some pets allowed, no-smoking floors* ▭ *AE, D, DC, MC, V.*

$$$–$$$$ ⊞ **Prescott Hotel.** Although not as famous as many other hotels in the area, this relatively small establishment provides extremely personalized service, as well as preferred reservations at Postrio, the Wolfgang Puck restaurant attached to its lobby. Rooms, which are filled with cherry-wood furniture, are handsomely decorated in dark autumn colors and have bathrooms with marble-top sinks. Complimentary coffee and evening wine are offered by a flickering fireplace in the living room. ⊠ *545 Post St., Union Sq., 94102* ☎ *415/563–0303* 🖷 *415/563–6831* ⊕ *www.prescotthotel.com* 🛏 *132 rooms, 33 suites* ⚥ *Restaurant, room service, in-room fax, in-room safes, minibars, cable TV with movies and video games, some in-room VCRs, in-room data ports, gym, bar, concierge, concierge floor, Internet room, business services, meeting rooms, parking (fee), some pets allowed, no-smoking floors* ▭ *AE, D, DC, MC, V.*

★ **$$–$$$$** ⊞ **Hotel Nikko.** The vast marble lobby of this Japan Airlines–owned hotel is airy and serene, and its rooms are among the most handsome in the city. Look for gold drapes; wheat-color wall coverings; furniture with clean, elegant lines; and ingenious window shades that screen the sun while allowing views of the city. The excellent, complimentary 5th-floor fitness facility has traditional *ofuros* (Japanese soaking tubs), a *kamaburo* (Japanese sauna), and a glass-enclosed rooftop pool and whirlpool. A multilingual staff provides attentive, sincere service. ⊠ *222 Mason St., Union Sq., 94102* ☎ *415/394–1111 or 800/645–5687* 🖷 *415/421–*

0 | 1/4 mile
0 | 400 meters

Chestnut St.
Lombard St.
Octavia St.
Gough St.
Franklin St.
Van Ness Ave.
Polk St.
Larkin St.
Hyde St.
Leavenworth St.

❷

❶

RUSSIAN HILL

Green St.
Vallejo St.
Broadway

PACIFIC HEIGHTS

Broadway

Leavenworth St.

Pacific St.
Jackson St.
Washington St.

Alta Plaza

Lafayette Park

Clay St.
Sacramento St.
California St.

Scott St.
Pierce St.
Steiner St.
Fillmore St.
Webster St.
Buchanan St.
Laguna St.
Octavia St.
Gough St.
Franklin St.
Van Ness Ave.
Polk St.
Larkin St.

Jones St.

Pine St.
Bush St.
Sutter St.

JAPANTOWN

Hyde St.

Post St.
Geary St.
O'Farrell St.

TENDERLOIN

Ellis St.
Eddy St.
Turk St.
Golden Gate Ave.

HAYES VALLEY

McAllister St.

City Hall ◆

United Nations Plaza ◆

❷❾

Fulton St.

❷❽

CIVIC CENTER

Market St.

❸⓿ Alamo Square

Alamo Square

Grove St.

7th St.

8th St.

Hayes St.

Where to Stay
In & Around
Downtown
San Francisco

Chestnut St.

Lombard St.

Coit Tower

❸-❺

Greenwich St.

Filbert St.

Union St.

TELEGRAPH HILL

Columbus Ave.

Grant Ave.

Mason St.

NORTH BEACH

❻

Pier 17

Pier 15

Front St.

Pier 9

Embarcadero

Pier 7

Pier 5

Pier 3

Pier 1

San Francisco Bay

Tunnel

Taylor St.

Powell St.

Stockton St.

Montgomery St.

Sansome St.

Battery St.

Davis St.

Drumm St.

Transamerica Pyramid

Justin Herman Plaza

NOB HILL

CHINATOWN

Kearny St.

Embarcadero Center

Davis St.

Audiffred Building

Halleck St.

Front St.

Spear St.

Steuart St.

❼

❶❷

❶❸

FINANCIAL DISTRICT

❽

❿

❾ **Chinatown Gate**

Main St.

Beale St.

Fremont St.

❶❹

❶❶

1st St.

❶❺

❶❼

❶❻

❶❽

UNION SQUARE

Maiden Ln.

Market St.

New Montgomery St.

2nd St.

Pier 24

❶❾ ❷⓿

❷❶

Pier 26

❷❷

❷❸

3rd St.

Pier 28

Visitor Information Center

❷❹

Yerba Buena Gardens

Hawthorn St.

80

Bryant St.

Pier 30

Mission St.

4th St.

Moscone Convention Center

Pier 32

5th St.

Howard St.

Brannan St.

Pier 34

SO MA

Folsom St.

Pier 36

6th St.

Harrison St.

TO AIRPORT

❷❺-❷❼

Townsend St.

Pier 38

Pier 40

0455 ⊕ www.hotelnikkosf.com ⇌ 516 rooms, 16 suites ⚐ Restaurant, room service, some in-room fax, some in-room safes, some in-room hot tubs, some kitchenettes, minibars, refrigerators, cable TV with movies and video games, in-room data ports, indoor pool, gym, hair salon, Japanese baths, massage, sauna, bar, lobby lounge, babysitting, dry cleaning, laundry service, concierge, concierge floor, Internet room, business services, meeting rooms, car rental, parking (fee), some pets allowed (fee), no-smoking floors ⊟ AE, D, DC, MC, V.

★ $$–$$$ 🏨 **Hotel Adagio.** The gracious, Spanish-colonial facade of this 16-story, theater-row hotel complements its chic, modern interior. Walnut furniture, bronze light fixtures, and brown and deep-orange hues dominate the spacious rooms, half of which have city views—and two penthouse suites have terraces looking out on the neighborhood. ⊠ *550 Geary St., Union Sq., 94102 ☎ 415/775–5000 or 800/228–8830 ⊟ 415/775–9388 ⊕ www. thehoteladagio.com ⇌ 169 rooms, 2 suites ⚐ Restaurant, room service, fans, in-room safes, minibars, refrigerators, room TVs with movies and video games, in-room data ports, gym, bar, lounge, babysitting, dry cleaning, laundry service, Internet room, business services, meeting rooms, parking (fee), no-smoking floors; no a/c ⊟ AE, D, DC, MC, V.*

$–$$$ 🏨 **Hotel Rex.** Literary and artistic creativity are celebrated at this styl-
Fodor's Choice   ish place named after writer Kenneth Rexroth. Shelves of antiquarian
★   books line the 1920s-style lobby lounge, where the proprietors often hold book readings and roundtable discussions. Although the spacious rooms evoke the spirit of 1920s salon society with muted checkered bedspreads, striped carpets, and restored period furnishings, they also have modern touches such as CD players, and complimentary Aveda hair and skin products. ⊠ *562 Sutter St., Union Sq., 94102 ☎ 415/433–4434 or 800/433–4434 ⊟ 415/433–3695 ⊕ www.thehotelrex.com ⇌ 92 rooms, 2 suites ⚐ Café, room service, minibars, refrigerators, cable TV with movies, in-room data ports, bar, lobby lounge, babysitting, dry cleaning, laundry service, concierge, Internet room, business services, meeting rooms, parking (fee), no-smoking floors ⊟ AE, D, DC, MC, V.*

★ $–$$ 🏨 **Hotel Beresford Arms.** Surrounded by fancy molding and 10-foot-tall windows, the red-carpeted lobby of this ornate brick Victorian shows why the building is on the National Register of Historic Places. Rooms with dark-wood antique-reproduction furniture vary in size and setup: junior suites have sitting areas and either a wet bar or kitchenette, and full suites have two queen beds, a Murphy bed, and a kitchen. All suites have a bidet in the bathroom. ⊠ *701 Post St., Union Sq., 94109 ☎ 415/ 673–2600 or 800/533–6533 ⊟ 415/929–1535 or 800/533–5349 ⊕ www. beresford.com ⇌ 83 rooms, 12 suites ⚐ Fans, some in-room hot tubs, some kitchens, some kitchenettes, minibars, some microwaves, refrigerators, cable TV, in-room VCRs, in-room data ports, dry cleaning, laundry service, concierge, Internet room, business services, parking (fee), some pets allowed, no-smoking floors; no a/c ⊟ AE, D, DC, MC, V ⓘ CP.*

¢–$ 🏨 **Grant Plaza Hotel.** Amazingly low room rates make this hotel a find
Fodor's Choice   for budget travelers wanting views of the striking architecture and fas-
★   cinating street life of Chinatown. Small modern rooms are sparkly clean, with newer, slightly more expensive digs on the top floor and quieter quarters in the back. Even if you're not on the top floor, take the elevator up anyway to view two large, beautiful stained-glass windows.

✉ *465 Grant Ave., Chinatown, 94108* ☎ *415/434–3883 or 800/472–6899* 📠 *415/434–3886* ⊕ *www.grantplaza.com* 🛏 *71 rooms, 1 suite* 🛎 *Some fans, some in-room VCRs, some in-room data ports, Internet room, business services, parking (fee), no-smoking rooms; no a/c* 🖃 *AE, D, DC, MC, V.*

Financial District

$$$$ 🏨 **Mandarin Oriental.** Two towers connected by glass-enclosed sky bridges
FodorśChoice compose the top 11 floors of San Francisco's third-tallest building. There
★ are spectacular panoramas from every room, and windows open so you
can hear the "ding ding" of the cable cars some 40 floors below. The
Mandarin Rooms have extra-deep tubs next to picture windows so you
can enjoy the views while soaking. All rooms have Egyptian-cotton
sheets, two kinds of robes (terry and waffle-weave), and terry slippers.
✉ *222 Sansome St., Financial District, 94104* ☎ *415/276–9888* 📠 *415/433–0289* ⊕ *www.mandarinoriental.com* 🛏 *154 rooms, 4 suites* 🛎 *Restaurant, room service, in-room safes, some in-room hot tubs, some kitchenettes, minibars, cable TV with movies and video games, some in-room VCRs, in-room data ports, gym, massage, lobby lounge, piano, babysitting, dry cleaning, laundry service, concierge, Internet room, business services, convention center, meeting rooms, parking (fee), some pets allowed (fee), no-smoking rooms* 🖃 *AE, D, DC, MC, V.*

★ **$$–$$$$** 🏨 **Hyatt Regency.** The 20-story gray concrete structure, at the foot of
Market Street, is the focal point of the Embarcadero Center. The spec-
tacular 17-story atrium lobby (listed by Guinness World Records as the
largest hotel lobby in the world) is a marvel, with sprawling trees, a shim-
mering stream, and a huge fountain. Glass elevators whisk you up to
Equinox, the city's only revolving rooftop restaurant. Rooms—all with
city or bay views, and some with bay-view balconies—have an attrac-
tive, contemporary look, with light-color walls and carpets, handsome
cherry furniture, and ergonomic desk chairs. ✉ *5 Embarcadero Cen-
ter, Embarcadero, 94111* ☎ *415/788–1234 or 800/233–1234* 📠 *415/398–2567* ⊕ *http://sanfranciscoregency.hyatt.com* 🛏 *776 rooms, 29 suites* 🛎 *2 restaurants, café, dining room, room service, in-room safes, mini-bars, cable TV with movies, in-room data ports, gym, 2 bars, lobby lounge, dry cleaning, laundry service, concierge, business services, convention center, meeting rooms, car rental, parking (fee), no-smoking floors* 🖃 *AE, D, DC, MC, V.*

SoMa

$$$$ 🏨 **Four Seasons Hotel San Francisco.** On floors 5–17 of a skyscraper, this
FodorśChoice luxurious hotel is sandwiched between multimillion-dollar condos, elite
★ shops, and a premier sports-and-fitness complex—and while you're
here, you can indulge in a little surreptitious celebrity hunting. Elegant
rooms with contemporary artwork and fine linens have floor-to-ceiling
windows overlooking Yerba Buena Gardens, the bay, or the city. All have
deep soaking tubs and glass-enclosed showers. Take the elevator to the
vast Sports Club/LA, where you have free use of the junior Olympic pool,
full-size indoor basketball court, and the rest of the magnificent facili-
ties, classes, and spa services. ✉ *757 Market St., SoMa, 94103* ☎ *415/*

633–3000 🖨 *415/633–3009* ⊕ *www.fourseasons.com/sanfrancisco*
↪ *222 rooms, 55 suites* ♿ *Restaurant, room service, in-room safes, minibars, cable TV with movies and video games, some in-room VCRs, in-
room data ports, indoor pool, health club, sauna, spa, steam room,
basketball, volleyball, bar, dry cleaning, laundry service, concierge, Internet room, business services, meeting rooms, parking (fee), some pets
allowed, no-smoking floors* ▭ *AE, D, DC, MC, V.*

★ **$$$$** 🏨 **Hotel Palomar.** The top five floors of the green-tiled and turreted
1908 Pacific Place Building provide a luxurious oasis above the busiest
part of town. A softly lighted lounge area with plush sofas gives way to
the Fifth Floor restaurant, which serves modern French cuisine. Rooms
have muted leopard-pattern carpeting, drapes with bold navy-and-
cream stripes, and sleek furniture echoing a 1930s moderne sensibility.
Sparkling bathrooms provide a "tub menu" with various herbal and
botanical infusions to tempt adventurous bathers. In-room spa services
are arranged through Equilibrium Spa. ✉ *12 4th St., SoMa, 94103* ☎ *415/
348–1111* 🖨 *415/348–0302* ⊕ *www.hotelpalomar.com* ↪ *185 rooms,
13 suites* ♿ *Restaurant, room service, in-room fax, in-room safes, some
in-room hot tubs, minibars, cable TV with movies and video games, some
in-room VCRs, in-room data ports, gym, massage, bar, lounge, babysitting, dry cleaning, laundry service, concierge, Internet room, business
services, meeting rooms, parking (fee), some pets allowed (fee), no-
smoking floors* ▭ *AE, D, DC, MC, V.*

$$$$ 🏨 **Palace Hotel.** This landmark hotel was the world's largest and most
Fodor's Choice luxurious when it opened in 1875. Completely rebuilt after the earth-
★ quake and fire of 1906, the splendid hotel has a stunning entryway and
the fabulous belle-epoque Garden Court restaurant, with its graceful chandeliers and stained-glass domed ceiling. Rooms, with twice-daily maid
service and nightly turndown, have 14-foot ceilings, traditional mahogany
furnishings, and marble bathrooms. ✉ *2 New Montgomery St., SoMa,
94105* ☎ *415/512–1111* 🖨 *415/543–0671* ⊕ *www.sfpalace.com* ↪ *518
rooms, 34 suites* ♿ *3 restaurants, room service, in-room safes, some in-
room hot tubs, refrigerators, cable TV with movies and video games,
in-room data ports, indoor pool, gym, hot tub, sauna, spa, steam room,
bar, dry cleaning, laundry service, concierge, business services, meeting
rooms, parking (fee), no-smoking floors* ▭ *AE, D, DC, MC, V.*

★ **$$$–$$$$** 🏨 **Harbor Court.** The exemplary service of the friendly staff earns high
marks for this cozy hotel overlooking the Embarcadero and within
shouting distance of the Bay Bridge. Guest rooms are smallish but have
double sets of soundproof windows and include nice touches such as
wall-mounted 27-inch flat-screen TVs, brightly colored throw pillows
on beds with 320-thread-count sheets, and tub-showers with curved
shower curtain rods for more elbow room. Some rooms have bay (and
bridge) views. The hotel provides free use of the adjacent YMCA and
free weekday limo service within the Financial District. ✉ *165 Steuart
St., SoMa, 94105* ☎ *415/882–1300* 🖨 *415/882–1313* ⊕ *www.
harborcourthotel.com* ↪ *130 rooms, 1 suite* ♿ *In-room fax, minibars,
room TVs with movies and video games, in-room data ports, bar, dry
cleaning, laundry service, concierge, Internet room, business services,
meeting room, parking (fee), some pets allowed, no-smoking rooms* ▭*AE,
D, DC, MC, V.*

Nob Hill

★ **$$$$** 🏨 **Fairmont San Francisco.** The history of the hotel, which commands the top of Nob Hill like a European palace, includes triumph over the 1906 earthquake and the creation of the United Nations Charter here in 1945. Architect Julia Morgan's 1907 lobby design includes alabaster walls and gilt-embellished ceilings supported by Corinthian columns. Gracious rooms, done in pale color schemes, have high ceilings, fine dark-wood furniture, colorful Chinese porcelain lamps, and marble bathrooms. Rooms in the Tower are generally larger and have better views. An array of amenities and services (including free chicken soup if you're under the weather) keeps loyal (and royal) guests coming back. ⊠ *950 Mason St., Nob Hill, 94108* 🕿 *415/772–5000* 🖷 *415/772–5086* ⊕ *www.fairmont.com* ⤳ *526 rooms, 65 suites* ₰ *2 restaurants, room service, in-room safes, minibars, cable TV with movies and video games, in-room data ports, health club, hair salon, spa, steam room, 2 bars, lobby lounge, lounge, nightclub, shops, babysitting, dry cleaning, laundry service, concierge, Internet room, business services, convention center, meeting rooms, car rental, parking (fee), some pets allowed (fee), no-smoking floors* ▤ *AE, D, DC, MC, V.*

★ **$$$$** 🏨 **The Huntington Hotel.** The venerable ivy-covered hotel has provided gracious personal service to everyone from Bogart and Bacall to Picasso and Pavarotti. Rooms and suites, many of which have great views of Grace Cathedral, the bay, or the city skyline, are large because they used to be apartments. Most rooms have wet bars; all have large antique desks. The elegant Nob Hill Spa complex has panoramic city views, numerous spa services, and spa cuisine served by white-jacketed waiters around an indoor pool with a fireplace lounge area. ⊠ *1075 California St., Nob Hill, 94108* 🕿 *415/474–5400 or 800/227–4683* 🖷 *415/474–6227* ⊕ *www. huntingtonhotel.com* ⤳ *100 rooms, 35 suites* ₰ *Restaurant, room service, in-room fax, in-room safes, some in-room hot tubs, some kitchenettes, minibars, some refrigerators, cable TV with movies, in-room data ports, indoor pool, hot tub, gym, massage, sauna, spa, steam room, bar, piano, dry cleaning, laundry service, concierge, business services, meeting rooms, parking (fee), no-smoking floors* ▤ *AE, D, DC, MC, V.*

$$$$ 🏨 **Ritz-Carlton, San Francisco.** This hotel is a stunning tribute to beauty
Fodor's Choice and attentive, professional service. Beyond the Ionic columns of the neo-
★ classic facade, crystal chandeliers illuminate Georgian antiques and museum-quality 18th- and 19th-century paintings in the lobby. All rooms have featherbeds with 300-thread-count Egyptian cotton Frette sheets and down comforters. Afternoon tea in the Lobby Lounge—overlooking the beautifully landscaped garden courtyard—is a San Francisco institution. ⊠ *600 Stockton St., at California St., Nob Hill, 94108* 🕿 *415/ 296–7465* 🖷 *415/291–0288* ⊕ *www.ritzcarlton.com* ⤳ *294 rooms, 42 suites* ₰ *2 restaurants, room service, in-room safes, minibars, refrigerators, cable TV with movies and video games, some in-room VCRs, in-room data ports, indoor pool, exercise equipment, gym, hot tub, massage, steam room, 3 bars, lobby lounge, piano bar, shop, babysitting, dry cleaning, laundry service, concierge, concierge floor, Internet room, business services, meeting rooms, parking (fee), some pets allowed, no-smoking floors* ▤ *AE, D, DC, MC, V.*

$–$$$ 🏨 **Executive Hotel Vintage Court.** This Napa Valley–inspired hotel two blocks from Union Square has inviting rooms named after California wineries. Some have sunny window seats, and all have large writing desks, dark-wood venetian blinds, and steam heat. Bathrooms are small, some with tub-showers and some with stall showers. The Wine Country theme extends to complimentary local vintages served nightly in front of the fireplace in the chocolate-color lobby, where long couches invite lingering. ⊠ *650 Bush St., Nob Hill, 94108* 🕾 *415/392–4666* 🖷 *415/433–4065* ⊕ *www.executivehotels.net* ➷ *106 rooms, 1 suite* ♨ *Restaurant, some in-room hot tubs, minibars, refrigerators, cable TV with movies and video games, in-room data ports, bar, dry cleaning, concierge, Internet room, meeting rooms, parking (fee), some pets allowed (fee); no smoking* 🖃 *AE, D, DC, MC, V* ❜⚬❜ *CP.*

Fisherman's Wharf/North Beach

$$–$$$$
FodorsChoice
★ 🏨 **Argonaut Hotel.** When this four-story brick building was a fruit-and-vegetable-canning complex in 1907, boats docked right up against the building. Today it's a tribute to nautical chic—anchors, ropes, compasses, and a row of cruise-ship deck chairs find their way into the lively lobby decor. Spacious rooms, many of which have a sitting area with a sofa bed, have exposed-brick walls, wood-beamed ceilings, and whitewashed wooden furniture that evokes a beach mood. Windows are open to the sea air and the sounds of the waterfront, and many have unimpeded views of the bay. Suites come with extra-deep whirlpool tubs and telescopes for close-up views of passing ships. ⊠ *495 Jefferson St., at Hyde St., Fisherman's Wharf, 94109* 🕾 *415/563–0800* 🖷 *415/563–2800* ⊕ *www.argonauthotel.com* ➷ *239 rooms, 13 suites* ♨ *Restaurant, room service, in-room safes, some in-room hot tubs, minibars, refrigerators, cable TV with movies and video games, in-room VCRs, in-room data ports, gym, bar, lounge, babysitting, dry cleaning, laundry service, concierge, Internet room, convention center, meeting rooms, parking (fee), some pets allowed, no-smoking rooms* 🖃 *AE, D, DC, MC, V.*

★ **$$–$$$** 🏨 **Radisson Hotel Fisherman's Wharf.** Directly facing Alcatraz, this city block–size hotel and shopping area at Fisherman's Wharf has vast, clear views of the bay. Contemporary rooms, most of which have water vistas, are decorated with cherrywood furniture and black-and-tan-stripe drapes. About half the rooms (those with king-size beds) let you adjust the firmness of each side of the bed individually. A landscaped courtyard and heated pool are in the center of the hotel complex, which provides the closest accommodations to Pier 39 and the bay cruise docks. ⊠ *250 Beach St., Fisherman's Wharf, 94133* 🕾 *415/392–6700* 🖷 *415/986–7853* ⊕ *www.radisson.com/sanfranciscoca_wharf* ➷ *355 rooms* ♨ *In-room safes, some refrigerators, cable TV with movies and video games, in-room data ports, pool, gym, dry cleaning, laundry service, concierge, business services, meeting rooms, parking (fee), no-smoking rooms* 🖃 *AE, D, DC, MC, V.*

$$ 🏨 **Hotel Bohème.** This small hotel in historic North Beach takes you back in time with cast-iron beds, large mirrored armoires, and memorabilia recalling the Beat generation. Allen Ginsberg stayed here many times and could be seen in his later years sitting in a window, tapping away on his laptop computer. Screenwriters from Francis Ford Coppola's nearby American Zoetrope studio stay here often, as do poets and other artists. Rooms have a bistro table, two chairs, and tropical-style mosquito netting over the bed; bathrooms have cheerful yellow tiles and tiny showers. Rooms in the rear are quieter, especially on weekends. ⊠ *444 Columbus Ave., North Beach, 94133* 🕾 *415/433–9111* 📠 *415/362–6292* ⊕ *www.hotelboheme.com* ➟ *15 rooms* ♨ *Fans, cable TV, in-room data ports, concierge; no a/c, no smoking* 🖃 *AE, D, DC, MC, V.*

¢–$
Fodor'sChoice
★
🖾 **San Remo Hotel.** A few blocks from Fisherman's Wharf, this three-story 1906 Italianate Victorian was once home to longshoremen and Beat poets. A narrow stairway from the street leads to the front desk and labyrinthine hallways. Rooms are small but charming, with lace curtains, forest-green-painted wood floors, brass beds, and other antique furnishings. About a third of the rooms have sinks, and all rooms share scrupulously clean black-and-white-tile shower and toilet facilities with pull-chain toilets. ⊠ *2237 Mason St., North Beach, 94133* 🕾 *415/776–8688 or 800/352–7366* 📠 *415/776–2811* ⊕ *www.sanremohotel.com* ➟ *64 rooms with shared baths, 1 suite* ♨ *Fans, laundry facilities, Internet room, parking (fee); no a/c, no room phones, no room TVs, no smoking* 🖃 *AE, MC, V.*

Cow Hollow

$$–$$$$
Fodor'sChoice
★
🖾 **Union Street Inn.** With the help of precious family antiques and unique artwork, innkeepers Jane Bertorelli and David Coyle (who was a chef for the Duke and Duchess of Bedford) turned this green-and-cream 1902 Edwardian into a delightful B&B. Equipped with candles, fresh flowers, wineglasses, and fine linens, rooms are popular with honeymooners and romantics. The Carriage House, with its whirlpool tub, is set off from the main house by an old-fashioned English garden with lemon trees. ⊠ *2229 Union St., Cow Hollow, 94123* 🕾 *415/346–0424* 📠 *415/922–8046* ⊕ *www.unionstreetinn.com* ➟ *6 rooms* ♨ *Cable TV, parking (fee); no a/c in some rooms, no smoking* 🖃 *AE, MC, V* ⥮ *BP.*

★ ☾ $–$$
🖾 **Hotel Del Sol.** Once a typical 1950s-style motor court, the Del Sol is now an atypical artistic statement. The sunny yellow-and-blue, three-story building and courtyard are a riot of stripes and bold colors. Rooms, some with brick fireplaces, open onto the courtyard's heated pool and hammock under towering palm trees and evoke a beach-house mood with plantation shutters, tropical-stripe bedspreads, and rattan chairs. Family suites have child-friendly furnishings and games. Ask about the hotel's 15-style "pillow library." ⊠ *3100 Webster St., Cow Hollow, 94123* 🕾 *415/921–5520 or 877/433–5765* 📠 *415/931–4137* ⊕ *www.thehoteldelsol.com* ➟ *46 rooms, 11 suites* ♨ *In-room safes, some kitchenettes, some microwaves, some refrigerators, cable TV, some in-room VCRs, in-room data ports, pool, bicycles, dry cleaning, laundry service, concierge, free parking, no-smoking rooms; no a/c in some rooms* 🖃 *AE, D, DC, MC, V* ⥮ *CP.*

Civic Center/Van Ness

$–$$$
🖾 **The Archbishop's Mansion.** Everything in this stately 1904 French chateau–style mansion is extravagantly romantic, starting with the cav-

ernous common areas, where a chandelier used in the movie *Gone With the Wind* hangs above a Bechstein grand piano once owned by Noël Coward. Guest rooms here are grand, too; they're individually decorated with ornately carved antiques, and many have whirlpool tubs or fireplaces. Have complimentary Continental breakfast served to you in your canopied bed if you wish, then stroll past the famous Victorian "Painted Ladies" homes that share your Alamo Square location. ✉ *1000 Fulton St., Western Addition, 94117* ☎ *415/563–7872 or 800/543–5820* 🖷 *415/885–3193* 🌐 *www.thearchbishopsmansion.com* *10 rooms, 5 suites* *Dining room, some fans, some in-room hot tubs, cable TV, in-room VCRs, in-room data ports, piano, dry cleaning, concierge, meeting room, some free parking; no a/c, no smoking* 💳 *AE, D, MC, V* 🍽 *CP.*

★ **$–$$** **Alamo Square Inn.** A large, 1895 Queen Anne home and an 1896 Tudor-revival mansion combine to form this extravagantly romantic B&B overlooking the terraced, grassy hilltop park for which it is named. Elaborate wainscoting and period antiques decorate the four parlors, two dining rooms, hallways, and guest rooms. One suite has peaked ceilings and a sunken whirlpool tub; another has bookcases with hundreds of old volumes and a fireplace. Oriental carpets cover lustrous hardwood floors, and there are four fireplaces, three pianos, and a regulation billiards table to discover in the rambling common areas. ✉ *719 Scott St., at Fulton St., Western Addition, 94117* ☎ *415/922–2055 or 888/886–8803* 🖷 *415/931–1304* 🌐 *www.alamoinn.com* *9 rooms, 3 suites* *Some in-room hot tubs, some refrigerators, 3 pianos, babysitting, dry cleaning, laundry facilities, Internet room, business services, meeting room, free parking, no-smoking rooms; no a/c, no TV in some rooms* 💳 *AE, MC, V* 🍽 *BP.*

$ **Inn at the Opera.** Within a block or so of Davies Symphony Hall and the War Memorial Opera House, this hotel has played host to such music, dance, and opera stars as Luciano Pavarotti and Mikhail Baryshnikov. Beyond the genteel marble-floor lobby, modern and compact standard rooms have dark-wood furnishings, queen-size pillow-top beds with 250-thread-count sheets, and terry robes. ✉ *333 Fulton St., Van Ness/Civic Center, 94102* ☎ *415/863–8400 or 800/325–2708* 🖷 *415/861–0821* 🌐 *www.innattheopera.com* *30 rooms, 18 suites* *Restaurant, room service, fans, some kitchenettes, some microwaves, some refrigerators, cable TV, some in-room VCRs, in-room data ports, bar, babysitting, dry cleaning, concierge, business services, parking (fee); no a/c, no smoking* 💳 *AE, DC, MC, V* 🍽 *CP.*

The Airport

★ **$$$–$$$$** **Hotel Sofitel–San Francisco Bay.** Set on a lagoon in a business park with several big-name corporate headquarters nearby, the hotel is a warm, inviting haven within this somewhat sterile area. Parisian lampposts, a métro sign, and a poster-covered kiosk bring an unexpected French theme to the public spaces, and the light, open feeling extends to the luxurious rooms. Done in pale earth tones, accommodations include fine linens and bath products, complimentary turndown service, Evian water, and fresh orchids. Many staff members speak both French and English. ✉ *223 Twin Dolphin Dr., Redwood City 94065* ☎ *650/598–9000*

⌖ 650/598–0459 ⊕ *www.accorhotels.com/sofitel_san_francisco_bay. htm* ⌦ *400 rooms, 21 suites ⟠ Restaurant, coffee shop, picnic area, room service, in-room fax, minibars, cable TV with movies and video games, in-room data ports, pool, gym, bar, lobby lounge, piano bar, shop, dry cleaning, laundry service, concierge, Internet room, business services, meeting rooms, airport shuttle, free parking, some pets allowed (fee), no-smoking rooms ▭ AE, DC, MC, V.*

★ **$$** ▦ **Embassy Suites San Francisco Airport, Burlingame.** This pink California Mission–style hostelry is one of the most lavish hotels in the airport area. Set on the bay, with clear views of airplanes flying above distant San Francisco, the building centers on a nine-story atrium and tropical garden replete with towering palms, bamboo and banana plants, koi-filled ponds, and a waterfall. This is an all-suites property, and each unit has a living room with a work area and a sleeper sofa, a bedroom, and a kitchenette between the two rooms. All suites have views of either the bay or a lagoon. ⊠ *150 Anza Blvd., Burlingame 94010* ☎ *650/ 342–4600* ⌖ *650/343–8137* ⊕ *www.embassyburlingame.com* ⌦ *340 suites ⟠ Restaurant, kitchenettes, microwaves, refrigerators, cable TV with movies and video games, in-room data ports, indoor pool, gym, hot tub, sauna, bar, dry cleaning, laundry service, concierge, Internet room, business services, meeting rooms, airport shuttle, free parking, some pets allowed (fee), no-smoking floors; no kids under 18* ▭ *AE, DC, MC, V* ⫶⊙⫶ *BP.*

NIGHTLIFE & THE ARTS

Updated by
John A.
Vlahides

From ultrasophisticated piano bars to come-as-you-are dives that reflect the city's gold-rush past, San Francisco has a tremendous variety of evening entertainment. Enjoy a night out at the opera in the Civic Center area or hit the hip SoMa neighborhood for straight-up rock or retro jazz. Except at a few skyline lounges, you're not expected to dress up. Nevertheless, jeans are the exception and stylish dress is the norm at most nightspots.

The Arts

The best guide to arts and entertainment events in San Francisco is the "Datebook" section, printed on pink paper, in the *San Francisco Sunday Chronicle*. Also consult any of the free alternative weeklies.

City Box Office (⊠ 180 Redwood St., Suite 100, off Van Ness Ave. between Golden Gate Ave. and McAllister St., Civic Center ☎ 415/392–4400 ⊕ www.cityboxoffice.com), a charge-by-phone service, offers tickets for many concerts and lectures. You can buy tickets in person at its downtown location. You can charge tickets for everything from jazz concerts to Giants games by phone or online through **Tickets.com** (☎ 415/478–2277 or 800/955–5566 ⊕ tickets.com). Half-price, same-day tickets for many local and touring stage shows go on sale (cash only) at 11 AM Tuesday through Saturday at the **TIX Bay Area** (⊠ Powell St. between Geary and Post Sts., Union Sq. ☎ 415/433–7827 ⊕ www.theatrebayarea. org/tix/tix.shtml) booth on Union Square. TIX is also a full-service ticket agency for theater and music events around the Bay Area.

Dance

★ **San Francisco Ballet.** Under artistic director Helgi Tomasson, both classical and contemporary works have won admiring reviews. Tickets and information are available at the **War Memorial Opera House.** ✉ *War Memorial Opera House, 301 Van Ness Ave., Civic Center* ☎ *415/865–2000* ⊕ *www.sfballet.org.*

Music

★ **San Francisco Opera.** Founded in 1923, this world-renowned company has resided in the Civic Center's War Memorial Opera House since the building's completion, in 1932. Over its split season—September through January and June through July—the opera presents about 70 performances of 10 to 12 operas. Translations are projected above the stage during almost all non-English operas. Long considered a major international company and the most important operatic organization in the United States outside New York, the opera frequently embarks on productions with European opera companies. Ticket prices are about $25–$195. The full-time box office is at 199 Grove Street, at Van Ness Avenue. ✉ *War Memorial Opera House, 301 Van Ness Ave., at Grove St., Civic Center* ☎ *415/864–3330 tickets* ⊕ *www.sfopera.com.*

★ **San Francisco Symphony.** One of America's top orchestras, the symphony performs from September through May, with additional summer performances of light classical music and show tunes. Michael Tilson Thomas, who is known for his innovative programming of 20th-century American works (most notably his Grammy Award–winning Mahler cycle), is the music director, and he and his orchestra often perform with soloists of the caliber of Andre Watts, Gil Shaham, and Renée Fleming. Tickets run about $15–$100. ✉ *Davies Symphony Hall, 201 Van Ness Ave., at Grove St., Civic Center* ☎ *415/864–6000* ⊕ *www. sfsymphony.org.*

Theater

★ **American Conservatory Theater.** Not long after its founding in the mid-1960s, the city's major nonprofit theater company became one of the nation's leading regional theaters. During its season, which runs from early fall to late spring, ACT presents approximately eight plays, from classics to contemporary works, often in rotating repertory. In December ACT stages a much-loved version of Charles Dickens's *A Christmas Carol.* The **ACT ticket office** (✉ 405 Geary St., Union Sq. ☎ 415/749–2228) is next door to Geary Theater, the company's home. ✉ *Geary Theater, 425 Geary St., Union Sq.* ⊕ *www.act-sfbay.org.*

Magic Theatre. Once Sam Shepard's favorite showcase, the Magic presents works by rising American playwrights, such as Matthew Wells, Karen Hartman, and Claire Chafee. ✉ *Fort Mason, Bldg. D, Laguna St. at Marina Blvd.* ☎ *415/441–8822* ⊕ *www.magictheatre.org.*

Nightlife

For information on who's performing where, check out the "Datebook" insert of the *San Francisco Chronicle,* or consult the free *San Francisco Bay Guardian,* which lists neighborhood, avant-garde, and budget-priced events. The *SF Weekly,* also free, blurbs nightclubs and music venues and is packed with information on arts events around town.

Another handy reference is the weekly *Where* magazine, offered free in most major hotel lobbies and at Hallidie Plaza (Market and Powell streets).

Bars

★ **Beach Chalet.** The restaurant-microbrewery, in a historic building filled with Works Project Administration murals from the 1930s, has a stunning view overlooking the Pacific Ocean. ⊠ *1000 Great Hwy., near Martin Luther King Jr. Dr., Golden Gate Park* ☎ *415/386–8439.*

Big 4 Bar. This is the sort of place where you could linger all night talking philosophy or tapping your toe to Broadway standards expertly played by a gray-templed pianist. ⊠ *The Huntington Hotel, 1075 California St., Nob Hill* ☎ *415/474–5400.*

Buena Vista Café. The Buena Vista packs 'em in for its famous Irish coffee, which made its U.S. debut here in 1952. ⊠ *2765 Hyde St., at Beach St., Fisherman's Wharf* ☎ *415/474–5044.*

Carnelian Room. Only birds get a better view of the San Francisco skyline than you will from the 52nd floor of the Bank of America Building. ⊠ *555 California St., at Kearny St., Financial District* ☎ *415/433–7500.*

★ **Eos Restaurant and Wine Bar.** A narrow and dimly lighted space with more than 400 wines by the bottle and 40-plus by the glass offers two different wine flights, one red and one white, every month. ⊠ *901 Cole St., at Carl St., Haight* ☎ *415/566–3063.*

★ **Harry Denton's Starlight Room.** Velvet booths and romantic lighting help re-create the 1950s high life on the 21st floor of the Sir Francis Drake Hotel. ⊠ *Sir Francis Drake Hotel, 450 Powell St., between Post and Sutter Sts., Union Sq.* ☎ *415/395–8595.*

Jade Bar. This narrow trilevel space with floor-to-ceiling windows, a 15-foot waterfall, and stylish sofas and banquettes attracts a near-capacity crowd even midweek. ⊠ *650 Gough St., between McAllister and Fulton Sts., Hayes Valley* ☎ *415/869–1900.*

Laszlo. At this nightspot attached to the Foreign Cinema restaurant, a bilevel design, dim lighting, and candles on each table set the scene for a romantic tête-à-tête over a classy cocktail or single-malt whiskey. ⊠ *2532 Mission St., between 21st and 22nd Sts., Mission* ☎ *415/401–0810.*

Ovation. A crackling fire sets the mood for quiet conversation over cognac at this restaurant-lounge at the Inn at the Opera. ⊠ *Inn at the Opera, 333 Fulton St., near Franklin St., Hayes Valley* ☎ *415/553–8100 or 415/305–8842.*

Fodor'sChoice **Redwood Room.** Originally opened in 1933 and updated by über-hip de-★ signer Philippe Starck in 2001, the Redwood Room at the Clift Hotel is a San Francisco icon. ⊠ *Clift Hotel, 495 Geary St., at Taylor St., Union Sq.* ☎ *415/929–2372 for table reservations, 415/775–4700.*

Ritz-Carlton Lobby Lounge. A harpist plays during high tea (about 1–5:15), and a jazz pianist performs in the evening at this ever-so-civilized lobby lounge. ⊠ *600 Stockton St., at California St., Nob Hill* ☎ *415/296–7465.*

Seasons Bar. Discreet staff members in dark suits serve cocktails and salty nibbles while a piano player entertains Tuesday through Saturday evenings. ⊠ *Four Seasons Hotel San Francisco, 757 Market St., between 3rd and 4th Sts., SoMa* ☎ *415/633–3000.*

Specs'. If you're bohemian at heart, you'll groove on this hidden hangout for artists, poets, and heavy-drinking lefties. ⊠ *12 William Saroyan*

Pl., off Columbus Ave., between Pacific Ave. and Broadway, North Beach ☎ *415/421–4112.*

Top of the Mark. A famous magazine photograph immortalized this place, on the 19th floor of the Mark Hopkins Inter-Continental, as a hot spot for World War II servicemen on leave or about to ship out. ✉ *Mark Hopkins Inter-Continental, 999 California St., at Mason St., Nob Hill* ☎ *415/616–6916.*

Tosca Café. This charmer has an Italian flavor, with opera, big-band, and Italian standards on the jukebox, plus an antique espresso machine that's nothing less than a work of art. ✉ *242 Columbus Ave., near Broadway, North Beach* ☎ *415/391–1244.*

★ **Vesuvio Café.** The 2nd-floor balcony of this boho hangout, little altered since its 1960s heyday, is a fine vantage point for watching the colorful Broadway-Columbus intersection. ✉ *255 Columbus Ave., at Broadway, North Beach* ☎ *415/362–3370.*

Cabaret

asiaSF. The entertainment, as well as gracious food service, is provided by "gender illusionists." These gorgeous men don daring dresses and strut in impossibly high heels on top of the bar, which serves as a catwalk. ✉ *201 9th St., at Howard St., SoMa* ☎ *415/255–2742.*

Fodor'sChoice ★ **Club Fugazi.** Its claim to fame is *Beach Blanket Babylon,* a wacky musical send-up of San Francisco moods and mores that has run since 1974 and become the longest-running show of its genre. Order tickets as far ahead as possible. ✉ *678 Green St., at Powell St., North Beach* ☎ *415/ 421–4222.*

Dance Clubs

DNA Lounge. The sounds change nightly at this venerable dance club, with psychedelic-trance (aka psytrance), deep house, and Gothic music well represented. ✉ *375 11th St., between Harrison and Folsom Sts., SoMa* ☎ *415/626–1409.*

Fodor'sChoice ★ **El Rio.** Acts at this casual spot range from funk and soul DJs on Monday to pan-Arabian dance music on Thursday and a packed world-music dance party on Friday; bands play on Saturday. ✉ *3158 Mission St., between Cesar Chavez and Valencia Sts., Mission* ☎ *415/282–3325.*

★ **111 Minna Gallery.** A gallery by day and bar and dance club by night, this unpretentious warehouse space is often full of artsy young San Franciscans who prefer it to some of the glitzier dance clubs. Call for details. ✉ *111 Minna St., bordered by Mission and Howard and 2nd and New Montgomery Sts., SoMa* ☎ *415/974–1719.*

Roccapulco. With live music and salsa dancing on Friday and Saturday, this cavernous dance hall and restaurant knows how to bring 'em in. ✉ *3140 Mission St., between Precita and Cesar Chavez Sts., Mission* ☎ *415/648–6611.*

Gay & Lesbian

MEN **Café Flore.** More of a daytime destination, this café attracts a mixed crowd, including poets, students, and fashionistas. ✉ *2298 Market St., at Noe St., Castro* ☎ *415/621–8579.*

The Cinch. The Wild West–theme neighborhood bar has pinball machines, pool tables, and a smoking patio, and it's not the least bit trendy.

✉ *1723 Polk St., between Washington and Clay Sts., Van Ness/Polk*
☎ *415/776–4162.*

Divas. In the rough-and-tumble Tenderloin, around the corner from the
Polk Street bars, this is *the* place for trannies (transvestites and trans-
sexuals) and their admirers. ✉ *1081 Post St., at Larkin St., Tenderloin*
☎ *415/928–6006.*

★ **Eagle Tavern.** Bikers are courted with endless drink specials and, increasingly, live rock music at this humongous indoor-outdoor watering hole,
one of the few SoMa bars remaining from the days before AIDS and gentrification. ✉ *398 12th St., at Harrison St., SoMa* ☎ *415/626–0880.*

★ **Martuni's.** A mixed crowd enjoys cocktails in the semirefined environment of this elegant bar at the intersection of the Castro, the Mission,
and Hayes Valley. Variations on the martini are a specialty. ✉ *4 Valencia St., at Market St., Mission* ☎ *415/241–0205.*

Midnight Sun. One of the Castro's longest-running bars is popular with
the polo-shirt-and-khakis crowd and has giant video screens playing
episodes of *Will and Grace, The Simpsons, Queer Eye for the Straight
Guy,* and other TV shows, as well as musicals and comedy. ✉ *4067 18th
St., at Castro St., Castro* ☎ *415/861–4186.*

The Stud. Nearly four decades after its opening in 1966, this bar is still
going strong seven days a week. Each night's music is different—from
funk, soul, and hip-hop to 1980s tunes and disco favorites. ✉ *399 9th
St., at Harrison St., SoMa* ☎ *415/252–7883.*

WOMEN **Lexington Club.** According to its slogan, "every night is ladies' night" at
★ this all-girl club geared toward urban alterna-dykes in their twenties and
thirties (think piercings and tattoos, not lipstick). ✉ *3464 19th St., at
Lexington St., Mission* ☎ *415/863–2052.*

Jazz

Bruno's. The long bar and the plush red booths are both comfortable
places to indulge in a swanky cocktail. ✉ *2389 Mission St., at 20th St.,
Mission* ☎ *415/648–7701.*

Cafe du Nord. You can hear some of the coolest jazz, blues, rock, and
alternative sounds in town at this basement bar. ✉ *2170 Market St.,
between Church and Sanchez Sts., Castro* ☎ *415/861–5016.*

★ **Jazz at Pearl's.** Dim lighting, plush 1930s supper-club style, and great
straight-ahead jazz make it ideal for a romantic evening. Cover is
$5–$10. ✉ *256 Columbus Ave., at Broadway, North Beach* ☎ *415/291–
8255.*

Rock, Pop, Folk & Blues

★ **Bimbo's 365 Club.** The plush main room and adjacent lounge of this club,
here since 1951, retain a retro vibe perfect for the "Cocktail Nation"
programming that keeps the crowds entertained. ✉ *1025 Columbus Ave.,
at Chestnut St., North Beach* ☎ *415/474–0365.*

Fodor'sChoice **Boom Boom Room.** Top-notch blues acts attract old-timers and hipsters
★ alike. ✉ *1601 Fillmore St., at Geary Blvd., Japantown* ☎ *415/673–8000.*

Fillmore. San Francisco's most famous rock-music hall serves up a varied menu of national and local acts: rock, reggae, grunge, jazz, folk, acid
house, and more. ✉ *1805 Geary Blvd., at Fillmore St., Western Addition* ☎ *415/346–6000.*

tion ☎ *415/346–6000.*

Fodor'sChoice ★ **Great American Music Hall.** You can find top-drawer entertainment at this great, eclectic nightclub; acts run the gamut from the best in blues, folk, and jazz to alternative rock and American roots music. ☒ *859 O'Farrell St., between Polk and Larkin Sts., Tenderloin* ☎ *415/885–0750.*

Last Day Saloon. Rising local bands as well as major acts perform blues, hip-hop, rock, funk, country, or jazz at this club, open since 1973. ☒ *406 Clement St., between 5th and 6th Aves., Richmond* ☎ *415/387–6343.*

The Saloon. Hard-drinkin' North Beach locals in the know favor this raucous blues and rock spot. ☒ *1232 Grant Ave., near Columbus Ave., North Beach* ☎ *415/989–7666.*

Slim's. National touring acts—mostly classic rock, blues, jazz, and world music—are the main event at this venue, one of SoMa's most popular nightclubs. ☒ *333 11th St., between Harrison and Folsom Sts., SoMa* ☎ *415/522–0333.*

SPORTS & THE OUTDOORS

Updated by
John A.
Vlahides

Temperatures rarely drop below 50°F, so it's no surprise that visitors and residents alike are drawn outdoors in San Francisco. The captivating views are a major part of the appeal, as are the city's 3,500 acres of parks and open spaces. On the best days, even longtime city dwellers marvel at the sun sparkling on the bay and the cool, crisp air blowing right off the Pacific Ocean.

Beaches

Nestled in a quiet cove between the lush hills adjoining Fort Mason, Ghirardelli Square, and Fisherman's Wharf, **Aquatic Park** (⊕ www.nps.gov/safr) has a tiny, ¼-mi-long sandy beach with gentle water. Facilities include restrooms and showers. **Baker Beach** (☒ Gibson Rd., off Bowley St., southwest corner of Presidio), with gorgeous views of the Golden Gate Bridge and the Marin Headlands, is a local favorite. The pounding surf and strong currents make swimming a dangerous prospect. **China Beach,** one of the city's safest swimming beaches, is a 600-foot strip of sand, south of the Presidio and Baker Beach. It has gentle waters as well as changing rooms, bathrooms, showers, grills, drinking water, and picnic tables. Although **Ocean Beach** isn't the city's cleanest shore, this wide, sandy expanse stretches for more than 3 mi along the Great Highway, south of the Cliff House, making it ideal for long walks and runs. Because of extremely dangerous currents, swimming isn't recommended.

Baseball

Home field for the National League's **San Francisco Giants** (☒ SBC Park, 24 Willie Mays Plaza, between 2nd and 3rd Sts., China Basin ☎ 415/972–2000 or 800/734–4268 ⊕ sanfrancisco.giants.mlb.com) is downtown's **SBC Park. Tickets.com** (☎ 510/762–2255 Baseball Line, 415/478–2277 or 800/955–5566 ⊕ www.tickets.com) sells game tickets over the phone. Its Baseball Line charges a per-ticket fee of $2–$10, plus a per-call processing fee of up to $5.

Football

The **San Francisco 49ers** (✉ Monster Park, 490 Jamestown Ave., Bayview Heights ☎ 415/656–4900 ⊕ www.sf49ers.com) play at **Monster Park,** which locals stubbornly call by its original name of **Candlestick Park,** near the San Mateo County border. Single-game tickets, available via **Ticketmaster** (☎ 415/421–8497 ⊕ www.ticketmaster.com), almost always sell out far in advance.

SHOPPING

Shopping Neighborhoods

Updated by
Sharron Wood

The Castro/Noe Valley. Often called the gay capital of the world, it's also a major shopping destination for nongay travelers, filled with men's clothing boutiques, home-accessories stores, and various specialty shops.

Chinatown. The intersection of Grant Avenue and Bush Street marks the gateway to 24 blocks of shops, restaurants, and markets. Dominating the exotic cityscape are the sights and smells of food. Racks of Chinese silks, toy trinkets, colorful pottery, baskets, and carved figurines are displayed chockablock on the sidewalks.

Fisherman's Wharf. Sightseers crowd this area and with good reason: Pier 39, the Anchorage, Ghirardelli Square, and the Cannery. Each has shops and restaurants, as well as outdoor entertainment—musicians, mimes, and magicians. Best of all are the wharf's view of the bay and its proximity to cable-car lines.

The Haight. Haight Street is a perennial attraction for visitors, if only to see the sign at Haight and Ashbury streets. These days chain stores such as The Gap and Ben & Jerry's have taken over large storefronts near the famous intersection, but it's still possible to find high-quality vintage clothing, funky shoes, and folk art from around the world in this always-busy neighborhood.

Jackson Square. Elegant Jackson Square, on the northeastern edge of the Financial District, is home to a dozen or so of San Francisco's finest retail antiques dealers, many of which occupy Victorian-era buildings.

North Beach. Although it's sometimes compared to New York City's Greenwich Village, North Beach is only a fraction of the size, clustered tightly around Washington Square and Columbus Avenue. Most of its businesses are small eateries, cafés, and shops selling clothing, antiques, and vintage wares.

Pacific Heights. Pacific Heights residents seeking fine items for their luxurious homes head straight for Fillmore Street between Post Street and Pacific Avenue, and Sacramento Street between Lyon and Maple streets, where private residences alternate with fine clothing and gift shops and housewares stores.

SoMa. High San Francisco rents mean there aren't many discount outlets in the city, but a few do exist in the semi-industrial zone south of Market Street (SoMa). At the other end of the spectrum is the gift shop of the San Francisco Museum of Modern Art, which sells handmade jewelry, upscale and offbeat housewares, and other great gift items.

Union Square. Serious shoppers head straight to San Francisco's main shopping area and the site of most department stores, as well as the Virgin Megastore, the Disney Store, Borders Books and Music, and Frette. Nearby are the pricey international boutiques of Tiffany, Yves Saint Laurent, Cartier, Emporio Armani, Gucci, Hermès of Paris, Louis Vuitton, and Gianni Versace.

Malls & Department Stores

Crocker Galleria. Forty or so mostly upscale shops and restaurants a few blocks east of Union Square are housed in this complex beneath a glass dome. (⊠ 50 Post St., at Kearny St., Financial District ☎ 415/393–1505)

Embarcadero Center. Four sprawling buildings of shops, restaurants, offices, and a popular art movie theater—plus the Hyatt Regency hotel—make up the Embarcadero Center, downtown at the end of Market Street. Most of the stores are branches of upscale national chains, such as Ann Taylor, Banana Republic, and Pottery Barn. It's one of the few major shopping centers with an underground parking garage. ⊠ *Clay and Sacramento Sts. between Battery and Drumm Sts.* ☎ *415/772–0734.*

Japan Center. The three-block complex includes an 800-car public garage and three shop-filled buildings. Especially worthwhile are the Kintetsu and Kinokuniya buildings, where shops and showrooms sell bonsai trees, tapes and records, jewelry, antique kimonos, *tansu* (Japanese chests), electronics, and colorful glazed dinnerware and teapots. (⊠ Bordered by Laguna, Fillmore, and Post Sts. and Geary Blvd. ☎ No phone)

★ **Gump's.** Stocked with large decorative vases, sumptuous housewares that look too luxe for everyday use, and extravagant jewelry, this airy store exudes a museumlike aura. A small collection of luxurious bed linens is upstairs. ⊠ *135 Post St., between Grant Ave. and Kearny St., Union Sq.* ☎ *415/982–1616.*

Macy's. Downtown has two behemoth branches of this retailer. One—with entrances on Geary, Stockton, and O'Farrell streets—houses the women's, children's, furniture, and housewares departments. The men's department occupies its own building, across Stockton Street. ⊠ *170 O'-Farrell St., at Stockton St., Union Sq.* ☎ *415/397–3333* ⊠ *Men's branch:* ⊠ *50 O'Farrell St., entrance on Stockton St., Union Sq.* ☎ *415/397–3333.*

Neiman Marcus. The surroundings, which include a Philip Johnson–designed checkerboard facade, gilded atrium, and stained-glass skylight, are as high class as the goods showcased in them. The mix includes designer men's and women's clothing and accessories as well as posh household wares. ⊠ *150 Stockton St., at Geary Blvd., Union Sq.* ☎ *415/362–3900.*

★ **Nordstrom.** This service-oriented store specializes in designer fashions, accessories, cosmetics, and, most notably, shoes. The space, with spiral escalators circling a four-story atrium, is stunning. ⊠ *San Francisco Shopping Centre, 865 Market St., between 4th and 5th Sts., Union Sq.* ☎ *415/243–8500.*

San Francisco Shopping Centre. The center, across from the cable-car turnaround at Powell and Market streets, has spiral escalators that wind up through the sunlit atrium. Inside are 65 retailers, including Nordstrom and Godiva. (⊠ 865 Market St., between 4th and 5th Sts. ☎ 415/495–5656)

Saks Fifth Avenue. A central escalator ascends past a series of designer boutiques, which give Saks the feel of an exclusive multilevel mall. ⊠ *384 Post St., at Powell St., Union Sq.* ☎ *415/986–4300.*

SIDE TRIPS FROM SAN FRANCISCO

Updated by John A. Vlahides

One of San Francisco's best assets is its surroundings. To the north is Marin County, where the lively waterfront town of Sausalito has bougainvillea-covered hillsides, an expansive yacht harbor, and an artists' colony. To the east is Berkeley, a colorful university town. Explore a bit beyond the city limits and you're bound to discover what makes the Bay Area such a coveted place to live.

Sausalito

Like much of San Francisco, Sausalito had a raffish reputation before it went upscale. Discovered in 1775 by Spanish explorers and named Sausalito ("Little Willow") for the trees growing around its springs, the town served as a port for whaling ships during the 19th century. By the mid-1800s wealthy San Franciscans were making Sausalito their getaway across the bay. They built lavish Victorian summer homes in the hills, many of which still stand. In 1875 the railroad from the north connected with ferryboats to San Francisco, bringing the merchant and working classes with it. This influx of hardworking, fun-loving folk polarized the town into "wharf rats" and "hill snobs," and the waterfront area grew thick with saloons, gambling dens, and bordellos.

Sausalito developed its bohemian flair in the 1950s and '60s, when a group of artists established an artists' colony and a houseboat community here. Today more than 450 houseboats are docked in Sausalito, which has since also become a major yachting center. The ferry is the best way to get to Sausalito from San Francisco; you get more romance (and less traffic) and disembark in the heart of downtown.

☾ The U.S. Army Corps of Engineers uses the **Bay Model** to reproduce the rise and fall of tides, the flow of currents, and the other physical forces at work on the bay. ⊠ *2100 Bridgeway, at Marinship Way* ☎ *415/332–3870* ⊕ *www.spn.usace.army.mil/bmvc* ☒ *Free* ☉ *Memorial Day–Labor Day, Tues.–Fri. 9–4, weekends 10–5; rest of yr, Tues.–Sat. 9–4.*

☾ The **Bay Area Discovery Museum** fills five former military buildings with entertaining and enlightening hands-on exhibits related to science and the arts. Kids and their families can fish from a boat at the indoor wharf, imagine themselves as marine biologists in the Wave Workshop, and play outdoors at Lookout Cove, a 2.5-acre bay-in-miniature made up of scaled-down sea caves, tide pools, and even a re-created shipwreck. Toddlers and preschoolers should head to Tot Zone, a dedicated indoor-outdoor interactive play area. From San Francisco take the Alexander Avenue exit from U.S. 101 and follow signs to East Fort Baker. ⊠ *557 McReynolds Rd., at East Fort Baker* ☎ *415/339–3900* ⊕ *www.badm.org* ☒ *8.50* ☉ *Tues.–Fri. 9–4, weekends 10–5.*

Where to Stay & Eat

★ $-$$$ ✕ **Poggio.** One of the few restaurants in Sausalito to attract both food-savvy locals and tourists, Poggio serves modern Tuscan cuisine in a handsome, open-walled space that spills onto the street in the style of restaurants on the Italian Riviera. Expect dishes such as grilled lamb chops with roasted eggplant, braised artichokes with polenta, feather-light gnocchi, and pizzas from the open kitchen's wood-fired oven. ✉ *777 Bridgeway* ☎ *415/332–7771* ⟡ *Reservations essential* ▭ *AE, D, MC, V.*

★ ☺ $-$$ ✕ **Fish.** For fresh seafood, you can't beat this gleaming dockside fish house a mile north of downtown. Order at the counter, and then grab a seat by the floor-to-ceiling windows or at a picnic table on the pier, overlooking the yachts and fishing boats. Most of the fish is caught locally and hauled in from boats right on the dock. Try the ceviche, crab Louis, cioppino, barbecue oysters, or anything fresh that day that's being grilled over the oak-wood fire. ✉ *350 Harbor Dr.* ☎ *415/331–3474* ⟡ *Reservations not accepted* ▭ *No credit cards* ☉ *Closed Mon. and Tues.*

$$$$ ⌂ **Casa Madrona.** What began as a small inn with a handful of historic accommodations in a 19th-century landmark house has expanded over the decades to incorporate a variety of lodgings and a top-notch spa, all tiered down the hill in the center of town. The design in the original rooms and suites ranges from the cutesiness of what's called the Artist's Loft to elegant Mediterranean and Asia-inspired motifs. An adjacent three-story building contains newer rooms that are uniformly contemporary, with wet bars, sunken tubs, and bay windows; some have balconies overlooking Richardson Bay. ✉ *801 Bridgeway, 94965* ☎ *415/332–0502 or 800/567–9524* ▤ *415/332–2537* ⊕ *www.casamadrona.com* ↝ *56 rooms, 7 suites* ⟡ *Restaurant, minibars, cable TV, in-room VCRs, in-room data ports, hot tub, spa, dry cleaning, laundry service, concierge, meeting rooms; no a/c, no smoking* ▭ *AE, D, DC, MC, V* ¶◎ *CP.*

$-$$ ⌂ **Hotel Sausalito.** Soft yellow, green, and orange tones create a warm Mediterranean feel at this well-run inn with handmade furniture and tasteful original art and reproductions. The rooms, some of which have harbor or park views, range from small quarters good for budget-minded travelers to commodious suites. ✉ *16 El Portal, 94965* ☎ *415/332–0700 or 888/442–0700* ▤ *415/332–8788* ⊕ *www.hotelsausalito.com* ↝ *14 rooms, 2 suites* ⟡ *Cable TV, in-room data ports, concierge; no a/c, no smoking* ▭ *AE, DC, MC, V* ¶◎ *CP.*

Berkeley

Although Berkeley has grown alongside the University of California, which dominates its history and contemporary life, the university and the town are not synonymous. The city of 100,000 facing San Francisco across the bay has other interesting attributes. It's culturally diverse and politically adventurous, a breeding ground for social trends, a bastion of the counterculture, and an important center for Bay Area writers, artists, and musicians.

The **Berkeley Visitor Information Center** (✉ University Hall, Room 101, 2200 University Ave., at Oxford St. ☎ 510/642–5215) is the starting point for the free, student-guided tours of the campus, which last 1½ hours and start at 10 on weekdays.

1

The **University of California, Berkeley Art Museum & Pacific Film Archive** has an interesting collection of works that spans five centuries, with an emphasis on contemporary art. Changing exhibits line the spiral ramps and balcony galleries. Don't miss the museum's series of vibrant paintings by abstract expressionist Hans Hofmann. On the ground floor, the Pacific Film Archive has programs of historic and contemporary films, and the exhibition theater is at 2575 Bancroft Way, near Bowditch Street. ☒ *2626 Bancroft Way* ☎ *510/642–0808, 510/642–1124 film-program information* ⊕ *www.bampfa.berkeley.edu* ☒ *$8* ☉ *Wed. and Fri.–Sun. 11–5, Thurs. 11–7.*

About 13,500 species of plants from all over the world flourish in the 34-acre **University of California Botanical Garden.** Free garden tours are given Thursday, Saturday, and Sunday at 1:30. Benches and shady picnic tables make this a relaxing alternative to the busy main campus. ☒ *200 Centennial Dr.* ☎ *510/643–2755* ⊕ *botanicalgarden.berkeley.edu* ☒ *$3, free Thurs.* ☉ *Memorial Day–Labor Day, Mon. and Tues. 9–5, Wed.–Sun. 9–8; rest of yr, daily 9–5. Closed 1st Tues. of month.*

☙ At the fortresslike **Lawrence Hall of Science,** a dazzling hands-on science center, kids can look at insects under microscopes, solve crimes using chemical forensics, and explore the physics of baseball. ☒ *Centennial Dr. near Grizzly Peak Blvd.* ☎ *510/642–5132* ⊕ *www. lawrencehallofscience.org* ☒ *$8.50* ☉ *Daily 10–5.*

Where to Stay & Eat

$$–$$$$ ✕ **Café Rouge.** You can recover from 4th Street shopping in this spacious two-story bistro, complete with zinc bar, skylights, and festive lanterns. The short, seasonal menu ranges from the sophisticated, such as rack of lamb and juniper-berry-cured pork chops, to the homey, such as spit-roasted chicken or pork loin, or cheddar-topped burgers. ☒ *1782 4th St.* ☎ *510/525–1440* ▤ *MC, V* ☉ *No dinner Mon.*

$$–$$$$
Fodor'sChoice
★   ✕ **Chez Panisse Café & Restaurant.** The downstairs portion of Alice Waters's legendary eatery is noted for its formality and personal service. Here, the daily-changing multicourse dinners are prix fixe and pricey ($$$$), although the cost is slightly lower on weekdays. Upstairs, in the informal café, the crowd is livelier, the prices are lower ($$), and the ever-changing menu is à la carte. The food is simpler, too: penne with new potatoes, arugula, and sheep's-milk cheese; fresh figs with Parmigiano-Reggiano cheese and arugula; and grilled tuna with savoy cabbage, for example. ☒ *1517 Shattuck Ave., north of University Ave.* ☎ *510/ 548–5525 restaurant, 510/548–5049 café* ⬧ *Reservations essential* ▤ *AE, D, DC, MC, V* ☉ *Closed Sun. No lunch in restaurant.*

$$–$$$ ✕ **Rivoli.** Italian-inspired dishes using fresh, mostly organic California ingredients star on a menu that changes every three weeks. Typical meals include fresh line-caught fish, pastas, and inventive offerings such as its trademark portobello fritters with aioli. ☒ *1539 Solano Ave.* ☎ *510/526–2542* ⬧ *Reservations essential* ▤ *AE, D, DC, MC, V* ☉ *No lunch.*

¢–$ ✕ **Bette's Oceanview Diner.** Buttermilk pancakes are just one of the specialties at this 1930s-inspired diner, complete with checkered floors and burgundy booths. The wait for a seat can be long. If you're starving, head to Bette's to Go, next door, for takeout. ⊠ *1807 4th St.* ☎ *510/ 644–3230* ⚠ *Reservations not accepted* ▭ *MC, V* ⊘ *No dinner.*

$$$$ 🏨 **Claremont Resort and Spa.** Straddling the Oakland-Berkeley border,
Fodor'sChoice the hotel beckons like a gleaming white castle in the hills. Traveling ex-
★ ecutives come for the guest rooms' business amenities, including T-1 In-
ternet connections, guest e-mail addresses, and oversize desks. The
Claremont also shines for leisure travelers, drawing honeymooners and
families alike with its luxurious suites, therapeutic massages, and per-
sonalized yoga workouts at the on-site spa. ⊠ *41 Tunnel Rd., at Ashby
and Domingo Aves., 94705* ☎ *510/843–3000 or 800/323–7500* 🖷 *510/
843–6629* ⊕ *www.claremontresort.com* 🛏 *262 rooms, 17 suites* ⚐ *2
restaurants, café, in-room safes, some in-room hot tubs, some minibars,
some refrigerators, cable TV, in-room VCRs, in-room data ports, 10 ten-
nis courts, 2 pools, health club, hair salon, hot tub, sauna, spa, steam
room, 2 bars, children's programs (ages 6 wks–10 yrs), dry cleaning,
laundry service, concierge, Internet room, business services, meeting
rooms, parking (fee), no-smoking floor* ▭ *AE, D, DC, MC, V.*

$$ 🏨 **Hotel Durant.** Long the mainstay of parents visiting their children at
U.C. Berkeley, the hotel is a good option for those who want to be a
short walk from campus and from the restaurants and shops of Telegraph Avenue. Rooms, accented with dark wood set against deep jewel
tones, are small without feeling cramped. ⊠ *2600 Durant Ave., 94704*
☎ *510/845–8981* 🖷 *510/486–8336* ⊕ *www.hoteldurant.com* 🛏 *135
rooms, 5 suites* ⚐ *Restaurant, room service, some refrigerators, cable
TV with movies, in-room data ports, sports bar, dry cleaning, laundry
service, concierge, business services, meeting room, parking (fee), no-
smoking floors; no a/c* ▭ *AE, D, DC, MC, V.*

$ 🏨 **French Hotel.** The only hotel in north Berkeley, this three-level brick
structure has a certain pensione feel. Rooms have pastel or brick walls
and modern touches such as white wire baskets in lieu of dressers. Balconies make the rooms seem larger than their modest dimensions.
⊠ *1538 Shattuck Ave., 94709* ☎ *510/548–9930* 🖷 *510/548–9930*
🛏 *18 rooms* ⚐ *Café, room service, cable TV with movies, dry cleaning, laundry service, concierge, business services, free parking; no a/c*
▭ *AE, D, DC, MC, V.*

SAN FRANCISCO A TO Z

*To research prices, get advice from other travelers, and book travel arrange-
ments, visit www.fodors.com.*

AIR TRAVEL
Heavy fog is infamous for causing chronic delays into and out of San
Francisco. If you're heading to the East Bay, make every effort to fly into
Oakland International Airport, which is easy to navigate and accessible
by public transit. Of the major carriers, Alaska, America West, Ameri-
can, Continental, Delta, Southwest, United, and US Airways fly into both
Oakland and San Francisco. JetBlue Airways services Oakland. North-
west flies into San Francisco but not Oakland. Midwest Express and Frontier Airlines, two smaller carriers, both fly into San Francisco. *See* Air
Travel *in* Smart Travel Tips A to Z for airline phone numbers.

AIRPORTS & TRANSFERS

The major gateway to San Francisco is San Francisco International Airport (SFO), off U.S. 101 15 mi south of the city. Oakland International Airport (OAK) is across the bay, not much farther away from downtown San Francisco (via I–880 and I–80), but rush-hour traffic on the Bay Bridge may lengthen travel times considerably.

🚹 Oakland International Airport (OAK) ☎ 510/577-4000 ⊕ www.flyoakland.com. San Francisco International Airport (SFO) ☎ 650/761-0800 ⊕ www.flysfo.com.

TRANSFERS **From San Francisco International Airport:** A taxi ride to downtown costs $35–$40. Airport shuttles are inexpensive and generally efficient. The SFO Airporter ($14) picks up passengers at baggage claim (lower level) and serves selected downtown hotels. Lorrie's Airport Service and SuperShuttle both stop at the upper-level traffic islands and take you anywhere within the city limits of San Francisco. They charge $14–$17, depending on your destination. Lorrie's also sells tickets online, at a $2 discount. Shuttles to the East Bay, such as BayPorter Express, also depart from the upper-level traffic islands; expect to pay around $35. You can **take BART directly to downtown San Francisco;** the trip takes about 30 minutes and costs less than $5. Trains leave from the international terminal every 15 minutes on weekdays and every 20 minutes on weekends. Another inexpensive way to get to San Francisco is via two SamTrans buses: No. 292 (55 minutes, $1.25–$2.50) and the KX (35 minutes, $3.50; only one small carry-on bag permitted). Board the SamTrans buses at the north end of the lower level.

From Oakland International Airport: A taxi to downtown San Francisco costs $35–$40. BayPorter Express and other shuttles serve major hotels and provide door-to-door service to the East Bay and San Francisco. Marin Door to Door serves Marin County for a flat $50 fee. The best way to get to San Francisco via public transit is to take the AIR BART bus ($2) to the Coliseum/Oakland International Airport BART station (BART fares vary depending on where you're going; the ride to downtown San Francisco costs $3.15).

🚹 American Airporter ☎ 415/202-0733 ⊕ americanairporter.com. BayPorter Express ☎ 415/467-1800 ⊕ www.bayporter.com. East Bay Express Airporter ☎ 510/547-0404. Lorrie's Airport Service ☎ 415/334-9000 ⊕ www.sfovan.com. Marin Door to Door ☎ 415/457-2717 ⊕ www.marindoortodoor.com. SamTrans ☎ 800/660-4287 ⊕ www.samtrans.com. SFO Airporter ☎ 877/877-8819 or 650/624-0500 ⊕ www.sfoairporter.com. South & East Bay Airport Shuttle ☎ 408/559-9477. SuperShuttle ☎ 800/258-3826 or 415/558-8500 ⊕ www.supershuttle.com. VIP Airport Shuttle ☎ 800/235-8847, 408/885-1800, or 408/986-6000 ⊕ www.yourairportride.com.

BOAT & FERRY TRAVEL

Blue & Gold Fleet operates a number of lines, including service to Alcatraz ($11.50–$16), Angel Island ($13), Sausalito ($7.25 one-way), and Tiburon ($7.25 one-way). Tickets are sold at Pier 41 (next to Fisherman's Wharf), where the boats depart (except the ferry to Tiburon, which departs from the Ferry Building). Golden Gate Ferry runs daily to and from Sausalito and Larkspur (each are $6.15 one-way), leaving from Pier 1, behind the San Francisco Ferry Building at the foot of Market Street on the Embarcadero.

🚢 **Blue & Gold Fleet** ☎ 415/705-5555 ⊕ www.blueandgoldfleet.com. **Golden Gate Ferry** ☎ 415/923-2000 ⊕ www.goldengateferry.org.

BUS TRAVEL TO & FROM SAN FRANCISCO

Greyhound, the only long-distance bus company serving San Francisco, operates buses to and from most major cities in the country.

🚌 **Greyhound** ✉ 425 Mission St., between Fremont and 1st Sts., SoMa ☎ 800/231-2222 or 415/495-1569 ⊕ www.greyhound.com.

BUS & TRAIN TRAVEL WITHIN SAN FRANCISCO

BART: Bay Area Rapid Transit (BART) trains, which run until midnight, connect San Francisco with Oakland, Berkeley, Pittsburgh/Bay Point, Richmond, Fremont, Dublin/Pleasanton, and other small cities and towns in between. Within San Francisco, stations are limited to downtown, the Mission, and a couple of outlying neighborhoods. Trains also travel south from San Francisco as far as Millbrae. The BART-SFO Extension Project connects downtown San Francisco to San Francisco International Airport; a ride is $4.95. Intra-city San Francisco fares are $1.25; intercity fares are $2.15–$7.45.

Bus: Outside the city, AC Transit serves the East Bay, and Golden Gate Transit serves Marin County.

Caltrain: Caltrain connects San Francisco to Palo Alto, San Jose, Santa Clara, and many smaller cities en route. In San Francisco, trains leave from the main depot, at 4th and King streets, and a rail-side stop at 22nd and Pennsylvania streets. One-way fares are $1.75–$8, depending on the number of zones through which you travel. Trips last 1 to 1¾ hours.

Muni: The San Francisco Municipal Railway, or Muni, operates light-rail vehicles, the historic F-line streetcars along Fisherman's Wharf and Market Street, trolley buses, and the world-famous cable cars. On buses and streetcars, the fare is $1.25. Exact change is required, and dollar bills are accepted in the fare boxes. For all Muni vehicles other than cable cars, 90-minute transfers are issued free upon request at the time the fare is paid. Transfers are valid for two additional transfers in any direction. Cable cars cost $3 and include no transfers.

🚌 **AC Transit** ☎ 510/839-2882 ⊕ www.actransit.org. **Bay Area Rapid Transit** (BART) ☎ 650/992-2278 ⊕ www.bart.gov. **Caltrain** ☎ 800/660-4287 ⊕ www.caltrain.com. **Golden Gate Transit** ☎ 415/923-2000 ⊕ www.goldengate.org. **San Francisco Caltrain Station** ✉ 700 4th St., at King St. ☎ 800/660-4287.

San Francisco Municipal Railway System (Muni) ☎ 415/673-6864 ⊕ www.sfmuni.com.

CAR RENTAL

All of the national car-rental companies have offices at the San Francisco and Oakland airports. *See* Car Rental *in* Smart Travel Tips A to Z for national rental agency phone numbers.

CAR TRAVEL

Driving in San Francisco can be a challenge because of the hills, one-way streets, and traffic. Take it easy and, to avoid getting a ticket, remember to curb your wheels when parking on hills—turn wheels away from the curb when facing uphill, toward the curb when facing downhill.

PARKING On certain streets, parking is forbidden during rush hours. Look for the warning signs; illegally parked cars are towed immediately. Downtown parking lots are often full, and most are expensive. Large hotels often have parking available, but it doesn't come cheap; many charge as much as $40 a day for the privilege.

LODGING

The San Francisco Convention and Visitors Bureau publishes a free lodging guide with a map and listings of San Francisco and Bay Area hotels. You can also reserve a room, by phone or via the Internet, at more than 60 bureau-recommended hotels. San Francisco Reservations, in business since 1986, can arrange reservations at more than 200 Bay Area hotels, often at special discounted rates. Hotellocators.com also offers online and phone-in reservations at special rates.

🚹 **Hotellocators.com** ✆ 9 Sumner St., San Francisco 94103 ☎ 800/576-0003 🖷 858/581-1730 ⊕ www.hotellocators.com. **San Francisco Convention and Visitors Bureau** ☎ 415/391-2000 general information, 415/283-0177, 888/782-9673 lodging service ⊕ www.sfvisitor.org. **San Francisco Reservations** ☎ 800/677-1500 ⊕ www.hotelres.com.

TAXIS

Taxi service is notoriously bad in San Francisco, and hailing a cab can be frustratingly difficult in some parts of the city, especially on weekends. In a pinch, hotel taxi stands are an option, as is calling for a pickup. But be forewarned: taxi companies frequently don't answer the phone during peak periods. Taxis in San Francisco charge $2.85 for the first ⅓ mi, 45¢ for each additional ⅓ mi, and 45¢ per minute in stalled traffic. There is no charge for additional passengers; there is no surcharge for luggage.

🚹 **City Wide Cab** ☎ 415/920-0700. **DeSoto Cab** ☎ 415/970-1300. **Luxor Cab** ☎ 415/282-4141. **Veteran's Taxicab** ☎ 415/552-1300. **Yellow Cab** ☎ 415/626-2345.

SIGHTSEEING TOURS

BUS & VAN In addition to bus and van tours of the city, most tour companies run TOURS excursions to various Bay Area and Northern California destinations, such as Marin County. City tours generally last 3½ hours and cost $38–$40. Great Pacific Tours conducts city tours in passenger vans (starting at $40). San Francisco Sightseeing (Gray Line), a much larger, corporately owned outfit, operates 42-passenger motor coaches and motorized cable cars ($17–$57). For about $15 more, either tour operator can supplement a city tour with a bay cruise.

🚹 **Great Pacific Tours** ☎ 415/626-4499 ⊕ www.greatpacifictour.com. **San Francisco Sightseeing** ☎ 415/558-9400 ⊕ www.graylinesanfrancisco.com.

WALKING TOURS The best way to see San Francisco is to hit the streets. Tours of various San Francisco neighborhoods generally cost $15–$40. Some tours explore culinary themes, such as Chinese food or coffeehouses: lunch and snacks are often included. Others focus on architecture or history.

🚹 Architecture Tours **"Victorian Home Walk"** ☎ 415/252-9485 ⊕ www.victorianwalk.com.

🚹 Culinary Tours **"Chinatown with the Wok Wiz"** ☎ 415/981-8989 ⊕ www.wokwiz.com. **"Javawalk"** ☎ 415/673-9255 ⊕ www.javawalk.com.

🎦 General Interest Tours **City Guides** ☎ 415/557-4266 ⊕ www.sfcityguides.org. **San Francisco Visitor Information Center** ✉ Hallidie Plaza, lower level, Powell and Market Sts., Union Sq. ☎ 415/391-2000, 415/392-0328 TDD ⊕ www.sfvisitor.org.
🎦 Historic Tours **Chinese Culture Center** ☎ 415/986-1822 ⊕ www.c-c-c.org. **Trevor Hailey** ☎ 415/550-8110 ⊕ www.webcastro.com/castrotour.

TRAIN TRAVEL TO & FROM SAN FRANCISCO

Amtrak trains travel to the Bay Area from some cities in California and the United States. The *Coast Starlight* travels north from Los Angeles to Seattle, passing the Bay Area along the way. Amtrak also has several inland routes between San Jose, Oakland, and Sacramento. The *California Zephyr* route travels from Chicago to the Bay Area. San Francisco doesn't have an Amtrak station, but there is one in Emeryville, just over the Bay Bridge, as well as in Oakland. A free shuttle operates between these two stations and the Ferry Building, the Caltrain station, and several other points in downtown San Francisco.
🎦 **Amtrak** ☎ 800/872-7245 ⊕ www.amtrak.com.

VISITOR INFORMATION

🎦 **Berkeley Convention and Visitors Bureau** ✉ 2015 Center St., Berkeley 94704 ☎ 800/847-4823 or 510/549-7040 ⊕ www.berkeleycvb.com. **San Francisco Convention and Visitors Bureau** 🖅 201 3rd St., Suite 900, 94103 ☎ 415/391-2000, 415/392-0328 TDD ⊕ www.sfvisitor.org. **San Francisco Visitor Information Center** ✉ Hallidie Plaza, lower level, Powell and Market Sts., Union Sq. ☎ 415/391-2000, 415/392-0328 TDD ⊕ www.sfvisitor.org.

The Wine Country

Updated by
Sharron Wood

IN 1862, AFTER AN EXTENSIVE TOUR of the wine-producing areas of Europe, Count Agoston Haraszthy de Mokcsa reported a promising prognosis about his adopted California: "Of all the countries through which I passed, not one possessed the same advantages that are to be found in California. . . . California can produce as noble and generous a wine as any in Europe; more in quantity to the acre, and without repeated failures through frosts, summer rains, hailstorms, or other causes."

The "dormant resources" that the father of California's viticulture saw in the balmy days and cool nights of the temperate Napa and Sonoma valleys have come to fruition today. The wines produced here are praised and savored by connoisseurs throughout the world. The area also continues to be a proving ground for the latest techniques of grape growing and wine making.

Ever more competitive, vintners constantly hone their skills, aided by the scientific expertise of graduates of the nearby University of California at Davis and by the practical knowledge of the grape growers. They experiment with high-density vineyard planting, canopy management (to control the amount of sunlight that reaches the grapes), and filtration of the wine.

For many, wine making is a second career. Any would-be winemaker can rent the cumbersome, costly machinery needed to stem and press the grapes. Many say making wine is a good way to turn a large fortune into a small one, but that hasn't deterred the doctors, former college professors, publishing tycoons, entertainers, and others who come here to try their hand at it.

In 1975 Napa Valley had no more than 20 wineries; today there are more than 280—although exhausted travelers will be thankful to learn that not all of these have tasting rooms open to the public. In Sonoma County, where the web of vineyards is looser, there are well over 150 wineries, and development is now claiming the cool Carneros region, at the head of the San Francisco Bay, deemed ideal for growing the chardonnay grape. Nowadays many individual grape growers produce their own wines instead of selling their grapes to larger wineries. As a result, smaller "boutique" wineries harvest excellent, reasonably priced wines that have caught the attention of connoisseurs and critics, while the larger wineries consolidate land and expand their varietals.

This state-of-the-art viticulture has also given rise to an equally robust passion for food. Inspired by the creative spirit that produces the region's great wines, nationally and regionally famous chefs have opened restaurants both extravagant and modest, sealing the area's reputation as one of the finest destinations for dining in the nation.

In addition to great food and wine, you'll find a wealth of California history in the Wine Country. The town of Sonoma is filled with remnants of Mexican California and the solid, ivy-covered, brick wineries built by Haraszthy and his followers. Calistoga is a virtual museum of Steamboat Gothic architecture, replete with the fretwork and clapboard beloved of gold-rush prospectors and late-19th-century spa goers. A later architectural fantasy, the beautiful art-nouveau mansion of the Beringer

GREAT ITINERARIES

Because the Wine Country is expansive, and traveling between the Napa and Sonoma valleys usually requires a winding drive through a small mountain range, it's best to plan shorter, separate trips over the course of several days. You can get a feel for the area's towns and vineyards by taking to the open road over a weekend. Along the way you can stop at a winery or two, have a picnic lunch, and watch the countryside glide past your windshield. Four or five days gives you enough time to explore more towns and wineries and also indulge in dining adventures. You might even bike the Silverado Trail or fish the Russian River. A full week allows time for all of the above, plus pampering at the region's hot springs and mud baths, a round of golf, and a hot-air balloon ride.

Numbers in the text correspond to numbers in the margin and on the Napa Valley and Sonoma Valley maps.

IF YOU HAVE 2 DAYS. Start at the circa-1857 **Buena Vista Winery** 45 ▶ just outside Sonoma. From there, take Route 12 north to the Trinity Road/Oakville Grade. Drive east over the Mayacamas Mountains, taking time to admire the views as you descend into the Napa Valley. Take Route 29 north into ☒ **St. Helena** for lunch. After lunch in St. Helena, take the 30-minute tour of **Beringer Vineyards** 27. The next day continue north on Route 29 to **Calistoga** for an early-morning balloon ride, an afternoon trip to the mud baths, and a visit to **Clos Pegase** 34 before heading back to St. Helena for dinner at Greystone—the beautiful West Coast campus and highly acclaimed restaurant of the **Culinary Institute of America** 28.

IF YOU HAVE 4 DAYS. Concentrate on the Napa Valley north of Yountville. Make your first stop in **Oakville** ▶, where the circa-1880s **Oakville Grocery** 12—once a Wells Fargo Pony Express stop—is indisputably the most popular place for picnic supplies and an espresso. Enjoy the picnic grounds at **Robert Mondavi** 14 before touring the winery and tasting the wine. If time permits, spend the night in the town of ☒ **Rutherford** and visit either **Round Pond** 16, where you can learn about locally made olive oil, or the **Niebaum-Coppola Estate** 17, or continue north to ☒ **St. Helena.** Take a look at the nearby Silverado Museum and visit the shopping complex surrounding the **Freemark Abbey Winery** 29. On your third day drive to ☒ **Calistoga** for a balloon ride before heading north to **Old Faithful Geyser of California** 36; then continue on to **Robert Louis Stevenson State Park** 38, which encompasses the summit of Mount St. Helena. On the fourth day take Route 29 just north of Calistoga proper, head west on Petrified Forest Road, and then go south on Calistoga Road, which runs into Route 29. Follow Route 12 southeast to rustic **Glen Ellen** for a taste of the Sonoma Valley. Visit **Jack London State Historic Park** 47, and then loop back north on Bennett Valley Road to beautiful **Matanzas Creek Winery** 53 in Santa Rosa.

brothers, is in St. Helena. Modern architecture is the exception rather than the rule, but one standout exception is the postmodern extravaganza of Clos Pegase winery, in Calistoga.

The area's natural beauty draws a continuous flow of tourists—from the late winter, when the vineyards bloom yellow with wild mustard and mist shrouds the mountains encircling the valleys, to the fall, when the grapes are ripe.

Exploring the Wine Country

The Wine Country is composed of two main areas—the Napa Valley and the Sonoma Valley—but also includes the Carneros district, which straddles southern Sonoma and Napa counties. Five major paths cut through both valleys: U.S. 101 and Routes 12 and 121 through Sonoma County, and Route 29 north from Napa. The 25-mi Silverado Trail, which runs parallel to Route 29 north from Napa to Calistoga, is a more scenic, less crowded route with a number of distinguished wineries.

One of the most important viticultural areas in the Wine Country spreads across southern Sonoma and Napa counties. The Carneros region has a long, cool growing season tempered by maritime breezes and lingering fogs off the San Pablo Bay—optimum slow-growing conditions for pinot noir and chardonnay grapes. So exotic looking are the misty Carneros marshlands that Francis Ford Coppola chose them as the location for scenes of the Mekong Delta in his 1979 movie *Apocalypse Now.* When the sun is shining, however, Carneros looks like a sprawling and scenic expanse of quintessential Wine Country, where wildflower meadows and vineyards stretch toward the horizon.

About the Restaurants

Many star chefs from urban areas throughout the United States have migrated to the Wine Country, drawn by the area's renowned produce and superlative wines—the products of fertile soil and near-perpetual sun during the growing season. As a result of this marriage of imported talent and indigenous bounty, food now rivals wine as the principal attraction of the region. Although excellent cuisine is available throughout the region, the little town of Yountville has become something of an epicurean crossroads. If you don't succeed at getting a much-coveted reservation at Thomas Keller's French Laundry, often described as one of the best restaurants in the country, then the more casual Bistro Jeanty and Bouchon, as well as a host of other restaurants in and around Yountville, are excellent choices.

Such high quality often means high prices, but you can also find appealing, inexpensive eateries. High-end delis serve superb picnic fare, and brunch is a cost-effective strategy at pricey restaurants.

With few exceptions (which are noted in individual restaurant listings), dress is informal. Where reservations are indicated as essential, you may need to make them a week or more ahead. In summer and early fall you may need to book several weeks ahead.

PLEASURES & PASTIMES

GALLERIES & MUSEUMS. Artists and art dealers have discovered the Napa Valley as a showplace for original works of art. Internationally famous artists and local artists exhibit their work side by side in galleries that showcase artistic styles to suit every taste. Shows at most galleries are scheduled throughout the year, and exhibitions change frequently.

HOT-AIR BALLOONING. Day after day, colorful balloons fill the morning sky high above the Wine Country's valleys. To aficionados, peering down at vineyards from the vantage point of the clouds is the ultimate California experience. Balloon flights usually take place soon after sunrise, when the calmest, coolest conditions offer maximum lift and soft landings. Prices vary slightly according to the duration of the flight, number of passengers, and services, but you should expect to pay about $200, considerably more if you want a balloon without any other passengers. Some companies provide such extras as pickup at your lodging, and most include a champagne brunch after the flight.

SPAS & MUD BATHS. Mineral-water soaks, mud baths, and massage are rejuvenating local traditions. Calistoga, known worldwide as the Hot Springs of the West, is famous for its warm, springwater-fed mineral tubs and mud baths full of volcanic ash. Sonoma, St. Helena, Napa, and other towns also have full-service spas. Many hotels have full-service spas, open either to the public or to guests only. Even hotels without a spa can usually arrange for a massage therapist to visit your hotel room with notice of a day or two.

WONDERFUL WORLD OF WINE. Wine tasting can be an educational, fascinating, and even mysterious ritual. The sight of polished glasses and uniquely labeled bottles lined up in a row, the tour guide's commentary on the character of each wine, and the aroma of the oak casks and fermenting grapes combine to create an anticipation that's gratified with the first sip of wine. Learning about the origin of the grapes, the terraces on which they're grown, the weather that nurtured them, and the methods by which they're transformed into wine will give you a new appreciation of wine—and a great afternoon (or all-day) diversion. For those new to the wine-tasting game, Robert Mondavi and Korbel Champagne Cellars give general tours geared toward teaching novices the basics on how wine and champagne are made and what to look for when tasting.

There are more than 400 wineries in Sonoma and Napa, so it pays to be selective when planning your visit. Better to mix up the wineries with other sights and diversions—a picnic, trips to local museums, a ride in a hot-air balloon—than attempt to visit too many in one day. Unless otherwise noted, the wineries in this chapter are open daily year-round and charge no fee for admission, tours, or tastings. In general, fees tend to be $5 to $10 in the Napa and Sonoma valleys, although these are often refundable with the purchase of a bottle of wine. Smaller wineries farther off the beaten track, such as in the Russian River or Alexander valleys, generally have free tastings.

About the Hotels

Ranging from unique to utterly luxurious, the area's many inns and hotels are usually exquisitely appointed. Most of the bed-and-breakfasts have historical Victorian and Spanish architecture and include a full breakfast highlighting local produce. The newer hotels tend to have a more modern, streamlined aesthetic, and many have state-of-the-art spas with massage treatments or spring-water pools. Numerous hotels and B&Bs have top-quality restaurants on their grounds, and all that don't still have spots providing gastronomic bliss just a short car ride away.

However, all of this comes with a hefty price tag. As the cost of vineyards and grapes has risen, so have lodging rates. Santa Rosa, the largest population center in the area, has the widest selection of moderately priced rooms. Try there if you've failed to reserve in advance or have a limited budget. In general, all accommodations in the area often have considerably lower rates on weeknights, and prices are about 20% lower in winter.

On weekends, two- or even three-night minimum stays are commonly required, especially at smaller inns and B&Bs. If you'd prefer to stay a single night, though, innkeepers are usually more flexible during winter. Many B&Bs book up long in advance of the summer and fall seasons, and they're often not suitable for children.

WHAT IT COSTS				
$$$$	$$$	$$	$	¢
RESTAURANTS over $30	$23–$30	$15–$22	$10–$14	under $10
HOTELS over $250	$200–$250	$150–$199	$90–$149	under $90

Restaurant prices are per person for a main course at dinner. Hotel prices are for two people in a standard double room in high season.

Timing

Crush, the term used to indicate the season when grapes are picked and crushed, usually takes place in September or October, depending on the weather. From September until November the entire Wine Country celebrates its bounty with street fairs and festivals. The Sonoma County Harvest Fair, with its famous grape stomp, is held the first weekend in October. Golf tournaments, wine auctions, and art and food fairs occur throughout the fall.

In season (April through October), Napa Valley draws crowds of tourists, and traffic along Route 29 from St. Helena to Calistoga is often backed up on weekends. The Sonoma Valley, Santa Rosa, and Healdsburg are less crowded. In season and over holiday weekends it's best to book lodging, restaurant, and winery reservations well in advance. Many wineries give tours at specified times and require appointments.

To avoid crowds, visit the Wine Country during the week and get an early start (most wineries open around 9 or 10). Because many wineries close as early as 4 or 4:30—and almost none is open past 5—you'll need to get a reasonably early start if you want to fit in more than one or two, especially if you're going to enjoy the leisurely lunch customary in the Wine Country. Summer is usually hot and dry, and autumn can be even hotter, so pack a sun hat if you go during these times.

THE NAPA VALLEY

2

With more than 280 wineries, the Napa Valley is the undisputed capital of American wine production. Famed for its unrivaled climate and neat rows of vineyards, the area is made up of small, quirky towns whose Victorian Gothic architecture—narrow, gingerbread facades and pointed arches—is reminiscent of a distant world. Yountville, in the lower Napa Valley, is compact and redolent of American history yet is also an important culinary hub. St. Helena, in the middle of the valley, is posh, with tony shops and elegant restaurants. Calistoga, near the north border of Napa County, feels a bit like an Old West frontier town, with wooden-plank storefronts and a more casual feel than many Wine Country towns.

Napa

46 mi from San Francisco via I–80 east and north, Rte. 37 west, and Rte. 29 north.

Established in 1848 and with a population of about 120,000, Napa is the oldest town as well as the largest city in the valley. It has been undergoing a cultural rebirth that has encompassed the 2001 opening of Copia: The American Center for Wine, Food & the Arts, the sprucing up of the downtown area, and the reopening of the glamorous 1880 Napa Valley Opera House after years of renovations.

The commercial hub for one of the richest wine-producing regions in the world, the city itself is urban and busy. But it's surrounded by some of California's prettiest agricultural lands. Most destinations in both the Napa and Sonoma valleys are easily accessible from here. For those seeking an affordable alternative to the hotels and B&Bs in the heart of the Wine Country, Napa is a good option. But choose lodgings right downtown or on the north side of town near Yountville, because parts of Napa are downright seedy.

★ ❶ **Domaine Carneros** occupies a 138-acre estate dominated by a classic château inspired by Champagne Taittinger's Château de la Marquetterie in France. Carved into the hillside beneath the winery, Domaine Carneros's cellars produce sparkling wines reminiscent of the Taittinger style and using only Carneros grapes. (It's in the Carneros wine district.) At night the château is a glowing beacon rising above the dark vineyards. Flights of wines (in which small amounts of several different wines are poured) and accompanying cheese plates and caviar can be ordered from tables inside or on the terrace overlooking the vineyards. ✉ *1240 Duhig Rd.* ☎ *707/257–0101* ⊕ *www.domainecarneros.com* ✉ *Tastings $5.50–$13.50, 40-min tour free* ☉ *Daily 10–6; tours daily at 10:15, 11, noon, 1, 2, 3, and 4.*

❷ **Artesa Vineyards & Winery,** formerly called Codorniu Napa, is bunkered into a Carneros hilltop. The Spanish owners produce primarily still wines

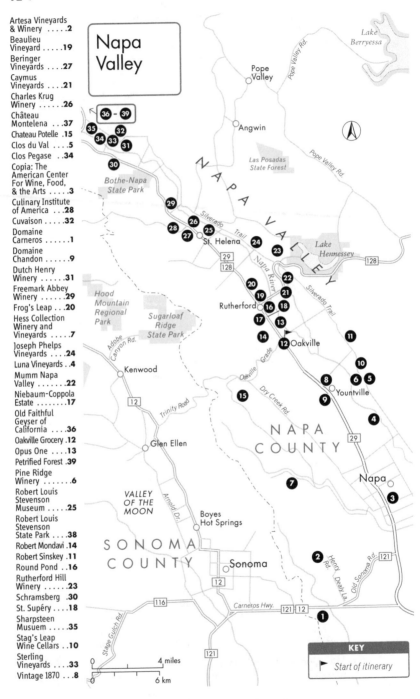

Napa Valley

2

under the talented winemaker Don Van Staaveren. With a modern, minimalist look in the tasting room and contemporary sculptures and fountains on the property, this place is a far cry from the many faux French châteaux and rustic Italian-style villas in the region. Two rooms off the tasting room display exhibits on the Carneros region's history and geography, as well as antique wine-making tools. ✉ *1345 Henry Rd., north off Old Sonoma Rd. and Dealy La.* ☎ *707/224–1668* ⊕ *www.artesawinery.com* ⌨ *Tastings $2 and up, ½-hr tour free* ☉ *Daily 10–5; tours daily at 11 and 2.*

❸ **Copia: The American Center for Wine, Food & the Arts,** named after the
FodorsChoice goddess of abundance, is a shrine to American food and wine. An enor-
★ mous variety of food-related art exhibits, video screenings, food and wine tastings, and tours are scheduled daily (pick up a list from the informa-tion desk near the front door). The entry fee (halved on Wednesday) al-lows access to the exhibitions, informative tours, gift shop, and a daily wine tasting. One-hour tours of the ever-changing gardens are very popular. Special programs, such as a luncheon exploration of wine and cheese pairings, are fantastic (additional fee required). ✉ *500 1st St.* ☎ *707/259–1600* ⊕ *www.copia.org* ⌨ *$12.50* ☉ *Wed.–Mon. 10–5.*

❹ **Luna Vineyards,** the southernmost winery on the Silverado Trail, was es-tablished in 1995 by veterans of the Napa wine industry intent on mak-ing less-conventional wines, particularly Italian varieties. (Their whites are styled after those from Fruili, the reds after those from Tuscany.) They've planted pinot grigio on the property and also produce Sangiovese and merlot. ✉ *2921 Silverado Trail* ☎ *707/255–2474* ⊕ *www. lunavineyards.com* ⌨ *Tastings $5–$10, tour $5–$10* ☉ *Daily 10–5; tours by appointment.*

❺ **Clos du Val,** founded by French owner Bernard Portet, produces a cele-brated reserve cabernet. It also makes zinfandel, pinot noir, and chardon-nay. Although the winery itself is austere, the French-style wines age beautifully. Anyone is welcome to try a hand at the boccie-style game of pétanque. ✉ *5330 Silverado Trail* ☎ *707/259–2200* ⊕ *www.closduval. com* ⌨ *Tastings and tour $5* ☉ *Daily 10–5; tours by appointment.*

❻ Small **Pine Ridge Winery,** in the Stags Leap district, makes estate-bottled wines, including chardonnay, chenin blanc, and merlot, as well as a first-rate cabernet. Tours (by appointment) include barrel tastings in the winery's caves. ✉ *5901 Silverado Trail* ☎ *707/252–9777* ⊕ *www. pineridgewinery.com* ⌨ *Tastings $10–$20, tour $20* ☉ *Daily 10:30–4:30; tours at 10, noon, and 2.*

❼ The **Hess Collection Winery and Vineyards** is a delightful discovery on
FodorsChoice Mt. Veeder 9 mi northwest of the city of Napa. (Don't give up; the road
★ leading to the winery is long and winding.) The simple, rustic limestone structure, circa 1903, contains Swiss owner Donald Hess's personal art collection, including mostly large-scale works by such contemporary Eu-ropean and American artists as Robert Motherwell, Francis Bacon, and Frank Stella. Cabernet sauvignon is the real strength here, though Hess also produces some fine chardonnays. The winery and the art collec-tion are open for self-guided tours (free). ✉ *4411 Redwood Rd., west*

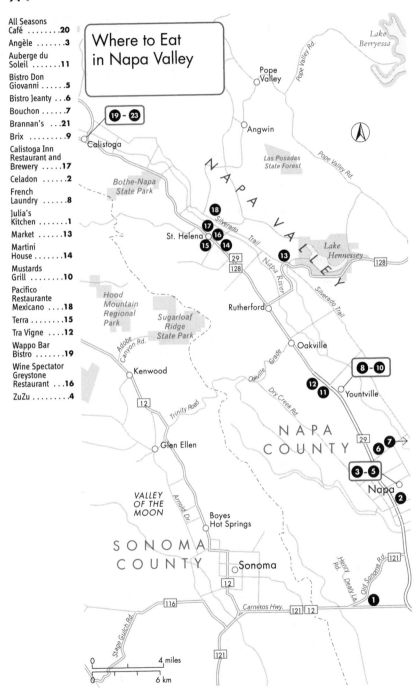

Where to Eat in Napa Valley

of Rte. 29 ☎ *707/255–1144* ⊕ *www.hesscollection.com* ☒ *Tastings $3* ⊙ *Daily 10–4.*

Where to Stay & Eat

$$–$$$$ ✕ **Pilar.** A small, subdued dining room, stylish though not unusually impressive, is one of the hottest dining destinations in downtown Napa, the project of celebrity chef Pilar Sanchez and husband chef Didier Lenders. California cuisine is accented by French and Latin flavors. Rack of lamb is a hearty choice; the lighter steamed mussels with *romesco* sauce (a thick combination of red pepper, tomato, almonds, and garlic) and Spanish chorizo hint at Pilar's Spanish and Mexican heritage. California line up alongside their Continental counterparts on the unusual wine list. ☒ *807 Main St.* ☎ *707/252–4474* ⚄ *Reservations essential* ☱ *AE, D, MC, V* ⊙ *Closed Sun. No lunch weekends.*

$$–$$$ ✕ **Julia's Kitchen.** Named for Julia Child, the restaurant at Copia serves French-California cuisine that relies on the freshest regional ingredients, as well as on the skills of acclaimed chef Victor Scargle. Salad greens and many other vegetables come from Copia's 3½ acres of organic gardens, just outside the door. Grilled quail might be accompanied by frisée and pancetta, and arctic char might be poached in olive oil to wonderfully tender, flaky effect. Diners can watch the chefs at work in the open kitchen. Unusual desserts, such as strawberry mascarpone meringue, show off the talents of the inventive pastry chef. ☒ *500 1st St.* ☎ *707/265–5700* ☱ *AE, MC, V* ⊙ *No lunch Tues. No dinner Mon.–Wed.*

$–$$$ ✕ **Angèle.** Vaulted wood-beam ceilings, dim lights, and candles on every table set a romantic mood at this congenial and cozy French bistro. Classic dishes such as French onion soup and blanquette *de veau* (of veal) are well executed and served by an attentive staff. The charmingly rustic restaurant is housed in the Hatt Building, part of a complex of riverside structures in downtown Napa. ☒ *540 Main St.* ☎ *707/252–8115* ☱ *AE, D, DC, MC, V.*

★ **$–$$$**   ✕ **Bistro Don Giovanni.** Terra-cotta tile floors and high ceilings surround this lively, festive bistro. The Italian food with a Californian spin is simultaneously inventive and comforting: risotto with squab and radicchio, pizza with pear and prosciutto, and rabbit braised in cabernet. Whole, wood-oven-roasted fish is an unusual specialty. Seats on the covered patio are coveted in fair weather. ☒ *4110 Howard La./Rte. 29* ☎ *707/224–3300* ☱ *AE, D, DC, MC, V.*

$–$$$ ✕ **Boon Fly Cafe.** This newcomer to the Carneros region, west of downtown Napa, has a rural charm–meets–industrial chic theme. Outside, rocking chairs and swings occupy the porch of a modern red barn; inside, high ceilings and galvanized steel tabletops set a sleek and stylish mood. The small menu of modern California cuisine includes dishes such as roast organic chicken with sautéed mushrooms and artisanal cheese plates. Though the wine list is impressive for such a moderately priced spot, kids' dishes such as "Cheese Pizza the Adults Can't Have" hint that the proprietors don't take themselves too seriously. ☒ *4048 Sonoma Hwy.* ☎ *707/299–4872* ⚄ *Reservations not accepted* ☱ *AE, D, MC, V.*

$–$$$ ✕ **Celadon.** Venture into downtown Napa for chef-owner Greg Cole's creative and enticing "global comfort food." Dishes such as flash-fried calamari with a chipotle-ginger glaze and a Moroccan-inspired lamb shank served with almond couscous make this an ideal place to sample contemporary cuisine accompanied by any of the dozen wines available by the glass. ⊠ *500 Main St.* ☎ *707/254–9690* ▤ *AE, D, DC, MC, V* ⊘ *No lunch weekends.*

$–$$$ ✕ **ZuZu.** Spanish glass lamps, a faded tile floor, and hammered-tin ceiling panels set the tone for a menu composed almost entirely of tapas. These little dishes so common in Spain are a rarity in the Wine Country, which may be why the in-crowd immediately adopted this lively place where there's usually a wait on weekend nights (they don't take reservations). White anchovies with endive, ratatouille, salt cod with garlic croutons, and paella are typical fare. ⊠ *829 Main St.* ☎ *707/224–8555* ▤ *AE, MC, V* ⊘ *No lunch weekends.*

$$$$ 🏠 **Carneros Inn.** Although from the exterior the freestanding cottages
Fodor'sChoice at this luxury resort look simple, even spartan, inside the ethereal beds
★ are piled high with fluffy pillows and covered with Frette linens and pristine white down comforters. High-tech amenities include DVD players, flat-panel TVs, and heated slate bathroom floors. Each cottage also has a wood-burning fireplace and French doors opening onto a private courtyard with a gas-fired heater. The infinity pool invites impromptu dips day and night, and the hilltop dining room serves cocktails and dinner (guests only) overlooking the vineyards. ⊠ *4048 Sonoma Hwy., 94559* ☎ *707/299–4900* 🖷 *707/299–4950* ⊕ *www.thecarnerosinn.com* ⬭ *76 rooms, 10 suites* ⌂ *2 restaurants, dining room, room service, refrigerators, cable TV, in-room VCRs, in-room data ports, pool, gym, hot tub, spa, bar, dry cleaning, laundry service, concierge, meeting rooms* ▤ *AE, D, DC, MC, V.*

★ **$$$$** 🏠 **Milliken Creek Inn.** Soft jazz and complimentary port set a romantic mood in the intimate lobby, with its terrace overlooking the Napa River and the inn's lavishly landscaped lawn. The feeling extends to the chic rooms, which replicate the style of British-colonial Asia. Khaki- and cream-color walls surround rattan furniture, hydrotherapy spa tubs, and some of the fluffier beds in the Wine Country. Adirondack chairs and umbrellas are an invitation to lazy afternoons on the lawn in fair weather, and a tiny deck overlooking the river is the spot for massages and private yoga classes. All of the treatment rooms at the serene spa, including one used for popular couples' treatments, have river views. ⊠ *1815 Silverado Trail, 94558* ☎ *707/255–1197 or 888/622–5775* ⊕ *www.millikencreekinn.com* ⬭ *12 rooms, 7 suites* ⌂ *Minibars, refrigerators, cable TV, in-room VCRs, in-room data ports, spa, dry cleaning, concierge; no kids, no smoking* ▤ *AE, D, DC, MC, V* ⊩ *CP.*

$$$–$$$$ 🏠 **La Résidence.** Most of these deluxe accommodations, romantic and secluded amid extensive landscaping, are in two buildings: the French Barn and the Mansion, a renovated 1870s Gothic-revival manor house built by a riverboat captain from New Orleans. Towering oaks bathe the entire property in shade. The spacious rooms have floral bedspreads and curtains, period antiques, and fireplaces, and most have double French doors that open onto verandas or patios. In addition to an elegant breakfast, you are treated to a sumptuous spread of appetizers and wine every evening. ⊠ *4066 Howard La., 94558* ☎ *707/253–0337* 🖷 *707/253–0382* ⊕ *www.laresidence.com* ⬭ *22 rooms, 1 suite* ⌂ *Some*

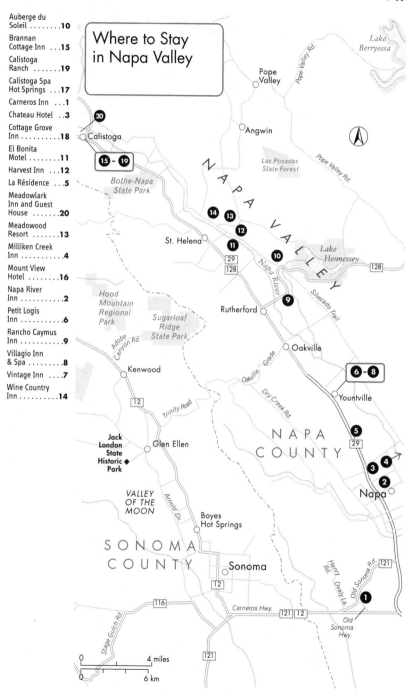

Auberge du
Soleil **10**

Brannan
Cottage Inn ...**15**

Calistoga
Ranch **19**

Calistoga Spa
Hot Springs ...**17**

Carneros Inn ...**1**

Chateau Hotel ..**3**

Cottage Grove
Inn **18**

El Bonita
Motel **11**

Harvest Inn ...**12**

La Résidence ...**5**

Meadowlark
Inn and Guest
House **20**

Meadowood
Resort **13**

Milliken Creek
Inn **4**

Mount View
Hotel **16**

Napa River
Inn **2**

Petit Logis
Inn **6**

Rancho Caymus
Inn **9**

Villagio Inn
& Spa **8**

Vintage Inn **7**

Wine Country
Inn **14**

Where to Stay in Napa Valley

refrigerators, some cable TV, pool, hot tub; no TV in some rooms, no smoking ⊟ *AE, D, DC, MC, V* ⦿⦿ *BP.*

$$–$$$$ 🏨 **Napa River Inn.** A 2½-acre complex includes restaurants, shops, a spa, and this waterfront inn. Accommodations in the 1884 Hatt Building maintain original architectural details, including maple hardwood floors; some rooms have canopy beds, fireplaces, and artwork depicting an 1880s river town. Brighter colors dominate in the adjacent Embarcadero building, where some rooms have small balconies and the decor has an understated nautical theme. ⊠ *500 Main St., 94559* ☎ *707/251–8500 or 877/251–8500* 🖷 *707/251–8504* ⊕ *www.napariverinn.com* ⇲ *65 rooms, 1 suite* ♨ *2 restaurants, café, patisserie, refrigerators, cable TV with video games, in-room VCRs, in-room data ports, spa, bicycles, wine bar, shops, dry cleaning, laundry service, concierge, Internet room, business services, meeting rooms, some pets allowed (fee); no smoking* ⊟ *AE, D, DC, MC, V* ⦿⦿ *CP.*

$–$$ 🏨 **Chateau Hotel.** Despite the name, this is a fairly simple motel that makes only the barest nod to France. Clean rooms, its location at the entrance to the Napa Valley, the adjacent restaurant, and free stays for children under age 12 are conveniences that make up for the rooms' lack of charm. New conference facilities mean it's a popular place for business travelers. ⊠ *4195 Solano Ave., west of Rte. 29, exit at Trower Ave., 94558* ☎ *707/253–9300, 800/253–6272 in CA* 🖷 *707/253–0906* ⊕ *www.napavalleychateauhotel.com* ⇲ *109 rooms, 6 suites* ♨ *Some refrigerators, cable TV, pool, hot tub* ⊟ *AE, D, DC, MC, V* ⦿⦿ *CP.*

The Arts

In 1995, former telecommunications tycoon and vintner William Jarvis and his wife transformed a stone winery building in downtown Napa into the **Jarvis Conservatory,** an excellent venue for baroque ballet and Spanish operetta known as zarzuela. Performances open to the public are held in conjunction with workshops and festivals centered on these two art forms. The conservatory presents opera nights featuring local talent the first Saturday of each month. ⊠ *1711 Main St.* ☎ *707/255–5445* ⊕ *www.jarvisconservatory.com.*

Sports & the Outdoors

BICYCLING Thanks to the long country roads that wind through the region, bicycling is a popular pastime. The Silverado Trail, with its very gently rolling hills, is more scenic than Route 29, which nevertheless tempts some bikers with its pancake-flat aspect. **Napa Valley Bike Tours** (⊠ 68 Coombs St., Suite I-1, Napa ☎ 707/251–8687 or 800/707–2453) rents bikes for $10–$15 per hour or $30–$50 per day. One-day winery tours are $115, including lunch and van support.

GOLF The 18-hole course at the **Chardonnay Golf Club** (⊠ 2555 Jameson Canyon Rd. ☎ 707/257–8950) is a favorite among Bay Area golfers. The greens fee, $70 weekdays and $90 weekends in high season, includes a cart. Within the vicinity of the Silverado Trail, the **Silverado Country Club** (⊠ 1600 Atlas Peak Rd. ☎ 707/257–5444) has two challenging 18-hole courses designed by Robert Trent Jones Jr. The greens fee ranges from $70 to $155, depending on the day of week and the time of year.

Yountville

13 mi north of the town of Napa on Rte. 29.

Founded in 1831 by George Calvert Yount, who is credited with planting the first grapevines in the Napa Valley, Yountville has become the valley's boomtown. No other small town in the Wine Country has as many inns, shops, or internationally celebrated restaurants. Particularly **8** popular is **Vintage 1870** (✉ 6525 Washington St. ☎ 707/944–2451), a 26-acre complex of boutiques, restaurants, and fancy-food stores. The vine-covered brick shops, built in 1870, once housed a winery, livery stable, and distillery. The property's original mansion is now the Mexican-style Compadres Bar and Grill. Nearby, the Pacific Blues Café is set in the 1868 train depot built by Samuel Brannan for his privately owned Napa Valley Railroad.

At the intersection of Madison and Washington streets is **Washington Square,** a complex of boutiques and restaurants. **Pioneer Cemetery**, the final resting place of town founder George Yount, is on the far side of Washington Street.

9 French-owned **Domaine Chandon** claims one of Yountville's prime pieces of real estate, on a knoll west of downtown. Tours of the sleek, modern facilities on the beautifully landscaped property include sample flutes of the *méthode champenoise* sparkling wine. Champagne is $4–$12 per glass, hors d'oeuvres are available, and an elegant restaurant has been garnering rave reviews for its innovative cuisine. ✉ *1 California Dr., west of Rte. 29* ☎ *707/944–2280* ⊕ *www.chandon.com* 🖃 *Tour free* ☉ *Apr.–Nov., daily 10–6; Dec.–Mar., daily 10–5. Call for tour times.*

10 It was the 1973 cabernet sauvignon produced by **Stag's Leap Wine Cellars** that put the winery—and the California wine industry—on the map by placing first in the famous Paris tasting of 1976. Today, Stag's Leap makes cabernet, as well as chardonnay, sauvignon blanc, Riesling, and merlot. ✉ *5766 Silverado Trail* ☎ *707/265–2441* ⊕ *www.cask23.com* 🖃 *Tastings $10–$30; tour $20* ☉ *Daily 10–4:30; tours by appointment.*

11 **Robert Sinskey Vineyards** makes renowned estate-bottled wines, including chardonnay, cabernet, and merlot, but is best known for its pinot noir. The open kitchen in the dramatic tasting room is the site of occasional cooking classes and demos; call ahead for a schedule. ✉ *6320 Silverado Trail* ☎ *707/944–9090* 🖷 *707/994–9092* ⊕ *www.robertsinskey.com* 🖃 *Tastings $10; tour free* ☉ *Daily 10–4:30; 1-hr tours by appointment.*

Where to Stay & Eat

$$$$ ✕ **French Laundry.** An old stone building houses the most acclaimed **Fodor'sChoice** restaurant in Napa Valley—and, indeed, one of the most highly re- ★ garded in the country. The prix-fixe menus ($125–$150), one of which is vegetarian, include five or nine courses. A full three hours will likely pass before you reach dessert. Chef Thomas Keller, with two James Beard awards, doesn't lack for admirers. Reservations are hard won and not accepted more than two months in advance (call two months ahead to the day). Didn't get a reservation? Call on the day you'd like to dine here to be considered if there's a cancellation. ⊠ *6640 Washington St.* ☎ *707/944–2380* ⚲ *Reservations essential* ☲ *AE, MC, V* ☉ *Closed 1st 2 wks in Jan. No lunch Mon.–Thurs.*

$$–$$$$ ✕ **Brix.** The spacious dining room has artisan glass, fine woods, and an entire wall of west-facing windows that overlooks vineyards. Many of the herbs used in the kitchen are grown in the adjacent garden. Mains might include fresh fettuccine with sugar snap peas or grilled Atlantic salmon with chanterelles and vanilla beurre blanc. Pizzas are cooked in a wood-burning oven. ⊠ *7377 St. Helena Hwy./Rte. 29* ☎ *707/944–2749* ☲ *AE, D, DC, MC, V.*

$$–$$$ ✕ **Bistro Jeanty.** Philippe Jeanty's menu draws its inspiration from the cooking of his French childhood. His traditional cassoulet will warm those nostalgic for France, and the bistro classic steak frites might be served with a decadent béarnaise sauce. The scene here is Gallic through and through, with a small bar and a handful of tables in two crowded, noisy rooms. The best seats are in the back room, near the fireplace. ⊠ *6510 Washington St.* ☎ *707/944–0103* ☲ *MC, V.*

$$–$$$ ✕ **Bouchon.** The team that brought the French Laundry to its current
Fodor'sChoice pinnacle is behind this place, where everything from the snazzy zinc bar
★ to the black vests on the waiters to the traditional French onion soup could have come straight from a Parisian bistro. *Boudin noir* (blood sausage) with potato puree and leg of lamb with white beans are among the hearty dishes served in the high-ceiling room. Late-night meals are served from a limited menu until 12:45 AM. ⊠ *6534 Washington St.* ☎ *707/944–8037* ☲ *AE, MC, V.*

★ **$–$$$** ✕ **Mustards Grill.** There's not an ounce of pretension at the first restaurant of owner-chef Cindy Pawlcyn, despite the fact that it's booked solid almost nightly with fans of her hearty cuisine. The menu mixes updated renditions of traditional American dishes such as grilled fish, steak, and lemon meringue pie with innovative choices such as seared ahi tuna on homemade sesame crackers with wasabi crème fraîche. A black-and-white marble tile floor, dark-wood wainscoting, and upbeat artwork set a scene that's casual but refined. ⊠ *7399 St. Helena Hwy./Rte. 29, 1 mi north of town* ☎ *707/944–2424* ⚲ *Reservations essential* ☲ *AE, D, DC, MC, V.*

★ **$$$$** ⊞ **Villagio Inn & Spa.** Villalike buildings cluster around fountains that are arranged on the property to evoke a canal. This plush inn in the heart of Yountville provides guest rooms in which streamlined furnishings, subdued color schemes, and high ceilings enhance a sense of spaciousness. Each room has a fireplace and, beyond louvered doors, a balcony or patio. A youthful vibe infuses the pool area, where live music is sometimes played on summer afternoons and automated misters cool sunbathers. The full-service spa has its own pool and whirlpool. Rates include afternoon tea, a bottle of wine, and a generous champagne buffet breakfast. ⊠ *6481 Washington St., 94599* ☎ *707/944–8877 or 800/351–1133* ⊟ *707/944–8855* ⊕ *www.villagio.com* ⊠ *86 rooms, 26 suites* ⚲ *Room service, in-room hot tubs, cable TV, in-room VCRs, in-room data ports, 2 tennis courts, pool, outdoor hot tub, spa, bicycles,* *boccie, lobby lounge, shops, dry cleaning, laundry service, concierge, business services, meeting rooms; no smoking* = *AE, D, DC, MC, V* ❚O❙ *CP.*

$$$$ 🏨 **Vintage Inn.** Rooms in this luxurious inn are housed in two-story villas scattered around a lush, landscaped 3½-acre property. French fabrics and plump upholstered chairs outfit spacious, airy guest rooms with vaulted beamed ceilings, all of which have a private patio or balcony, a fireplace, and a whirlpool tub in the bathroom. Some private patios have vineyard views. You're treated to a bottle of wine, a champagne buffet breakfast, and afternoon tea and scones. ✉ *6541 Washington St., 94599* ☎ *707/944–1112 or 800/351–1133* 📠 *707/944–1617* ⊕ *www.vintageinn. com* ➦ *68 rooms, 12 suites* & *Room service, in-room hot tubs, refrigerators, cable TV, in-room VCRs, in-room data ports, 2 tennis courts, pool, outdoor hot tub, bicycles, lobby lounge, shop, dry cleaning, laundry service, concierge, business services, meeting rooms, some pets allowed (fee), no-smoking rooms* = *AE, D, DC, MC, V* ❚O❙ *CP.*

$$ 🏨 **Petit Logis Inn.** Murals and 11-foot-high ceilings infuse a European charm into the rooms of this small, understated one-story inn, which was formerly a row of shops. Though the individually decorated rooms generally recall the 19th century, bathrooms have modern luxuries such as whirlpool baths big enough for two. Breakfast, included in the room rate, is provided by one of two nearby restaurants. The inn's proximity to many of Yountville's best restaurants (within walking distance) is another plus. ✉ *6527 Yount St., 94599* ☎ *707/944–2332 or 877/944–2332* 📠 *707/944–2388* ⊕ *www.petitlogis.com* ➦ *5 rooms* & *Refrigerators, cable TV, in-room data ports; no smoking* = *AE, MC, V* ❚O❙ *BP.*

Oakville

2 mi west of Yountville on Rte. 29.

There are three reasons to visit the town of Oakville: its grocery store, its scenic mountain road, and its magnificent, highly exclusive winery.

⑫ The **Oakville Grocery** (✉ 7856 St. Helena Hwy./Rte. 29 ☎ 707/944–8802), built in 1881 as a general store, carries a surprisingly wide range of unusual and upscale groceries and prepared foods despite its tiny size. It's a popular place to sit on a bench out front and sip an espresso between winery visits. Along the mountain range that divides Napa and Sonoma, the **Oakville Grade** (✉ West of Rte. 29) is a twisting half-hour route with breathtaking views of both valleys. Although the surface of the road is good, it can be difficult to negotiate at night, and those driving trucks are advised not to attempt it at any time.

⑬ **Opus One,** the combined venture of California winemaker Robert Mondavi and the late French baron Philippe de Rothschild, is famed for its vast (1,000 barrels side by side on a single floor), semicircular cellar modeled on the Château Mouton Rothschild winery in France. The futuristic building, which seems to be pushing itself out of the earth, is the work of the architects responsible for San Francisco's Transamerica Pyramid. The state-of-the-art facilities produce about 20,000 cases of ultra-premium Bordeaux-style red wine from grapes grown in the estate's vineyards and in the surrounding area. ✉ *7900 St. Helena Hwy./Rte.*

29 ☎ 707/944–9442 ⊕ www.opusonewinery.com ✉ Tastings $25; tour free ⊙ Daily 10–4; tastings and tours by appointment.

⑭ At **Robert Mondavi,** perhaps the best-known winery in the United States, you're encouraged to take the 75- to 90-minute vineyard and winery tour followed by a seated wine tasting. Longer tours ($50–$75) allow visitors to learn more about the sensory evaluation of wine or the art of making cabernet sauvignon. Afterward, visit the art gallery, or, in summer, stick around for a concert (from jazz to pop and world music). ✉ *7801 St. Helena Hwy./Rte. 29 ☎ 888/766–6328 ⊕ www. robertmondaviwinery.com ✉ Tastings $5–$30, tour $20 ⊙ Daily 10–5; tours by appointment.*

★ **⑮** **Chateau Potelle,** an out-of-the-way spot at nearly 2,000 feet on the slopes of Mt. Veeder, produces acclaimed estate zinfandel, chardonnay, and cabernet sauvignon. Jean-Noël and Marketta Fourmeaux were official tasters for the French government before establishing this winery in 1988, which they named for the château in the Champagne region belonging to Jean-Noël's family. The friendly, casual atmosphere and location away from the crowds in the valley below make it an ideal spot for a picnic. ✉ *3875 Mt. Veeder Rd., 4 mi west of Rte. 29 off Oakville Grade ☎ 707/255–9440 ⊕ www.chateaupotelle.com ✉ Tastings $5 ⊙ Nov.–mid-Apr., daily 11–5; mid-Apr.–Oct., daily 11–6.*

Rutherford

1 mi northwest of Oakville on Rte. 29.

From a fast-moving car, Rutherford is a quick blur of dark forest, a rustic barn or two, and maybe a country store. But don't speed by this tiny hamlet. With its singular microclimate and soil, this is an important viticultural center.

⑯ Five varieties of Italian olives and three types of Spanish olives are grown on 12 acres at **Round Pond.** Within an hour of being handpicked (sometime between October and February), the olives are crushed in the mill on the property to produce pungent, peppery oils that are later blended and sold. Call a day in advance to arrange a tour of the mill followed by an informative tasting, during which you can sample several types of oil, both alone and with Round Pond's own red wine vinegars and other tasty foods. ✉ *877 Rutherford Rd. ☎ 707/963–7555 ⊕ www. roundpond.com ✉ Tour $20 ⊙ Tours by appointment.*

⑰ In the 1970s, filmmaker Francis Ford Coppola bought the old Niebaum
Fodor'sChoice property, a part of the world-famous Inglenook estate. He resurrected
★ an early Inglenook-like red with his first bottle of Rubicon, released in 1985. Since then, the **Niebaum-Coppola Estate** has consistently received high ratings, and in 1995 Coppola purchased the other half of the Inglenook estate; the ancient, ivy-covered château; and an additional 95 acres. A small museum in the château has displays documenting the history of the Inglenook estates as well as Coppola movie memorabilia, which include Don Corleone's desk and chair from *The Godfather* and costumes from *Bram Stoker's Dracula.* ✉ *1991 St. Helena Hwy./Rte.*

29 ☎ 707/963–9099 ⊕ *www.niebaum-coppola.com* ⌨ *Tastings $10, tour $20* ☉ *Daily 10–5; Memorial Day–Labor Day, open until 6 Fri. and Sat.; château tours daily at 10:30, 12:30, and 2:30; vineyard tours daily at 11, weather permitting.*

⑱ Fine sauvignon blancs, merlots, chardonnays, and cabernet sauvignons are among the wines at which **St. Supéry** excels. Although the tasting room is less atmospheric than most, an excellent free self-guided tour allows you a peek at the barrel and fermentation rooms, as well as a restored home from 1882. ⊠ *8440 St. Helena Hwy. S/Rte. 29* ☎ *707/963–4507* ⊕ *www.stsupery.com* ⌨ *Tastings $5–$10, tour free–$12* ☉ *May–Sept., daily 10–5:30; Oct.–Apr., daily 10–5; tours at 1 and 3.*

⑲ **Beaulieu Vineyard** still uses the same wine-making process, from crush to bottle, as it did the day it opened in 1900. The winery's cabernet is a benchmark of the Napa Valley. The Georges de Latour Private Reserve cabernet sauvignon consistently garners high marks from major wine publications. ⊠ *1960 St. Helena Hwy./Rte. 29* ☎ *707/967–5200* ⊕ *www.bvwines.com* ⌨ *Tastings $5–$25* ☉ *Daily 10–5, tours daily on the hr 11–4.*

⑳ **Frog's Leap** is the perfect place for wine novices to begin their education. Owners John and Julie Williams maintain a sense of humor and a humble attitude that translates into an informative and satisfying experience. They also happen to produce some very fine zinfandel, cabernet sauvignon, merlot, and sauvignon blanc. ⊠ *8815 Conn Creek Rd.* ☎ *707/963–4704* ⊕ *www.frogsleap.com* ⌨ *Tastings and tour free* ☉ *Mon.–Sat. 10–4; tours and tastings by appointment.*

FodorsChoice
★

㉑ **Caymus Vineyards** is run by wine master Chuck Wagner, who started making wine on the property in 1972. His family, however, had been farming in the valley since 1906. Today a 100% cabernet sauvignon special selection is the winery's claim to fame. Reserve to taste. ⊠ *8700 Conn Creek Rd.* ☎ *707/963–4204* ⊕ *www.caymus.com* ⌨ *Tastings free* ☉ *Sales daily 10–4; tastings by appointment.*

㉒ A joint venture of Mumm—the French champagne house—and Seagram, **Mumm Napa Valley** is considered one of California's premier sparkling-wine producers. Its Napa Brut Prestige and ultrapremium Vintage Reserve are the best known. The excellent tour and comfortable tasting room are two more reasons to visit. A photography gallery contains a permanent exhibit of Ansel Adams photographs as well as rotating exhibits of works by others. ⊠ *8445 Silverado Trail* ☎ *707/967–7700* ⊕ *www.mummnapavalley.com* ⌨ *Tastings $5–$12, tour free* ☉ *Daily 10–5; tours daily on the hr 10–3.*

㉓ The wine at **Rutherford Hill Winery** is aged in French oak barrels stacked in more than 44,000 square feet of caves—one of the largest winery cave systems in the United States. Tours of the caves can be followed by a picnic in oak, olive, or madrone orchards. ⊠ *200 Rutherford Hill Rd., east of Silverado Trail* ☎ *707/963–7194* ⊕ *www.rutherfordhill.com* ⌨ *Tastings $5–$10, tour $10–$15* ☉ *Daily 10–5; tours daily at 11:30, 1:30, and 3:30.*

Where to Stay & Eat

★ **$$$$** ✕🏠 **Auberge du Soleil.** Every room at this renowned hotel has at least a small terrace, from which you can take in the views of the stunning property and its steep, olive tree–studded slopes. Guest rooms are dressed in a spare and elegant style. Bathrooms are truly grand (as expected at this price level), many of them equipped with whirlpool tubs. The Auberge du Soleil restaurant has a masterful wine list and serves a menu that relies largely on local produce, and the bar serves moderately priced fare until 11 PM. ⊠ *180 Rutherford Hill Rd., off Silverado Trail north of Rte. 128, 94573* ☎ *707/963–1211 or 800/348–5406* 🖷 *707/ 963–8764* ⊕ *www.aubergedusoleil.com* ⇥ *18 rooms, 32 suites* ♨ *2 restaurants, kitchenettes, refrigerators, cable TV, in-room VCRs, in-room data ports, tennis court, pool, gym, hot tub, massage, sauna, spa, bar, concierge, business services, meeting rooms* ▭ *AE, D, DC, MC, V.*

★ **$$$–$$$$** ✕🏠 **Rancho Caymus Inn and La Toque.** California-Spanish in style, this cozy inn has large suites with kitchens and whirlpool baths. Well-chosen details include wrought-iron lamps, tile murals, stoneware basins, and window seats. But even if you don't stay here, come for dinner at the understated La Toque, which gives Yountville's French Laundry its toughest competition for Wine Country diners' haute-cuisine dollars. Reservations are essential, and jackets are preferred for men. Chef-owner Ken Frank's changing prix-fixe menu ($$$$) is loaded with intense flavors; dishes might include seared Sonoma foie gras with dates and roasted boneless quail with winter vegetables. ⊠ *1140 Rutherford Rd., east of Rte. 29, 94573* ☎ *707/963–1777, 800/845–1777 inn, 707/963–9770 restaurant* 🖷 *707/963–5387* ⊕ *www.ranchocaymus.com* ⇥ *27 suites* ♨ *Restaurant, dining room, minibars, refrigerators, cable TV, in-room data ports, wine bar; no smoking* ▭ *AE, DC, MC, V* ⊗ *Restaurant closed Mon., Tues., and 1st 2 wks in Jan. No lunch* ❮❯❮ *CP.*

St. Helena

2 mi northwest of Oakville on Rte. 29.

By the time pioneer winemaker Charles Krug planted grapes in St. Helena around 1860, quite a few vineyards already existed in the area. Today the town greets you with its abundant selection of wineries, many of which lie along the route from Yountville to St. Helena, and its wonderful restaurants, including Greystone, on the West Coast campus of the Culinary Institute of America. Many Victorian and false-front buildings dating from the late 19th and early 20th centuries distinguish the downtown area. Arching sycamore trees bow across Main Street (Route 29) to create a pleasant, shady drive.

②④ Bordeaux blends, Rhône varietals, and a cabernet sauvignon are the house specialties at **Joseph Phelps Vineyards.** One of Napa's top wineries, it first hit the mark with Johannisberg Riesling. ⊠ *200 Taplin Rd.* ☎ *707/963– 2745* ⊕ *www.jpvwines.com* 🖾 *Tastings $5–$10* ⊗ *Tastings and tours by appointment only.*

②⑤ For some nonalcoholic sightseeing, visit the **Robert Louis Stevenson Museum** (⊠ *1490 Library La.* ☎ *707/963–3757* ⊗ *Tues.–Sun. noon–4*), next door to the public library. Its eponymous memorabilia consists of more than 8,000 artifacts, including first editions, manuscripts, and photographs. The museum is free (donation suggested).

26 The first winery founded in the Napa Valley, **Charles Krug Winery** opened in 1861 when Count Haraszthy lent Krug a small cider press. Today the Peter Mondavi family runs it. At this writing, tours have been suspended indefinitely because a major earthquake retrofit project is in the works, but you can still come for tastings. ✉ *2800 N. Main St.* ☎ *707/963–5057* ⊕ *www.charleskrug.com* ☰ *Tastings $5–$8* ☉ *Daily 10:30–5.*

★ **27** Arguably the most beautiful winery in Napa Valley, the 1876 **Beringer Vineyards** is also the oldest continuously operating property. In 1883 Frederick and Jacob Beringer built the Rhine House Mansion, where tastings are held among pieces of Belgian art-nouveau hand-carved oak and walnut furniture and stained-glass windows. The introductory tour departs every hour. Longer tours and seminars on special topics such as wine-and-cheese pairings occur occasionally. ✉ *2000 Main St./Rte. 29* ☎ *707/963–4812* ⊕ *www.beringer.com* ☰ *Tastings and tour $5–$30* ☉ *May 30–Oct. 23, daily 10–6; Oct. 24–May 29, daily 10–5; tours daily every hr 10–4.*

28 The West Coast headquarters of the **Culinary Institute of America,** the country's leading school for chefs, are in the **Greystone Winery,** a National Historic Landmark and, at 117,000 square feet, once the largest stone winery in the world. The campus consists of 30 acres of herb and vegetable gardens, a 15-acre merlot vineyard, and a Mediterranean-inspired restaurant, which is open to the public. Also on the property are a well-stocked culinary store, a quirky corkscrew display, and a culinary library. Daily one-hour cooking demonstrations begin at 1:30 and 3:30, with an extra class at 10:30 on weekend mornings. ✉ *2555 Main St.* ☎ *800/333–9242* ⊕ *www.ciachef.edu* ☰ *Free, demonstrations $12.50* ☉ *Restaurant Sun.–Thurs. 11:30–9, Fri. and Sat. 11:30–10; store and museum daily 10–6.*

29 **Freemark Abbey Winery** was originally called the Tychson Winery, after Josephine Tychson, the first woman to establish a winery in California. It has long been known for its cabernets, whose grapes come from the fertile Rutherford Bench. A much-touted late-harvest Riesling, known as Edelwein Gold, is produced when the climate and conditions allow. ✉ *3022 St. Helena Hwy. N/Rte. 29* ☎ *707/963–9694* ⊕ *www.freemarkabbey.com* ☰ *Tastings $5* ☉ *Daily 10–5; tours by appointment.*

Where to Stay & Eat

★ **$$–$$$$** ✕**Martini House.** Beautiful and boisterous, St. Helena's hottest new restaurant resides in a converted 1923 Craftsman-style home, where earthy colors (designer Pat Kuleto was inspired by Native American motifs) are made even warmer by the glow of three fireplaces. Woodsy ingredients such as chanterelles or juniper berries might accompany sweetbreads or a hearty grilled pork chop. Inventive salads and delicate desserts such as the blood orange sorbet demonstrate chef Todd Humphries's range. The patio, where lights sparkle in the trees, is as attractive as the interior. ✉ *1245 Spring St.* ☎ *707/963–2233* ☰ *AE, D, DC, MC, V* ☉ *No lunch Mon.–Thurs.*

$$–$$$$ ✕ **Wine Spectator Greystone Restaurant.** The Culinary Institute of America runs this place in the handsome old Christian Brothers Winery. Century-old stone walls house a large and bustling restaurant, with cooking, baking, and grilling stations in full view. The menu has a Mediterranean spirit and emphasizes locally grown produce. Typical main courses include crispy striped bass with braised leeks and winter-vegetable potpie. ⊠ *2555 Main St.* ☎ *707/967–1010* ▭ *AE, D, DC, MC, V.*

$$–$$$ ✕ **Terra.** A romantic, candlelit restaurant housed in an 1884 fieldstone
Fodor'sChoice   building, Terra is especially known for its exquisite Mediterranean-in-
  ★   spired dishes, many with Asian touches. The duck rillettes with Belgian endive, grilled lobster with saffron risotto, and spaghettini with tripe are memorable. Inventive desserts might include a rose crème brûlée served with a pear poached in pomegranate molasses. ⊠ *1345 Railroad Ave.* ☎ *707/963–8931* ♨ *Reservations essential* ▭ *DC, MC, V* ☉ *Closed Tues. No lunch. Closed 1st 2 wks in Jan.*

$$–$$$ ✕ **Tra Vigne.** A fieldstone building has been transformed into a striking trattoria with a huge wood bar, 30-foot ceilings, and plush banquettes. Homemade mozzarella, dressed with olive oil and vinegar, and house-cured pancetta and prosciutto are preludes to rustic Tuscan specialties such as oak-grilled rabbit with fava beans. The outdoor courtyard in summer and fall is a sun-splashed Mediterranean vision of striped umbrellas and awnings, crowded café tables, and rustic pots overflowing with flowers. ⊠ *1050 Charter Oak Ave., east of Rte. 29* ☎ *707/963–4444* ▭ *D, DC, MC, V.*

$–$$ ✕ **Market.** The fieldstone walls and friendly service would set a homey mood here even if the menu didn't present comfort food's greatest hits, from fried chicken with mashed potatoes to their signature macaroni and cheese. A top-notch team, with experience working at some of San Francisco's finest restaurants, has made this an exceedingly popular spot for casual food that's excellently prepared. ⊠ *1347 Main St.* ☎ *707/ 963–3799* ▭ *AE, MC, V.*

★ **$$$$**   ✕▥ **Meadowood Resort.** Luxurious accommodations are housed in a rambling lodge and several bungalows scattered on a sprawling property at the end of a quiet road off the Silverado Trail. Airy rooms, many with views of the trees through their large windows, have a simple but chic style. Supremely comfortable beds will defy you to rise early enough to indulge in the golf, tennis, hiking, spa treatments, and other activities that are available here. The elegant dining room, open at dinner only, specializes in California Wine Country cooking. The Grill, a less formal, less expensive restaurant, serves a lighter menu of pizzas and spa food. ⊠ *900 Meadowood La., 94574* ☎ *707/963–3646 or 800/458–8080* ☐ *707/963–5863* ⊕ *www.meadowood.com* ☞ *40 rooms, 45 suites* ⌂ *2 restaurants, room service, refrigerators, cable TV, in-room data ports, 9-hole golf course, 7 tennis courts, 2 pools, health club, hot tub, massage, sauna, steam room, croquet, hiking, bar, concierge, business services, meeting rooms; no smoking* ▭ *AE, D, DC, MC, V.*

$$$$ ▥ **Harvest Inn.** Most rooms in this Tudor-esque inn on lushly landscaped grounds have wet bars, antique furnishings, and fireplaces. Some of the rooms are housed in cottages scattered around 8 acres. Pets are allowed in two rooms for a $75 fee. Complimentary breakfast is served in the breakfast room and on the patio overlooking the vineyards, or you can have it delivered to your room. ⊠ *1 Main St., 94574* ☎ *707/ 963–9463 or 800/950–8466* 🖷 *707/963–4402* ⊕ *www.harvestinn.com* 🛏 *51 rooms, 3 suites* ⚭ *Refrigerators, cable TV, in-room VCRs, in-room data ports, 2 pools, 2 hot tubs, spa, bicycles, wine bar, shop, concierge, meeting rooms, some pets allowed (fee)* ⊟ *AE, D, DC, MC, V* ⧫⊙⧫ *CP.*

$$$–$$$$ 🏨 **Wine Country Inn.** A pastoral landscape of hills surrounds this peace-ful New England–style retreat. Rooms are filled with comfortable coun-try-style furniture, and many have a wood-burning fireplace, a private hot tub, or a patio or balcony overlooking the vineyards. A hearty country breakfast is served buffet-style in the sun-splashed common room. Wine tastings are scheduled in the afternoon. ⊠ *1152 Lodi La., east of Rte. 29, 94574* ☎ *707/963–7077* 🖷 *707/963–9018* ⊕ *www. winecountryinn.com* 🛏 *24 rooms, 5 suites* ⚭ *Refrigerators, pool, hot tub, business services; no room TVs, no smoking* ⊟ *MC, V* ⧫⊙⧫ *BP.*

$–$$ 🏨 **El Bonita Motel.** Landscaped grounds with picnic tables are some of the pleasant touches at this motel, where rooms vary in style but lean toward a simple country look. Its location right on Route 29 makes it convenient, but light sleepers should ask for rooms farthest from the road. Family-friendly pluses include roll-away beds and cribs for a mod-est extra charge. ⊠ *195 Main St./Rte. 29, 94574* ☎ *707/963–3216 or 800/541–3284* 🖷 *707/963–8838* ⊕ *www.elbonita.com* 🛏 *37 rooms, 4 suites* ⚭ *Kitchenettes, microwaves, refrigerators, cable TV, in-room data ports, pool, hot tub, sauna, Internet room, business services, some pets allowed (fee); no smoking* ⊟ *AE, D, DC, MC, V* ⧫⊙⧫ *CP.*

Shopping

The **Spice Island Marketplace** (⊠ Culinary Institute of America, 2555 Main St. ☎ 888/424–2433) is the place to shop for all things related to preparing and cooking food, from cookbooks to copper bowls. **Dean & Deluca** (⊠ 607 St. Helena Hwy. S/Rte. 29 ☎ 707/967–9980), a branch of the famous Manhattan store, is crammed with everything you need in the kitchen—including terrific produce and deli items—as well as a huge wine selection. Many of the cheeses sold here are produced locally. The airy **I. Wolk Gallery** (⊠ 1354 Main St. ☎ 707/963–8800) has works by established and emerging American artists—everything from ab-stract and contemporary realist paintings to high-quality works on paper and sculpture. Chocolates handmade on the premises are displayed like miniature works of art at **Woodhouse Chocolate** (⊠ 1367 Main St. ☎ 707/963–8413). **On the Vine** (⊠ 1234 Main St. ☎ 707/963–2209) sells wearable art and unique jewelry such as whimsical purses that could easily be mistaken for a bouquet of flowers. Many pieces have a food or wine theme. Italian ceramics, tableware, cutlery, and other high-quality home accessories fill **Vanderbilt & Company** (⊠ 1429 Main St. ☎ 707/963–1010). Bargain hunters delight in designer labels such as Escada and Coach at the **St. Helena Premier Outlets** (⊠ 3111 St. Helena Hwy. N/Rte. 29 ☎ 707/963–7282) complex, across the street from Freemark Abbey Winery.

Calistoga

3 mi northwest of St. Helena on Rte. 29.

In addition to its wineries, Calistoga is noted for its mineral water, hot mineral springs, mud baths, steam baths, and massages. The Calistoga Hot Springs Resort was founded in 1859 by maverick entrepreneur Sam Brannan, whose ambition was to found "the Saratoga of California." He reputedly tripped up the pronunciation of the phrase at a formal banquet—it came out "Calistoga"—and the name stuck.

30 **Schramsberg,** perched on a wooded knoll on the southeast side of Route 29, is one of Napa's oldest wineries, with caves that were dug by Chinese laborers in 1880. Eight distinct sparkling wines come in several price ranges. If you want to taste, you must tour first. ✉ *1400 Schramsberg Rd.* ☎ *707/942–4558* ⊕ *www.schramsberg.com* 🖃 *Tastings and tour $20* ⊙ *Daily 10–4; tastings and tours by appointment.*

31 It's worth taking a slight detour off the main artery to find the family-owned and -operated **Dutch Henry Winery,** where wines are available only on-site or through mail order (they produce only about 5,000 cases annually). Tastings are held in a working winery, where winemakers explain the process. This is a good place to try cabernet sauvignon and merlot. ✉ *4300 Silverado Trail* ☎ *707/942–5771* ⊕ *www.dutchhenry. com* 🖃 *Tastings $5* ⊙ *Daily 10–4:30; tastings by appointment.*

32 Of the wines produced by **Cuvaison,** 65% are chardonnays, with pinot noir, cabernet sauvignon, and merlot rounding out the choices. Picnic grounds with a view of the valley are shaded by 350-year-old oak trees. ✉ *4550 Silverado Trail* ☎ *707/942–6266* ⊕ *www.cuvaison.com* 🖃 *Tastings $8–$10, tour $15* ⊙ *Apr.–Nov., daily 10–5; Dec.–Mar., Sun.–Thurs. 11–4, Fri. and Sat. 10–5; tours by appointment.*

33 **Sterling Vineyards** sits on a hilltop 1 mi south of Calistoga, its pristine white Mediterranean-style buildings reached by an aerial tramway from the valley floor. The view from the tasting room is superb, and the gift shop is one of the best in the valley. ✉ *1111 Dunaweal La., east off Rte. 29* ☎ *707/942–3300* ⊕ *www.sterlingvineyards.com* 🖃 *$15, including tramway, self-guided tour, and tastings* ⊙ *Daily 10:30–4:30.*

34 Designed by postmodern architect Michael Graves, the **Clos Pegase** winery is a one-of-a-kind "temple to wine and art" packed with unusual art objects from the collection of owner and publishing entrepreneur Jan Shrem, from sculptures made of Italian glass, to huge contemporary canvases, to a 19th-century courtyard fountain of Bacchus. Cheese and other foods are for sale in the visitor center, ready to take to the shady picnic area. ✉ *1060 Dunaweal La., east off Rte. 29* ☎ *707/ 942–4981* ⊕ *www.clospegase.com* 🖃 *Tastings $5–10* ⊙ *Daily 10:30–5; tours daily at 11 and 2.*

Fodor'sChoice
★

35 The **Sharpsteen Museum,** in the center of town, has a magnificent diorama of the Calistoga Hot Springs Resort in its heyday. Other permanent and rotating exhibits are dedicated to the region's past, from its prehistory to World War II, and might document the history of the Wappo, the original inhabitants of the area, or typical family life in the 19th century. ☒ *1311 Washington St.* ☎ *707/942–5911* ⊕ *www.sharpsteen-museum.org* ☒ *$3 donation* ⊙ *Daily 11–4.*

Indian Springs, an old-time spa, has welcomed clients to mud baths, mineral pools, and steam rooms, all supplied with mineral water from its three geysers, since 1871. Today it continues to offer a wide variety of spa treatments and volcanic-ash mud baths, and has an Olympic-size mineral-water pool, kept at 90°F to 102°F, depending on the season. The spa rents 16 bungalows ($$$–$$$$) ranging from a studio duplex to a three-bedroom house. Reservations are recommended for spa treatments. ☒ *1712 Lincoln Ave./Rte. 29* ☎ *707/942–4913* ⊕ *www.indianspringscalistoga.com* ⊙ *Daily 9–8.*

☾ ➌➏ Many families bring children to Calistoga to see **Old Faithful Geyser of California** blast its 60- to 100-foot tower of steam and vapor about every 45 minutes. One of just three regularly erupting geysers in the world, it's fed by an underground river that's heated by molten magma deep beneath the earth's surface. Picnic facilities are available, and a small exhibit hall explains geothermal processes. ☒ *1299 Tubbs La., 1 mi north of Calistoga* ☎ *707/942–6463* ⊕ *www.oldfaithfulgeyser.com* ☒ *$8* ⊙ *Apr.–Sept., daily 9–6; Oct.–Mar., daily 9–5.*

➌➐ **Château Montelena** is a vine-covered stone French château constructed circa 1882 and set amid Chinese-inspired gardens, complete with a man-made lake with gliding swans and islands crowned by Chinese pavilions. Its wines include chardonnays, cabernet sauvignons, and a limited-production Riesling. ☒ *1429 Tubbs La.* ☎ *707/942–5105* ⊕ *www.montelena.com* ☒ *Tastings $10–$25, tour $25* ⊙ *Daily 9:30–4; Mar.–Oct., tours at 9:30, 1:30, and by appointment; Nov.–Feb., tours at 2 by appointment.*

☾ ➌➑ **Robert Louis Stevenson State Park** encompasses the summit of **Mount St. Helena.** It was here, in the summer of 1880, in an abandoned bunkhouse of the Silverado Mine, that Stevenson and his bride, Fanny Osbourne, spent their honeymoon. The stay inspired Stevenson's "The Silverado Squatters," and Spyglass Hill in *Treasure Island* is thought to be a portrait of Mount St. Helena. The park's approximately 3,600 acres are mostly undeveloped except for a fire trail leading to the site of the bunkhouse—which is marked with a marble tablet—and to the summit beyond. ☒ *Rte. 29, 7 mi north of Calistoga* ☎ *707/942–4575* ⊕ *www.parks.ca.gov* ☒ *Free* ⊙ *Daily sunrise–sunset.*

☾ ➌➒ The **Petrified Forest** contains the remains of the volcanic eruptions of Mount St. Helena 3.4 million years ago. The force of the explosion uprooted the gigantic redwoods, covered them with volcanic ash, and infiltrated the trees with silica and minerals, causing petrifaction. Explore the museum, and then picnic on the grounds. ☒ *4100 Petrified Forest Rd., 5 mi west of Calistoga* ☎ *707/942–6667* ⊕ *www.petrifiedforest.org* ☒ *$6* ⊙ *Mid-Apr.–mid-Sept., daily 9–6; mid-Sept.–mid-Apr., daily 9–5.*

Where to Stay & Eat

$$–$$$$ ✕ **Brannan's.** Arts and Crafts–style lamps cast a warm glow over the booths and tables at Calistoga's popular spot for hearty dishes. Look for beef tenderloin, served with garlic mashed potatoes, or roast chicken, served with butternut squash risotto. An attractive, well-stocked bar provides a congenial setting for cocktails or for desserts such as chèvre cheesecake with pears and pecans. ✉ *1374 Lincoln Ave.* ☎ *707/942–2233* ▭ *AE, D, MC, V.*

$$–$$$ ✕ **All Seasons Café.** Bistro cuisine takes a California spin in this sun-filled space, where tables topped with flowers sit upon a black-and-white checkerboard floor. The seasonal menu, which includes homemade breads and dessert, might include organic greens, hand-rolled tagliatelle, pan-seared salmon, or braised lamb shank. Attentive service contributes to the welcoming atmosphere. ✉ *1400 Lincoln Ave.* ☎ *707/942–9111* ▭ *D, MC, V* ☉ *Closed Mon. No lunch most Mon.–Wed.; call for additional lunch dates in summer and fall.*

$$–$$$ ✕ **Calistoga Inn Restaurant and Brewery.** A tree-shaded patio on the banks of the Napa River draws diners to a lovely setting where meals are prepared with flair. Lunches are light, focusing on soups, salads, and sandwiches, and hearty main courses at dinner include grilled skirt steak with blue-cheese butter and braised lamb shank with tapenade. ✉ *1250 Lincoln Ave.* ☎ *707/942–4101* ▭ *AE, MC, V.*

★ ¢–$$ ✕ **Pacifico Restaurante Mexicano.** At first glance it looks like a Mexican chain restaurant, but be assured that the quality and ingenuity of the food exceed that of the standard franchises. Many choices showcase the regional cuisines of Mexico, such as the sweet and spicy fare of Oaxaca. The chiles rellenos *pacificos* (grilled, cheese-drizzled poblano chilies filled with onions, mushrooms, spinach, and peanuts) make a delicious, inventive dish. Hefty margaritas come in several varieties. ✉ *1237 Lincoln Ave.* ☎ *707/942–4400* ▭ *MC, V.*

¢–$$ ✕ **Wappo Bar Bistro.** This colorful restaurant is an adventure in international dining. The menu covers the world, with dishes ranging from tandoori chicken and Thai coconut curry with prawns and vegetables to chiles rellenos and Turkish meze. ✉ *1226 S. Washington St.* ☎ *707/942–4712* ▭ *AE, MC, V* ⌕ *Reservations not accepted* ☉ *Closed Tues.*

★ $$$$ ▤ **Calistoga Ranch.** The outdoors comes indoors at this posh resort that opened in the hills just south of Calistoga in 2004. Freestanding cedar-shingle cabins throughout the sprawling wooded property have outdoor living areas, and even the restaurant, spa, and reception area have outdoor seating areas and fireplaces. Though the service is friendly and cabins are luxurious, with soaking tubs and both indoor and outdoor showers in every room, the overall result still has a casual ranchlike feel rather than the refined sheen of some similarly priced places. ✉ *580 Lommel Rd., 94515* ☎ *707/254–2820 or 800/942–4220* 🖷 *707/254–2888* ⊕ *www.calistogaranch.com* ➘ *47 rooms* ♿ *2 restaurants, room service, minibars, refrigerators, cable TV, in-room VCRs, pool, gym, hot tub, sauna, spa, steam room, boccie, hiking, bar, shop, concierge; no smoking* ▭ *AE, D, MC, V.*

★ $$$–$$$$ ▤ **Cottage Grove Inn.** Elm trees shade 16 contemporary, individually decorated cottages. Cozy, skylit rooms come with plush furnishings, as well as wood-burning fireplaces, CD players, extra-deep two-person whirlpool tubs, and porches with wicker rocking chairs. Spas and restaurants are

2

within walking distance. Rates include afternoon wine and cheese. ⊠ *1711 Lincoln Ave., 94515* ☎ *707/942–8400 or 800/799–2284* 🖷 *707/942–2653* ⊕ *www.cottagegrove.com* 🛏 *16 rooms* ⚘ *In-room safes, minibars, refrigerators, cable TV, in-room VCRs, in-room data ports; no smoking* ☰ *AE, D, DC, MC, V* ❙❙❙ *CP.*

$$–$$$$
FodorsChoice
★

🏠 **Meadowlark Inn and Meadow Guest House.** Twenty hillside acres just north of downtown Calistoga surround this decidedly laid-back and sophisticated inn, where innkeepers Kurt and Richard train horses on the property when they're not attending to their guests. Rooms in the main house and guest wing each have their own charms: one has a four-poster bed and opens onto a private garden, and others have a deck with a view of the mountains. Many rooms have fireplaces, and most have whirlpool tubs large enough for two. A spacious two-story guesthouse opens directly onto the clothing-optional pool and sauna area (open to all guests). ⊠ *601 Petrified Forest Rd., 94515* ☎ *707/942–5651 or 800/ 942–5651* 🖷 *707/942–5023* ⊕ *www.meadowlarkinn.com* 🛏 *5 rooms, 5 suites* ⚘ *Some kitchens, some refrigerators, cable TV, in-room VCRs, pool, hot tub, sauna, Internet room, some pets allowed; no smoking* ☰ *AE, MC, V* ❙❙❙ *BP.*

$$–$$$
🏠 **Mount View Hotel & Spa.** A National Historic Landmark, the Mount View conjures up Calistoga's 19th-century heyday with its late-Victorian decor. A full-service European spa provides state-of-the-art pampering, and three cottages are each equipped with a private redwood deck, whirlpool tub, and wet bar. The hotel's location on Calistoga's main drag, plus the excellent restaurant and the bar in the same building, mean you won't need to go far if your spa treatment has left you too indolent to drive. ⊠ *1457 Lincoln Ave., 94515* ☎ *707/942–6877 or 800/816–6877* 🖷 *707/942–6904* ⊕ *www.mountviewhotel.com* 🛏 *20 rooms, 12 suites* ⚘ *Restaurant, some refrigerators, cable TV, pool, hot tub, spa, bar, concierge, Internet room; no smoking* ☰ *AE, D, MC, V* ❙❙❙ *CP.*

$–$$
🏠 **Brannan Cottage Inn.** The pristine Victorian cottage with lacy white fretwork, large windows, and a shady porch is the only one of Sam Brannan's 1860 resort cottages still standing on its original site. Each room has individual touches such as a four-poster bed, a claw-foot tub, or a velvet settee, in keeping with the inn's Greek-revival Victorian style. ⊠ *109 Wapoo Ave., 94515* ☎ *707/942–4200* ⊕ *www.brannancottageinn.com* 🛏 *6 rooms* ⚘ *Refrigerators; no TV in some rooms, no smoking* ☰ *AE, MC, V* ❙❙❙ *BP.*

$–$$
🏠 **Calistoga Spa Hot Springs.** Though the rooms are standard motel issue, their well-equipped kitchenettes and the property's four outdoor heated mineral pools make this a popular spot for those who want to enjoy Calistoga's famed waters on a budget. An on-site spa offers mud baths, massage, and other services at reasonable rates, and its location on a quiet side street one block from Calistoga's main drag is another plus. ⊠ *1006 Washington St., 94515* ☎ *707/942–6269* 🖷 *707/942– 4214* ⊕ *www.calistogaspa.com* 🛏 *51 rooms, 1 suite* ⚘ *Snack bar, kitchenettes, cable TV, 2 pools, wading pool, fitness classes, gym, outdoor hot tub, massage, spa, laundry facilities, meeting room; no smoking* ☰ *MC, V.*

Sports & the Outdoors

Calistoga Bikeshop (✉ 1318 Lincoln Ave. ☎ 866/942–2453) rents bicycles, including tandem bikes.

Shopping

For connoisseurs seeking hard-to-find wines, the **All Seasons Wine Shop** (✉ 1400 Lincoln Ave. ☎ 707/942–6828), open when the All Seasons Café is open, is the place to visit. The **Calistoga Wine Stop** (✉ 1458 Lincoln Ave., No. 2 ☎ 707/942–5556), inside California's second-oldest existing train depot, carries more than 1,000 wines. Handcrafted beeswax candles are for sale at **Hurd Beeswax Candles** (✉ 1255 Lincoln Ave. ☎ 707/963–7211). Unusual tapers twisted into spiral shapes are a specialty.

THE SONOMA VALLEY

Although the Sonoma Valley may not have quite the cachet of the neighboring Napa Valley, wineries here entice with their unpretentious attitude and smaller crowds. Sonoma's landscape seduces, too, its roads gently climbing and descending on their way to wineries hidden from the road by trees. Its name is Miwok for "many moons," but writer Jack London's nickname for the region—Valley of the Moon—is more fitting. The scenic valley, bounded by the Mayacamas Mountains on the east and Sonoma Mountain on the west, extends north from San Pablo Bay nearly 20 mi to the eastern outskirts of Santa Rosa. The varied terrain, soils, and climate (cooler in the south because of the bay influence and hotter toward the north) allow grape growers to raise cool-weather varietals such as chardonnay and pinot noir as well as merlot, cabernet sauvignon, and other heat-seeking vines. The valley is home to dozens of wineries, many of them on or near Route 12, a California Scenic Highway that runs the length of the valley, which is near the Sonoma-Napa county border.

Sonoma

14 mi west of Napa on Rte. 12; 45 mi from San Francisco, north on U.S. 101, east on Rte. 37, and north on Rte. 121/12.

Sonoma is the oldest town in the Wine Country. Its town plaza is the site of the last and the northernmost of the 21 missions established by the Franciscan order of Father Junípero Serra. It also includes the largest group of old adobes north of Monterey.

On your way into town from the south, you pass through the Carneros wine district, which straddles the southern sections of Sonoma and Napa counties. Sam Sebastiani, of the famous Sebastiani family, and his 40 wife, Vicki, have established their own hilltop winery, **Viansa**, in the Carneros district. Reminiscent of a Tuscan villa, the winery's ocher-color building is surrounded by olive trees and overlooks the valley. The grapes grown here depart from the traditionally Californian and include Sangiovese, Dolcetto, and Tocai Friulano. The Italian Marketplace on the premises sells delicious specialty sandwiches and salads to complement Viansa's Italian-style wines. The adjacent Wine Country Visitor

Center has brochures and information. ✉ *25200 Arnold Dr.* ☎ *707/935–4700* ⊕ *www.viansa.com* 🖃 *Tour free* ☉ *Daily 10–5; tours daily at 11 and 2.*

④ The sparkling and still wines at **Gloria Ferrer Champagne Caves** originated with a 700-year-old stock of Ferrer grapes. The method here is to age the wines in a *cava,* or cellar, where several feet of earth maintain a constant temperature—an increasingly popular alternative to temperature-controlled warehouses. Call the day of your visit to confirm that tours will be conducted as scheduled. ✉ *23555 Carneros Hwy./Rte. 121* ☎ *707/996–7256* ⊕ *www.gloriaferrer.com* 🖃 *Tastings $2–$3, tour free* ☉ *Daily 10:30–5:30; tours daily at noon, 2, and 4.*

④ In town, the **Mission San Francisco Solano,** whose chapel and school were used to bring Christianity to the Native Americans, is now a museum with a fine collection of 19th-century watercolors. ✉ *114 Spain St. E* ☎ *707/938–9560* 🖃 *$2, including Sonoma Barracks on the central plaza and Lachryma Montis* ☉ *Daily 10–5.*

④ A tree-lined driveway leads to **Lachryma Montis,** which General Mariano G. Vallejo, the last Mexican governor of California, built for his large family in 1852; the state purchased the home in 1933. The Victorian Gothic house, insulated with adobe, represents a blend of Mexican and American cultures. Opulent furnishings, including white-marble fireplaces and a French rosewood piano, are particularly noteworthy. Free tours are occasionally conducted by docents on the weekend; call ahead for a schedule. ✉ *W. Spain St., near 3rd St. E* ☎ *707/938–9559* 🖃 *$2, tour free* ☉ *Daily 10–5.*

④ Originally planted by Franciscans of the Sonoma Mission in 1825, the **Sebastiani Vineyards** were bought by Samuele Sebastiani in 1904. In addition to the regularly scheduled historical tours of the winery, a trolley tour provides an informative glimpse of the vineyards Friday and Saturday at 2. Red wine is king here. ✉ *389 4th St. E* ☎ *707/938–5532* ⊕ *www.sebastiani.com* 🖃 *Tour $5* ☉ *Daily 10–5; tours daily at 11 and 3.*

④ **Buena Vista Winery** is the oldest continuously operating winery in California. It was here, in 1857, that Count Agoston Haraszthy de Mokcsa laid the basis for modern California wine making, bucking the conventional wisdom that vines should be planted on well-watered ground by instead planting on well-drained hillsides. Chinese laborers dug tunnels 100 feet into the hillside, and the limestone they extracted was used to build the main house. The winery, which is surrounded by redwood and eucalyptus trees, has a specialty-foods shop, an art gallery, and picnic areas. The guided tour, which includes a tasting of premium wines, is $15, but the self-guided tour is free. ✉ *18000 Old Winery Rd., off Napa Rd., follow signs from plaza* ☎ *707/938–1266 or 800/678–8504* ⊕ *www.buenavistawinery.com* 🖃 *Tastings $5–$10, tour $15* ☉ *Daily 10–5; tours weekdays at 2, weekends at 11 and 2.*

④ **Ravenswood,** dug into the mountains like a bunker, is famous for its zinfandel. The merlot should be tasted as well. Tours include barrel tastings of wines in progress in the cellar. ✉ *18701 Gehricke Rd., off E.*

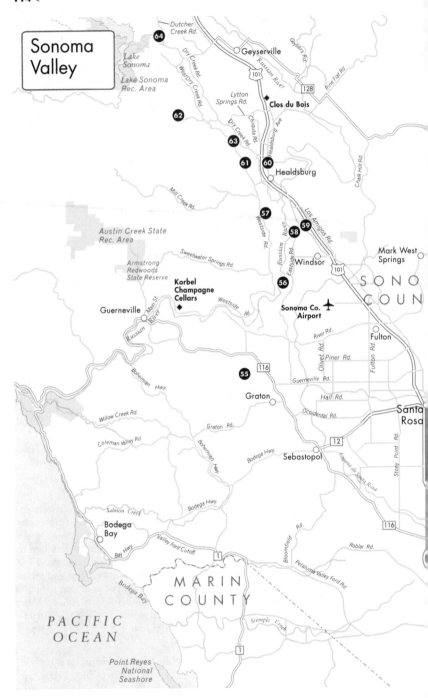

Sonoma
Valley

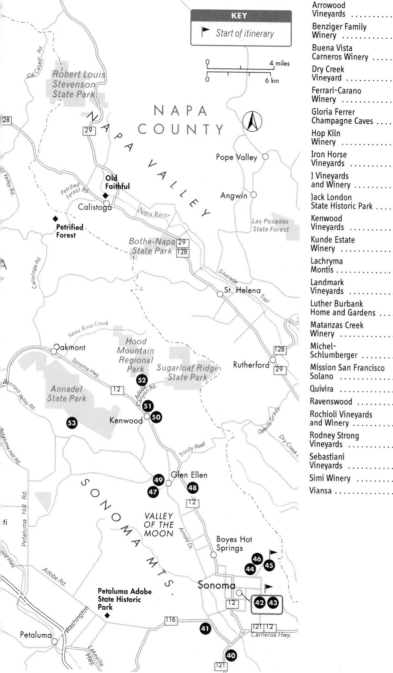

Spain St. ☎ *707/938–1960* ⊕ *www.ravenswood-wine.com* ✉ *Tastings $5, tour $10* ☙ *Daily 10–5; tours at 10:30 by appointment.*

Where to Stay & Eat

$$–$$$$ ✕ **Santé.** In the Fairmont Sonoma Mission Inn's formal restaurant, creative fare is served in a dining room that's both rustic (wrought-iron chandeliers) and elegant (Frette table linens). Chef Bruno Tison takes local seasonal ingredients and gives them a twist. Foie gras, for instance, might be coupled with a savory flan. Main courses could include thick lamb chops, Muscovy duck breast, or even ostrich. ⊠ *Fairmont Sonoma Mission Inn & Spa, 100 Boyes Blvd./Rte. 12 at Boyes Blvd., 2 mi north of Sonoma, Boyes Hot Springs* ☎ *707/939–2415* ▭ *AE, DC, MC, V* ☙ *No lunch.*

$$–$$$ ✕ **Cafe La Haye.** In a postage-stamp-size kitchen, skillful chefs turn out half a dozen main courses that star on a small but worthwhile menu emphasizing local ingredients. Chicken, beef, pasta, fish, and risotto get deluxe treatment without fuss or fanfare. The offbeat dining room, hung with large, abstract paintings, turns out some of the best food for the price in the Wine Country. ⊠ *140 E. Napa St.* ☎ *707/935–5994* ▭ *AE, MC, V* ☙ *Closed Sun. and Mon. No lunch.*

$$–$$$ ✕ **Harmony Club.** This stylish, urbane spot has French doors thrown open to Sonoma's main plaza in fair weather and a large fireplace aglow in the evening. Dishes are unusual twists on California cuisine: Brie fondue, duck confit with creamy lentils, or pan-roasted quail with grilled tomato polenta, pine nuts, and currants. The extensive wine list includes many choices from the Ledson Winery. Listen to nightly jazz and blues music played on the grand piano. ⊠ *480 1st St. E* ☎ *707/996–9779* ▭ *AE, D, MC, V* ☙ *Closed Tues.*

$$–$$$ ✕ **LaSalette.** Chef-owner Manny Azevedo, born in the Azores and raised in Sonoma, found culinary inspiration in his travels. The flavors of his dishes, such as prawns with tomato-peanut sauce and coconut rice or salt cod baked with white onions, stand strong while complementing each other. The variety of ports on the wine list emphasizes Azevedo's Portuguese heritage. ⊠ *452 E. 1st St.* ☎ *707/938–1927* ▭ *AE, MC, V* ☙ *Closed Mon.*

$–$$$ ✕ **The Girl & the Fig.** The popular restaurant was in Glen Ellen before migrating to the Sonoma Hotel, where it has revitalized the barroom with cozy banquettes and inventive French country cuisine. A seasonally changing menu may include something with figs, duck confit with green lentils, steak frites, or Provençale shellfish stew. The wine list is notable for its inclusion of Rhône and other less-common varietals. ⊠ *Sonoma Hotel, Sonoma Plaza, 110 W. Spain St.* ☎ *707/938–3634* ▭ *AE, D, DC, MC, V.*

$$ ✕ **Meritage.** A fortuitous blend of southern French and northern Italian cuisine is the backbone of this restaurant, where chef Carlo Cavallo works wonders with house-made pastas. The warmly lighted dining room, with its sea of unusual sculpted glass light fixtures, is more romantic than the lively bar area, where an oyster bar augments the menu's extensive seafood choices. Vegetarians can enjoy a special tasting menu, which can be adapted for vegans. ⊠ *165 Napa St. W* ☎ *707/938–9430* ▭ *AE, MC, V* ☙ *Closed Tues.*

Spas of Every Stripe

THE WINE COUNTRY WAS in the forefront of America's love affair with hot springs, mud baths, and spa treatments. Blessed with natural mineral ash from nearby volcanoes and mineral springs, areas around Calistoga and Sonoma were popular with Native Americans long before the stressed-out white man arrived. Today you can find spas of every stripe throughout the area.

Though its surroundings are less luxurious than some, **Calistoga Spa Hot Springs** is the best choice if you have several hours to lounge around. A house special is "The Works" ($120), a two-hour marathon of mud bath, mineral whirlpool, steam bath, blanket wrap, and massage. If you're booking any treatment, you can pay $5 and get all-day pool access as well. You can try relaxing in four pools of varying size and temperature until you decide on a favorite. ✉ *1006 Washington St., Calistoga* ☏ *707/942-6269* ⊕ *www.calistogaspa.com.*

Dr. Wilkinson's is the oldest spa in Calistoga. Best known for its mud baths, it is perhaps the least chic of the bunch. ✉ *1507 Lincoln Ave., Calistoga* ☏ *707/942-4102* ⊕ *www.drwilkinson.com.*

The **Fairmont Sonoma Mission Inn & Spa** is the best-known sybaritic hot spot in the Wine Country, with a vast facility sprawling over 43,000 square feet. Arrive at least 45 minutes in advance of your appointment to spend some time in the bathing ritual room. ✉ *100 Boyes Blvd./Rte. 12, Boyes Hot Springs* ☏ *707/938-9000* ⊕ *www.sonomamissioninn.com.*

Treatments at the **Garden Spa at MacArthur Place** are based on single ingredients—herbs, flowers, or minerals—rather than a blend of two or three. The two-hour "Rose Garden" treatment ($199) includes a bath in rose petals, a rose-petal body polish, and an essential oil massage. ✉ *29 E. MacArthur St., Sonoma* ☏ *707/933-3193* ⊕ *www.macarthurplace.com.*

Facilities at **Kenwood Inn & Spa** claim the prettiest spa setting in the Wine Country, thanks to the vineyards across the road and the Mediterranean style of the inn. A specialty is "vinotherapie" treatments, which incorporate the use of grape-seed and grapevine extracts. ✉ *10400 Sonoma Hwy./Rte. 12, Kenwood* ☏ *707/833-1293* ⊕ *www.kenwoodinn.com.*

Lincoln Avenue Spa occupies a 19th-century bank building, a history suggested by elegant woodwork and a tiled steam room. House specialties include a body mud and salt scrub combo ($140). ✉ *1339 Lincoln Ave., Calistoga* ☏ *707/942-5296* ⊕ *www.lincolnavenuespa.com.*

The **Mount View Spa** is the most elegant in town. This retreat at the rear of the Mount View Hotel lobby is one of the best places for facials. ✉ *1457 Lincoln Ave., Calistoga* ☏ *707/942-5789* ⊕ *www.mountviewspa.com.*

The spacious **Spa at Villagio** features the popular Napa River Stone Massage, in which warm stones are placed on your body to melt away tension. In addition to a dry sauna and a steam room, you have access to a 40-foot outdoor lap pool. ✉ *6481 Washington St., Yountville* ☏ *707/948-5050.*

$–$$ ✕ **Della Santina's.** A longtime favorite with a charming, enclosed brick patio out back serves the most authentic Italian food in town. Daily fish and veal specials provide an alternative to other classic northern Italian pastas such as linguine with pesto and lasagna Bolognese. Of special note are the roasted meat dishes and, when available, petrale sole and sand dabs. ✉ *133 E. Napa St.* ☎ *707/935–0576* ▤ *AE, D, MC, V.*

$–$$ ✕ **Piatti.** A beautiful room opens onto one of the finest patios in the valley at this restaurant, the first in a minichain of trattorias. Pizza from the wood-burning oven and northern Italian specials (spit-roasted chicken, ravioli with spinach-ricotta filling) are served on the terrace or in a rustic space with an open kitchen. ✉ *El Dorado Hotel, 405 1st St. W* ☎ *707/996–2351* ▤ *AE, MC, V.*

¢–$$ ✕ **La Casa.** Whitewashed stucco and red tiles evoke Old Mexico at this spot around the corner from Sonoma's plaza. There are bar seating, a patio, and an extensive menu of traditional Mexican food: chimichangas and snapper Veracruz (with tomatoes, peppers, onions, and olives) for entrées, sangria for drink, and flan for dessert. The food isn't really the draw here; locals love the casual atmosphere and the margaritas. ✉ *121 E. Spain St.* ☎ *707/996–3406* ▤ *AE, D, DC, MC, V.*

$$$$ ⌂ **The Fairmont Sonoma Mission Inn & Spa.** California Mission–style architecture combines with the elegance of a European luxury spa at this beautifully landscaped estate. Although not large, standard rooms are supremely comfortable. Some larger rooms have fireplaces and patios or balconies. The real draw is the 43,000-square-foot spa, where you can enjoy a vast array of treatments. Warm mineral water is pumped up from beneath the property to feed the inn's pools. ✉ *100 Boyes Blvd./Rte. 12, 2 mi north of Sonoma, Boyes Hot Springs 95476* ☎ *707/938–9000* 🖷 *707/938–4250* ⊕ *www.sonomamissioninn.com* ⇔ *168 rooms, 60 suites △ 2 restaurants, room service, in-room safes, minibars, refrigerators, cable TV, in-room data ports, 18-hole golf course, pro shop, 3 pools, fitness classes, gym, hair salon, hot tub, sauna, spa, bicycles, 2 bars, shops, babysitting, dry cleaning, laundry service, concierge, business services, meeting rooms; no smoking* ▤ *AE, DC, MC, V.*

$$$$ ⌂ **Ledson Hotel.** The hotel's brickwork and wrought-iron balconies recall an opulent 19th-century home, and its six rooms are lavish in every way. King-size beds, piled high with pillows and silk bedding, sit on beautifully inlaid wooden floors. All rooms have enormous Jacuzzi tubs and balconies; three front rooms overlook Sonoma's main plaza. ✉ *480 1st St. E, 95476* ☎ *707/996–9779* 🖷 *707/996–9776* ⊕ *www.ledsonhotel. com* ⇔ *6 rooms △ Restaurant, refrigerators, cable TV, in-room data ports, wine bar, dry cleaning, laundry service; no smoking* ▤ *AE, D, MC, V* ⦿ *BP.*

$$$$ ⌂ **MacArthur Place.** Chic country colors such as olive and lemon distinguish the accommodations at this sprawling complex. Rooms are in a renovated 19th-century mansion as well as in contemporary two-story structures tucked into the back of the property. Beyond the extensively landscaped grounds is a full-service spa, adjacent to the pool. ✉ *29 E. MacArthur St., 95476* ☎ *707/938–2929 or 800/722–1866* 🖷 *707/ 933–9833* ⊕ *www.macarthurplace.com* ⇔ *35 rooms, 29 suites △ Restau-*

CLOSE UP

Wine Tasting 101

IF ONE OF YOUR REASONS for visiting the Wine Country is to learn about wine, your best friend should be the person who is pouring in a winery tasting room. The people who do this are only too happy to share their knowledge. Though wine bars and shops abound, the best way to learn about wines is to visit the wineries themselves. True, you'll get to taste only one product line, but because most wineries make 5 or 10 or even more types, you can make a lot of headway after visiting one or two wineries.

Why do people make such a big deal about tasting wine? Because it's the only way to learn the differences among varieties of wines and styles of wine making. Contrary to the cartoon image, tasting wine is by no means an effete exercise. As long as you don't act pretentious—say, by tilting your glass with your pinkie finger in the air—you won't look silly.

So how do you go about tasting wine? You start by looking at it. Usually the pourer gives you between 1 and 1½ ounces of each wine you try. You can hold the glass by the stem or by the bowl; the former grip keeps the wine from heating up, but the latter is a good idea if the tasting room is so crowded you fear getting jostled. If you can hold the glass to the light, all the better. You're looking for clues to the grape variety as well as to the wine's age. Connecting the color with the wine grape is part of the sensory experience and is likely to help you

remember the aromas and flavors better. As for age, remember that red wines pale with time, whereas white wines get darker.

Sniff once or twice to see if you smell anything recognizable. Next, swirl the wine gently in the glass. Aerating the wine this way releases more aromas. (This step works with just about every type of wine except the sparkling kind.) Don't be afraid to stick your nose in the glass. The receptor nerve cells in your nose can detect every scent and forward them to the brain's olfactory bulb. Those cells tire quickly, however, so be sure to assess the aromas as quickly as possible.

At this point, it is time to taste. Although smell plays an enormous role in taste memory, so can "mouth-feel," or the weight of the wine on your tongue. Is it light or watery? Is it rich like milk? Mentally record these impressions, along with any other tactile sensations such as smoothness or silkiness. Hold the wine in your mouth for a few seconds to give your taste buds a chance to pick up as many flavors as possible. Wines carry an almost infinite range of flavors, from butter to olives, mint to chocolate, pineapple to vanilla, or cherry to blackberry. If you can still perceive flavor well after you've swallowed the wine, you can say it has a long finish. And you can be assured that it's a wine you will remember.

—Marty Olmstead

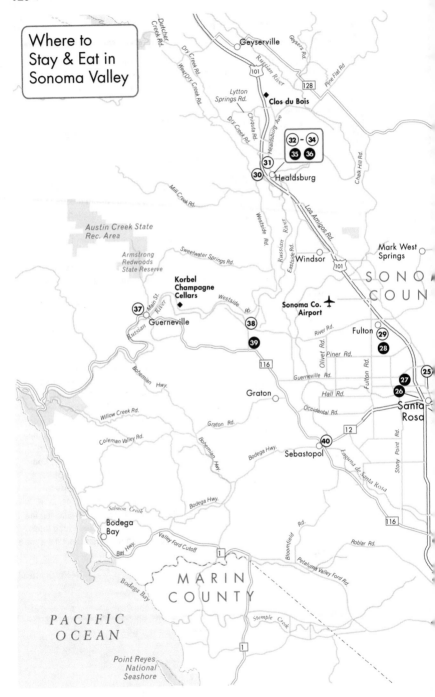

Where to
Stay & Eat in
Sonoma Valley

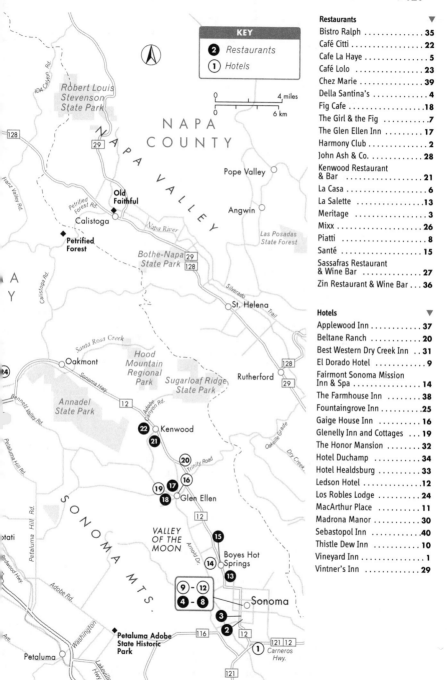

KEY

2 Restaurants
1 Hotels

0   4 miles
0   6 km

NAPA COUNTY

NAPA VALLEY

Restaurants ▼

Bistro Ralph **35**
Café Citti **22**
Cafe La Haye **5**
Café Lolo **23**
Chez Marie **39**
Della Santina's **4**
Fig Cafe **18**
The Girl & the Fig **7**
The Glen Ellen Inn **17**
Harmony Club **2**
John Ash & Co. **28**
Kenwood Restaurant
& Bar **21**
La Casa **6**
La Salette **13**
Meritage **3**
Mixx **26**
Piatti **8**
Santé **15**
Sassafras Restaurant
& Wine Bar **27**
Zin Restaurant & Wine Bar . . . **36**

Hotels ▼

Applewood Inn **37**
Beltane Ranch **20**
Best Western Dry Creek Inn . . **31**
El Dorado Hotel **9**
Fairmont Sonoma Mission
Inn & Spa **14**
The Farmhouse Inn **38**
Fountaingrove Inn **25**
Gaige House Inn **16**
Glenelly Inn and Cottages . . . **19**
The Honor Mansion **32**
Hotel Duchamp **34**
Hotel Healdsburg **33**
Ledson Hotel **12**
Los Robles Lodge **24**
MacArthur Place **11**
Madrona Manor **30**
Sebastopol Inn **40**
Thistle Dew Inn **10**
Vineyard Inn **1**
Vintner's Inn **29**

rant, room service, some refrigerators, cable TV, in-room VCRs, in-room data ports, pool, gym, hot tub, sauna, spa, croquet, bar, shop, dry cleaning, laundry service, concierge, Internet room, business services; no smoking ⊟ *AE, D, MC, V* ⑩ *CP.*

★ $$–$$$ ⊞ **Thistle Dew Inn.** The living room and dining room of this pair of turn-of-the-20th-century Victorian homes half a block from Sonoma Plaza are filled with collector-quality Arts and Crafts furnishings and photos of the innkeepers' family. Guest rooms maintain a similar style, with a quilt on every bed. Some rooms have fireplaces; some have whirlpool tubs. Most have private entrances and decks, and rooms in the rear house open onto a garden. Welcome bonuses include a hot tub in the backyard and free use of the inn's bicycles. ⊠ *171 W. Spain St., 95476* ☎ *707/938–2909, 800/382–7895 in CA* 🖷 *707/938–2129* ⊕ *www.thistledew.com* ⇥ *4 rooms, 1 suite* ⚘ *In-room data ports, hot tub, bicycles, some pets allowed (fee); no room TVs, no smoking* ⊟ *AE, D, MC, V* ⑩ *BP.*

$–$$$ ⊞ **Vineyard Inn.** Built as a roadside motor court in 1941, this inn with red-tile roofs brings a touch of Mexican village charm to an otherwise lackluster and somewhat noisy location at the junction of two main highways. It's across from two vineyards and is the closest lodging to Sears Point Raceway. Rooms have queen-size beds, and Continental breakfast is included. ⊠ *23000 Arnold Dr., at junction of Rtes. 116 and 121, 95476* ☎ *707/938–2350 or 800/359–4667* 🖷 *707/938–2353* ⊕ *www.sonomavineyardinn.com* ⇥ *19 rooms, 2 suites* ⚘ *Cable TV, in-room data ports, pool; no smoking* ⊟ *AE, MC, V* ⑩ *CP.*

$$ ⊞ **El Dorado Hotel.** A modern hotel in a remodeled 1843 building, this place has spare and simply elegant accommodations. Rooms reflect Sonoma's Mission era, with Mexican-tile floors and white walls. The best rooms are Nos. 3 and 4, which have larger balconies that overlook Sonoma Plaza. At this writing the hotel had been closed for several months for renovation but was scheduled to reopen in 2005. ⊠ *405 1st St. W, 95476* ☎ *707/996–3030 or 800/289–3031* 🖷 *707/996–3148* ⊕ *www.hoteleldorado.com* ⇥ *26 rooms* ⚘ *Restaurant, room service, refrigerators, cable TV, in-room VCRs, in-room data ports, pool, bar, shops, laundry service; no smoking* ⊟ *AE, MC, V* ⑩ *CP.*

Nightlife & the Arts

The **Sebastiani Theatre** (⊠ 476 1st St. E ☎ 707/996–2020), on Sonoma Square, schedules first-run movies.

Shopping

Half-Pint (⊠ Sonoma Plaza, 450 1st St. E ☎ 707/938–1722) carries fashionable clothing and accessories for infants and children. Several shops in the four-block **Sonoma Plaza** (⊠ Between E. Napa and E. Spain Sts. and 1st St. W and 1st St. E) attract food lovers from miles around. The **Sonoma Cheese Factory and Deli** (⊠ Sonoma Plaza, 2 Spain St. ☎ 707/996–1931), run by the same family for four generations, makes Sonoma Jack cheese and the tangy Sonoma Teleme. It has everything you could possibly need for a picnic. **Shushu Fufu** (⊠ Sonoma Plaza, 452 1st St. E ☎ 707/938–3876) is a chic clothing boutique that specializes in fashionable footwear, including fine French walking shoes.

Glen Ellen

7 mi north of Sonoma on Rte. 12.

Jack London lived in Sonoma Valley for many years. The craggy, quirky, and creek-bisected town of Glen Ellen commemorates him with place-names and nostalgic establishments. In the Jack London Village complex, the **Olive Press** (⊠ 14301 Arnold Dr. ☎ 707/939–8900) not only carries many local olive oils, serving bowls, books, and dining accessories but also presses fruit for a number of local growers, usually in the late fall. You can taste a selection of olive oils that have surprisingly different flavors. Built in 1905, the **Jack London Saloon** (⊠ 13740 Arnold Dr. ☎ 707/996–3100 ⊕ www.jacklondonlodge.com) is decorated with photos of London and other London memorabilia.

In the hills above Glen Ellen—known as the Valley of the Moon—lies
47 **Jack London State Historic Park.** The author's South Seas artifacts and other personal effects are on view at the House of Happy Walls museum. The ruins of Wolf House, which London designed and which mysteriously burned down just before he was to move in, are close to the House of Happy Walls. Also restored and open to the public are a few farm outbuildings. London is buried on the property. ⊠ *2400 London Ranch Rd.* ☎ *707/938–5216* ⊡ *Parking $6* ☽ *Park Nov.–Mar., daily 9:30–5; Apr.–Oct., daily 9:30–7. Museum daily 10–5.*

48 **Arrowood Vineyards & Winery** is neither as old nor as famous as some of its neighbors, but winemakers and critics are quite familiar with the wines produced here, especially the chardonnays, cabernet sauvignons, and syrahs. The winery's harmonious architecture overlooking the Valley of the Moon earned it an award from the Sonoma Historic Preservation League, and the wine-making equipment is state-of-the-art. A stone fireplace in the tasting room makes this an especially enticing destination in winter. The winery has been owned by Robert Mondavi since 2000, but winemaker Richard Arrowood has stayed on. ⊠ *14347 Sonoma Hwy./Rte. 12* ☎ *707/935–2600* ⊕ *www.arrowoodvineyards.com* ⊡ *Tastings $5–$10, tour $10 (includes tasting)* ☽ *Daily 10–4:30; tours by appointment.*

As you drive along Route 12, you see orchards and rows of vineyards flanked by oak-covered mountain ranges. One of the best-known local
★ **49** wineries is **Benziger Family Winery,** situated on a sprawling estate in a bowl with 360-degree sun exposure. Among the first wineries to identify certain vineyard blocks for particularly desirable flavors, Benziger is noted for its merlot, pinot blanc, chardonnay, and fumé blanc. Tram tours through the vineyards cover everything from regional microclimates and geography to a glimpse of the extensive cave system. Tours depart several times a day, weather permitting. ⊠ *1883 London Ranch Rd.* ☎ *707/935–3000* ⊕ *www.benziger.com* ⊡ *Tastings $5–$10, tour $10* ☽ *Daily 10–5.*

Where to Stay & Eat

$$–$$$ ✕ **Glen Ellen Inn Restaurant.** Recommended for romantic evenings, this restaurant adjusts its seafood and pasta offerings according to seasonal availability. Look for braised lamb shank with homemade pasta and seafood risotto. Desserts such as warm pumpkin bread pudding are large enough to share. Seats on the covered patio are more attractive than those inside. ⊠ *13670 Arnold Dr.* ☎ *707/996–6409* ▤ *AE, MC, V* ✆ *No lunch Wed. or Thurs.*

$–$$ ✕ **The Fig Cafe.** Celadon booths, yellow walls, and a sloping high ceiling make the latest in the string of Sondra Bernstein's popular Napa Valley restaurants feel summery and airy even in the middle of winter. Artisanal cheese plates and fried calamari are popular appetizers, and entrées such as braised pot roast and grilled hanger steak tend to be hearty. Don't forget to look on the chalkboard for frequently changing desserts, such as butterscotch pot de crème. The unusual no-corkage-fee policy makes it a great place to drink the wine you just discovered down the road. ⊠ *13690 Arnold Dr.* ☎ *707/938–2130* ▤ *AE, D, MC, V* ⚓ *Reservations not accepted* ✆ *Closed Tues. and Wed. No lunch.*

$$$$ 🏨 **Gaige House Inn.** The elegant comfort of a 19th-century residence is
Fodor'sChoice enhanced with contemporary, uncluttered furnishings and Asian details
★ at this country inn with gracious service. Eight cottages completed in 2005, the most lavish of the accommodations, have the most pronounced Japanese influence, with 2,500-pound granite soaking tubs overlooking small private gardens and shoji screens hiding a wet bar; four of the cottages overlook Calabasas Creek. Rooms in the main house, some with fireplaces, have their own appeal; one opens onto the pool. The manicured lawn, striped awnings, and magnolias around the pool conjure up genteel refinement in the midst of rustic Glen Ellen. ⊠ *13540 Arnold Dr., 95442* ☎ *707/935–0237 or 800/935–0237* 🖷 *707/935–6411* ⊕ *www.gaige.com* ⇌ *12 rooms, 11 suites* ⚒ *Some in-room safes, refrigerators, cable TV, in-room data ports, pool, hot tub; no smoking* ▤ *AE, D, DC, MC, V* ⦿ *BP.*

$$–$$$ 🏨 **Glenelly Inn and Cottages.** On a quiet side street a few blocks from the center of sleepy Glen Ellen, this sunny little establishment offers quiet respite from Wine Country crowds. It was built as an inn in 1916, and the rooms, each individually decorated, tend toward a simple country style. Many have four-poster beds and touches such as a wood-burning stove or antique oak dresser; some have whirlpool tubs. All have fluffy down comforters. Breakfast is served in front of the common room's cobblestone fireplace, as are cookies or other snacks in the afternoon. Innkeeper Kristi Hallamore Jeppesen has two children of her own, so this is an unusually kid-friendly inn. ⊠ *5131 Warm Springs Rd., 95442* ☎ *707/996–6720* 🖷 *707/996–5227* ⊕ *www.glenelly.com* ⇌ *10 rooms* ⚒ *Some refrigerators, some in-room VCRs, outdoor hot tub, laundry facilities; no a/c in some rooms, no phones in some rooms, no TV in some rooms, no smoking* ▤ *AE, D, MC, V* ⦿ *BP.*

$–$$ 🏨 **Beltane Ranch.** On a slope of the Mayacamas range just a few miles from Glen Ellen, this 1892 ranch house stands on 1,600 acres. All of the charmingly old-fashioned rooms, decorated with antiques and supplied with quilts, have separate entrances, and some open onto a wraparound balcony ideal for whiling away lazy afternoons. The detached cottage, once the gardener's quarters, has a small sitting room. Formerly a turkey farm, the spread is traversed by an 8-mi hiking trail that's popular with guests. ⊠ *11775 Sonoma Hwy./Rte. 12, 95442* ☎ *707/996–*

6501 ⊕ *www.beltaneranch.com* ⇆ *3 rooms, 3 suites* ⚲ *Tennis court, hiking; no a/c, no room TVs* ⊟ *No credit cards* ⦙⊙⦙ *BP.*

Kenwood

3 mi north of Glen Ellen on Rte. 12.

Kenwood has a historic train depot and several restaurants and shops that specialize in locally produced goods. Its inns, restaurants, and winding roads nestle in soothing bucolic landscapes.

⑤⓪ **Kunde Estate Winery & Vineyards** lies on 2,000 acres and is managed by the fourth generation of Kunde-family grape growers and winemakers. The standard tour of the grounds includes its extensive caves. A tasting and dining room lies 175 feet below a chardonnay vineyard. Tastings usually include viognier, chardonnay, cabernet sauvignon, and zinfandel. ✉ *10155 Sonoma Hwy./Rte. 12* ☎ *707/833–5501* ⊕ *www.kunde.com* ⌣ *Tastings $5–$10, tour free* ⊙ *Daily 10:30–4:30, tours hourly Fri.–Sun. 11–3.*

⑤① The beautifully rustic grounds at **Kenwood Vineyards** complement the tasting room and artistic bottle labels. Although Kenwood produces wine from many varietals, the winery is best known for its Jack London Vineyard reds—pinot noir, zinfandel, merlot, and a unique Artist Series cabernet. Most weekends the winery offers a free food-and-wine pairing, but there are no tours. ✉ *9592 Sonoma Hwy./Rte. 12* ☎ *707/833–5891* ⊕ *www.kenwoodvineyards.com* ⌣ *Tastings free* ⊙ *Daily 10–4:30.*

⑤② The landscaping and design of **Landmark Vineyards,** established by the heirs of John Deere, are as classical as the winery's wine-making methods. Those methods include two fermentations in French oak barrels and the use of the yeasts present in the skins of the grapes rather than the addition of manufactured yeasts to create the wine. Landmark's chardonnays have been particularly well received, as has the winery's pinot noir. ✉ *101 Adobe Canyon Rd., off Sonoma Hwy.* ☎ *707/833–1144 or 800/452–6365* ⊕ *www.landmarkwine.com* ⌣ *Tastings $5–$10, tour free* ⊙ *Daily 10–4:30; horse-drawn-wagon vineyard tours Apr.–Sept., Sat.*

Where to Eat

$–$$$ ✕ **Kenwood Restaurant & Bar.** One of the enduring favorites in an area known for fine dining, this is where Napa and Sonoma chefs eat on their nights off. You can indulge in French-inspired California cuisine in the sunny, South of France–style dining room or head through the French doors to the patio for a memorable view of the vineyards. Dishes might include crispy roast duck or beef bourguignon with mashed potatoes. ✉ *9900 Sonoma Hwy./Rte. 12* ☎ *707/833–6326* ⊟ *MC, V* ⊙ *Closed Mon. and Tues.*

★ **¢–$** ✕ **Café Citti.** Opera tunes in the background and a friendly staff (as well as a roaring fire when the weather's cold) keep this no-frills roadside café from feeling too spartan. Order dishes such as roast chicken, pasta, and slabs of tiramisu from the counter and they're delivered to your table. An ample array of prepared salads and sandwiches means they do a brisk business in takeout for picnic packers. ✉ *9049 Sonoma Hwy./Rte. 12* ☎ *707/833–2690* ⊟ *MC, V.*

ELSEWHERE IN SONOMA COUNTY

At nearly 1,598 square mi, Sonoma is far too large a county to cover in one or two days. The landmass extends from San Pablo Bay south to Mendocino County and from the Mayacamas Mountains on the Napa side west to the Pacific Ocean. Although wineries and restaurants are around almost every bend in the road near Sonoma and Glen Ellen, the western stretches of the county are populated by little more than the occasional ranch.

Within this varied terrain are hills and valleys, rivers, creeks, lakes, and tidal plains that beg to be explored. To be sure, Sonoma offers much more than wine, though the county, with 60,000 acres of vineyards, contributes to the north coast's $4 billion–a–year wine industry. And Sonoma, though less famous than Napa, in fact has more award-winning wines.

In addition to the Sonoma Valley, the major grape-growing appellations include the Alexander and Dry Creek valleys, close to Healdsburg, along with the Russian River Valley to the west of U.S. 101. The last has been gaining an international reputation for its pinot noir, which thrives in the valley climate cooled by the presence of morning and evening fog.

Guerneville, a popular summer destination for gays and lesbians, and neighboring Forestville are in the heart of the Russian River Valley. Dozens of small, winding roads and myriad wineries make this region a delight to explore, as do small towns such as Occidental.

After meandering westward for miles, the Russian River arrives at its destination at Jenner, one of several towns on Sonoma's 62 mi of coastline. A number of state beaches offer tide-pooling and fishing. Although less dramatic than the beaches on the far north coast, those along Sonoma's coast offer cooling summer winds. Rustic restaurants and hotels here are more utilitarian than the sophisticated spots so prevalent in the Sonoma and Napa valleys.

Santa Rosa

8 mi northwest of Kenwood on Rte. 12.

Santa Rosa is the Wine Country's largest city and a good bet for moderately priced hotel rooms, especially for those who have not reserved in advance.

★ ⑤ **Matanzas Creek Winery** specializes in three varietals—sauvignon blanc, merlot, and chardonnay. The visitor center is a far cry from the faux French châteaus and Tuscan villas popular elsewhere in the Wine Country, and instead has an understated Japanese aesthetic, with a tranquil fountain and koi pond. Huge windows overlook a vast field of fragrant lavender plants. After you taste the wines, ask for the self-guided garden-tour book before taking a stroll. ⊠ *6097 Bennett Valley Rd.* ☎ *707/ 528–6464 or 800/590–6464* ⊕ *www.matanzascreek.com* ✉ *Tastings $5, tour free* ☉ *Daily 10–4:30; tours weekdays at 10:30 and 2:30, weekends at 10:30, by appointment.*

54 The **Luther Burbank Home and Gardens** commemorates the great botanist who lived and worked on these grounds for 50 years, single-handedly developing the modern techniques of hybridization. Arriving as a young man from New England, he wrote: "I firmly believe . . . that this is the chosen spot of all the earth, as far as nature is concerned." The Santa Rosa plum, Shasta daisy, and lily of the Nile agapanthus are among the 800 or so plants he developed or improved. In the music room of his house, a Webster's dictionary of 1946 lies open to a page on which the verb *burbank* is defined as "to modify and improve plant life." ⊠ *Santa Rosa and Sonoma Aves.* ☎ *707/524–5445* ⊕ *www.lutherburbank.org* 🖾 *Gardens free, guided tour of house and greenhouse $4* ☉ *Gardens daily 8–dusk; tours Apr.–Oct., Tues.–Sun. 10–3:30.*

Where to Stay & Eat

$$–$$$$ ✕ **John Ash & Co.** Patio seating, views out over vineyards, and a cozy indoor fireplace make this slightly formal restaurant a draw on both summer and winter evenings. The California cuisine incorporates a bit of France, Italy, and even Asia, but the ingredients are largely local: Hog Island oysters come from Tomales Bay, and the goat cheese in the ravioli comes from Laura Chenel, local cheese maker extraordinaire. Entrées may include Dungeness crab cakes or pan-seared ahi tuna. The wine list is impressive even by Wine Country standards. A café menu offers bites between meals. ⊠*4330 Barnes Rd., River Rd. exit west from U.S. 101* ☎ *707/527–7687* ▭ *AE, D, DC, MC, V* ☉ *Closed Jan.–Mar. No lunch Mon.–Sat.*

★ $$ ✕ **Café Lolo.** This small and boisterous spot is the territory of chef and co-owner Michael Quigley, who has single-handedly made downtown Santa Rosa a culinary destination. His dishes stress fresh ingredients and an eye for presentation. Popular choices include grilled hanger steak and penne with sausage and pecorino. ⊠ *620 5th St.* ☎ *707/576–7822* ▭ *AE, MC, V* ☉ *Closed Sun. No lunch weekends.*

$$ ✕ **Sassafras Restaurant & Wine Bar.** Chef Jack Mitchell changes the modern American menu frequently to reflect what's fresh at the market. The wine list is heavy on California vintages but also includes Canadian and East Coast labels. Dishes that sound familiar get a contemporary twist: pizza is topped with spicy shrimp and cilantro pesto, and quail is served with pinto beans and mole. ⊠ *1229 N. Dutton Ave.* ☎ *707/578–7600* ▭ *AE, D, DC, MC, V* ☉ *No lunch weekends.*

$–$$ ✕ **Mixx.** Great service and an eclectic mix of dishes made with locally grown ingredients define this small restaurant with large windows, high ceilings, and a hand-carved bar made in Italy in the 19th century. House-made ravioli, grilled Cajun prawns, and short ribs with mashed potatoes are among the favorites of the many regulars, and the kids' menu makes it a favorite with families. The frequently changing wine list includes more than a dozen choices by the glass. ⊠ *135 4th St., at Davis St., behind mall on Railroad Sq.* ☎ *707/573–1344* ▭ *AE, D, MC, V* ☉ *Closed Sun.*

$$$–$$$$ 🏨 **Vintners Inn.** Set on almost 100 acres of vineyards, this French provincial inn has large rooms, all with a patio or balcony and many with wood-burning fireplaces, and a trellised sundeck. Breakfast is complimentary, and the nearby John Ash & Co. restaurant is tempting for other meals.

Discount passes to an affiliated health club are available. ⊠ *4350 Barnes Rd., River Rd. exit west from U.S. 101, 95403* ☎ *707/575–7350 or 800/421–2584* 🖷 *707/575–1426* ⊕ *www.vintnersinn.com* ↪ *38 rooms, 6 suites ⚭ Restaurant, room service, in-room safes, minibars, refrigerators, cable TV, in-room data ports, hot tub, lounge, dry cleaning, laundry service, concierge, business services, meeting room; no smoking* ▭ *AE, D, DC, MC, V* ⎟◉⎟ *BP.*

★ **$–$$** 🏨 **Fountaingrove Inn.** A redwood sculpture and a wall of cascading water distinguish the lobby at this comfortable hotel and conference center. Dark blue bedspreads and light wood furnishings give the rooms an uncluttered look, and artwork on the walls echoes the equine theme of the lobby and restaurant. A restaurant and bar has piano music and specializes in steak. Though the property is close to the highway, fences and landscaping minimize its effect. ⊠ *101 Fountaingrove Pkwy., near U.S. 101, 95403* ☎ *707/578–6101 or 800/222–6101* 🖷 *707/544–3126* ⊕ *www.fountaingroveinn.com* ↪ *88 rooms, 36 suites ⚭ Restaurant, room service, refrigerators, cable TV, in-room data ports, golf privileges, pool, hot tub, wine bar, dry cleaning, laundry service, Internet room, business services, meeting rooms, some pets allowed (fee), no-smoking rooms* ▭ *AE, D, DC, MC, V* ⎟◉⎟ *CP.*

¢–$ 🏨 **Los Robles Lodge.** Many of the rooms at this bare-bones hotel overlook a pool at the center of the complex. Though they tend to be rather dark, those that are better located catch the sun on their patios, outside sliding glass doors. Some of the rooms have whirlpool tubs, and pets are permitted in others. ⊠ *1985 Cleveland Ave., Steele La. exit west from U.S. 101, 95401* ☎ *707/545–6330 or 800/255–6330* 🖷 *707/ 575–5826* ↪ *104 rooms ⚭ Restaurant, coffee shop, in-room safes, some microwaves, refrigerators, cable TV with movies, in-room data ports, pool, wading pool, gym, hot tub, sauna, bar, laundry facilities, some pets allowed (fee), no-smoking rooms* ▭ *AE, D, DC, MC, V.*

Nightlife & the Arts

The **Luther Burbank Center for the Arts** (⊠ 50 Mark West Springs Rd. ☎ 707/546–3600) presents concerts, plays, and other performances by locally and internationally known artists. For symphony, ballet, and other live theater performances throughout the year, call the **Spreckels Performing Arts Center** (⊠ 5409 Snyder La. ☎ 707/588–3400) in Rohnert Park.

Russian River Valley

5 mi northwest of Santa Rosa.

The Russian River flows all the way from Mendocino to the Pacific Ocean, but in terms of wine making, the Russian River Valley is centered on a triangle with points at Healdsburg, Guerneville, and Sebastopol. Tall redwoods shade many of the two-lane roads that access this scenic area, where, thanks to the cooling marine influence, pinot noir and chardonnay are the king and queen of grapes. For a free map of the area, contact **Russian River Wine Road** (🖃 Box 46, Healdsburg 95448 ☎ 800/723–6336 ⊕ www.wineroad.com).

55 Tucked into Green Valley, **Iron Horse Vineyards** is as successful at making still wine as it is the sparkling type. Three hundred acres of rolling, vine-covered hills seem a world away from the much more developed Napa Valley. Tours are available by appointment on weekdays. ⊠ *9786 Ross Station Rd., near Sebastopol* ☎ *707/887–1507* ⊕ *www. ironhorsevineyards.com* 🎫 *Tour $5* ☽ *Daily 10–3:30.*

⑤⑥ Rochioli Vineyards and Winery claims one of the prettiest picnic sites in the area, with tables overlooking vineyards, which are also visible from the airy little tasting room hung with modern artwork. The winery makes one of the county's best chardonnays but is especially known for its pinot noir. ⊠ *6192 Westside Rd.* ☎ *707/433–2305* 🎫 *Tastings free* ☽ *Feb.–Oct., daily 10–5; Nov.–Jan., daily 11–4.*

★ ⑤⑦ At **Hop Kiln Winery,** you can easily spot the triple towers of the old hop kiln, built in 1905 and now a California state historical landmark. One of the friendliest wineries in the Russian River area, Hop Kiln has a rustic, barnlike tasting room steps away from a duck pond where you can picnic. This is a good place to try light wines such as A Thousand Flowers (a fruity Gewürztraminer blend), but be sure to try some of the big-bodied zinfandels and cabernets as well. ⊠ *6050 Westside Rd., Healdsburg* ☎ *707/433–6491* ⊕ *www.hopkilnwinery.com* 🎫 *Tastings free* ☽ *Daily 10–5.*

⑤⑧ Of the 225 acres of Russian River Vineyards belonging to **J Vineyards and Winery,** 150 are planted with pinot noir grapes. Since the winemakers here believe that wine should be experienced with food, your tasting fee brings you a flight of four wines, each matched with two bites of hors d'oeuvres. Dry sparkling wines are a specialty. ⊠ *11447 Old Redwood Hwy.* ☎ *707/431–3646* 🎫 *Tastings $10* ⊕ *www.jwine.com* ☽ *Daily 11–5.*

Old Vine zinfandel, along with chardonnay and pinot noir, is top of the **⑤⑨** line at **Rodney Strong Vineyards.** A walkway around the tasting room provides views of the tanks and barrels below, and placards explain the history of the winery and the art of making casks. Picnic areas overlook the vineyards. ⊠ *11455 Old Redwood Hwy.* ☎ *707/433–6511* ⊕ *www. rodneystrong.com* 🎫 *Tastings and tour free* ☽ *Daily 10–5; tours daily at 11 and 3.*

OFF THE BEATEN PATH

KORBEL CHAMPAGNE CELLARS – To be called champagne, a wine must be made in the French region of Champagne or it's just sparkling wine. But despite the objections of the French, champagne has entered the lexicon of California winemakers, and many refer to their sparkling wines as champagne. Whatever you call it, Korbel produces a tasty, reasonably priced wine as well as its own beer, which is available at a brewpub on the premises. The wine tour, one of the best in Sonoma County, clearly explains the process of making sparkling wine. The winery's 19th-century buildings and gorgeous rose gardens are a delight in their own right. Call the wine shop at 707/824-7316 for times of the garden tours, which run mid-April through mid-October. ⊠ *13250 River Rd., Guerneville* ☎ *707/824-7000* ⊕ *www.korbel.com* 🎫 *Tastings and tour free* ☽ *Oct.–Apr., daily 9-4:30; May–Sept., daily 9-5; tours Oct.–Apr., daily on the* *hr 10–3; May–Sept., weekdays every 45 min 10–3:45, weekends at 10, 11, noon, 12:45, 1:30, 2:15, 3, and 3:45.*

Where to Stay & Eat

$–$$ ✕ **Chez Marie.** Forestville is light on places to eat, so Chez Marie fills up with locals familiar with the rustic French specialties, such as cassoulet and *ris de veau* (veal sweetbreads). Desserts tend to reflect the chef's New Orleans heritage; look for pecan pie in addition to crème brûlée. ⊠ *6675 Front St., Forestville* ☎ *707/887–7503* ☉ *Closed Mon. and Tues. No lunch.*

★ **$$–$$$$** ⌂ **Applewood Inn.** On a knoll in the shelter of towering redwoods, this hybrid inn has two distinct types of accommodations. Those in the original Belden House are comfortable but modest in scale. Most of the 10 accommodations in the newer buildings are larger and airier. The buildings cluster around a Mediterranean-style courtyard complete with gurgling fountains. Cooking classes are available at an on-site cooking school, La Buona Forchetta. ⊠ *13555 Rte. 116, Guerneville 95421* ☎ *707/869–9093 or 800/555–8509* 🖷 *707/869–9170* ⊕ *www.applewoodinn.com* 🛏 *19 rooms* ⌂ *Restaurant, cable TV, in-room data ports, pool, outdoor hot tub; no a/c in some rooms, no smoking* ▭ *AE, MC, V* ⧉ *BP.*

★ **$$–$$$** ⌂ **The Farmhouse Inn.** This pale yellow 1873 farmhouse and adjacent cottages house eight individually decorated rooms with luxurious touches such as featherbeds and down comforters, whirlpool tubs, and canopy beds. Most of the rooms have wood-burning fireplaces and even their own private little sauna, which makes this place especially inviting during the rainy winter months. The restaurant ($$$), open for dinner Thursday through Sunday, is renowned for its refined take on rustic dishes, such as root vegetables accompanied by white truffles and lavender salt–encrusted rack of lamb. ⊠ *7871 River Rd., Forestville 95436* ☎ *707/887–3300 or 800/464–6642* 🖷 *707/887–3311* ⊕ *www.farmhouseinn.com* 🛏 *6 rooms, 2 suites* ⌂ *Restaurant, refrigerators, pool, sauna, spa, boccie, croquet, concierge, meeting rooms; no room TVs, no smoking* ▭ *AE, D, DC, MC, V* ⧉ *BP.*

$–$$ ⌂ **Sebastopol Inn.** Simple but stylish rooms in a California country–style are tucked behind an old train station; some have views over a wetlands preserve. The offbeat coffeehouse Coffee Catz, on the property, is convenient for light meals. ⊠ *6751 Sebastopol Ave., Sebastopol 95472* ☎ *707/829–2500* 🖷 *707/823–1535* ⊕ *www.sebastopolinn.com* 🛏 *29 rooms, 2 suites* ⌂ *Coffee shop, microwaves, refrigerators, cable TV, in-room data ports, pool, hot tub, spa, dry cleaning, laundry facilities, laundry service; no smoking* ▭ *AE, D, DC, MC, V.*

Healdsburg

17 mi north of Santa Rosa on U.S. 101.

The countryside around Dry Creek Valley and Healdsburg is a fantasy of pastoral bliss—beautifully overgrown and in constant repose. Alongside the relatively untrafficked roads, country stores offer just-plucked fruits and vine-ripened tomatoes. Wineries here are barely visible, tucked behind groves of eucalyptus or hidden high on fog-shrouded hills.

Healdsburg itself is centered on a fragrant plaza surrounded by shady trees, upscale antiques shops, spas, and restaurants. A whitewashed bandstand is the venue for free summer concerts, where the music ranges from jazz to bluegrass.

Where to Stay & Eat

$$–$$$ ✕ **Bistro Ralph.** Ralph Tingle has discovered a formula for success with his California home-style cuisine, serving a small menu that changes weekly. Typical dishes include osso buco with saffron risotto and sautéed mahimahi with hedgehog mushrooms. The stark industrial space includes a stunning, gracefully curved wine rack, concrete floors, and a painted brick wall. Take a seat at the bar and chat with the locals, who love this place just as much as out-of-towners do. ⊠ *109 Plaza St., off Healdsburg Ave.* ☎ *707/433–1380* ▤ *MC, V* ⊗ *Closed Sun.*

$$–$$$ ✕ **Zin Restaurant and Wine Bar.** Concrete walls and floors, large canvases on the walls, and servers in jeans and white shirts give the restaurant a casual, industrial, and slightly artsy feel. The American cuisine—such as smoked pork chop with homemade applesauce or the red beans and rice with andouille sausage—is hearty and highly seasoned. True to the restaurant's name, the wine list includes dozens of zinfandels, including half a dozen by the glass. ⊠ *344 Center St.* ☎ *707/473–0946* ▤ *AE, DC, MC, V* ⊗ *No lunch weekends.*

★ **$$$$** ✕🏨 **Hotel Healdsburg.** Across the street from Healdsburg's tidy town plaza is a spare and sophisticated spot that caters to style-conscious travelers. The attention to detail is striking, from the sleek, modern decor to the 6-foot-long bathtubs, the Frette bathrobes, and the wide, uncarpeted hallways. The attached restaurant, Dry Creek Kitchen, serves celebrity chef Charlie Palmer's cuisine in an elegant and subdued setting. ⊠ *25 Matheson St., 95448* ☎ *707/431–2800 or 800/889–7188* 🖷 *707/431–0414* ⊕ *www.hotelhealdsburg.com* ⇌ *45 rooms, 10 suites* △ *Restaurant, room service, refrigerators, cable TV, in-room VCRs, in-room data ports, pool, gym, hot tub, spa, bar, dry cleaning, laundry service, concierge, Internet room, business services, meeting rooms, some pets allowed (fee); no-smoking rooms* ▤ *AE, DC, MC, V* ⦿⧫ *CP.*

★ **$$$$** 🏨 **Hotel Duchamp.** Six identical, freestanding villas are archetypes of spare design, with concrete floors, white walls, and furniture composed strictly of right angles. Luxe lily-white bedding keeps the rooms from feeling spartan, as do CD players loaded with groovy global dance music. Bathrooms decked out in stainless steel and white tile have showers that could fit four and have just as many showerheads. The four cottages named after artists are larger and less minimalist, with mostly mid-century furniture and quirky, artsy touches. ⊠ *421 Foss St.* ☎ *707/431–1300 or 800/431–9341* 🖷 *707/431–1333* ⊕ *www.duchamphotel.com* ⇌ *8 rooms, 2 suites* △ *In-room safes, minibars, refrigerators, cable TV, in-room VCRs, in-room data ports, pool, hot tub, wine bar, some pets allowed (fee); no smoking* ▤ *AE, MC, V* ⦿⧫ *CP.*

$$$–$$$$ 🏨 **The Honor Mansion.** Each room is unique at this photogenic 1883 Italianate Victorian. Rooms in the main house preserve a sense of the building's Victorian heritage, whereas the larger suites out back are comparatively understated. Luxurious touches such as lovely antiques and featherbeds are found in every room, and suites have the added advantage of private outdoor hot tubs and a deck. ⊠ *14891 Grove St., 95448* ☎ *707/433–4277 or 800/554–4667* ☎ *707/431–7173* ⊕ *www. honormansion.com* ☞ *5 rooms, 9 suites* ⟡ *Refrigerators, cable TV, some in-room VCRs, in-room data ports, putting green, tennis court, pool, hot tub, basketball, boccie, shop* ⊟ *AE, MC, V* ⊙ *Closed 1 wk around Christmas* ⊚ *BP.*

$$$–$$$$ ⊡ **Madrona Manor.** The oldest continuously operating inn in the area, this 1881 Victorian mansion, surrounded by 8 acres of wooded and landscaped grounds, is straight out of a storybook. Rooms in the splendid three-story mansion, the carriage house, and the two separate cottages are elegant and ornate, with mirrors in gilt frames and paintings covering every wall. Each bed is piled high with silk- and velvet-clad pillows. Romantic candlelight dinners are served in the formal dining rooms Wednesday through Sunday, and there's jazz on the veranda on Saturday evenings from May through July, plus on Friday from August through October. ⊠ *1001 Westside Rd., central Healdsburg exit off U.S. 101 and then left on Mill St., 95448* ☎ *707/433–4231 or 800/258–4003* ☎ *707/433–0703* ⊕ *www.madronamanor.com* ☞ *17 rooms, 5 suites* ⟡ *Restaurant, in-room data ports, pool, bar, meeting rooms; no room TVs, no smoking* ⊟ *MC, V* ⊚ *BP.*

Shopping

Oakville Grocery (⊠ 124 Matheson St. ☎ 707/433–3200) has a bustling Healdsburg branch filled with wine, condiments, and deli items. A terrace with ample seating makes a good place for an impromptu picnic. For a good novel, children's literature, and books on interior design and gardening, head to **Levin & Company** (⊠ 306 Center St. ☎ 707/433–1118), which also stocks a lot of CDs and tapes and has a small art gallery upstairs.

Every Saturday morning from early May through November, Healdsburg locals gather at the open-air **Farmers' Market** (⊠ North Plaza parking lot, North and Vine Sts. ☎ 707/431–1956) to pick up supplies from local producers of vegetables, fruits, flowers, cheeses, and olive oils. An additional market takes place Tuesday 4–6:30 PM from June through October.

Dry Creek & Alexander Valleys

On the west side of U.S. 101, Dry Creek Valley remains one of the least-developed appellations in Sonoma. Zinfandel grapes flourish on the benchlands, whereas the gravelly, well-drained soil of the valley floor is better known for chardonnay and, in the north, sauvignon blanc. The wineries in this region tend to be smaller and clustered in bunches.

The Alexander Valley, which lies east of Healdsburg, has a number of family-owned wineries. Most can be found right on Highway 28, which runs through this scenic, diverse region where zinfandel and chardonnay grow particularly well.

Giuseppe and Pietro Simi, two brothers from Italy, began growing
⑥⓪ grapes in Sonoma in 1876. Though the operations at **Simi Winery,** in the Alexander Valley, are strictly high-tech these days, the winery's tree-stud-

ded entrance area and stone buildings recall a more genteel era. The tour highlights the winery's rich history. ⊠ *16275 Healdsburg Ave., Dry Creek Rd. exit off U.S. 101* ☎ *707/433–6981* ⊕ *www.simiwinery.com* ⌂ *Tastings $5–$10, tour $3* ☉ *Daily 10–5. Tours Feb.–Nov., daily at 11, 1, and 3; Dec. and Jan., daily at 11 and 2.*

❻❶ Dry Creek Vineyard, whose fumé blanc is an industry benchmark, is also earning notice for its reds, especially zinfandels. Picnic beneath the flowering magnolias and soaring redwoods. ⊠ *3770 Lambert Bridge Rd.* ☎ *707/433–1000* ⊕ *www.drycreekvineyard.com* ⌂ *Tastings free–$5* ☉ *Daily 10:30–4:30; tours by appointment.*

Housed in a California Mission–style complex in Wine Creek Canyon, **❻❷ Michel-Schlumberger** produces ultrapremium wines including chardonnay, merlot, and pinot blanc, but its reputation is based on the exquisite cabernet sauvignon. The family of owner Jacques Schlumberger has been making wine in Alsace, France, for more than 400 years. ⊠ *4155 Wine Creek Rd.* ☎ *707/433–7427 or 800/447–3060* ⊕ *www. michelschlumberger.com* ⌂ *Tastings and tours free* ☉ *Tastings and tours at 11 and 2, by appointment.*

❻❸ An unassuming winery in a wood–and–cinder block barn, **Quivira** produces some of the most interesting wines in Dry Creek Valley. Though it is known for its exquisitely balanced and fruity zinfandel, the spicy syrahs and dry mourvèdre rosé are also worth checking out. Redwood and olive trees shade the picnic area. ⊠ *4900 W. Dry Creek Rd.* ☎ *707/431–8333* ⊕ *www.quivirawine.com* ⌂ *Tastings free; tour $1* ☉ *Daily 11–5; tours by appointment.*

❻❹ Noted for its beautiful Italian villa–style winery and visitor center, **Ferrari-Carano Winery** produces mostly zinfandels, chardonnays, fumé blancs, and merlots. Tours cover not only the wine-making facilities and underground cellar, but also the lush gardens. ⊠ *8761 Dry Creek Rd., Dry Creek Valley* ☎ *707/433–6700* ⊕ *www.ferrari-carano.com* ⌂ *Tastings $3, tour free* ☉ *Daily 10–5; tours Mon.–Sat. at 10 AM, by appointment.*

OFF THE BEATEN PATH

CLOS DU BOIS – Some of the best wines from Clos du Bois, 5 mi north of Healdsburg on Route 116, are somewhat unusual because they are made from 100% cabernet sauvignon grapes (which are more often blended with other types of grapes). Their tempranillo is also atypical for the region (it's more common in Spain). Chardonnay, pinot noir, and merlot are other specialties. ⊠ *19410 Geyserville Ave., Geyserville* ☎ *707/857–3100 or 800/222–3189* ⊕ *www. closdubois.com* ⌂ *Tastings free–$5, tour $10* ☉ *Daily 10–4:30; tours daily at 11 and 2, by appointment.*

Where to Stay

$–$$ 🏨 **Best Western Dry Creek Inn.** Continental breakfast and a bottle of wine are complimentary at this three-story Spanish Mission–style motel. Midweek discounts are available. A casual family restaurant is next door. Deluxe rooms are slightly more spacious and muted in color than the standard rooms. ⊠ *198 Dry Creek Rd., Healdsburg 95448* ☎ *707/433–*

0300 *or* 800/222–5784 🖶 707/433–1129 ⊕ *www.drycreekinn.com*
↪ *103 rooms* 🍽 *Restaurant, refrigerators, cable TV, in-room data
ports, pool, hot tub, gym, laundry facilities, some pets allowed (fee), no-
smoking rooms* □ *AE, D, DC, MC, V* 🍽 *CP.*

WINE COUNTRY A TO Z

*To research prices, get advice from other travelers, and book travel arrange-
ments, visit www.fodors.com.*

BUS TRAVEL

Greyhound runs buses from the Transbay Terminal at 1st and Mission
streets in San Francisco to Sonoma, Napa, Santa Rosa, and Healdsburg.
Sonoma County Transit offers daily bus service to points all over the
county. VINE (Valley Intracity Neighborhood Express) provides bus service within the city of Napa and between other Napa Valley towns.

📌 Bus Lines **Greyhound** ☎ 800/231-2222. **Sonoma County Transit** ☎ 707/576-7433
or 800/345-7433. **VINE** (Valley Intracity Neighborhood Express) ☎ 707/255-7631.

CAR TRAVEL

Although traffic on the two-lane country roads can be heavy during summer and early fall, the best way to get around the sprawling Wine
Country is by car.

From San Francisco, cross the Golden Gate Bridge, and then go north
on U.S. 101, east on Route 37, and north and east on Route 121. For
Sonoma wineries, head north at Route 12; for Napa, turn left (to the
northwest) when Route 121 runs into Route 29.

From Berkeley and other East Bay towns, take Interstate 80 north to
Route 37 west to Route 29 north, which will take you directly up the
middle of the Napa Valley. To reach Sonoma County, take Route 121
west off Route 29 south of Napa (the city). From points north of the
Wine Country, take U.S. 101 south to Geyserville and take Route 128
southeast to Calistoga and Route 29. Most Sonoma County wine regions are clearly marked and accessible off U.S. 101; to reach the
Sonoma Valley, take Route 12 east from Santa Rosa.

LODGING

📌 **Bed & Breakfast Association of Sonoma Valley** ✉ 3250 Trinity Rd., Glen Ellen 95442
☎ 707/938-9513 or 800/969-4667 ⊕ www.sonomabb.com. **The Wine Country Bed and
Breakfast Inns of Sonoma County** ☎ 800/946-3268 ⊕ www.winecountryinns.com.

TOURS

Full-day guided tours of the Wine Country usually include lunch and
cost about $57–$77 per person. The guides, some of whom are winery
owners themselves, know the area well and may show you some lesser-
known cellars. Reservations are usually required.

Gray Line (✉ Pier 43½ Embarcadero, San Francisco 94133 ☎ 415/434–
8687 or 888/428–6937 ⊕ www.graylinesanfrancisco.com) has buses that
tour the Wine Country. **Great Pacific Tour Co.** (✉ 518 Octavia St., Civic
Center, San Francisco 94102 ☎ 415/626–4499 ⊕ www.greatpacifictour.

com) operates full-day tours of Napa and Sonoma, including a restaurant or picnic lunch, in passenger vans that seat 14. **HMS Travels Food and Wine Trail** (✉ 707-A 4th St., Santa Rosa 95404 ☎ 707/526–2922 or 800/367–5348 ⊕ www.foodandwinetrails.com) runs customized tours of the Wine Country for six or more people, by appointment only. The **Napa Valley Wine Train** (✉ 1275 McKinstry St., Napa 94559 ☎ 707/253–2111 or 800/427–4124 ⊕ www.winetrain.com) allows you to enjoy lunch, dinner, or weekend brunch on one of several restored 1915–17 Pullman railroad cars that run between Napa and St. Helena. Prices start at $75 for brunch and $80 for lunch and go up to $85 for dinner. Special gourmet events and murder-mystery packages are more expensive. Frequency varies according to the season and demand.

HOT-AIR BALLOONING — For views of the ocean coast, the Russian River, and San Francisco on a clear day, Above the Wine Country operates out of Santa Rosa. The cost is $195 per person, including a champagne brunch. Balloons Above the Valley is a reliable organization; rides are $195 per person, including a champagne brunch after the flight. Bonaventura Balloon Company schedules flights out of Calistoga or, depending on weather conditions, St. Helena, Oakville, or Rutherford. Flights cost $175 to $198 per person, depending on the breakfast option you choose. Pilots are well versed in Napa Valley lore. Napa Valley Balloons charges $185 per person, including a picnic brunch.

Above the Wine Country ☎ 707/538-7359 or 888/238-6359 ⊕ www.balloontours. com. **Balloons Above the Valley** ☎ 707/253-2222, 800/464-6824 in CA ⊕ www. balloonrides.com. **Bonaventura Balloon Company** ☎ 707/944-2822 or 800/359-6272 ⊕ www.bonaventuraballoons.com. **Napa Valley Balloons** ☎ 707/944-0228, 800/253-2224 in CA ⊕ www.napavalleyballoons.com.

VISITOR INFORMATION

Napa Valley Conference and Visitors Bureau ✉ 1310 Napa Town Center, Napa 94559 ☎ 707/226-7459 ⊕ www.napavalley.com. **Sonoma County Tourism Program** ✉ 520 Mendocino Ave., Suite 210, Santa Rosa 95401 ☎ 707/565-5383 or 800/576-6662 ⊕ www.sonomacounty.com. **Sonoma Valley Visitors Bureau** ✉ 453 1st St. E, Sonoma 95476 ☎ 707/996-1090 ⊕ www.sonomavalley.com.

The North Coast

From Coastal Marin County to Crescent City

WORD OF MOUTH

"Garberville is a small logging town in the middle of wonderful scenery—it is really the gateway to the best of the north coast redwoods. We drove the Avenue of the Giants, stopped in several groves, and went to Ferndale, where there are some of the most beautiful Victorian houses in northern California."

—janisj

Updated by
Constance
Jones

THE 386 MILES between the Golden Gate and the Oregon state line is a land of spectacular scenery, secret beaches, and uncrowded national, state, and local parks. Migrating whales and other sea mammals swim within sight of the dramatic bluffs that make the shoreline north of San Francisco one of the most photographed landscapes in the country.

In between lonely stretches of cypress- and redwood-studded highway, it's a pleasant surprise to find small, funky towns—many of which contain art galleries, small inns, and imaginative restaurants whose menus highlight locally grown produce. Only a handful of towns in this sparsely populated region have more than 1,000 inhabitants.

Note: The beaches of the North Coast are beautiful, but many of them aren't safe for swimming. Year-round, frigid waters are hazardous for those without wet suits. Some stretches experience pounding surf, and rip currents are wickedly strong. "Sneaker" or "sleeper" waves—huge waves that appear without warning even out of calm seas—can reach far up onto the beach and sweep you out to deep water. Never turn your back on the sea, and heed posted warnings.

About the Restaurants

A few restaurants with national reputations, plus several more of regional note, entertain palates on the North Coast. Even the workaday local spots have access to abundant fresh seafood and locally grown (often organic) vegetables and herbs. Dress is usually informal, though dressy casual is the norm at the pricier establishments. As in many rural areas, plan to dine early: many kitchens close at 8 or 8:30 and virtually no one serves past 9:30.

About the Hotels

Restored Victorians, rustic lodges, country inns, and vintage motels are among the accommodations available along the North Coast. Hardly any have air-conditioning (the ocean breezes make it unnecessary), and many have no phones or TVs. Several towns have only one or two places to spend the night, but some of these lodgings are destinations in themselves. Make summer and weekend bed-and-breakfast reservations as far ahead as possible—rooms at the best inns often sell out months in advance. In winter you're likely to find reduced rates and nearly empty inns and B&Bs. For some of the area's most noteworthy lodging options, check out ⊕ www.uniquenorthwestinns.com.

WHAT IT COSTS				
$$$$	**$$$**	**$$**	**$**	**¢**
RESTAURANTS over $30	$23–$30	$16–$22	$10–$15	under $10
HOTELS over $250	$176–$250	$121–$175	$90–$120	under $90

Restaurant prices are for a main course at dinner, excluding sales tax of 7¼% (depending on location). Hotel prices are for two people in a standard double room in high season, excluding service charges and 8%–10% tax.

Exploring the North Coast

Without a car (or motor coach), it is all but impossible to explore the Northern California coast. Highway 1 is a beautiful if sometimes slow and nerve-racking drive. You should stop frequently to appreciate the views, and on many portions of the highway you can't drive faster than 20–40 mph. You can still have a fine trip even if you don't have much time, but be realistic and don't plan to drive too far in one day. The itineraries below proceed north from Marin County, just north of San Francisco.

Timing

The North Coast is a year-round destination, though when you go determines what you will see. The migration of the Pacific gray whales is a wintertime phenomenon, which lasts roughly from mid-December to early April. In July and August views are often obscured by fog. The coastal climate is quite similar to San Francisco's, although winter nights are colder than in the city.

COASTAL MARIN COUNTY

North over the Golden Gate Bridge from San Francisco lies Marin County, where a collection of hamlets is strung along the coast within an hour's drive of the city. Nearly half of the county, including the majority of the shoreline, is protected parkland encompassing rocky bluffs, beaches, forest, chaparral, and grassland. The beauty of the countryside draws hikers, cyclists, kayakers, families, and urbanites seeking a break from busy streets.

The Marin Headlands

❶ *1 mi north of the Golden Gate Bridge on Hwy. 101; first exit north of the bridge.*

The Marin Headlands stretch from the north end of the Golden Gate Bridge to Muir Beach. Part of the Golden Gate National Recreation Area, the headlands are a dramatic stretch of windswept hills that plunge down to the ocean, threaded with scenic roads and trails. Photographers flock to the southern headlands for shots of the city, with the bridge in the foreground and the skyline on the horizon.

The **Marin Headlands Visitor Center** (✉ Fort Barry, Field and Bunker Rds., Bldg. 948 ☎ 415/331–1540 ⊕ www.nps.gov/goga/mahe), open daily 9:30–4:30, has exhibits on headlands history and ecology and posts the latest wildlife sightings. It distributes a map of hiking trails as well as the park newspaper, which lists a calendar of events, including a schedule of guided walks. The bookstore sells a large selection of titles on local and regional flora and fauna, hiking, camping, and history.

The headlands' strategic position at the mouth of San Francisco Bay made them a logical site for military installations. Today you can explore the crumbling World War II concrete batteries where naval guns protected the approaches from the sea. The now defunct **Nike Missile Site** (✉ Field Rd., off Bunker Hill Rd. ☎ 415/331–1453 or 415/331–1540) gives

GREAT ITINERARIES

Numbers in the text correspond to numbers on the North Coast maps.

IF YOU HAVE 3 DAYS. Some of the finest redwoods in California are found less than 20 mi north of San Francisco in **Muir Woods National Monument** ❷ ▶ . After walking through the woods, stop for an early lunch in Point Reyes Station (on the eastern edge of Point Reyes National Seashore) or continue on Highway 1 to **Fort Ross State Historic Park** ❾. Catch the sunset and stay the night in ▦ **Gualala** ⓫. On Day 2 drive to ▦ **Mendocino** ⓯. Spend the next day and a half browsing in the many galleries and shops and visiting the historic sites, beaches, and parks of this cliffside enclave. Return to San Francisco via Highway 1, or the quicker (3½ hours, versus up to 5) and less winding route of Highway 128 east to U.S. 101 south.

IF YOU HAVE 7 DAYS. Early on your first day, walk through **Muir Woods National Monument** ❷ ▶. Then visit **Stinson Beach** ❹ for a walk on the shore and lunch. In springtime and early summer head north on Highway 1 to Bolinas Lagoon, where you can see birds nesting at Audubon Canyon Ranch. At other times of the year (or after you've visited the ranch) continue north on Highway 1 to **Point Reyes National Seashore** ❺.

Tour the reconstructed Miwok village near the visitor center and drive out to Point Reyes Lighthouse. Spend the night in Inverness or one of the other gateway towns. The next day stop at Goat Rock State Beach and **Fort Ross State Historic Park** ❾ on the way to ▦ **Mendocino** ⓯. On your third morning head toward **Fort Bragg** ⓰ for a visit to the Mendocino Coast Botanical Gardens. If you're in the mood to splurge, continue north to ▦ **Garberville** ⓱ and spend the night at the Benbow Inn. Otherwise, linger in the Mendocino area and drive on the next morning. On Day 4 continue north through **Humboldt Redwoods State Park** ⓲, including the Avenue of the Giants. Stop for the night in the Victorian village of ▦ **Ferndale** ⓳ and visit the Ferndale Museum. On Day 5 drive to ▦ **Eureka** ⓴. Have lunch in the old downtown, visit the shops, and stop in at the Clarke Memorial Museum. Begin Day 6 by driving to **Patrick's Point State Park** ㉓ to enjoy stunning views of the Pacific from a point high above the surf. Have a late lunch overlooking the harbor in **Trinidad** ㉒ before returning to Eureka for the night. Return to San Francisco on Day 7. The drive back takes six hours on U.S. 101; it's nearly twice as long if you take Highway 1.

you a firsthand view of menacing Hercules missiles and missile-tracking radar. The site is open Wednesday through Friday, 12:30–3:30 (closed in bad weather), with guided walks starting on the hour.

At the end of Conzelman Road is the **Point Bonita Lighthouse,** a restored beauty that is still guiding ships to safety with its original 1855 refractory lens. The steep ½-mi walk from the parking area down to the lighthouse takes you through a rock tunnel and across a suspension bridge. It's open Saturday through Monday, 12:30–3:30.

♨ The **Marine Mammal Center** (✉ 1065 Fort Cronkhite, north side of Rodeo Lagoon ☎ 415/289–7325 ⊕ www.marinemammalcenter.org), a hospital for rescued seals, sea lions, dolphins, and otters, is open daily 10–4. There's no charge to see the animals convalescing in the pens and pools out front, but the nonprofit heartily appreciates donations. Construction to expand and improve the center is ongoing through 2007 and may necessitate occasional closures; call ahead to check.

Muir Woods National Monument

★ ♨ ❷ *10 mi northwest of the Marin Headlands off Panoramic Hwy.*

The 550 acres of Muir Woods National Monument contain some of the most majestic redwoods in the world—some nearly 250 feet tall and 1,000 years old. The stand of old-growth *Sequoia sempervirens* became one of the country's first national monuments in 1905; environmental naturalist John Muir, for whom the site was named, declared it "the best tree lover's monument that could be found in all of the forests of the world."

The hiking trails here vary in difficulty and distance. One of the easiest is the 2-mi, wheelchair-accessible **loop trail,** which crosses streams and passes ferns and azaleas, as well as magnificent redwood groves. The most popular are **Bohemian Grove** and the circular formation called **Cathedral Grove,** where crowds of tourists can often be heard oohing and aahing in several languages. If you prefer a little more serenity, consider the challenging **Dipsea Trail,** which climbs west from the forest floor to soothing views of the ocean and the Golden Gate Bridge.

The weather in Muir Woods is usually cool and often wet, so wear warm clothes and shoes appropriate for damp trails. Picnicking and camping aren't allowed, and pets aren't permitted. Parking can be difficult here—the lots are small and the crowds are large—so try to come early in the morning or late in the afternoon. The small **Muir Woods Visitor Center** has exhibits on redwood trees and the history of Muir Woods, plus a selection of books and gifts; the large gift shop within the park sells all manner of souvenirs.

To get here from the Golden Gate Bridge, take U.S. 101 north to the Mill Valley–Stinson Beach exit and follow Highway 1 north to Panoramic Highway. ✉ *Muir Woods Rd., 2 mi north of Hwy. 1 via Panoramic Hwy.* ☎ *415/388–2595* ⊕ *www.nps.gov/muwo* ☞ *$3* ⊙ *Daily 8 AM–sunset.*

▌OFF THE BEATEN PATH

MUIR BEACH – A small but scenic sheltered cove off Highway 1, Muir Beach is a good place to stretch your legs. Locals often walk their dogs here, and anglers and boogie-boarders share the gentle surf. At one end of the strand is a cluster of waterfront homes, and at the other are the bluffs of the northern Marin Headlands. From Muir Woods, drive south on Muir Woods Road about 3 mi to Highway 1 and jog south (left) to the right-hand turnoff for the beach.

Where to Stay & Eat

$$$ ✕⌂ **Pelican Inn.** From its slate roof to its whitewashed plaster walls, this inn looks so Tudor that it's hard to believe it was built in the 1970s. The Pelican is English to the core, with its smallish guest rooms up-

PLEASURES & PASTIMES

BEACHES. The waters of the Pacific Ocean along the North Coast are fine for seals, but most humans find the temperatures downright arctic. When it comes to spectacular cliffs and seascapes, though, the North Coast beaches are second to none. You can explore tidal pools, watch seabirds and sea lions, or dive for abalone—and you'll often have the beach all to yourself. South to north, Stinson Beach, Limantour Beach (at Point Reyes National Seashore), the beaches in Manchester and Van Damme state parks, and the 10-mi strand in MacKerricher State Park are among the most notable.

HIKING. Gorgeous landscape, cool year-round weather, and numerous state and national parks make the North Coast an ideal hiking destination. Whatever your fitness level, you can enjoy the diverse beauty of this region on foot, whether on the hilly trails of the Marin Head-

lands and Mt. Tamalpais, the ocean-front bluff walks in Point Reyes National Seashore and Salt Point State Park, or the primeval forest tracks of Humboldt Redwoods State Park and Redwoods National and State Parks. Always be sure to carry water, and check carefully for ticks after your hike.

WHALE-WATCHING. From any number of excellent observation points along the coast, you can watch gray whales during their annual winter migration season (mid-December to early April). In summer and fall, you can see blue or humpback whales. Point Reyes Lighthouse, Gualala Point Regional Park, Point Arena Lighthouse, and Patrick's Point State Park are just a few of the places where you stand a good chance of spotting one of the giant sea creatures. Whale-watching cruises operate out of several towns, including Bodega Bay and Fort Bragg.

stairs (no elevator), high half-tester beds draped in heavy fabrics, and bangers and grilled tomatoes for breakfast. Downstairs, the little pub pours ales and ports, and "the snug" is a private fireplace lounge for overnight guests. At dinner in the tavernlike or solarium dining rooms ($$–$$$), keep it simple with fish-and-chips, roasted hen, or prime rib and focus on the well-crafted wine list. Lunch is served, too, a good thing since your nearest alternatives are miles away via slow, winding roads. ⊠ *10 Pacific Way at Hwy. 1, Muir Beach 94965* ☎ *415/383–6000* 🖨 *415/383–3424* ⊕ *www.pelicaninn.com* 🛏 *7 rooms* ⚒ *Restaurant, pub, no-smoking rooms; no a/c, no room phones, no room TVs* ⊟ *MC, V* ⦿ *BP.*

Mt. Tamalpais State Park

❸ *6 mi northwest of Muir Woods National Monument on Panoramic Hwy.*

At 2,571 feet, Mt. Tamalpais affords views of the entire Bay Area and the Pacific Ocean. The mountain was sacred to Native Americans, who saw in its profile the silhouette of a sleeping maiden. Within the 6,300-acre park are more than 200 mi of hiking trails, some rugged but many

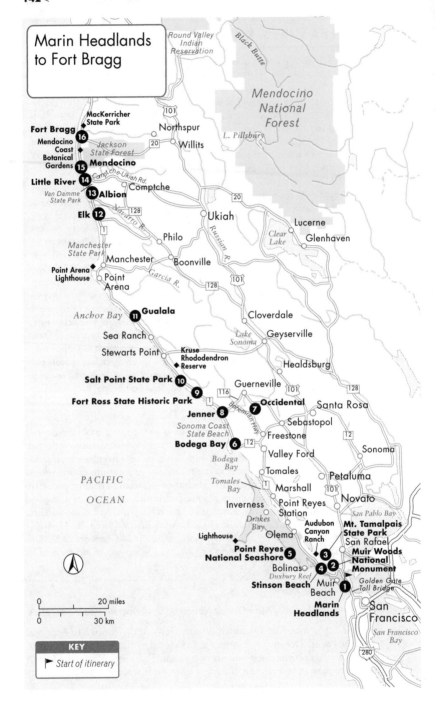

Marin Headlands to Fort Bragg

Round Valley Indian Reservation

Black Butte

Mendocino National Forest

L. Pillsbury

MacKerricher State Park

101

Northspur

Fort Bragg 16

Mendocino Coast Botanical Gardens

20

Willits

Jackson State Forest

15 **Mendocino**

Little River 14

Comptche-Ukiah Rd.

20

Van Damme State Park

13 **Albion**

Comptche

128

Ukiah

Elk 12

Navarro R.

Philo

Russian R.

Lucerne

Clear Lake

Glenhaven

Manchester State Park

Manchester

Boonville

Point Arena Lighthouse

Point Arena

Garcia R.

128

US 101

Anchor Bay

11 **Gualala**

Cloverdale

Lake Sonoma

Geyserville

Sea Ranch

Stewarts Point

Kruse Rhododendron Reserve

Healdsburg

128

Salt Point State Park 10

Guerneville

101

Fort Ross State Historic Park 9

116

Occidental 7

Santa Rosa

Jenner 8

Bohemian Hwy.

Sonoma Coast State Beach

Sebastopol

12

Sonoma

Bodega Bay 6

12

Freestone

Bodega Bay

Valley Ford

PACIFIC

Tomales

Petaluma

OCEAN

Tomales Bay

Marshall

101

Novato

Inverness

Point Reyes Station

San Pablo Bay

Drakes Bay

Audubon Canyon Ranch

Mt. Tamalpais State Park

San Rafael

Lighthouse

Olema

Point Reyes National Seashore 5

Bolinas

3

Muir Woods National Monument

Duxbury Reef

4 2

Stinson Beach

Muir Beach

1

Golden Gate Toll Bridge

Marin Headlands

San Francisco

San Francisco Bay

| 0 | 20 miles |
| 0 | 30 km |

280

KEY

► *Start of itinerary*

good for easy walking through meadows and forests and along creeks. Mountain bikers toil up and whiz down Mt. Tam's winding roads.

The park's major thoroughfare, the Panoramic Highway, snakes its way up from Highway 1 to the **Pantoll Ranger Station** (⊠ 3801 Panoramic Hwy., at Pantoll Rd. ☎ 415/388–2070). Pan Toll Road branches off the highway at the station, connecting up with Ridgecrest Boulevard. Along these roads are numerous parking areas, picnic spots, scenic overlooks, and trailheads. Parking is free along the roadside, but there is a fee at the ranger station and other parking lots.

★ $$$–$$$$ ✕⊡ **Mountain Home Inn.** Next door to 40,000 acres of state and national parks, the inn stands at the foot of Mt. Tamalpais. Its multilevel, airy wooden building nests high up in the trees, with pristine wilderness on one side and an unparalleled view of the bay on the other. Rooms are built for romance, each mixing huge views with some combination of balcony, fireplace, and whirlpool tub. For full-moon nights book far in advance. The on-site wine bar and dining room (closed Monday and Tuesday) serves lunch on the deck and a terrific $38 prix-fixe dinner of American regional cuisine inside by the fire. ⊠ 810 Panoramic Hwy., 94941 ☎ 415/381–9000 ☎ 415/381–3615 ⊕ www.mtnhomeinn.com ☜ 10 rooms ♿ Restaurant, lounge; no a/c, no room TVs, no smoking ⊟ AE, MC, V ¶⊙ BP.

Stinson Beach

❹ 4 mi west of Mt. Tamalpais State Park on Panoramic Hwy.; 20 mi northwest of Golden Gate Bridge on Hwy. 1.

Stinson Beach is the most expansive stretch of sand in Marin County. When it's not fogged in, the village clustered by this strand resembles a stereotypical Southern California beach town. On any hot summer weekend every road to Stinson Beach is jam-packed, so factor this into your plans.

Late May through early October, the professional **Shakespeare at Stinson** company performs each Friday, Saturday, and Sunday evening in its outdoor 155-seat theater. Tickets run $25 for adults, $14 for children 16 and under; some Fridays two kids are admitted free with each paying adult. ⊠ Calle Del Mar and Hwy. 1 ☎ 415/868–1115 ⊕ www.shakespeareatstinson.org.

Where to Stay & Eat

$–$$ ✕ **Parkside Cafe.** Most people know the Parkside for its snack bar (¢, cash only) beside the beachfront park, but inside is the best restaurant in Stinson Beach. The food is classic Cal cuisine, with appetizers such as day-boat scallops ceviche and mains such as lamb with goat cheese–stuffed red peppers. Breakfast, a favorite among locals, is served until 2. Eat on the sunny patio or by the fire in the contemporary dining room. ⊠ 43 Arenal Ave. ☎ 415/868–1272 ⊟ D, MC, V.

$–$$ ✕ **Sand Dollar.** Old salts have been coming here since 1921, but these days they sip microbrews at a handsome bar or beneath market umbrellas on the heated deck. The American food—panfried sand dabs, pear salad with blue cheese—is good, but the real draw is the lively atmosphere. On sunny afternoons the deck is packed, and on weekends there's live music. ⊠ *3458 Hwy. 1* ☎ *415/868–0434* ▭ *AE, MC, V.*

¢–$$$ ▣ **Stinson Beach Motel.** Built in the 1930s, this motel surrounds three courtyards that burst with flowering greenery. Rooms are immaculate, simple, and summery, with freshly painted walls, good mattresses, and some kitchenettes. The motel is conveniently on the main drag, so it can get loud on busy weekends. Weekday room rates ($85–$125) are a bargain for Marin. ⊠ *3416 Hwy. 1, 94970* ☎ *415/868–1712* ⎙ *415/868–1790* ⊕ *www.stinsonbeachmotel.com* ⌨ *8 rooms* ♢ *Some kitchenettes, cable TV; no a/c, no room phones* ▭ *D, MC, V.*

⌐ EN ROUTE **Audubon Canyon Ranch,** a 1,000-acre wildlife sanctuary along the Bolinas Lagoon, gets the most traffic during late spring, when great blue herons and egrets come to nest. It's a spectacular sight, these large birds and their young roosting in the hillside evergreens and swooping between treetop and lagoon. Trails provide fabulous birding through strategically placed telescopes, as well as tremendous vistas of Bolinas Lagoon and Stinson Beach. Naturalists are sometimes on hand, and docents give half-day nature walks some Saturdays—well worth it if you can get a space. A small museum, open all year, surveys the region's geology and natural history. ⊠ *4900 Hwy. 1, between Stinson Beach and Bolinas* ☎ *415/868-9244* ⊕ *www.egret.org* ⊠ *$10 suggested donation* ⊗ *Mid-Mar.–mid-July, weekends 10–4; Tues.–Fri. by appointment.*

The tiny waterfront town of **Bolinas** attracts potters, poets, and peace lovers to its quiet streets. With a fine-arts gallery, a general store selling organic produce, and a saloon where you can hear live music, the main thoroughfare looks like a hippie-fied version of Main Street USA. The Coast Cafe serves dependable American fare indoors and out. Residents have torn down signs to the isolated town, but Bolinas isn't difficult to find, and it is a gateway to the southernmost portion of Point Reyes National Seashore. Heading north on Highway 1 about 5 mi north from Stinson Beach, make the first left (Bolinas-Olema Road) just past Bolinas Lagoon, then turn left at the stop sign. The road dead-ends smack dab in the middle of the hamlet, so drive slowly lest you come face-to-face with an angry local.

Point Reyes National Seashore

❺ *15 mi north of Stinson Beach on Hwy. 1.*

Fodor's Choice
★

One of the Bay Area's most spectacular treasures and the only national seashore on the West Coast, the 66,500-acre Point Reyes National Seashore (⊕ www.nps.gov/pore) encompasses secluded beaches, rugged chaparral and grasslands, and dense forest as well as **Point Reyes**, a triangular peninsula that juts into the Pacific. The hills and dramatic cliffs afford hikers, whale-watchers, and solitude seekers magnificent views of the sea.

A few tiny towns along its eastern boundary serve as gateways to the national seashore. **Olema,** a crossroads with a couple of fine restaurants and small inns, is where you'll find the main visitor center. Two miles north on Highway 1 is **Point Reyes Station,** the biggest burg in the area. A mix of upscale, counterculture, and mom-and-pop shops and eateries line several old-timey blocks, and numerous B&Bs lie north of town. On Sir Francis Drake Boulevard, which parallels Highway 1 up the opposite shore of Tomales Bay, **Inverness** overlooks the water from a forested hillside. You can eat and sleep humbly or extravagantly here.

The **Bear Valley Visitor Center** (⊠ Bear Valley Rd. west of Hwy. 1 in Olema ☎ 415/464–5100), open weekdays 9–5 and weekends 8–5, has exhibits about park history and wildlife. Rangers here dispense information about beaches, whale-watching, hiking trails, and camping. The infamous San Andreas Fault runs along the eastern edge of the park and up the center of Tomales Bay; take the short **Earthquake Trail** from the visitor center to see the impact near the epicenter of the 1906 earthquake that devastated San Francisco. A ½-mi path from the visitor center leads to **Kule Loklo,** a brilliantly reconstructed Miwok village that illustrates the daily lives of the region's first inhabitants. From here, trails also lead to the park's free campgrounds (camping permits are required).

The **Point Reyes Lighthouse** (⊠ Western end of Sir Francis Drake Blvd. ☎ 415/669–1534 ⊙ Thurs.–Mon. 10–4:30, except in very windy weather), in operation since December 1, 1870, occupies the tip of Point Reyes. The drive here, 22 mi from the Bear Valley Visitor Center, is a scenic 45-minute trip over hills scattered with old cattle ranches. Half a mile from the parking lot, 308 steps—the equivalent of 30 stories—lead down to (and back up from) the lighthouse: the view is worth it. On busy whale-watching weekends (late December through mid-April), parking may be restricted and shuttle buses ($5) put in service from Drakes Beach. You don't have to walk down the stairs to have a view of the whales.

In late winter and spring, wildlife enthusiasts should make a stop at **Chimney Rock,** just before the lighthouse, and take the short walk to the Elephant Seal Overlook. Even from up on the cliff, the males look enormous as they spar for the resident females.

Along the park's northernmost finger of land, the 4.7-mi (one way) **Tomales Point Trail** follows the spine of a ridge through Tule Elk Preserve, providing spectacular ocean views from high bluffs. Expect to see lots of elk, but keep your distance from the animals. To reach the fairly easy hiking trail, head north out of Inverness on Sir Francis Drake Boulevard and turn right on Pierce Point Road. Park at the end of the road by the old ranch buildings.

In the southernmost part of the park, near the town of Bolinas, the free **Point Reyes Bird Observatory** (PRBO; ⊠ Mesa Rd. ☎ 415/868–0655 ⊕ www.prbo.org) is a treat for birders. The compact visitor center, open daily sunrise–5 PM, has excellent interpretive exhibits, including a comparative display of real birds' talons. What really warrants a visit, though, are the surrounding woods, which harbor nearly 225 bird species. As you hike the quiet trails through forest and along ocean cliffs, you're likely to see biologists at work.

Where to Stay & Eat

$–$$$ ✕ **Station House Cafe.** In good weather hikers fresh from the park fill the adjoining garden for alfresco dining, and on weekends there's not a spare seat on the banquettes in the wide-open dining room. The focus is on traditional American food—fresh popovers hit the table as soon as you arrive—and there's a little of everything on the menu. Grilled salmon, barbecued oysters, and burgers are all predictable hits. The place is also open for breakfast. ⊠ *11180 Hwy. 1, Point Reyes Station* ☎ *415/663–1515* ▭ *D, MC, V* ☙ *Closed Wed.*

★ ¢–$ ✕ **Tomales Bay Foods and Indian Peach Food.** A renovated hay barn houses this collection of food shops. Watch workers making Cowgirl Creamery cheese, then buy some at a counter that sells exquisite artisanal cheeses from around the world. Tomales Bay Foods showcases local organic fruits and vegetables and premium packaged foods, and the kitchen at Indian Peach Food turns the best ingredients into creative sandwiches, salads, and soups. You can eat at a café table or on the lawn, or take it away. The shops are open until 6 PM. ⊠ *80 4th St., Point Reyes Station* ☎ *415/663–9335 cheese shop, 415/663–8478 deli* ▭ *MC, V* ☙ *Closed Mon. and Tues.*

¢ ✕ **Café Reyes.** In a triangular, semi-industrial room with glazed concrete floors and ceilings high enough to accommodate market umbrellas, you can mix and match Californian and international flavors. Burritos filled with Latin- and Asian-tinged medleys, such as a shrimp-and-vegetable stir-fry with ginger sauce and chutney, are a specialty. Sandwiches and salads are generous. A big deck beckons on nice days. ⊠ *11101 Hwy. 1, Point Reyes Station* ☎ *415/663–9493* ▭ *No credit cards.*

¢ ✕ **Priscilla's Pizza Café.** This casual eatery in Inverness is a good stop for a quick bite: pizza, sandwiches, salad, pastries, and espresso. They'll stretch the crust thin for you if you ask. ⊠ *12781 Sir Francis Drake Blvd., Inverness* ☎ *415/669–1244* ▭ *AE, MC, V.*

$$$–$$$$ ✕▥ **Manka's Inverness Lodge.** Chef-owner Margaret Grade realizes a
Fodor's Choice rustic fantasy in her 1917 hunting lodge and cabins, where everywhere
★ mica-shaded lamps cast an amber glow and bearskin rugs warm wide-planked floors. Each detail—featherbeds, deep leather armchairs, huge soaking tubs—bespeaks sensuous indulgence, but this is a private hideout, not a swanky resort. The centerpiece restaurant ($$$$) ranks among California's best. Grade prepares nearly everything over a wood fire with ingredients from within 15 mi, creating boldly flavorful dishes daily according to what comes in from farmers, fishermen, and foragers. Succulent meats reign, but vegetarians can ask for adjustments to the prix-fixe menu. ⊠ *30 Callendar Way, at Argyll Way, Inverness 94937* ☎ *415/669–1034* ⊕ *www.mankas.com* ⇨ *8 rooms, 2 suites, 4 cabins* ⚹ *Restaurant, some in-room hot tubs, some kitchenettes, piano; no a/c, no phones in some rooms, no room TVs, no smoking* ▭ *MC, V* ☙ *No lunch. Restaurant closed Wed. year-round, Mon.–Thurs. Jan.–Mar.* ¶❂ *BP.*

$$–$$$ ✕▥ **Olema Inn & Restaurant.** Built in 1876, the inn retains its original architectural charm but has been updated in a sophisticated, uncluttered style. The understated rooms have antique armoires and sumptuous beds

with crisp linens; the white-tile baths have gleaming fixtures. But the main attraction is the top-notch Northern California cooking served in the restaurant ($$$, reservations essential). The preparations of organic, local, and free-range ingredients include fresh oysters with a panoply of cold and hot toppings, pork chops with apple-cider glaze, and house-made ricotta gnocchi. Come on Monday, locals' night, when the place hops with live music and you can browse a delectable small-plates menu. ⊠ *10000 Sir Francis Drake Blvd., Olema 94950* ☎ *415/663–9559* 🖷 *415/663–8783* ⊕ *www.theolemainn.com* 🗘 *6 rooms* 🐾 *Some pets allowed; no a/c, no room phones, no smoking* ⊟ *AE, MC, V* ⊗ *No lunch weekdays, no dinner Tues.* ⦿| *BP.*

$$$–$$$$ 🏨 **Blackthorne Inn.** There's no other inn quite like the Blackthorne, a combination of whimsy and sophistication tucked on a hill in the woods. The giant tree-house-like structure has spiral staircases, a 3,500-square-foot deck, and a fireman's pole. The solarium was made with timbers from San Francisco wharves, and the outer walls are salvaged doors from a railway station. The best room is aptly named the Eagle's Nest, perched as it is in the glass-sheathed octagonal tower that crowns the inn. ⊠ *266 Vallejo Ave., Inverness Park 94937* ☎ *415/663–8621* ⊕ *www. blackthorneinn.com* 🗘 *3 rooms, 1 suite* 🐾 *Dining room, hot tub; no a/c, no room phones, no room TVs, no kids, no smoking* ⊟ *MC, V* ⦿| *BP.*

$$–$$$ 🏨 **Ten Inverness Way.** With its stone fireplace, comfy couches, and window seats, the generous 2nd-floor common room of this low-key inn is an appealing spot to plop down for complimentary wine and cheese or fresh-baked cookies. Upstairs, four rooms under the eaves are snug with patchwork quilts and waffle-weave robes; Room 1 is largest, with skylights and a tub. On the ground floor, a suite with a separate entrance can accommodate three adults or two adults plus two children. The full breakfast, made from scratch using many ingredients grown in the backyard garden, is ample fuel for a day in the great outdoors. ⊠ *10 Inverness Way, 94937* ☎ *415/669–1648* 🖷 *415/669–7403* ⊕ *www. teninvernessway.com* 🗘 *4 rooms, 1 suite* 🐾 *1 kitchenette, hot tub, library, shop; no a/c, no room phones, no room TVs* ⊟ *D, MC, V* ⦿| *BP.*

$–$$ 🏨 **Motel Inverness.** This roadside row of rooms has everything a small-town motel should offer: friendly management; spotless, thoughtfully maintained accommodations (some quite small); and extras that add real value. The lodge, a window-lined common room with skylighted cathedral ceiling, has a fireplace, big-screen TV, billiards table, and kitchenette. Sliding glass doors open to a deck overlooking Tomales Bay. For $400, you can have the two-story suite (sleeps four) and its two decks, full kitchen, fireplace, and jetted tub; $500 rents you the ornate Dacha, a three-bedroom Russian-style house on stilts over the bay. ⊠ *12718 Sir Francis Drake Blvd., Inverness 94937* ☎ *415/669–1081 or 888/669–6909* 🖷 *415/669–1906* ⊕ *www.motelinverness.com* 🗘 *6 rooms, 2 suites, 1 house* 🐾 *Some kitchens, some kitchenettes, cable TV, billiards; no a/c, no room phones, no smoking* ⊟ *MC, V.*

CAMPING Within the Point Reyes National Seashore are four hike-in campgrounds in isolated wilderness areas 3–6½ mi from trailheads. All sites have barbecue pits, picnic tables, pit toilets, and food-storage lockers; the water isn't potable and dogs are not allowed. The fee is $12 per night for up to six people. Reservations are essential spring through fall and can be booked up to three months in advance; to reserve call ☎ 415/663–8054 weekdays between 9 and 2 or inquire in person at the Bear Valley Visitor Center. For detailed information about camping, call the park at ☎ 415/464–5100 or visit ⊕ www.nps.gov/pore.

Sports & the Outdoors

On Tomales Bay, **Blue Waters Kayaking** (✉ 12938 Sir Francis Drake Blvd., Inverness ☎ 415/669–2600 ⊕ www.bwkayak.com) provides guided morning, full-day, sunset, full-moon, and overnight camping paddles. They also rent out kayaks and offer beginner through advanced lessons. **Five Brooks Stables** (✉ 8001 Hwy. 1, Olema ☎ 415/663–1570 ⊕ www. fivebrooks.com) rents horses and equipment. Trails from the stables wind through Point Reyes National Seashore and along the beaches. Rides run from one to six hours and cost $35–$165.

EN ROUTE
Marshall, on the stretch of Highway 1 that hugs the east shore of Tomales Bay, is a good place to stop for some of the bay's famous oysters. Since 1909 **Tomales Bay Oyster Company** (✉ 15479 Hwy. 1, Marshall ☎ 415/663–1242 ☽ Daily 8–6) has farmed oysters. Families buy them by the dozen and eat at the picnic tables, usually barbecuing the bivalves on the grills. Bring your shucking knife, fixings, and charcoal. On weekends, when foodies from San Francisco make the pilgrimage to **Hog Island Oyster Company** (✉ 20215 Hwy. 1, Marshall ☎ 415/ 663–9218 ☽ Wed.–Sun. 9–5) to party, reservations for the picnic tables are a must. You're given use of a shucking knife, but you have to supply your own sides, drinks, and charcoal for the grills. There's an $8 per head, per table charge. The giant barbecued and fried oysters at ramshackle **Tony's Seafood** (✉ 18663 Hwy. 1, Marshall ☎ 415/663–1107 ☽ Fri.–Sun. and Mon. holidays noon–8) are so good that it doesn't matter that they aren't local.

THE SONOMA COAST

Heading up through northwestern Marin into Sonoma County, Highway 1 traverses gently rolling pastureland. North of Bodega Bay dramatic shoreline scenery takes over. The road snakes up, down, and around sheer cliffs and steep inclines—some without guardrails—where cows seem to cling precariously. Stunning vistas (or cottony fog) and hairpin turns make this one of the most exhilarating drives north of San Francisco.

Bodega Bay

❻ *34 mi north of Point Reyes National Seashore on Hwy. 1.*

From the busy harbor here, commercial boats pursue fish and Dungeness crab. There's nothing cutesy about this working town without a center—it's just a string of businesses along several miles of Highway 1. But tourists still come to see where Alfred Hitchcock shot *The Birds* in 1962. The buildings in the movie are all gone, but in nearby Bodega you can find Potter Schoolhouse. A major (now unrecognizable) *Birds* location, the **Tides Wharf** (✉ 801 Hwy. 1 ☎ 707/875–2751) complex is cheesy but convenient, with a sit-down restaurant, an enormous snack bar, a souvenir shop, and a wine-and-food shop. The same owners operate the Inn at the Tides across the road.

For a closer look at Bodega Bay itself, visit the **Bodega Marine Laboratory** (✉ 2099 Westside Rd. ☎ 707/875–2211), a 326-acre reserve on Bodega Head. Fridays from 2 to 4 PM, docents give free tours and peeks at intertidal invertebrates, such as sea stars and sea anemones (suggested donation $2).

Where to Stay & Eat

$–$$ ✕ **Sandpiper Restaurant.** A local favorite for breakfast, this friendly café on the marina does a good job for a fair price. Peruse the board for the day's fresh catches or order a menu regular such as crab stew or wasabi tuna; clam chowder is the house specialty. There's often live jazz Friday and Saturday evening. ✉ *1410 Bay Flat Rd.* ☎ *707/875–2278* 🖃 *MC, V.*

$$$–$$$$ ✕🏠 **Bodega Bay Lodge & Spa.** Looking out to the ocean across a wetland, a group of shingle-and-river-rock buildings houses Bodega Bay's finest accommodations. Capacious rooms with masculine country-club decor are appointed with high-quality bedding, fireplaces, and patios or balconies; some have vaulted ceilings and jetted tubs. In the health complex, state-of-the-art fitness equipment sparkles and the spa provides a full roster of pampering treatments. The quiet Duck Club restaurant ($$–$$$$), a notch or two above most places in town, hits more than it misses; try the Dungeness crab cakes with tomato-ginger chutney. ✉ *103 Hwy. 1, 94923* ☎ *707/875–3525 or 800/368–2468* 🖶 *707/875–2428* ⊕ *www.bodegabaylodge.com* ⤳ *78 rooms, 5 suites* ⌂ *Restaurant, room service, refrigerators, cable TV with movies, in-room data ports, pool, gym, outdoor hot tub, sauna, spa, concierge, laundry facilities, meeting rooms* 🖃 *AE, D, DC, MC, V.*

¢ 🏠 **Bodega Harbor Inn.** As humble as can be, this is one of the few places on this stretch of the coast where you can get a room for less than $100 a night. Renovated rooms have tile floors and a few antiques; unrenovated rooms are more generic, with wall-to-wall carpeting. All are small and clean. You can also rent an apartment or house nearby for $110–$300. The motel is at the north end of town on a side street off Highway 1, behind Pelican Plaza shopping center. ✉ *1345 Bodega Ave., 94923* ☎ *707/875–3594* 🖶 *707/875–9468* ⊕ *www. bodegaharborinn.com* ⤳ *14 rooms* ⌂ *Cable TV; no a/c, no room phones, no smoking* 🖃 *MC, V.*

Sports & the Outdoors

Bodega Bay Sportfishing (✉ Bay Flat Rd. ☎ 707/875–3344) charters ocean-fishing boats and rents equipment. The operators of the 400-acre **Chanslor Guest Ranch** (✉ 2660 Hwy. 1 ☎ 707/875–2721 ⊕ www. chanslorranch.com) lead guided horseback rides, some along the beach. At the incredibly scenic oceanfront **Links at Bodega Harbour** (✉21301 Heron

Dr. ☎ 707/875–3538 or 800/503–8158 ⊕ www.bodegaharbourgolf. com) you can play an 18-hole Robert Trent Jones–designed course.

EN ROUTE
Sonoma Coast State Beach (☎ 707/875–3483 or 707/865–2391) stretches along the shoreline from Bodega Head to a point several miles north of Jenner. Rock Point, Duncan's Landing, and Wright's Beach, clustered at about the halfway mark, have picnic areas.

Occidental

❼ *14 mi northeast of Bodega Bay on Bohemian Hwy.*

A village surrounded by redwood forests, orchards, and vineyards, Occidental is a former logging hub with a bohemian feel. In 19th-century downtown are a top-notch B&B, good eats, and a handful of art galleries and crafts and clothing boutiques. To reach Occidental take Highway 12 (Bodega Highway) east 5 mi from Highway 1. Take a left onto Bohemian Highway, where you'll find minuscule Freestone; another 3½ mi and you'll be in Occidental.

A traditional Japanese detoxifying treatment awaits you at **Osmosis–The Enzyme Bath Spa,** the only such facility in America. Your bath is a deep redwood tub of damp cedar shavings and rice bran, naturally heated to 140° by the action of enzymes. Serene attendants bury you up to the neck and during the 20-minute treatment ($75 weekdays, $80 weekends) bring you sips of water and place cool cloths on your forehead. After a shower, lie down and listen to brain-balancing music through headphones or have a massage, perhaps in one of the creekside pagodas. A stroll through the meditation garden tops off the experience. ⊠ *209 Bohemian Hwy., Freestone* ☎ *707/823–8231* ⊕ *www.osmosis.com* ☉ *Daily 9–8.*

Where to Stay & Eat

¢–$$ ✕ **Willow Wood Market Café.** About 5 mi east of Occidental in the village of Graton is one of the best-kept secrets in the Wine Country. Tucked among the market merchandise are a number of tables and a counter where casually dressed locals sit down to order the signature creamy polenta, freshly made soups and salads, dinner plates, and gingerbread cake. ⊠ *9020 Graton Rd., Graton* ☎ *707/522–8372* ⟐ *Reservations not accepted* ⊟ *MC, V.*

$$$–$$$$
Fodor'sChoice
★
▦ **The Inn at Occidental.** Quilts, folk art, and original paintings and photographs fill this colorful and friendly inn. Some rooms—such as the Cirque du Sonoma Room, with a bright yellow-and-red color scheme—brim with personality and others are more sedate; all are comfortable and have fireplaces. Most guest rooms are spacious and have private decks and jetted tubs. An air of relaxed refinement prevails amid the whimsical antiques and fine Asian rugs in the ground-floor living room, where guests gather for evening hors d'oeuvres and wine. The two-bedroom Sonoma Cottage, which allows pets for an additional fee, goes for $625 a night. ⊠ *3657 Church St., 95465* ☎ *707/874–1047 or 800/522–6324* 🖷 *707/874–1078* ⊕ *www.innatoccidental.com* ⇗ *13*

rooms, 3 suites, 1 cottage ⚒ 1 in-room hot tub, some refrigerators, in-room data ports, Internet room, some pets allowed (fee); no room TVs, no smoking ▤ AE, D, DC, MC, V ⱓ BP.

Jenner

❽ *10 mi north of Bodega Bay on Hwy. 1.*

The broad, lazy Russian River empties into the Pacific Ocean at Jenner, a wide spot in the road where the houses are sprinkled up a mountainside high above the sea. Facing south, the village looks across the river's mouth to **Goat Rock State Beach**, home to a colony of sea lions for most of the year; pupping season is March through June. The beach, accessed for free off Highway 1 a couple of miles south of town, is open daily from 8 AM to sunset. Bring binoculars and walk north from the parking lot to view the sea lions.

A 10-minute drive up the Russian River Valley via Highway 116, **Duncans Mills** is a restored 19th-century railroad town with a small history museum. A few browsable shops and galleries, a bakery, and a café make it easy to spend an hour or two here; a kayaking outfitter can take you out on the river. In the evening, the Blue Heron Tavern (☎ 707/865–9135), with a popular dinner-only restaurant and a serious lineup of blues, folk, and acoustic artists, is the place to be.

Where to Stay & Eat

$$–$$$$ ✕ **River's End.** A magnificent ocean view makes lunch or an evening here memorable. Come for cocktails and Hog Island oysters on the half shell and hope for a splashy sunset. If you stay for dinner, choose from elaborate entrées such as grilled wild king salmon on cucumber noodles or elk with a red-wine-poached pear and Gorgonzola. The execution may not always justify the prices and the dining room is plain-jane, but just look at that view. Open hours sometimes vary, so call to confirm. River's End also rents out a few ocean-view rooms and cabins ($–$$$). ✉ *11048 Hwy. 1* ☎ *707/865–2484* ▤ *MC, V* ⊘ *Closed Tues. and Wed. Apr.–June and Sept. and Oct. Closed Mon.–Thurs. Nov.–Mar. Closed Jan. 3–early Feb.*

$–$$$$ ⌂ **Jenner Inn.** Checking into one of the rooms or cottages scattered around town is like arriving at someone's home: the decor is a hodgepodge of mismatched furniture, antiques, and patterned fabrics. One room might have cedar-plank walls and a wraparound deck, another might have bay windows and a fireplace. Accommodations range from comfortable to shabby: if possible, look at a few rooms before you commit. Guests gather in the rambling main lodge for breakfast in the window-lined salon, yoga classes in the circular studio, and drinks on the vintage velvet couches of the Fireside Lounge. The Mystic Isle Cafe serves healthful fare. ✉ *10400 Hwy. 1, 95450* ☎ *707/865–2377 or 800/732–2377* ⊕ *www.jennerinn.com* ⇨ *10 rooms, 10 suites, 6 cottages, 1 house ⚒ Restaurant, some in-room hot tubs, some kitchens, some kitchenettes, fitness classes, outdoor hot tubs, massage, boccie, bar, Internet room, meeting rooms, some pets allowed (fee); no phones in some rooms, no room TVs ▤ AE, MC, V* ⱓ *CP.*

Fort Ross State Historic Park

🐾 **9** *12 mi north of Jenner on Hwy. 1.*

Fort Ross, established in 1812, became Russia's major outpost in California, meant to produce crops and other supplies for northerly fur-trading operations. The Russians brought Aleut sea-otter hunters down from Alaska. By 1841 the area was depleted of seals and otters, and the Russians sold their post to John Sutter, later of gold-rush fame. After a local Anglo rebellion against the Mexicans, the land fell under U.S. domain, becoming part of California in 1850. The state park service has reconstructed Fort Ross, including its Russian Orthodox chapel, a redwood stockade, the officers' barracks, and a blockhouse. The excellent museum here documents the history of the fort and this part of the North Coast. ⊠ *19005 Hwy. 1* ☎ *707/847–3286* ✉ *$4 per vehicle* ☉ *Daily 10–4:30* ☞ *No dogs allowed past parking lot and picnic area.*

Where to Stay & Eat

$–$$$$ ✕🏠 **Timber Cove Inn.** Take a funky 1970s ski lodge, slip it into a weathered redwood-and-glass skin, anchor it to a craggy Sonoma Coast cliff, and you're here. Some guest rooms open onto a gallery suspended from the cross-beamed ceiling over the soaring lobby, where a long bar sidles up to a massive rock fireplace. Most rooms offset dated appointments and clunky furniture with ocean views and raw wood flourishes. The best have freestanding fireplaces and big Jacuzzis tucked into tiled corners or placed before sliding-glass doors; the worst have seen better days. A crew of resident raccoons waddles boldly about, as if they own the place. Picture-windowed and rock-walled, the restaurant ($$–$$$$) is the only one between Jenner and Sea Ranch. ⊠ *21780 Hwy. 1, 3 mi north of Fort Ross State Historic Park, Jenner 95450* ☎ *707/847–3231 or 800/987–8319* 🖶 *707/847–3704* ⊕ *www.timbercoveinn.com* ⇨ *50 rooms* ♨ *Restaurant, in-room hot tubs, cable TV, in-room data ports, hiking, lobby lounge, piano, shop; no a/c, no smoking* ▭ *AE, MC, V.*

Salt Point State Park

10 *6 mi north of Fort Ross on Hwy. 1.*

For 5 mi, Highway 1 winds through this park, 6,000 acres of forest washed by the sound of surf pounding on the rocky shore. Hiking trails lead past seals sunning themselves at Gerstle Cove, and through meadows where birds flit through wild brush. Don't miss the unusual *tafonis*—honeycomb patterns in the sandstone caused by centuries of wind and rain erosion—at Fisk Mill Cove in the north end of the park. A five-minute walk uphill from the parking lot leads to a dramatic view of Sentinel Rock, an excellent spot for sunsets. South Gerstle Cove's picnic area overlooks the water. ⊠ *20705 Hwy. 1* ☎ *707/847–3221* ✉ *$4 per vehicle* ☉ *Daily sunrise–sunset.*

Adjacent to Salt Point State Park, thousands of rhododendrons bloom in late spring within **Kruse Rhododendron State Reserve.** To reach the peaceful 317-acre evergreen preserve you must drive 4 mi of narrow, unpaved road. ✉ *Kruse Ranch Rd. off Hwy. 1, north of Fisk Mill Cove* ☎ *707/847–3221* 🖾 *Free.*

Where to Stay & Eat

★ **$$$–$$$$** ✕🛏 **Sea Ranch Lodge.** Wide-open vistas and minimalist design keep the focus on nature at this tranquil lodge 8 mi north of Salt Point State Park. Picture windows—some with window seats—overlook trails along the bluff and out to a lofty point. Plank-paneled walls and ceilings, goose-down comforters, and robes make large rooms cozy on foggy nights, though bathrooms are small. The noteworthy restaurant ($$–$$$) serves such seasonal fare as wild mushroom risotto with baby leek and fennel confit and braised venison with creamy herbed polenta; there is also a bar menu. A lobby office handles vacation rentals in surrounding Sea Ranch, 10 mi of coastline where architects designed the homes to harmonize with the environment. ✉ *60 Sea Walk Dr., Sea Ranch 95497* ☎ *707/785–2371 or 800/732–7262* 🖨 *707/785–2917* ⊕ *www.searanchlodge.com* 📑 *20 rooms* ♿ *Restaurant, 18-hole golf course, massage, beach, hiking, bar, lounge, shop, babysitting, concierge, business services, meeting rooms, some pets allowed; no TV in some rooms, no smoking* 🖃 *AE, MC, V* 🍴 *BP.*

⚠ **Salt Point State Park Campgrounds.** There are two excellent campsites in the park. Gerstle Cove campground, on the west side of Highway 1, is set on a wooded hill with some sites overlooking the ocean. Woodside campground offers more trees and protection from the wind; it is on the east side of Highway 1. Woodside is closed December–March 15. Reservations are accepted March–October. ♿ *Flush toilets, drinking water, fire grates, picnic tables* 📑 *Gerstle Cove, 30 sites; Woodside, 79 sites* ✉ *20705 Hwy. 1, 95450* ☎ *800/444–7275* 🖾 *$25.*

THE MENDOCINO COAST

The timber industry gave birth to most of the small towns strung along this stretch of the California coastline. Although tourism now drives the economy, the region has retained much of its old-fashioned charm. The beauty of the coastal landscape, of course, has not changed.

Gualala

⓫ *16 mi north of Salt Point State Park on Hwy. 1.*

This former lumber port on the Gualala River has become an appealing headquarters for exploring the coast. The busiest town between Bodega Bay and Mendocino, it has all the basic services plus a number of galleries and gift shops. Stop by the **Gualala Arts Center** (✉ 46501 Gualala Rd. ☎ 707/884–1138 ⊕ www.gualalaarts.org ⊙ Weekdays 9–4, weekends noon–4) to see free rotating exhibits of regional art. The third weekend in August the center is the site of Art in the Redwoods, a festival that includes a juried exhibition.

Gualala Point Regional Park (✉ 1 mi south of Gualala on Hwy. 1 ☎ 707/785–2377 ⊙ Daily 8 AM–sunset) has picnic areas ($3 day-use fee) and is an excellent whale-watching spot December through April.

Where to Stay & Eat

$$$ ✕ **Pangaea.** Some of Gualala's best organic, seasonal food is prepared in the artsy jewel-colored dining rooms of this little log cabin. The well-traveled chef serves imaginative dishes such as lavender duck breast with gold beets and rainbow chard and wood oven–roasted pork chop with peach-mango salsa. If available, a plate of braised artichokes with preserved lemon and celery root is an auspicious start. Intelligent and well priced, the wine list balances local and European selections. ✉ *39165 Hwy. 1* ☎ *707/884–9669* ▭ *MC, V* ⊙ *No lunch seasonally. Closed Mon. and Tues.*

¢ ✕ **Café LaLa.** Under the clock tower in the Cypress Village shopping center, you can have breakfast or lunch with an ocean view. Along with the standards, choose from bagels stuffed with whatever you want, a long menu of salads, and creative sandwiches. Sip your espresso or chai on the patio. ✉ *39150 Ocean Dr.* ☎ *707/884–1104* ▭ *No credit cards* ⊙ *No dinner.*

$–$$$$ ✕▣ **St. Orres.** Resembling a traditional Russian dacha, with two onion-domed towers, this intriguing lodge stands on 42 acres of redwood forest and meadow scattered with an eclectic collection of cottages. Woodsy to grand, each has different amenities, such as ocean views, fireplaces or woodstoves, saunas, and Jacuzzis. Fetchingly snug wood-lined rooms in the main building share large baths. In the tower dining room, a spectacular atrium beneath an onion dome, locally farmed and foraged ingredients appear as garlic flan with black chanterelles, Dijon-crusted rack of lamb, and the like. Prix fixe ($40) includes soup and salad but not appetizer or dessert (available à la carte). ✉ *36601 Hwy. 1, 3 mi north of Gualala, 95445* ☎ *707/884–3303* ▤ *707/884–1840* ⊕ *www.saintorres.com* ⇨ *8 rooms with shared bath, 13 cottages* ⌂ *Restaurant, some in-room hot tubs, some kitchenettes, some refrigerators, hot tub, sauna, beach; no room phones, no room TVs, no smoking* ▭ *MC, V* ⊙ *No lunch* ⦿ *BP.*

¢–$ ✕▣ **Gualala Hotel.** The yellow, porch-fronted hotel in the center of town has operated since 1903. Decorated to evoke the early 20th century, the public spaces and small rooms are furnished with antiques and accented with period wallpaper and lace curtains. Rates are low because most rooms share old-fashioned baths. In the dining room (¢–$$), all-American breakfast and lunch menus give way to red-sauce Italian favorites at dinner. The scruffy first-floor saloon is the town's main watering hole. ✉ *39301 Hwy. 1* ☎ *707/884–3441 or 888/482–5252* ▤ *707/884–1054* ⊕ *www.gualalahotel.com* ⇨ *19 rooms, 14 with shared bath* ⌂ *Restaurant, Wi-Fi, billiards, bar, piano; no room TVs, no room phones* ▭ *AE, D, MC, V.*

$$–$$$ ▣ **Mar Vista Cottages.** The dozen 1930s cottages at Mar Vista have been beautifully restored. Intentionally slim on modern gadgetry (no TV, phone, radio, or even a clock), the thoughtfully appointed and sparkling clean cottages are big on retro charm: windows are hung with embroidered drapes, coffee percolates on a white enamel stove in the full, if diminutive, kitchen, and straw sun hats hang from hooks, ready for your walk down to Fish Rock Beach. Some have wood-burning or gas stoves. Outside, where benches overlook the blustery coastline, you can snip fresh greens from the organic garden for your supper. ✉ *35101 S. Hwy 1, 5 mi north of Gualala, 95445* ☎ *707/884–3522 or 877/855–3522*

☏ *707/884–4861* ⊕ *www.marvistamendocino.com* ⇆ *8 1-bedroom cottages, 4 2-bedroom cottages* ⚲ *Kitchens, outdoor hot tub, beach; no room phones, no room TVs, no smoking* ☰ *AE, MC, V.*

$$ ⌂ **Seacliff on the Bluff.** Wedged behind a downtown shopping center it's not much to look at, and the interiors are motel standard, but you'll spend your time here staring at the Pacific panorama. Surprising extras ice the cake: take the binoculars out to your balcony or patio; stay in and watch the sunset from your jetted tub; snuggle into a robe and pop that complimentary champagne before your gas fireplace. Upstairs rooms have cathedral ceilings. ✉ *39140 Hwy. 1, 95445* ☏ *707/884–1213 or 800/ 400–5053* ☐ *707/884–1731* ⊕ *www.seacliffmotel.com* ⇆ *16 rooms* ⚲ *Cable TV, refrigerators, Internet room, airport shuttle* ☰ *MC, V.*

3

EN ROUTE For a dramatic view of the surf and, in winter, migrating whales, take the marked road off Highway 1 north of the fishing village of Point Arena to the 115-foot **Point Arena Lighthouse** (☏ 707/882–2777). The lighthouse is open for tours daily from 10 until 3:30, until 4:30 in summer; admission is $5. As you continue north on Highway 1 toward Elk, you'll pass several beaches, most notably the one at **Manchester State Park,** 3 mi north of Point Arena.

Elk

⑫ *33 mi north of Gualala on Hwy. 1.*

There's not much happening on the streets of this former timber town, but that's exactly why people love it. The beautiful, rocky coastline is the perfect place for romance or quiet escape.

Where to Stay & Eat

★ **$$$$** ✕ **Inn at Victorian Gardens.** Among the most coveted dinner reservations on the North Coast are those you need to dine at this big white country inn 13 mi south of Elk. Luciano and Pauline Zamboni present authentic multicourse celebrations of Italian regional cuisine ($150 per couple, including wines) that feel more like intimate parties than restaurant meals. There are four inn rooms upstairs, which are lovely but nearly impossible to book; it's a better idea to call a month in advance for a dinner reservation and expect to stay somewhere else. ✉ *14409 S. Hwy. 1, Manchester, 95459* ☏ *707/882–3606* ⊕ *www.innatvictoriangardens. com* ☰ *MC, V* ⊘ *Closed Mon. No lunch* ⚲ *Reservations essential.*

$$$$ ✕⌂ **Harbor House.** Constructed in 1916, this redwood Craftsman-style house is as elegant as its location is rugged. Rooms in the main house are decorated with antiques and have gas fireplaces. The newer cottages are luxurious; each has a fireplace and deck. Room rates include breakfast and a four-course dinner (except on weeknights during January and February, when the rates drop drastically). The ocean-view restaurant ($$$$; reservations essential), which serves California cuisine on a prix-fixe menu, is excellent, but seating for nonguests is limited. ✉ *5600 S. Hwy. 1, 95432* ☏ *707/877–3203 or 800/720–7474* ⊕ *www. theharborhouseinn.com* ⇆ *6 rooms, 4 cottages* ⚲ *Restaurant; no room phones, no room TVs* ☰ *AE, MC, V* ⦿ *MAP.*

★ **$$–$$$$**   ✕🖼 **Elk Cove Inn & Spa.** Perched on a bluff above pounding surf and a driftwood-strewn beach, this property has stunning views from most rooms. Spread among four cottages and a grand main house, accommodations are each unique and decorated in soothing tones. Suites have stereos and fireplaces; most have wood-burning stoves. A stone-and-cedar-shingle Arts-and-Crafts–style building houses plush spa suites ($370–$395) with cathedral ceilings. Relax with a massage in the small spa or a cocktail at the bar. 'Zebo restaurant fuses California, Southern, and international flavors. ✉ *6300 S. Hwy. 1, 95432* ☎ *707/877–3321 or 800/ 275–2967* 🖷 *707/877–1808* ⊕ *www.elkcoveinn.com* 🛏 *7 rooms, 4 suites, 4 cottages* ♨ *Some in-room hot tubs, some microwaves, some refrigerators, spa, beach, bar; no room TVs* ▤ *AE, D, MC, V* ⦿⊦ *BP.*

Albion

⓭ *10 mi north of Elk on Hwy. 1.*

A hamlet nestled next to its namesake river, Albion has played host to many visitors—from the original settlers, the Pomo Indians, to Sir Francis Drake in the late 16th century, to Russian fur traders three centuries later. Over the years fires have destroyed most of the town's historical buildings, so the town today is defined by its most recent settlers, many of whom are staunch environmentalists. It is quieter and less touristy than the neighboring towns to the north.

Where to Stay & Eat

$$–$$$ ✕ **Ledford House.** The only thing separating this bluff-top wood-and-glass restaurant from the Pacific Ocean is a great view. Entrées evoke the flavors of southern France and include hearty bistro dishes— stews, cassoulets, and pastas—and large portions of grilled meats and freshly caught fish. The long bar, with its unobstructed water view, is a scenic spot for a sunset aperitif. ✉ *3000 N. Hwy. 1* ☎ *707/937– 0282* ⊕ *www.ledfordhouse.com* ▤ *AE, DC, MC, V* ⊘ *Closed Mon. and Tues. No lunch.*

$$$–$$$$ ✕🖼 **Albion River Inn.** Contemporary New England–style cottages at this inn overlook the dramatic bridge and seascape where the Albion River empties into the Pacific. All but two have decks facing the ocean. Six have spa tubs with ocean views; all have fireplaces. The traditional, homey rooms are filled with antiques; at the glassed-in restaurant ($$–$$$), the grilled meats and fresh seafood are as captivating as the views. ✉ *3790 N. Hwy. 1, 95410* ☎ *707/937–1919 or 800/479–7944* 🖷 *707/ 937–2604* ⊕ *www.albionriverinn.com* 🛏 *22 rooms* ♨ *Restaurant, some in-room hot tubs, refrigerators, concierge; no smoking* ▤ *AE, D, DC, MC, V* ⊘ *No lunch* ⦿⊦ *BP.*

Little River

⓮ *4 mi north of Albion on Hwy. 1.*

Van Damme State Park is best known for its beach and for being a prime abalone diving spot. Upland trails lead through lush riparian habitat and the bizarre Pygmy Forest, where acidic soil and poor drainage have produced mature cypress and pine trees that are no taller than a person.

The visitor center has displays on ocean life and Native American history. There's a $4 day-use fee. ⊠ *Hwy. 1* ☎ *707/937–5804 for park, 707/937–4016 for visitor center* ⊕ *www.parks.ca.gov.*

Where to Stay & Eat

$$–$$$ ✕ **Restaurant at Little River Inn.** There are fewer than a dozen entrées on this inn's menu, but they're all very good; if you're lucky, the choices might include loin of California lamb, locally caught salmon, or grilled polenta with vegetables. Main courses come with soup or salad. Less expensive lighter fare is served in the ocean-view Ole's Whale Watch Bar. Swedish hotcakes are the specialty at breakfast. The adjoining resort ($–$$$$) has a wide variety of accommodations, from small inn rooms to oceanfront suites with hot tubs on ocean-view decks. ⊠ *7901 N. Hwy. 1* ☎ *707/937–5942 or 888/466–5683* ▤ *AE, MC, V* ⊘ *No lunch.*

$$–$$$$ ✕▣ **Heritage House.** Every part of this rambling oceanside resort has a stunning view. The decor ranges from frilly to tastefully spare. The real draw is the amenities—many units have private decks, fireplaces, and whirlpool tubs. The restaurant's ($$$–$$$$) old-world formality is unusual on the North Coast. Cioppino or a veal porterhouse chop might precede the elegant desserts. The restaurant is closed from early December through mid-February. ⊠ *5200 N. Hwy. 1, 95456* ☎ *707/937–5885 or 800/235–5885* 🖷 *707/937–0318* ⊕ *www.heritagehouseinn.com* 🛏 *56 rooms, 10 suites* ⌂ *Restaurant, some in-room hot tubs, massage, beach, lounge, concierge; no room phones, no room TVs* ▤ *AE, MC, V* ⊘ *No lunch* ▯◌▯ *BP.*

★ **$$–$$$$** ▣ **Glendeven Inn.** If Mendocino is the New England village of the West Coast, then Glendeven is the local country manor. The main house was built in 1867 and is surrounded by acres of gardens. Inside are five guest rooms, three with fireplaces. A converted barn holds an art gallery. The 1986 Stevenscroft building, with its high gabled roof, contains four rooms with fireplaces. The carriage-house suite makes for a romantic retreat. La Bella Vista, a two-bedroom house, is the only accommodation appropriate for families. ⊠ *8205 N. Hwy. 1, 95456* ☎ *707/937–0083 or 800/822–4536* 🖷 *707/937–6108* ⊕ *www.glendeven.com* 🛏 *6 rooms, 4 suites, 1 house* ⌂ *Wi-Fi, shop; no room phones, no TVs in some rooms* ▤ *AE, D, MC, V* ▯◌▯ *BP.*

Mendocino

⓯ *3 mi north of Little River on Hwy. 1; 153 mi from San Francisco, north on U.S. 101, west on Hwy. 128, and north on Hwy. 1.*

Many of Mendocino's original settlers came from the Northeast and built houses in the New England style. Thanks to the logging boom the town flourished for most of the second half of the 19th century. As the timber industry declined, many residents left, but the town's setting was too beautiful to be ignored. Artists and craftspeople began flocking here in the 1950s, and Elia Kazan chose Mendocino as the backdrop for his 1955 film adaptation of John Steinbeck's *East of Eden,* starring James Dean. As the arts community thrived, restaurants, cafés, and inns started to open. Today, the small downtown area consists almost entirely of places to eat and shop.

The restored **Ford House,** built in 1854, serves as the visitor center for Mendocino Headlands State Park. The house has a scale model of Mendocino as it looked in 1890, when the town had 34 water towers and a 12-seat public outhouse. From the museum, you can head out on a 3-mi trail across the spectacular seaside cliffs that border the town. ⊠ *Main St. west of Lansing St.* ☎ *707/937–5397* 🎫 *Free, $2 donation suggested* ⊘ *Daily 11–4.*

An 1861 structure holds the **Kelley House Museum,** whose artifacts include Victorian-era furniture and historical photographs of Mendocino's logging days. ⊠ *45007 Albion St.* ☎ *707/937–5791* ⊕ *mendocinohistory.org* 🎫 *$2* ⊘ *June–Sept., daily 1–4; Oct.–May, Fri.–Mon. 1–4.*

The **Mendocino Art Center** (⊠ 45200 Little Lake St. ☎ 707/937–5818 or 800/653–3328 ⊕ www.mendocinoartcenter.org), which has an extensive program of workshops, also mounts rotating exhibits in its galleries and is the home of the Mendocino Theatre Company.

Where to Stay & Eat

$$$–$$$$ ✕ **Cafe Beaujolais.** The Victorian cottage that houses this popular restaurant is surrounded by a garden of heirloom and exotic plantings. A commitment to the freshest possible organic, local, and hormone-free ingredients guides the chef here. The menu is eclectic and ever-evolving, but often includes free-range fowl, line-caught fish, and edible flowers. The bakery turns out several delicious varieties of bread from a wood-fired oven. The restaurant typically closes for a month or more in winter. ⊠ *961 Ukiah St.* ☎ *707/937–5614* ⊕ *www.cafebeaujolais.com* ▭ *D, MC, V* ⊘ *No lunch.*

FodorsChoice
★

$$–$$$$ ✕ **955 Ukiah Street Restaurant.** A homey, woodsy interior and creative California cuisine make this spot a perennial favorite. Specialties of the house include fresh fish—depending on the catch, weekly offerings change—peppercorn New York steak, and spinach-and–red chard ravioli. When available, flourless chocolate-rum torte is a dangerous way to end the evening. ⊠ *955 Ukiah St.* ☎ *707/937–1955* ⊕ *www.955restaurant.com* ▭ *MC, V* ⊘ *Closed Mon. and Tues. No lunch.*

★ $$$$ ✕▥ **Stanford Inn by the Sea.** This woodsy yet luxurious family-run property a few minutes south of town feels like the Northern California version of an old-time summer resort. Several lodge buildings house guest rooms that range from cozy to chic, many with ocean views, fireplaces, and paintings by local artists. On the spacious, dog-friendly grounds you'll find organic gardens, llamas, and a sandy river beach where you can rent a kayak or canoe and head 8 mi upstream. Yoga classes and in-room massages and body wraps are complemented by the sophisticated vegetarian cuisine at The Ravens restaurant ($$–$$$). Breakfast is vegetarian, too. ⊠ *Comptche-Ukiah Rd. east of Hwy. 1, 95460* ☎ *707/937–5615 or 800/331–8884* 🖷 *707/937–0305* ⊕ *www.stanfordinn.com* 🛏 *31 rooms, 10 suites* ⚘ *Restaurant, refrigerators, cable TV with movies, in-room VCRs, in-room data ports, Wi-Fi, indoor pool, hot tub, massage, sauna, beach, bicycles, bar, Internet room, business services, pets allowed (fee); no smoking* ▭ *AE, D, DC, MC, V* ⅋️ *BP.*

$$-$$$
Fodor's Choice
★ ✕⌂ **MacCallum House.** Rosebushes, some planted by the original owner in the late 1800s, dot the inn's 2 acres in the middle of town. Rooms in the several buildings vary in character: the main house feels genteel, the cottages are bright and honeymoon-y, and the renovated barn and water tower are cedar walled. Suites ($265–$350) are more lavish yet; two cottages and a two-bedroom house ($350) give you complete privacy. At the excellent restaurant ($$$–$$$$; reservations essential), the dishes highlight local ingredients and are prepared daily from scratch. The informal café serves lighter fare. The restaurant is closed early January through mid-February. ⊠ *45020 Albion St., 95460* ☏ *707/937–0289 or 800/609–0492* ⊕ *www.maccallumhouse.com* ⚲ *15 rooms, 9 suites, 2 cottages, 1 house* ⚭ *Restaurant, cafe, cable TV, in-room DVD, some in-room broadband, in-room data ports, Wi-Fi, outdoor hot tub, massage, bicycles, bar, concierge, Internet room, pets allowed (fee)* ▭ *AE, D, MC, V* ☾ *No lunch* ⦿ *BP.*

$$-$$$$ ✕⌂ **Mendocino Hotel & Garden Suites.** From the outside, this hotel's period facade and wide balcony make it look like something out of the Wild West. Inside, though, the stained-glass lamps, polished wood, and Persian rugs are more lumber-baron. Stay in an atmospheric room in the restored 1878 main building or in a larger, modern garden room out back; these rooms have TV and some have a fireplace. The wood-paneled restaurant ($$$–$$$$), fronted by a solarium, serves fine fish entrées and the best deep-dish ollalieberry pie in California. ⊠ *45080 Main St., 95460* ☏ *707/937–0511 or 800/548–0513* ⊟ *707/937–0513* ⊕ *www.mendocinohotel.com* ⚲ *45 rooms, 14 with shared bath; 6 suites* ⚭ *Restaurant, room service, cable TV, bar, meeting rooms; no TV in some rooms* ▭ *AE, MC, V.*

$$-$$$$ ⌂ **Alegria.** A pathway from the back porch to Big River Beach makes this the only oceanfront lodging in Mendocino. Each room has something special and unique: beautiful bamboo floors; a woodstove; sunset views from a perfectly positioned window seat. Despite its central location, the property is more private than others in town; it feels like a quiet retreat. The hot tub, surrounded by jasmine vines, is wonderful at night. ⊠ *44781 Main St., 95460* ☏ *707/937–5150 or 800/780–7905* ⊕ *www.oceanfrontmagic.com* ⚲ *7 rooms* ⚭ *Some kitchenettes, some microwaves, refrigerators, cable TV, in-room DVD/VCR, outdoor hot tub, beach* ▭ *AE, MC, V* ⦿ *BP.*

$$-$$$ ⌂ **Blackberry Inn.** It sounds hokier than it is: each unit here has a false front with an Old West theme—bank, saloon, sheriff's office, Belle's Place (of hospitality), and the like. Within, though, the frontier motif gives way to cheery, spacious rooms with only a vaguely Western flavor. Most have wood-burning stoves or fireplaces and at least partial ocean views. The inn is a short drive east of town down a quiet side street. ⊠ *44951 Larkin Rd., 95460* ☏ *707/937–5281 or 800/950–7806* ⊕ *www.blackberryinn.biz* ⚲ *16 rooms, 1 cottage* ⚭ *Some kitchenettes, some refrigerators, cable TV, in-room data ports, some pets allowed (fee); no smoking* ▭ *MC, V* ⦿ *CP.*

Nightlife & the Arts

Mendocino Theatre Company (⊠ Mendocino Art Center, 42500 Little Lake St. ☏ 707/937–4477 ⊕ www.mcn.org/1/mtc) has been around for nearly three decades. Their repertoire ranges all over the contemporary map, including works by David Mamet, Neil Simon, and local playwrights. Performances take place Thursday through Sunday evenings, with some Sunday matinees.

Patterson's Pub (⊠ 10485 Lansing St. ☎ 707/937–4782), an Irish-style watering hole, is a friendly gathering place day (there's garden seating) or night, though it becomes boisterous as the evening wears on. Bands entertain on Friday night.

Sports & the Outdoors

Catch-A-Canoe and Bicycles Too (⊠ Stanford Inn by the Sea, Comptche-Ukiah Rd., off Hwy. 1 ☎ 707/937–0273) rents kayaks and regular and outrigger canoes as well as mountain and suspension bicycles.

Fort Bragg

🔞 *10 mi north of Mendocino on Hwy. 1.*

The commercial center of Mendocino County, Fort Bragg has undergone quite a few changes in the past several years, largely because the declining timber industry has been steadily replaced by booming tourism. The city has also attracted many artists, some of whom have left Mendocino seeking coastal serenity at a lower price.

★ The **Mendocino Coast Botanical Gardens** has something for nature lovers in every season. Even in winter, heather and camellias bloom. Along 2 mi of trails with ocean views and observation points for whale-watching is a splendid profusion of flowers. The rhododendrons are at their peak from April through June, and the dahlias are spectacular in August. ⊠ *18220 N. Hwy. 1, 1 mi south of Fort Bragg* ☎ *707/964–4352* ⊕ *www.gardenbythesea.org* 🎟 *$7.50* ☉ *Mar.–Oct., daily 9–5; Nov.–Feb., daily 9–4.*

Back in the 1920s, a fume-spewing gas-powered train car used to shuttle passengers along a rail line dating from the logging days of the 1880s. Nicknamed the **Skunk Train**, it traversed redwood forests inaccessible to automobiles. The reproduction that you can ride today travels the same route, making a 3½-hour round-trip between Fort Bragg and the town of Northspur, 21 mi inland. The schedule varies depending on the season and in summer includes evening barbecue excursions and wine parties. ⊠ *Foot of Laurel St. (west of Main St.)* ☎ *707/964–6371 or 800/866–1690* ⊕ *www.skunktrain.com* 🎟 *$20–$55.*

★ **MacKerricher State Park** includes 9 mi of sandy beach and several square miles of dunes. The headland is a good place for whale-watching from December to mid-April. Fishing (at a freshwater lake stocked with trout), canoeing, hiking, jogging, bicycling, beachcombing, camping, and harbor seal–watching at Laguna Point are among the popular activities, many of which are accessible to the mobility-impaired. Rangers lead nature hikes in summer. ⊠ *Hwy. 1, 3 mi north of Fort Bragg* ☎ *707/964–9112* 🎟 *Free.*

Where to Stay & Eat

$$–$$$ ✕ **Rendezvous Inn.** Applying sophisticated European technique to fresh seasonal ingredients, chef Kim Badenhop turns out a Northern California interpretation of country French cooking. To start you might try Dungeness crab bisque finished with brandy, then follow with pheasant pot-au-feu with black chanterelles and glazed fall root vegetables. A sense of well-being prevails in the redwood-paneled dining room, where service is never rushed. ✉ *647 N. Main St.* ☎ *707/964–8142 or 800/491–8142* ▭ *D, MC, V* ☺ *Closed Mon. and Tues. No lunch.*

¢–$$ ✕ **Mendo Bistro.** The constant buzz from this popular restaurant spills out from the second floor of the Company Store complex downtown. Pasta is made fresh on the premises here; a house specialty is rigatoni with Italian sausage, capers, and roasted peppers. Order an entrée off the menu or choose your protein (meat, fish, tofu), cooking method (grilling, roasting, etc.), and sauce; your masterpiece will arrive with the evening's mashed potatoes or polenta and seasonal vegetables. ✉ *301 N. Main St.* ☎ *707/964–4974* ▭ *AE, D, DC, MC, V* ☺ *No lunch.*

$$–$$$ ▦ **Weller House Inn.** Rooms in this 1886 mansion are decorated with Victorian-style wallpaper and furnishings; the baths have hand-painted tiles. The third-floor breakfast room, which is 900 square feet and paneled in California redwood, was once a ballroom. Newer accommodations are in a water tower on the property—at 51 feet the tallest building in town—topped by a hot tub with spectacular ocean views. Guest rooms have jacks but no phones; request one if you need a lifeline. ✉ *524 Stewart St., 95437* ☎ *707/964–4415 or 877/893–5537* ▤ *707/961–1281* ⊕ *www.wellerhouse.com* ⇝ *9 rooms* ♿ *Some microwaves, some refrigerators, hot tub; no room phones, no TV in some rooms, no smoking* ▭ *AE, D, DC, MC, V* ¶❋ *BP.*

$–$$$ ▦ **Surf and Sand Lodge.** As its name implies, this hotel sits practically right on the beach; pathways lead from the property down to the rock-strewn shore. All rooms are bright and clean, although the six least expensive don't have views. The nicest of the second-story rooms have jetted tubs and fireplaces. ✉ *1131 N. Main St., 95437* ☎ *707/964–9383 or 800/964–0184* ▤ *707/964–0314* ⊕ *www.surfsandlodge.com* ⇝ *30 rooms* ♿ *Refrigerators, cable TV, in-room VCRs, beach; no smoking* ▭ *AE, D, MC, V.*

⚠ **MacKerricher State Park.** The campsites here are in woodsy spots about a quarter mile from the ocean. There are no hookups. Make reservations for summer weekends as early as possible (reservations are taken April–mid-October), unless you want to try your luck getting one of the 25 sites that are available on a first-come, first-served basis each day. ♿ *Flush toilets, drinking water, showers, fire pits, picnic tables* ⇝ *150 sites* ✉ *Hwy. 1, 3 mi north of Fort Bragg* ☎ *800/444–7275 for reservations* ▩ *$20.*

Nightlife

Caspar Inn (✉ *14957 Caspar Rd.* ☎ *707/964–5565*) presents DJs or live blues, rock, hip-hop, and alternative rock. If you feel like staying over after a show, there are simple, inexpensive rooms upstairs.

Sports & the Outdoors

All Aboard Adventures (⊠ 32400 N. Harbor Dr. ☎ 707/964–1881 ⊕ www.allaboardadventures.com) operates whale-watching trips from December through mid-April, as well as fishing excursions all year. **Ricochet Ridge Ranch** (⊠ 24201 N. Hwy. 1 ☎ 707/964–7669 ⊕ www.horse-vacation.com) guides private and group trail rides through redwood forest and on the beach.

EN ROUTE

North of Fort Bragg, civilization thins out considerably along the coast. After about 16 mi Highway 1 passes through the mill town of Westport. Before continuing into the wilderness, make a stop at the **Lost Coast Inn** (⊠ 38921 Hwy. 1, Westport ☎ 707/964–5584), a B&B whose bar-coffeehouse has a chess set and friendly resident dog. Highway 1 cuts inland some 15 mi north of Westport to skirt the rugged King Range. Known as the **Lost Coast,** the area bypassed by Highway 1 almost all the way up to Eureka is mostly protected and all but undeveloped. Highway 1 joins U.S. 101 at Leggett. To the north, **Richardson Grove State Park** contains the southernmost of the truly giant redwoods.

REDWOOD COUNTRY
FROM GARBERVILLE TO CRESCENT CITY

The majestic redwoods that grace California's coast become more plentiful as you head north. Their towering ancient presence defines the landscape.

Garberville

⑰ *67 mi north of Fort Bragg and 204 mi north of San Francisco on U.S. 101.*

Although it's the largest town in the vicinity of Humboldt Redwoods State Park, Garberville hasn't changed much since timber was king. The town is a pleasant place to stop for lunch, pick up picnic provisions, or poke through arts-and-crafts stores. A few miles below Garberville is an elegant Tudor resort, the Benbow Inn. Even if you are not staying there, stop in for a drink or a meal; the architecture and gardens are lovely.

Where to Stay & Eat

¢ ✕ **Woodrose Cafe.** This modest eatery serves basic breakfast items until 1 PM on the weekends and breakfast and healthful lunches every weekday. Dishes include chicken, big salads, burritos, and vegetarian specials. ⊠ *911 Redwood Dr.* ☎ *707/923–3191* ▭ *No credit cards* ☺ *No dinner.*

★ $$–$$$$ ✕▥ **Benbow Inn.** South of Garberville alongside the Eel River, this Tudor-style manor resort is the equal of any in the region. The most luxurious of the antiques-filled rooms are on the terrace, with fine river views; some rooms have fireplaces. You have canoeing, tennis, golf, and pool privileges at an adjacent property. The wood-paneled restaurant ($$$) serves American cuisine and specializes in locally caught salmon and trout. ⊠ *445 Lake Benbow Dr., 95542* ☎ *707/923–2124 or 800/355–3301* ⊟ *707/923–2897* ⊕ *www.benbowinn.com* ⇆ *43 rooms, 1 cottage*

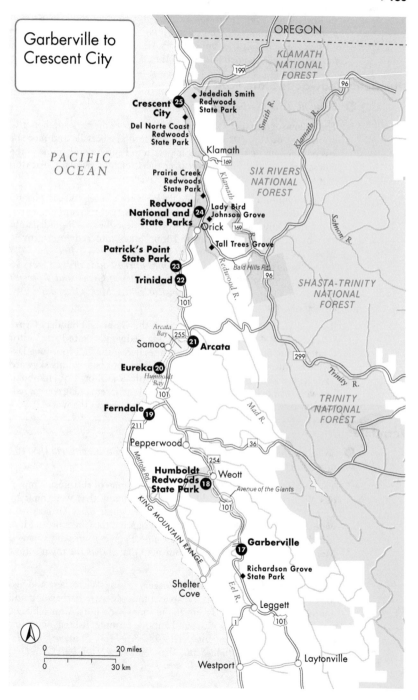

Garberville to
Crescent City

⚘ *Restaurant, some refrigerators, cable TV, some in-room VCRs, golf privileges, lake, massage, bicycles, hiking, lounge, meeting rooms; no TVs in some rooms, no smoking* ▤ *AE, D, MC, V* ⊘ *Closed early Jan.–late Mar. No lunch mid-Sept.–May.*

Humboldt Redwoods State Park

🐾 ⑱ *20 mi north of Garberville on U.S. 101.*

The **Avenue of the Giants** (Highway 254) traverses the park south–north, branching off U.S. 101 about 7 mi north of Garberville and more or less parallelling that road for 33 mi north to Pepperwood. Some of the tallest trees on the planet tower over the stretch of two-lane blacktop that follows the south fork of the Eel River.

At the **Humboldt Redwoods State Park Visitor Center** you can pick up information about the redwoods, waterways, and recreational activities in the 53,000-acre park. One brochure describes a self-guided auto tour of the park, with short and long hikes into redwood groves. ⊠ *Ave. of the Giants, 2 mi south of Weott* ☎ *707/946–2409 park, 707/946–2263 visitor center* ⊕ *www.humboldtredwoods.org* ⊠ *Free; $6 day-use fee for parking and facilities in Williams Grove and Women's Federation Grove* ⊘ *Park daily; visitor center Mar.–Oct., daily 9–5; Nov.–Feb., daily 10–4.*

Reached via a ½-mi trail off Avenue of the Giants is **Founders Grove** (⊠ Hwy. 254, 4 mi north of Humboldt Redwoods State Park Visitor Center). One of the most impressive trees here—the 362-foot-long Dyerville Giant—fell to the ground in 1991; its root base points skyward 35 feet. **Rockefeller Forest** (⊠ Mattole Rd., 6 mi north of Humboldt Redwoods State Park Visitor Center) is the largest remaining coastal redwood forest. It contains 40 of the 100 tallest trees in the world.

Ferndale

⑲ *35 mi northwest of Weott, 57 mi northwest of Garberville via U.S. 101 north to Hwy. 211 west.*

The residents of this stately town maintain some of the most sumptuous Victorian homes in California. Of the many that were built by 19th-century Scandinavian, Swiss, and Portuguese dairy farmers who were drawn to the area's mild climate, the queen is the Gingerbread Mansion, built in 1899. The mansion, now a B&B, gives tours daily noon–4. Many shops carry a self-guided tour map that shows the town's most interesting historical buildings.

The main building of the **Ferndale Museum** exhibits Victoriana and historical photographs and has a display of an old-style barbershop and another of Wiyot Indian baskets. In the annex are a horse-drawn buggy, a re-created blacksmith's shop, and antique farming, fishing, and dairy equipment. ⊠ *515 Shaw Ave.* ☎ *707/786–4466* ⊕ *www.ferndale-museum.org* ⊠ *$1* ⊘ *June–Sept., Tues.–Sat. 11–4, Sun. 1–4; Oct.–Dec. and Feb.–May, Wed.–Sat. 11–4, Sun. 1–4.*

Eel River Delta Tours (✉ 285 Morgan Slough Rd. ☎ 707/786–4187) conducts two-hour boat trips that examine the wildlife and history of the Eel River's estuary and salt marsh.

Where to Stay

$$–$$$$ ⌂ **Gingerbread Mansion.** This beautifully restored Victorian is dazzling enough to rival San Francisco's "painted ladies." The exterior has detailed spindlework, turrets, and gables; inside, the guest rooms are decorated in plush, flowery period splendor. Some rooms have views of the mansion's English garden; one has side-by-side bathtubs. One particularly posh suite is the Veneto, which has hand-painted scenes of Venice on the walls and ceiling as well as marble floors. ✉ 400 Berding St., off Brown St., 95536 ☎ 707/786–4000 or 800/952–4136 ⊕ www. gingerbread-mansion.com ⌁ 11 rooms, 4 suites ⌂ No room phones, no room TVs, no smoking ⊟ AE, MC, V ⊙ BP.

Shopping

Among the shops along Main Street, **Golden Gait Mercantile** (✉ 421 Main St. ☎ 707/786–4891) seems to have been left back in time; it sells Burma Shave products and old-fashioned long johns as well as penny candy.

Eureka

⓴ 18 mi north of Ferndale, 66 mi north of Garberville on U.S. 101.

With a population of 26,381, Eureka is the North Coast's largest city. Over the past century, it has gone through several cycles of boom and bust—first with mining and later with timber and fishing—but these days, tourism is becoming a healthy industry. The town's nearly 100 Victorian buildings have caused some to dub it "the Williamsburg of the West." Shops draw people to the renovated downtown, and a walking pier reaches into the harbor.

At the **Eureka Chamber of Commerce** you can pick up maps with self-guided driving tours of Eureka's architecture, and also learn about organized tours. ✉ 2112 Broadway ☎ 707/442–3738 or 800/356–6381 ⊕ www. eurekachamber.com ⊙ Weekdays 8:30–5, Sat. 10–4.

The Native American Wing of the **Clarke Memorial Museum** contains a beautiful collection of northwestern California basketry. Artifacts from Eureka's Victorian, logging, and maritime eras fill the rest of the museum. ✉ 240 E St. ☎ 707/443–1947 ⊕ www.clarkemuseum.org ⌁ Donations suggested ⊙ Tues.–Sat. 11–4.

☝ The structure that gave **Fort Humboldt State Historic Park** its name was built in response to conflicts between white settlers and Native Americans. It no longer stands, but on its grounds are some reconstructed buildings, fort and logging museums, and old logging locomotives. Demonstrators steam up the machines on third Saturdays, May through September. The park is a good place for a picnic. ✉ 3431 Fort Ave. ☎ 707/445–6567 or 707/445–6547 ⊕ www.parks.ca.gov ⌁ Free ⊙ Daily 8–5, museum and fort 8–4:30.

Where to Stay & Eat

¢–$$ ✕ **Cafe Waterfront.** This airy local landmark serves a solid basic menu of burgers and steaks, but the real standouts are the daily seafood specials—lingcod, shrimp, and other treats fresh from the bay across the street. The building, listed on the National Register of Historic Places, was a saloon and brothel until the 1950s. Named after former ladies of the house, two Victorian-style B&B rooms ($$) are available upstairs. ⊠ *102 F St.* ☎ *707/443–9190* ▤ *MC, V.*

✪ ¢–$ ✕ **Samoa Cookhouse.** A longtime logger's hangout, this eatery serves up family-style meals at its long wooden tables. Each day a different main dish—fried chicken, baked ham, or another homey standard—is the centerpiece of the pre-set menu, which also includes soup, salad, and dessert. It's worth saving room (if you can) for sweets such as home-made apple pie or strawberry shortcake. ⊠ *Cookhouse Rd.; from U.S. 101 cross Samoa Bridge, turn left onto Samoa Rd., then left 1 block later onto Cookhouse Rd.* ☎ *707/442–1659* ▤ *AE, D, MC, V.*

★ $$–$$$$ ✕▥ **Carter House & Restaurant 301.** According to owner Mark Carter, his staff has been trained always to say "Yes." Whether it's breakfast in bed or an in-room massage, someone here will make sure you get what you want. Richly painted and aglow with wood detailing, rooms blend modern and antique furnishings in two main buildings and several cottages. Eureka's most elegant restaurant ($$$) uses ingredients hand-selected from the farmers' market, local cheese makers and ranchers, and the on-site gardens. Dishes are prepared with a delicate hand and a sensuous imagination—the ever-changing menu has featured sturgeon with house-made mushroom pasta, braised fennel, and white wine sauce. ⊠ *301 L St., 95501* ☎ *707/444–8062 or 800/404–1390* ☎ *707/444–8067* ⊕ *www.carterhouse.com* ➵ *32 rooms, 15 suites* ⚍ *Restaurant, some kitchens, cable TV, in-room VCRs, in-room broadband, massage, shop, laundry service, concierge, meeting rooms; no smoking* ▤ *AE, D, DC, MC, V* ✸ *No lunch* ⵙ *BP.*

$–$$$ ▥ **Abigail's Elegant Victorian Mansion.** This meticulously restored East-lake mansion in a residential neighborhood lives up to its name. Each room is completely decked out in period furnishings, down to the carved-wood beds, fringed lamp shades, and pull-chain commodes. You can rent from a library of 1920s, '30s, and '40s movies, or play croquet on the rosebush-encircled lawn. You can also arrange for a guided tour of local Victoriana in an antique automobile. The lowest rates do not include breakfast. ⊠ *1406 C St., 95501* ☎ *707/444–3144* ☎ *707/442–3295* ⊕ *www. eureka-california.com* ➵ *4 rooms, 2 with shared bath* ⚍ *Tennis court, sauna, bicycles, croquet, laundry service; no smoking* ▤ *MC, V* ⵙ *BP.*

Nightlife

Lost Coast Brewery & Cafe (⊠ 617 4th St. ☎ 707/445–4480), a bustling microbrewery, is the best place in town to relax with a pint of ale or porter. Soups, salads, and light meals are served for lunch and dinner.

Sports & the Outdoors

Hum-Boats (⊠ A Dock, Woodley Island Marina ☎ 707/444–3048 ⊕ www.humboats.com) provides sailing and kayaking tours, rentals, and lessons.

Shopping

Eureka has several art galleries in the district running from C to I streets between 2nd and 3rd streets. Specialty shops in Eureka's Old Town include **Gepetto's** (✉ 416 2nd St. ☎ 707/443–6255) toy shop. **Flying Tiki Trading** (✉ 630 2nd St. ☎ 707/441–1234) stocks a stash of folk art. The original **Restoration Hardware** (✉ 417 2nd St. ☎ 707/443–3152) is a good place to find stylish yet functional home and garden accessories and clever polishing and cleaning products.

Arcata

㉑ *7 mi north of Eureka on U.S. 101.*

The home of Humboldt State University centers around a town square. For a self-guided tour of Arcata that includes some of its restored Victorian buildings, pick up a map from the **chamber of commerce** (✉ 1635 Heindon Rd. ☎ 707/822–3619 ⊕ www.arcatachamber.com), open daily 9–5.

Where to Stay & Eat

$–$$$ ✕ **Abruzzi.** Salads and hearty pasta dishes take up most of the menu at this upscale Italian restaurant, in the lower level of Jacoby's Storehouse on the town square. Don't miss the linguine *pescara,* with a spicy seafood-and-tomato sauce. ✉ *H and 8th Sts.* ☎ 707/826–2345 ▬ *AE, D, MC, V* ⊘ *No lunch.*

¢–$ ✕ **Crosswinds.** Tasty breakfast and lunch fare at reasonable prices make this place popular with university students. Hit the sunny Victorian dining room shortly after the 7:30 AM opening, though, and you'll have the place to yourself. ✉ *10th and I Sts.* ☎ 707/826–2133 ▬ *D, MC, V* ⊘ *Closed Mon. No dinner.*

¢–$$ ▦ **Hotel Arcata.** Rooms at this historic landmark overlooking the town square are clean and modest, but flowered bedspreads and claw-foot bathtubs lend them a bit of character. You get free access to a nearby gym with an indoor pool, hot tub, and yoga classes when you stay here. Tomo ($), the restaurant on the ground floor, serves sushi as well as other Japanese dishes. ✉ *708 9th St., 95521* ☎ 707/826–0217 or 800/344–1221 ⊟ 707/826–1737 ⊕ *www.hotelarcata.com* ⌂ *32 rooms* ⚭ *Restaurant, meeting room, no-smoking rooms* ▬ *AE, D, DC, MC, V* ❢⊘❢ *CP.*

Trinidad

㉒ *14 mi north of Arcata on U.S. 101.*

Trinidad got its name from the Spanish mariners who entered the bay on Trinity Sunday, June 9, 1775. The town became a principal trading post for the mining camps along the Klamath and Trinity rivers. Mining and whaling have faded from the scene, and now Trinidad is a quiet and genuinely charming community with enough sights and activities to entertain visitors.

Where to Stay & Eat

$$–$$$ ✕ **Larrupin' Cafe.** Locals consider this restaurant one of the best places to eat on the North Coast. Set in a two-story house on a quiet country road north of town, it's often thronged with people enjoying fresh seafood, Cornish game hen, or mesquite-grilled ribs. The garden setting and candlelight stir thoughts of romance, though service can be rushed. ⊠ *1658 Patrick's Point Dr.* ☎ *707/677–0230* ◬ *Reservations essential* ⊟ *No credit cards* ⊙ *Closed Tues. and Wed. in winter, Tues. in summer. No lunch.*

¢–$ ✕ **Katy's Smokehouse.** Purchase delectable picnic fixings at this tiny shop that has been doing things the same way since the 1940s, curing day-boat, line-caught fish with its original smokers. Salmon cured with brown sugar, albacore jerky, and smoked scallops are popular. Buy bread and drinks in town and walk to the waterside for alfresco snacking. Katy's closes at 6 PM. ⊠ *740 Edwards St.* ☎ *707/677–0151* ⊕ *www.katyssmokehouse.com* ⊟ *MC, V.*

$$$ ⊡ **Turtle Rocks Oceanfront Inn.** This comfortable inn has the best view in Trinidad, and the builders have made the most of it. Each room's private, glassed-in deck overlooks the ocean and rocks where sea lions lie sunning. Interiors are spare and contemporary. The surrounding landscape has been left wild and natural; tucked among the low bushes are sundecks for winter whale-watching and summer catnaps. Patrick's Point State Park is a short walk away. ⊠ *3392 Patrick's Point Dr., 4½ mi north of town, 95570* ☎ *707/677–3707* ⊕ *www.turtlerocksinn.com* ↪ *6 rooms, 1 suite* ⬡ *Cable TV* ⊟ *AE, D, MC, V* ⫶⊙⫶ *BP.*

Patrick's Point State Park

★ ㉓ *5 mi north of Trinidad on U.S. 101.*

On a forested plateau almost 200 feet above the surf, Patrick's Point has stunning views of the Pacific, great whale- and sea lion–watching in season, picnic areas, bike paths, and hiking trails through old-growth spruce forest. There are also tidal pools at Agate Beach, a re-created Yurok Indian village, and a small museum with natural-history exhibits. Because the park is far from major tourist hubs, there are few visitors (most are local surfers), which leaves the land sublimely quiet. ☎ *707/677–3570* ⊕ *www.parks.ca.gov* ⊡ *$6 per vehicle.*

Where to Stay

⚠ **Patrick's Point State Park Campgrounds.** In spruce and alder forest above the ocean (just a handful of sites have sea views), the park's three campgrounds have all amenities except RV hookups. In summer, it's best to reserve in advance. ⬡ *Flush toilets, drinking water, showers, bear boxes, fire pits* ↪ *124 sites* ⊠ *U.S. 101, 4150 Patrick's Point Dr.* ☎ *800/444–7275 for reservations* ⊕ *www.reserveamerica.com* ⊙ *Year-round* ⊡ *$19.*

Redwood National & State Parks

☾ ㉔ *Orick entrance 16 mi north of Patrick's Point State Park on U.S. 101.*

After 115 years of intensive logging, this 106,000-acre parcel of towering trees came under government protection in 1968. Redwood National and State Parks encompasses one national and three state parks and is more than 40 mi long. There is no admission fee to the national park, but the state parks charge a $5 day-use fee.

At the **Thomas H. Kuchel Information Center,** open daily 9–5, you can get brochures, advice, and a free permit to drive up the access road to Tall Trees Grove. Whale-watchers will find the deck of the visitor center an excellent observation point, and bird-watchers will enjoy the nearby Freshwater Lagoon, a popular layover for migrating waterfowl. ⊠ *Off U.S. 101, Orick* ☏ *707/464–6101 Ext. 5265* ⊕ *www.nps.gov/redw.*

About 3 mi north of Kuchel Information Center, turn east off U.S. 101 onto Bald Hills Road. In a couple of miles you will reach **Lady Bird Johnson Grove,** where a short circular trail leads through splendid redwoods. Continue on Bald Hills Road to Redwood Creek Overlook; the steep, 17-mi road (the last 6 mi are gravel) to **Tall Trees Grove** branches off just beyond. At the grove, a 3-mi round-trip hiking trail leads to the world's tallest redwood, as well as its third- and fifth-tallest ones.

To reach the entrance to **Prairie Creek Redwoods State Park,** leave U.S. 101 at the Newton B. Drury Scenic Parkway. The 10-mi drive through this old-growth redwood forest leads to numerous trailheads that access a 70-mi network of trails; it then rejoins U.S. 101. From the visitor center, a fully accessible trail leads to a meadow grazed by an imposing herd of Roosevelt elk. ⊠ *Visitor Center: Newton B. Drury Scenic Pkwy. off U.S. 101* ☏ *707/464–6101 Ext. 5300* ⊙ *Mar.–Oct. daily 9–5; Nov.–Feb. daily 10–4.*

U.S. 101 passes through **Del Norte Coast Redwoods State Park** on its way north to Crescent City. Close to the ocean, the immense trees in this cool, often misty area shelter lush undergrowth. Damnation Creek Trail descends a photogenic 1,000 feet through an old-growth forest to the water; expect a strenuous round-trip hike of at least three hours. ⊠ *Crescent City Information Center: 1111 Second St., Crescent City* ☏ *707/464–6101 Ext. 5064* ⊙ *Daily 9–5.*

Take U.S. 101 north out of Crescent City and head east on Highway 199 to reach **Jedediah Smith Redwoods State Park,** the northernmost section of Redwood National and State Parks. Rivers and streams thread through the groves here. Howland Hill Road, a 6-mi improved gravel road, gives access to trails such as the riverside Stout Grove Loop, an easy ½-mi walk. ⊠ *Hiouchi Information Center: U.S. 199, Hiouchi* ☏ *707/464–6101 Ext. 5067* ⊙ *Mid-June–mid-Sept., daily 9–5.*

Crescent City

㉕ *41 mi north of Orick on U.S. 101.*

Named for the shape of its harbor, Del Norte County's largest town (population 7,542) was an important steamship stop in the 1800s. A tsunami demolished half the city in 1964, taking with it most of the older architecture. Today commercial fishing drives the economy. At low tide from April through October, you can walk from the pier across the ocean floor to the **Battery Point Lighthouse** (☏ 707/464–3089). Poke around the small museum and take a tour ($3) of the 1856 structure Wednesday through Sunday between 10 and 4, tide permitting. The nonprofit **North Coast Marine Mammal Center** (⊠ Beachfront Park, 424 Howe Dr. ☏ 707/

465–6265) rehabilitates rescued sea lions, seals, and other marine mammals in a facility that you can visit daily 10–5, donation requested.

THE NORTH COAST A TO Z

To research prices, get advice from other travelers, and book travel arrangements, visit www.fodors.com.

AIRPORTS & TRANSFERS

The only North Coast airport with commercial air service, Arcata/Eureka Airport (ACV) receives United Express and Alaska Airlines flights from San Francisco. The airport is in McKinleyville, which is 16 mi from Eureka. *See* Air Travel *in* Smart Travel Tips A to Z for airline phone numbers. A taxi costs about $40 and takes roughly 20 minutes. Door to Door Airport Shuttle costs $17/$20 to Arcata and Trinidad, $20/$25 to Eureka, and $45/$45 to Ferndale for one/two people.

🛪 **Arcata/Eureka Airport** ✉ 3561 Boeing Ave., McKinleyville ☎ 707/839-5401. **Door to Door Airport Shuttle** ☎ 707/442-9266 or 888/338-5497 ⊕ www.doortodoorairporter.com.

BUS TRAVEL

Greyhound buses travel along U.S. 101 from San Francisco to Seattle, with regular stops in Eureka and Arcata. Bus drivers will stop in other towns along the route if you specify your destination when you board. Humboldt Transit Authority connects Eureka, Arcata, Scotia, Fortuna, and Trinidad.

🚌 **Greyhound** ☎ 800/231-2222 ⊕ www.greyhound.com. **Humboldt Transit Authority** ☎ 707/443-0826 ⊕ www.hta.org.

CAR RENTAL

Alamo, Avis, Hertz, and National rent cars at the Arcata/Eureka Airport, but call the reservation desk in advance if your flight will arrive late in the evening—the desks tend to close early, especially on weekends. *See* Car Rental *in* Smart Travel Tips A to Z for national rental agency phone numbers.

CAR TRAVEL

Although there are excellent services along U.S. 101, long, lonesome stretches separate towns (with their gas stations and mechanics) along Highway 1, and services are even fewer and farther between on the smaller roads. If you're running low on fuel and see a gas station, stop for a refill. Driving directly to Mendocino from San Francisco is quicker if, instead of driving up the coast on Highway 1, you take U.S. 101 north to Highway 128 west (from Cloverdale) to Highway 1 north. The quickest way to the far North Coast from the Bay Area is a straight shot up U.S. 101 to its intersection with Highway 1 near Eureka. Weather sometimes forces closure of parts of Highway 1. For information on the condition of roads in Northern California, call the Caltrans Highway Information Network's voice-activated system.

🚗 Road Conditions **Caltrans Highway Information Network** ☎ 800/427-7623 ⊕ www.dot.ca.gov/hq/roadinfo.

EMERGENCIES

In an emergency dial 911. In state and national parks, park rangers serve as police officers and will help you in any emergency. Bigger towns along the coast have hospitals, but for major medical emergencies you will need to go to San Francisco. Note that cell phones don't work along large swaths of the North Coast.

🛈 **General Hospital** ✉ 2200 Harrison St., Eureka ☎ 707/445-5111. **Mendocino Coast District Hospital** ✉ 700 River Dr., Fort Bragg ☎ 707/961-1234. **Palm Drive Hospital** ✉ 501 Petaluma Ave., Sebastopol ☎ 707/823-8511. **Sutter Coast Hospital** ✉ 800 E. Washington Blvd., Crescent City ☎ 707/464-8511.

VISITOR INFORMATION

🛈 **Humboldt County Convention and Visitors Bureau** ✉ 1034 2nd St., Eureka 95501 ☎ 707/443-5097 or 800/346-3482 ⊕ www.redwoodvisitor.org. **Fort Bragg-Mendocino Coast Chamber of Commerce** ✉ 332 N. Main St., Fort Bragg 95437 ☎ 707/961-6300 or 800/726-2780 ⊕ www.mendocinocoast.com. **Mendocino County Alliance** ✉ 525 S. Main St., Ukiah 95482 ☎ 707/462-7417 or 866/466-3636 ⊕ www.gomendo.com. **Redwood Empire Association** ✉ 825 Geary St., Suite 701, San Francisco 94109 ☎ 415/292-5527 or 800/619-2125 ⊕ www.redwoodempire.com. **Sonoma County Tourism Program** ✉ 520 Mendocino Ave., Suite 210, Santa Rosa 95401 ☎ 707/565-5383 ⊕ www.sonomacounty.com. **West Marin Chamber of Commerce** ☎ 415/663-9232 ⊕ www.pointreyes.org.

The Peninsula & South Bay

South of San Francisco

4

WORD OF MOUTH

"I never knew that San Jose had such a great little Egyptian Museum! And the architecture of the Park (replicas of Egyptian temples) is very impressive. My family and I stumbled across this treasure and want to go back. A must see!"

—Lisa

"I love the Tech Museum of Innovation. I guess I am just a kid at heart!"

—jcorrea

Updated by
Lisa M.
Hamilton

TWO PARALLEL WORLDS LIE SOUTH OF SAN FRANCISCO. On the fog-shrouded San Mateo County coast, rural towns perch between undeveloped hills and rugged coastline. Most of the hamlets that dot the coast are no more than a few blocks long, with just enough room for a couple of bed-and-breakfasts, restaurants, and boutiques or galleries. As you wind your way from one to the other, past pumpkin patches and stunning beaches, you'll find that the pace of life is slower here than in the rest of the Bay Area.

Over the Santa Cruz Mountains from the coast, the Inland Peninsula pulses with prosperity and creative energy. Many visitors to the Bay Area associate the Peninsula with traffic congestion and suburban sprawl, and indeed, much of the region from Santa Clara County to San Francisco is clogged with office complexes and strip-mall shopping centers. But a closer look at the Peninsula reveals redwood forests, and vast stretches of tawny hills where hawks soar overhead. Stanford University's bucolic campus is wonderful to visit, as are the wooded former country estates built by 19th-century mining and transportation "bonanza kings"—early adopters who realized the area's potential long before the "dot.com" boom.

Farther south is the heart of Silicon Valley, the birthplace of the tiny electronic chips and circuits that support the information age. Beyond what seems to be an endless sprawl of office parks, intertwined highways, shopping centers, and high-rises, the South Bay contains old-fashioned neighborhoods and abundant green hills. There are diverse towns such as Santa Clara, with its 200-year-old mission; Saratoga, with its fine antiques stores and posh restaurants; and San Jose—the third-largest city on the West Coast—with its flourishing downtown center, its many micro-neighborhoods, and a growing ribbon of urban green connecting the city from north to south.

Exploring the Peninsula & South Bay

You'll need a car to get around. The stretch of Highway 1 that leads north from the Monterey Bay area passes through a sparsely populated landscape punctuated by only a few small towns. By contrast, the Inland Peninsula and South Bay is a tangle of freeways. Public transportation can get you far here, but if you are in a car, it's best to avoid driving during rush hour.

About the Restaurants

Gone are the days when Peninsula and South Bay food lovers had to drive to San Francisco for an exceptional meal. Today some of the country's greatest chefs have recognized the area's appeal, opening trendy bistros and eateries, especially in San Jose's revitalized downtown. In the area's more progressive communities, particularly Palo Alto and Saratoga, the best chefs follow the farm-to-table ideals that guide Northern California's best restaurants. Dining in the South Bay might be a little less formal than in San Francisco—and a little less expensive—but that doesn't mean you won't need reservations. Along the coast, however, restaurants are strictly casual, and unless otherwise noted, you can generally walk in without waiting for a table.

About the Hotels

Along the coastal peninsula, accommodations tend to have homegrown character and cater to San Franciscans and weekend visitors here for a romantic getaway. Because of the weekend demand on the coast you'd be wise to make reservations as far in advance as possible. Inland Peninsula and South Bay lodgings generally attract business travelers—most are chain motels and hotels, though a number of B&Bs have popped up in recent years. During the week, when business conventions are in full swing, many of these hotels are booked up to two weeks in advance. However, some are nearly empty on weekends—and this is when rates plummet and package deals abound.

	WHAT IT COSTS				
	$$$$	**$$$**	**$$**	**$**	**¢**
RESTAURANTS	over $30	$23–$30	$16–$22	$10–$15	under $10
HOTELS	over $250	$176–$250	$121–$175	$90–$120	under $90

Restaurant prices are for a main course at dinner, excluding sales tax of 8¼% (depending on location). Hotel prices are for two people in a standard double room in high season, excluding service charges and 10% tax.

Timing

The hills that separate the Santa Clara Valley from the coast keep summertime fog from blowing into the Inland Peninsula and South Bay. This means that there are usually drastic variations in temperature between the coast and the inland area from April through October. In July you can expect foggy weather and temperatures in the mid-60s along the coastline, whereas just inland the days are sunny, with temperatures in the mid-80s. The rainy season runs from about November through March, and temperatures are generally constant across the region; daytime highs are ordinarily in the 50s and 60s.

THE COASTAL PENINSULA
UP HIGHWAY 1 FROM AÑO NUEVO TO MOSS BEACH

The coastal towns between Santa Cruz and San Francisco were founded in the late 18th century by Spanish explorer Gaspar de Portola. After Mexico won its independence from Spain in 1822, the peninsula was used by its new residents to raise food for the Mission Dolores in San Francisco. The agriculture industry began with simple cattle ranching, but the following century saw the advent of vegetable farms and fruit orchards. As food production grew, so did the building of lighthouses and ships, to ease the transport of goods to San Francisco. Drive north from Santa Cruz (Chapter 10) to San Francisco along scenic Highway 1, hugging the twists and turns of the coast, or venture 11 mi inland at Half Moon Bay, over hilly Route 92 to San Mateo.

GREAT ITINERARIES

Numbers in the text correspond to numbers in the margin and on the Peninsula & South Bay and Downtown San Jose maps.

IF YOU HAVE 1 DAY Spend your morning in ☞ **Palo Alto** ⑥, taking a look around town and a tour of Stanford University. In the afternoon head for ⬛ **San Jose** ⑩–㉑ and the **Tech Museum of Innovation** ⑭, the **Rosicrucian Egyptian Museum** ⑱, and the **Winchester Mystery House** ⑳. Depending on your taste, have an evening of symphony, ballet, or theater at San Jose's Center for Performing Arts.

IF YOU HAVE 3 DAYS Spend your first day on the coast, noodling around ☞ **Año Nuevo State Reserve** ①, **Pescadero State Beach** ②, Half

Moon Bay ③, and **Moss Beach** ④. After overnighting in a Half Moon Bay B&B, drive Route 92 through the countryside to I–280 and head south to **Woodside** ⑤, where you can tour Filoli (except Monday November–January). Drive south on I–280 to the Sand Hill Road exit and take that route to the central campus of Stanford University. Take an afternoon tour of the university and its Iris and B. Gerald Cantor Center for Visual Arts, then have dinner in ⬛ **Palo Alto** ⑥. On your third day stop in **Santa Clara** ⑦ to see Mission Santa Clara de Asis, or if you have kids in tow, you might want to treat them to a morning at Paramount's Great America. Devote your afternoon to ⬛ **San Jose** ⑩–㉑ and its attractions, then take a sunset drive to **Saratoga** ⑨.

Año Nuevo State Reserve

☞ ❶ *21 mi north of Santa Cruz on Hwy. 1.*

At the most southerly point of the San Mateo County Coast, Año Nuevo is the world's only approachable mainland rookery for elephant seals. If you know you'll be in the area between mid-December and March, make reservations early for a 2½-hour guided walking tour to view the huge (up to 2½ tons), furry elephant seals mating or birthing, depending on the time of year. Tours stay on schedule even in bad weather, so bring a raincoat just in case. From April through November the seals are less active, but you can still see them lounging on the beach. The area's visitor center has natural history exhibits and a fascinating film about the seals. ⊠*Hwy. 1, 13 mi south of Pescadero* ☎ *650/879–0227, 800/444–4445 for tour reservations* ✉ *$4, parking $5* ☉ *Tours leave every 15 min, daily 8:45–3.*

EN ROUTE

About 6 mi north of Año Nuevo State Reserve stands the 115-foot **Pigeon Point Lighthouse,** one of the tallest on the West Coast. Built in 1872, it has been used as a backdrop in numerous TV shows and commercials. The light from the 8,000-pound Fresnel lens can be seen from 20 mi out at sea. The former coast guard quarters have been converted to a youth hostel. You can still visit the park, but the lighthouse itself is closed indefinitely for repairs. ⊠ *Pigeon Point Rd. and Hwy. 1* ☎ *650/879-2120* ✉ *$2* ☉ *Daily 8-sunset, tours late May–early Sept. and weather permitting rest of yr, Fri.-Sun. 10:30-4.*

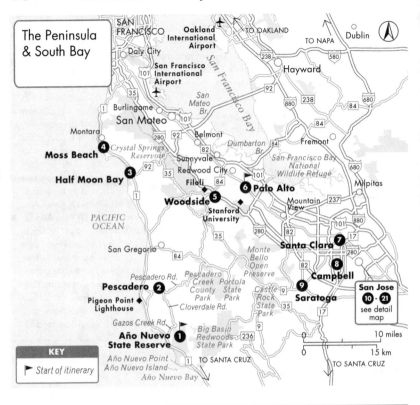

Pescadero

12 mi north of Año Nuevo State Reserve on Hwy. 1.

As you walk down Stage Road, Pescadero's main street, it's hard to be-lieve you're only 30 minutes from Silicon Valley. If you could block out the throngs of weekend cyclists, the downtown area could almost serve as the backdrop for a western movie. (In fact, with few changes, Duarte's Tavern could fill in as the requisite saloon.) This is a good place to stop for a bite or to browse for antiques. The town's real attractions, though, are its spectacular beaches and hiking.

★ ❷ If a quarantine is not in effect (watch for signs), from November through April you can look for mussels at **Pescadero State Beach** amid tidal pools and rocky outcroppings, then roast them at the barbecue pits. Any time of year is good for exploring the beach, the north side of which has sev-eral secluded spots along sandstone cliffs. Across U.S. 101, the **Pescadero Marsh Natural Preserve** has hiking trails that cover 600 acres of marsh-land. Early spring and fall are the best times to come, when there are lots of migrating birds and other wildlife to see. ⊠ *14½ mi south of Half Moon Bay on Hwy. 1* ☎ *650/879–2170* ⌑ *Free, parking $5* ☉ *Daily 8 AM–sunset.*

PLEASURES & PASTIMES

BEACHES. The main draw of coastal San Mateo County is its beaches. From Montara to Pescadero the strands accessible from Highway 1 are surprisingly uncrowded. Fog and cool weather may keep many people out of the water for large portions of the year, but the unspoiled beauty and wildlife make these beaches a treasure of the Bay Area. Some standouts are San Gregorio and Pomponio for strolling and sunbathing; windy Waddell Creek for windsurfing and kite-surfing; and Fitzgerald Marine Preserve for tide pooling. Then again, since nearly three-quarters of the county (70%) is open space, there's enough beach that you can usually find a good one by simply pulling over wherever you see a patch of sand.

HISTORIC HOMESTEADS. The communities of the Peninsula and South Bay have worked hard to preserve their parklands and turn-of-the-20th-century homesteads. In Woodside, Filoli stands as one of the great California country houses that remain intact. The Winchester Mystery House, in San Jose, may be the best-known site, but look beyond the tales of ghosts to see the sprawling farmhouse it once was. You can also visit former vineyards and historic homes in the Santa Cruz Mountains, notably Villa Montalvo and the Mountain Winery in Saratoga.

If you prefer mountain trails to sand dunes, head for **Pescadero Creek County Park,** an 8-acre expanse of shady, old-growth redwood forests, grasslands, and mountain streams. The park is actually composed of three smaller ones: Heritage Grove Redwood Preserve, Sam McDonald Park, and San Mateo Memorial County Park. The Old Haul Road Trail, 6½ mi long, runs the length of the park. Campsites cost $18 per night. ⊠ *Pescadero Road off Hwy. 1* ☎ *650/879–0238* ⊡ *Daily 8 AM–sunset.*

Where to Eat

¢–$$$ ✕ **Duarte's Tavern.** This 19th-century roadhouse serves simple American fare, with a menu based on locally grown vegetables and fresh fish. The house specialty is the abalone ($40), but other terrific choices include artichoke soup and old-fashioned berry pie à la mode. The restaurant's bar dates back to 1894, and is a great place to sip a whiskey; because it's also the local liquor store, however, don't be surprised if some locals ask for their orders to go. ⊠ *202 Stage Rd.* ☎ *650/879–0464* ⊟ *AE, MC, V.*

EN ROUTE In addition to beautiful scenery and expansive state beaches, one thing you'll pass on your way from Pescadero to Half Moon Bay is the town of San Gregorio and its idiosyncratic **San Gregorio General Store** (⊠ Rte. 84 at Stage Rd., 1 mi east of Hwy. 1 ☎ 650/726–0565). Part old-time saloon, part hardware store, part grocery, the place has been a fixture in town since the late 1800s. The current Spanish-style structure replaced the original wooden building when it burned down in 1930. Come to browse through the hodgepodge of items—camp stoves, books, and boots, to name just a few—or to listen to Irish music and bluegrass on weekend afternoons.

Half Moon Bay

❸ *16 mi north of Pescadero on Hwy. 1.*

The largest and most visited of the South Bay communities, Half Moon Bay is nevertheless a tiny town with a population of fewer than 10,000. Although the town doesn't look like much from the highway, once you turn onto Main Street, you'll find five blocks of vibrant galleries, shops, and cafés, many of which occupy renovated 19th-century buildings. The town comes to life on the third weekend in October, when 250,000 people gather for the **Half Moon Bay Art and Pumpkin Festival** (☎ 650/726–9652).

The 4-mi stretch of **Half Moon Bay State Beach** (⊠ Hwy. 1, west of Main St. ☎ 650/726–8819) is perfect for long walks, kite flying, and picnic lunches, though the 50°F water and dangerous currents make swimming inadvisable. There are three access points, one in Half Moon Bay and two south of town off the highway. To find them, look for road signs that have a picture of footsteps.

Where to Stay & Eat

$$–$$$$ ✕ **Cetrella.** This is the coast at its most dressed up. The restaurant is all polished wood and pressed tablecloths, and hits every gourmet mark—adventurous wine list, sumptuous cheese course, and live jazz and salsa music Thursday through Saturday. The menu—which features local organic ingredients—is largely Provençal, with some yummy Spanish surprises, such as a variety of tapas (small plates of different hors d'oeuvres). Seafood lovers, however, may want to order oysters directly from the raw bar. ⊠ *845 Main St.* ☎ *650/726–4090* ▤ *AE, MC, V.*

★ $$–$$$ ✕ **Pasta Moon.** At one of the best restaurants on the coast between San Francisco and Monterey, the staff is friendly and laid back, and the crowd is jovial and fun. Local produce flavors the seasonal menu, which includes such highlights as wood-fired-oven pizzas and grilled quail. Though the dining room can get slightly noisy on weekend nights, the food is worth it. ⊠ *315 Main St.* ☎ *650/726–5126* ▤ *AE, D, DC, MC, V.*

★ ¢–$$ ✕ **Sushi Main Street.** The coast's best sushi restaurant is the creation of a Japanese surfer and a California designer. The interior has been called "Bali meets sushi"—carved wood walls and spare branches are artfully lighted by eclectic lamps. The menu is traditional Japanese, with tempura, teriyaki, and clay-pot noodles, and the sushi is much less expensive than you'll find in nearby cities. For a special treat, try the banana tempura dessert. ⊠ *696 Mill St.* ☎ *650/726–6336* ⊕ *www.sushimainst. com* ▤ *AE, MC, V* ☉ *No lunch Sun.*

¢–$$ ✕ **Two Fools.** Big organic salads and burritos are the draw at this place, but some of the more unusual menu choices—such as the homemade nut loaf, and meat loaf topped with caramelized onions in a fresh-baked bun—are equally good. ⊠ *408 Main St.* ☎ *650/712–1222* ▤ *AE, D, MC, V* ☉ *No dinner Mon.*

$$$$ 🏨 **The Ritz-Carlton.** With its enormous but elegantly decorated rooms, secluded oceanfront property, and a staff that waits on guests hand and foot, this golf and spa resort defines opulence. Attention to detail is considered right down to the silver service, china, and 300-thread-count Egyptian cotton sheets. During cocktail hour, view the ocean from the plush conservatory bar, or while tucked under a heavy blanket on an Adirondack chair on the lawn. ⊠ *1 Miramontes Point Rd., 94019* ☎ *650/712–7000 or 800/241–3333* 🖷 *650/712–7070* ⊕ *www.ritzcarlton.com* 🛏 *261 rooms, 22 suites* ⚒ *2 restaurants, room service, in-room safes, some in-room hot tubs, cable TV with movies and video games, some in-room DVD, in-room broadband, in-room data ports, 2 18-hole golf courses, 6 tennis courts, fitness classes, health club, hair salon, 2 hot tubs, massage, sauna, spa, steam room, bicycles, 2 bars, shops, babysitting, children's programs (ages 4–12), dry cleaning, laundry service, concierge, concierge floor, Internet rooms, business services, meeting rooms, airport shuttle, some pets allowed (fee), no-smoking rooms* ⊟ *AE, D, DC, MC, V.*

$$–$$$$ 🏨 **Mill Rose Inn.** Luxurious extras at this B&B include fireplaces, brass beds stacked high with down comforters, coffee, cocoa, and fruit baskets in the guest rooms, as well as decanters of sherry and brandy in the parlor. The gardens are full of roses and climbing sweet peas. Room rates include champagne breakfast and afternoon snacks. ⊠ *615 Mill St., 94019* ☎ *650/726–8750 or 800/900–7673* 🖷 *650/726–3031* ⊕ *www.millroseinn.com* 🛏 *4 rooms, 2 suites* ⚒ *Some in-room hot tubs, refrigerators, cable TV, in-room VCRs, in-room broadband, Wi-Fi, hot tub, meeting room; no a/c, no smoking* ⊟ *AE, D, DC, MC, V* ⎹⊙⎸ *BP.*

★ **$$–$$$$** 🏨 **Old Thyme Inn.** The owners of this 1898 Princess Anne Victorian love herbs and flowers, and if you have a green thumb of your own, this is the place for you. The gardens alongside the house burst with blossoms year-round, guest rooms are filled with fragrant bouquets, and each room is named after an herb and decorated in its colors. Antiques, homemade breakfasts, complimentary sherry, and afternoon snacks enhance the sense of homeyness. ⊠ *779 Main St., 94019* ☎ *650/726–1616 or 800/720–4277* 🖷 *650/726–6394* ⊕ *www.oldthymeinn.com* 🛏 *7 rooms* ⚒ *Some in-room hot tubs, cable TV, in-room VCRs, in-room data ports, concierge; no a/c, no smoking* ⊟ *AE, D, MC, V* ⎹⊙⎸ *BP.*

Sports
The Bike Works (⊠ 20 Stone Pine Ctr. ☎ 650/726–6708) rents bikes and can provide information on organized rides up and down the coast. If you prefer to go it alone, try the 3-mi bike trail that leads from Kelly Avenue in Half Moon Bay to Mirada Road in Miramar.

Moss Beach

❹ *7 mi north of Half Moon Bay on Hwy. 1; 20 mi south of San Francisco on Hwy. 1.*

Moss Beach was a busy outpost during Prohibition, when regular shipments of liquid contraband from Canada were unloaded at the secluded beach and hauled off to San Francisco. The town stayed under the radar out of necessity, with only one local hotel and bar (now The Distillery) where Bay Area politicians and gangsters could go for a drink while waiting for their shipments. Today, although it has grown into a cheerful surfing town with charming shops and restaurants, it is still all but invisible from the highway—a good hideaway for those allergic to crowds.

The biggest Moss Beach attraction is the **Fitzgerald Marine Reserve** (✉ California and North Lake Sts. ☎ 650/728–3584), a 3-mi stretch of bluffs and tide pools. Since the reserve was protected in 1969, scientists have discovered 25 new aquatic species here; depending on the tide, you'll most likely find shells, anemones, or starfish.

Just off the coast at Moss Beach is **Mavericks.** When there's a big swell, it's one of the biggest surfing breaks in the world. Waves here have reportedly reached 60 feet in height, and surfers get towed out to them by Jet Skis. The break is a mile offshore, so seeing it from the coast can be tough and requires a demanding hike. The intrepid can get photocopied directions at The Distillery restaurant, then drive 3 mi south for the trail out of **Pillar Point Harbor.** Even if you're not hunting for waves, the harbor is a nice place to wander, with its laid-back restaurants and waters full of fishing boats and sea lions.

Built in 1928 after two horrible shipwrecks on the point, the **Point Montara Lighthouse** still has its original light keeper's quarters from the late 1800s. Gray whales pass this point during their migration from November through April, so bring your binoculars. Visiting hours coincide with morning and afternoon check-in and check-out times at the adjoining youth hostel ($18–$22 dorm beds, $57 private room). ✉ *16th St. at Hwy. 1, Montara* ☎ *650/728–7177* ☉ *Daily 8* AM–*sunset.*

Where to Stay & Eat

$$$–$$$$ ✕ **The Distillery.** Story has it that this Prohibition-era restaurant still harbors the ghost of a 1930s adultress, who appears from time to time. In its modern incarnation, the upstairs restaurant is candlelit and has a good surf-and-turf menu. Things are more casual (and less expensive) at the self-service lunch spot and bar on the deck downstairs. On chilly afternoons couples can cuddle under heavy woolen blankets on swinging benches and sip wine while watching the fog roll in. ✉ *140 Beach Way* ☎ *650/728–5595* ⊕ *www.mossbeachdistillery.com* ▤ *D, DC, MC, V.*

★ $–$$ ✕ **Cafe Gibraltar.** Chef-owner Jose Luiz Ugalde is a master of creative dishes, particularly the sweet and spicy (many sauces contain fruits such as apricots and currants). The flavors here are unexpected—calamari baked with cinnamon, lavender crème brûlée—and the atmosphere is sensual, with peach walls lighted by flickering candles and booths draped with curtains and lined with pillows. Located 2 mi south of Moss Beach on the east side of the highway, it's a bit hard to find, but worth the hunt. At signs for Pillar Point Harbor, turn inland onto Capistrano, then right onto Alhambra. ✉ *425 Avenue Alhambra, at Palma Ave., El Granada* ☎ *650/560–9039* ⊕ *www.cafegibraltar.com* ▤ *AE, MC, V* ☉ *Closed Mon. No lunch.*

¢ ✕ **Three–Zero Cafe.** This busy restaurant at the tiny Half Moon Bay Airport is a local favorite, especially for weekend breakfasts. The food is standard—eggs and pancakes for breakfast, burgers for lunch—but reliably good. Get a window table, and as you eat, watch two-seater planes take off and land on the runway 20 feet away. ⊠ *Hwy. 1, 2 mi south of Moss Beach, El Granada* ☎ *650/728–1411* ☐ *MC, V* ⊘ *No dinner.*

$$$ ▥ **Seal Cove Inn.** Travel writer Karen Brown has written guidebooks to inns all over the world, and this is what she has created at home. Her inn is modern but charming and warm, with all windows looking onto flower gardens and toward cypress trees that border the marine reserve. Rooms have antique bed frames and writing desks, plush mattresses, lounge chairs, and fireplaces. Upstairs rooms have cathedral ceilings and balconies. ⊠ *221 Cypress Ave., 94038* ☎ *650/728–4114 or 800/995–9987* ▤ *650/728–4116* ⊕ *www.sealcoveinn.com* ◲ *8 rooms, 2 suites* ♿ *Minibars, refrigerators, in-room VCRs; no a/c* ⦿ *BP* ☐ *AE, D, MC, V.*

$$–$$$ ▥ **The Goose and Turrets.** Artifacts from the international travels of innkeepers Raymond and Emily Hoche-Mong fill the shelves of this inn 8 mi north of Half Moon Bay. A full home-cooked breakfast, afternoon goodies, and homemade chocolate truffles are sure to make anyone feel at home. Some rooms have fireplaces. ⊠ *835 George St., Montara 94037* ☎ *650/728–5451* ▤ *650/728–0141* ⊕ *goose.montara.com* ◲ *5 rooms* ♿ *Boccie, piano; no a/c, no smoking* ☐ *AE, D, DC, MC, V* ⦿ *BP.*

THE INLAND PENINSULA

Much of your first impression of the Inland Peninsula will depend on where and when you enter. Take the 30-mi stretch of U.S. 101 from San Francisco along the eastern side of the Peninsula, and you'll see office complex after shopping center after corporate tower—and you'll likely get caught in horrific morning and evening commuter traffic. On the west side, however, the less crowded I–280 takes you past soul-soothing hills, lakes, and reservoirs.

Woodside

❺ *31 mi south of San Francisco via I–280.*

West of Palo Alto, Woodside is a tiny rustic town where weekend warriors stock up on espresso and picnic fare before charging off on their mountain bikes. Blink once, and you're past the town center. The main draw here is the wealth of surrounding lush parks and preserves.

★ One of the few great country houses in California that remains intact is **Filoli.** Built 1915–17 for wealthy San Franciscan William B. Bourn II, it was designed by Willis Polk in a Georgian-revival style, with red-brick walls and a tile roof. The name is Bourn's acronym for "fight, love, live." As interesting as the house are the 16 acres of formal gardens, which include a sunken garden and a teahouse in the Italian Renaissance style. From June through September Filoli is the site of a series of Sunday afternoon jazz concerts. Bring a picnic or buy a box lunch; Filoli provides tables, sodas, wine, fruit, and popcorn. In December the mansion is festively decorated for a series of holiday events: brunches, afternoon teas, Christmas concerts, and more. ⊠ *Cañada Rd. near Edgewood Rd.* ☎ *650/364–8300* ⊕ *www.filoli.org* ⊠ *$12* ⊘ *Mid-Feb.–Oct., Tues.–Sat. 9:30–3:30* ☞ *Reservations are essential for guided tours.*

Where to Eat

$$–$$$ ✕**Woodside Bakery and Café.** The bakery section of this bustling spot is perfect for a cup of hot cocoa and a fresh-baked pastry; the café area in the courtyard is equally pleasant for a glass of wine and a meal. Although the café menu focuses mostly on light pastas and salads, there are also a few more-substantial entrées such as oven-braised lamb shank and baked Dijon chicken. ⊠ *3052 Woodside Rd.* ☎ *650/851–0812* ⊟ *AE, MC, V.*

¢–$$$ ✕**Bucks in Woodside.** This casual restaurant typifies Silicon Valley's unusual approach to corporate culture. The walls may be decorated with giant plastic alligators and Elvis paintings, but the guy in bike shorts at the next table may well be a high-power tech executive. The menu is a grab bag of crowd pleasers: soups, sandwiches, burgers, and salads. For breakfast there's a "U-do-it" omelet in addition to standard choices. ⊠ *3062 Woodside Rd.* ☎ *650/851–8010* ⊟ *AE, D, MC, V.*

Palo Alto

▶ ❻ *34 mi south of San Francisco via I–280 or U.S. 101.*

Palo Alto's main attraction is the pastoral campus of Stanford University, which encompasses 8,200 acres of grassy hills. The university also serves as an emblem of the city's dual personality: at once cutting-edge techno-savvy and outspoken California liberal. For example, the entire city is equipped for Wi-Fi, which means you can walk down the street and search "vegetarian cuisine" on a handheld, then e-mail en route to one of the many dining options. A wander up and down University Avenue and its surrounding side streets will reveal myriad restaurants as well as attractions such as the 1920s-style Stanford Theatre.

Stanford University was former California governor Leland Stanford's horse-breeding farm, and the land is still known as the Farm. Founded in 1885 and opened in 1891, the university occupies a campus designed by Frederick Law Olmsted. Its unique California Mission—Romanesque sandstone buildings, joined by arcades and topped by red-tile roofs—are mixed with newer buildings in variations on Olmstead's style. The 285-foot Hoover Tower is a landmark and a tourist attraction; an elevator ($2) leads to an observation deck that provides sweeping views. Free one-hour **walking tours** (⊠ Serra St., opposite Hoover Tower ☎ 650/723–2560) of the Stanford campus leave daily at 11 and 3:15 from the visitor center in the front hall of Memorial Auditorium. ⊠ *Galvez St. at Serra St.* ☎ *650/723–2300* ⊕ *www.stanford.edu.*

★ **The Iris and B. Gerald Cantor Center for Visual Arts,** one of the most comprehensive and varied art collections in the Bay Area, includes works from pre-Columbian periods through the modern. Included is the world's largest collection—180 pieces—of Rodin sculptures outside Paris, many of them displayed in the outdoor garden (for a spectacular sight, visit these at night during a full moon). Other highlights include a bronze Buddha from the Ming dynasty, wooden masks and carved figurines from 18th- and 19th-century Africa, paintings by Georgia O'Keeffe, and sculpture by Willem de Kooning and Bay Area artist Robert Arneson. The exceptional café has a menu—all organic—and clientele that's savvy but unpretentious. You can sit in the airy dining room or on the sunny terrace overlooking the Rodin garden. ⊠ *328 Lomita Dr. and Museum Way, off Palm Dr. at Stanford University* ☎ *650/723–4177* ⊕ *ccva.stanford.edu* ☒ *Free* ⊗ *Wed., Fri.–Sun. 11–5, Thurs. 11–8.*

Tucked into a small, heavily wooded plot is the **Papua New Guinea Sculpture Garden,** filled with tall, ornately carved poles, drums, and stones—all created in the 1990s by 10 artists from Papua New Guinea. Complementing them are plants from Melanesia, including a huge, gorgeous Silk Oak tree. Detailed plaques explain the concept and the works. ⊠ *Santa Teresa St. and Lomita Dr., at Stanford University* ☒ *Free.*

Two-hour tours of the **Stanford Linear Accelerator Center (SLAC)** reveal the workings of the 2-mi-long electron accelerator, which is used by Stanford University scientists for research into elementary particles. Call for times and reservations. ⊠ *Sand Hill Rd., 3 mi west of the central campus* ☎ *650/926–2204.*

OFF THE BEATEN PATH

MUSEUM OF PEZ MEMORABILIA – The museum celebrates the collectible candy dispensers with an astounding array of their early incarnations, some actually worth thousands of dollars. ⊠ *214 California Dr., 17 miles north of Palo Alto on Hwy. 101 Burlingame* ☎ *650/347–2301* ☒ *$3* ⊗ *Tue.–Sat., 10–6.*

Where to Stay & Eat

$$–$$$$ ✕ **Spago.** Silicon Valley's best and brightest have made a hit out of Wolfgang Puck's splashy, dashing Spago. The fare is inventive Californian, the service flawless. Flat breads, bread sticks, and specialty loaves will tide you over until the real food arrives. Dinner might include roast chicken breast with ricotta gnocchi or grilled quail with a white-bean cassoulet. The tasty desserts are artistically presented; don't miss the satsuma parfait. ⊠ *265 Lytton Ave.* ☎ *650/833–1000* ⌚ *Reservations recommended* ☐ *AE, D, DC, MC, V* ⊗ *No lunch weekends.*

★ **$–$$$$** ✕ **Evvia.** This Greek restaurant is no shish-kebab joint. The dining rooms are decorated in the fashion of a (superbly tasteful) Greek country house, with copper pots and garlic wreaths lining the mantels. The menu is rustic yet elegant, and ranges from the familiar—roast chicken, Greek salad—to the adventurous—boar confit in phyllo with dried apricots and slow-cooked cabbage. ⊠ *420 Emerson St.* ☎ *650/326–0983* ⌚ *Reservations essential* ☐ *AE, D, DC, MC, V* ⊗ *No lunch weekends.*

★ **$$–$$$** ✕ **Flea Street Café.** The staff at this romantic, friendly restaurant has been on board for decades and takes great care in preparing and serving food. Ingredients are selected from farmers that owner Jesse Cool knows personally, and the dishes are fresh and inventive: the winter *fritto misto* (batter-fried vegetables) includes Meyer lemon slices; spring oysters are served with avocado and smoked trout. ✉ *3607 Alameda de las Pulgas* ☎ *650/854–1226* ▭ *AE, MC, V* ✆ *Closed Mon. No lunch.*

$–$$$ ✕ **Zibibbo.** The menu changes seasonally at this two-story Victorian establishment, where you can sit in a garden, a glassed-in atrium, or a dining room. Even the pickiest diner is likely to find something appealing on the unusually long menu, which includes such creative dishes as crispy saffron rice balls with chorizo, and pork loin with a pomegranate-molasses glaze. Vegetarians will be happy here, too; there are many tempting meat-free choices. ✉ *430 Kipling St.* ☎ *650/328–6722* ▭ *AE, DC, MC, V.*

$–$$ ✕ **Tamarine.** Bamboo place mats and paper lamps suggest the cultural roots of the Vietnamese cuisine here, but the menu is hardly traditional. Crab wontons are served in a lemongrass and coconut milk consommé; duck is glazed with *yuzu*, garlic, and orange juice. The tatami-mat interior is stylish, as is the perpetual crowd at the door. ✉ *546 University Ave.* ☎ *650/325–8500* ▭ *AE, DC, MC, V* ✆ *No lunch weekends.*

¢–$$ ✕ **Nola.** This festive, New Orleans–inspired restaurant has a lantern-lighted central courtyard and a whimsical folk art–filled interior. The food is California-Cajun: the grilled Cajun pork chop on garlic mashed potatoes is especially good, as are the jambalaya and shrimp étouffée. Almost all the wines are served by the glass as well as by the bottle. Save room for the homemade beignets. ✉ *535 Ramona St.* ☎ *650/328–2722* ▭ *AE, DC, MC, V* ✆ *No lunch weekends.*

$ ✕ **JZ Cool Eatery.** Comfort food favoring local organic ingredients—such as homemade meat loaf topped with caramelized onions—is the focus at this spot in downtown Menlo Park. Touches such as butcher-block tables and potato salad disguise the health-conscious bent; you might just forget the food here is supposed to be good for you. ✉ *827 Santa Cruz Ave., Menlo Park* ☎ *650/325–3665* ▭ *MC, V.*

¢ ✕ **Bay Leaf Café.** This place is about as eco-friendly as you can get. Organic ingredients and vegan cuisine are the fare here, and flavors range from grilled nondairy cheese to spicy tofu masala. The restaurant is calm, bright, and quiet, and is a favorite of South Bay herbivores. ✉ *520 Ramona St.* ☎ *650/321–7466* ▭ *MC, V* ✆ *Closed Mon.*

¢ ✕ **Pasta?** The most expensive pasta dish here—and there are many on the menu—is $9. This is good food, plain and simple, made with fresh seasonal ingredients and presented with care. In addition to such standard pasta dishes as salmon fettuccine, there are always a few lighter selections made without heavy oils, cheese, or salt. Naturally, the place does a brisk business with students. ✉ *326 University Ave.* ☎ *650/328–4585* ▭ *AE, MC, V.*

¢ ✕ **Pluto's.** This loud and lively restaurant is known for fresh, custom-made salads, sandwiches, and buffet-style hot meals. By visiting different serving stations, you can have a salad made with toppings such as grilled fennel and roasted peppers, or build your own sandwich with choices such as marinated flank steak and grilled eggplant. ✉ *482 University Ave.* ☎ *650/853–1556* ▭ *MC, V.*

★ $$$$ ▥ **Garden Court Hotel.** The outside of this boutique hotel looks like an Italian villa, with columns and arches, a dormer roof, and bougainvillea-draped balconies. Inside, though, the feeling is more modern California, with gauzy bed canopies and and colorful walls. Some rooms overlook a lush central courtyard, others have fireplaces or four-poster beds; all suites have private terraces. ⊠ *520 Cowper St., 94301* ☎ *650/ 322–9000 or 800/824–9028* 🖷 *650/324–3609* ⊕ *www.gardencourt.com* 🍴 *50 rooms, 12 suites* 👌 *Restaurant, room service, in-room safes, some in-room hot tubs, minibars, refrigerators, cable TV with movies, in-room broadband, in-room data ports, Wi-Fi, gym, bar, laundry service, concierge, Internet room, business services, meeting rooms, some pets allowed (fee), no-smoking rooms* ▤ *AE, D, DC, MC, V* 🍽 *CP.*

$$$$ 🏨 **The Westin Palo Alto.** Though it's near the highway and Stanford Shopping Center (in the interest of its business clientele), this upscale hotel is relatively quiet. The elegant decor is tastefully spare, including clean, white beds and simple, Audubon-inspired framed prints. Outside are several inviting courtyards, cooled by arbors and olive trees. The prices can drop by nearly half on weekends. ⊠ *675 El Camino Real, 94301* ☎ *650/321–4422 or 800/937–8461* 🖷 *650/321–5522* ⊕ *www. westin.com* 🍴 *163 rooms, 21 suites* 👌 *2 restaurants, room service, cable TV with movies and video games, in-room broadband, in-room data ports, Wi-Fi, pool, gym, hot tub, massage, bar, dry cleaning, laundry facilities, laundry service, concierge, Internet room, business services, meeting rooms, some pets allowed; no smoking* ▤ *AE, D, DC, MC, V.*

$$–$$$$ 🏨 **Stanford Park Hotel.** The interior of this stately hotel takes its cues from an English hunt club, with its antiques, oil paintings, and a forest-green color scheme. The grand lobby is focused around a fireplace surrounded by armchairs, and the formal Duck Club restaurant ($$$–$$$$) is decorated with paintings of waterfowl. The warm rooms follow suit, featuring tapestry-print bedspreads and plaid armchairs. The staff is delightful. ⊠ *100 El Camino Real, 94025* ☎ *650/322–1234 or 800/368– 2468* 🖷 *650/322–0975* ⊕ *www.woodsidehotels.com* 🍴 *155 rooms, 8 suites* 👌 *Restaurant, minibars, cable TV with movies and video games, in-room data ports, Wi-Fi, pool, gym, hot tub, bar, lobby lounge, library, dry cleaning, laundry service, concierge, Internet room, business services, meeting rooms; no smoking* ▤ *AE, D, DC, MC, V.*

$$–$$$$ 🏨 **The Victorian on Lytton.** Only a block from downtown Palo Alto, this inn attracts business travelers who want comfort and amenities without too many frills. The innkeepers gutted the building—a former apartment complex—and renovated the interior to accommodate spacious rooms, some with canopy beds. Complimentary breakfast is ordered the night before and brought to your room in the morning. ⊠ *555 Lytton Ave., 94301* ☎ *650/322–8555* 🖷 *650/322–7141* ⊕ *www. victorianonlytton.com* 🍴 *10 rooms* 👌 *In-room data ports, Wi-Fi; no smoking* ▤ *AE, MC, V* 🍽 *CP.*

$$–$$$ 🏨 **Atherton Inn.** Over the border in a residential neighborhood, this inn is meant to feel like a home. You can lounge by the fireplace in armchairs or sit among flowers on the patio, and the do-it-yourself kitchen is open 24 hours a day. Rooms are simple but plush, with European down pillows and cherrywood armoires. A bonus for those with physical limitations: this B&B also has an elevator. ⊠ *1201 W. Selby La., Redwood City 94061* ☎ *650/474–2777, 800/603–8105* 🖷 *650/474–0733* ⊕ *www. athertoninn.com* 🍴 *5 rooms* 👌 *Some in-room hot tubs, cable TV with DVD and VCR, piano; no smoking* ▤ *AE, D, DC, MC, V* 🍽 *BP.*

¢–$$ 🏠 **Cowper Inn.** This former Victorian home in a quiet residential neighborhood is one of the least expensive lodging options around, and it's charming to boot. The cozy parlor has a brick fireplace, a piano, and a big window looking out on tree-lined Cowper Street. Breakfast includes homemade muffins and granola and fresh-squeezed orange juice. ⊠ *705 Cowper St., 94301* ☎ *650/327–4475* 🖷 *650/329–1703* ⊕ *www. cowperinn.com* 🖙 *14 rooms, 12 with bath* ⚲ *Fans, cable TV, in-room VCRs, Wi-Fi, piano; no a/c, no smoking* 🖃 *AE, MC, V* ⍟⎮ *CP.*

SOUTH BAY
WEST OF SAN JOSE

To many the South Bay is synonymous with Silicon Valley, the center of high-tech research and the corporate headquarters of such giants as Apple, Sun Microsystems, Oracle, and Hewlett-Packard. But Silicon Valley is more a state of mind than a place—it's an attitude held by the legions of software engineers, programmers, and computerphiles who call the area home. That home is becoming increasingly visitor-friendly; within the sprawl are appealing towns whose histories stretch back centuries, a thriving arts scene, and shops and restaurants to satisfy the most discerning tastes.

Santa Clara

❼ *40 mi south of San Francisco on Hwy. 101.*

Santa Clara has two major attractions at opposite ends of the sightseeing spectrum: Mission Santa Clara de Asis, founded in 1777, and Paramount's Great America, Northern California's answer to Disneyland. Although many visitors head straight to the amusement park, Santa Clara has plenty of history and is worthy of a visit—despite its ubiquitous shopping malls and sterile business parks.

Santa Clara University, founded in 1851 by Jesuits, was California's first college. The campus's **de Saisset Art Gallery and Museum** shows a permanent collection that includes California mission artifacts and gold-rush-era pieces, California-theme artwork, and contemporary Bay Area art, especially prints. ⊠ *500 El Camino Real* ☎ *408/554–4528* ⊕ *www. scu.edu/desaisset* 🎟 *Free* ⊗ *Tues.–Sun. 11–4.*

In the center of Santa Clara University's campus is the **Mission Santa Clara de Asis,** the first of California's original missions to honor a female saint. In 1926 the mission chapel was destroyed by fire. Roof tiles of the current building, a reproduction of the original, were salvaged from earlier structures, which dated from the 1790s and 1820s. Early adobe walls and a spectacular rose garden with 4,500 roses—many of the varieties classified as antique—remain intact as well. Part of the wooden Memorial Cross, from 1777, is set in front of the church. ⊠ *500 El Camino Real* ☎ *408/554–4023* ⊕ *www.scu.edu/visitors/mission* 🎟 *Free* ⊗ *Self-guided tours daily 1–sundown.*

☾ At the gigantic theme park **Paramount's Great America,** each section recalls a familiar part of North America: Hometown Square, Yukon Territory, Yankee Harbor, or County Fair. Popular attractions include the Drop Zone Stunt Tower, the tallest free-fall ride in North America; a *Top Gun* movie-theme roller coaster, whose cars travel along the outside of a 360-degree loop track; and Nickelodeon Splat City, 3 acres of obstacle courses apparently designed for kids who love to get wet and dirty. You can get to the park via Valley Transit Authority, Caltrain, and BART. ⊠ *Great America Pkwy. between U.S. 101 and Rte. 237, 6 mi north of San Jose* ☎ *408/988–1776* ⊕ *www.pgathrills.com* ☞ *$49.99, parking $10* ☉ *Apr., May, Sept., and Oct. weekends; June–Aug., daily; opens 10 AM, closing times vary* ⊟ *AE, D, MC, V.*

The **Carmelite Monastery** is a fine example of Spanish ecclesiastical architecture. Built in 1917, it's on the grounds of a mission-era ranch crossed by shady walkways and dotted with benches perfect for quiet contemplation. ⊠ *1000 Lincoln St.* ☎ *408/296–8412* ⊕ *members.aol.com/ santaclaracarmel* ☞ *Free* ☉ *Grounds daily 6:30–4:15.*

Skylights cast natural light for viewing the exhibitions in the **Triton Museum of Art.** A permanent collection of 19th- and 20th-century sculpture by Bay Area artists is displayed in the garden, which you can see through a curved-glass wall at the rear of the building. Indoor galleries present excellent, eclectic shows of contemporary Native American work. ⊠ *1505 Warburton Ave.* ☎ *408/247–3754* ⊕ *www.tritonmuseum. org* ☞ *$2 suggested donation* ☉ *Fri.–Wed. 11–5, Thurs. 11–9.*

The **Harris-Lass Historic Museum** is built on Santa Clara's last farmstead. A restored house, summer kitchen, and barn convey what life was like on the farm from the early 1900s through the 1930s. Guided tours take place every half hour until 3:30. ⊠ *1889 Market St.* ☎ *408/249–7905* ☞ *$3* ☉ *Weekends noon–4.*

Where to Stay & Eat

$$–$$$$ ✕ **Birk's.** Silicon Valley's businesspeople come to this sophisticated American grill to unwind. High-tech sensibilities will appreciate the modern open kitchen and streamlined, multilevel dining area—yet the menu is traditional, strong on steaks and chops. An oyster bar adds a lighter element, as do the simply prepared but high-quality organic vegetable dishes such as garlic mashed potatoes and creamed spinach. ⊠ *3955 Freedom Cir., at Hwy. 101 and Great America Pkwy.* ☎ *408/980–6400* ⊟ *AE, D, DC, MC, V* ☉ *No lunch weekends.*

¢–$$ ✕ **Mio Vicino.** Mio's is a small, bare-bones, checkered-tablecloth Italian bistro in Old Santa Clara. The menu includes a long list of classic and contemporary pastas—and if you don't see it on the menu, just ask. The house specialties are shellfish pasta and chicken cannelloni. ⊠ *1290 Benton St.* ☎ *408/241–9414* ⊟ *MC, V* ☉ *No lunch weekends.*

¢–$ ✕ **Chez Sovan.** This Cambodian jewel is a departure from the average South Bay restaurant—and a reliable one. The noodle dishes, grilled meats, and curries are all excellently flavored. Specialties of the house are the spring rolls and the rice noodles in tamarind sauce. ⊠ *2425 S. Bascom Ave.* ☎ *408/371–7711* ⊟ *AE, MC, V.*

$$–$$$ ⊞ **Embassy Suites.** This upper-end chain hotel attracts Silicon Valley business travelers—but because the rates plummet on the weekends, it's even better suited to families bound for Paramount's Great America. Nearly all the accommodations here are two-room suites, and rates include cooked-to-order breakfasts and evening beverages. ✉ *2885 Lakeside Dr., 95054* ☎ *408/496–6400 or 800/362–2779* 🖷 *408/988–7529* ⊕ *www.embassy-suites.com* ➟ *17 rooms, 240 suites* ♧ *Restaurant, room service, refrigerators, cable TV with movies and video games, in-room data ports, Wi-Fi, pool, gym, hot tub, sauna, bar, shop, dry cleaning, laundry facilities, laundry services, Internet room, business services, meeting rooms, airport shuttle, free parking, no-smoking rooms* 🖶 *AE, D, DC, MC, V* ⭑◎⭒ *BP.*

¢–$ 🏩 **Madison Street Inn.** At this Queen Anne Victorian, complimentary afternoon refreshments and a full breakfast are served on a brick garden patio with a bougainvillea-draped trellis. The inn feels like a private home, with its green-and-red-trimmed facade and individually styled rooms that range from homey to fancy. ✉ *1390 Madison St., 95050* ☎ *408/249–5541 or 800/491–5541* 🖷 *408/249–6676* ⊕ *www.madisonstreetinn.com* ➟ *5 rooms, 3 with bath, 1 suite* ♧ *Some fans, some microwaves, some refrigerators, cable TV with movies, some in-room DVD, in-room VCRs, in-room broadband, in-room data ports, Wi-Fi, pool, hot tub, sauna, bicycles, library, dry cleaning, laundry service, Internet room, meeting room, some pets allowed (fee); no a/c in some rooms, no TV in some rooms, no smoking* 🖶 *AE, D, DC, MC, V* ⭑◎⭒ *BP.*

Campbell

❽ *6 mi southwest of Santa Clara on Hwy. 17.*

Buried in the heart of metropolitan Santa Clara County 10 minutes south of San Jose on Highway 17, the town of Campbell has a small-town center with a friendly neighborhood mood. Within a couple of blocks are the city hall, an old fruit cannery that now houses offices, and a handful of galleries, boutiques, and restaurants.

On Campbell's Civic Center Plaza, the Tudor-revival **Ainsley House** gives a glimpse of South Bay life in the 1920s and '30s, when it was owned by the valley's founding canner. The structure was moved in one piece from its previous location a half mile away, after descendants of the owners donated it to the city for preservation. Admission includes access to the Campbell Historical Museum down the street. ✉ *300 Grant St.* ☎ *408/866–2119* 🖭 *$6 for Ainsley House; $8 includes admission to Campbell Historical Museum* ⊙ *Guided tours Thurs.–Sun. noon–4; gardens daily sunrise–sunset.*

Committed to exploring themes in Americana, the **Campbell Historical Museum** presents exhibits on life in Silicon Valley in the age before computers. ✉ *51 N. Central Ave.* ☎ *408/866–2119* 🖭 *Museum $4; $8 includes admission to Ainsley House* ⊙ *Thurs.–Sun. noon–4.*

Where to Stay & Eat

¢ ✕ **Orchard Valley Coffee.** At this favorite local hangout, the large-pane front windows open wide on spring and summer days. Despite the propensity of laptops (taking advantage of free Wi-Fi), the café keeps its cozy feel with well-worn pillows and benches you're comfortable putting your feet on. The menu includes light meals, salads, soups, and pastries. ⊠ *349 E. Campbell Ave.* ☎ *408/374–2115* ⊟ *AE, MC, V.*

$$ 🏨 **Campbell Inn.** There are plenty of reasons to stay 10 minutes from downtown San Jose at this creek-side inn. You can play tennis, swim in the pool, ride one of the inn's bicycles on a nearby trail, or simply relax in the lobby, which has large, comfortable chairs and a fireplace. Suites have whirlpool tubs and saunas, and all room rates include a complimentary breakfast buffet. ⊠ *675 E. Campbell Ave., 95008* ☎ *408/ 374–4300 or 800/582–4449* 🖷 *408/379–0695* ⊕ *www.campbell-inn. com* 🛏 *85 rooms, 10 suites* ⚑ *Some in-room hot tubs, refrigerators, cable TV with movies, in-room VCRs, in-room data ports, Wi-Fi, tennis court, pool, outdoor hot tub, bicycles, airport shuttle, no-smoking rooms* ⊟ *AE, D, DC, MC, V* ⬤ *BP.*

Saratoga

❾ *12 mi southwest of Santa Clara on Hwy. 85.*

A 10-mi detour southwest of San Jose's urban core puts you in the heart of Saratoga, at the foot of the Santa Cruz Mountains. Once an artists' colony, the town is now home to many Silicon Valley CEOs, whose mansions dot the hillsides. Spend a slow-paced afternoon exploring Big Basin Way, the ⅓-mi main drag of the Village, as the downtown area is locally known. Here you'll find antiques stores, galleries, spas, and a handful of worthwhile restaurants.

Just up the hill from town, **Saratoga Historical Musem** has a small but interesting collection of photographs and artifacts pertaining to the history of Saratoga and the surrounding mountains. You can dig through their extensive research files for information on the Ohlone Indians, fruit orchards, and more. ⊠ *20450 Saratoga–Los Gatos Rd.* ☎ *408/867– 4311* 🎟 *Free* 🕙 *Fri.–Sun. 1–4.*

★ Built in 1912 by former governor James Phelan, **Villa Montalvo** is a striking white mansion presiding over an expansive lawn. You can picnic on the lawn amidst sculptures or stroll through the gallery, whose changing exhibits feature work by local artists and artists-in-residence. Additional draws are a gift shop and 175-acre park with hiking trails, as well as a summer concert series and year-round literary events. ⊠ *15400 Montalvo Rd.* ☎ *408/961–5800* ⊕ *www.villamontalvo.org* 🎟 *Free* 🕙 *Park May–Sept., Mon.–Thurs. 8–7, Fri.–Sun. 9–5; Oct.–Apr., weekdays 8–5, weekends 9–5. Gallery Wed.–Sat. 1–4, Sun. 10–4.*

★ For a quick driving tour of the hills with their sweeping valley views, drive south out of Saratoga on Big Basin Way, which is **Scenic Highway 9.** The road leads into the Santa Cruz Mountains, all the way to the coast at the city of Santa Cruz. But you can take in some great views about 1½ mi out of town by taking a right on Pierce Road and driving out to the **Mountain Winery.** Built by Paul Masson in 1905 and now listed on the National Register of Historic Places, it is constructed of masonry and oak to resemble a French country château. Although it no longer serves its original purpose, the Mountain Winery now hosts winemaker dinners and a summer concert series. Walking tours are available for free if you call in advance.

Where to Stay & Eat

$$$–$$$$ ⌖✕ **Sent Sovi.** Chef Josiah Slone picks the best local produce and natural meats, then creates dishes around them that let the ingredients speak for themselves. The French-inspired menu includes porcini mushroom–dusted scallops with freshly shelled peas and lemon-infused beets with pistachios. With copper-paneled walls, wooden floors, and candlelight, the dining room is among the most formal in town. ✉ *14583 Big Basin Way* ☎ *408/867–3110* ◈ *Reservations essential* ▤ *AE, MC, V* ⊘ *Closed Mon. No lunch.*

★ **$–$$$** ✕ **The Basin.** Organic produce, meats, and fresh fish are the starting points for this long, imaginative menu of American cuisine. Aside from a few flights of fancy, familiar favorites—pork and beans, beet salad, spaghetti carbonara—take on a personality all their own. The dim, clubby dining room and bar feels more like Manhattan than small-town California. ✉ *14572 Big Basin Way* ☎ *408/867–1906* ▤ *AE, DC, MC, V* ⊘ *No lunch.*

$$–$$$ ▥ **Inn at Saratoga.** This European-style inn is only 20 minutes from San Jose, but its aura of calm makes it feel far from the Silicon Valley buzz. The furnishings are rather lacklustre—reminiscent of an upscale motel—but each room's view of a creek makes for a relaxing stay. In the evening wine and hors d'oeuvres are set out in the cozy lobby, and although modern business conveniences are available, they are discreetly hidden. ✉ *20645 4th St., 95070* ☎ *408/867–5020 or 800/543–5020* ▣ *408/741–0981* ⊕ *www.innatsaratoga.com* ⤶ *42 rooms, 3 suites* ♻ *Refrigerators, some in-room hot tubs, cable TV, in-room VCRs, in-room broadband, in-room data ports, Wi-Fi, exercise equipment, babysitting, dry cleaning, laundry service, Internet room, business services, meeting room; no smoking* ▤ *AE, DC, MC, V* ⦿ *CP.*

$–$$$ ▥ **Saratoga Oaks Lodge.** The towering namesake trees shade the property and provide a spot for birds to sing from their branches. Furnishings are neat and classic, with wooden armoires and steam showers in most rooms. Up the hill in back are several bungalows, the patios of which look onto a soothing fountain. ✉ *14626 Big Basin Way, 95070* ☎ *408/867–3307 or 888/867–3588* ▣ *408/867–6765* ⊕ *www.saratogaoakslodge.com* ⤶ *15 rooms, 5 suites* ♻ *Microwaves, refrigerators, cable TV with movies, some in-room DVD, in-room VCRs, in-room data ports, Wi-Fi; no smoking* ▤ *AE, D, MC, V* ⦿ *CP.*

SAN JOSE

For years San Jose has played second fiddle to its more celebrated cousin just up the highway, but in truth this city of nearly 1 million people has a lot to offer. The city has nationally recognized art and science museums, and its own ballet and repertory companies. It's also a city of great diversity, for no ethnic group holds the majority here. Residents speak a total of 46 languages, and alongside machines vending the *San Jose Mercury News,* you'll find *Nuevo Mundo* and the *Chinese World Jour-*

nal. The city is also one of the safest in the country, with the lowest crime rate for any city over 500,000 people.

The diversity extends to San Jose's various neighborhoods. Downtown has wide streets and several parks for enjoying the usually warm weather from March to October. The SoFA (South of First Area) district, along 1st and 2nd streets south of San Carlos Avenue, is the best spot for nightlife, with its numerous music clubs. Japantown, around Jackson and Taylor streets between 4th and 6th streets, has modern shops and restaurants and many historical buildings. Willow Glen (Lincoln Avenue between Willow and Minnesota streets) is a place of boutiques, small cafés, and tree-lined streets—a welcome counter to downtown's urbanity.

Downtown can be easily explored by foot, and Guadalupe River Park, a 3-mi belt of trees and gardens, connects downtown with the Children's Discovery Museum to the south. A 21-mi light-rail system links downtown to the business district and Paramount's Great America to the north, but you will still need a car to get to such sights as the Egyptian Museum and the Winchester Mystery House.

A walking tour of downtown San Jose is detailed in a brochure available from the Convention and Visitors Bureau. Vintage trolleys operate in downtown San Jose from 10:30 to 5:30 in summer and on some holidays throughout the year. You can buy trolley tickets at vending machines in any transit station.

Downtown San Jose & Vicinity

4 mi east of Santa Clara on Hwy. 82; 55 mi south of San Francisco on Hwy. 101 or I–280.

A GOOD TOUR

Much of downtown San Jose can be toured easily on foot. Start at the ► **Children's Discovery Museum** ⑩ and be sure to wander around the outside of this outrageously purple building. Crossing through the surrounding park, take a stroll through the "herd" of larger-than-life animal sculptures facing San Carlos Street. The nearby steps lead down to Guadalupe Creek and a parallel walking path; a good detour heads north to the San Jose Arena and the **Guadalupe River Park** ⑪, with a carousel and children's playground.

Back at the sculpture park, continue east on San Carlos Street into the heart of downtown San Jose. Immediately on the left is the Center for Performing Arts, home to the city's ballet and symphony. San Jose's McEnery Convention Center and the visitor center are diagonally across the road. In front of the center an outdoor skating rink (open daily) is set up from mid-November to mid-January.

Continue down San Carlos Street and turn left on Market Street; ahead is Plaza de Cesar Chavez. On the square's northeast corner are the must-see **San Jose Museum of Art** ⑫ and adjacent **Cathedral Basilica of St. Joseph** ⑬. On the square's western edge at Park Avenue is the **Tech Museum of Innovation** ⑭, with its children-friendly hands-on exhibits.

Follow Market Street north from the plaza and turn left on Santa Clara Street. For a glimpse of the Hotel De Anza, walk four blocks ahead to

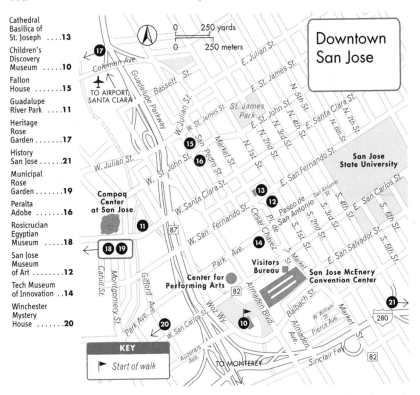

Downtown
San Jose

the corner of North Almaden Boulevard. Otherwise, walk one block, turn right on San Pedro Street, and continue two blocks—past the sidewalk cafés and restaurants—to St. John Street and turn left. The **Fallon House** 15 will be on your right, the **Peralta Adobe** 16 on your left. At this point you can turn around and go east three blocks on St. John Street and board the light-rail to return to your starting point.

Pick up your car and drive northwest from the center of town on Coleman Avenue. At Taylor Street take a right to reach **Heritage Rose Garden** 17. After you've strolled the grounds, head southwest on Taylor Street, which turns into Naglee Avenue at Alameda. Naglee will take you to the **Rosicrucian Egyptian Museum** 18 and, across the street, the **Municipal Rose Garden** 19. When you're finished there, continue southwest on Naglee until it turns into Forest Avenue, which intersects Winchester Boulevard. Turn left onto Winchester Boulevard to reach **Winchester Mystery House** 20. Finally, take I–280 east to Highway 82 (Monterey Road) south and turn left on Phelan Avenue. At Kelley Park you can visit **History San Jose** 21. To return to downtown, backtrack to Monterey Road and turn right to drive north.

TIMING   The walking portion of this tour can easily be completed in about two hours. However, if you decide to spend time in the museums or at a café along San Pedro Street, give yourself at least four hours. The length of the driving tour depends on how long you spend at each sight. Plan on anywhere from three to six hours.

What to See

⑬ Cathedral Basilica of St. Joseph. This Renaissance-style cathedral embodies the idea of resurrection: it is the fifth church of St. Joseph built in San Jose (the fourth on this site). All its predecessors have perished in earthquakes and other natural disasters. The original adobe church began serving the residents of the pueblo of San Jose in 1803. The current and longest-standing incarnation, built in 1877, is a grand cathedral with stained-glass windows and murals. ⊠ *80 S. Market St.* ☎ *408/283–8100* ⊕ *www.stjosephcathedral.org.*

☾ ⚑ ⑩ Children's Discovery Museum of San Jose. You can't miss this angular purple building that seems to rise from the creek across from the convention center. Exhibits here explore the world of how things work, from why water gushes to why springs go *boing.* Everything is hands-on, so kids can blow gigantic bubbles, dress up in old-timey clothes, or climb on the oversize animal sculptures outside while tired parents picnic on the lawn. The gallery shows art by children from all over the world. ⊠ *180 Woz Way, at Auzerais St.* ☎ *408/298–5437* ⊕ *www.cdm.org* ⊠ *$7* ☉ *Tues.–Sat. 10–5, Sun. noon–5.*

⑮ Fallon House. San Jose's seventh mayor, Thomas Fallon, built this Victorian mansion in 1855. The house's period-decorated rooms can be viewed on a 90-minute tour that includes the Peralta Adobe and a screening of a video about the two houses. ⊠ *175 W. St. John St.* ☎ *408/993–8300* ⊕ *www.historysanjose.org* ⊠ *$5, includes admission to Peralta Adobe* ☉ *Guided tours weekends noon–5, last tour at 3:30.*

☾ ⑪ Guadalupe River Park. This downtown park includes the Arena Green, next to the sports arena, with a carousel, children's playground, and artwork honoring five champion figure skaters from the area. The River Park path, which stretches for 3 mi, starts at the Children's Discovery Museum and runs north, ending at the Arena Green. ⊠ *345 W. Santa Clara St.* ☎ *408/277–5904* ⊕ *www.grpg.org* ⊠ *Free.*

⑰ Heritage Rose Garden. The newer of the city's two rose gardens has won national acclaim for its 5,000 rosebushes and trees. This quiet, 4-acre retreat has ample benches and is alongside the Historic Orchard, which has fruit trees indigenous to the Santa Clara Valley. The garden is northwest of downtown, near the airport. ⊠ *Taylor and Spring Sts.* ☎ *408/298–7657* ⊠ *Free* ☉ *Daily dawn–dusk.*

㉑ History San Jose. Southeast of the city center, occupying 25 acres of Kelley Park, this outdoor "museum" highlights the history of San Jose and the Santa Clara Valley. You can see 28 historic and reconstructed buildings, hop an antique trolley, observe letterpress printing, and grab a snack at O'Brien's Ice Cream Parlor and Candy Store. On weekdays admission is free, but the buildings are closed except for the galleries, Pacific Hotel, and the candy store. ⊠ *1650 Senter Rd., at Phelan Ave.* ☎ *408/287–2290* ⊕ *www.historysanjose.org* ⊠ *Free* ☉ *Tues.–Sun. noon–5; call for weekend tour times.*

Ira F. Brilliant Center for Beethoven Studies. This museum holds endless scores of music—including original scores hand-written by the composer—as well as thousands of books, a 19th-century Viennese fortepiano, and—in true rock star fashion–a lock of Beethoven's hair. ⊠ *Dr. Martin Luther King Jr. Library One Washington Sq. San Jose* ☎ *408/808–2058* ✉ *Free* ⊙ *Mon.–Fri., 1–5.* **Municipal Rose Garden.** Installed in 1931, the Municipal Rose Garden is one of several outstanding green spaces in the city's urban core—and certainly the most fragrant. West of downtown San Jose you'll find 5½ acres of roses here, with 4,000 shrubs and trees in 189 well-labeled beds, as well as walkways, fountains, and trellises. Some of the neighboring homes in the Rose Garden district date to the time of the city's founding. ⊠ *Naglee and Dana Aves.* ☎ *408/277-2757* ⊕ *www.sjparks.org.* ✉ *Free* ⊙ *Daily 8 AM–sunset.*

⑯ Peralta Adobe. California pepper trees shade the last remaining structure (circa 1797) from the Pueblo de Guadalupe, the original settlement from which the modern city of San Jose was born. This whitewashed, two-room house has been furnished to show what home life was like during the Spanish occupation and the Mexican rancho era. ⊠ *184 W. St. John St.* ☎ *408/993–8300* ⊕ *www.historysanjose.org* ✉ *$5, includes admission to Fallon House* ⊙ *Guided tours weekends noon–5.*

Phantom Galleries. Free art abounds in the storefronts of downtown San Jose courtesy of this program. Exhibits rotate bimonthly in empty storefronts beginning at the corner of San Fernando Street and South 1st Street, down to Santa Clara Street. Call to find out about the latest installations. ☎ *408/271–5151.*

⑱ Rosicrucian Egyptian Museum. Owned by the Rosicrucian Order (a modern-day group devoted to the study of metaphysics for self-improvement), this museum exhibits the West Coast's largest collection of Egyptian and Babylonian antiquities, including mummies, and an underground reproduction of a rock tomb. The planetarium gives related presentations daily. The complex, 3 mi from downtown, is surrounded by a garden filled with palms, papyrus, and other plants recalling ancient Egypt. ⊠ *1342 Naglee Ave., at Park Ave.* ☎ *408/947–3635* ⊕ *www.egyptianmuseum. org* ✉ *$9* ⊙ *Tues.–Fri. 10–5, weekends 11–6.*

⑫ San Jose Museum of Art. Housed in a former post office building, this museum doesn't attempt to compete with the larger, swankier art museums in San Francisco. Instead, it does its own thing. The permanent collection of paintings, sculpture, photography, and large-scale multimedia installations is solid, with an emphasis on cutting-edge California and Latino artists. The massive Dale Chihuly glass sculpture hanging above the lobby hints at the appreciation for futuristic, high-tech pieces. ⊠ *110 S. Market St.* ☎ *408/294–2787* ⊕ *www.sjmusart.org* ✉ *Free* ⊙ *Tues.–Sun. 11–5.*

San Jose Institute of Contemporary Art. The best art in San Jose is at this white-walled gallery, which shows groundbreaking work by Bay Area artists. ⊠ *451 S. 1st St.* ☎ *408/283–8155* ✉ *Free* ⊙ *Tues., Wed., and Fri. 10–5, Thurs. 10–8, Sat. noon–5.*

A Fruitful Past

THERE WAS A TIME– not so long ago, in fact–when the Silicon Valley was known by a very different name: "The Valley of Heart's Delight."

The name came from the Valley's rich soil, which proved perfect for growing sweet, "delightful" fruit of all kinds. Orchardists first settled in the area in the 1860s, but it wasn't until the transcontinental railroad arrived in 1869 that the industry blossomed, giving the Valley its "fruit basket" identity that would remain in place for almost a century.

At the height of the industry in the 1940s and 1950s, there were 5 million fruit trees in the Valley– so many, it's said, that in the springtime, the area between Mt. Hamilton and the Santa Cruz Mountains looked like a snowdrift for all the white blossoms there.

Today no commercial orchards remain; real estate values have priced out agricultural operations, and so office parks and housing have replaced the once-fertile fields. However, the tradition is upheld in a few public places around the South Bay. In 1998 the town of Sunnyvale broke ground on **Orchard Heritage Park** (⊠ 550 E. Remington Dr. ☎ 408/749–0220), a working apricot orchard open to the public. In San Jose, Guadalupe Gardens includes **The Historic Orchard** (⊠ 715 Spring St. ☎ 408/ 298–7657). The 3.3 acres commemorate the diversity of the valley's agricultural past, with 250 trees growing apples, apricots, pomegranates, persimmons, and other kinds of fruit. You may also catch glimpses of the valley's fruitful past in neighborhood backyards– where flowering lemon and plum trees still delight at least a few hearts.

Tech Museum of Innovation. Designed by renowned architect Ricardo Legorreta of Mexico City, this museum of technology is both high-tech and hands-on. Exhibits allow you to create an action movie in a video-editing booth, solve the story behind a crime scene using real forensic techniques, and talk with a roaming robot named Zaza. Another highlight is the 299-seat Hackworth IMAX Dome Theater. ⊠ 201 S. Market St., at Park Ave. ☎ 408/294–8324 ⊕ www.thetech.org ⊠ Museum $9.50, IMAX $9.50, combination ticket $16 ☉ Daily 10–5.

FodorśChoice
★

Winchester Mystery House. Convinced that spirits would harm her if construction on her house ever stopped, the late Sarah Winchester kept carpenters working for 38 years to create this bizarre 160-room labyrinth. Today the 19th-century house (which is on the National Register of Historic Places) is a favorite family attraction, and though the grounds are no longer overgrown, the place retains an air of mystery. You can explore the house on the 65-minute mansion tour or the 50-minute behind-the-scenes tour (these depart every 20–30 minutes); each Friday the 13th there's also a special nighttime flashlight tour. ⊠ 525 S. Winchester Blvd., between Stevens Creek Blvd. and I–280 ☎ 408/247–2101 ⊕ www.winchestermysteryhouse.com ⊠ Mansion tour $19.95, behind-the-scenes tour $16.95, combination ticket $24.95 ☉ June–Sept., daily 9–7; May and Oct., Sun.–Thurs. 9–5, Fri. and Sat. 9–7; Nov.–Apr., daily 9–5.

OFF THE
BEATEN
PATH

LACE MUSEUM – This muesum goes far beyond doilies; here you'll find a vest tatted from human hair, lace decorated with beetle shells, an intricate flaxen piece that required days' work for every square inch, as well as just plain beautiful quilts, tablecloths, and handkerchiefs dating back through the 1900s. ☒ *552 S. Murphy Ave., 12 mi east of Palo Alto on Hwys. 101 and 87, Sunnyvale* ☎ *408/730-4695* ☜ *Free, donation requested* ☺ *Tue.–Sat., 11–4.*

Where to Stay & Eat

$$–$$$$ ✗ **A. P. Stump's.** Tin ceilings, low lights, and high-walled booths set the tone of this chophouse, favorite of local power brokers. The platinum-card feel is reinforced with such dishes as filet mignon with baked lobster tail and oyster shooters in a house-made Absolut citron sauce. In summer, ask for a table on the airy back patio. ☒ *163 W. Santa Clara St.* ☎ *408/292–9928* ▭ *AE, D, DC, MC, V* ☺ *No lunch weekends.*

★ **$$–$$$$** ✗ **Emile's Restaurant.** In a city that's gone through numerous changes, Emile's has remained a solidly popular downtown dining spot for decades. The menu, which focuses on European-influenced California cuisine, is given a slightly decadent edge by Swiss chef-owner Emile Mooser: duck a l'orange is flavored with Grand Marnier; beef tournedo is wrapped in bacon and served with Béarnaise sauce. Half portions allow you to create your own tasting menu. ☒ *545 S. 2nd St.* ☎ *408/289–1960* ▭ *AE, D, DC, MC, V* ☺ *No lunch. Closed Sun. and Mon.*

$$–$$$$ ✗ **Menara Moroccan Restaurant.** The delicious cumin- and coriander-spiced cuisine is only part of what makes dining here an exotic experience. Arched entryways, lazily spinning ceiling fans, and a tile fountain all evoke a glamorous Moroccan palace. If sitting on jewel-tone cushions and feasting on lamb with honey, delicately spiced chicken kebabs, or hare with paprika doesn't make you feel like you've traveled to a distant land, then just wait until the belly dancers arrive for their nightly performance. ☒ *41 E. Gish Rd.* ☎ *408/453–1983* ▭ *AE, D, MC, V* ☺ *No lunch.*

$$–$$$$ ✗ **Paolo's.** This Italian restaurant is run by the fourth generation of a family that arrived in California in 1917. The menu is mainly classics with a few surprises, such as buckwheat pasta stuffed with potato, cheese, and caramelized savoy cabbage. Italophiles will love the wine list, which has more than 450 vintages—most of them, naturally, from the mother country. ☒ *333 W. San Carlos St.* ☎ *408/294–2558* ▭ *AE, D, DC, MC, V* ☺ *Closed Sun. No lunch Sat.*

$$–$$$ ✗ **7 Restaurant & Lounge.** People come to this flashy restaurant and lounge as much to eat as to feel glamorous at the tight bar and in the high-ceilinged, industrial-chic dining room. Case in point: there are only five entrées on the menu. Better to choose from the long list of small plates, share with friends, and get ready to people-watch. Crabcakes served with Napa cabbage slaw and black bean vinaigrette is a top choice, as is the pasta with prosciutto, asparagus, and smoked mozzarella. ☒ *754 The Alameda* ☎ *408/280–1644* ▭ *AE, D, DC, MC, V* ☺ *Closed Sun. No lunch Sat.*

$–$$$ ✗ **Henry's World-Famous Hi-Life.** Locals agree this is hands-down the best steak house in town. But unlike the shiny new restaurants downtown, this place has character (and grit) instead of glitz, built over 43 years in business. The dining room's decoration is a picket fence running along the wall. There are no menus; dinner selections are written on the wall, and only the prices have changed over the years. You can choose from pork chops, ribs, or chicken, but really, the whole point is to order one of the nine varieties of steak that have made this place "famous." ⊠ *301 W. St. John St.* ☎ *408/295–5414* 🖃 *AE, MC, V.*

★ **$–$$$** ✗ **71 Saint Peter.** This is among the prettiest restaurants in San Jose: ceramic tile floors, skylights, and rough wood walls give it the feel of an elegant farmhouse. Chef Mark Tabak prepares each dish carefully— you can even watch him do so in the glass-walled kitchen, which takes an unpretentious center stage here. Try the five-part tasting menu, which changes often to reflect the best of local ingredients. In summer, the menu might include a Mission fig strudel with dolce gorgonzola and duck prosciutto, or honey-lavender grilled apricots for dessert. ⊠ *71 N. San Pedro St.* ☎ *408/971–8523* 🖃 *AE, D, DC, MC, V* ⊗ *Closed Sun. No lunch Sat.*

$–$$ ✗ **Paragon.** At this cosmopolitan spot, the lighting is low and the soul music is constant (even in the courtyard lounge, where it's piped in through faux rocks). The dining room is grand and plush, though a row of high-tables lined with stools down the center gives it a casual feel. The food complements—duck confit with dried cherries, pancetta-wrapped monk-fish—though plenty of diners also order the smashing side order of mac and cheese. This is also a great place for cocktails. ⊠ *211 S. First St.* ☎ *408/282–8888* 🖃 *AE, D, DC, MC, V* ⊗ *No lunch weekends.*

★ **¢–$$** ✗ **Citronelle.** If you can endure the distance from downtown (6 mi), you'll find that this Vietnamese restaurant is special. A bouquet of flowers from the owner's garden graces each table, and the seasonal menu is based on natural meats and organic produce. Specialties include the traditional clay-pot catfish and the chef's very own lemongrass pork chop. ⊠ *826 S. Winchester Blvd.* ☎ *408/244–2528* ⊕ *www.citronellemv.com.* 🖃 *MC, V.*

¢–$ ✗ **Tacqueria la Mordida.** At this authentic tacqueria, choices range from standard burritos to such house creations as Shrimp à la Diabla. Portions are huge across the board. Bright yellow decor, Mexican pop music, and a weekend margarita bar complete the experience. ⊠ *86 N. Market St.* ☎ *408/298–9357* 🖃 *MC, V.*

¢ ✗ **La Villa.** People come from all over the South Bay to take home the house-made ravioli that made this deli locally famous. You can taste them or any of the other Italian specialties for lunch at tables outside on the street. This is also a good place for picnic supplies such as deli salads, cheese, and sausage. ⊠ *1319 Lincoln Ave.* ☎ *408/295–7851* 🖃 *AE, MC, V* ⊗ *Closed Sun. and Mon.*

¢ ✗ **Tofoo Com Chay.** This bare-bones vegetarian restaurant is a favorite of college students and local hipsters. There's no table service—order from the counter from a selection of sandwiches and simple entrées— but the food is reliably good, as well as super cheap. ⊠ *388 E. Santa Clara St.* ☎ *408/286–6335* 🖃 *No credit cards* ⊗ *Closed Sun.*

¢ ✗ **White Lotus.** The Southeast Asian–influenced meatless dishes at this slightly worn but popular restaurant are deliciously prepared using fresh ingredients. Choose from an extensive menu of vegetable and meat-substitute entrées, such as soft, chewy, pan-fried rice noodles with tofu and crisp vegetables; curry "chicken"; or spicy garlic eggplant. Start your meal with an order of crunchy imperial rolls or Thai sweet-and-sour soup. ☒ *80 N. Market St.* ☎ *408/977–0540* ▭ *MC, V* ⊘ *Closed Tues.*

$$–$$$$ ▣ **The Fairmont.** This downtown gem is as opulent as its sister property in San Francisco. Get lost in the lavish lobby sofas under dazzling chandeliers, or dip your feet in the 4th-floor pool, which is surrounded by exotic palms. Rooms have every imaginable comfort, from down pillows and custom-designed comforters to oversize bath towels changed twice a day. ☒ *170 S. Market St., 95113* ☎ *408/998–1900 or 800/257–7544* 🖶 *408/287–1648* ⊕ *www.fairmont.com* ✏ *718 rooms, 77 suites* ♨ *3 restaurants, room service, some in-room faxes, in-room safes, minibars, refrigerators, cable TV with movies and video games, in-room broadband, in-room data ports, Wi-Fi, pool, health club, hair salon, massage, steam room, bar, lobby lounge, dry cleaning, laundry service, concierge, Internet room, business services, meeting rooms, some pets allowed (fee), no-smoking rooms, no-smoking floor* ▭ *AE, D, DC, MC, V.*

$$–$$$$ ▥▣ **Hotel Montgomery.** Wall Street Journal meets Wallpaper magazine is the feel at this boutique hotel, which opened in 2004. It's the hippest place to stay in San Jose—evident even as you enter the lobby through an outdoor lounge complete with martinis, bocce courts, and either hip-hop or soul music playing at all times. The rooms are stylish, with an emphasis on texture rather than bright color: faux-fur throw pillows, woven wool blankets, leather headboards, and even leather-textured wallpaper. But for all the hipness, no congeniality is sacrificed. The staff is young and friendly, and little perks like the CD lending library give the hotel a welcoming vibe. ☒ *211 S. 1st St., 95113* ☎ *408/282–8800, 800/738–7477* 🖶 *408/282–8850* ⊕ *www.montgomeryhotelsj.com* ✏ *80 rooms, 6 suites* ♨ *Restaurant, room service, in-room safes, minibars, refrigerators, cable TV with movies, in-room broadband, in-room data ports, Wi-Fi, exercise equpiment, bocce, bar, dry cleaning, laundry service, concierge, Internet room, business services, meeting rooms, no smoking floors* ▭ *AE, D, DC, MC, V.*

★ $$–$$$ ▣ **Hotel De Anza.** This lushly appointed art deco hotel has hand-painted ceilings, a warm coral-and-green color scheme, and an enclosed terrace with towering palms and dramatic fountains. Business travelers will appreciate the many amenities, including a full-service business center and personal voice-mail services—not to mention the fireside lounge, where jazz bands often play. ☒ *233 W. Santa Clara St., 95113* ☎ *408/286–1000 or 800/843–3700* 🖶 *408/286–0500* ⊕ *www.hoteldeanza.com* ✏ *90 rooms, 10 suites* ♨ *Restaurant, some in-room hot tubs, minibars, refrigerators, cable TV with movies, in-room VCRs, in-room broadband, in-room data ports, Wi-Fi, exercise equipment, bar, dry cleaning, laundry service, concierge, Internet room, business services, no-smoking floors* ▭ *AE, D, DC, MC, V.*

Nightlife & the Arts

NIGHTLIFE **Agenda** (☒ 399 S. 1st St. ☎ 408/380–3042) is one of the most popular nightspots downtown, with a restaurant on the main floor, a bar upstairs, and a nightclub on the bottom floor. Pick up a pool cue at trendy **South First Billiards** (☒ 420 S. 1st St. ☎ 408/294–7800), amid the burgeoning cluster of small clubs in the SoFA district. Also in the neighborhood is **Pete Escovedo's Latin Jazz Club** (☒ 400 S. 1st St. ☎ 408/947–7500), run by the legendary jazz percussionist, with nightly music ranging from jazz to reggae. Just west of downtown, the **Garden City Lounge** (☒ 360 S. Saratoga Ave. ☎ 408/244–3333) has jazz nightly with no cover charge.

THE ARTS The **Center for Performing Arts** (☒ 255 Almaden Blvd. ☎ 408/277–3900) is the city's main performance venue. **American Musical Theatre of San Jose** (☎ 408/453–7108) presents a half dozen musicals per year. **Ballet San Jose Silicon Valley** (☎ 408/288–2800) performs from November through May. **San Jose Repertory Theatre** (☒ 101 Paseo de San Antonio ☎ 408/367–7255) occupies a contemporary four-story, 528-seat theater, dubbed the Blue Box because of its angular blue exterior. **City Lights Theater Co.** (☒ 529 S. 2nd St. ☎ 408/295–4200) presents progressive and traditional programs in an intimate 99-seat theater.

Sports & the Outdoors

GOLF **San Jose Municipal Golf Course** (☒ 1560 Oakland Rd. ☎ 408/441–4653) is an 18-hole course. Greens fees are $32 on weekdays and $46 on weekends. Cart rental is $25 extra. **Cinnabar Hills Golf Club** (☒ 23600 McKean Rd. ☎ 408/323–5200) is a 27-hole course. Greens fees are $80 on weekdays and $100 on weekends until 2 PM; late-afternoon fees are considerably lower.

SPECTATOR The 17,496-seat **HP Pavilion at San Jose** (☒ Santa Clara St. at Autumn
SPORTS St. ☎ 408/287–9200, 408/998–8497 for tickets), known locally as the Shark Tank (even just "the Tank"), is home to the National Hockey League's **San Jose Sharks**. The building looks like a giant hothouse, with its glass entrance, shining metal armor, and skylight ceiling. Inside, hockey alternates with other sporting events and concerts. The **Hellyer Velodrome** (☒ 985 Hellyer Ave. ☎ 408/226–9716) attracts national-class cyclists and Olympians in training to races from May through August.

THE PENINSULA & SOUTH BAY A TO Z

To research prices, get advice from other travelers, and book travel arrangements, visit www.fodors.com.

AIRPORTS & TRANSFERS

All the major airlines serve San Francisco International Airport, and most of them fly to San Jose International Airport. South & East Bay Airport Shuttle can transport you between the airport and Saratoga, Palo Alto, and other destinations. *See* Air Travel *in* Smart Travel Tips A to Z for airline and airport phone numbers.

🚹 **South & East Bay Airport Shuttle** ☎ 408/225–4444 or 800/548–4664.

BUS TRAVEL

SamTrans buses travel to Moss Beach and Half Moon Bay from the Daly City BART (Bay Area Rapid Transit) station. Another bus connects Half Moon Bay with Pescadero. Each trip takes approximately one hour. Call for schedules, because departures are infrequent. The Valley Transportation Authority (VTA) shuttle links downtown San Jose to the CalTrain station, across from the Arena Green, every 20 minutes during morning and evening commute hours.

🛈 **SamTrans** ☎ 800/660-4287 ⊕ www.samtrans.org. **VTA Shuttle** ☎ 408/321-2300, 800/894-9908 ⊕ www.vta.org.

CAR RENTAL

You can rent a car at the San Jose airport from any of the many major agencies. Specialty Rentals offers standard cars and luxury vehicles; it has an office in Palo Alto and will deliver a car to you anywhere on the Peninsula or at the airport. *See* Car Rental *in* Smart Travel Tips A to Z for national rental agency phone numbers.

🛈 Local Agencies **Specialty Rentals** ☎ 650/856-9100 or 800/400-8412.

CAR TRAVEL

Public transportation to coastal areas is limited, so it's best to drive. To get to Moss Beach or Half Moon Bay, take Highway 1, also known as the Coast Highway, south along the length of the San Mateo coast. When coastal traffic is heavy, especially on summer weekends, you can also reach Half Moon Bay via I–280, the Junipero Serra Freeway; follow it south as far as Route 92, where you can turn west toward the coast. To get to Pescadero, drive south 16 mi on Highway 1 from Half Moon Bay. For Año Nuevo continue south on Highway 1 another 12 mi.

By car the most pleasant route down the Inland Peninsula to Palo Alto, Woodside, Santa Clara, and San Jose is I–280, which passes along Crystal Springs Reservoir. U.S. 101, also known as the Bayshore Freeway, is more direct but also more congested. To avoid the often-heavy commuter traffic on Highway 101, use I–280 during rush hours.

To reach Saratoga, take I–280 south to Highway 85 and follow Highway 85 south toward Gilroy. Exit on Saratoga–Sunnyvale Road, go south, and follow the signs to the Village—about 2½ mi. Signs will also direct you to Hakone Gardens, Villa Montalvo, and on concert nights, the Mountain Winery.

EMERGENCIES

In an emergency dial 911.

🛈 Hospitals **San Jose Medical Center** ✉ 675 E. Santa Clara St., San Jose ☎ 408/998-3212. **Stanford Hospital** ✉ 300 Pasteur Dr., Palo Alto ☎ 650/723-4000.

TRAIN TRAVEL

CalTrain runs from 4th and Townsend streets in San Francisco to Palo Alto ($4.25 each way); from there take the free Marguerite shuttle bus to the Stanford campus and the Palo Alto area. Buses run about every 15 minutes from 6 AM to 7:45 PM and are timed to connect with trains and public transit buses.

CalTrain service continues south of Palo Alto to Santa Clara's Railroad and Franklin streets stop, near Santa Clara University ($5.50 one-way), and to San Jose's Rod Diridon station ($5.50 one-way). The trip to Santa Clara takes approximately 1¼ hours; to San Jose, it's about 1½ hours.

Valley Transportation Authority buses run efficiently throughout the Santa Clara Valley, although not as frequently as you might like. Operators can help you plan routes.

In San Jose, light-rail trains run 24 hours a day and serve most major attractions, shopping malls, historic sites, and downtown. Trains run every 10 minutes weekdays from 6 AM to 8 PM and vary during weekends and late-night hours from every 15 minutes to once an hour. Tickets are valid for two hours; they cost $1.40 one-way or $4 for a day pass. Buy tickets at vending machines in any transit station. For more information call or visit the Downtown Customer Service Center.

🚊 **CalTrain** ☎ 800/660-4287 ⊕ www.caltrain.com. **Downtown Customer Service Center** Light Rail ⊠ 2 N. 1st St., San Jose ☎ 408/321-2300. **Marguerite Shuttle** ☎ 650/723-9362. **Valley Transportation Authority** ☎ 408/321-2300 or 800/894-9908 ⊕ www.vta.org.

VISITOR INFORMATION

🚊 **California State Parks** ☎ 800/777-0369. **Half Moon Bay Chamber of Commerce** ⊠ 520 Kelly Ave., Half Moon Bay 94019 ☎ 650/726-8380 ⊕ www.halfmoonbaychamber. org. **Palo Alto Chamber of Commerce** ⊠ 122 Hamilton Ave., Palo Alto 94301 ☎ 650/ 324-3121 ⊕ www.paloaltochamber.com. **San Jose Convention and Visitors Bureau** ⊠ 408 Almaden Blvd., 3rd fl., San Jose 95110 ☎ 800/726-5673, 408/295-2265, or 408/ 295-9600 ⊕ www.sanjose.org. **Santa Clara Chamber of Commerce and Convention and Visitors Bureau** ⊠ 1850 Warburton Ave., Santa Clara 95050 ☎ 408/244-9660 ⊕ www.santaclarachamber.org. **Saratoga Chamber of Commerce** ⊠ 14485 Big Basin Way, Saratoga 95070 ☎ 408/867-0753 ⊕ www.saratogachamber.org. **Woodside Town Hall** ⊠ 2955 Woodside Rd., Woodside 94062 ☎ 650/851-6790 ⊕ www. woodsidetown.org.

Monterey Bay
From Carmel to Santa Cruz

WORD OF MOUTH

"The Monterey Bay Aquarium is a great experience for young kids and adults. Venues for the sea creatures are very well done. It is quite a fun and an educational experience. I suggest going early in the day to avoid the lines. Either way, it's well worth the wait."

—Tom

"The beauty of Point Lobos State Reserve was so stunning, I could not believe it. Here you have a mix of tall cliffs, crashing waves, gorgeous wild flowers, abundant wildlife (seals, sea otters, deer), and sheltered emerald-green coves with white sandy beaches."

—Birder

Updated by
Lisa M.
Hamilton

THERE IS NO SINGLE HISTORY OF THE MONTEREY PENINSULA. John Steinbeck saw a community built on the elbow grease of farm laborers in the Salinas Valley and fishermen along Cannery Row in Monterey. Military buffs see centuries of battles to decide which nation would control this land. Biologists use the natural history here to determine how we might interact with the ocean in a more sustainable way for the future. Native Americans appreciate the area through a history that reaches thousands of years into the past.

But what all these histories have in common is a binding element inherent to nearly every experience of the Monterey Bay area—abundance. It's certainly apparent today: in the good life of coast-side towns and luxurious resorts that ring the bay; in the resplendent marine habitat stretching to the horizon.

The Ohlone Indians, the first human inhabitants, thrived here for thousands of years because of the natural year-round supply of food. Plants, animals, and sea creatures contributed to the generous diet. In fact, accounts by early visitors recall that wildlife was so profuse as to be a "nuisance." So great were the mounds of discarded shells in abandoned camps that European settlers used them to pave roads.

This same natural bounty captivated explorer Juan Rodríguez Cabrillo, when he arrived in 1542 and claimed the peninsula for Spain. Sixty years after Cabrillo, explorer Sebastián Vizcaíno named the bay for his Mexican viceroy, the Count of Monte Rey. The people who followed were first Mexican settlers in search of a better life, followed by Spanish missionaries and military men who claimed the rich land for the king.

In 1770 Monterey became the capital of the Spanish territory of Alta California. Commander Don Gaspar de Portola established the first of California's four Spanish presidios here, and Father Junípero Serra founded the second of 21 Franciscan missions (he later moved it to Carmel). Mexico revolted against Spain in 1810; a decade later, a treaty was signed and the newly independent Mexico claimed Alta California as its own. By the mid-1840s Monterey had grown into a lively seaport that attracted Yankee sea traders, and land from California to Texas was coveted by the United States. On July 7, 1846, Commodore John Sloat raised the flag of the United States over the Custom House.

The development that followed laid the foundation for the modern wealth of Monterey County. In the rich, deep soil of the Salinas Valley agriculture flourished, spurred on by the arrival of the railroad in 1872. Likewise, dairy farms thrived in the mild climate of Carmel Valley. In Monterey, fishing for sardines and other seafood built an industry whose structure remains today.

California's constitution was framed in Monterey's Colton Hall, but the town was nearly forgotten once gold was discovered at Sutter's Mill on the American River. After the gold rush, the state capital moved to Sacramento, while in Monterey the whaling industry boomed until the early 1900s. Tourists began to arrive at the turn of the 20th century with the opening of the Del Monte Hotel, the most palatial resort the West Coast had ever seen. Writers and artists such as John Steinbeck, Henry Miller,

Robinson Jeffers, and Ansel Adams also discovered Monterey Bay, adding their legacy to the region while capturing its magic on canvas, paper, and film. In the 1920s and 1930s Cannery Row's sardine industry took off, but by the late 1940s and early 1950s the fish had disappeared. The causes are still in dispute, though overfishing, water contamination, and a change in ocean currents were the likely culprits.

Today the Monterey Peninsula's diverse cultural and maritime heritage is evident in all the sights visitors come to see. Cannery Row has been reborn as a tourist attraction with shops, restaurants, hotels, and the Monterey Bay Aquarium. The downtowns of Carmel, Salinas, San Juan Bautista, and Monterey are walks through history. The bay itself is protected by the Monterey Bay National Marine Sanctuary, the nation's largest undersea canyon—which is bigger and deeper than the Grand Canyon. And of course, the natural wonder that fostered them all still thrives through the area, as the view from almost anywhere along Highway 1 will show you.

Exploring Monterey Bay

The individual charms of its towns complement Monterey Bay's natural beauty. Santa Cruz sits at the northern tip of the crescent formed by Monterey Bay; the Monterey Peninsula, including Monterey, Pacific Grove, and Carmel, occupies the southern end. In between, Highway 1 (sometimes also called the Pacific Coast Highway) cruises along the coastline, passing windswept beaches piled high with sand dunes. Along the route are artichoke fields and the towns of Watsonville and Castroville. Inland towns such as working-class Salinas and sun-drenched San Juan Bautista are less touristy.

About the Restaurants
Between San Francisco and Los Angeles, some of the finest dining to be found is around Monterey Bay. The surrounding waters are full of fish, wild game roams the foothills, and the inland valleys are some of the most fertile in the country—local chefs draw on this bounty for their fresh, truly California cuisine. Except at beachside stands and inexpensive eateries, where anything goes, casual but neat resort wear is the norm. The few places where more formal attire is required are noted.

About the Hotels
Monterey-area accommodations range from no-frills motels to luxurious resorts. Many of the area's small inns and bed-and-breakfasts pamper the traveler in grand style, serving not only full breakfasts but afternoon or early evening wine and hors d'oeuvres. Pacific Grove has quietly turned itself into the region's B&B capital; Carmel also has charming inns in residential areas. Truly lavish resorts, with everything from featherbeds to heated floors, cluster in exclusive Pebble Beach and pastoral Carmel Valley. Many of these accommodations are not suitable for children, so if you're traveling with kids, be sure to ask before you book.

Around Monterey Bay high season runs April through October. Rates during winter, especially at the larger hotels, may drop by 50% or more,

GREAT ITINERARIES

Although it's compact, the Monterey Peninsula is chock-full of diversions. In Carmel you can shop till you drop, and when summer and weekend hordes overwhelm the town's clothing boutiques, art galleries, housewares outlets, and gift shops, you can slip off to enjoy the coast. Fans of Victorian architecture will want to search out the many fine examples in Pacific Grove. If you have an interest in California history and historic preservation, the place to start is Monterey, with its adobe buildings along the downtown Path of History.

Numbers in the text correspond to numbers in the margin and on the Monterey Bay and Monterey maps.

IF YOU HAVE 3 DAYS   Start in ► ⌖ **Carmel ❶** to visit Carmel Mission and Tor House if it's open. Leave yourself plenty of time to browse the shops of Ocean Avenue, then stroll over to Scenic Road and spend time on Carmel Beach before dinner. On the following day, motor up **17-Mile Drive ❸** in the morning, stopping at Point Lobos State Reserve to take in the views. That afternoon visit a few of the buildings in the state historic park

in ⌖ **Monterey ❺–⓱**. Spend your final day along Cannery Row and **Fisherman's Wharf ⓱**. Don't miss the **Monterey Bay Aquarium ⓲**. Catch the sunset from the bustling wharf or slip into the serene bar at the Monterey Plaza Hotel and Spa.

IF YOU HAVE 5 DAYS   Spend your first day and second morning following the itinerary above, but instead of continuing to Monterey on your second afternoon, explore the shoreline and Victorian houses of ⌖ **Pacific Grove ❹**. Start Day 3 at the **Monterey Bay Aquarium ⓲** and enjoy the afternoon either relaxing on the waterfront in ⌖ **Monterey ❺–⓱** or getting a glimpse of the city's fascinating past at Monterey State Historic Park. The next morning, get up-close and personal with Monterey Bay marine life by boarding a whale-watching or other cruise vessel at **Fisherman's Wharf ⓱**. Spend the afternoon on the wharf and along Cannery Row. On your last day, head up the Monterey–Salinas Highway and stop for a taste of wine at Ventana Vineyards, then visit **San Juan Bautista ㉑**, a classic mission village.

5

and B&Bs often offer midweek specials in the off-season. However, even the simplest of the area's lodgings are expensive, and most properties require a two-night stay on weekends.

	WHAT IT COSTS				
	$$$$	$$$	$$	$	¢
RESTAURANTS	over $30	$23–$30	$16–$22	$10–$15	under $10
HOTELS	over $250	$176–$250	$121–$175	$90–$120	under $90

Restaurant prices are for a main course at dinner, excluding sales tax of 7½%–8¼% (depending on location). Hotel prices are for two people in a standard double room in high season, excluding service charges and 10%–10½% tax.

Timing

Summer is peak season, with crowds everywhere and generally mild weather. A sweater or windbreaker is nearly always necessary along the coast, where a cool breeze usually blows and fog is on the way in or out. Inland, temperatures in Salinas or Carmel Valley can be 15 or 20 degrees warmer than those in Carmel and Monterey. Off-season, from November through April, fewer people visit and the mood is mellower. Rainfall is heaviest in January and February.

MONTEREY PENINSULA

If you want to see small towns and spectacular vistas, be sure to visit the stretch of coast between Big Sur and Monterey. Each of the communities here is distinct, and you'll see everything from thatch-roofed cottages to palatial estates, rolling hills to craggy cliffs.

Carmel

▶ ❶ *26 mi north of Big Sur on Hwy. 1.*

Although the community has grown quickly through the years and its population quadruples with tourists on weekends and in summer, Carmel retains its identity as a quaint village. Self-consciously charming, the town is populated by many celebrities, major and minor, and has more than its share of quirky ordinances. For instance, women wearing high heels do not have the right to pursue legal action if they trip and fall on the cobblestone streets; drivers who hit a tree and leave the scene are charged with hit-and-run; live music is banned in local watering holes; and ice-cream parlors are not allowed to sell cones—only cups—because children might drop them, leaving unsightly puddles on the pretty streets. Buildings still have no street numbers (street names are written on discreet white posts) and consequently no mail delivery (if you really want to see the locals, go to the post office). Artists started this community, and their legacy is evident in the numerous galleries. Wandering the side streets off Ocean Avenue, where you can poke into hidden courtyards and stop at cafés for tea and crumpets, is a pleasure. For a look past the shops and into the town's colorful history, the **Carmel Heritage Society** (✉ Lincoln St. at 6th Ave. ☎ 831/624–4447) leads 1½-hour walking tours every Saturday at 9:30 AM.

Downtown Carmel's chief lure is shopping, especially along its main street, **Ocean Avenue,** between Junipero Avenue and Camino Real; the architecture here is a mishmash of ersatz Tudor, Mediterranean, and other styles. **Carmel Plaza** (✉ Ocean and Junipero Aves. ☎ 831/624–0138), in the east end of the village proper, holds more than 50 shops and restaurants.

Long before it became a shopping and browsing destination, Carmel was an important religious center during the establishment of Spanish California. That heritage is preserved in the Mission San Carlos Borroméo del Rio Carmelo, more commonly known as the **Carmel Mission.** Founded in 1771, it served as headquarters for the mission system in California under Father Junípero Serra. Adjoining the stone church is

PLEASURES & PASTIMES

FINE DINING. In California you can eat well, and around Monterey Bay you can eat very, very well. Thanks to the abundance of local produce, meats, seafood, and wine, the best cuisine here is that which doesn't stray too far from home. Monterey and Carmel fairly burst at the seams with such restaurants, with Monterey's Montrio Bistro—a temple of California cuisine—leading the pack. Carmel's restaurants are guided by their worldly chefs, most notably the inventive Walter Manske at intimate L'Auberge Carmel. And although Santa Cruz is not famed for its restaurants, it is famous for its organic farmers; the best place to taste the fruits of their labor is at Theo's, which specializes in seasonal American dishes.

GREAT GOLF. Since the opening of the Del Monte Golf Course in 1897, golf has been an integral part of the Monterey Peninsula's social and recreational scene. Pebble Beach's championship courses host prestigious tournaments, and though the greens fees at these courses can run well over $200, elsewhere on the peninsula you'll find less expensive—but still challenging and scenic—options. Many hotels will help with golf reservations or have golf packages; inquire when you book your room.

WHALE-WATCHING. On their annual migration between the Bering Sea and Baja California, thousands of gray whales pass close by the Monterey coast. They are sometimes visible through binoculars from shore, but a whale-watching cruise is the best way to get a close look at these magnificent mammals. The migration south takes place from December through March. January is prime viewing time. The migration north occurs from March through June. In addition, some 2,000 blue whales and 600 humpbacks pass the coast and are easily spotted in late summer and early fall. Smaller numbers of minke whales, orcas, sperm whales, and fin whales have been sighted in mid-August. Even if no whales surface, bay cruises almost always encounter other enchanting sea creatures, such as sea otters, sea lions, and porpoises.

a tranquil garden planted with California poppies. Museum rooms at the mission include an early kitchen, Serra's spartan sleeping quarters, and the first college library in California. ✉ *3080 Rio Rd., at Lasuen Dr.* ☎ *831/624–3600* ⊕ *www.carmelmission.org* ✉ *$5* ☉ *Weekdays 9:30–5, weekends 10:30–5.*

Scattered throughout the pines in Carmel are houses and cottages originally built for the writers, artists, and photographers who discovered the area decades ago. Among the most impressive dwellings is **Tor House**, a stone cottage built in 1919 by poet Robinson Jeffers on a craggy knoll overlooking the sea. Portraits, books, and unusual art objects fill the low-ceiling rooms. The highlight of the small estate is Hawk Tower, a detached edifice set with stones from the Carmel coastline—as well as one from the Great Wall of China. The docents who lead tours (six people maximum) are well informed about the poet's work and life. Reservations for tours are recommended. ✉ *26304 Ocean View Ave.* ☎ *831/*

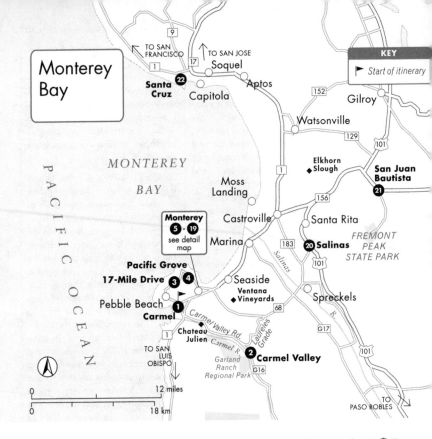

Monterey Bay

KEY

▶ Start of itinerary

TO SAN FRANCISCO

TO SAN JOSE

9

1

17

Soquel

Aptos

Santa Cruz 22

Capitola

152

Gilroy

Watsonville

129

101

MONTEREY

BAY

Moss Landing

Elkhorn Slough

San Juan Bautista 21

1

156

Santa Rita

FREMONT PEAK STATE PARK

Monterey 5 · 19 see detail map

Castroville

Marina

183

20 **Salinas** *PEAK*

101

Pacific Grove

17-Mile Drive 3 4

Seaside

Ventana Vineyards

Spreckels

68

Pebble Beach

Carmel 1

Carmel Valley Rd.

G17

Laureles Grade

101

Chateau Julien

Carmel R.

2 **Carmel Valley**

Garland Ranch Regional Park

G16

TO SAN LUIS OBISPO

1

TO PASO ROBLES

0 _____ 12 miles

0 _____ 18 km

PACIFIC OCEAN

624–1813 ⊕ *www.torhouse.org* ☜$7 ☞ *No children under 12* �⏱ *Tours on the hr Fri. and Sat. 10–3.*

Carmel's greatest beauty is its rugged coastline, with pine and cypress forests and countless inlets. **Carmel Beach** (⊠ End of Ocean Ave.), an easy walk from downtown shops, has sparkling white sands and magnificent sunsets. **Carmel River State Beach** stretches for 106 acres along Carmel Bay. The sugar-white beach is adjacent to a bird sanctuary, where you might spot pelicans, kingfishers, hawks, and sandpipers. ⊠ *Off Scenic Rd. south of Carmel Beach* ☎ *831/624–4909 or 831/649–2836* ⊕ *www.cal-parks.ca.gov* ☜ *Parking $8.* ⏱ *Apr.–Oct., daily 9–7; Nov.–Mar., daily 9–5.*

★ **Point Lobos State Reserve,** a 350-acre headland harboring a wealth of marine life, lies a few miles south of Carmel. The best way to explore the reserve is to walk along one of its many trails. The Cypress Grove Trail leads through a forest of Monterey cypress (one of only two natural groves remaining), which clings to the rocks above an emerald-green cove. Sea Lion Point Trail is a good place to view sea lions. From those and other trails you may also spot otters, harbor seals, and (during winter and spring) migrating whales. An additional 750 acres of the reserve is an undersea marine park open to qualified scuba divers. Arrive early (or in late afternoon) to avoid crowds; the parking lots fill up. No pets are allowed. ⊠ *Hwy. 1* ☎ *831/624–4909, 831/624–8413 for scuba-diving reservations* ⊕ *www.pointlobos.org* 🎫 *$8 per vehicle* ☉ *Apr.–Oct., daily 9–7; Nov.–Mar., daily 9–4:30.*

Where to Stay & Eat

$$$–$$$$ ✕ **Anton and Michel.** Carefully prepared European cuisine is the menu at this airy restaurant. The rack of lamb is carved at the table, the duck prosciutto is cured in-house, and the desserts are set aflame before your eyes. In summer, you (and your dog!) can have lunch served in the courtyard; inside, the dining room looks onto a lighted fountain. ⊠ *Mission St. and 7th Ave.* ☎ *831/624–2406* ⚄ *Reservations essential* 🖃 *AE, D, DC, MC, V.*

★ **$$$–$$$$** ✕ **Casanova.** Built in a former home, this cozy restaurant inspires European-style celebration and romance—chairs are painted in all colors, accordions hang from the walls, tiny party lights dance along the low ceilings. All entrées include antipasti and your choice of appetizers, which all but mandate you to sit back and enjoy a long meal. The food consists of delectable seasonal dishes from southern France and northern Italy. Private dining and a special menu are offered at Van Gogh's Table, a special table imported from France's Auberge Ravoux, the artist's final residence. ⊠ *5th Ave. between San Carlos and Mission Sts.* ☎ *831/625–0501* ⚄ *Reservations essential* 🖃 *AE, MC, V.*

$$–$$$$ ✕ **Kurt's Carmel Chop House.** This is the Carmel version of a classic steak house. The menu is all prime cuts prepared traditionally, augmented by such specialties as Assyrian lamb chops in pomegranate juice or the sage-and-apple-brined pork chops. Similarly, you can get a simple martini, but you can also have one made with Godiva chocolate liqueur or nine other imaginative twists. ⊠ *5th Ave. and San Carlos St.* ☎ *831/625–1199* ⚄ *Reservations essential* 🖃 *AE, MC, V* ☉ *No lunch.*

★ **$$–$$$** ✕ **Bouchee.** Prepared by a kitchen staff coming from such places as Bettina in Los Angeles and New York's Le Cirque, the food here is tailored for fanciful gourmands. Each dish presents an innovative take on local ingredients, such as a Reuben sandwich made with veal sweetbreads or parsnip ravioli with crispy pancetta. With its copper bar the dining room feels more urban than most of Carmel, perhaps why this is the "cool" place in town to dine. ⊠ *Mission St. between Ocean and 7th Aves.* ☎ *831/626–7880* ⚄ *Reservations essential.* 🖃 *AE, MC, V* ☉ *Closed Mon. No lunch.*

$$–$$$ ✕ **Flying Fish.** Simple in appearance yet bold with its flavors, this Japanese-California seafood restaurant has quickly established itself as one of Carmel's most inventive eateries. Among the best entrées is the almond-crusted sea bass served with Chinese cabbage and rock shrimp stir-fry. For the entrance, look underground at the gates to Carmel Plaza. ⊠ *Mission St. between Ocean and 7th Aves.* ☎ *831/625–1962* 🖃 *AE, D, MC, V* ☉ *Closed Tues. No lunch.*

$$–$$$ ✕ **Grasing's Coastal Cuisine.** Chef Kurt Grasing's contemporary adaptations of European provincial and American cooking include artichoke lasagna that's rolled and graced with roasted tomato sauce. Since he opened his chop house around the corner, this restaurant has come to

5

focus on fish and vegetarian dishes (though red meat and poultry still appear daily). ⊠ *6th Ave. and Mission St.* ☎ *831/624–6562* ⚑ *Reservations essential* ⊟ *AE, D, DC, MC, V.*

$$–$$$ ✕ **L'Escargot.** Chef-owner Kericos Loutas personally cares for each plate of food served at this romantic and thankfully unpretentious French restaurant. Take his recommendation and order the duck confit in puff pastry or the bone-in steak in truffle butter; or, if you can't decide, choose the three-course prix-fixe dinner. Service is warm and attentive. ⊠ *Mission St. between 4th and 5th Aves.* ☎ *831/620–1942* ⚑ *Reservations essential* ⊟ *AE, DC, MC, V* ☺ *Closed Tues. No lunch.*

$–$$$ ✕ **Bahama Billy's.** The energy is electric at this always-bustling Caribbean bar and restaurant. An excellent and diverse menu combined with a lively crowd makes this a prime spot for fun and good eating in Carmel. Particularly good is the ahi tuna, which is rolled in Jamaican jerk seasoning, seared, and served with aioli. Because it's outside the area covered by the town's strict zoning laws, there is often live music in the bar. ⊠ *Barnyard Shopping Center, Hwy. 1 and Carmel Valley Rd.* ☎ *831/626–0430* ⚑ *Reservations essential* ⊟ *AE, D, MC, V.*

$–$$$ ✕ **Caffè Napoli.** Redolent of garlic and olive oil, this small, atmospheric Italian restaurant is a favorite of locals, who come for the crisp-crusted pizzas, house-made pastas, and fresh seafood. The grilled artichokes and fresh salmon are specialties of the house, but it's hard to go wrong with anything on the menu. There's also a good Italian wine list. ⊠ *Ocean Ave. and Lincoln St.* ☎ *831/625–4033* ⚑ *Reservations essential* ⊟ *MC, V.*

¢–$$$ ✕ **Jack London's.** If anyone's awake after dinner in Carmel, he's at Jack London's. This publike local hangout is the only Carmel restaurant to serve food until midnight. The menu includes everything from snacks such as nachos to steaks. ⊠ *Su Vecino Court on Dolores St. between 5th and 6th Aves.* ☎ *831/624–2336* ⊟ *AE, D, DC, MC, V.*

$–$$ ✕ **The Cottage Restaurant.** If you're looking for the best breakfast in Carmel, this is the place: the menu offers six different preparations of eggs Benedict, and all kinds of sweet and savory crepes. Sandwiches and homemade soups are served at lunch, and there are dinner specials on weekends, but you'll have the best meals here in the morning. ⊠ *Lincoln St. between Ocean and 7th Aves.* ☎ *831/625–6260* ⊟ *MC, V* ☺ *No dinner Sun.–Wed.*

$–$$ ✕ **Lugano Swiss Bistro.** Fondue is the centerpiece here. The house specialty is a version made with Gruyère, Emmentaler, and Appenzeller. Rotisserie-broiled meats are also popular, and include rosemary chicken, plum-basted duck, and fennel pork loin. Ask for a table in the back room, which contains a hand-painted street scene of Lugano. ⊠ *The Barnyard, Hwy. 1 and Carmel Valley Rd.* ☎ *831/626–3779* ⊟ *AE, DC, MC, V* ☺ *Closed Mon.*

¢–$ ✕ **Em Le's.** Easy and unpretentious is the style at this old-time restaurant and soda fountain. Thanks to the big selection of "early bird" dinner specials, you can get spaghetti with meatballs or lamb shank for less than $10 between 4:30 and 7 each day. For breakfast try the French toast. ⊠ *Dolores St. between 5th and 6th Aves.* ☎ *831/625–6780* ⊟ *D, DC, MC, V.*

¢–$ ✕ **Tuck Box.** This bright little restaurant is in a cottage right out of a fairy tale, complete with a stone fireplace that's lighted on rainy days. Handmade scones are the house specialty, and are good for breakfast or afternoon tea. ⊠ *Dolores St. between Ocean and 7th Aves.* ☎ *831/624–6365* ▭ *No credit cards* ☽ *No dinner.*

$$$$ ✕▦ **L'Auberge Carmel.** Stepping through the doors of this elegant inn
Fodor'sChoice is like being transported to a little European village. The rooms are lux-
★ urious yet understated, with Italian sheets and huge, classic soaking tubs;
sitting in the sun-soaked brick courtyard makes you feel like a movie
star. To eat and sleep here is a weekend in itself, but even those staying
elsewhere should consider splurging on the intimate restaurant ($$$$).
The single, prix-fixe tasting menu consists of endless courses, each one
a marvel in itself imagined by chef Walter Manske. The deconstructed
lobster taco, for example, consists of a tortilla strip balanced atop a tiny
glass of clear tomato and cilantro essence, a cube of lobster, and a shot
of lime ice drenched in fine tequila. ⊠ *Monte Verde at 7th Ave., 93921*
☎ *831/624–8578* ▤ *831/626–1018* ⊕ *www.laubergecarmel.com* ⇋ *20*
⌂ *In-room safes, in-room DVD, lobby lounge, concierge; no smoking.*
▭ *AE, D, MC, V.*

$$$–$$$$ ✕▦ **Park Hyatt Carmel Highlands Inn.** High on a hill overlooking the Pa-
cific, this place has superb views. Accommodations include king rooms
with fireplaces, suites with personal Jacuzzis, and full town houses with
all the perks. The excellent prix-fixe menus at the inn's Pacific's Edge
restaurant ($$$$; jackets recommended) blend French and California
cuisine; the sommelier helps choose the perfect wines. ⊠ *120 Highlands
Dr., 93921* ☎ *831/620–1234 or 800/682–4811, 831/622–5445 for
restaurant* ▤ *831/626–1574* ⊕ *highlandsinn.hyatt.com* ⇋ *48 rooms,
105 suites* ⌂ *2 restaurants, room service, in-room safes, some in-room
hot tubs, some kitchenettes, refrigerators, cable TV with movies, some
in-room VCRs, in-room data ports, pool, gym, 3 hot tubs, bicycles, 3
lounges, babysitting, laundry service, concierge, Wi-Fi, business serv-
ices, meeting rooms; no a/c, no smoking* ▭ *AE, D, DC, MC, V.*

$$$$ ▦ **Tickle Pink Inn.** Atop a towering cliff, this inn has views of the Big Sur
coastline, which you can contemplate from your private balcony. After
falling asleep to the sound of surf crashing below, you'll wake to a Con-
tinental breakfast and the morning paper in bed. If you prefer the com-
pany of fellow travelers, breakfast is also served buffet-style in the
lounge, as is complimentary wine and cheese in the afternoon. Many
rooms have wood-burning fireplaces, and there are six luxurious spa
suites. ⊠ *155 Highlands Dr., 93923* ☎ *831/624–1244 or 800/635–4774*
▤ *831/626–9516* ⊕ *www.ticklepink.com* ⇋ *24 rooms, 11 suites*
⌂ *Some in-room hot tubs, refrigerators, cable TV, in-room VCRs, in-
room data ports, outdoor hot tub, concierge; no a/c, no smoking* ▭ *AE,
DC, MC, V* ❍ *CP.*

★ **$$$$** ▦ **Tradewinds Inn.** This hotel has been around long enough to have
been a favorite of Bing Crosby's, but it has never looked like this be-
fore. The 1950s-era property reopened in fall 2003 with a new, glam-
orous decor inspired by the South Seas. Each room has a tabletop
fountain and orchids, and the courtyard houses waterfalls and a med-
itation garden. Amazingly, this chic boutique hotel has been owned by
the same family since it opened in 1959. It's one of the few of its kind
in downtown Carmel. ⊠ *Mission St. at 3rd Ave., 93921* ☎ *831/624–
2776 or 800/624–6665* ▤ *831/624–0634* ⊕ *www.carmeltradewinds.
com* ⇋ *26 rooms, 2 suites* ⌂ *Some in-room hot tubs, cable TV, in-room*

data ports, massage, concierge, business services, meeting room, some pets allowed (fee); no a/c, no smoking ▭ *AE, MC, V* ⍩ *CP.*

$$–$$$$ ⌂ **Carmel River Inn.** Besides attracting those looking for a relative bargain in pricey Carmel, this half-century-old inn appeals to travelers who enjoy a bit of distance from the madding crowd. There are 10 acres of gardens on the property, but area beaches are only 1½ mi away. The blue-and-white motel at the front of the property contains units with cable TV, small refrigerators, and coffeemakers. Cabins out back sleep up to six; some have fireplaces and kitchens. ⊠ *Hwy. 1 at Carmel River Bridge, 93922* ☎ *831/624–1575 or 800/882–8142* 📠 *831/624–0290* ⊕ *www.carmelriverinn.com* ⇆ *19 rooms, 24 cabins* ♨ *Some microwaves, refrigerators, cable TV, pool, Internet room, some pets allowed (fee), no-smoking rooms; no a/c* ▭ *MC, V.*

$$–$$$$ ⌂ **Cypress Inn.** The decorating style here is luxurious but refreshingly simple. Rather than chintz and antiques, there are wrought-iron bed frames, wooden armoires, and rattan armchairs. Some rooms have fireplaces, some hot tubs, and one (Room 215) even has its own sunny veranda that looks out on the ocean. The in-town location makes walking to area attractions easy, and pet owners will be pleased to hear that in the spirit of the dog-loving owner (and movie star) Doris Day, animal companions are always welcome. ⊠ *Lincoln St. and 7th Ave., Box Y, 93921* ☎ *831/624–3871 or 800/443–7443* 📠 *831/624–8216* ⊕ *www.cypress-inn.com* ⇆ *39 rooms, 5 suites* ♨ *Fans, some in-room hot tubs, cable TV, in-room data ports, bar, laundry service, concierge, some pets allowed (fee); no a/c in some rooms, no smoking* ▭ *AE, D, DC, MC, V* ⍩ *CP.*

$$–$$$$ ⌂ **La Playa Hotel.** Norwegian artist Christopher Jorgensen built this property's original structure in 1902 for his bride, a member of the Ghirardelli chocolate clan. The property has since undergone many additions and now resembles a Mediterranean estate. Rooms are small but comfortable, with furnishings in muted colors; some have views of gardens or the ocean. You can also opt for a cottage; most have full kitchens and wood-burning fireplaces, and all have patios or terraces. ⊠ *Camino Real at 8th Ave., 93921* ☎ *831/624–6476 or 800/582–8900* 📠 *831/624–7966* ⊕ *www.laplayahotel.com* ⇆ *75 rooms, 5 cottages* ♨ *Restaurant, refrigerators, cable TV, Wi-Fi, pool, massage, bar, laundry service, business services, meeting rooms; no a/c, no smoking* ▭ *AE, DC, MC, V.*

$$–$$$$ ⌂ **Tally Ho Inn.** Since a major face-lift in 2005, this inn is nearly all suites, many of which have floor-to-ceiling glass walls that open onto ocean-view patios. All rooms have spa tubs and marble bathrooms. Evening aperitifs are served in the English garden courtyard, where a fire blazes on chilly nights. ⊠ *Monte Verde St. and 6th Ave., 93921* ☎ *831/624–2232 or 877/482–5594* 📠 *831/624–2661* ⊕ *www.tallyho-inn.com* ⇆ *1 room, 11 suites* ♨ *Some fans, some in-room data ports, laundry service; no a/c, no TV in some rooms, no smoking* ▭ *AE, D, DC, MC, V* ⍩ *CP.*

$–$$$$ ⌂ **Mission Ranch.** The property at Mission Ranch is gorgeous and includes a sprawling sheep pasture, bird-filled wetlands, and a sweeping view of the ocean. The ranch is nicely decorated but low-key, with a 19th-century farmhouse as the central building. Other accommodations include rooms in a converted barn, and several cottages, many with fireplaces. Though the ranch belongs to movie star Clint Eastwood, relaxation, not celebrity, is the focus here. ✉ *26270 Dolores St., 93923* ☎ *831/624–6436 or 800/538–8221* 🖷 *831/626–4163* ➺ *31 rooms* ⟁ *Restaurant, fans, some in-room hot tubs, some refrigerators, cable TV, in-room data ports, 6 tennis courts, pro shop, gym, piano bar; no a/c, no smoking* ▤ *AE, MC, V* ¶◎¶ *CP.*

★ **$$–$$$** 🖭 **Cobblestone Inn.** Stones from the Carmel River cover the exterior walls of this English-style country inn; inside, the work of local painters is on display. Guest rooms have stone fireplaces, as well as thick quilts on the beds. Antiques in the cozy sitting room, and afternoon wine and hors d'oeuvres, contribute to the homey feel. ✉ *Junipero Ave., between 7th and 8th Aves., 93921* ☎ *831/625–5222 or 800/833–8836* 🖷 *831/625–0478* ⊕ *www.foursisters.com* ➺ *22 rooms, 2 suites* ⟁ *Refrigerators, cable TV, in-room data ports, bicycles; no a/c, no smoking* ▤ *AE, DC, MC, V* ¶◎¶ *BP.*

$$–$$$ 🖭 **Pine Inn.** A favorite with generations of Carmel visitors, the Pine Inn has Victorian-style furnishings, complete with grandfather clock, padded fabric wall panels, antique tapestries, and marble tabletops. Only four blocks from the beach, the property includes a brick courtyard of specialty shops and a modern Italian restaurant. ✉ *Ocean Ave. and Monte Verde St., 93921* ☎ *831/624–3851 or 800/228–3851* 🖷 *831/624–3030* ⊕ *www.pine-inn.com* ➺ *43 rooms, 6 suites* ⟁ *Restaurant, fans, some refrigerators, cable TV, some in-room data ports, bar, laundry service, meeting room; no a/c, no smoking* ▤ *AE, D, DC, MC, V.*

$–$$ 🖭 **Lobos Lodge.** The white-stucco motel units here are set amid cypress, oaks, and pines on the edge of the business district. All accommodations have fireplaces, and some have private patios. ✉ *Monte Verde St. and Ocean Ave., 93921* ☎ *831/624–3874* 🖷 *831/624–0135* ⊕ *www.loboslodge.com* ➺ *28 rooms, 2 suites* ⟁ *Fans, refrigerators, cable TV, in-room data ports, no-smoking rooms; no a/c* ▤ *AE, MC, V* ¶◎¶ *CP.*

$–$$ 🖭 **Sea View Inn.** In a residential area a few hundred feet from the beach, this restored 1905 home has a double parlor with two fireplaces, Oriental rugs, canopy beds, and a spacious front porch. Afternoon tea and evening wine and cheese are offered daily. Because of the fragile furnishings and quiet atmosphere, families with kids will likely be more comfortable elsewhere. ✉ *Camino Real between 11th and 12th Aves., 93921* ☎ *831/624–8778* 🖷 *831/625–5901* ⊕ *www.seaviewinncarmel.com* ➺ *8 rooms, 6 with private bath* ⟁ *No a/c, no room phones, no room TVs, no smoking* ▤ *AE, MC, V* ¶◎¶ *CP.*

The Arts

Carmel Bach Festival (☎ 831/624–2046 ⊕ www.bachfestival.org) has presented the works of Johann Sebastian Bach and his contemporaries in concerts and recitals since 1935. The festival runs for three weeks, starting mid-July. **Monterey County Symphony** (☎ 831/624–8511 ⊕ www.montereysymphony.org) performs classical concerts from October through May at the Sunset Community Cultural Center.

The **Pacific Repertory Theater** (☎ 831/622–0700 ⊕ www.pacrep.org) puts on the Carmel Shakespeare Festival from August through October and performs contemporary dramas and comedies at several area venues from February through July. **Sunset Community Cultural Center** (✉ San Carlos St. at 9th Ave. ☎ 831/624–3996), which presents concerts, lectures, and headline performers, is the Monterey Bay area's top venue for the performing arts.

Shopping

ART GALLERIES **Carmel Art Association** (⊠ Dolores St. between 5th and 6th Aves. ☎ 831/624–6176 ⊕ www.carmelart.org) exhibits the paintings, sculptures, and prints of local artists. **Galerie Pleine Aire** (⊠ Dolores St. between 5th and 6th Aves. ☎ 831/625–5686) showcases oil paintings by a group of seven local artists. **Masterpiece Gallery** (⊠ Dolores St. and 6th Ave. ☎ 831/624–2163) shows early California impressionist art. **Photography West Gallery** (⊠ Ocean Ave. and Dolores St. ☎ 831/625–1587) exhibits photography by Ansel Adams and other 20th-century artists. Run by the family of the late Edward Weston, **Weston Gallery** (⊠ 6th Ave. between Dolores and Lincoln Sts. ☎ 831/624–4453) is hands-down the best photography gallery around, with contemporary color photography complemented by classic black-and-whites.

SPECIALTY SHOPS **Bittner** (⊠ Ocean Ave. between Mission and San Carlos Sts. ☎ 831/626–8828) has a fine selection of collectible and vintage pens from around the world. **Intima** (⊠ Mission St. between Ocean and 7th Aves. ☎ 831/625–0599) is the place to find European lingerie that ranges from lacy to racy. **Jan de Luz** (⊠ Dolores St. between Ocean and 7th Aves. ☎ 831/622–7621) monograms and embroiders fine linens (including bathrobes) while you wait. **Madrigal** (⊠ Carmel Plaza and Mission St. ☎ 831/624–3477) carries sportswear, sweaters, and accessories for women. **Mischievous Rabbit** (⊠ Lincoln Ave. between 7th and Ocean Aves. ☎ 831/624–6854) sells toys, nursery accessories, books, music boxes, china, and children's clothing, and specializes in Beatrix Potter items.

Carmel Valley

② *10 mi east of Carmel, Hwy. 1 to Carmel Valley Rd.*

Carmel Valley Road, which heads inland from Highway 1 south of Carmel, is the main thoroughfare through this valley, a secluded enclave of horse ranchers and other well-heeled residents who prefer the area's sunny climate to the fog and wind on the coast. Once thick with dairy farms, the valley has recently proved itself as a venerable wine appellation. Tiny Carmel Valley Village, about 13 mi southeast of Carmel via Carmel Valley Road, has several crafts shops and art galleries, as well as tasting rooms for numerous local wineries. At **Bernardus Tasting Room,** you can sample many of the wines—including older vintages and reserves—from the nearby Bernardus Winery and Vineyard. ⊠ *5 W. Carmel Valley Rd.* ☎ *800/223–2533* ☉ *Daily 11–5.*

Garland Ranch Regional Park (⊠ Carmel Valley Rd., 9 mi east of Carmel ☎ 831/659–4488) has hiking trails across nearly 4,500 acres of property that includes meadows, forested hillsides, and creeks. The beautiful **Château Julien** winery, recognized internationally for its chardonnays and merlots, gives tours on weekdays at 10:30 and 2:30 and weekends at 12:30 and 2:30, all by appointment. The tasting room is open daily. ⊠ *8940 Carmel Valley Rd.* ☎ *831/624–2600* ⊕ *www.chateaujulien.com* ☉ *Weekdays 8–5, weekends 11–5.*

Where to Stay & Eat

$$–$$$$ ✕ **Will's Fargo.** On the main street of Carmel Valley since the 1920s, this restaurant has also been a tearoom and a roadhouse. Today it calls itself a "dressed-up saloon," with steerhorns and gilt-frame paintings adorning the walls. The menu is mainly steaks, including a 24-ounce porterhouse. ✉ *16 E. Carmel Valley Rd.* ☎ *831/659–2774* 🖃 *AE, DC, MC, V.* ☉ *No lunch Mon.–Thurs.*

$–$$ ✕ **Café Rustica.** Italian-inspired country cooking is the focus at this lively roadhouse. Specialties include roasted meats, pastas, and pizzas from the wood-fired oven. Because of the tile floors, it can get quite noisy inside; opt for a table outside if you want a quieter meal. ✉ *10 Delfino Pl.* ☎ *831/659–4444* ⚇ *Reservations essential* 🖃 *MC, V* ☉ *Closed Wed.*

¢ ✕ **Wagon Wheel Coffee Shop.** This local hangout decorated with wagon wheels, cowboy hats, and lassos serves up terrific hearty breakfasts, including date-walnut-cinnamon French toast and a plate of trout and eggs. The lunch menu includes a dozen different burgers and other sandwiches. ✉ *Valley Hill Center, Carmel Valley Rd. next to Quail Lodge* ☎ *831/ 624–8878* 🖃 *No credit cards* ☉ *No dinner.*

$$$$ ✕🏨 **Bernardus Lodge.** Even before you check in at this luxury spa resort, the valet hands you a glass of chardonnay. And that's only the beginning. Spacious guest rooms have vaulted ceilings, featherbeds, fireplaces, patios, and bathtubs for two. The restaurant ($$$$; jacket recommended) is perhaps the best in the Monterey Bay area, with a menu that changes daily to highlight local meats and produce. Reserve the chef's table in the main kitchen and you can talk to the chef as he prepares your meal. ✉ *415 Carmel Valley Rd., 93924* ☎ *831/659–3131 or 888/ 648–9463* 🖷 *831/659–3529* ⊕ *www.bernardus.com* ⇆ *54 rooms, 3 suites* ⚇ *2 restaurants, room service, in-room safes, minibars, refrigerators, cable TV with movies, in-room DVD, Wi-Fi, 2 tennis courts, pool, gym, hair salon, hot tub, sauna, spa, steam room, croquet, lawn bowling, bar, lobby lounge, laundry service, concierge, Internet room, meeting room; no smoking* 🖃 *AE, DC, MC, V.*

Fodor's Choice
★

★ **$$$$** ✕🏨 **Quail Lodge.** What began as the Carmel Valley Country Club—a hangout for Frank Sinatra, among others—is now a private golf club and resort in the valley's west side. Winding around swimming pools and putting greens, the buildings' exteriors recall the old days, but indoors the luxury is totally updated with a cool, modern feel: plasma TVs swing out from the walls, the toiletries include giant tea bags to infuse your bath with herbs, and each room has a window seat overlooking a private patio. The Covey at Quail Lodge ($$–$$$$; jacket recommended) serves contemporary California cuisine in a romantic lakeside dining room. ✉ *8205 Valley Greens Dr., 93923* ☎ *831/624–1581 or 800/538–9516* 🖷 *831/624–3726* ⊕ *www.quaillodge.com* ⇆ *83 rooms, 14 suites* ⚇ *2 restaurants, room service, in-room safes, minibars, refrigerators, cable TV with movies and video games, in-room data ports, Wi-Fi, 18-hole golf course, putting green, 4 tennis courts, pro shop, 2 pools, gym, hot tub, spa, steam room, bicycles, hiking, lawn bowling, 2 bars, babysitting, laundry service, concierge, Internet room, business services, meeting rooms, no-smoking rooms* 🖃 *AE, DC, MC, V.*

5

$$$$ 🏨 **Stonepine Estate Resort.** Set on 330 pastoral acres, this former estate
Fodor'sChoice of the Crocker banking family has been converted to an ultraluxurious
★ inn. The oak-paneled main château holds eight elegantly furnished
rooms and suites, and a dining room for guests (although with advance
reservations, it is also possible for nonguests to dine here). The property's "cottages" are equally opulent, each with its own luxurious identity (the Hermes House has four fireplaces and a 27-foot-high living room
ceiling). Fresh flowers, afternoon tea, and evening champagne are offered daily. This is a quiet property, best suited to couples traveling without children. ⊠ *150 E. Carmel Valley Rd., 93924* ☎ *831/659–2245*
🖨 *831/659–5160* ⊕ *www.stonepinecalifornia.com* ⤳ *6 rooms, 2 suites,
3 cottages* ⚐ *Dining room, room service, fans, some in-room safes, in-
room hot tubs, some minibars, cable TV, in-room DVD/VCR, in-room
data ports, Wi-Fi, 9-hole golf course, 2 tennis courts, 2 pools, gym, massage, mountain bikes, archery, croquet, hiking, horseback riding, library,
piano, recreation room, laundry service, concierge, Internet room; no
a/c, no smoking* ⊟ *AE, MC, V* ⦿ *BP.*

$$$–$$$$ 🏨 **Carmel Valley Lodge.** This small inn has rooms surrounding a garden
patio, and separate one- and two-bedroom cottages with fireplaces and
full kitchens. ⊠ *8 Ford Rd., at Carmel Valley Rd., 93924* ☎ *831/659–
2261 or 800/641–4646* 🖨 *831/659–4558* ⊕ *www.valleylodge.com* ⤳ *19
rooms, 4 suites, 8 cottages* ⚐ *Fans, some kitchenettes, refrigerators,
cable TV, in-room VCRs, in-room data ports, Wi-Fi, pool, exercise equip-
ment, hot tub, sauna, horseshoes, Ping-Pong, Internet room, some pets
allowed (fee), no-smoking rooms; no a/c* ⊟ *AE, MC, V* ⦿ *CP.*

The Arts

The **Magic Circle Center** (⊠ 8 El Caminito ☎ 831/659–1108) presents
three comedies, two dramas, and a music series annually in an intimate
60-seat theater. **Hidden Valley Performing Arts Institute** (⊠ Carmel Valley
Road at Ford Rd. ☎ 831/659–3115) gives classes for promising young
musicians and holds a year-round series of classical and jazz concerts
by students, masters, and the Monterey Peninsula Choral Society.

Sports & the Outdoors

The **Golf Club at Quail Lodge** (⊠ 8000 Valley Greens Dr. ☎ 831/624–
2770) incorporates several lakes into its course. Depending on the sea-
son and day of the week, greens fees range from $115 to $140 for guests
and $125 to $175 for nonguests, including cart rental. **Rancho Cañada
Golf Club** (⊠ 4860 Carmel Valley Rd., 1 mi east of Hwy. 1 ☎ 831/624–
0111) is a public course with 36 holes, some of them overlooking the
Carmel River. Fees range from $35 to $80, plus $34 for cart rental, de-
pending on course and tee time.

17-Mile Drive

❸ *Off North San Antonio Rd. in Carmel or off Sunset Dr. in Pacific Grove.*
Fodor'sChoice
★ Primordial nature resides in quiet harmony with palatial late-20th-cen-
tury estates along 17-Mile Drive, which winds through an 8,400-acre
microcosm of the Monterey coastal landscape. Dotting the drive are rare
Monterey cypress, trees so gnarled and twisted that Robert Louis Steven-
son described them as "ghosts fleeing before the wind." Some sightseers

balk at the $8.50-per-car fee collected at the gates—this is the only private toll road west of the Mississippi—but most find the drive well worth the price. An alternative is to grab a bike: cyclists tour for free, as do those with confirmed lunch or dinner reservations at one of the hotels.

You can take in views of the impeccable greens at **Pebble Beach Golf Links** (⊠ 17-Mile Dr. near the Lodge at Pebble Beach ☎ 800/654–9300 ⊕ www.pebblebeach.com) over a drink or lunch at the Lodge at Pebble Beach. The ocean plays a major role in the 18th hole of the famed golf course. Each winter the course is the main site of the AT&T Pebble Beach Pro-Am (formerly the Bing Crosby Pro-Am), where show business celebrities and golf pros team up for one of the nation's most glamorous tournaments.

Many of the stately homes along 17-Mile Drive reflect the classic Monterey or Spanish Mission style typical of the region. A standout is the **Crocker Marble Palace,** about a mile south of the Lone Cypress (*see below*). It's a private waterfront estate inspired by a Byzantine castle, easily identifiable by its dozens of marble arches.

Bird Rock, the largest of several islands at the southern end of the Monterey Country Club's golf course, teems with harbor seals, sea lions, cormorants, and pelicans. Sea creatures and birds—as well as some very friendly ground squirrels—also make use of **Seal Rock,** the largest of a group of islands south of Bird Rock. The most-photographed tree along 17-Mile Drive is the weather-sculpted **Lone Cypress,** which grows out of a precipitous outcropping above the waves about 2 mi south of Seal Rock. You can stop for a view of the Lone Cypress at a parking area, but you can't walk out to the tree.

Where to Stay & Eat

$$$$ ✕🏨 **Inn at Spanish Bay.** This resort sprawls across a breathtaking stretch of shoreline, and has lush, 600-square-foot rooms. Peppoli's restaurant ($$–$$$), which serves Tuscan cuisine, overlooks the coast and the golf links; Roy's Restaurant ($$–$$$$) serves more casual and innovative Euro-Asian fare. When you stay here, you're also allowed privileges at the Lodge at Pebble Beach, which is under the same management. ⊠ 2700 17-Mile Dr., Pebble Beach 93953 ☎ 831/647–7500 or 800/654–9300 🖷 831/644–7960 ⊕ www.pebblebeach.com ➴ 252 rooms, 17 suites ♿ 3 restaurants, room service, minibars, refrigerators, cable TV with movies, in-room VCRs, in-room broadband, in-room data ports, 18-hole golf course, 8 tennis courts, pro shop, pool, hot tub, fitness classes, health club, sauna, steam room, beach, bicycles, bar, lobby lounge, laundry service, concierge, Internet room, business services, meeting rooms; no a/c, no smoking ⊟ AE, D, DC, MC, V.

★ **$$$$** ✕🏨 **Lodge at Pebble Beach.** All rooms have fireplaces and many have wonderful ocean views at this circa 1919 resort. The golf course, tennis club, and equestrian center are posh. Overlooking the 18th green, the intimate Club XIX restaurant ($$$$; jackets recommended) serves expertly prepared French cuisine. When staying here, you also have privileges at the Inn at Spanish Bay. ⊠ 1700 17-Mile Dr., Pebble Beach 93953 ☎ 831/624–3811 or 800/654–9300 🖷 831/644–7960 ⊕ www.

pebblebeach.com ⌐ *142 rooms, 19 suites* ♤ *3 restaurants, coffee shop, some in-room hot tubs, minibars, refrigerators, cable TV with movies and video games, some in-room DVD/VCR, in-room broadband, in-room data ports, 18-hole golf course, 12 tennis courts, pro shop, pool, gym, health club, sauna, spa, beach, bicycles, horseback riding, 2 bars, lobby lounge, laundry service, concierge, Internet room, business services, meeting rooms, some pets allowed; no a/c, no smoking* 🖃 *AE, D, DC, MC, V.*

★ **$$$$** ▣ **Casa Palmero.** This exclusive spa resort evokes a stately Mediterranean villa. Rooms are decorated with sumptuous fabrics and fine art; each has a wood-burning fireplace and heated floor, and some have private outdoor patios with in-ground Jacuzzis. Complimentary cocktail service is offered each evening in the main hall and library. The spa is state-of-the-art, and you have use of all facilities at the Lodge at Pebble Beach and the Inn at Spanish Bay. ⌧ *1518 Cypress Dr., Pebble Beach 93953* ☎ *831/622–6650 or 800/654–9300* 🖷 *831/622–6655* ⊕ *www. pebblebeach.com* ⌐ *21 rooms, 3 suites* ♤ *Room service, some in-room hot tubs, minibars, refrigerators, cable TV with movies and video games, in-room VCRs, in-room data ports, 18-hole golf course, pool, spa, bicycles, billiards, lounge, laundry service, concierge, meeting rooms; no a/c, no smoking* 🖃 *AE, D, DC, MC, V.*

Sports & the Outdoors

GOLF The **Links at Spanish Bay** (⌧ 17-Mile Dr., north end ☎ 831/624–3811, 831/624–6611, or 800/654–9300), which hugs a choice stretch of shoreline, is designed in the rugged manner of a traditional Scottish course, with sand dunes and coastal marshes interspersed among the greens. Greens fees are $215, plus $25 per person for cart rental (cart included for resort guests); nonguests can reserve tee times up to two months in advance.

Pebble Beach Golf Links (⌧ 17-Mile Dr. near the Lodge at Pebble Beach ☎ 831/624–3811, 831/624–6611, or 800/654–9300) attracts golfers from around the world, despite greens fees of $395, plus $25 per person for an optional cart (complimentary cart for guests of the Pebble Beach and Spanish Bay resorts). Nonguests can reserve a tee time only one day in advance on a space-available basis (up to a year for groups); resort guests can reserve up to 18 months in advance.

Peter Hay (⌧ 17-Mile Dr. ☎ 831/625–8518 or 831/624–6611), a 9-hole, par-3 course, charges $20 per person, no reservations necessary. **Poppy Hills** (⌧ 3200 Lopez Rd., at 17-Mile Dr. ☎ 831/625–2035), a splendid 18-hole course designed in 1986 by Robert Trent Jones Jr., has greens fees of $130–$150; an optional cart costs $30. Individuals may reserve up to one month in advance, groups up to a year.

Spyglass Hill (⌧ Stevenson Dr. and Spyglass Hill Rd. ☎ 831/624–3811, 831/624–6611, or 800/654–9300) is among the most challenging Pebble Beach courses. With the first 5 holes bordering on the Pacific and the other 18 reaching deep into the Del Monte Forest, the views offer some consolation. Greens fees are $265, and an optional cart costs $25 (the cart is complimentary for resort guests). Reservations are essential and may be made up to one month in advance (18 months for guests).

HORSEBACK
RIDING

The **Pebble Beach Equestrian Center** (✉ Portola Rd. and Alva La. ☏ 831/624–2756) offers guided trail rides along the beach and through 26 mi of bridle trails in the Del Monte Forest.

Pacific Grove

❹ *3 mi north of Carmel on Hwy. 68.*

This picturesque town, which began as a summer retreat for church groups more than a century ago, recalls its prim and proper Victorian heritage in its host of tiny board-and-batten cottages and stately mansions. Today, though, it is the breathtaking outdoors that inspires residents. Indeed, even before the church groups flocked here, Pacific Grove had been receiving thousands of annual pilgrims in the form of bright orange-and-black monarch butterflies. Known as Butterfly Town USA, Pacific Grove is the winter home of monarchs that migrate south from Canada and the Pacific Northwest to take residence in pine and eucalyptus groves from October through March. The sight of a mass of butterflies hanging from the branches like a long, fluttering veil is unforgettable.

A prime way to enjoy Pacific Grove is to walk or bicycle along its 3 mi of city-owned shoreline, a cliff-top area following Ocean View Boulevard that is landscaped with native plants and has benches on which to sit and gaze at the sea. You can spot many types of birds here, including colonies of web-foot cormorants crowding the massive rocks rising out of the surf.

Among the Victorians of note is the **Pryor House** (✉ 429 Ocean View Blvd.), a massive, shingled, private residence with a leaded- and beveled-glass doorway. **Green Gables** (✉ 5th St. and Ocean View Blvd. ☏ 831/375–2095), a romantic Swiss Gothic–style mansion with peaked gables and stained-glass windows, is a B&B.

☾ The view of the coast is gorgeous from **Lovers Point Park** (☏ 831/648–5730), on Ocean View Boulevard midway along the waterfront. The park's sheltered beach has a children's pool and picnic area, and the

☾ main lawn has a sandy volleyball court and snack bar. At the 1855-vintage **Point Pinos Lighthouse,** the oldest continuously operating lighthouse on the West Coast, you can learn about the lighting and foghorn operations and wander through a small museum containing U.S. Coast Guard memorabilia. ✉ *Lighthouse Ave. off Asilomar Blvd.* ☏ *831/648–5716* ⊕ *www.pgmuseum.org* 🎟 *$2* ☉ *June–Sept., 11:30–5 daily; Oct.–May, Thurs.–Mon. 1–4.*

Monarchs sometimes vary their nesting sites from year to year, but the **Monarch Grove Sanctuary** (✉ 1073 Lighthouse Ave., at Ridge Rd. ⊕ www.pgmuseum.org) is a fairly reliable spot for viewing the butterflies between October and February. If you are in Pacific Grove when the monarch butterflies aren't, you can view the well-crafted butterfly tree

☾ exhibit at the **Pacific Grove Museum of Natural History.** The museum also displays 400 mounted birds and has a touch gallery for children. ✉ *165 Forest Ave.* ☏ *831/648–3116* ⊕ *www.pgmuseum.org* 🎟 *Free* ☉ *Tues.–Sun. 10–5.*

Asilomar State Beach (☎ 831/372–4076), a beautiful coastal area, is on Sunset Drive between Point Pinos and the Del Monte Forest in Pacific Grove. The 100 acres of dunes, tidal pools, and pocket-size beaches form one of the region's richest areas for marine life—including surfers, who migrate here most winter mornings.

Where to Stay & Eat

$$$$ ✕ **Robert's White House.** The culinary experience of chef-owner Robert Kincaid (the man behind Fresh Cream, in Monterey) stretches from California to Europe and Japan. And it's this experience that is reflected in his three-course, prix-fixe menus, which might include Hungarian goulash, roast duckling with black currant sauce, or shrimp cake with pineapple rum and dill sauce. The restaurant itself, housed in a stately Victorian downtown, provides an elegant showcase for his sophisticated cuisine. ⊠ *649 Lighthouse Ave.* ☎ *831/375–9626* ▱ *MC, V* ☾ *Closed Mon.*

$$–$$$$ ✕ **Old Bath House.** This romantic converted bathhouse overlooks the water at Lovers Point. The menu makes the most of local produce and seafood (such as Monterey Bay shrimp) and specializes in game meats. There is also a less expensive menu for late-afternoon diners. ⊠ *620 Ocean View Blvd.* ☎ *831/375–5195* ▱ *AE, D, DC, MC, V* ☾ *No lunch.*

$$–$$$ ✕ **Joe Rombi's.** Pastas, fish, and veal are the specialties at this modern trattoria, which is the best in town for Italian food. The look is spare and clean, with colorful antique wine posters decorating the white walls. ⊠ *208 17th St.* ☎ *831/373–2416* ▱ *AE, MC, V* ☾ *Closed Mon. and Tues.*

$–$$$ ✕ **Fandango.** The menu here is mostly European provincial, with such dishes as calves' liver and onions and paella served in a skillet. The decor follows suit: stone walls and country furniture give the restaurant the earthy feel of a southern European farmhouse. So it's fitting that this is where locals come when they want to have a big dinner with friends— drink wine, have fun, and generally feel at home. ⊠ *223 17th St.* ☎ *831/ 372–3456* ▱ *AE, D, DC, MC, V.*

$–$$$ ✕ **Red House Café.** Set inside a little red house, this cozy restaurant feels a bit like Grandma's house. When it's nice out, sun pours through big windows and across tables on the porch; when fog rolls in, the fireplace is lighted. The menu is simple but selective, including grilled lamb fillets atop mashed potatoes for dinner and a huge Dungeness crab cake over salad for lunch. Breakfast on weekends is a local favorite. ⊠ *662 Lighthouse Ave.* ☎ *831/643–1060* ▱ *AE, D, DC, MC, V* ☾ *Closed Mon.*

$–$$ ✕ **Fifi's Café.** Candles illuminate this small bistro, known for its generous wine pouring and carefully selected music. French cuisine guides the menu, with such traditional dishes as escargot and beef bourguignon, but you'll also find American creations such as baked trout and Caesar salad. ⊠ *1188 Forest Ave.* ☎ *831/372–5325* ⊕ *www.fifiscafe.com* ⚱ *Reservations essential* ▱ *AE, D, DC, MC, V* ☾ *No lunch Wed.*

$–$$ ✕ **Passion Fish.** South American artwork and artifacts decorate the room, but both Latin and Asian flavors infuse the dishes here. Chef Ted Wolters shops at local farmers' markets several times a week to find the best produce available. He pairs it with fresh local fish and creative sauces; try the crispy squid with spicy orange-cilantro vinaigrette. ⊠ *701 Lighthouse Ave.* ☎ *831/655–3311* ▱ *AE, D, MC, V* ☾ *Closed Tues. No lunch.*

$–$$ ✕ **Taste Café and Bistro.** A favorite of locals, Taste serves hearty European-inspired California cuisine in a casual, airy room with high ceilings and an open kitchen. Meats are excellent here, particularly the marinated lamb fillets and the filet mignon. ✉ *1199 Forest Ave.* ☎ *831/ 655–0324* 🖃 *AE, MC, V* ☉ *Closed Mon.*

¢–$$ ✕ **Fishwife.** Fresh fish with a Latin accent makes this a favorite of locals for lunch or a casual dinner. Good bets are the green-lipped mussels (steamed and served with velouté sauce and salsa) and—for large appetites—any of the fisherman's bowls, which feature fresh fish served with rice, beans, spicy cabbage, salsa, vegetables, and a tortilla. ✉ *1996½ Sunset Dr., at Asilomar Blvd.* ☎ *831/375–7107* 🖃 *AE, D, MC, V.*

¢–$$ ✕ **Peppers Mexicali Cafe.** This cheerful white-walled restaurant serves fresh seafood and traditional dishes from Mexico and Latin America. The entrées are complemented by excellent red and green salsas (made fresh throughout the day) and the large selection of beers. ✉ *170 Forest Ave.* ☎ *831/373–6892* 🖃 *AE, D, DC, MC, V* ☉ *Closed Tues. No lunch Sun.*

$$$–$$$$ 🏨 **Martine Inn.** The glassed-in parlor and many guest rooms at this Mediterranean-style villa have stunning ocean views. The inn is furnished with exquisite antiques, including an 1860 Chippendale Revival four-poster bed, movie costume designer Edith Head's entire bedroom suite, and the owner's collection of classic race cars on display in the patio area. Lavish breakfasts—and elaborate dinners of up to 12 courses—are served on lace-clad tables set with china, crystal, and silver. Because of the fragility of the antiques, the inn is not suitable for children. ✉ *255 Ocean View Blvd., 93950* ☎ *831/373–3388 or 800/852–5588* 🖷 *831/373–3896* ⊕ *www.martineinnn.com* ⇌ *24 rooms* ♤ *Some fans, refrigerators, in-room data ports, hot tub, Internet room, meeting rooms, no-smoking rooms; no a/c, no room TVs* 🖃 *AE, D, MC, V* ⍟ *BP.*

$$–$$$ 🏨 **The Inn at 213 Seventeen Mile Drive.** Set in a residential area just past town, this carefully restored 1920s Craftsman-style home and cottage has spacious, well-appointed rooms. The innkeepers offer complimentary wine and hors d'oeuvres in the evening and tea and snacks throughout the day. Redwood, cypress, and eucalyptus trees tower over the garden and outdoor hot tub. ✉ *213 17-Mile Dr., 93950* ☎ *831/642–9514 or 800/526–5666* 🖷 *831/642–9546* ⊕ *www.innat17.com* ⇌ *14 rooms* ♤ *Some fans, cable TV, in-room data ports, hot tub; no a/c, no smoking* 🖃 *AE, MC, V* ⍟ *BP.*

$–$$$ 🏨 **Gosby House Inn.** Though in the town center, this turreted yellow Queen Anne Victorian has an informal country feel. The two most private rooms are in the rear carriage house; they have fireplaces, balconies, and whirlpool tubs. Buffet breakfast is served in the parlor or garden. ✉ *643 Lighthouse Ave., 93950* ☎ *831/375–1287 or 800/527–8828* 🖷 *831/655– 9621* ⊕ *www.foursisters.com* ⇌ *22 rooms, 20 with bath* ♤ *Some fans, some in-room hot tubs, some refrigerators, some cable TV, some in-room VCRs, in-room data ports; no a/c, no TV in some rooms, no smoking* 🖃 *AE, DC, MC, V* ⍟ *BP.*

★ $–$$$ 🏨 **Green Gables Inn.** Stained-glass windows and ornate interior details compete with spectacular ocean views at this Queen Anne–style mansion, built by a businessman for his mistress in 1888. Rooms in a carriage house perched on a hill out back are larger, have more modern amenities, and afford more privacy, but rooms in the main house have more charm. Afternoon wine and cheese are served in the parlor. ⊠ *301 Ocean View Blvd., 93950* ☏ *831/375–2095 or 800/722–1774* 🖷 *831/ 375–5437* ⊕ *www.foursisters.com* 🗦 *7 rooms, 3 with bath; 4 suites* ♨ *Some in-room hot tubs, some cable TV, some in-room VCRs, some in-room data ports, bicycles; no a/c, no smoking* ⊟ *AE, D, DC, MC, V* ⊠ *BP.*

¢–$$$ ▦ **Lighthouse Lodge and Suites.** Near the tip of the peninsula, this complex straddles Lighthouse Avenue—the lodge is on one side, the all-suites facility on the other. With daily afternoon barbecues, it's a woodsy alternative to downtown Pacific Grove's B&B scene. Suites have fireplaces and whirlpool tubs. Standard rooms are simple, but they're decently sized and much less expensive. ⊠ *1150 and 1249 Lighthouse Ave., 93950* ☏ *831/655–2111 or 800/858–1249* 🖷 *831/655–4922* ⊕ *www.lhls.com* 🗦 *64 rooms, 31 suites* ♨ *Fans, minibars, microwaves, refrigerators, cable TV with movies, in-room data ports, pool, hot tub, meeting rooms, some pets allowed (fee); no a/c, no smoking* ⊟ *AE, D, DC, MC, V* ⊠ *BP.*

$–$$ ▦ **Asilomar Conference Center.** This former YWCA retreat, set in a woodsy, 105-acre oceanfront state park, may bring back fond memories of summer camp. There's Ping-Pong in the lodge, volleyball and campfires outside—but thankfully, no bunk beds. The rooms are tasteful and modern, if simple, and spread among different buildings separated by woods and sandy paths. Rooms are available to the general public only when not booked for conferences. ⊠ *800 Asilomar Blvd., 93950* ☏ *831/ 372–8016* 🖷 *831/372–7227* ⊕ *www.visitasilomar.com* 🗦 *313 rooms* ♨ *Dining room, pool, beach, bicycles, billiards, Ping-Pong, volleyball, business services, Wi-Fi, meeting rooms; no a/c, no room phones, no room TVs, no smoking* ⊟ *AE, MC, V* ⊠ *BP.*

Sports & the Outdoors

GOLF Greens fees at the 18-hole **Pacific Grove Municipal Golf Links** (⊠ 77 Asilomar Blvd. ☏ 831/648–5777) run between $32 and $38 (you can play 9 holes for between $18 and $20), with an 18-hole twilight rate of $20. Optional carts cost $30. The course has spectacular ocean views on its back 9. Tee times may be reserved up to seven days in advance.

TENNIS The **Pacific Grove Municipal Courts** (⊠ 515 Junipero St. ☏ 831/648–5729) are available for public play for a small hourly fee. The pro shop here rents rackets and offers lessons.

MONTEREY

Early in the 20th century Carmel Martin, the first mayor of the city of Monterey, saw a bright future for his town: "Monterey Bay is the one place where people can live without being disturbed by manufacturing and big factories. I am certain that the day is coming when this will be the most desirable place in the whole state of California." It seems that Mayor Martin was not far off the mark.

Historic Monterey

2 mi southeast of Pacific Grove via Lighthouse Ave.; 2 mi north of Carmel via Hwy. 1.

A GOOD
TOUR

You can glimpse Monterey's early history in the well-preserved adobe buildings at **Monterey State Historic Park.** Far from being a hermetic period museum, the park facilities are an integral part of the day-to-day business life of the town—within some of the buildings are a store, a theater, and government offices. Some of the historic houses are graced with gardens that are worthy sights themselves. Free guided tours of Casa Soberanes, Larkin House, Cooper-Molera Adobe, and Stevenson House are given on an erratic schedule (call for current tour times), but when the buildings are open, you're welcome to wander through on your own. Spend the first day of your Monterey visit exploring the historic park, starting at ▶ **Stanton Center ❺**, which also houses the **Maritime Museum of Monterey ❻**. Take the guided 90-minute tour of the park (call for times), after which you can tour some or all of the following adobes and their gardens. Start next door to the Maritime Museum at **Pacific House ❼** and cross the plaza to the **Custom House ❽**. It's a short walk up Scott Street to **California's First Theatre ❾**, then one block down Pacific to **Casa Soberanes ❿**. Afterward, see the **Stevenson House ⓫, Cooper-Molera Adobe ⓬, Larkin House ⓭**, and **Colton Hall ⓮**. Stop in at the **Monterey Museum of Art ⓯**, and finish the day at **La Mirada ⓰**.

Start Day 2 on **Fisherman's Wharf ⓱**, then head for the **Presidio of Monterey Museum ⓲**. Spend the rest of the day on **Cannery Row,** which has undergone several transformations since it was immortalized in John Steinbeck's 1945 novel of the same name. The street that Steinbeck described was crowded with sardine canneries processing, at their peak, nearly 200,000 tons of the smelly silver fish a year. During the mid-1940s, however, the sardines disappeared from the bay, causing the canneries to close. Through the years the old tin-roof canneries have been converted into restaurants, art galleries, and malls with shops selling T-shirts, fudge, and plastic sea otters. Recent tourist development along the row has been more tasteful, however, and includes several stylish inns and hotels. The **Monterey Plaza Hotel and Spa,** on the site of a historic estate at 400 Cannery Row, is a great place to relax over a drink and watch for sea otters. Wisps of the neighborhood's colorful past appear at **651 Cannery Row,** whose tile Chinese dragon roof dates to 1929.

Next, head to 800 Cannery Row, a weathered wooden building that was the site of **Pacific Biological Laboratories.** Edward F. Ricketts, the inspiration for Doc in *Cannery Row,* did much of his marine research here. The **Wing Chong Building,** at 835 Cannery Row, is the former Wing Chong Market that Steinbeck called Lee Chong's Heavenly Flower Grocery in *Cannery Row.* Step back into the present at the spectacular **Monterey Bay Aquarium ⓳** and commune with the marine life.

TIMING

Depending on how quickly you tour (it's easy to spend a couple of hours at both the maritime museum and the art museum), Day 1 will be a long one, but all of the park sites are in a small area. Monterey Museum of Art and La Mirada are a short drive or taxi ride from the park. Day 2

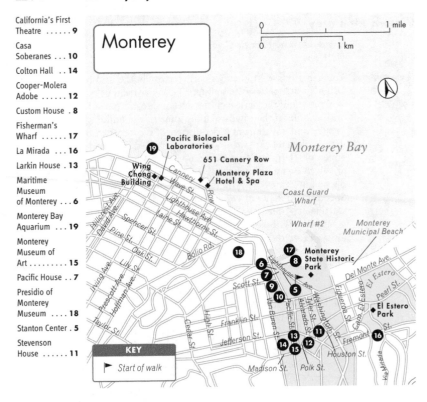

Monterey

KEY

► *Start of walk*

will also be full; it's easy to linger for hours at Fisherman's Wharf and the aquarium.

What to See

⑨ California's First Theatre. This adobe began its life in 1846 as a saloon and lodging house for sailors. Four years later stage curtains were fashioned from army blankets, and some U.S. officers staged plays to the light of whale oil lamps. As of this writing, the building is currently closed for renovations. ⊠ *Monterey State Historic Park, Scott and Pacific Sts.* ☎ *831/657–6348* 🎟 *Free* ⊙ *Call for hrs.*

⑩ Casa Soberanes. A classic low-ceiling adobe structure built in 1842, this was once a Custom House guard's residence. Exhibits at the house survey life in Monterey from the era of Mexican rule to the present. The building is open only during tours, but in back the peaceful garden, with a lovely rose-covered arbor and sitting benches, is open daily 10–4. ⊠ *Monterey State Historic Park, 336 Pacific St.* ☎ *831/657–6348* 🎟 *Free* ⊙ *Call for hrs.*

⑭ Colton Hall. A convention of delegates met in 1849 to draft the first state constitution at California's equivalent of Independence Hall. The stone building, which has served as a school, a courthouse, and the county seat, is a museum furnished as it was during the constitutional convention. The extensive grounds outside the hall surround the Old Monterey Jail. The museum closes each day from noon to 1. ⊠ *500 block of Pacific St., between Madison and Jefferson Sts.* ☎ *831/646–5640* ⊠ *Free* ⊗ *Mon.–Sat. 10–4, Sun. 11–3.*

⑫ Cooper-Molera Adobe. The restored 2-acre complex includes a house dating from the 1820s, a visitor center, a bookstore, and a large garden enclosed by a high adobe wall. The mostly Victorian-era antiques and memorabilia that fill the house provide a glimpse into the life of a prosperous early sea merchant's family. The building is open only during organized tours. ⊠ *Monterey State Historic Park, Polk and Munras Sts.* ☎ *831/657–6348* ⊠ *Free* ⊗ *Call for hrs.*

❽ Custom House. This adobe structure built by the Mexican government in 1827—now California's oldest standing public building—was the first stop for sea traders whose goods were subject to duties. At the beginning of the Mexican-American War, in 1846, Commodore John Sloat raised the American flag over the building and claimed California for the United States. The house's lower floor displays cargo from a 19th-century trading ship. ⊠ *Monterey State Historic Park, 1 Custom House Plaza, across from Fisherman's Wharf* ☎ *831/649–2909* ⊠ *Free* ⊗ *Mon. and Thurs.–Sat., 10–3, Sun. 11–3.*

⑰ Fisherman's Wharf. The mournful barking of sea lions provides a steady sound track all along Monterey's waterfront, but the best way to actually view the whiskered marine mammals is to walk along one of the two piers across from Custom House Plaza. Fisherman's Wharf is lined with souvenir shops, seafood restaurants, and whale-watching tour boats. It's undeniably touristy, but still a lively and entertaining place. Up the harbor to the right is Wharf No. 2, a working municipal pier where you can see fishing boats unloading their catches to one side, and fishermen casting their lines into the water on the other. The pier has a couple of low-key restaurants, from whose seats lucky customers may spot otters and harbor seals. ⊠ *At the end of Calle Principal* ☎ *831/ 373–0600* ⊕ *www.montereywharf.com.*

⑯ La Mirada. Asian and European antiques fill this 19th-century adobe house. A newer 10,000-square-foot gallery space, designed by Charles Moore, houses Asian and California regional art. Outdoors are magnificent rose and rhododendron gardens. The entrance fee for La Mirada includes admission to the Monterey Museum of Art. ⊠ *720 Via Mirada, at Fremont St.* ☎ *831/372–3689* ⊠ *$5* ⊗ *Wed.–Sat. 11–5, Sun. 1–4.*

NEED A BREAK? El Estero Park's **Dennis the Menace Playground** (⊠ Pearl St. and Camino El Estero ☎ 831/646–3866) is an imaginative play area designed by the late Hank Ketcham, the well-known cartoonist. The equipment is on a grand scale and made for daredevils; there's a roller slide, a clanking suspension bridge, and a real Southern Pacific steam locomotive. You can rent a rowboat or a paddleboat for cruising around U-shape Lake El Estero, populated with an assortment of ducks, mud hens, and geese. The park is open 10–dusk and closed Monday except for holidays.

The Underwater Kingdom

ALTHOUGH MONTEREY'S COASTAL LANDSCAPES ARE STUNNING, their beauty is more than equaled by the wonders that lie offshore. The huge Monterey Bay National Marine Sanctuary—which stretches 276 mi, from north of San Francisco almost all the way down to Santa Barbara—teems with abundant life, and has a topography as diverse as that above ground.

The preserve's 5,322 square mi include vast submarine canyons, which reach down 10,663 feet at their deepest point. They also encompass dense forests of giant kelp—a kind of seaweed that can grow more than a hundred feet from its roots on the ocean floor. These kelp forests are especially robust off Monterey.

The sanctuary was established in 1992, to protect the habitat in which these species thrive. Some animals can be seen quite easily from land. In summer and winter you might glimpse the offshore spray of gray whales as they migrate between their summer feeding grounds in Alaska and their breeding grounds in Baja. Clouds of marine birds—including white-faced ibis, three types of albatross, and more than 15 types of gull—skim above the waves, or roost in the rock islands along 17-Mile Drive. Sea otters dart and gambol in the calmer waters of the bay; and of course, you can watch the sea lions—and hear their round-the-clock barking—on the wharves in Santa Cruz and Monterey.

The sanctuary supports many other creatures, however, that remain unseen by most on-land visitors. Some of these are enormous, such as the giant blue whales that arrive to feed on plankton during the summer months; others, like the more than 22 species of red algae in these waters, are microscopic. So whether you choose to visit the Monterey Bay Aquarium, take a whale-watch trip, or look out to sea with your binoculars, remember—you are seeing just a small part of a vibrant underwater kingdom.

For a little down time, kick off your shoes at **Del Monte Beach** (⊠ North of Del Monte Ave., east of Wharf No. 2), where the shallow waters are usually warm and calm enough for wading. It's a favorite spot for beginning divers, who come to see the sandy-bottom ecosystem, which is unusual for the area. Depending on the tides, this can be a great place for finding sand dollars.

⓭ **Larkin House.** A veranda encircles the 2nd floor of this architecturally significant two-story adobe built in 1835, whose design bears witness to the Mexican and New England influences on the Monterey style. The rooms are furnished with period antiques, many of them brought from New Hampshire by the building's namesake, Thomas O. Larkin, an early California statesman. The building is open only during organized tours. ⊠ Monterey State Historic Park, 510 Calle Principal, between Jefferson and Pacific Sts. ☎ 831/657–6348 ⬚ Free ☉ Call for hrs.

⓺ **Maritime Museum of Monterey.** This collection of maritime artifacts belonged to Allen Knight, who was Carmel's mayor from 1950 to 1952.

Highlights are a collection of outstanding scrimshaw, including fully jointed pocket knives and a toy guillotine, and a lively movie from 1943 chronicling a day in the life of the cannery that used to stand where the aquarium is. The jewel in the museum's crown is the enormous, multifaceted Fresnel lens from the lighthouse at Point Sur Light Station. ⊠ *Monterey State Historic Park, 5 Custom House Plaza* ☎ *831/372–2608* 🖃 *$8* ☉ *Thurs.–Tues. 10–5.*

🅒 ⑲ **Monterey Bay Aquarium.** The minute you hand over your ticket at this
FodorśChoice extraordinary aquarium you are surrounded by sea creatures; right at
★ the entrance, you can see dozens of them swimming in a three-story-tall, sunlit kelp forest tank. The beauty of the exhibits here is that they are all designed to give a sense of what it's like to be in the water with the animals—sardines swim around your head in a circular tank, and jellyfish drift in and out of view in dramatically lighted spaces that suggest the ocean depths. A petting pool gives you a hands-on experience with bat rays, and the million-gallon "Outer Bay" tank shows the vast variety of creatures (from sharks to placid-looking turtles) that live in the Eastern Pacific. The only drawback to the experience is that it must be shared with the throngs of people that crowd the place daily; most think it's worth it. ⊠ *886 Cannery Row* ☎ *831/648–4888, 800/756–3737 in CA for advance tickets* ⊕ *www.montereybayaquarium.org* 🖃 *$19.95* ☉ *Late May–early Sept., daily 9:30–6; early Sept.–late May, daily 10–6.*

⑮ **Monterey Museum of Art.** Photographs by Ansel Adams and Edward Weston, as well as works by other artists who have spent time on the peninsula, are on display here. There is also a colorful collection of international folk art; the pieces range from Kentucky hearth brooms to Tibetan prayer wheels. The entrance fee for the Monterey Museum of Art includes admission to La Mirada. ⊠ *559 Pacific St., across from Colton Hall* ☎ *831/372–5477* ⊕ *www.montereyart.org* 🖃 *$5* ☉ *Wed.–Sat. 11–5, Sun. 1–4.*

❼ **Pacific House.** Once a hotel and saloon, this visitor center and museum now commemorates early-California life with gold-rush relics and photographs of old Monterey. The upper floor displays Native American artifacts, including gorgeous baskets and pottery. ⊠ *Monterey State Historic Park, 10 Custom House Plaza* ☎ *831/657–6348* 🖃 *Free* ☉ *Call for hrs.*

⑱ **Presidio of Monterey Museum.** This spot has been significant for centuries as a town, a fort, and the site of several battles, including the skirmish in which the pirate Hipoleto Bruchard conquered the Spanish garrison that stood here. Its first incarnation was as a Native American village for the Rumsien tribe; then it became known as the landing site for explorer Sebastien Vizcaíno in 1602, and father of the California missions, Father Serra, in 1770. The indoor museum tells the stories; the outdoor sites are marked with plaques. ⊠ *Corporal Ewing Rd., lower Presidio Park, Monterey Presidio* ☎ *831/646–3456* ⊕ *www.monterey.org/museum/pom* 🖃 *Free* ☉ *Mon. 10–1, Thurs.–Sat. 10–4, Sun. 1–4.*

▶ ❺ **Stanton Center.** This is the place to go to load up on maps and area information. You can also view a free 20-minute film about Monterey State

Historic Park and take a 90-minute walking tour along the 2-mi Path of History, marked by round gold tiles set into the sidewalk. The tour passes several landmark buildings and details their history and significance. Admission to most sites along the walk is free, and most are open daily. ⊠ *Monterey State Historic Park, 5 Custom House Plaza* ☎ *831/372–2608* ⊕ *www.mbay.net/~mshp* ⊴ *Free; park tours $5* ۞ *Thurs.–Sat. 10–4, Sun. 1–4.*

⑪ **Stevenson House.** This house was named in honor of author Robert Louis Stevenson, who boarded here briefly in a tiny upstairs room. Items from his family's estate furnish Stevenson's room; period-decorated chambers elsewhere in the house include a gallery of the author's memorabilia and a children's nursery stocked with Victorian toys and games. The building is open only during organized tours. ⊠ *Monterey State Historic Park, 530 Houston St.* ☎ *831/657–6348* ⊴ *Free* ۞ *Tours Mon., Fri., and Sat. at 2.*

OFF THE BEATEN PATH

VENTANA VINEYARDS – A short drive from downtown Monterey leads to this winery, which is known for its chardonnays and Rieslings. Ventana's knowledgeable and hospitable owners, Doug and LuAnn Meador, invite you to bring a lunch to eat while tasting wines on the patio. ⊠ *2999 Monterey–Salinas, at Hwy. 68* ☎ *831/372–7415* ⊕ *www.ventanawines.com* ۞ *Daily 11–5.*

Where to Stay & Eat

$$$–$$$$ ✕ **Fresh Cream.** For years this has been one of the most refined dining experiences in Monterey. The wine list is carefully chosen, the service is attentive yet restrained, and everything carries an air of luxury. The menu centers around imaginative variations on classic French cuisine, such as roast duck in black-currant sauce, but the standout here is the view of glittering Heritage Harbor. Though there is no requirement for dress, men will feel more comfortable in a jacket. ⊠ *99 Pacific St., Suite 100C* ☎ *831/375–9798* ⌂ *Reservations essential* ▭ *AE, D, DC, MC, V* ۞ *No lunch.*

$–$$$$ ✕ **Monterey's Fish House.** Casual yet stylish, and removed from the hubbub of the wharf, this always-packed seafood restaurant attracts locals and frequent visitors to the city. If the dining room is full, you can wait at the bar and savor deliciously plump oysters on the half shell. The bartenders and waitstaff will gladly advise you on the perfect wine to go with your poached, blackened, or oak-grilled seafood. ⊠ *2114 Del Monte Ave.* ☎ *831/373–4647* ▭ *AE, D, DC, MC, V* ۞ *No lunch weekends.*

$–$$$ ✕ **Montrio Bistro.** This quirky, converted firehouse, with its rawhide
Fodor'sChoice walls and iron indoor trellises, has a wonderfully sophisticated menu.
★ Chef Tony Baker uses organic produce and meats to create imaginative dishes that reflect the local agriculture, such as baby artichoke risotto and whole stuffed quail with savory French toast and apple-blackberry reduction. Likewise, the wine list draws primarily on California, and many come from the Monterey area. ⊠ *414 Calle Principal* ☎ *831/648–8880* ⌂ *Reservations essential* ▭ *AE, D, DC, MC, V* ۞ *No lunch.*

$–$$$ ✕ **Stokes Restaurant & Bar.** This 1833 adobe building has housed, in the past, the first wood-fired oven in California; the printer that cranked out the state's first newspaper; and a ballroom, bakery, and private residence. Now, in its latest incarnation as a restaurant, it serves California-style cuisine along with comfort-food standbys (such as calzones and pork chops). ⊠ *500 Hartnell St.* ☎ *831/373–1110* ▤ *AE, D, DC, MC, V* ✷ *No lunch.*

¢–$$$ ✕ **Tarpy's Roadhouse.** Fun, dressed-down roadhouse lunches and dinners are served in this renovated farmhouse from the early 1900s. The kitchen serves all the favorites Mom used to make—ribs, meat loaf, steak—only better. Eat indoors by a fireplace or outdoors in the courtyard. ⊠ *2999 Monterey–Salinas Hwy., at Hwy. 68* ☎ *831/647–1444* ▤ *AE, D, DC, MC, V.*

$–$$ ✕ **Old Monterey Café.** Breakfast here gets constant local raves. Its fame rests on such familiar favorites in many incarnations: a dozen kinds of omelets, and pancakes from blueberry to cinnamon-raisin-pecan. The lunch and dinner menus have good soups, salads, and sandwiches, and this is a great place to relax with an afternoon cappuccino. ⊠ *489 Alvarado St.* ☎ *831/646–1021* ⌀ *Reservations not accepted* ▤ *AE, D, MC, V.*

¢–$ ✕ **Thai Bistro.** This cheery mom-and-pop restaurant serves excellent, authentic Thai cuisine from family recipes. Though technically just over the city line in Pacific Grove, it is within walking distance of Cannery Row and the Monterey Bay Aquarium. ⊠ *159 Central Ave., Pacific Grove* ☎ *831/372–8700* ▤ *AE, D, MC, V.*

¢ ✕ **Café Noir.** Attached to the lobby of Monterey's art-house cinema, this café is a stylish place to eat a light lunch, drink coffee, or choose a pot of tea from the extensive selection. Menu items include simple sandwiches, hummus, and green salads. Most patrons bring their laptops for the free Wi-Fi, so for the sake of space most tables are shared. It also serves as a good alternative to the nighttime bar scene, because it's open until midnight on weekends and 10 PM otherwise. ⊠ *365 Calle Principal* ☎ *831/ 649–6647* ▤ *No credit cards.*

$$$$ 🏨 **Old Monterey Inn.** This three-story manor house was originally the
Fodor's Choice home of the first mayor of Monterey, and today it remains a private en-
★ clave within walking distance of downtown. Lush gardens are shaded by huge old oak, pine, and redwood trees and bordered by a creek. Rooms are individually decoratedwith tasteful antiques; many have fireplaces, and all have featherbeds and sitting areas. Those with private entrances have split doors, which means guests often open the top half to let in cool air and the sound of birds. The extensive breakfast is delivered to the rooms, and wine, cheese, and cookies are served each afternoon in the parlor. ⊠ *500 Martin St., 93940* ☎ *831/375–8284 or 800/350–2344* 📠 *831/375–6730* ⊕ *www.oldmontereyinn.com* ⇆ *7 rooms, 2 suites, 1 cottage* ⌂ *Some in-room hot tubs, cable TV, in-room VCRs, in-room broadband, in-room data ports, hot tub, concierge; no a/c, no smoking* ▤ *MC, V* ⦿ *BP.*

$$$–$$$$ 🏨 **Hotel Pacific.** A few blocks from the historic park, this modern hotel has a cool, adobe style. All rooms are junior suites, with featherbeds, hardwood floors, fireplaces, patios, and separate showers and tubs. The rates include afternoon tea, and wine and cheese. ⊠ *300 Pacific St., 93940* ☎ *831/373–5700 or 800/554–5542* 📠 *831/373–6921* ⊕ *www.hotelpacific.com* ⇆ *105 rooms* ⌂ *Some fans, refrigerators,*

cable TV with movies, in-room VCRs, in-room data ports, in-room broadband, 2 hot tubs, meeting rooms; no a/c, no smoking ⊟ AE, D, DC, MC, V ⦵ CP.

★ **$$$–$$$$** ⌕ **Monterey Plaza Hotel and Spa.** This full-service hotel and spa commands a waterfront location on Cannery Row, where frolicking sea otters can be observed from the wide outdoor patio and many room balconies. The architecture blends early California and Mediterranean styles, and also echoes elements of the old cannery design. The property is meticulously maintained and offers both simple and luxurious accommodations. The Duck Club serves contemporary cuisine for dinner and breakfast and is particularly romantic at night, with its view of the waterfront. ⊠ *400 Cannery Row, 93940* ☎ *831/646–1700 or 800/368–2468* ⊟ *831/646–0285* ⊕ *www.montereyplazahotel.com* ⟿ *280 rooms, 10 suites △ 2 restaurants, room service, fans, minibars, cable TV with movies, some in-room DVD, in-room data ports, health club, spa, laundry service, concierge, Internet room, business services, meeting rooms; no a/c, no smoking ⊟ AE, D, DC, MC, V.*

$$$–$$$$ ⌕ **Spindrift Inn.** This boutique hotel on Cannery Row, under the same management as the Hotel Pacific and the Monterey Bay Inn, has beach access and a rooftop garden that overlooks the water. Spacious rooms with sitting areas, hardwood floors, fireplaces, and down comforters are among the indoor pleasures. This is an adults-only property. ⊠ *652 Cannery Row, 93940* ☎ *831/646–8900 or 800/841–1879* ⊟ *831/646–5342* ⊕ *www.spindriftinn.com* ⟿ *42 rooms △ Minibars, refrigerators, cable TV, in-room VCRs, in-room broadband, in-room data ports, Wi-Fi, concierge; no a/c, no smoking ⊟ AE, D, DC, MC, V ⦵ CP.*

$$–$$$$ ⌕ **Cypress Tree Inn.** Spacious and immaculate rooms here (about 2 mi from downtown) cost much less than in hotels adjacent to the wharf area. Many rooms have hot tubs; some have their own fireplaces. ⊠ *2227 N. Fremont St., 93940* ☎ *831/372–7586 or 800/446–8303* ⊟ *831/372–2940* ⊕ *www.cypresstreeinn.com* ⟿ *55 rooms △ Some in-room hot tubs, some kitchenettes, microwaves, refrigerators, cable TV, in-room data ports, hot tub, sauna, laundry facilities; no a/c, no smoking ⊟ AE, D, DC, MC, V.*

¢–$$$$ ⌕ **The Beach Resort.** The rooms here may be nondescript, but this Best Western hotel has a great waterfront location about 2 mi north of town that affords views of the bay and the city skyline. The grounds are pleasantly landscaped, and there's a large pool with a sunbathing area. ⊠ *2600 Sand Dunes Dr., 93940* ☎ *831/394–3321 or 800/242–8627* ⊟ *831/393–1912* ⊕ *www.montereybeachresort.com* ⟿ *196 rooms △ Restaurant, refrigerators, cable TV with movies, in-room data ports, Wi-Fi, pool, exercise equipment, hot tub, beach, lounge, business services, meeting rooms, some pets allowed (fee); no smoking ⊟ AE, D, DC, MC, V.*

$$–$$$ ⌕ **Monterey Hotel.** The rooms in this restored Victorian building are clean and reliable. The decor is reproduction antique, and as long as you're not allergic to pink (the property's dominant hue), this is a good value. The location right downtown is particularly good for those wanting to be out on the town at night. ⊠ *406 Alvarado St., 93940* ☎ *831/375–3184 or 800/727–0960* ⊟ *831/373–2899* ⊕ *www.montereyhotel.com* ⟿ *39 rooms, 6 suites △ Fans, some refrigerators, cable TV, in-room data ports; no a/c, no smoking ⊟ AE, D, DC, MC, V ⦵ CP.*

⚙ **$–$$** ▦ **Monterey Bay Lodge.** Location (on the edge of Monterey's El Estero Park) and superior amenities give this motel an edge over others along the busy Munras Avenue motel row. Indoor plants and a secluded courtyard with a heated pool are other pluses at this cheerful facility. ⊠ *55 Camino Aguajito, 93940* ☎ *831/372–8057 or 800/558–1900* ☒ *831/655–2933* ⊕ *www.montereybaylodge.com* ⥯ *43 rooms, 2 suites* ⚘ *Restaurant, refrigerators, cable TV, some in-room VCRs, in-room data ports, Wi-Fi, pool, hot tub, some pets allowed (fee), no-smoking rooms* ▭ *AE, D, DC, MC, V.*

¢–$$ ▦ **Quality Inn Monterey.** This attractive motel has a friendly, country-inn feeling. Rooms are light and airy, some have fireplaces—and the price is right. ⊠ *1058 Munras Ave., 93940* ☎ *831/372–3381* ☒ *831/372–4687* ⊕ *www.qualityinnmonterey.com* ⥯ *55 rooms* ⚘ *Microwaves, re-frigerators, cable TV, in-room VCRs, some in-room data ports, indoor pool, hot tub; no smoking* ▭ *AE, D, DC, MC, V* ⦿ *CP.*

Nightlife & the Arts

NIGHTLIFE **Bluefin** (⊠ 685 Cannery Row ☎ 831/375–7000) has 19 pool tables, and welcomes all ages until 9 PM nightly. **Planet Gemini** (⊠ 625 Cannery Row ☎ 831/373–1449) presents comedy shows on weekends and dancing to a DJ or live music most nights. **Sly McFly's** (⊠ 700-A Cannery Row ☎ 831/372–3225) has live jazz and blues every night.

THE ARTS **Dixieland Monterey** (☎831/633–5053 or 888/349–6879 ⊕www.dixieland-monterey.com), held on the first full weekend of March, presents traditional jazz bands at waterfront venues on the harbor. The **Monterey Bay Blues Festival** (☎ 831/394–2652 ⊕ www.montereyblues.com) draws blues fans to the Monterey Fairgrounds the last weekend in June. The **Monterey Jazz Festival** (☎ 831/373–3366 ⊕ www.montereyjazzfestival.org), the world's oldest, attracts jazz and blues greats from around the world to the Monterey Fairgrounds on the third full weekend of September.

Near Cannery Row, **Barbary Coast Theater** (⊠ 324 Hoffman ☎831/655–4992) performs vaudeville acts and spoofy comedy-melodramas. Audience participation is encouraged. **Monterey Bay Theatrefest** (☎ 831/622–0700) presents free outdoor performances at Custom House Plaza on weekend afternoons and evenings from late June to mid-July. The **Wharf Theater** (⊠ Fisherman's Wharf ☎ 831/649–2332) focuses on American musicals past and present.

Sports & the Outdoors

Throughout most of the year, the Monterey Bay area is a haven for those who love the outdoors. Residents are an active bunch; tennis, golf, surfing, fishing, biking, hiking, scuba diving, and kayaking are popular activities. Golf and tennis are less popular, however, in the rainy winter months—when the waves grow larger and adventurous surfers flock to the water.

BICYCLING For bicycle rentals, visit **Bay Bikes** (⊠ 640 Wave St. ☎ 831/646–9090). **Adventures by the Sea, Inc.** (⊠ 299 Cannery Row ☎ 831/372–1807) rents tandem and standard bicycles.

FISHING **Randy's Fishing Trips** (⊠ 66 Fisherman's Wharf ☎ 831/372–7440 or 800/251–7440) has been operating under the same skippers since 1958.

Tom's Sportfishing (✉ Moss Landing Harbor, Moss Landing ☎ 831/ 633–2564) leads trips for salmon and rockfish seasonally.

GOLF   Greens fees at the 18-hole **Del Monte Golf Course** (✉ 1300 Sylvan Rd. ☎ 831/ 373–2700) are $95, plus $20 per person for an optional cart. The $25 twilight special (plus cart rental) begins two hours before sunset.

KAYAKING   **Monterey Bay Kayaks** (✉ 693 Del Monte Ave. ☎ 831/373–5357, 800/ 649–5357 in CA ✉ 2390 Hwy. 1, Moss Landing ☎ 800/649–5357 ⊕ www.montereybaykayaks.com) rents equipment and conducts classes and natural-history tours. Their Moss Landing store, about 20 mi north of Monterey, offers the same services and is a good departure point for exploration of the Elkhorn Slough.

SCUBA DIVING   Monterey Bay waters never warm to the temperatures of their southern California counterparts (the warmest they get is low 60s), but that's one reason why the marine life here is so extraordinary. All but the faintest of heart will want to throw on a wet suit and explore this underwater ecosystem, one of the world's most diverse. The Monterey Bay National Marine Sanctuary, home to mammals, seabirds, fishes, invertebrates, and plants, encompasses a 276-mi shoreline and 5,322 square mi of ocean. The staff at **Aquarius Dive Shop** (✉ 2040 Del Monte Ave. ☎ 831/375– 1933) gives diving lessons and tours, and rents equipment. Their **scuba- diving conditions information line** (☎ 831/657–1020) is updated daily.

SKATING   **Del Monte Gardens** (✉ 2020 Del Monte Ave. ☎ 831/375–3202) is an old-fashioned rink for roller-skating and in-line skating. **Monterey Skate Park** (✉ Next to Lake El Estero behind Sollecito Ballpark ☎ 831/646– 3866) is an unsupervised park open daily from 9 AM to dusk.

WALKING   From Custom House Plaza, you can walk along the coast in either direction on the 29-mi-long **Monterey Bay Coastal Trail** (☎ 831/372–3196 ⊕ www.mprpd.org/parks/coastaltrail.html) for spectacular views of the sea. It runs all the way from north of Monterey to Pacific Grove, with sections continuing around Pebble Beach.

WHALE-   **Sanctuary Cruises** (✉ A Dock, Moss Landing ☎ 831/643–0128) leads
WATCHING   eco-conscious trips, some on catamarans and others on boats that use bio-diesel. **Monterey Bay Whale Watch** (✉ 84 Fisherman's Wharf ☎ 831/ 375–4658), which operates out of Sam's Fishing at Fisherman's Wharf, gives three-to-five-hour tours led by marine biologists. **Monterey Whale Watch** (✉ 96 Fisherman's Wharf #1 ☎ 831/372–2203, 800/200–2203) provides shorter, somewhat less expensive tours on large, 75-foot boats.

Shopping

Shopping is not the central activity in Monterey, but still, window-shoppers are not relegated to the gift shops of Cannery Row. Try strolling among the many boutiques along Alvarado Street, in Monterey, and Lighthouse Avenue, in Pacific Grove. **Old Monterey Book Co.** (✉ 136 Bonifacio Pl., off Alvarado St. ☎ 831/372–3111) specializes in antiquarian books and prints. For new books, try **Bay Books & Coffeehouse** (✉ 316 Alvarado St. ☎ 831/375–0277)

Antiques and reproductions of merchandise popular in Monterey in the 1850s are available at **The Boston Store** (✉ Monterey State Historic

Park, 1 Custom House Plaza, across from Fisherman's Wharf ☎ 831/649–3364). **The Cooper Store** (⊠ Polk and Munras Sts., in the Cooper-Molera Adobe ☎ 831/649–7111) is an 1800s-themed shop that is dedicated to the preservation of antiquities in the Monterey State Historic Park. Bargain hunters can sometimes find little treasures at the **Cannery Row Antique Mall** (⊠ 471 Wave St. ☎ 831/655–0264), which houses 150 local vendors under one roof. Historical Society–operated, **The Pickett Fence** (⊠ Monterey State Historic Park, 1 Custom House Plaza, across from Fisherman's Wharf ☎ 831/649–3364) sells high-end garden accessories and furnishings.

SANTA CRUZ COUNTY

Less manicured than its upscale Monterey Peninsula neighbors to the south, Santa Cruz is the big city on this stretch of the California coast. A haven for people opting out of the rat race and a bastion of 1960s-style counterculture, Santa Cruz has been at the forefront of such quintessential "left coast" trends as organic food, medicinal marijuana, and environmentalism. (Indeed, many salty locals contend that "S.C." also stands for Surf City.) Between Santa Cruz and the Monterey Peninsula, the quieter towns of Capitola, Soquel, and Aptos have their own high-quality restaurants, small inns, resorts, and antiques shops.

Salinas

 17 mi east of Monterey via Hwy. 68.

Salinas is the locus of a rich agricultural valley where fertile soil, an ideal climate, and a good water supply produce optimum growing conditions for crops such as lettuce, broccoli, strawberries, and flowers. This unpretentious town may lack the sophistication and scenic splendors of the coast, but it will interest literary and architectural buffs. Turn-of-the-20th-century buildings have been the focus of ongoing renovation, much of it centered on the handsome stone storefronts in the original downtown area of South Main Street. The memory and literary legacy of John Steinbeck, Salinas native (and winner of Pulitzer and Nobel prizes), are honored here.

The **National Steinbeck Center** is an imaginative museum and archive that brings to life the history of John Steinbeck and the local communities that inspired his books. The exhibits are inventive and often interactive: highlights include reproductions of the green pickup-camper from *Travels with Charley* and the bunkroom from *Of Mice and Men,* and you can watch actors read from Steinbeck's books on video screens throughout the museum. The Valley of the World exhibit explores the valley's agriculture, from its inception in the 1800s to the issues facing farmworkers and organic farmers today. The center has information about Salinas's annual Steinbeck Festival, in August, and about tours of area landmarks mentioned in his novels. Stop by for a free self-guided walking tour of Oldtown Salinas. ⊠ *1 Main St.* ☎ *831/796–3833* ⊕ *www. steinbeck.org* ☑ *$11* ⊗ *Daily 10–5.*

The **Jose Eusebio Boronda Adobe,** former home of a high-profile Juan Bautista consort, has been impeccably maintained. The furniture and decorations inside—some of them original—depict the California lifestyle of the 1840s. ⊠ *333 Boronda Rd.* ☎ *831/757–8085* ☜ *Free; donation requested* ☉ *Weekdays 10–2; weekends by appointment.*

A Taste of Monterey Wine Tasting Visitors Center holds regular wine tastings from 35 local vintners. Those who want to visit the wineries themselves can get a map here (and at the center's other location, in Monterey's Fisherman's Wharf) for the self-guided driving tour of 20 wineries between Monterey and King City. ⊠ *700 Cannery Row* ☎ *831/646–5446* ☉ *Daily 11–6.*

Where to Eat

$–$$$ ✕ **Hullabaloo.** Despite elegant lighting and white tablecloths, this local hangout still feels relaxed and fun. You can get great lunchtime burgers here, and dinner highlights include filet mignon over white truffle grits and baby back ribs glazed with Guinness stout. The wine list is good, with all California vintages (mostly from Carmel and Salinas), but locals come for the martinis and wild cocktails such as one called the Pineapple Upside-Down Cake. ⊠ *228 S. Main St.* ☎ *831/757–3663* ▤ *AE, D, DC, MC, V* ☉ *No lunch weekends.*

$ ✕ **Steinbeck House.** John Steinbeck's birthplace, a Victorian frame house, has been converted into a lunch-only (11:30–2) eatery run by the volunteer Valley Guild. The restaurant displays some Steinbeck memorabilia. There's no à la carte service; the set menu includes soup or salad, vegetable, main dish, and nonalcoholic beverage. Dishes such as zucchini lasagna and spinach crepes are created using locally grown produce. ⊠ *132 Central Ave.* ☎ *831/424–2735* ▤ *MC, V* ☉ *Closed Sun. and 3 wks in late Dec. and early Jan.*

¢ ✕ **One Main Street Café.** Inside the Steinbeck Center, this bright café is a good pick for lunch in Salinas. The menu is based on ingredients grown in the surrounding valley, and portions are huge and hearty. The house specialty is artichokes, which you can order fire-roasted, deep-fried, or served with a jalapeño spread. ⊠ *1 Main St.* ☎ *831/775–4738* ▤ *AE, MC, V* ☉ *No dinner.*

San Juan Bautista

㉑ *U.S. 101, 20 mi north of Salinas.*

Sleepy San Juan Bautista has been protected from development since 1933, when much of the town became a state park. This is about as close to early-19th-century California as you can get. Small antiques shops and art galleries line the side streets, and throughout the year the town is the site of weekend events—including a Victorian ball, an American Indian festival, and the Peddler's Faire, an open-air bazaar of crafts and antiques.

The centerpiece of **San Juan Bautista State Historic Park** is a wide green plaza ringed by historic buildings: a restored blacksmith shop, a stable, a pioneer cabin, and a jailhouse. The **Castro-Breen Adobe,** furnished with Spanish-colonial antiques, gives a glimpse of mid-19th-century domestic life in the village. Running along one side of the town square is **Mission San Juan Bautista** (✉ 408 S. 2nd St. ☎ 831/623–2127 ☉ Cemetery daily 9:30–5 ☜ Cemetery $2), founded by Father Fermin de Lasuen in 1797. Adjoining the long, low, colonnaded structure is the mission cemetery, where more than 4,300 Native Americans who converted to Christianity are buried in unmarked graves.

★ ☾ After the mission era, San Juan Bautista became an important crossroads for stagecoach travel. The principal stop in town was the **Plaza Hotel,** a collection of adobe buildings with furnishings from the 1860s. On **Living History Day,** which takes place on the first Saturday of each month, costumed volunteers engage in quilting bees, tortilla making, butter churning, and other frontier activities. ✉ *2nd and Franklin Sts. off Hwy. 156* ☎ *831/623–4881 or 831/623–4526* ⊕ *www.cal-parks.ca.gov* ☜ *$2* ☉ *Daily 10–4:30.*

Fremont Peak Observatory is located at 3,000 feet—which means that even when the fog rolls into Monterey Bay, the sky here is usually dark and clear. From late April through October the observatory holds public stargazing events through its 30-inch telescope every Saturday night (except when there's a full moon); on the first Saturday afternoon of each month, you can also observe the sun through a special solar telescope. ✉ *Fremont State Park, Hwy. 156, 11 mi south of San Juan Bautista* ☎ *831/623–2465* ☜ *Free.*

EN ROUTE

★ About halfway between Monterey and Santa Cruz, east of the tiny harbor town of Moss Landing, is one of only two federal research reserves in California, the **Elkhorn Slough at the National Estuarine Research Reserve** (✉ 1700 Elkhorn Rd., Watsonville ☎ 831/728–2822 ⊕ www.elkhornslough.org ☜ $2.50 ☉ Wed.–Sun. 9–5). Its 1,400 acres of tidal flats and salt marshes form a complex environment that supports some 300 species of birds. A walk along the meandering waterways and wetlands can reveal hawks, white-tailed kites, owls, herons, and egrets. On weekends guided walks to the heron rookery begin at 10 and 1.

Santa Cruz

 34 mi northwest of Salinas; 48 mi north of Monterey on Hwy. 1.

The surrounding mountains shelter the beach town of Santa Cruz from the coastal fog and from the smoggy skies of the San Francisco Bay area and Silicon Valley. The climate here is mild, and it is usually sunnier than other northerly coastal areas.

The heart of downtown Santa Cruz is along Pacific Avenue south of Water Street, where you'll find shops, restaurants, and other establishments in the outdoor **Pacific Garden Mall.**

Santa Cruz gets some of its youthful spirit from the nearby **University of California at Santa Cruz.** The school's redwood buildings are perched on the forested hills above town; with its sylvan setting and sweeping ocean vistas, the campus is tailor-made for the contemplative life. ⊠ *Bay and High Sts.* ☎ *831/459–0111* ⊕ *www.ucsc.edu.*

Santa Cruz has been a seaside resort since the mid-19th century. The Looff carousel and classic wooden Giant Dipper roller coaster at the ☾ **Santa Cruz Beach Boardwalk** date from the early 1900s. Elsewhere along the boardwalk, the Casino Fun Center has its share of video-game technology. But this is still primarily a place for good old-fashioned family fun: rides, games, corn dogs, and chowder fries. ⊠ *Along Beach St. west from San Lorenzo River* ☎ *831/423–5590 or 831/426–7433* ⊕ *www. beachboardwalk.com* ⊠ *$26.95, day pass for unlimited rides* ☉ *Late May–early Sept., daily; early Sept.–late May, weekends only, weather permitting, call for hrs.*

The **Santa Cruz Municipal Wharf** (☎ 831/420–6025 ⊕ www. santacruzwharf.com), just up the beach from the boardwalk, is lined with restaurants, shops, and seafood takeout windows. The barking sea lions that lounge in heaps under the wharf's pilings enliven the area.

Drive southwest from the municipal wharf on West Cliff Drive about ¾ mi to the promontory at **Seal Rock,** where you can watch pinnipeds hang out, sunbathe, and occasionally frolic. The **Mark Abbott Memorial Lighthouse,** adjacent to the promontory, was built in 1868. Aside from ★ being the site of a fabulous view, it's worth a stop for the **Santa Cruz Surfing Museum** on its ground floor. The historical photographs are fun, and the display of boards from over the years includes a heavy redwood plank (from before the days of fiberglass) and the remains of a modern board that was munched by a great white shark. ⊠ *701 W. Cliff Dr.* ☎ *831/420–6289* ⊕ *www.santacruzmuseums.org* ⊠ *Free* ☉ *Wed.–Mon. noon–4.*

☾ About 1¾ mi west of the lighthouse is secluded **Natural Bridges State Beach,** a stretch of soft sand with tidal pools and a natural rock bridge nearby. From October to early March a colony of monarch butterflies resides here. ⊠ *2531 W. Cliff Dr.* ☎ *831/423–4609* ⊕ *www.parks.ca.gov* ⊠ *Parking $3* ☉ *Park daily 8 AM–sunset. Visitor center Oct.–Feb., daily 10–4; Mar.–Sept., weekends 10–4.*

Where to Stay & Eat

★ **$$$–$$$$** ✕ **Theo's.** Set on a quiet side street in a residential neighborhood, Theo's serves mainly three- and five-course prix-fixe dinners. Seasonal standouts include duck with garden vegetables and currants, as well as rack of lamb with ratatouille. Much of the produce comes from the ¾-acre organic garden behind the restaurant (where you can stroll between courses); the rest comes from area farmers and ranchers. Service is gracious and attentive, and the wine list has won awards from *Wine Spectator* 14 years in a row. ⊠ *3101 N. Main St., Soquel* ☎ *831/462–3657* ⌀ *Reservations essential* ▤ *AE, MC, V* ☉ *Closed Sun. and Mon. No lunch.*

$–$$$$ ✕ **Shadowbrook.** To get to this romantic spot overlooking Soquel Creek, you can take a cable car or walk the stairs down a steep, fern-lined bank beside a running waterfall. Dining room options include the rooftop Redwood Room, the wood-paneled Wine Cellar, and the airy, glass-enclosed Garden Room. Prime rib and grilled seafood are the stars of the simple menu. A cheaper menu of light entrées is available in the lounge. Champagne brunch is served on Sunday. ⊠ *1750 Wharf Rd., Capitola* ☎ *831/475–1571 or 800/975–1511* ⊟ *AE, D, DC, MC, V* ☺ *No lunch.*

★ ¢–$$$$ ✕ **Bittersweet Bistro.** A large old tavern with cathedral ceilings houses this popular bistro, where chef-owner Thomas Vinolus draws culinary inspiration from the Mediterranean. The menu changes seasonally, but regular highlights include the outstandingly fresh fish specials, grilled vegetable platter, seafood puttanesca (pasta with a spicy sauce of garlic, tomatoes, anchovies, and olives), and grilled lamb tenderloin. The decadent chocolate desserts are not to be missed. Lunch is available to go from the express counter. ⊠ *787 Rio Del Mar Blvd., off Hwy. 1, Aptos* ☎ *831/662–9799* ⊟ *AE, MC, V.*

$$–$$$ ✕ **Oswald's.** Intimate and stylish, this tiny courtyard bistro serves sophisticated yet unpretentious European-inspired California cooking. The menu changes seasonally, but might include such items as perfectly prepared sherry-steamed mussels or sautéed veal livers. ⊠ *1547-E Pacific Ave.* ☎ *831/423–7427* ⊟ *AE, D, DC, MC, V* ☺ *Closed Mon. No lunch.*

$–$$$ ✕ **Gabriella Café.** This tiny, intimate café displays the work of local artists, and the seasonal Italian menu features organic produce from area farms. Highlights include the steamed mussels, braised lamb shank, and grilled portobello mushrooms. ⊠ *910 Cedar St.* ☎ *831/457–1677* ⊟ *AE, MC, V.*

☺ ¢–$ ✕ **Seabright Brewery.** Great burgers, seafood, and stellar house-made microbrews make this a favorite local hangout. Sit outside on the large patio or inside at one of the comfortable, spacious booths. ⊠ *519 Seabright Ave.* ☎ *831/426–2739* ⊟ *AE, MC, V.*

¢ ✕ **Zachary's.** With its mostly young clientele, this noisy café defines the funky essence of Santa Cruz. It also dishes up great breakfasts: omelets, sourdough pancakes, artichoke frittatas, and "Mike's Mess"—eggs scrambled with bacon, mushrooms, and home fries, then topped with sour cream, melted cheese, and fresh tomatoes. ⊠ *819 Pacific Ave.* ☎ *831/427–0646* ⌂ *Reservations not accepted* ⊟ *MC, V* ☺ *Closed Mon. No dinner.*

$$$$ ▦ **Coast Santa Cruz Hotel.** Just a short stroll from the boardwalk and wharf, this resort opens right onto Cowell Beach. Though the hotel is a concrete monolith, all rooms have private balconies or patios overlooking the Pacific. If it's too cold to swim in the ocean, you can head for the heated swimming pool and hot tub. ⊠ *175 W. Cliff Dr., 95060* ☎ *831/426–4330 or 800/663–1144* ⊟ *831/427–2025* ⇴ *147 rooms, 16 suites* ⌂ *Restaurant, room service, in-room safes, refrigerators, cable TV with movies and video games, Wi-Fi, pool, hot tub, bar, laundry service, Internet room, business services, no-smoking rooms* ⊟ *AE, D, DC, MC, V.*

☺ $$$$ ▦ **Seascape Resort.** On a bluff overlooking Monterey Bay, Seascape is a perfect place to unwind. The spacious suites sleep from two to six people; each has a kitchenette and fireplace, and many have ocean-view patios with barbecue grills. Treat yourself to an in-room manicure, facial, or massage. The resort is about 9 mi south of Santa Cruz. ⊠ *1 Seascape Resort Dr., Aptos 95003* ☎ *831/688–6800 or 800/929–7727* ⊟ *831/685–0615* ⊕ *www.seascaperesort.com* ⇴ *285 suites* ⌂ *Restaurant, room* *service, some kitchens, some kitchenettes, cable TV with movies and video games, some in-room DVD, in-room data ports, Wi-Fi, golf privileges, 3 pools, health club, 3 hot tubs, spa, beach, children's programs (ages 5–10), laundry service, Internet room, business services, convention center, meeting room; no a/c, no smoking* ⊟ *AE, D, DC, MC, V.*

$$$–$$$$ 🖼 **Inn at Depot Hill.** This inventively designed B&B in a former rail depot sees itself as a link to the era of luxury train travel. Each double room or suite, complete with fireplace and featherbeds, is inspired by a different destination—Italy's Portofino, France's Côte d'Azur, Japan's Kyoto. One suite is decorated like a Pullman car for a railroad baron. Some accommodations have private patios with hot tubs. This is a great place for an adults-only weekend. ⊠ *250 Monterey Ave., Capitola 95010* ☎ *831/462–3376 or 800/572–2632* 🖷 *831/462–3697* ⊕ *www. innatdepothill.com* ⟿ *8 rooms, 4 suites* ⚲ *Fans, cable TV, in-room VCRs, in-room data ports, hot tub; no a/c, no smoking* ⊟ *AE, D, MC, V.*

$$$–$$$$ 🖼 **Pleasure Point Inn.** Tucked in a residential neighborhood at the east end of town, this modern Mediterranean-style B&B sits right across the street from the ocean and a popular surfing beach (where surfing lessons are available). The rooms are handsomely furnished and include such deluxe amenities as wireless Internet access and dimmer switches; some rooms have fireplaces. You have use of the large rooftop sundeck and hot tub, which overlook the Pacific. Because this is a popular romantic getaway spot, it's best not to bring kids. ⊠ *2–3665 E. Cliff Dr., 95062* ☎ *831/475–4657 or 877/557–2567* 🖷 *831/479–1347* ⊕ *www. pleasurepointinn.com* ⟿ *4 rooms* ⚲ *Fans, in-room safes, some in-room hot tubs, minibars, refrigerators, cable TV, in-room data ports, hot tub, beach; no a/c, no smoking* ⊟ *MC, V* ⏻⏐ *CP.*

$$$ 🖼 **Babbling Brook Inn.** Though it's smack in the middle of Santa Cruz, this B&B has lush gardens, a running stream, and tall trees that make you feel like you're in a secluded wood. All rooms have fireplaces (though a few are electric) and featherbeds; most have private patios. Complimentary wine, cheese, and fresh-baked cookies are available in the afternoon. ⊠ *1025 Laurel St., 95060* ☎ *831/427–2456 or 800/866–1131* 🖷 *831/427–2457* ⊕ *www.babblingbrookinn.com* ⟿ *11 rooms, 2 suites* ⚲ *Some in-room hot tubs, cable TV, in-room VCRs; no a/c, no smoking* ⊟ *AE, D, DC, MC, V* ⏻⏐ *BP.*

★ $$$ 🖼 **Historic Sand Rock Farm.** On the site of a former winery, this century-old Arts and Crafts–inspired farmhouse, surrounded by 10 acres of forest and meadow, has been beautifully restored and modernized. There are comfortable, spacious rooms here, and sumptuous breakfasts are served. Most rooms have their own Jacuzzi tubs; if yours doesn't, there's also a large outdoor hot tub. ⊠ *6901 Freedom Blvd., Aptos 95003* ☎ *831/688–8005* 🖷 *831/688–8025* ⊕ *www.sandrockfarm.com* ⟿ *3 rooms, 2 suites* ⚲ *Fans, some in-room hot tubs, cable TV, in-room VCRs, in-room broadband, outdoor hot tub; no a/c, no smoking* ⊟ *D, DC, MC, V* ⏻⏐ *BP.*

The Arts

Shakespeare Santa Cruz (⊠ Performing Arts Complex, University of California at Santa Cruz ☎ 831/459–2121 ⊕ www.shakespearesantacruz. org) stages a six-week Shakespeare festival in July and August that may also include the occasional modern dramatic performance. Most performances are outdoors in the striking Redwood Glen. A holiday program is also performed in December.

Sports & the Outdoors

BICYCLING To go local you can park the car and rent a beach cruiser at **Bike Shop Santa Cruz** (⊠ 1325 Mission St. ☎ 831/454–0909). Mountain bikers should head to **Another Bike Shop** (⊠ 2361 Mission St. ☎ 831/427–2232) for tips on the best trails around and a look at cutting-edge gear made and tested locally.

BOATS & **Chardonnay Sailing Charters** (☎ 831/423–1213) accommodates 49 pas-
CHARTERS sengers for year-round cruises on Monterey Bay. The 70-foot *Chardonnay II* leaves from the yacht harbor in Santa Cruz. Food and wine are served on many of their cruises, and appearances by guest chefs and local astronomers are common. Reservations are essential. **Original Stagnaro Fishing Trips** (⊠ Center of Santa Cruz Municipal Wharf ☎ 831/427–2334) operates salmon-, albacore-, and rock-cod-fishing expeditions; the fees ($55–$65) include bait. The company also runs whale-watching cruises ($28) between December and April.

SURFING **Manresa State Beach** (⊠ Manresa Dr., La Selva Beach ☎ 831/761–1795), south of Santa Cruz, has premium surfing conditions, but the currents can be treacherous; campsites are available if you're brave enough to stay. The surf at **New Brighton State Beach** (⊠ 1500 State Park Dr., Capitola ☎ 831/464–6330) has challenging surf and campsites. Surfers gather for spectacular waves and sunsets at **Pleasure Point** (⊠ E. Cliff and Pleasure Point Drs.). **Steamer Lane,** near the lighthouse on West Cliff Drive, has a decent break. The area plays host to several competitions in summer.

The most welcoming place in town for surf gear is **Paradise Surf Shop** (⊠ 3961 Portola Dr. ☎ 831/462–3880). The shop is owned by local amateur longboarder Sally Smith and run by women who aim to help everyone feel comfortable on the water. Boards, suits, and other gear can be bought and rented here. **Cowell's Beach 'n' Bikini Surf Shop** (⊠ 30 Front St. ☎ 831/427–2355) rents surfboards and wet suits and offers lessons.

MONTEREY BAY A TO Z

To research prices, get advice from other travelers, and book travel arrangements, visit www.fodors.com.

AIRPORTS & TRANSFERS

Monterey Peninsula Airport is 3 mi east of downtown Monterey (take Olmstead Road off Highway 68). It is served by America West, American, American Eagle, United, and United Express. *See* Air Travel *in* Smart Travel Tips A to Z for airline phone numbers. Taxi service is available for about $9–$10, and Monterey–Salinas Transit has buses to and from the airport Monday through Saturday.

🚖 **Carmel Taxi** ☎ 831/624–3885. **Monterey Airport Taxi** ☎ 831/626–3385. **Monterey Peninsula Airport** ⊠ 200 Fred Kane Dr., Monterey ☎ 831/648–7000 ⊕ www. montereyairport.com. **Monterey-Salinas Transit** ☎ 831/899-2555. **Yellow Checker Cabs** ☎ 831/646-1234.

BUS TRAVEL

Greyhound serves Santa Cruz and Monterey from San Francisco three or four times daily. The trips take about 3 and 4½ hours, respectively. Monterey-Salinas Transit provides frequent service between the peninsula's towns and many major sightseeing spots and shopping areas. The base fare is $1.75, with an additional $1.75 for each zone you travel into. A day pass costs $3.50–$7, depending on how many zones you'll be traveling through. Monterey-Salinas Transit also runs the WAVE shuttle, which links major attractions on the Monterey waterfront. The free shuttle operates late May through early September, daily from 9 to 6:30.

🚍 **Greyhound** ☎ 800/231-2222 ⊕ www.greyhound.com. **Monterey-Salinas Transit** ☎ 831/899-2555 or 888/678-2871 ⊕ www.mst.org.

CAR RENTAL

Most of the major agencies have locations in downtown Santa Cruz and at the Monterey Airport. *See* Car Rental *in* Smart Travel Tips A to Z for national car-rental agency phone numbers.

CAR TRAVEL

Parking is especially difficult in Carmel and in the heavily touristed areas of Monterey.

Two-lane Highway 1 runs north–south along the coast, linking the towns of Santa Cruz, Monterey, and Carmel. Highway 68 runs east from Pacific Grove toward Salinas at U.S. 101. North of Salinas, the freeway (U.S. 101) links up with Highway 156 to San Juan Bautista. The drive south from San Francisco to Monterey can be made comfortably in three hours or less. The most scenic way is to follow Highway 1 down the coast past flower, pumpkin, and artichoke fields and the seaside communities of Pacifica, Half Moon Bay, and Santa Cruz. Unless you drive on sunny weekends when locals are heading for the beach, the two-lane coast highway may take no longer than the freeway.

A sometimes faster route is I–280 south from San Francisco to Highway 17, north of San Jose. Highway 17 crosses the redwood-filled Santa Cruz Mountains between San Jose and Santa Cruz, where it intersects with Highway 1. The traffic can crawl to a standstill, however, heading into Santa Cruz. Another option is to follow U.S. 101 south through San Jose to Prunedale and then take Highway 156 west to Highway 1 south into Monterey.

From Los Angeles the drive to Monterey can be made in five to six hours by heading north on U.S. 101 to Salinas and then west on Highway 68. The spectacular but slow alternative is to take U.S. 101 to San Luis Obispo and then follow the hairpin turns of Highway 1 up the coast. Allow about three extra hours if you take this route.

EMERGENCIES

In the event of an emergency, dial 911. The Monterey Bay Dental Society provides dentist referrals, and the Monterey County Medical Society can refer you to a doctor. There is a 24-hour Walgreens pharmacy in Seaside, about 4 mi northeast of Monterey via Highway 1.

🏥 Hospitals **Community Hospital of Monterey Peninsula** ✉ 23625 Holman Hwy., Monterey ☎ 831/624-5311. **Dominican Hospital** ✉ 1555 Soquel Dr., Santa Cruz ☎ 831/462-7700.

🏥 Pharmacies **Walgreens** ✉ 1055 Fremont Blvd., Seaside ☎ 831/393-9231.

🏥 Referrals **Monterey Bay Dental Society** ☎ 831/658-0168. **Monterey County Medical Society** ☎ 831/455-1008.

LODGING

Bed and Breakfast Innkeepers of Santa Cruz County is an association of innkeepers that can help you find a B&B. Monterey County Conventions and Visitors Bureau Visitor Services operates a lodging referral line and publishes an informational brochure with discount coupons that are good at restaurants, attractions, and shops. Monterey Peninsula Reservations will assist you in booking lodgings.

🏥 **Bed and Breakfast Innkeepers of Santa Cruz County** ☎ 831/688-0444 ⊕ www. santacruzbnb.com. **Monterey County Conventions and Visitors Bureau Visitor Services** ☎ 888/221-1010 ⊕ www.montereyinfo.org. **Monterey Peninsula Reservations** ☎ 888/655-3424 ⊕ www.monterey-reservations.com.

TOURS

California Parlor Car Tours operates motor-coach tours from San Francisco that include one or two days in the Monterey Peninsula. Ag Venture Tours runs wine-tasting, sightseeing, and agricultural tours in the Monterey, Salinas, Carmel Valley, and Santa Cruz areas.

🏥 **Ag Venture Tours** ☎ 831/643-9463 ⊕ www.agventuretours.com. **California Parlor Car Tours** ☎ 415/474-7500 or 800/227-4250 ⊕ www.calpartours.com.

TRAIN TRAVEL

Amtrak's *Coast Starlight,* which runs between Los Angeles, Oakland, and Seattle, stops in Salinas. Connecting Amtrak Thruway buses serve Monterey and Carmel.

🏥 **Amtrak** ✉ 30 Railroad Ave., Salinas ☎ 800/872-7245 ⊕ www.amtrakcalifornia.com.

VISITOR INFORMATION

🏥 **Monterey County Convention & Visitors Bureau** ☎ 888/221-1010 ⊕ www. montereyinfo.org. **Monterey County Vintners and Growers Association** ☎ 831/375-9400 ⊕ www.montereywines.org. **Monterey Peninsula Visitors and Convention Bureau** ✉ 462 Webster St., #4, Monterey 93940 ☎ 831/372-9323 ⊕ www.monterey.com. **Salinas Valley Chamber of Commerce** ✉ 119 E. Alisal St., Salinas 93901 ☎ 831/424-7611 ⊕ www.salinaschamber.com. **Santa Cruz County Conference and Visitors Council** ✉ 1211 Ocean St., Santa Cruz 95060 ☎ 831/425-1234 or 800/833-3494 ⊕ www.scccvc. org. **Santa Cruz Mountain Winegrowers' Association** ✉ 7605-A Old Dominion Ct., Aptos 95003 ☎ 831/479-9463 ⊕ www.scmwa.com.

The Central Valley

Highway 99 from Bakersfield to Lodi

WORD OF MOUTH

"A trip through the Forestiere Underground Gardens is a near-magical experience. The tunnels, the exotic trees, the grottoes—it's amazing to think someone actually lived here."

—marie606

Updated by
Reed Parsell

AMONG THE WORLD'S MOST FERTILE working lands, the Central Valley is also California's heartland. Lush fields and orchards crisscrossed by miles of back roads define the landscape of this sunbaked region, and a number of rivers and creeks provide relief from the flat farmland that carpets most of the valley. The agriculturally rich area is home to a diversity of wildlife. Many telephone posts are crowned by a hawk or kestrel hunting the land below. Humans, in turn, have created a profusion of vineyards, dairy farms, orchards, and pastures that stretch to the horizon. In the towns, historical societies display artifacts of the valley's eccentric past; concert halls and restored theaters showcase samplings of contemporary culture; and museums provide a blend of both. Whether on back roads or main streets, people are not only friendly but proud to help outsiders explore the Central Valley.

If the well-populated Central Valley appears at first glance to be a traveler's void, it's because most folks never leave the highway. Many choose to drive boring I–5 instead of Highway 99, which is framed by farms, vineyards, and dairies. The valley's history of being passed over dates back hundreds of years. Until the mid-19th century, the area was a desert. Gold discoveries, starting in the 1850s, sparked the birth of some towns; the arrival of the railroad in following decades spurred the development of others. But it was the coming of water, courtesy of private dams and, in the 1930s, the Central Valley Project, that transformed this land into the country's most vital agricultural region.

As soon as irrigation gave potential to the valley's open acres, the area became a magnet for farmers, ranchers, developers, World War II refugees, and immigrants from places as diverse as Portugal, China, Armenia, and Laos. Today refugees from the state's big cities come in search of cheaper real estate, safer neighborhoods, and more space. With development has come some unsightly sprawl, air pollution, and pressure on crucial water supplies. Nevertheless, the valley retains many of its traditional charms. The region's cultural diversity and agricultural roots have woven a textured social fabric that has been chronicled by some of the country's finest writers, including Fresno native William Saroyan, Stockton native Maxine Hong Kingston, and *Grapes of Wrath* author John Steinbeck.

Just as these authors found inspiration in a place you cannot view while speeding down the highway, you must invest time and footwork to appreciate the Central Valley. The rewards can be surprising, relaxing . . . even poetic.

Exploring the Central Valley

The 225-mi Central Valley cuts through Kern, Tulare, Kings, Fresno, Madera, Merced, Stanislaus, and San Joaquin counties. It is bounded on the east by the mighty Sierra Nevada and on the west by the smaller coastal ranges. I–5 runs south–north through the valley, as does Highway 99.

About the Restaurants

Fast-food places and chain restaurants dominate valley highways, but away from the main drag, independent and family-owned eateries will awaken your taste buds. Many bistros and fine restaurants take advantage of the local produce and locally raised meats that are the cornerstone of California cuisine. Even simple restaurants produce hearty, tasty fare that often reflects the valley's ethnic mix. Some of the nation's best Mexican restaurants call the valley home. Chinese, Italian, Armenian, and Basque restaurants also are abundant; many serve massive, many-course meals. Although dress at most valley eateries is casual, diners at some of the finer establishments won't feel out of place in jacket and tie or cocktail dress.

About the Hotels

The Central Valley has many chain motels and hotels, but independently owned hotels and bed-and-breakfasts also can be found. There's a large selection of upscale lodgings, Victorian-style B&Bs, and places that are simply utilitarian but clean and comfortable.

	WHAT IT COSTS				
	$$$$	**$$$**	**$$**	**$**	**¢**
RESTAURANTS	over $30	$23–$30	$16–$22	$10–$15	under $10
HOTELS	over $250	$176–$250	$121–$175	$90–$120	under $90

Restaurant prices are for a main course at dinner, excluding sales tax of 7%–10% (depending on location). Hotel prices are for two people in a standard double room in high season, excluding service charges and 8%–13% tax.

Timing

Spring, when wildflowers are in bloom and the scent of fruit blossoms is in the air, and fall, when the air is brisk and leaves turn red and gold, are the best times to visit. Many of the valley's biggest festivals take place during these seasons. (If you suffer from allergies, though, beware of spring, when stone-fruit trees blossom.) Summer, when temperatures often top 100°F, can be oppressive. June–August, though, are great months to visit area water parks and lakes or to take in the museums, where air-conditioning provides a reprieve from the heat. Many attractions close in winter, which can get cold and dreary. Thick, ground-hugging fog, called tule fog by locals, is a common driving hazard November–February.

SOUTHERN CENTRAL VALLEY

BAKERSFIELD & KERNVILLE

When gold was discovered in Kern County in the 1860s, settlers flocked to the southern end of the Central Valley. Black gold—oil—is now the area's most valuable commodity; the county provides 64% of California's oil production. Kern is also among the country's five most productive agricultural counties. From the flat plains around Bakersfield, the landscape grows gently hilly and then graduates to mountains as it nears Kernville, which lies in the Kern River valley.

GREAT ITINERARIES

Numbers in the text correspond to numbers in the margin and on the Central Valley and Fresno Area maps.

IF YOU HAVE 1 DAY Touring the Fresno area is a good strategy if you have only a day to spend in the valley. ☞ **Roeding Park** ❻ has a striking tropical rain forest within Chaffee Zoological Gardens; the park's Playland and Storyland are great stops if you're traveling with children. Don't miss the **Forestiere Underground Gardens** ⑫, on Shaw Avenue. In springtime take the self-guided **Blossom Trail** driving tour through orchards, vineyards, and fields. Along the trail in Reedley is the Mennonite Quilt Center. Depending on your mood and the weather, you can spend part of the afternoon at Wild Water Adventures or visit the **Fresno Metropolitan Museum** ❼, whose highlights include an exhibit about author William Saroyan.

IF YOU HAVE 3 DAYS Start your trip through the Central Valley in ☞ **Bakersfield** ❶, with a visit to the Kern

County Museum. Drive north on Highway 99 and west on Highway 122 to drive to **Colonel Allensworth State Historic Park** ❸, which is on the site of a now-deserted town founded by African-Americans in 1908. Continue north on Highway 34 to ⊞ **Hanford** ❺ and stroll around Courthouse Square and China Alley. The next morning proceed to ⊞ **Fresno** ❻–⑬ via Highways 43 and 99 north and spend the day there, as in the one-day itinerary above. In the evening take in a show at Roger Rocka's or the Tower Theatre, both in Fresno's Tower District. On Day 3 continue up Highway 99 and stop off at the Castle Air Museum, north of **Merced** ⑭ in Atwater. **Modesto** ⑮ is a good place to stop for lunch. In the afternoon, choose from a rafting trip on the Stanislaus River near **Oakdale** ⑯, an hour or two of art appreciation at the Haggin Museum in **Stockton** ⑰, and a tour of the wineries around **Lodi** ⑱. Lodi is a pleasant place to overnight.

6

Bakersfield

☞ ❶ *110 mi north of Los Angeles on I–5 and Hwy. 99; 110 mi west of Ridgecrest via Hwy. 14 south and Hwy. 58 west.*

Bakersfield's founder, Colonel Thomas Baker, arrived with the discovery of gold in the nearby Kern River valley in 1851. Now Kern County's biggest city (it has a population of 279,000, which includes the largest Basque community in the United States), Bakersfield probably is best known as Nashville West, a country-music haven and hometown of performers Buck Owens and Merle Haggard. It also has its own symphony orchestra and two good museums.

★ � The **Kern County Museum and Lori Brock Children's Discovery Center** form one of the Central Valley's top museum complexes. The indoor-outdoor Kern County Museum is set up as an open-air, walk-through historic village with more than 50 restored or re-created buildings dating from the 1860s–1940s. "Black Gold: The Oil Experience," a permanent exhibit that opened in November 2002, shows how oil is created, discovered, and extracted. The Children's Discovery Center has hands-on displays and activities. ✉ *3801 Chester Ave.* ☎ *661/852–5000* 🌐 *www.kcmuseum.org* 🎟 *$8* ⏲ *Mon.–Sat. 10–5, Sun. noon–5.*

★ 👶 At the **California Living Museum,** a combination zoo, botanical garden, and natural-history museum, the emphasis is on zoo. All animal and plant species displayed are native to the state. Within the reptile house lives every species of rattlesnake found in California. The landscaped grounds—in the hills about a 20-minute drive northeast of Bakersfield—also shelter captive bald eagles, tortoises, coyotes, mountain lions, black bears, and foxes. ✉ *10500 Alfred Harrell Hwy., Hwy. 178 east, then 3½ mi northwest on Alfred Harrell Hwy.* ☎ *661/872–2256* 🌐 *www.calmzoo.org* 🎟 *$4.50* ⏲ *Tues.–Sun. 9–5.*

Where to Stay & Eat

$–$$$ ✕ **Uricchio's Trattoria.** This downtown restaurant draws everyone from office workers to oil barons—all attracted by the tasty food and casual atmosphere. *Panini* (Italian pressed sandwiches, served at lunch only), pasta, and Italian-style chicken dishes dominate the menu; the chicken piccata outsells all other offerings. ✉ *1400 17th St.* ☎ *661/326–8870* 💳 *AE, D, DC, MC, V* ⏲ *Closed Sun. No lunch Sat.*

$–$$ ✕ **Woolgrower's Restaurant.** Thick lamb chops, roast lamb, oxtail stew, and shrimp scampi have made this spot popular with locals. All meals are served family-style, so you might share your table with diners you don't know. Meals include vegetables and a potato or rice dish. ✉ *620 E. 19th St.* ☎ *661/327–9584* 💳 *AE, D, MC, V* ⏲ *Closed Sun.*

¢ ✕ **Jake's Tex Mex Cafe.** Don't let the cafeteria-style service fool you; this is probably the best lunch place in Bakersfield. The chicken burritos and the chili fries (with meaty chili ladled on top) are superb. For dessert, try the Texas sheet cake or the homemade chocolate chip cookies. It's open for dinner, too. ✉ *1710 Oak St.* ☎ *661/322–6380* ✍ *Reservations not accepted* 💳 *AE, D, MC, V* ⏲ *Closed Sun.*

$–$$$ 🏨 **Four Points by Sheraton.** Fountains, lush lawns, and exotic plants provide a spectacular setting for this hotel. Occupying 7.5 acres in Bakersfield's business district, it's a mile west of Highway 99. The large rooms come equipped with coffeemakers, irons, hair dryers, and DSL connections. The pool is just shy of Olympic size. ✉ *5101 California Ave., 93309* ☎ *661/325–9700 or 800/368–7764* 📠 *661/323–3508* 🌐 *www.fourpoints.com* 🛏 *198 rooms* 👍 *Cable TV, in-room data ports, pool, gym, hot tub, meeting rooms, airport shuttle, no-smoking rooms* 💳 *AE, D, DC, MC, V.*

¢ 🏨 **Quality Inn.** Near downtown in a relatively quiet location off Highway 99, this two-story motel offers good value. Most rooms have king- or queen-size beds, and all have HBO. Some have refrigerators and a patio or a balcony overlooking the heated pool. Complimentary coffee is available all day. ✉ *1011 Oak St., 93304* ☎ *661/325–0772 or 877/424–6423* 📠 *661/325–4646* 🌐 *www.qualityinn.com* 🛏 *89 rooms* 👍 *Some refrigerators, cable TV, pool, gym, hot tub, laundry facilities* 💳 *AE, D, DC, MC, V* 🍽 *BP.*

PLEASURES & PASTIMES

FESTIVALS, TOURS & TASTINGS. The Central Valley is a great destination for anyone who likes produce fresh from the fields. As billboards announce, fruit and nut orchards as well as cheese factories offer educational tours that include tastings. Better yet, there are farmers' markets in virtually every town, and roadside stands in between. Good places to find produce stands are Highway 198 between Visalia and Hanford, Herndon Avenue in Fresno and Clovis, and Highway 12 in Lodi. Prime season for farmers' markets is May through October, though many larger ones are open year-round, including those held every Saturday in Bakersfield, Fresno, Merced, Stockton, and Visalia. Especially in fall check with chambers of commerce for festivals celebrating everything from the asparagus and raisin crops to residents' Chinese, Greek, and Swedish roots.

SPORTS & THE OUTDOORS. Several cities and towns serve as convenient starting points for white-water rafting trips on the Stanislaus, Merced, Kings, and Kern rivers. Fishing in the rivers and lakes is another favored activity; the lakes are also prime spots for boating and swimming. Stockton is a popular rental area for houseboating on the Sacramento River delta, and Bakersfield is a center for NASCAR racing. The San Francisco Giants' Triple-A team, the Fresno Grizzlies, plays in a stadium opened in 2002 in Fresno. Wildlife refuges are excellent sites for watching birds, especially migrating waterfowl.

6

Nightlife & the Arts

The **Bakersfield Symphony Orchestra** (✉ 1328 34th St., Suite A ☎ 661/323–7928 ⊕ www.bakersfieldsymphony.org) performs classical music concerts at the convention center from October through May.

Buck Owens' Crystal Palace (✉ 2800 Buck Owens Blvd. ☎ 661/328–7560 ⊕ www.buckowens.com) is a combination nightclub, restaurant, and showcase of country music memorabilia. Country-and-western singers perform here, including Buck Owens and the Buckaroos. A dance floor beckons customers who can still twirl after sampling the menu of steaks, burgers, nachos, and gooey desserts. Entertainment is free on most weeknights; on Friday and Saturday nights when Owens performs, there's a cover charge (usually $6–$12); there's also a cover for some of the more well-known entertainers.

Sports & the Outdoors

CAR RACING At **Bakersfield Speedway** (✉ 5001 N. Chester Extension ☎ 661/393–3373 ⊕ www.bakersfieldspeedway.com), stock and sprint cars race around a ⅓-mi clay oval track. **Mesa Marin Raceway** (✉ 11000 Kern Canyon Rd. ☎ 661/366–5711 ⊕ www.mesamarin.com) presents high-speed stock-car, Craftsman Truck, and NASCAR racing on a ½-mi paved oval course.

SKATING The free skate park at **Beach Park** (✉ Oak and 21st Sts. ☉ Daily 5 AM–10 PM) has good street skating as well as a relaxing grassy area.

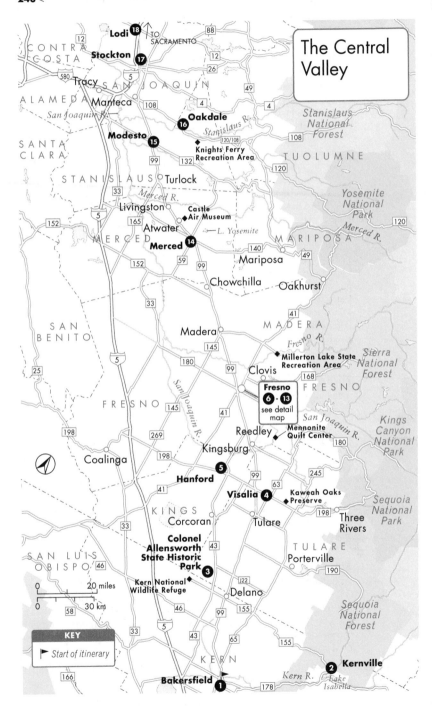

The Central Valley

TO SACRAMENTO

Lodi **18**
Stockton **17**
Tracy
Manteca
Modesto **15**
Oakdale **16**
Merced **14**
Fresno **6** - **13**
see detail map
Hanford **5**
Visalia **4**
Colonel Allensworth State Historic Park **3**
Kernville **2**
Bakersfield **1**

CONTRA COSTA
SAN JOAQUIN
ALAMEDA
SANTA CLARA
STANISLAUS
Turlock
Livingston
Atwater
MERCED
Chowchilla
SAN BENITO
Madera
MADERA
Clovis
FRESNO
Reedley
Kingsburg
Coalinga
KINGS
Corcoran
Tulare
TULARE
Porterville
Delano
KERN

Knights Ferry Recreation Area
Castle Air Museum
L. Yosemite
Mariposa
Oakhurst
Millerton Lake State Recreation Area
Mennonite Quilt Center
Kaweah Oaks Preserve
Three Rivers
Kern National Wildlife Refuge

Stanislaus National Forest
TUOLUMNE
Yosemite National Park
MARIPOSA
Merced R.
Sierra National Forest
San Joaquin R.
Kings Canyon National Park
Sequoia National Park
Sequoia National Forest

San Joaquin R.
Stanislaus R.
Merced R.
Fresno R.
Kern R.
Lake Isabella

SAN LUIS OBISPO

0   20 miles
0   30 km

KEY
▶ Start of itinerary

Shopping

Many antiques shops are on 18th and 19th streets between H and R streets, and on H Street between Brundage Lane and California Avenue. **Central Park Antique Mall** (⊠ 701 19th St. ☎ 661/633–1143) has a huge selection. The **Great American Antiques** (⊠ 625 19th St. ☎ 661/322–1776) is full of treasures.

Dewar's Candy Shop (⊠ 1120 Eye St. ☎ 661/322–0933) was founded in 1909 and has been owned by the Dewar family ever since. The hand-dipped chocolate cherries are delicious; so are the Dewar's Chews, a mouth-watering taffy concoction available in peanut butter, peppermint, caramel, and almond flavors. There's also an old-fashioned soda fountain.

Kernville

❷ *50 mi from Bakersfield, northeast on Hwy. 178 and north on Hwy. 155.*

The wild and scenic Kern River, which flows through Kernville en route from Mount Whitney to Bakersfield, delivers some of the most exciting white-water rafting in the state. Kernville (population 1,700) rests in a mountain valley on both banks of the river and also at the northern tip of Lake Isabella (a dammed portion of the river used as a reservoir and for recreation). A center for rafting outfitters, Kernville has lodgings, restaurants, and antiques shops. The main streets are lined with Old West–style buildings, reflecting Kernville's heritage as a rough-and-tumble gold-mining town once known as Whiskey Flat. (Present-day Kernville dates from the 1950s, when it was moved upriver to make room for Lake Isabella.) The road from Bakersfield includes portions with the rushing river on one side and granite cliffs on the other.

Where to Stay & Eat

$ ✕ **That's Italian.** For northern Italian cuisine in a typical trattoria, this is the spot. Try the braised lamb shanks in a Chianti wine sauce or the linguine with clams, mussels, calamari, and shrimp in a white-wine clam sauce. ⊠ *9 Big Blue Rd.* ☎ *760/376–6020* ▤ *AE, D, MC, V* ☉ *No lunch Nov.–Apr.*

$$-$$$$ ▥ **Whispering Pines Lodge.** Perched on the banks of the Kern River, this 8-acre property gives you a variety of overnight options. All units are housed in bungalows. Some have full kitchens, fireplaces, queen-size sleepers, and whirlpool tubs; all have coffeemakers and king-size beds. ⊠ *13745 Sierra Way, 93238* ☎ *760/376–3733 or 877/241–4100* ▤ *760/376–6513* ⊕ *www.kernvalley.com/whisperingpines* ⇗ *17 rooms* ♿ *Some kitchenettes, refrigerators, cable TV, pool* ▤ *AE, D, MC, V* ▥ *BP.*

Sports & the Outdoors

BOATING & WINDSURFING   The Lower Kern River, which extends from Lake Isabella to Bakersfield and beyond, is open for fishing year-round. Catches include rainbow trout, catfish, smallmouth bass, crappie, and bluegill. Lake Isabella is popular with anglers, water-skiers, sailors, and windsurfers. Its shoreline marinas have boats for rent, bait and tackle, and moorings. **North Fork Marina** (☎ 760/376–1812) is in Wofford Heights, on the lake's west shore. **French Gulch Marina** (☎ 760/379–8774) nestles in a cove on Lake Isabella's north shore.

WHITE-WATER RAFTING
The three sections of the Kern River—known as the Lower Kern, Upper Kern, and the Forks—add up to nearly 50 mi of white water, ranging from Class I (easy) to Class V (expert). The Lower and Upper Kern are the most popular and accessible sections. Organized trips can last from one hour (for as little as $20) to more than two days. Rafting season usually runs from late spring until the end of summer. **Kern River Tours** (☎ 800/844–7238 ⊕ www.kernrivertours.com) leads several rafting tours from half-day trips to three days of navigating Class V rapids, and also arranges for mountain-bike trips. **Mountain & River Adventures** (☎ 760/376–6553 or 800/861–6553 ⊕ www.mtnriver.com) gives calm-water kayaking tours as well as white-water rafting trips. Half-day Class II and III white-water rafting trips are emphasized at **Sierra South** (☎ 760/376–3745 or 800/457–2082 ⊕ www.sierrasouth.com), which also offers kayaking classes and calm-water excursions.

MID-CENTRAL VALLEY
FROM VISALIA TO FRESNO

The Mid-Central Valley extends over three counties—Tulare, Kings, and Fresno. Historic Hanford and bustling Visalia are unadvertised but worthwhile discoveries. From Visalia, Highway 198 winds east 35 mi to Generals Highway, which leads into Sequoia and Kings Canyon national parks. Highway 180 snakes east 55 mi to Sequoia and Kings Canyon. From Fresno, Highway 41 leads north 95 mi to Yosemite National Park.

Colonel Allensworth State Historic Park

★ ❸ *45 mi north of Bakersfield on Hwy. 43.*

A former slave who became the country's highest-ranking black military officer of his time founded Allensworth—the only California town settled, governed, and financed by African-Americans—in 1908. After enjoying early prosperity, the town was plagued by hardships and was eventually deserted. Its rebuilt buildings reflect the era when it thrived. Festivities each October commemorate the town's rededication. ✉ *4129 Palmer Ave.* ☎ *661/849–3433* ⊕ *www.cal-parks.ca.gov* 🚗 *$4 per car* ☉ *Daily sunrise–sunset, visitor center open daily 10–4, buildings open by appointment.*

OFF THE BEATEN PATH
KERN NATIONAL WILDLIFE REFUGE – Snowy egrets, peregrine falcons, warblers, dozens of types of ducks, and other birds inhabit the marshes and wetlands here from November through April. Follow the 6½-mi loop drive (pick up maps at the entrance) to find good viewing spots, but beware that waterfowl hunting is allowed October through January. ✉ *10811 Corcoran Rd., 18 mi west of Delano on Hwy. 155 (Garces Hwy.); from Allensworth take Hwy. 43 south to Hwy. 155 west* ☎ *661/725-2767* ⊕ *www.natureali.org/knwrvisitors.htm* 🚗 *Free* ☉ *Daily sunrise–sunset.*

Visalia

❹ *40 mi north of Colonel Allensworth State Historic Park on Hwy. 99 and east on Hwy. 198; 75 mi north of Bakersfield via Hwy. 99 north and Hwy. 198 east.*

Visalia's combination of a reliable agricultural economy and civic pride has yielded perhaps the most vibrant downtown in the Central Valley. A clear day's view of the Sierra from Main Street is spectacular, and even Sunday night can find the streets busy with pedestrians, many coming from Bakersfield and Fresno for the good restaurants that abound here. Founded in 1852, the town contains many historic homes; ask for a free guide at the **visitor center** (⊠ 720 W. Mineral King Ave., 93921 ☎ 559/ 734–5876 ☽ Weekdays 8:30–5).

The **Chinese Cultural Center,** housed in a pagoda-style building, mounts exhibits about Asian art and culture. ⊠ *500 S. Akers Rd., at Hwy. 198* ☎ *559/625–4545* ⊠ *Free* ☽ *Call for hrs.*

☾ In oak-shaded **Mooney Grove Park** you can picnic alongside duck ponds, rent a boat for a ride around the lagoon, and view a replica of the famous *End of the Trail* statue. The original, designed by James Earl Fraser for the 1915 Panama-Pacific International Exposition, is now in the Cowboy Hall of Fame in Oklahoma. ⊠ *27000 S. Mooney Blvd., 5 mi south of downtown* ☎ *559/733–6291* ⊠ *$6 per car, free in winter, dates vary* ☽ *Late May–early Sept., weekdays 8–7, weekends 8 AM–9 PM; early Sept.–Oct. and Mar.–late May, Mon., Thurs., and Fri. 8–5, weekends 8–7; Nov.–Feb., Thurs.–Mon. 8–5.*

The indoor-outdoor **Tulare County Museum** contains several re-created environments from the pioneer era. Also on display are Yokuts tribal artifacts (basketry, arrowheads, clamshell-necklace currency) as well as saddles, guns, dolls, quilts, and gowns. ⊠ *Mooney Grove Park, 27000 S. Mooney Blvd., 5 mi south of downtown* ☎ *559/733–6616* ⊠ *Free* ☽ *Late May–Sept., Thurs.–Mon. 10–4; Oct.–late May, Mon., Tues., and Fri. 10–4, weekends 1–4.*

Trails at the 300-acre **Kaweah Oaks Preserve,** a wildlife sanctuary off the main road to Sequoia National Park, lead past oak, sycamore, cottonwood, and willow trees. Among the 125 bird species you might spot are hawks, hummingbirds, and great blue herons. Lizards, coyotes, and cottontails also live here. ⊠ *Follow Hwy. 198 for 7 mi east of Visalia, turn north on Rd. 182, and proceed ½ mi to gate on left side.* ☎ *559/738– 0211* ⊕ *www.sequoiariverlands.org* ⊠ *Free* ☽ *Daily sunrise–sunset.*

Where to Stay & Eat

★ **$$–$$$$** ✕ **The Vintage Press.** Built in 1966, the Vintage Press is the best restaurant in the Central Valley. Cut-glass doors and bar fixtures decorate the artfully designed rooms. The California-Continental cuisine includes dishes such as crispy veal sweetbreads with a port wine sauce, and a baconwrapped filet mignon stuffed with mushrooms. The chocolate Grand Marnier cake is a standout among the homemade desserts and ice creams. The wine list has more than 900 selections. ⊠ *216 N. Willis St.* ☎ *559/733–3033* ▭ *AE, DC, MC, V.*

¢–$$ ✕ **Café 225.** This downtown favorite combines high ceilings and warm yellow walls with soft chatter and butcher-papered tables to create an elegance that's relaxed enough for kids. The basic menu of pastas and grilled items is highlighted with unusual treats, such as scusami (calzone with melting Gorgonzola and tomato, basil, and garlic). ⊠ *225 W. Main St.* ☎ *559/733–2967* ▭ *AE, D, DC, MC, V.*

¢–$ ✕ **Henry Salazar's.** Traditional Mexican food with a contemporary twist is served at this restaurant that uses fresh ingredients from local farms. Bring your appetite if you expect to finish the Burrito Fantastico, a large flour tortilla stuffed with your choice of meat, beans, and chili sauce, and smothered with melted Monterey Jack cheese. Another signature dish is grilled salmon with lemon-butter sauce. Colorfully painted walls, soft reflections from candles in wall niches, and color-coordinated tablecloths and napkins make the atmosphere cozy and restful. ⊠ *123 W. Main St.* ☎ *559/741–7060* ▭ *AE, D, MC, V.*

$ ▣ **Ben Maddox House.** Housed in a building dating to 1876, this homey B&B offers the best of all worlds: plush beds, a cool swimming pool, and excellent service remind you you're on vacation; private bathrooms and dining tables on the sunny porch make the surroundings homey and comfortable. The Water Tower Room has its own sitting area, and all rooms have wireless Internet access. ⊠ *601 N. Encina St., 93291* ☎ *559/739–0721 or 800/401–9800* ᨨ *559/625–0420* ⊕ *www.benmaddoxhouse.com* ↰ *5 rooms* ♨ *Cable TV, in-room data ports, pool; no smoking* ▭ *AE, D, MC, V* ⦿ *BP.*

¢–$ ▣ **The Spalding House.** This restored colonial revival B&B is decked out with antiques, Oriental rugs, handcrafted woodwork, and glass doors. The house, built in 1901, has suites with separate sitting rooms and private baths. The quiet neighborhood, also home to the Ben Maddox House, offers a place for one of life's simple pleasures: an evening walk on lovely, tree-lined streets. ⊠ *631 N. Encina St., 93291* ☎ *559/739–7877* ᨨ *559/625–0902* ⊕ *www.thespaldinghouse.com* ↰ *3 suites* ♨ *No-smoking, no room phones, no room TVs* ▭ *AE, MC, V* ⦿ *BP.*

Hanford

★ ❺   *20 mi west of Visalia on Hwy. 198; 43 mi north of Colonel Allensworth State Historic Park on Hwy. 43.*

Founded in 1877 as a Southern Pacific Railroad stop, Hanford had one of California's largest Chinatowns—the Chinese came to help build the railroads and stayed on to farm. You can take a self-guided walking tour with the help of a free brochure, or take a driving tour in a restored 1930s Studebaker fire truck ($35 for up to 15 people) through the **Hanford Visitor Agency** (☎ *559/582–5024* ⊕ *www.visithanford.com*). One tour explores the restored buildings of Courthouse Square, whose Hanford Auditorium is a visual standout; another heads to narrow China Alley. If you have specific interests, a tour can also be designed for you.

The **Hanford Carnegie Museum** displays fashions, furnishings, toys, and military artifacts that tell the region's story. The living-history museum is inside the former Carnegie Library, a Romanesque building dating from 1905. ⊠ *109 E. 8th St.* ☎ *559/584–1367* 🖃 *$2* ⊘ *Wed.–Sat. 10–2.*

A 1st-floor museum in the 1893 **Taoist Temple** displays photos, furnishings, and kitchenware from Hanford's once-bustling Chinatown. The 2nd-floor temple, largely unchanged for a century, contains altars, carvings, and ceremonial staves. You can visit as part of a guided tour or by calling the temple and making an appointment two weeks in advance. ⊠ *12 China Alley* ☎ *559/582–4508* 🖃 *Free; donations welcome.*

Where to Stay & Eat

$$–$$$ ✕ **Imperial Dynasty.** Despite its name and elegant Chinese teak and porcelain accents, Imperial Dynasty serves primarily Continental cuisine. This is one of the better restaurants in the valley and fills up quickly on weekends. For a memorable meal start with the garlicky escargots and continue with the veal sweetbreads or rack of lamb. The extensive wine list contains many prized vintages. ⊠ *China Alley, 7th and Green Sts.* ☎ *559/582–0196* 🖃 *AE, D, MC, V* ⊘ *Closed Mon. No lunch.*

¢–$ ✕ **La Fiesta.** Mexican-American families, farmworkers, and farmers all eat here, polishing off traditional Mexican dishes such as enchiladas and tacos. The Fiesta Special—for two or more—includes nachos, garlic shrimp, shrimp in a spicy red sauce, clams, and two pieces of top sirloin. ⊠ *106 N. Green St.* ☎ *559/583–8775* 🖃 *AE, D, MC, V.*

★ ¢–$$ 🏠 **Irwin Street Inn.** This inn is one of the few lodgings in the valley that warrant a detour. Four tree-shaded, restored Victorian homes have been converted into spacious accommodations with comfortable rooms and suites. Most have antique armoires, dark-wood detailing, lead-glass windows, and four-poster beds; bathrooms have old-fashioned tubs, brass fixtures, and marble basins. ⊠ *522 N. Irwin St., 93230* ☎ *559/583–8000 or 866/583–7378* 🖷 *559/583–8793* ⊕ *www.irwinstreetinn.com* 🛏 *24 rooms, 3 suites* ⏧ *Restaurant, pool* 🖃 *AE, D, DC, MC, V* ⏝ *CP.*

Nightlife & the Arts

The restored Moorish-Castilian–style **Hanford Fox Theatre** (⊠ 326 N. Irwin St. ☎ 559/584–7823 ⊕ www.foxhanford.com) was built as a movie palace in 1929. The 1,000-seat venue now is host to a variety of live performances, including jazz, country, pop, and comedy.

Fresno

35 mi north of Hanford via Hwys. 43 and 99 north.

Sprawling Fresno, with more than 450,000 people, is the center of the richest agricultural county in America. Cotton, grapes, and tomatoes are among the major crops; poultry and milk are other important products. One of the city's most important products, Pulitzer Prize–winning playwright and novelist William Saroyan (*The Time of Your Life, The Human Comedy*), was born here in 1908. About 75 ethnic groups, including Armenians, Laotians, and Indians, call Fresno home. The city has a burgeoning arts scene, several public parks, and an abundance of low-priced restaurants serving tasty food. The Tower District, with its chic restaurants, coffeehouses, and boutiques, is the trendy spot.

6

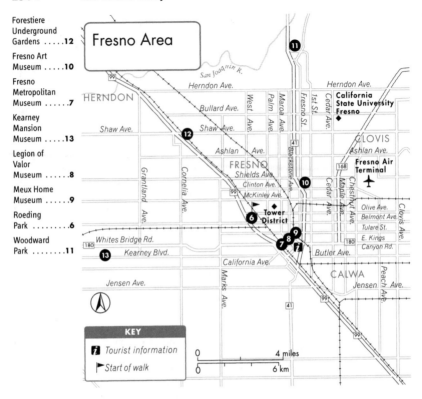

Fresno Area

KEY

i *Tourist information*
► *Start of walk*

0   4 miles
0   6 km

🔥 ► **6** Tree-shaded **Roeding Park** is a place of respite on hot summer days; it has picnic areas, playgrounds, tennis courts, horseshoe pits, and a zoo. The most striking exhibit at **Chaffee Zoological Gardens** (☎ 559/498–2671 ⊕ www.chaffeezoo.org ☑ $7 ☉ Feb.–Oct., daily 9–4; Nov.–Jan., daily 10–3) is the tropical rain forest, where you'll encounter exotic birds along the paths and bridges. Elsewhere you'll find tigers, grizzly bears, sea lions, tule elk, camels, elephants, and hooting siamangs. Also here are a high-tech reptile house and a petting zoo. A train, little race cars, paddleboats, and other rides for kids are among the amusements that operate March–November at **Playland** (☎ 559/233–3980 ☉ Wed.–Fri. 11–5, weekends 10–6). Children can explore attractions with fairy-tale themes at **Storyland** (☎ 559/264–2235 ☉ Weekdays 11–5, weekends 10–6), which is also open March–November. ⊠ *Olive and Belmont Aves.* ☎ *559/498–1551* ☑ *$1 per vehicle park entrance; Playland rides require tokens; $4 for Storyland.*

🔥 **7** The **Fresno Metropolitan Museum** mounts art, history, and hands-on science exhibits, many of them quite innovative. The William Saroyan History Gallery presents a riveting introduction in words and pictures to the author's life and times. ⊠ *1515 Van Ness Ave.* ☎ *559/441–1444* ⊕ *www.fresnomet.org* ☑ *$8, $1 Thurs. nights after 5* ☉ *Tues., Wed., and Fri.–Sun. 11–5, Thurs. 11–8.*

8 The **Legion of Valor Museum** is a real find for military history buffs of all ages. It has German bayonets and daggers, a Japanese Namby pistol, a Gatling gun, and an extensive collection of Japanese, German, and American uniforms. The staff is extremely enthusiastic. ✉ *2425 Fresno St.* ☎ *559/498–0510* 🌐 *www.legionofvalor.com/museum.php* 🎫 *Free* ⏲ *Mon.–Sat. 10–3.*

9 Inside a restored 1889 Victorian, the **Meux Home Museum** displays furnishings typical of early Fresno. Guided tours proceed from the front parlor to the backyard carriage house. ✉ *Tulare and R Sts.* ☎ *559/233–8007* 🌐 *www.meux.mus.ca.us* 🎫 *$5* ⏲ *Fri.–Sun. noon–3:30.*

10 The **Fresno Art Museum** exhibits American, Mexican, and French art; highlights of the permanent collection include pre-Columbian works and graphic art from the postimpressionist period. The 152-seat Bonner Auditorium is the site of lectures, films, and concerts. ✉ *Radio Park, 2233 N. 1st St.* ☎ *559/441–4221* 🌐 *www.fresnoartmuseum.org* 🎫 *$4; free Tues.* ⏲ *Tues., Wed., and Fri.–Sun. 11–5, Thurs. 11–8.*

★ 11 **Woodward Park,** 300 acres of jogging trails, picnic areas, and playgrounds in the northern reaches of the city, is especially pretty in the spring, when plum and cherry trees, magnolias, and camellias bloom. Outdoor concerts take place in summer. The **Shinzen Friendship Garden** has a teahouse, a koi pond, arched bridges, a waterfall, and Japanese art. ✉ *Audubon Dr. and Friant Rd.* ☎ *559/621–2900* 🎫 *$3 per car Feb.–Oct.; additional $3 for Shinzen Garden* ⏲ *Apr.–Oct., daily 7 AM–10 PM; Nov.–Mar., daily 7–7.*

6

★ 12 Sicilian immigrant Baldasare Forestiere spent four decades (1906–46) carving out the **Forestiere Underground Gardens,** a subterranean realm of rooms, tunnels, grottoes, alcoves, and arched passageways that extends for more than 10 acres beneath busy, mall-pocked Shaw Avenue. Only a fraction of Forestiere's prodigious output is on view, but you can tour his underground living quarters, including bedrooms (one with a fireplace), the kitchen, living room, and bath, as well as a fishpond and an aquarium. Skylights allow exotic full-grown fruit trees, including one that bears seven kinds of citrus as a result of grafting, to flourish more than 20 feet belowground. Reservations are recommended. ✉ *5021 W. Shaw Ave., 2 blocks east of Hwy. 99* ☎ *559/271–0734* 🎫 *$9* ⏲ *Tours weekends at noon and 2. Call for other tour times.*

13 The drive along palm-lined Kearney Boulevard is one of the best reasons to visit the **Kearney Mansion Museum,** which stands in shaded 225-acre **Kearney Park.** The century-old home of M. Theo Kearney, Fresno's onetime "raisin king," is accessible only by taking a guided 45-minute tour. ✉ *7160 W. Kearney Blvd., 6 mi west of Fresno* ☎ *559/441–0862* 🎫 *museum $5, park entrance $3, waived for museum visitors* ⏲ *Park 7 AM–10 PM; museum tours Fri.–Sun. at 1, 2, and 3.*

OFF THE BEATEN PATH

BLOSSOM TRAIL – This 62-mi self-guided driving tour takes in Fresno-area orchards, citrus groves, and vineyards during spring blossom season. Pick up a route map at the Fresno City & County Convention and Visitors Bureau (✉ 848 M St., Fresno 93721 ☎ 559/233–0836 or 800/788–0836 🌐 www.fresnocvb.

org). The route passes through small towns and past rivers, lakes, and canals. The most colorful and aromatic time to go is from late February to mid-March, when almond, plum, apple, orange, lemon, apricot, and peach blossoms shower the landscape with shades of white, pink, and red. Directional and crop identification signs mark the trail. Allow at least two to three hours for the tour.

Along the Blossom Trail, roughly halfway between Fresno and Visalia, the colorful handiwork of local quilters is on display at the **Mennonite Quilt Center** (⊠ 1012 G St. [take Manning Ave. exit off Hwy. 99 and head east 12 mi], Reedley ☎ 559/638–3560). The center is open weekdays 9:30–4:30 and Saturday 10–4, but try to visit on Monday (except holidays) between 8 and noon, when two dozen quilters stitch, patch, and chat over coffee. Prime viewing time—with the largest number of quilts—is in February and March, before the center's early-April auction. Ask a docent to take you to the locked upstairs room, where most of the quilts hang; she'll explain the fine points of patterns such as the Log Cabin Romance, the Dahlia, and the Snowball-Star. Admission is free.

Where to Stay & Eat

$–$$$ ✕ **La Rocca's Ristorante Italiano.** The sauces that top these pasta and meat dishes will make your taste buds sing. The rich tomato sauce, which comes with or without meat, is fresh and tangy. The marsala sauce—served on either chicken or veal—is rich but not overpowering. Typical red-sauce dishes such as spaghetti, rigatoni, and lasagna are offered here, but you'll also be happily surprised with more adventurous offerings such as the bowtie pasta with cream, peas, bacon, tomato sauce, and olive oil. Pizzas also are served. ⊠ 6735 N. 1st St. ☎ 559/431–1278 ▤ AE, MC, V ⊗ No lunch weekends.

$–$$$ ✕ **Tahoe Joe's.** This restaurant is known for its steaks; other selections include the slow-roasted prime rib, center-cut pork chops, and chicken breast served with a whiskey peppercorn sauce. But if it's a steak you want, all cuts, including sirloin, rib eye, strip, and filet mignon, will satisfy. The baked potato that accompanies almost every dish is loaded tableside with your choice of butter, sour cream, chives, and bacon bits. Tahoe Joe's has two Fresno locations. ⊠ 7006 N. Cedar Ave. ☎ 559/299–9740 ⌕ Reservations not accepted ▤ AE, D, MC, V ⊠ 2700 W. Shaw Ave. ☎ 559/277–8028 ⌕ Reservations not accepted ▤ AE, D, MC, V ⊗ No lunch.

$ ✕ **Irene's.** Downtown workers pack this Tower District restaurant at lunchtime. Handmade, half-pound burgers are the most popular, and most filling, items on the menu. Other popular dishes include the smoked ham and melted Swiss cheese sandwich served on a hard roll, and fresh salads. For breakfast, homemade granola, huge buttermilk pancakes, and the Denver omelet (with ham, onions, and green peppers) will fill up even those with the most hearty appetites. ⊠ 747 E. Olive Ave. ☎ 559/237–9919 ▤ AE, D, MC, V.

$ ▦ **Piccadilly Inn Shaw.** This two-story property has 7½ attractively landscaped acres and a big swimming pool. The sizable rooms have king- and queen-size beds, robes, ironing boards, and coffeemakers; some have fireplaces and wireless Internet access. ⊠ *2305 W. Shaw Ave., 93711* ☎ *559/226–3850* 🖨 *559/226–2448* ⊕ *www.piccadilly-inn.com/west-shaw* ⏩ *194 rooms, 5 suites* ⚘ *Restaurant, some microwaves, refrigerators, cable TV, in-room data ports, pool, gym, hot tub, laundry facilities, laundry service, business services, meeting rooms, no-smoking rooms* ➡ *AE, D, DC, MC, V.*

¢–$ 🔲 **La Quinta Inn.** Rooms are ample at this basic three-story motel near downtown. Most rooms have large desks that prove helpful for business travelers. ⊠ *2926 Tulare St., 93721* ☎ *559/442–1110 or 866/725–1661* 🖨 *559/237–0415* ⏩ *129 rooms* ⚘ *Some microwaves, some refrigerators, cable TV, in-room data ports, pool, gym, no-smoking rooms* ➡ *AE, D, DC, MC, V* 🍴 *CP.*

Nightlife & the Arts

The **Fresno Philharmonic Orchestra** (☎ 559/261–0600 ⊕ www.fresnophil. org) performs classical concerts (sometimes pops) on weekends, usually at the **William Saroyan Theatre** (⊠ 700 M St.), from September through June. **Roger Rocka's Dinner Theater** (⊠ 1226 N. Wishon Ave. ☎ 559/266–9494 or 800/371–4747), in the Tower District, stages six Broadway-style musicals a year. The **Tower Theatre for the Performing Arts** (⊠ 815 E. Olive Ave. ☎ 559/485–9050 ⊕ www.towertheatrefresno.org) has given its name to the trendy Tower District of theaters, clubs, restaurants, and cafés. The restored 1930s art deco movie house presents theater, ballet, concerts, and other cultural events year-round.

Sports & the Outdoors

Kings River Expeditions (⊠ 211 N. Van Ness Ave. ☎ 559/233–4881 or 800/846–3674 ⊕ www.kingsriver.com) arranges one- and two-day white-water rafting trips on the Kings River. **Wild Water Adventures** (⊠ 11413 E. Shaw Ave., Clovis ☎ 559/299–9453 or 800/564–9453 ⊕ www.wildwater.net 🎟 $22, $16 after 4 PM), a 52-acre water theme park about 10 mi east of Fresno, is open from late May to early September.

Shopping

Old Town Clovis (⊠ Upper Clovis Ave., Clovis) is an area of restored brick buildings with numerous antiques shops and art galleries (along with restaurants and saloons). Be warned, though: not much here is open on Sunday. Head east on Fresno's Herndon Avenue about 10 mi, and then turn right onto Clovis Avenue.

NORTH CENTRAL VALLEY
FROM MERCED TO LODI

The northern section of the valley cuts through Merced, Madera, Stanislaus, and San Joaquin counties, from the flat, abundantly fertile terrain between Merced and Modesto north to the edges of the Sacramento River delta and the fringes of the Gold Country. If you're heading to Yosemite National Park from northern California, chances are you'll pass through (or very near) at least one of these gateway cities.

Merced

14 *50 mi north of Fresno on Hwy. 99.*

Thanks to a branch of the University of California opening in 2005 and an aggressive community redevelopment plan, the downtown of county seat Merced is coming back to life. The transformation is not yet complete, but there are promising signs: a brewpub, several boutiques, a multiplex, the restoration of numerous historic buildings, and foot traffic won back from outlying strip malls.

Even if you don't go inside, be sure to swing by the **Merced County Courthouse Museum.** The three-story former courthouse, built in 1875, is a striking example of Victorian Italianate style. The upper two floors are a museum of early Merced history. Highlights include ornate restored courtrooms and an 1870 Chinese temple with carved redwood altars. ⊠ *21st and N Sts.* ☎ *209/723–2401* ☺ *Free* ⊘ *Wed.–Sun. 1–4.*

The **Merced Multicultural Arts Center** displays paintings, sculpture, and photography. The Big Valley Arts & Culture Festival, which celebrates the area's ethnic diversity and children's creativity, is held here on the first weekend in October. ⊠ *645 W. Main St.* ☎ *209/388–1090* ⊕ *www. artsmerced.org* ☺ *Free* ⊘ *Weekdays 9–5, Sat. 10–2.*

OFF THE
BEATEN
PATH

MILLERTON LAKE STATE RECREATION AREA – This lake at the top of Friant Dam is a great place for boating, fishing, camping, and summertime swimming. The lake and its surrounding hills are wintering grounds for bald eagles, and boat tours are available to view the birds between December and February. ⊠ *5290 Millerton Rd., 20 mi northeast of Fresno via Hwy. 41 and Hwy. 145, Friant* ☎ *559/822–2225* ☺ *$8 per car* ⊘ *Daily Oct.–Mar., 6 AM–6 PM; Apr.–Sept., 6 AM–10 PM.*

Where to Stay & Eat

$$–$$$ ✕ **The Branding Iron.** Beef is what this restaurant is all about. The juicy cut of prime rib paired with potato and Parmesan-cheese bread will satisfy diners with even the most ravenous appetites. This restaurant is a favorite among farmers and ranchers looking for a place to refuel as they travel through cattle country. California cattle brands decorate the walls, and when the weather is nice, cooling breezes refresh diners on the outdoor patio. ⊠ *640 W. 16th St.* ☎ *209/722–1822* ☐ *AE, MC, V* ⊘ *No lunch weekends.*

★ **$–$$$** ✕ **DeAngelo's.** This restaurant isn't just the best in Merced—it's one of the best in the Central Valley. Chef Vincent DeAngelo, a graduate of the Culinary Institute of America, brings his considerable skill to everything from basic ravioli to calamari steak topped with two prawns. Half the restaurant is occupied by a new bar-bistro with its own menu, which includes brick-oven pizza. The delicious crusty bread comes from the Golden Sheath bakery, in Watsonville. ⊠ *350 W. Main St.* ☎ *209/383–3020* ☐ *AE, D, MC, V* ⊘ *No lunch weekends.*

¢–$ ✕ **Main Street Café.** This bright downtown café dishes up tasty breakfast and lunch fare. Sandwiches (try "The Chicago"—beef is topped with onion, roasted red pepper, garlic, mayonnaise, provolone, and pepperoncini) are served with tasty side salads. You can also get pastries, along with espresso or cappuccino. ⊠ *460 W. Main St.* ☎ *209/725–1702* ☐ *AE, MC, V* ⊘ *Closed Sun. No dinner.*

$–$$ ⚏ **Hooper House Bear Creek Inn.** This 1931 neocolonial home stands regally at the corner of M Street. The immaculately landscaped 1½-acre property has fruit trees and grapevines, and the house is appointed in well-chosen antiques and big, soft beds. Breakfast (which can be served in your room) is hearty and imaginative, featuring locally grown foods such as fried sweet potatoes and black walnuts. Across the street is a walking/bicycling trail that runs for a few miles beside the creek. ⊠ *575 W. N. Bear Creek Dr., at M St., 95348* ☎ *209/723–3991* 🖷 *209/723–7123* ⊕ *www.hooperhouse.com* 🛏 *3 rooms, 1 suite, 1 cottage* ⚏ *Cable TV, in-room data ports; no-smoking rooms* ☐ *AE, D, MC, V* ⏀| *BP.*

Sports & the Outdoors

At **Lake Yosemite Regional Park** (⊠ N. Lake Rd. off Yosemite Ave., 5 mi northeast of Merced ☎ 209/385–7426 ⊠ $5 per car late May–early Sept.), you can boat, swim, windsurf, water-ski, and fish on a 387-acre reservoir. Paddleboat rentals and picnic areas are available.

| EN ROUTE ⟁ | Heading north on Highway 99 from Merced, stop at the outdoor **Castle Air Museum,** adjacent to the former Castle Air Force Base (now Castle Airport). You can stroll among fighter planes and other historic military aircraft. The 46 restored vintage war birds include the B-25 Mitchell medium-range bomber (best known for the Jimmy Doolittle raid on Tokyo after the attack on Pearl Harbor) and the speedy SR-71 Blackbird, used for reconnaissance over Vietnam and Libya. E Santa Fe Ave. and Buhach Rd. (6 mi north of Merced, take the Buhach Rd. exit off Hwy. 99 in Atwater and follow signs), Atwater ☎ 209/723–2178 ⊠ $8 ⊘ Apr.–Sept., daily 9–5; Oct.–Mar., Wed.–Mon. 10–4. |

Modesto

⑮ *38 mi north of Merced on Hwy. 99.*

Modesto, a gateway to Yosemite and the southern reaches of the Gold Country, was founded in 1870 to serve the Central Pacific Railroad. The frontier town was originally to be named Ralston, after a railroad baron, but as the story goes, he modestly declined—thus the name Modesto. The Stanislaus County seat, a tree-lined city of 180,000, is perhaps best known as the site of the annual Modesto Invitational Track Meet and Relays and birthplace of film producer-director George Lucas, creator of the *Star Wars* film series.

The **Modesto Arch** (⊠ 9th and I Sts.) bears the city's motto: WATER, WEALTH, CONTENTMENT, HEALTH. The prosperity that water brought to Modesto has attracted people from all over the world. The city holds a well-attended **International Festival** (☎ 209/521–3852) in early October that celebrates the cultures, crafts, and cuisines of many nationalities. You can witness the everyday abundance of the Modesto area at the **Blue Diamond Growers Store** (⊠ 4800 Sisk Rd. ☎ 209/545–3222), which offers free samples, shows a film about almond growing, and sells many roasts and flavors of almonds, as well as other nuts.

★ A rancher and banker built the 1883 **McHenry Mansion,** the city's sole surviving original Victorian home. The Italianate-style mansion has been decorated to reflect Modesto life in the late 19th century. Its period-appropriate wallpaper is especially impressive. ⊠ *15th and I Sts.* ☎ *209/577–5341* ⊕ *www.mchenrymuseum.org* 🎟 *Free* ☉ *Sun.–Thurs. 12:30–4.*

The **McHenry Museum of Arts** is a jumbled repository of early Modesto and Stanislaus County memorabilia, including re-creations of an old-time dentist's office, a blacksmith's shop, a one-room schoolhouse, an extensive doll collection, and a general store stocked with period goods such as hair crimpers and corsets. ⊠ *14th and I Sts.* ☎ *209/577–5366* 🎟 *Free* ☉ *Tues.–Sun. noon–4.*

Where to Stay & Eat

$$–$$$$ ✕ **Hazel's Elegant Dining.** Hazel's is *the* special-occasion restaurant in Modesto. The seven-course dinners include Continental entrées served with appetizer, soup, salad, pasta, and dessert. Members of the Gallo family, which owns much vineyard land in the Central Valley, eat here often, perhaps because the wine cellar's offerings are so comprehensive. ⊠ *431 12th St.* ☎ *209/578–3463* 🖃 *AE, D, DC, MC, V* ☉ *Closed Sun. and Mon. No lunch Sat.*

$–$$ ✕ **St. Stan's.** Modesto's renowned microbrewery makes St. Stan's beers. The 14 on tap include the delicious Whistle Stop pale ale and Red Sky ale. The restaurant is casual and serves good corned-beef sandwiches loaded with sauerkraut as well as a tasty beer-sausage nibbler. ⊠ *821 L St.* ☎ *209/524–2337* 🖃 *AE, MC, V* ☉ *Closed Sun.*

$–$$ ✕ **Tresetti's World Café.** An intimate setting with white tablecloths and contemporary art draws diners to this eatery—part wineshop (with 500-plus selections), part restaurant—with a seasonally changing menu. For a small fee, the staff will uncork any wine you select from the shop. The Cajun-style crab cakes, served year-round, are outstanding. ⊠ *927 11th St.* ☎ *209/572–2990* 🖃 *AE, D, DC, MC, V* ☉ *Closed Sun.*

¢–$$ 🏨 **Doubletree Hotel.** Modesto's largest hotel rises 15 stories over the downtown area. Each room has a coffeemaker, hair dryer, iron, and desk. The convention center is adjacent, and St. Stan's brewpub is across the street. ⊠ *1150 9th St., 95354* ☎ *209/526–6000 or 800/222–8733* 🖶 *209/526–6096* ⊕ *www.doubletree.com* ⇥ *258 rooms* ⚘ *Café, room service, pool, gym, hair salon, hot tub, sauna, nightclub, laundry service, meeting rooms, airport shuttle, no-smoking rooms* 🖃 *AE, D, DC, MC, V.*

¢ 🏨 **Best Western Town House Lodge.** The downtown location is the primary draw for this hotel. The county's historical library is across the street, and the McHenry Mansion and the McHenry Museum are nearby. All rooms come equipped with a coffeemaker, hair dryer, and iron. ⊠ *909 16th St., 95354* ☎ *209/524–7261 or 800/772–7261* 🖶 *209/579–9546* ⊕ *www.bestwestern.com* ⇥ *59 rooms* ⚘ *Microwaves, refrigerators, cable TV, pool, hot tub, free parking, Internet, no-smoking rooms* 🖃 *AE, D, DC, MC, V* ⦿ *CP.*

The top attraction in Manteca, the largest town between Modesto and Stockton, is **Manteca Waterslides.** Kids usually head straight for the wild Thunder Falls, which has three three-story slides, and the V-Max, which stretches six stories tall. ⊠ 874 E. Woodward Ave., between I-5 and Hwy. 99 ☎ 209/249–2500 or 877/625–9663 ⊕ www.oakwoodlake.com ⊠ $25 C Daily May–Sept., call for specific hrs.

Oakdale

🔟 *15 mi northeast of Modesto on Hwy. 108.*

Oakdale is a bit off the beaten path from Modesto. You can sample the wares at **Oakdale Cheese & Specialties** (⊠ 10040 Hwy. 120 ☎ 209/848–3139 ⊕ www.oakdalecheese.com), which has tastings (try the aged Gouda) and cheese-making tours. There's a picnic area and a petting zoo.

If you're in Oakdale—home of a Hershey's chocolate factory—the third weekend in May, check out the **Oakdale Chocolate Festival** (☎ 209/847–2244), which attracts 50,000–60,000 people each year. The event's main attraction is Chocolate Avenue, where vendors proffer cakes, cookies, ice cream, fudge, and cheesecake.

★ The featured attraction at the **Knights Ferry Recreation Area** is the 355-foot-long Knights Ferry covered bridge. The beautiful and haunting structure, built in 1863, crosses the Stanislaus River near the ruins of an old gristmill. The park has picnic and barbecue areas along the riverbanks, as well as three campgrounds accessible only by boat, bicycle, or foot. You can hike, fish, canoe, and raft on 4 mi of rapids. ⊠ *Corps of Engineers Park, 17968 Covered Bridge Rd., Knights Ferry, 12 mi east of Oakdale via Hwy. 108* ☎ *209/881–3517* ⊠ *Free* ⊙ *Daily dawn–dusk.*

Sports & the Outdoors

Rafting on the Stanislaus River is a popular activity near Oakdale. **River Journey** (⊠ 14842 Orange Blossom Rd. ☎ 209/847–4671 or 800/292–2938 ⊕ www.riverjourney.com) will take you out for a few hours of fun. To satisfy your white-water or flat-water cravings, contact **Sunshine River Adventures** (☎ 209/848–4800 or 800/829–7238 ⊕ www.raftadventure.com).

Stockton

🔟 *29 mi north of Modesto on Hwy. 99.*

California's first inland port—connected since 1933 to San Francisco via a 60-mi-long deepwater channel—is wedged between I-5 and Highway 99, on the eastern end of the Sacramento River delta. Stockton, founded during the gold rush as a way station for miners traveling from San Francisco to the Mother Lode and now a city of 261,000, is where many of the valley's agricultural products begin their journey to other parts of the world. If you're here in late April, don't miss the **Stockton Asparagus Festival** (☎ 209/644–3740 ⊕ www.asparagusfest.com), at the Downtown Stockton Waterfront. The highlight of the festival is the food; organizers try to prove that almost any dish can be made with asparagus. A car show, kids' activity area, and musical entertainment also are part of the event.

★ The **Haggin Museum,** in pretty Victory Park, has one of the Central Valley's finest art collections. Highlights include landscapes by Albert Bierstadt and Thomas Moran, a still life by Paul Gauguin, a Native American gallery, and an Egyptian mummy. ⊠ *1201 N. Pershing Ave.* ☎ *209/940–6300* ⊕ *www.hagginmuseum.org* ✍ *$5* ◎ *Wed.–Sun. 1:30–5.*

Where to Stay & Eat

$$$–$$$$ ✕ **Le Bistro.** This upscale restaurant serves fairly standard Continental fare—rack of lamb, fillet of sole, sautéed shrimp, soufflé Grand Marnier—but you can count on high-quality ingredients and presentation with a flourish. ⊠ *Marina Center Mall, 3121 W. Benjamin Holt Dr., off I-5, behind Lyon's* ☎ *209/951–0885* ⊟ *AE, D, DC, MC, V* ◎ *No lunch weekends.*

¢–$ ✕ **On Lock Sam.** This Stockton landmark (it's been operating since 1898) is in a modern pagoda-style building with framed Chinese prints on the walls, a garden outside one window, and a sparkling bar area. One touch of old-time Chinatown remains: a few booths have curtains that can be drawn for complete privacy. The Cantonese food is among the best in the valley. ⊠ *333 S. Sutter St.* ☎ *209/466–4561* ⊟ *AE, D, MC, V.*

$ ▥ **La Quinta Inn.** Close to downtown and near many upscale restaurants, this is a good choice for business and pleasure travelers. The spacious and quiet rooms have large desks and televisions; if you're feeling active, you can get free passes to a nearby gym. ⊠ *2710 W. March La., 95219* ☎ *209/952–7800 or 866/725–1661* 🖷 *209/472–0732* ⊕ *www.laquinta.com* ➲ *151 rooms* ⟐ *Cable TV with movies, in-room data ports, pool, laundry service, meeting rooms, no-smoking rooms* ⊟ *AE, D, DC, MC, V.*

¢   ▥ **Best Western Stockton Inn.** Four miles from downtown, this large motel has a convenient location off Highway 99. The central courtyard with a pool and lounge chairs is a big plus on hot days. Most rooms are spacious. ⊠ *4219 Waterloo Rd., 95215* ☎ *209/931–3131 or 888/829–0092* 🖷 *209/931–0423* ⊕ *www.bestwesterncalifornia.com* ➲ *136 rooms, 5 suites* ⟐ *Restaurant, microwaves, refrigerators, cable TV, in-room data ports, pool, wading pool, hot tub, bar, laundry service, meeting room, no-smoking rooms* ⊟ *AE, D, DC, MC, V.*

Sports & the Outdoors

Several companies rent houseboats (of various sizes, usually for three, four, or seven days) on the Sacramento River delta waterways near Stockton. Houseboats, patio boats, fishing boats, and ski boats can be rented through the **Delta Houseboat Rental Hotline** (⊠ 6333 Pacific Ave., Suite 152 ☎ 209/477–1840). **Herman & Helen's Marina** (⊠ 15135 W. 8 Mile Rd. ☎ 209/951–4634) rents houseboats with hot tubs and fireplaces. **Paradise Point Marina** (⊠ 8095 Rio Blanco Rd. ☎ 209/952–1000) rents a variety of watercraft, including patio boats.

Lodi

⑱ *13 mi north of Stockton and 34 mi south of Sacramento on Hwy. 99.*

Founded on agriculture, Lodi was once the watermelon capital of the country, and today it is surrounded by fields of asparagus, pumpkins, beans, safflowers, sunflowers, kiwis, melons, squashes, peaches, and cherries. It also has become a wine-grape capital of sorts, producing zinfandel, merlot, cabernet sauvignon, chardonnay, and sauvignon blanc grapes. For years California wineries have built their reputations on the juice of grapes grown around Lodi. Now the area that includes Lodi, Lockeford, and Woodbridge is a wine destination boasting about 40 wineries, many offering tours and tastings. Lodi still retains an old rural charm. You can stroll downtown or visit a wildlife refuge, all the while benefiting from a Sacramento River delta breeze that keeps this microclimate cooler in summer than anyplace else in the area. With a short, mild winter and a long, rain-free summer, Lodi is ideal for outdoor recreation.

⟳ The 65-acre **Micke Grove Park and Zoo,** an oak-shaded county park off I–5, includes a Japanese garden, picnic areas, a golf course, and an agricultural museum with a collection of 94 tractors. Geckos and frogs, black-and-white ruffed lemurs, and hissing cockroaches found only on the African island of Madagascar inhabit "An Island Lost in Time," an exhibit at the **Micke Grove Zoo** (☎ 209/953–8840 ⊕ www.mgzoo.com ⊙ Daily 10–5). California sea lions bask on rocks much as they do off the coast of San Francisco in the "Islands Close to Home" exhibit, another highlight of this compact facility. Most rides and diversions at Micke Grove's **Funderwoods Playland** (☎209/368–1092 ⊙ Weekdays 11:30–6, weekends 10:30–6), a family-oriented amusement park, are geared toward children. ✉ *11793 N. Micke Grove Rd.* ☎ *209/331–7400* 🖾 *Zoo $2; parking $2 weekdays, $5 weekends and holidays.*

Stop by the **Lodi Wine & Visitor Center** (✉ 2545 W. Turner Rd. ☎ 209/365–0621) to see exhibits on Lodi's viticultural history. Here you can pick up a map of area wineries, as well as buy wine. One of the standout wineries in the area is **Jessie's Grove** (✉ 1973 W. Turner Rd. ☎ 209/368–0880 ⊕ www.jgwinery.com ⊙ Fri.–Sun. 11–4), a wooded horse ranch and vineyard that has been in the same family since 1863. In addition to producing outstanding old-vine zinfandels, it presents blues concerts on various Saturdays May–October. At the **Woodbridge Winery** (✉ 5950 E. Woodbridge Rd., Acampo ☎ 209/369–5861 ⊕ www.woodbridgewines.com ⊙ Tues.–Sun. 10:30–4:30), you can take a free 30-minute tour of the vineyard and aging room. At its homey facility, kid-friendly **Phillips Farms** (✉ 4580 W. Hwy. 12 ☎ 209/368–7384 ⊕ www.lodivineyards.com) offers tastings from its affordable Michael-David Vineyard. You can also cut flowers from the garden, pet the animals, eat breakfast or lunch at the café, and buy Phillips' produce. **Vino Piazza** (✉ 12470 Locke Rd., Lockeford ☎ 209/727–9770) is a sort of wine co-op housed in the old Lockeford Winery building, where 13 vineyards operate tasting rooms. If you don't have time to see the vineyards themselves, this is a good way to sample the area's many wines.

Where to Stay & Eat

$$-$$$ ✕ **Rosewood Bar & Grill.** In downtown Lodi, Rosewood offers fine dining without formality. Operated by the folks at Wine & Roses Hotel and Restaurant, this low-key spot serves American fare with a twist, such as meat loaf wrapped in bacon, and daily seafood specials. The bar has its own menu, and live music on Fridays and Saturdays. ⊠ *28 S. School St.* ☎ *209/369–0470* 🖃 *AE, D, DC, MC, V* ⊗ *No lunch.*

¢-$ ✕ **Habanero Hots.** If your mouth can handle the heat promised by the restaurant's name, try the tamales. If you want to take it easy on your taste buds, stick with the rest of the menu. ⊠ *1024 E. Victor Rd.* ☎ *209/369–3791* 🖃 *AE, MC, V.*

¢ ✕ **Angelo's.** Authentic Mexican dishes such as chili verde, steak ranchero, and all-meat chimichangas draw locals to this downtown eatery. The service is friendly and quick, and the atmosphere is casual. ⊠ *28 N. School St.* ☎ *209/366–2728* 🖃 *AE, DC, MC, V.*

★ $$-$$$ ✕🔳 **Wine & Roses Hotel and Restaurant.** Set on 7 acres amid a tapestry of informal gardens, this hotel has cultivated a sense of refinement typically associated with Napa or Carmel. Rooms are decorated in rich earth tones, and linens are imported from Italy. Some rooms have fireplaces; all have coffeemakers, irons, and hair dryers. Some of the bathrooms even have TVs. The restaurant ($$$) is *the* place to eat in Lodi. The Sunday buffet champagne brunch includes ham, prime rib, and made-to-order crepes and omelets. Afterward, consider heading to the spa for a facial or herbal body scrub. ⊠ *2505 W. Turner Rd., 95242* ☎ *209/334–6988* 🖶 *209/371–6049* ⊕ *www.winerose.com* 📭 *47 rooms, 4 suites* ♨ *Restaurant, room service, refrigerators, cable TV, in-room data ports, spa, bar, laundry service, no-smoking rooms* 🖃*AE, D, DC, MC, V* ⓘⓞⓘ*CP.*

$$-$$$ 🔳 **The Inn at Locke House.** Built in 1865, this B&B was a pioneer family's home and is on the National Register of Historic Places. Rooms are filled with antique furnishings, and all have fireplaces. The centerpiece of the Water Tower Suite is a queen canopy bed; it also has a deck and a private sitting room. In the oak-paneled parlor, you'll find books, games, historical artifacts, and an old pump organ. Refreshments are served when you arrive. ⊠ *19960 N. Elliott Rd., Lockeford 95237* ☎*209/727–5715* 🖶 *209/727–0873* ⊕ *www.theinnatlockehouse.com* 📭 *4 rooms, 1 suite* ♨ *Library, no-smoking rooms; no room TVs* 🖃 *AE, D, DC, MC, V* ⓘⓞⓘ*BP.*

¢ 🔳 **Lodi Comfort Inn.** This downtown motel has quiet rooms with contemporary furnishings and blow dryers in the bathrooms. It's easily accessible from Highway 99. Doughnuts, waffles, bagels, juice, and coffee make up the complimentary breakfast. ⊠ *118 N. Cherokee La.* ☎ *209/367–4848 or 877/424–6423* 🖶 *209/367–4898* ⊕ *www.comfortinn.com* 📭 *55 rooms* ♨ *Microwaves, refrigerators, cable TV, in-room data ports, pool, hot tub, laundry facilities, laundry service* 🖃 *AE, D, DC, MC, V* ⓘⓞⓘ *CP.*

Sports & the Outdoors

Even locals need respite from the heat of Central Valley summers, and **Lodi Lake Park** (⊠ 1101 W. Turner Rd. ☎ 209/333–6742 🎟 $5) is where they find it. The banks, shaded by grand old elms and oaks, are much cooler than other spots in town. Swimming, bird-watching, and picnicking are possibilities, as is renting a kayak, canoe, or pedal boat ($2–$4 per half hour, Tuesday–Sunday, late May–early September only).

THE CENTRAL VALLEY A TO Z

To research prices, get advice from other travelers, and book travel arrangements, visit www.fodors.com.

AIRPORTS & TRANSFERS

Fresno Yosemite International Airport is serviced by Alaska, Allegiant, America West, American and American Eagle, Continental, Delta, Hawaiian, Horizon, Northwest, Skywest, United, and United Express. Kern County Airport at Meadows Field is serviced by America West Express, Continental, and United Express. United Express flies from San Francisco to Modesto City Airport and from Los Angeles to Visalia Municipal Airport. *See* Air Travel *in* Smart Travel Tips A to Z for airline phone numbers.

🛪 **Fresno Yosemite International Airport** ✉ 4995 E. Clinton Way, Fresno ☎ 559/621-4500 ⊕ www.fresno.gov/flyfresno. **Kern County Airport at Meadows Field** ✉ 1401 Skyway Dr., Bakersfield ☎ 661/393-7990 ⊕ www.meadowsfield.com. **Modesto City Airport** ✉ 617 Airport Way, Modesto ☎ 209/577-5318 ⊕ www.modairport.com. **Visalia Municipal Airport** ✉ 9501 W. Airport Dr., Visalia ☎ 559/713-4201 ⊕ www.flyvisalia.com.

BUS TRAVEL

Greyhound provides service between major valley cities. Orange Belt Stages provides bus service, including Amtrak connections, to many valley locations, including Bakersfield, Fresno, Hanford, Modesto, Merced, and Stockton.

🛪 **Greyhound** ☎ 800/231-2222 ⊕ www.greyhound.com. **Orange Belt Stages** ☎ 800/266-7433 ⊕ www.orangebelt.com.

CAR RENTAL

Avis, Budget, Dollar, Enterprise, Hertz, and National rent cars at Fresno Yosemite International Airport. Avis, Budget, Hertz, and National rent cars at Kern County Airport at Meadows Field. Avis, Enterprise, and Hertz rent cars at Modesto City Airport. Avis, Budget, and Enterprise are represented at Visalia Municipal Airport. *See* Car Rental *in* Smart Travel Tips A to Z for national rental-agency phone numbers.

CAR TRAVEL

To reach the Central Valley from Los Angeles, follow I–5 north; Highway 99 veers north about 15 mi after entering the valley. To drive to the valley from San Francisco, take I–80 east to I–580 and then I–580 east to I–5, which leads south into the valley (several roads from I–5 head east to Highway 99); or continue east on I–580 to I–205, which leads to I–5 north to Stockton or (via Highway 120) east to Highway 99 at Manteca.

Highway 99 is the main route between the valley's major cities and towns. Interstate 5 runs roughly parallel to it to the west but misses the major population centers; its main use is for quick access from San Francisco or Los Angeles. Major roads that connect I–5 with Highway 99 are Highways 58 (to Bakersfield), 198 (to Hanford and Visalia), 152 (to Chowchilla, via Los Banos), 140 (to Merced), 132 (to Modesto), and 120 (to Manteca). For road conditions, call the California Department of Transportation hotline.

🚗 **California Department of Transportation** ☎ 800/266-6883 or 916/445-1534.

EMERGENCIES

In an emergency dial 911.

🚗 Hospitals **Bakersfield Memorial Hospital** ✉ 420 34th St., Bakersfield ☎ 661/327-4647. **St. Joseph's Medical Center** ✉ 1800 N. California St., Stockton ☎ 209/943-2000. **University Medical Center** ✉ 445 S. Cedar Ave., Fresno ☎ 559/459-4000.

TOURS

Central Valley Tours provides general and customized tours of the Fresno area and the valley, with special emphasis on the fruit harvests and Blossom Trail.

🚗 **Central Valley Tours** ☎ 559/276-4479 ⊕ www.angelfire.com/poetry/inc/valleytours.html.

TRAIN TRAVEL

Amtrak's daily *San Joaquin* travels between Bakersfield, San Jose, and Oakland, stopping in Hanford, Fresno, Madera, Merced, Modesto, and Stockton. Amtrak Thruway bus service connects Bakersfield with Los Angeles.

🚗 **Amtrak** ☎ 800/872-7245 ⊕ www.amtrakcalifornia.com.

VISITOR INFORMATION

🚗 **Fresno City & County Convention and Visitors Bureau** ✉ 848 M St., Fresno 93721 ☎ 559/233-0836 or 800/788-0836 ⊕ www.fresnocvb.org. **Greater Bakersfield Convention & Visitors Bureau** ✉ 515 Truxton Ave., Bakersfield 93301 ☎ 661/325-5051 or 866/425-7353 ⊕ www.bakersfieldcvb.org. **Hanford Visitor Agency** ✉ 200 Santa Fe Ave., Suite D, Hanford 93230 ☎ 559/582-5024 ⊕ www.visithanford.com. **Kern County Board of Trade** ✉ 2101 Oak St., Bakersfield 93301 ☎ 661/861-2367 or 800/500-5376 ⊕ www.co.kern.ca.us/boardoftrade. **Lodi Conference and Visitors Bureau** ✉ 2545 W. Turner Dr., Lodi 95242 ☎ 209/365-1195 or 800/798-1810 ⊕ www.visitlodi.com. **Merced Conference and Visitors Bureau** ✉ 710 W. 16th St., Merced 95340 ☎ 209/384-2791 ⊕ www.yosemite-gateway.org. **Modesto Convention and Visitors Bureau** ✉ 1150 9th St., Suite C, Modesto 95353 ☎ 209/526-5588 or 888/640-8467 ⊕ www.visitmodesto.com. **Stockton Visitors Bureau** ✉ 46 W. Fremont St., Stockton 95202 ☎ 209/937-5089 ⊕ www.visitstockton.org. **Visalia Chamber of Commerce and Visitors Bureau** ✉ 720 W. Mineral King Ave., Visalia 93291 ☎ 559/734-5876 ⊕ www.cvbvisalia.com.

Yosemite & the Southern Sierra
With Sequoia and Kings Canyon

WORD OF MOUTH

"Yosemite National Park is a garden of eden. I love it and have been here many times. The Waterfalls are FABULOUS! The meadow is green and breathtaking! . . . Wish my backyard was a paradise like this!"

—Jim Holseth

by John A.
Vlahides

VAST GRANITE PEAKS AND GIANT SEQUOIAS are among the mind-bog-
gling natural wonders of the Southern Sierra, many of which are protected in three national parks. Endowed with glacially carved valleys,
deep canyons, and towering peaks and trees, Kings Canyon and Sequoia
national parks abut each other and are easy to visit together. Yosemite,
the state's most famous national park, is renowned for its staggering U-
shape valleys and mile-high walls of granite formed during the Ice Age.
Outside the parks, pristine lakes, superb skiing, rolling hills, and small
towns complete the picture of the Southern Sierra.

Exploring the Yosemite & the Southern Sierra

For the full Sierra experience, explore the national forests as well as the
national parks. Stop at any of the ranger stations near the forests' borders and pick up information on lesser-known sights and attractions.
Spend a few nights in the small towns outside the parks. If, however,
you're tight on time and want to focus on the attractions that make the
region famous, then stay in the parks themselves instead of the gateway
towns in the foothills or the Central Valley; you won't want to lose time
shuttling back and forth.

Yosemite Valley is the primary destination for many visitors. Because
the valley is only 7 mi long and averages less than 1 mi wide, you can
visit its attractions in whatever order you choose and return to your favorites at different times of the day. Famous for plunging canyons and
the world's largest trees, Kings Canyon and Sequoia are more spread
out and don't pack the same instant wallop that Yosemite Valley does,
but they're no less gratifying, and you'll encounter fewer people.

About the Restaurants

Towns in the Sierra Nevada are small, but they usually have at least one
diner or restaurant. In the national parks, snack bars, coffee shops, and
cafeterias are not expensive. The three fanciest lodgings within Yosemite
National Park are prime dining spots, with hefty price tags to match.
With few exceptions, which are noted, dress is casual at the restaurants
listed in this chapter.

When you're traveling in the area, expect to spend a lot of time in the
car, so pick up snacks and drinks to keep with you, and keep the gas
tank full—especially in winter, when roads sometimes close because of
heavy snow (having tire chains or four-wheel drive in winter is also strongly
recommended). Stopping at a grocery store and filling the ice chest before you set out will also allow you to explore the national parks without having to worry about searching for food when you get hungry. With
picnic supplies on hand you can enjoy a meal under giant trees; just be
certain to leave no food or trash behind.

About the Hotels

Towns are few and far between in the Southern Sierra. Whenever possible, book lodging reservations in advance—especially in summer—or
plan to camp out. If you don't, you may find yourself driving long distances to find a place to sleep.

GREAT ITINERARIES

Numbers in the text correspond to numbers in the margin and on the Sequoia & Kings Canyon National Parks, Yosemite National Park, and Southern Sierra maps.

IF YOU HAVE 2 DAYS If your time is limited, explore Yosemite National Park. Use the Big Oak Flat Entrance on Highway 120, and head east toward ☞ ▣ **Yosemite Valley** ⑬–㉓. Once you reach the valley floor, traffic is diverted onto a one-way loop road. Continue east, following the signs to day-use parking, and ride the shuttle to **Yosemite Village** ⑬ and the Valley Visitor Center. Loop back west for a short hike near **Yosemite Falls** ⑭, the highest waterfall in North America. Hop back in the car and continue west for a valley view of famous **El Capitan** ⑮. This area is a good place for a picnic. Double back onto Southside Drive en route to Highway 41 southbound, stopping at misty **Bridalveil Fall** ⑰; then follow Highway 41/ Wawona Road south 14 mi to the Chinquapin junction and make a left turn onto Glacier Point Road. From **Glacier Point** ㉒ (road closed in winter) you'll get a phenomenal bird's-eye view of the entire valley, including **Half Dome** ㉑, **Vernal Fall** ⑲, and **Nevada Fall** ⑳. If you want to avoid the busloads of tourists at Glacier Point, stop at **Sentinel Dome** ㉓ instead.

On Day 2, head south again on Highway 41/Wawona Road and visit the **Mariposa Grove of Big Trees** ㉕ at the southern end of the park. Afterward, head north to the Wawona Hotel (closed in midwinter), where you can have lunch or a relaxing drink on the veranda or in the charming lobby bar. Afterward tour the Pioneer Yosemite History Center. Head back to Yosemite Valley on Wawona Road, and stop at the mouth of the tunnel on Highway 41, just before you drop into the valley, for one of the park's most famous and spectacular views. Plan to watch the sunset on **Half Dome** from Sentinel Bridge, and take in a ranger-led program in the early evening.

IF YOU HAVE 4 DAYS On your first day, stop briefly at the ☞ **Foothills Visitor Center** ③ in Sequoia National Park to pick up park information and tickets to **Crystal Cave** ⑤. After visiting the cave, stop to explore the museum at **Giant Forest** ④ and the park's other sights; if you're fit, be sure to climb Moro Rock. Spend the night in ▣ **Grant Grove** ⑩ or ▣ **Wuksachi Village** ⑦. On Day 2, explore the sights in Grant Grove, then (if you've started early) drive east along Kings Canyon Highway (Highway 180) to **Cedar Grove** ⑪. After lunch, double back on Highway 180, continuing west out of the park to Fresno, where you'll turn north onto Highway 41 toward Yosemite National Park. (It will take you three to four hours to reach the park.) Spend the night just south of the park in ▣ Oakhurst or just inside the south entrance gate at ▣ **Wawona** ㉔.

On your third morning, visit the Pioneer Yosemite History Center, and wander beneath the giant sequoias at the nearby **Mariposa Grove of Big Trees** ㉕. From here, head to ▣ **Yosemite Valley** ⑬–㉓, where you should stay the next two nights. Stop just past the tunnel on Highway 41 to take in the dramatic view of **Half Dome** ㉑. Dedicate Day 4 to exploring the valley.

Most accommodations inside Sequoia, Kings Canyon, and Yosemite national parks can best be described as "no frills"—many have no electricity or indoor plumbing. In Sequoia and Kings Canyon, lodging rates remain the same throughout the year. In winter, only some lodgings in Grant Grove remain open. Other than the Ahwahnee and Wawona hotels in Yosemite, lodgings tend to be basic motels or rustic cabins. Except during the off-peak season, from November through March, rates in Yosemite are pricey.

	WHAT IT COSTS				
	$$$$	$$$	$$	$	¢
RESTAURANTS	over $30	$23–$30	$16–$22	$10–$15	under $10
HOTELS	over $250	$176–$250	$121–$175	$90–$120	under $90

Restaurant prices are for a main course at dinner, excluding sales tax of 7¼%. Hotel prices are for two people in a standard double room in high season, excluding service charges and 9%–10% tax.

Timing

Summer is by far the busiest season for all the parks, though things never get as hectic at Sequoia and Kings Canyon as they do at Yosemite. During extremely busy periods, such as the Fourth of July, you may experience delays at the entrance gates. If you can make it here only when school is out, try to visit midweek. In winter, heavy snows occasionally cause road closures, and tire chains or four-wheel drive may be required on roads that remain open; trails in the backcountry and in wilderness areas aren't accessible (except on cross-country skis). To avoid these problems, visit between mid-April and late May, or early September to mid-October, when the parks are less busy and the weather is usually hospitable.

The falls at Yosemite are at their most spectacular in May and June. By the end of summer some will have dried up. They begin flowing again in late fall with the first storms, and during winter they may be hung with ice, a dramatic sight. "Spring" wildflowers can bloom late into the summer as you rise in elevation. Snow on the floor of Yosemite Valley is rarely deep, so you can often camp there even in winter (January highs are in the mid-40s, lows in the mid-20s). Tioga Road is usually closed from late October through May or June. Unless you ski or snowshoe in, you can't get to Tuolumne Meadows then. The road from the turnoff for Badger Pass to Glacier Point is not cleared in winter, but it is groomed for cross-country skiing, a 10-mi trek one-way.

SEQUOIA & KINGS CANYON

Naturalist John Muir declared in the early 20th century that the beauty of Sequoia and Kings Canyon national parks easily rivaled that of Yosemite; he described the sequoia trees here as "the most beautiful and majestic on Earth." The largest living things on the planet, *Sequoiadendron giganteum* trees are not as tall as the coast redwoods (*Sequoia sempervirens*), but they're more massive and, on average, older. Exhibits at

PLEASURES & PASTIMES

CAMPING. Camping in the Sierra Nevada means awakening to the sights of nearby meadows and streams and the unforgettable landscape of giant granite. Camping here also means gazing up at an awe-inspiring collection of constellations and spying a shooting star in the night sky. Dozens of campgrounds, from remote, tents-only areas to sprawling full-service facilities close to the main attractions, operate in the Southern Sierra's three national parks. Of the numerous campgrounds in Yosemite National Park, Tuolumne Meadows campground may be the prettiest of the easily accessible spots, so it's also among the most popular. Spectacular camping abounds outside the national parks, as well, at sites such as Lake Mary Campground in the Mammoth Lakes area.

HIKING & WALKING. Hiking is the primary outdoor activity in the Sierra Nevada. Whether you walk the paved loops that pass by major attractions in the national parks or head off the beaten path into the backcountry, a hike through groves and meadows or alongside streams and waterfalls will allow you to see, smell, and feel nature up close.

Some of the most popular trails are described briefly in this chapter; stop by the visitor centers for maps and advice from park rangers. No matter which trail you decide to take, always carry lots of water and a pocket-size emergency rain poncho for unexpected summer thunderstorms.

WINTER SPORTS. Famous for its incredible snowpack—some of the deepest anywhere on the North American continent—the Sierra Nevada has something for every winter-sports fan. Sequoia and Kings Canyon national parks are great places for snowshoeing and cross-country skiing. At Yosemite Mountaineering School you can learn how to snowshoe, cross-country ski, tele-mark ski, and skate-ski, and at Yosemite's Badger Pass Ski Area you can schuss down the slopes alpine-style. But Mammoth Mountain Ski Area is the star of the Southern Sierra winter sports scene. One of the biggest and best ski resorts in the western United States, Mammoth offers terrain to suit downhill skiers' every taste and ability level, plus great facilities for snowboarders.

7

the visitor centers explain why they can live so long and grow so big, as well as the special relationship between these trees and fire (their thick, fibrous bark helps protect them from flames and insects, and their seeds can't germinate until they first explode out of a burning pinecone).

A little more than 1.5 million people visit Sequoia and Kings Canyon annually, wandering trails through groves and meadows or tackling the rugged backcountry. The topography of the two parks runs the gamut from chaparral, at an elevation of 1,500 feet, to the giant sequoia belt, at 5,000–7,000 feet, to the towering peaks of the Great Western Divide and the Sierra crest. Mt. Whitney, the highest point in the contiguous United States, at 14,494 feet, is the crown jewel of the parks' less-crowded eastern side (the border between Sequoia National Park and John Muir Wilderness runs right through the summit of Mt. Whitney).

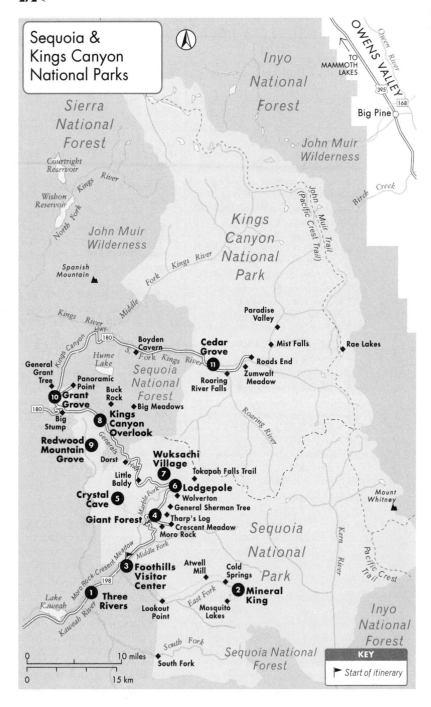

Sequoia &
Kings Canyon
National Parks

OWENS VALLEY

Inyo
National
Forest

TO
MAMMOTH
LAKES

395

168

Big Pine

Sierra
National
Forest

Courtright
Reservoir

Kings River

Wishon
Reservoir

North Fork

John Muir
Wilderness

John Muir
Wilderness

John Muir Trail
(Pacific Crest Trail)

Birch Creek

Spanish
Mountain

Fork Kings River

Kings
Canyon
National
Park

Kings River Hwy.

Middle

180

Boyden
Cavern

S. Fork Kings River

Hume
Lake

Cedar
Grove

11

Paradise
Valley

Mist Falls

Rae Lakes

Roads End

Zumwalt
Meadow

Roaring
River Falls

Roaring River

General
Grant
Tree

Panoramic
Point

Buck
Rock

180

10 Grant
Grove

Big
Stump

Big Meadows

8 Kings
Canyon
Overlook

Redwood
Mountain
Grove

9

Dorst

Generals Hwy.

Wuksachi
Village

7

Tokapah Falls Trail

Mount
Whitney

Little
Baldy

6 Lodgepole

Wolverton

Crystal
Cave

5

Marble Fork

General Sherman Tree

Giant Forest

4

Tharp's Log

Crescent Meadow

Moro Rock

Sequoia

Kern River

Moro Rock-Cresent Meadow

Middle Fork

Atwell
Mill

Cold
Springs

National

Pacific Crest Trail

3 Foothills
Visitor
Center

2 Mineral
King

Park

Lake
Kaweah

198

1 Three
Rivers

Kaweah River

Lookout
Point

East Fork

Mosquito
Lakes

Inyo
National
Forest

South Fork

0   10 miles

0   15 km

South Fork

Sequoia National
Forest

KEY

Start of itinerary

You cannot access Mt. Whitney from Sequoia's western side; you must circumnavigate the Sierra range via a 10-hour, nearly 400-mi drive outside the park (*see* Chapter 6, The Mojave Desert and Death Valley, *for* Mt. Whitney).

Sequoia and Kings Canyon national parks share their administration and are connected by the Generals Highway (Highway 198). Kings Canyon Highway (Highway 180) runs east from Grant Grove to Cedar Grove. The entrance fee to Sequoia and Kings Canyon (good for admission to both for seven consecutive days) is $10 per vehicle, or $5 per person for those who don't arrive by car. An information-packed quarterly newspaper and a map are handed out at the parks' entrances.

Three Rivers

❶ *200 mi north of Los Angeles via I–5 to Hwy. 99 to Hwy. 198; 8 mi south of Ash Mountain/Foothills entrance to Sequoia National Park on Hwy. 198.*

In the foothills of the Sierra along the Kaweah River, this sparsely populated hamlet serves as the parks' main gateway town. Its livelihood depends largely on tourism from the national parks, courtesy of two markets, several service stations, banks, a post office, and several lodgings, which are good spots to find a room when park accommodations are full.

Where to Stay & Eat

$–$$$ ✕ **Gateway Restaurant and Lodge.** The patio of this raucous roadhouse overlooks the roaring Kaweah River as it plunges out of the high country, and though the food is nothing special, the location makes up for it. Standouts include baby-back ribs and eggplant parmigiana; there's also a cocktail lounge, and guest rooms are available for overnight visitors. Breakfast isn't served weekdays; dinner reservations are essential on weekends. ✉ *45978 Sierra Dr.* ☎ *559/561–4133* ▭ *AE, D, MC, V.*

$–$$ ✕ **Main Fork Bistro.** The Kaweah River flows within view of the many windows at Three Rivers' best restaurant. The menu offers a good selection of eggs and pancakes for breakfast; salads, open-face sandwiches, and meat loaf for lunch; and steak and seafood for dinner. There's also a good vegetarian selection, and the soups are excellent. ✉ *41775 Sierra Dr.* ☎ *559/561–4917* ▭ *AE, D, MC, V.*

$–$$ ▣ **Lazy J Ranch Motel.** Surrounded by 12 acres of green lawns and a split-rail fence, the Lazy J is a modest, well-kept compound of freestanding cottages near the banks of the Kaweah River. Some rooms have gas fireplaces; all have coffeemakers. ✉ *39625 Sierra Dr., Hwy 198, 93271* ☎ *559/561–4449 or 888/315–2378* ▤ *559/561–4889* ⊕ *www.bvilazyj. com* ⇨ *11 rooms, 7 cottages* ♿ *Picnic area, BBQs, some kitchens, refrigerators, cable TV, in-room VCRs, pool, fishing, playground, laundry facilities, some pets allowed (fee), no-smoking rooms* ▭ *AE, D, DC, MC, V* ¶◉┤ *CP.*

$ ▣ **Buckeye Tree Lodge.** Every room at this two-story motel has a patio facing a sun-dappled grassy lawn, right on the banks of the Kaweah River. Accommodations are simple and well kept, and the lodge sits a mere quarter mile from the park gate. Book well in advance. ⊠ *46000 Sierra Dr. (Hwy. 198), 93271* ☎ *559/561–5900* ⊕ *www.buckeyetree.com* ⟿ *11 rooms, 1 cottage* ♿ *BBQs, cable TV, in-room VCRs, pool, fishing, hiking, some pets (fee); no-smoking rooms* ⊟ *AE, D, DC, MC, V* ⧯ *CP.*

$ ⧈ **Sequoia Motel.** An old-fashioned single-story mom-and-pop motel, the Sequoia stands out with such extra touches as country-style quilts and mismatched Americana furnishings that lend a retro charm to the rooms, which the on-site owners keep meticulously clean. There are also one- and two-bedroom cottages with full kitchens. ⊠ *43000 Sierra Dr. (Hwy. 198), Box 145, 93271* ☎ *559/561–4453* 🖷 *559/561–1625* ⊕ *www. sequoiamotel.com* ⟿ *11 rooms, 3 cottages* ♿ *BBQs, some kitchens, cable TV, some in-room VCRs, Wi-Fi, pool, laundry facilities; no room phones, no smoking* ⊟ *AE, D, MC, V.*

Sports & the Outdoors

Contact the **Sequoia Natural History Association** (⧉ HCR 89, Box 10, 93271 ☎ 559/565–3759 ⊕ www.sequoiahistory.org) for information on bird-watching in the Southern Sierra.

Kaweah White Water Adventures (☎ 559/561–1000 or 800/229–8658 ⊕ www.kaweahwhitewater.com) guides two-hour and full-day rafting trips, with some Class III rapids; longer trips may include some Class IV.

For hourly horseback rides or riding lessons, contact **Wood 'n' Horse Training Stables** (☎ 559/561–4268 ⊠ 42846 North Fork Dr.).

Mineral King

❷ *25 mi east of Three Rivers via Hwy. 198 and Mineral King Rd.*

Incorporated into Sequoia National Park in 1978, the Mineral King area is accessible from late May through October (depending on snowmelt) by a narrow, twisting, steep road (trailers and RVs are prohibited) off Highway 198, several miles outside the park entrance. This tough but exciting drive (budget 90 minutes each way) leads to an alpine valley, where there are two campgrounds and a ranger station. Facilities are limited, but some supplies are available. Many backpackers use this as a trailhead, and fine day-hiking trails lead from here as well.

Where to Stay

⟲ ¢–$$$ ⧈ **Silver City Resort.** High on the Mineral King Road, this resort provides an excellent alternative to the crowded properties at the parks' lower elevations. Lodgings range from modern Swiss-style chalets to traditional rustic alpine cabins with woodstoves and central bathing facilities. There is a small general store, a bakery serving homemade pies, and a modestly priced restaurant on-site, though the latter serves Thursday through Monday only. Some cabins share a central shower and bath. ⊠ *Mineral King Rd., 20 mi east of Hwy. 198, 93271* ☎ *559/561–3223 or 805/528–2730* ⊕ *www.silvercityresort.com* ⟿ *13 units, 8 with shared baths* ♿ *Restaurant, BBQs, kitchens, some refrigerators, some in-room data ports, fishing (nearby), hiking, horseshoes, Ping-Pong, playground; no a/c, no phones in some rooms, no room TVs, no smoking* ⊟ *MC, V* ⊗ *Closed Nov.–May.*

⚠ **Atwell Mill Campground.** Set at 6,650 feet, this tents-only campground is just south of the Western Divide. There are telephones and a general store ½ mi away at the Silver City Resort. Reservations are not accepted. ✉ *Mineral King Rd., 20 mi east of Hwy. 198* ☎ *559/565–3341* 💲 *$12* 🛏 *23 sites* ♿ *Pit toilets, drinking water, showers, bear boxes, fire grates, picnic tables* ☉ *Closed Nov.–Apr.*

Lodgepole & Giant Forest Area

16–27 mi northeast of the Foothills Visitor Center on Generals Hwy.

To see Sequoia National Park from the south, you drive on Generals Highway, which begins at the park's Ash Mountain/Foothills entrance. ▶ ❸ Before you venture into the park, it's helpful to stop at the **Foothills Visitor Center** for information and tickets to Crystal Cave. ✉ *Generals Hwy.* ☎ *559/565–3135* 💲 *Free* ☉ *Daily 8–4:30, 8–6 in summer.*

★ ❹ A 50-minute drive from Foothills, **Giant Forest** is known for its trails through a series of sequoia groves. You can get the best views of the big trees from the park's meadows, where flowers burst into bloom by June or July. The outstanding exhibits at the **Giant Forest Museum** trace the ecology of the giant sequoia. The **Big Trees Trail**, a ¾-mi paved trail, is easy to reach from the museum. ✉ *Generals Hwy., 16 mi northeast of Foothills Visitor Center* ☎ *559/565–4480 museum* ☉ *Museum: late May–mid-June, daily 8–5; mid-June–early Sept., daily 8–6; early Sept.–late May, daily 9–4:30.*

The **Moro Rock–Crescent Meadow Road** is a 3-mi spur road (closed in winter) that begins just south of the Giant Forest Museum and leads to Crescent Meadow, passing several landmarks along the way. The **Auto Log** is a wide fallen tree that visitors used to be able to drive their cars on; it's a great place to pose for photographs. The road also passes through the **Tunnel Log,** which is exactly that: a tunnel through a fallen sequoia tree. If your vehicle is too tall—7 feet 9 inches or more—a bypass is provided. (There is no standing drive-through Sequoia tree in the park. There used to be one in Yosemite, but it fell in 1969.) John Muir called **Crescent Meadow** the "gem of the Sierra"—brilliant wildflowers bloom here by midsummer; and a nearly 2-mi trail loops around the meadow. A 1½-mi round-trip trail that begins at Crescent Meadow leads to **Tharp's Log,** named for Hale Tharp, who built a pioneer cabin (still standing) out of a fire-hollowed sequoia.

★ **Moro Rock,** an immense granite monolith, stands along Moro Rock–Crescent Meadow Road, rising 6,725 feet above sea level, right from the edge of the Giant Forest. Four hundred steps lead to the top; the trail often climbs along narrow ledges over steep drops. The view from the top is stunning. To the southwest you look more than 4,000 vertical feet down the Kaweah River to Three Rivers, Lake Kaweah, and—on clear days—the Central Valley and the Coast Range. To the east stand the jagged peaks of the High Sierra. Regrettably, smog from Fresno may obscure the views.

The most famous sequoia in the Giant Forest area is the **General Sherman Tree** (✉ 1 mi north of the Giant Forest, off Generals Hwy.). Benches allow

7

you to sit and contemplate the tree's immensity: weighing in at 2.7 million pounds, it has the greatest volume of any living thing in the world. The first major branch is 130 feet above the ground. The paved **Congress Trail**, a popular 2-mi hike, starts at the General Sherman Tree and loops through the heart of the Giant Forest. In the one to two hours it takes to complete the loop you will pass groups of trees known as the House and Senate and individual trees called the President and McKinley.

★ ☾ ❺ Discovered in 1918 by two park employees, **Crystal Cave** is the best known of Sequoia's many caverns. Its interior, which was formed from limestone that metamorphosed into marble, is decorated with stalactites and stalagmites of various shapes, sizes, and colors. To visit the cave, you must first stop at the Foothills or Lodgepole Visitor Center to buy tickets; they are not sold at the cave. A narrow, twisting 7-mi road off the Generals Highway leads you 2.2 mi south of the old Giant Forest Village. From the parking area it's a 15-minute hike down a steep path to the cave's entrance. It's cool inside—48°F—so bring a sweater. ✉ *Crystal Cave Rd., off Generals Hwy.* ☎ *559/565-3759* ⊕ *www.sequoiahistory. org* ✆ *$11* ⊙ *May–mid-Nov., call for tour times.*

❻ **Lodgepole** sits in a canyon on the Marble Fork of the Kaweah River. Lodgepole pines, rather than sequoias, grow here because the U-shape canyon funnels in air from the high country that is too cold for the big trees. This area has a campground and a post office open year-round. A snack bar, market and deli, public laundry, and showers are open in the summer only. The **Lodgepole Visitor Center** has extensive exhibits, a small theater where you can watch an orientation slide show, and a first-aid center. You can buy tickets for the Crystal Cave, get advice from park rangers, purchase maps and books, and pick up wilderness permits. The **Tokopah Falls Trail** is an easy and rewarding 3½-mi round-trip hike from the Lodgepole Campground up the Marble Fork of the Kaweah River. The walk to the 1,200-foot falls, which flow down granite cliffs, is the closest you can get to the high country without substantial wear and tear on your hiking boots. Trail maps are available at the Lodgepole Visitor Center. Bring insect repellent during the summer; the mosquitoes can be ferocious. ✉ *Generals Hwy., 5 mi north of Giant Forest Museum* ☎ *559/565-4436* ✆ *Free* ⊙ *Visitor center mid-Apr.–mid-June, daily 9–4:30; mid-June–early Sept., daily 8–6; early Sept.–mid-Apr., weekends 9–4:30.*

❼ The dining and lodging facilities at **Wuksachi Village** (✉ Generals Hwy., 6 mi north of Lodgepole) have replaced the antiquated facilities of the old Giant Forest Village, most of which has been demolished. These are the nicest facilities in the area. There's also a gift shop.

Where to Stay & Eat

★ **$-$$$** ✕ **Wuksachi Village Dining Room.** In the high-ceiling dining room at Sequoia's only upscale restaurant, huge windows run the length of the room, providing a view of the surrounding trees. The dinner menu lists everything from sandwiches and burgers to steaks and pasta. Breakfast and lunch are also served. ✉ *Wuksachi Village* ☎ *559/565-4070* ✍ *Reservations essential* ▭ *AE, D, DC, MC, V.*

★ $$–$$$ ▣ **Wuksachi Village Lodge.** These cedar-and-stone lodge buildings, which blend with the landscape, house comfortable rooms with modern amenities. The village is 7,200 feet above sea level; many of the rooms have spectacular views of the surrounding mountains. ⊠ *Wuksachi Village* ☎ *559/565–4070 front desk, 559/253–2199, 888/252–5757 reservations* 🖶 *559/456–0542* ⊕ *www.visitsequoia.com* ➥ *102 rooms* ⟜ *Restaurant, fans, refrigerators, cable TV, in-room data ports, hiking, cross-country skiing, ski storage, bar, meeting room; no a/c, no smoking* ▭ *AE, D, DC, MC, V.*

⛺ **Lodgepole Campground.** The largest Lodgepole-area campground is also the noisiest, though things do quiet down at night. Restrooms are nearby. Lodgepole and Dorst (a mile or so to the west) are the two campgrounds within Sequoia that accept reservations (essential up to five months in advance for stays between mid-May and mid-October). ⊠ *Off Generals Hwy. beyond Lodgepole Village* ☎ *559/565–3341 Ext. 2 information, 800/365–2267 reservations* ⊕ *http://reservations. nps.gov* ▭ *$20* ➥ *214 sites (tent and RV)* ⟜ *Flush toilets, dump station (summer only), drinking water, guest laundry (summer only), showers (summer only), bear boxes, fire grates, picnic tables, public telephone, general store.*

Sports & the Outdoors

Hiking and backpacking are the top outdoor activities in Sequoia National Park (*see* Camping *in* the Southern Sierra A to Z). In winter you can cross-country ski, snowshoe, and sled, and in summer mule rides are available. The visitor centers have information on trail conditions, ranger-guided hikes, and snowshoe walks. Conditions permitting, you can rent winter sports equipment at **Wuksachi Village Lodge** (☎ 559/565–4070).

Sequoia National Forest

15–20 mi northwest of Lodgepole on Generals Hwy.

Though you may not even notice the change, on your way to Grant Grove, the Generals Highway leaves Sequoia National Park and passes through a section of Sequoia National Forest.

❽ **Kings Canyon Overlook,** a large turnout on the north side of the Generals Highway, has views across the canyon of mountain peaks and the backcountry. If you drive to Cedar Grove (about one hour east of Grant Grove on Highway 180, open summer only) along the south fork, you will see these spectacular canyons at much closer range.

★ ❾ The **Redwood Mountain Grove** is the largest grove of sequoias in the world. As you enter Kings Canyon on the Generals Highway, several paved turnouts allow you to look out over the grove (and into the smog of the Central Valley). The grove itself is accessible only on foot or horseback.

Where to Stay

$$–$$$ ▣ **Montecito-Sequoia Lodge.** A summer-camp atmosphere prevails all year long at this family-oriented resort just south of Kings Canyon Na-

tional Park. Specializing in all-inclusive vacations, it offers everything from skiing and snowboarding in winter to sailing and horseback riding in summer. From mid-June to early September there's normally a six-night minimum, but you can book a one-night stay on Saturdays. ⊠ *Generals Hwy., 11 mi south of Grant Grove* ☎ *559/565–3388 or 800/227–9900 (reservations)* ᗺ*650/967–0540* ⊕*www.montecitosequoia. com* ⇆ *32 rooms, 13 cabins* ⚒ *Dining room, snack bar, BBQs, tennis court, pool, lake, boating, waterskiing, fishing, bicycles, archery, hiking, horseback riding, volleyball, cross-country skiing, ice-skating, children's programs (ages 2–18); no a/c, no room phones, no room TVs* ⊟*AE, D, MC, V* ᐧ❍ᐧ *FAP.*

$$ 🏨 **Stony Creek.** Sitting at 6,800 feet among the peaceful pines, Stony Creek is on national forest land between Giant Forest and Grant Grove. Expect motel-style accommodations in the woods. A restaurant is adjacent to the lodge. ⊠ *Generals Hwy.* ☐ *Sequoia Kings Canyon Park Services Co., 5755 E. Kings Canyon Rd., Suite 101, Fresno 93727* ☎ *559/ 565–3909 or 866/522–6966* ᗺ *559/452–1353* ⊕ *www.sequoia-kingscanyon.com* ⇆ *11 rooms* ⚒ *Restaurant, cable TV, in-room data ports, Internet room; no a/c, no smoking* ⊟ *AE, D, MC, V* ⊘ *Closed Sept.–May* ᐧ❍ᐧ *CP.*

Grant Grove

⓾ *27 mi north of Lodgepole via Generals Hwy. to Kings Canyon Hwy.*

Kings Canyon's most developed area was designated General Grant National Park (the forerunner of Kings Canyon National Park) in 1890. This is another entry point to the national parks, and the **Kings Canyon Visitor Center** is the best place to gather information and to see exhibits on the park's three major resources: giant sequoias, the High Sierra, and Kings Canyon itself. ⊠ *Kings Canyon Hwy., Grant Grove Village* ☎ *559/565–4307* ᗺ *Free* ⊘ *May–mid-June and early Sept.–Oct., daily 8–8; mid-June–early Sept., daily 8–8; Nov.–Apr., daily 9–4:30.*

The visitor center is part of compact and often crowded **Grant Grove Village,** which also contains a grocery store, gift shop, campgrounds, a restaurant that has family dining, overnight lodging, and a post office. A walk along 1-mi **Big Stump Trail,** which starts near the park entrance, graphically demonstrates the toll heavy logging takes on wilderness. The **General Grant Tree Trail,** a paved ⅓-mi path, winds past the General Grant, an enormous, 2,000-year-old sequoia, the world's third-largest, which has been designated "the nation's Christmas tree." The **Gamlin Cabin,** an 1867 pioneer cabin, is listed on the National Register of Historic Places. Also within Grant Grove is the **Centennial Stump,** the remains of a huge sequoia cut for display at the 1876 Philadelphia Centennial Exhibition.

OFF THE
BEATEN
PATH

HUME LAKE – This reservoir, built by loggers in the early 1900s, is now the site of several church-affiliated camps, a gas station, and a public campground. Outside Kings Canyon's borders, the small lake has views of the mountains in the distance. ⊠ *Hume Lake Rd., off Kings Canyon Hwy., 8 mi northeast of Grant Grove.*

Where to Stay

$$ ▦ **John Muir Lodge.** This modern, timber-sided lodge is nestled in a wooded area near Grant Grove Village. The 24 rooms and six suites all have queen beds and private baths, and there's a comfortable lobby with low-pile carpeting and a stone fireplace where you can play cards and board games. The inexpensive, family-style Grant Grove Restaurant is a three-minute walk away. Though it's little more than a good motel, this is the best place to stay in Grant Grove. ⊠ *Kings Canyon Hwy., ¼ mi north of Grant Grove Village* ⊕ *Sequoia Kings Canyon Park Services Co., 5755 E. Kings Canyon Rd., Suite 101, Fresno 93727* ☎ *559/ 335–5500 or 866/522–6966* 🖷 *559/335–5507* ⊕ *www.sequoia-kingscanyon.com* ➷ *24 rooms, 6 suites* ♿ *Meeting room; no a/c, no room TVs* ▱ *AE, D, MC, V.*

⚠ **Azalea Campground.** One of three campgrounds in the Grant Grove area (the others are Sunset and Crystal Springs, both open May through September only), Azalea is open year-round. It sits at 6,500 feet amid giant sequoias, yet is close to restaurants, stores, and other facilities. Some sites at Azalea are wheelchair accessible. The campground can accommodate RVs up to 30 feet. Though it costs $18 May to mid-October— and reservations are not accepted—it's free the rest of the year. ⊠ *Kings Canyon Hwy., ¼ mi north of Grant Grove Village* ☎ *559/565–3341* ▱ *$18* ➷ *113 sites (tent or RV)* ♿ *Flush toilets, drinking water, showers, bear boxes, fire grates, picnic tables, public telephone, general store.*

Sports & the Outdoors

The primary activities in Kings Canyon are hiking and backpacking (*see* Camping *in* The Southern Sierra A to Z). Bicycling is discouraged, because the only paved roads outside village areas are the Kings Canyon and Generals highways, both winding mountain roads with heavy traffic. Horseback riding is an enjoyable alternative in summer. Winter snows turn the park into a playground for cross-country skiers and snowshoers, and there are dedicated areas for sledding. Check with the visitor center for conditions and trail maps.

HORSEBACK **Grant Grove Stables** (⊠ Grant Grove Village ☎ 559/335–9292 mid-
RIDING June–Sept., 559/594–9307 Oct.–mid-June) is the stable to choose if you want a short ride; for overnight trips, head to Cedar Grove (below).

EN
ROUTE
★
The spectacular 30-mi, hour-long descent along **Kings Canyon Highway** runs along the south fork of the Kings River. It cuts through dry hills covered with yuccas that bloom in summer and passes the scars where large groves of sequoias were felled at the beginning of the 20th century. There are amazing views into the deepest gorge in the United States—deeper even than the Grand Canyon—and up the canyons to the High Sierra, which remain snowcapped until midsummer, a thrilling sight. It takes about an hour from Grant Grove to Roads End, where you can hike or camp. Built by convict labor in the 1930s, the road (usually closed from mid-October through April) clings to some dramatic cliffs along the way: watch out for falling rocks, and though it may be difficult at times, keep your eye on the road.

Cedar Grove

⓫ *31 mi east of Grant Grove on Kings Canyon Hwy.*

Named for the incense cedars that grow in the area, Cedar Grove is nestled in a valley that snakes along the south fork of the Kings River. **Cedar Grove Village** (⊠ East end of Kings Canyon Hwy. ☎ 559/565–3793 visitor center) has campgrounds, lodgings, a small visitor center, a snack bar, a cafeteria, a convenience market, and a gift shop, but it's open only April to November, depending on snowfall.

About 4½ mi southeast of Cedar Grove Village, short trails circle grassy **Zumwalt Meadow,** which is surrounded by towering granite walls. Trails from Zumwalt Meadow lead to the base of **Roaring River Falls,** which run hardest in spring and early summer.

Where to Stay & Eat

$ ✕⌘ **Cedar Grove Lodge.** Although accommodations are close to the road, this lodge manages to deliver peace and quiet. Book far in advance— the lodge has only 21 rooms. Each has two queen-size beds, and three have kitchenettes and patios. You can order trout, hamburgers, hot dogs, and sandwiches at the snack bar (¢–$) and take them to one of the picnic tables along the river's edge. ⊠ *Kings Canyon Hwy.* ✇ *Sequoia Kings Canyon Park Services Co., 5755 E. Kings Canyon Rd., Suite 101, Fresno 93727* ☎ *559/335–5500 or 866/522–6966* ☒ *559/335–5507* ⊕ *www.sequoia-kingscanyon.com* ☞ *21 rooms* ♨ *Snack bar, some kitchenettes, hiking, laundry facilities; no room phones, no room TVs, no smoking* ▭ *AE, D, MC, V* ☉ *Closed mid-Oct.–mid-May.*

Sports & the Outdoors

For horseback rides and overnight pack trips into the wilderness, call **Cedar Grove Pack Station** (⊠ Cedar Grove Village ☎ 559/565–3464 mid-June–Sept., 559/337–2314 Oct.–mid-June).

SOUTH OF YOSEMITE
FROM OAKHURST TO EL PORTAL

Several gateway towns to the south and west of Yosemite National Park, most within an hour's drive of Yosemite Valley, have food, lodging, and other services. Highway 140 heads east from the San Joaquin Valley to El Portal and Yosemite's west entrance. Highway 41 heads north from Fresno to Oakhurst and Fish Camp to Yosemite's south entrance.

Oakhurst

40 mi north of Fresno and 23 mi south of Yosemite National Park's South Entrance on Hwy. 41.

Motels, restaurants, gas stations, and small businesses line both sides of Highway 41 as it cuts through Oakhurst. Though the town lacks much character, it's the last sizeable community before Yosemite and a good spot to find provisions. There are two major grocery stores near the intersection of Highways 41 and 49. Three miles north of town, then 6 mi east, honky-tonky Bass Lake is a popular spot in summer with motorboaters, jet-skiers, and families looking to cool off in the reservoir.

Where to Stay & Eat

$$$$ ✕ **Erna's Elderberry House.** Erna Kubin, the grande dame of Château du
Fodor'sChoice Sureau, has created a culinary oasis, stunning for its understated ele-
★ gance, gorgeous setting, and impeccable service. Red walls and dark beams accent the dining room's high ceilings, and arched windows reflect the glow of candles. The seasonal six-course prix-fixe dinner can be paired with superb wines, a must-do for oenophiles. When the waitstaff places all the plates on the table in perfect synchronicity, you know this will be a meal to remember. A small bistro menu is also served in the former wine cellar. ⊠ *48688 Victoria La.* ☎ *559/683–6800* ⌲ *Reservations essential* ⊟ *AE, D, MC, V* ⊘ *No lunch Mon.–Sat.*

¢–$ ✕ **Yosemite Fork Mountain House.** Bypass Oakhurst's greasy spoons and instead head to this family restaurant, 3 mi north of the Highway 49/Highway 41 intersection, with open-beamed ceiling and a canoe in the rafters. Portions are huge. Expect standard American fare: bacon and eggs at breakfast, sandwiches at lunch, and pastas and steaks at dinner. ⊠ *Hwy. 41 at the Bass Lake turnoff* ☎ *559/683–5191* ⌲ *Reservations not accepted* ⊟ *D, MC, V.*

$$$$ 🏨 **Château du Sureau.** This romantic inn, adjacent to Erna's Elderberry
Fodor'sChoice House, is straight out of a children's book. From the moment you drive
★ through the wrought-iron gates and up to the fairy-tale castle, you feel pampered. Every room is impeccably styled with European antiques, sumptuous fabrics, fresh-cut flowers, and oversize soaking tubs. After falling asleep by the glow of a crackling fire amid feather-light goose-down pillows and Italian linens, awaken to a hearty European breakfast in the dining room, then relax with a game of chess in the piano room beneath an exquisite ceiling mural. Cable TV is available by request only. ⊠ *48688 Victoria La., Box 577, 93644* ☎ *559/683–6860* 🖷 *559/683–0800* ⊕ *www.elderberryhouse.com* ⌁ *10 rooms, 1 villa* ⌂ *Restaurant, some in-room hot tubs, in-room data ports, golf privileges, pool, pond, boccie, bar, shop, laundry service, Internet room; no kids under 12, no smoking* ⊟ *AE, MC, V* ⊖I *BP.*

★ **$$–$$$** 🏨 **Homestead Cottages.** Serenity is the order of the day at this secluded getaway in Ahwahnee, 6 mi west of Oakhurst. On 160 acres of rolling hills that once held a Miwok village, these cottages have gas fireplaces, living rooms, fully equipped kitchens, and queen-size beds; the largest sleeps six. The cottages, hand-built by the owners out of real adobe bricks, are stocked with soft robes, oversize towels, and paperback books. If you're looking for a hideaway, this is the place. ⊠ *41110 Rd. 600, 2½ mi off Hwy. 49, Ahwahnee 93601* ☎ *559/683–0495 or 800/483–0495* 🖷 *559/683–8165* ⊕ *www.homesteadcottages.com* ⌁ *5 cottages, 1 loft* ⌂ *BBQs, kitchens, cable TV, hiking; no room phones, no smoking* ⊟ *AE, D, MC, V.*

☺ **$** 🏨 **Best Western Yosemite Gateway Inn.** Oakhurst's best motel has carefully tended landscaping and rooms with attractive dark-wood American colonial–style furniture and slightly kitsch hand-painted wall murals of Yosemite. Kids love choosing between the two pools. ⊠ *40530 Hwy.*

41, 93644 ☎ 559/683–2378 or 800/545–5462 ₰ 559/683–3813 ⊕ www.yosemitegatewayinn.com ⌨ 121 rooms, 12 suites ⚲ Restaurant, microwaves, refrigerators, cable TV, in-room broadband, in-room data ports, 2 pools (one indoors), hot tub, exercise equipment, bar, playground, laundry facilities, no-smoking rooms ▤ AE, D, MC, V.

Sports & the Outdoors

Bass Lake Water Sports and Marina (✉ Bass Lake Reservoir ☎ 559/642–3565), 3 mi north and 6 mi east of Oakhurst, rents ski boats, patio boats, and fishing boats. In summer, the noisy reservoir gets packed shortly after 8 AM, when it opens. There's also a restaurant and snack bar.

Fish Camp

⑫ *57 mi north of Fresno and 4 mi south of Yosemite National Park's South Entrance on Hwy. 41.*

As you climb in elevation along Highway 41 northbound, you see nothing but trees until you get to the small settlement of Fish Camp, where there's a post office and general store, but no gasoline (for gas, head 10 mi north to Wawona, in the park, or 17 mi south to Oakhurst).

↻ The **Yosemite Mountain Sugar Pine Railroad** has a narrow-gauge steam engine that chugs through the forest. It follows 4 mi of the route the Madera Sugar Pine Lumber Company cut through the forest in 1899 to harvest timber. The steam train runs daily May through September, and weekends and Wednesday April and October; call for schedules. Other times, Jenny railcars—open-air cars powered by Ford Model A engines—operate every half hour, 9:30 AM–3 PM. On Saturday (and Wednesday in summer), the Moonlight Special dinner excursion (reservations essential; BYOB) includes a picnic with toe-tappin' music by the Sugar Pine Singers, followed by a sunset steam-train ride. ✉ *56001 Hwy. 41* ☎ *559/683–7273* ⊕ *www.ymsprr.com* ✆ *$14; Moonlight Special $38* ☉ *Mar.–Oct., daily.*

Where to Stay & Eat

$$$$ ✕▦ **Tenaya Lodge.** One of the region's largest hotels, the Tenaya Lodge is ideal for people who enjoy wilderness treks by day but prefer creature comforts at night. The hulking prefab buildings and giant parking lot look out of place in the woods, but inside, the rooms have all the amenities of a modern, full-service hotel. The ample regular rooms are decorated in pleasant earth tones, deluxe rooms have minibars and other extras, and the suites have balconies. The Sierra Restaurant ($$–$$$$), with its high ceilings and giant fireplace, serves Continental cuisine. The more casual Jackalopes Bar and Grill ($–$$) has burgers, salads, and sandwiches. ✉ *1122 Hwy. 41* ⛺ *Box 159, 93623* ☎ *559/683–6555 or 888/514–2167* ₰ *559/683–0249* ⊕ *www. tenayalodge.com* ⌨ *244 rooms, 6 suites* ⚲ *2 restaurants, snack bar, room service, some minibars, cable TV with movies and video games, in-room data ports, Wi-Fi (fee), indoor pool, health club, hot tub, mountain bikes, hiking, cross-country skiing, bar, recreation room, babysitting, children's programs (ages 5–12), playground, laundry service, concierge, business services, meeting room; no smoking* ▤ *AE, D, DC, MC, V.*

★ **$–$$** ✕⃞ **Narrow Gauge Inn.** All of the rooms at this well-tended, family-owned property have balconies (some shared) and great views of the surrounding woods and mountains. For maximum atmosphere, book a room over-loooking the brook; for quiet, choose a lower-level room on the edge of the forest. All are comfortably furnished with old-fashioned accents and railroad memorabilia. Reserve way ahead. The restaurant ($–$$$; open Apr.–Oct., Wed.–Sun.), which is festooned with moose, bison, and other wildlife trophies, specializes in steaks and American fare, and merits a special trip. ⊠ *48571 Hwy. 41, 93623* ☎ *559/683–7720 or 888/ 644–9050* 🖷 *559/683–2139* ⊕ *www.narrowgaugeinn.com* ⇨ *25 rooms, 1 suite* ⚫ *Restaurant, cable TV, some in-room VCRs, in-room data ports, Wi-Fi (fee), pool, hot tub, bar, some pets allowed (fee); no a/c in some rooms, no smoking* ▭ *D, MC, V* ▯◯▯ *CP.*

El Portal

14 mi west of Yosemite Valley on Hwy. 140.

The market in town is a good place to pick up provisions before you get to Yosemite. There are also a post office and a gas station, but not much else.

Where to Stay

$$–$$$ ⃞ **Yosemite View Lodge.** The Yosemite View Lodge's prefab-motel de-sign aesthetic is ameliorated by its location right on the banks of the boulder-strewn Merced River and its proximity to the park entrance 2 mi east. Many rooms also have whirlpool baths, fireplaces, kitchenettes. The motel complex is on the public bus route to the park, and near fish-ing and river rafting. Ask for a riverside room. The lodge's sister prop-erty, the Cedar Lodge, sits 6 mi farther west and has similar-looking, less expensive rooms without river views. ⊠ *11136 Hwy. 140, 95318* ☎ *209/379–2681 or 888/742–4371* 🖷 *209/379–2704* ⊕ *www.yosemite-motels.com* ⇨ *276 rooms* ⚫ *Restaurant, pizzeria, some in-room hot tubs, some kitchenettes, cable TV, 2 pools (1 indoor), bar, laundry fa-cilities, meeting room, some pets allowed (fee), no-smoking rooms* ▭ *AE, MC, V.*

7

YOSEMITE NATIONAL PARK

▶ Of Yosemite's 1,189 square mi of parkland, 94.5% is undeveloped wilderness, most of it accessible only on foot or horseback. The west-ern boundary dips as low as 2,000 feet in the chaparral-covered foothills; the eastern boundary rises to 13,000 feet at points along the Sierra crest.

Yosemite is so large you can think of it as five different parks. Yosemite Valley, famous for waterfalls and cliffs, and Wawona, where the giant sequoias stand, are open all year. Hetch Hetchy, home of less-used back-country trails, closes after the first big snow and reopens in May or June. The subalpine high country, Tuolumne Meadows, is open for summer hiking and camping; in winter it's accessible only by cross-country skis or snowshoes. Badger Pass Ski Area is open in winter only. The fee to visit Yosemite National Park (good for seven days) is $20 per car, $10 per person if you don't arrive in a car. Within park boundaries, you can buy gasoline only in Wawona and Crane Flat, not the valley.

On entering the park, you'll receive a small glossy magazine with general information about the park, and a free monthly newspaper, *Yosemite Today,* which lists locations and times for ranger-led nature walks. Make it a point to read at least the newspaper for up-to-date visitors' information.

Yosemite Valley

214 mi east of San Francisco via I–80 to I–580 to I–205 to Hwy. 120; 330 mi northeast of Los Angeles via I–5 to Hwy. 99 to Hwy. 41.

Yosemite Valley has been so extravagantly praised (John Muir described it as "a revelation in landscape") and so beautifully photographed (by Ansel Adams, who said, "I knew my destiny when I first experienced Yosemite") that you may wonder if the reality can possibly measure up. For almost everyone it does. It's a true reminder of what *breathtaking* really means. The Miwok, the last of several Native American people to inhabit the Yosemite area (they were forced out by gold miners in 1851), named the valley Ahwahnee, which is thought to mean "the place of the gaping mouth."

It's important to remember a few things when visiting the valley. The roads at the eastern end of the valley are closed to private cars, but a free shuttle bus runs about every 15 minutes from the village (7 AM–10 PM May–September and approximately 9 AM–8:30 PM the rest of the year). Directions to the day-use parking lot, near the intersection of Sentinel and Northside drives, can be found on the back of *Yosemite Today,* along with a shuttle-bus map and current schedule. Bears are a huge problem in Yosemite; be sure to read pamphlets on the subject or speak with a ranger, and take proper precautions while in the park.

⑬ The center of activity in Yosemite Valley is **Yosemite Village,** which contains restaurants, stores, a post office, and a clinic; the Ahwahnee Hotel and Yosemite Lodge are nearby. You can get your bearings, pick up maps and books, and obtain information from park rangers at the village's **Valley Visitor Center;** the center's new exhibit hall is scheduled for completion in 2007. At the **Wilderness Center** you can find out everything you need to know about such backcountry activities as hiking and camping. The **Yosemite Museum** has a Native American cultural exhibit, with displays about the Miwok and Paiute people who lived in the region; there's a re-created Ahwahneechee village behind it. The **Ansel Adams Gallery** shows works of the master photographer and sells prints and camera equipment. ⊠ *Off Northside Dr.* ☎ *209/372–0200 visitor center, 209/372–4413 gallery* ☉ *Visitor center fall–spring, daily 9–5; summer, daily 8–6.*

⑭ Yosemite Valley is famed for its waterfalls, and the mightiest of them
Fodor'sChoice all is **Yosemite Falls,** the highest waterfall in North America and the sixth-
★ highest in the world. The upper fall (1,430 feet), the middle cascades (675 feet), and the lower fall (320 feet) combine for a total drop of 2,425 feet. In spring and early summer, when the falls run their hardest, you

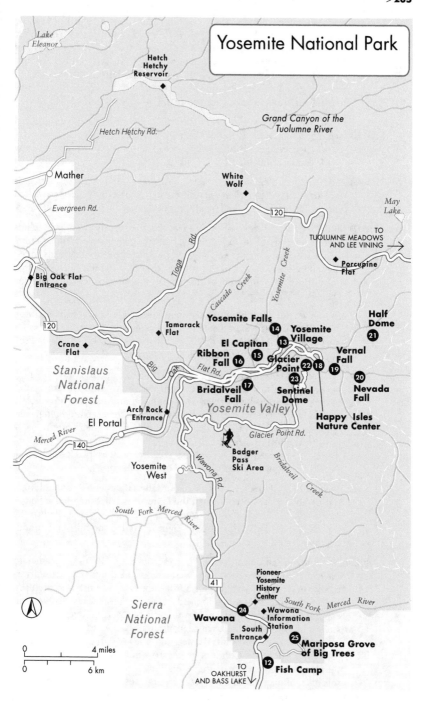

Yosemite National Park

Lake Eleanor

Hetch Hetchy Reservoir

Grand Canyon of the Tuolumne River

Hetch Hetchy Rd.

Mather

Evergreen Rd.

White Wolf

May Lake

120

TO TUOLUMNE MEADOWS AND LEE VINING →

Big Oak Flat Entrance

Tioga Rd.

Porcupine Flat

120

Cascade Creek

Yosemite Creek

Crane Flat

Tamarack Flat

Half Dome

21

Yosemite Falls

Stanislaus National Forest

Big Oak Flat Rd.

Ribbon Fall

16

El Capitan

15

14

Yosemite Village

13

Glacier Point

22 18

Vernal Fall

19

Nevada Fall

20

Bridalveil Fall

17

23

Sentinel Dome

Yosemite Valley

Happy Isles Nature Center

Arch Rock Entrance

El Portal

Merced River

140

Yosemite West

Glacier Point Rd.

Bridalveil Creek

Badger Pass Ski Area

Wawona Rd.

South Fork Merced River

Sierra National Forest

41

Pioneer Yosemite History Center

South Fork Merced River

Wawona

24

Wawona Information Station

South Entrance

25 Mariposa Grove of Big Trees

12 Fish Camp

TO OAKHURST AND BASS LAKE ↓

0   4 miles

0   6 km

can hear them thunder all across the valley. Peak flow is in May. (Be warned, though, that the falls slow to a trickle in winter.) The Upper Yosemite Fall Trail, a strenuous 3½-mi climb rising 2,700 feet, takes you above the top of the falls. It starts at Camp 4, formerly known as Sunnyside Campground. You cannot park at the falls, and the adjacent Yosemite Lodge parking is for lodge guests only (rangers will ticket illegally parked vehicles); park in the day-use area and ride the shuttle.

★ ⑮ Yosemite Valley's waterfalls tumble past magnificent geological scenery. **El Capitan,** rising 3,593 feet above the valley, is the largest exposed granite monolith in the world, almost twice the height of the Rock of Gibraltar.

⑯ At 1,612 feet, **Ribbon Fall** is the highest single fall in North America. It is also the first waterfall in the valley to dry up; the rainwater and melted snow that create the slender fall evaporate quickly at this height.

★ ⑰ **Bridalveil Fall,** a filmy fall of 620 feet that is often diverted as much as 20 feet one way or the other by the breeze, is the first view of Yosemite Valley for those who arrive via Wawona Road. Native Americans called the fall Pohono ("spirit of the puffing wind"). A ¼-mi trail leads to the base of the fall from the parking lot off the intersection of Southside Drive and Wawona Road.

🖑 ⑱ As you venture through the valley amid Yosemite's natural wonders, stop at the **Happy Isles Nature Center** to see ecology exhibits and find books for children. ✉ ½ mi east of Curry Village ☎ 209/372–0299 or 209/372–0200 ☼ May–Oct., daily 9–5 but may vary.

⑲ Fern-covered black rocks frame **Vernal Fall** (317 feet), and rainbows play in the spray at its base. The hike from the Happy Isles Nature Center to the bridge at the base of Vernal Fall is less than 1 mi long, on a paved trail, and only lightly strenuous. It's another steep (and often wet) ¾ mi up the Mist Trail—which is open only from late spring to early fall—to the top of Vernal Fall. Allow two to four hours for the 3-mi round-trip hike. In winter, the Mist Trail freezes with black ice; be sure to take the signed detour to the top of the fall.

⑳ **Nevada Fall** (594 feet) is the first major fall as the Merced River plunges out of the high country toward the eastern end of Yosemite Valley. A strenuous 2-mi section of the Mist Trail leads from Vernal Fall to the top of Nevada Fall. Allow six to eight hours for the full 7-mi round-trip hike.

★ ㉑ Astounding **Half Dome** rises 4,733 feet from the valley floor to a height 8,842 feet above sea level. The west side of the dome is fractured vertically and cut away to form a 2,000-foot cliff. For the best pictures, head to Sentinel Bridge late in the day, just before sunset, when you can capture the reflection of the mighty dome in the Merced River. The highly strenuous **John Muir Trail,** which incorporates the Mist Trail, leads from Yosemite Valley to the Half Dome Trail. The views from the top are astounding. Allow 10–12 hours for the 16¾-mi round-trip; start early in the morning and beware of afternoon thunderstorms. If you plan to take this hike, inquire about necessary preparations at one of the ranger stations; more injuries occur here than anywhere else in the park. There is no overnight camping on Half Dome.

㉒ **Glacier Point** yields what may be the most spectacular vista of the valley and the High Sierra that you can get without hiking, especially at sunset. Glacier Point Road splits off from Wawona Road (Highway 41) about 23 mi southwest of the valley; then it's a 16-mi drive through the woods into higher country. From the parking area walk a few hundred yards, and you'll be able to see Nevada, Vernal, and Yosemite Falls as well as Half Dome and other peaks. You can hike to the valley floor (3,214 feet below) via the Panorama or Four-Mile trails. To avoid a grueling round-trip, catch a ride to Glacier Point on one of the three daily **hikers' buses** (☎ 209/372–1240 reservations), which run from late spring through October; the cost is $15 one-way, $29.50 round-trip. Reservations are essential. In winter, Glacier Point Road is closed beyond the turnoff for the Badger Pass Ski Area, making Glacier Point inaccessible.

Fodor'sChoice
★

㉓ The view from **Sentinel Dome** is similar to that from Glacier Point, except you can't see the valley floor. A 1.1-mi path begins at a parking lot on Glacier Point Road a few miles below Glacier Point. The trail is long and steep enough to keep the crowds and tour buses away, but not overly rugged.

OFF THE
BEATEN
PATH

The **HETCH HETCHY RESERVOIR** – Supplier of water and hydroelectric power to San Francisco, the Hetch Hetchy is about 40 mi from Yosemite Valley via Big Oak Flat Road to Highway 120 to Evergreen Road to Hetch Hetchy Road. Some say John Muir died of heartbreak when the gates to the O'Shaughnessy Dam closed and flooded the valley beneath 300 feet of water in 1913. Muir would be thrilled to learn of the momentum gathering behind the movement to decommission the dam and restore the valley to its original splendor (for more on the restoration effort, pick up a copy of *The Battle Over Hetch Hetchy*, by Robert W. Righter, or see www.hetchhetchy.org).

TUOLUMNE MEADOWS – Spectacularly scenic Tioga Road is the only route to Tuolumne Meadows, which sits at 8,575 feet in altitude about 55 mi from Yosemite Valley. The largest subalpine meadow in the Sierra, it bursts with late-summer wildflowers; it's also the trailhead for many backpack trips into the High Sierra. The area contains campgrounds, a gas station, a store (with limited and expensive provisions), stables, a tent-cabin lodge, and a visitor center that is open from late June until early September from 9 to 5. Tioga Road (Highway 120) stays open until the first big snow of the year, usually about mid-October.

Where to Stay & Eat

Book in-park lodgings only through the Web sites and telephone numbers listed below to avoid unauthorized booking services that illegally buy blocks of rooms and resell them to unsuspecting travelers for inflated prices.

★ **$$–$$$** ✗ **Mountain Room Restaurant.** Though remarkably good, the food becomes secondary when you see Yosemite Falls through this dining room's wall of windows. Almost every table has a view of the falls. Grilled trout and salmon, steak, pasta, and several children's dishes are on the menu. ⊠ *Yosemite Lodge off Northside Dr.* ☎ *209/372–1281* ⌂ *Reservations essential* ▭ *AE, D, DC, MC, V* ⊗ *No lunch.*

$$$$ ✗▣ **Ahwahnee Hotel & Dining Room.** This grand 1920s-era mountain lodge, **Fodor'sChoice** designated a National Historic Landmark, is constructed of rocks and ★ sugar-pine logs. Some of the amenities found in a luxury hotel, including turn-down service and guest bathrobes, are standard here. The Dining Room ($$$–$$$$, jacket required, reservations essential), which has a 34-foot-tall beamed ceiling, full-length windows, and wrought-iron chandeliers, is by far the most impressive restaurant in the park, and one of the most beautiful rooms in California. Specialties include sautéed salmon, roast duckling, and prime rib. ⊠ *Ahwahnee Rd. north of Northside Dr., 95389* ⌂ *Yosemite Reservations, 5410 E. Home Ave., Fresno 93727* ☎ *559/252–4848 lodging reservations, 209/372–1489 restaurant* ⊕ *www.yosemitepark.com* ⌫ *99 rooms, 4 suites, 24 cottages* ⌂ *Restaurant, refrigerators, cable TV, in-room data ports, Wi-Fi, tennis court, pool, lounge, concierge; no a/c in some rooms, no smoking* ▭ *AE, D, DC, MC, V.*

★ ☾ **$–$$$** ✗▣ **Evergreen Lodge.** It feels like summer camp at the Evergreen, where you can ditch the valley's hordes for a cozy cabin in the woods 8 mi from Hetch Hetchy. The perfect blend of rustic charm and modern comfort, cabins have sumptuous beds, comfy armchairs, candy-cane-striped pull-out sofas, 3- by 4-foot topographic wall maps, and such retro-fun details as tree-stump end tables. The terrific roadhouse-style restaurant ($–$$) serves everything from buffalo burgers and rib eyes to rainbow trout and pastas. After dinner, shoot pool in the old-school rough-hewn-wood bar, melt s'mores, attend a lecture or film, or play Scrabble by the fire in the barnlike recreation center. ⊠ *33160 Evergreen Rd., 25 mi east of Groveland, 23 mi north of Yosemite Valley, Groveland 95321* ☎ *209/379–2606 or 800/935–6343* 🗄 *209/391–2390* ⊕ *www.evergreenlodge.com* ⌫ *66 cabins* ⌂ *Restaurant, snack bar, fans, refrigerators, Wi-Fi (in lobby), pool (nearby), massage, fishing, bicycles, badminton, basketball (nearby), billiards, boccie, hiking, horseback riding (nearby), horseshoes, Ping-Pong, bar, recreation room, children's programs (ages 5–12), playground, Internet room, meeting room; no a/c, no room phones, no room TVs, no smoking* ▭ *AE, D, DC, MC, V* ⊗ *Closed Jan. and Feb., weekdays.*

$–$$ ✗▣ **Yosemite Lodge.** This lodge near Yosemite Falls, which dates from 1915, once housed the U.S. Army cavalry. Today it looks like a 1950s motel-resort complex, with several brown-and-white buildings that blend in with the landscape. Rooms have two double beds, and larger rooms also have dressing areas and balconies. A few have views of the falls. Of the lodge's eating places, the Mountain Room Restaurant ($$–$$$) is the most formal. The cafeteria-style Food Court (¢–$) serves three meals a day and offers salads, soups, sandwiches, pastas, and roasted meats. ⊠ *Off Northside Dr., 95389* ⌂ *Yosemite Reservations, 5410 E. Home Ave., Fresno 93727* ☎ *559/252–4848* 🗄 *559/456–0542* ⊕ *www.yosemitepark.com* ⌫ *239 rooms* ⌂ *Restaurant, cafeteria, fans,* *in-room data ports, Wi-Fi (fee), pool, bicycles, bar, no-smoking rooms; no a/c ☰ AE, D, DC, MC, V.*

¢–$ 🏠 **Curry Village.** Opened in 1899 as a place where travelers could enjoy the beauty of Yosemite for a modest price, Curry Village has plain accommodations: standard motel rooms, cabins, and tent cabins, which have rough wood frames, canvas walls, and roofs. The latter are a step up from camping, with linens, blankets, and maid service provided. Some have heat. Most of the cabins share shower and toilet facilities. ⊠ *South side of Southside Dr., 95389* ⓓ *Yosemite Reservations, 5410 E. Home Ave., Fresno 93727* ☎ *209/372–8333 front desk, 559/252–4848 reservations* 🖷 *559/456–0542* ⊕ *www.yosemitepark.com* ⇆ *19 rooms; 182 cabins, 102 with bath; 427 tent cabins* ♿ *Cafeteria, pizzeria, pool, bicycles, ice-skating, no-smoking rooms; no a/c, no room phones, no room TVs ☰ AE, D, DC, MC, V.*

¢ 🏠 **Housekeeping Camp.** Set along the Merced River, these three-sided concrete units with canvas roofs may look a bit rustic, but they're good for travelers with RVs or those without a tent who want to camp. You can cook here on gas stoves rented from the front desk, or you can use the fire pits. Toilets and showers are in a central building, and there is a camp store for provisions. ⊠ *North side of Southside Dr., near Curry Village* ⓓ *Yosemite Reservations, 5410 E. Home Ave., Fresno 93727* ☎ *209/ 372–8338, 559/252–4848 reservations* 🖷 *559/456–0542* ⊕ *www. yosemitepark.com* ⇆ *226 units* ♿ *Picnic area, beach, laundry facilities; no a/c, no room phones, no room TVs ☰ AE, D, DC, MC, V* ⊗ *Closed early Oct.–late Apr.*

△ **Camp 4.** Formerly known as Sunnyside Walk-In, this is the only valley campground available on a first-come, first-served basis and the only one west of Yosemite Lodge. Open year-round, it is a favorite for rock climbers and solo campers, so it fills quickly and is typically sold out by 9 AM every day from spring through fall. ⊠ *Base of Yosemite Falls Trail, near Yosemite Lodge* ☎ *209/372–0265* ⊕ *www.nps.gov/yose* 🖷 *209/372– 0371* 🖂 *$5* ⇆ *35 sites* ♿ *Flush toilets, drinking water, showers, bear boxes, fire grates, picnic tables, public telephone, ranger station.*

△ **Lower Pines.** This moderate-size campground sits directly along the Merced River. It's a short walk to the trailheads for the Mirror Lake and Mist trails. Expect small sites and lots of people. ♿ *Flush toilets, drinking water, bear boxes, fire grates, picnic tables, public telephone, ranger station, swimming (river)* ⇆ *60 sites (tent or RV)* ⊠ *At east end of valley* ☎ *800/436–7275 or 209/372–0265* 🖷 *209/372–0371* ⊕ *reservations.nps.gov* 🖂 *$18* ♿ *Reservations essential ☰ AE, D, MC, V* ⊗ *Apr.–Oct.*

△ **Tuolumne Meadows.** In a wooded area at 8,600 feet, just south of its namesake meadow, this campground is one of the most spectacular and sought-after campgrounds in Yosemite. Hot showers can be used at the Tuolumne Meadows Lodge, though only at certain strictly regulated times. Half the sites are first-come, first-served, so arrive early or make reservations. The campground is open July–September. ⊠ *Hwy. 120, 46 mi east of Big Oak Flat entrance station* ☎ *209/372–0265 or 800/436–7275* 🖷 *209/372–0371* ⊕ *http://reservations.nps.gov* 🖂 *$18* ⇆ *314 sites (tent or RV)* ♿ *Flush toilets, dump station, drinking water, bear boxes, fire grates, picnic tables, public telephone, general store, ranger station.*

⚠️ **Upper Pines.** This is the valley's largest campground and is closest to the trailheads. Expect large crowds in the summer—and little privacy. ⛺ *Flush toilets, dump station, drinking water, showers, bear boxes, fire grates, picnic tables, public telephone, ranger station, swimming (river)* 🏕 *238 sites (tent or RV)* ⊠ *At east end of valley* ☎ *800/436–7275* ⊕ *reservations.nps.gov* 🍴 *$18* 🏕 *Reservations essential* ▭ *AE, D, MC, V* ☉ *Year-round.*

Sports & the Outdoors

BICYCLING You can explore the 12 mi of dedicated bicycle paths in Yosemite Valley or, if you don't mind traffic, ride the park's 196 mi of paved roads. **Yosemite Lodge** (☎ 209/372–1208) rents bicycles all year for $5.50 an hour or $21 per day. Rental bikes are available at **Curry Village** (☎ 209/372–8319) from April through October. Baby jogger strollers and bikes with child trailers are also available.

HIKING Yosemite's 840 mi of hiking trails range from short strolls to rugged multiday treks. The park's visitor centers have trail maps and information, and rangers will recommend easy trails to get you acclimated to the altitude. The staff at the **Wilderness Center** (⊠ Yosemite Village, near Ansel Adams Gallery ✉ Yosemite Wilderness Reservations, Box 545, Yosemite 95389 ☎ 209/372–0740 ⊕ www.nps.gov/yose) provides free wilderness permits, which are required for overnight camping (reservations are available for $5 and are highly recommended for popular trailheads from May through September and on weekends). They also provide maps and advice to hikers heading into the backcountry.

Yosemite Mountaineering School (☎ 209/372–8344 ⊕ www.yosemitepark. com), at the Curry Village Mountain Shop and other satellite locations, has guided half- and full-day treks, conducts rock-climbing and backpacking classes, and can design customized hikes for you.

HORSEBACK **Tuolumne Meadows Stables** (☎ 209/372–8427 ⊕ www.yosemitepark.com) RIDING runs two-, four-, and eight-hour trips, costing $51–$94, and High Sierra four- to six-day camping treks on mules beginning at $617. You can tour the valley and the start of the high country on two-hour, four-hour, and all-day rides at **Yosemite Valley Stables** (⊠ Near Curry Village ☎ 209/372–8348 ⊕ www.yosemitepark.com). You must reserve in advance.

ICE-SKATING The outdoor **ice-skating rink** (⊠ South side of Southside Dr., Curry Village ☎ 209/372–8319) is open from Thanksgiving through April, afternoons and evenings, with morning sessions on the weekends. Admission is $9.75, including skate rental.

SKIING California's first ski resort, **Badger Pass Ski Area** has nine downhill runs, 90 mi of groomed cross-country trails, and two excellent ski schools. Free shuttle buses from Yosemite Valley operate in ski season (December–early April, weather permitting). Lift tickets are $35, downhill equipment rents for $24, and snowboard rental is $35. The gentle slopes of Badger Pass make **Yosemite Ski School** (☎ 209/372–8430) an ideal spot for children and beginners to learn downhill skiing or snowboarding. The highlight of Yosemite's cross-country skiing center is a 21-mi loop from Badger Pass to Glacier Point. You can rent cross-country skis for $17 per day at the **Cross-Country Ski School** (☎ 209/372–

8444), which also rents snowshoes ($15 per day), telemarking equipment ($21.50), and skate-skis ($19.50). ⊠ *Badger Pass Rd., off Glacier Point Rd., 18 mi from Yosemite Valley* ☎ *209/372–8430* ⚲ *10 trails on 85 acres, rated 35% beginner, 50% intermediate, 15% advanced. Longest run ³/₁₀ mi, base 7,200′, summit, 8,000′. Lifts: 5.*

Yosemite Mountaineering School (⊠ Badger Pass Ski Area ☎ 209/372–8344 ⊕ www.yosemitepark.com) conducts snowshoeing, cross-country skiing, telemarking, and skate-skiing classes.

Wawona

㉔ *25 mi south of Yosemite Valley and 16 mi north of Fish Camp on Hwy. 41.*

The historic buildings in **Pioneer Yosemite History Center** were moved to Wawona from their original sites in the park. You can take a self-guided tour around their exteriors at any time, day or night. Wednesday through Sunday (hours sometimes vary; call ahead) in summer, costumed docents re-create 19th-century Yosemite life in a blacksmith's shop, a jail, and other buildings. At the nearby information center, you can ask about schedules of ranger-led walks and horse-drawn stage rides (alternatively, check *Yosemite Today*). ⊠ *Hwy. 41* ☎ *209/375–9531 or 209/ 379–2646* ⊠ *Free* ☉ *Grounds daily 24 hrs. Buildings mid-June–early Sept., Wed. 2–5, Thurs.–Sun. 10–1 and 2–5. Information center late May–early Sept., daily 8:30–4:30.*

㉕ **Mariposa Grove of Big Trees,** Yosemite's largest grove of giant sequoias, can be visited on foot—trails all lead uphill—or, in summer, on one-hour tram rides (reservations essential). The Grizzly Giant, the oldest tree here, is estimated to be 2,700 years old. In summer, a free shuttle connects Wawona to the Mariposa Grove between 9 and 6 (the last shuttle leaves Wawona at 4:30, the grove at 6). If the road to the grove is closed, which happens when Yosemite is crowded (or when there's been heavy snow), park in Wawona and take the free shuttle, which makes pickups near the gas station. You can also walk, snowshoe, or ski in, a worthwhile effort when the woods fall silent under a mantle of white. ⊠ *Off Hwy. 41, 2 mi north of South Entrance* ☎ *209/375–1621 or 209/375–6551* ⊠ *Free; tram tour $11* ☉ *Tram May–Oct., daily 9–5; shuttle late May–early Sept., daily 9–6.*

Where to Stay & Eat

$–$$ ✕▥ **Wawona Hotel and Dining Room.** This 1879 National Historic Landmark sits at Yosemite's southern end, near the Mariposa Grove of Big Trees. It's an old-fashioned New England–style estate, with whitewashed buildings, wraparound verandas, and pleasant, no-frills rooms decorated with period pieces (many share a bath; inquire when you book). In the romantic, candlelit dining room ($$–$$$), the smoky corn-trout soup hits the spot on cold winter nights. (The dining room is closed January–March, except holidays; call for hours.) Afterward, you can visit the cozy Victorian parlor, which has a fireplace, board games, and a pianist who plays ragtime most evenings. ⊠ *Hwy. 41* ☞ *Yosemite Reser-*

7

vations, 5410 E. Home Ave., Fresno 93727 ☎ 559/252–4848 lodging
reservations, 209/375–1425 dining reservations 🖶 559/456–0542
⊕ www.yosemitepark.com ☜ 104 rooms, 52 with bath ♨ Restaurant,
9-hole golf course, putting green, tennis court, pool, horseback riding,
bar; no a/c, no room phones, no room TVs, no smoking ▤ AE, D, DC,
MC, V ⊗ Closed Jan. and Feb.

🏕 **Wawona.** Near the Mariposa Grove, just downstream from a popular fishing spot, this year-round campground (reservations essential
May–September) has larger, less closely packed sites than campgrounds
in the valley, plus they're right by the river. The downside is that it's an
hour's drive to the valley's major attractions. ✉ Hwy. 41, 1 mi north
of Wawona ☎ 209/372–0265 or 800/436–7275 🖶 209/372–0371
⊕ http://reservations.nps.gov ✉ $18 ☜ 93 sites (tent or RV) ♨ Flush
toilets, dump station, drinking water, bear boxes, fire grates, picnic tables, ranger station, swimming (river).

Sports & the Outdoors
Wawona Stables (☎ 209/375–6502) has several rides, starting at $51 reser-
vations essential.

MAMMOTH AREA

A jewel in the vast eastern Sierra Nevada, the Mammoth Lakes area lies
just east of the Sierra crest, on the back side of Yosemite and the Ansel
Adams Wilderness. It's a place of rugged beauty, where giant sawtooth
mountains drop into the vast deserts of the Great Basin. In winter
11,053-foot-high Mammoth Mountain provides the finest skiing and
snowboarding south of Lake Tahoe—sometimes as late as June or even
July. Once the snows melt, Mammoth transforms itself into a warm-
weather playground, with fishing, mountain biking, golfing, hiking,
and horseback riding. Nine deep-blue lakes are spread through the
Mammoth Lakes Basin, and another 100 lakes dot the surrounding countryside. Crater-pocked Mammoth Mountain hasn't had a major eruption for 50,000 years, but the region is alive with hot springs, mud pots,
fumaroles, and steam vents.

Mammoth Lakes

㉖ 30 mi south of eastern edge of Yosemite National Park on U.S. 395.

Much of the architecture in the ordinary hub town of Mammoth Lakes
(elevation 7,800 feet) is of the faux-alpine variety. You'll find mostly basic
dining and lodging options here—although international real-estate developers have recently joined forces with Mammoth Mountain Ski Area
and are working hard to transform the once sleepy town into a chic ski
destination. Highway 203 heads west from U.S. 395, becoming Main Street
as it passes through the town of Mammoth Lakes, and later Minaret Road
(which makes a right turn) as it continues west to the Mammoth Mountain ski area and Devils Postpile National Monument.

The lakes of the **Mammoth Lakes Basin,** reached by Lake Mary Road off
Highway 203 southwest of town, are popular for fishing and boating

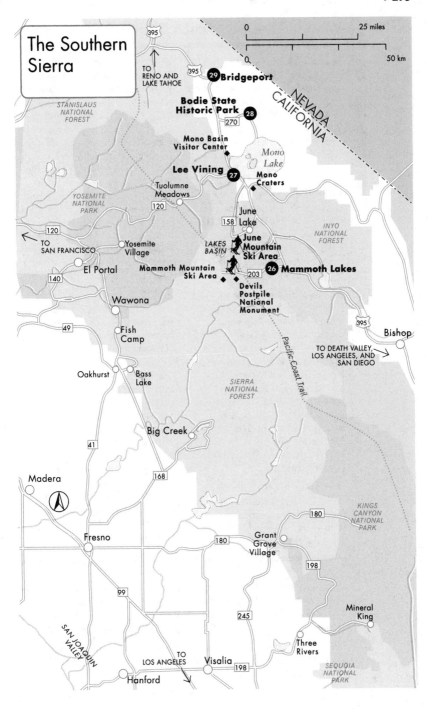

The Southern Sierra

0   25 miles

0   50 km

NEVADA

CALIFORNIA

395

TO RENO AND LAKE TAHOE

395

29 **Bridgeport**

STANISLAUS NATIONAL FOREST

Bodie State Historic Park **28**

270

Mono Basin Visitor Center

Mono Lake

Lee Vining **27**

Mono Craters

Tuolumne Meadows

YOSEMITE NATIONAL PARK

120

June Lake

158

INYO NATIONAL FOREST

120

TO SAN FRANCISCO

Yosemite Village

LAKES BASIN

June Mountain Ski Area

El Portal

Mammoth Mountain Ski Area

203 **26** **Mammoth Lakes**

140

Devils Postpile National Monument

Wawona

49

Fish Camp

Pacific Coast Trail

395

Bishop

TO DEATH VALLEY, LOS ANGELES, AND SAN DIEGO

Oakhurst

Bass Lake

SIERRA NATIONAL FOREST

41

Big Creek

Madera

168

Fresno

99

180

Grant Grove Village

KINGS CANYON NATIONAL PARK

180

198

245

Mineral King

SAN JOAQUIN VALLEY

TO LOS ANGELES

Visalia **198**

Three Rivers

SEQUOIA NATIONAL FOREST

Hanford

Why Is There So Much Snow?

THE SIERRA NEVADA MOUNTAINS receive some of the deepest snow anywhere in North America. In winter, houses literally get buried, and home owners have to build tunnels to their front doors (though many install enclosed wooden walkways). In the high country, it's not uncommon for a single big storm to bring 10 feet of snow and for 30 feet of snow to accumulate at the height of the season. In the enormous bowls of Mammoth Mountain, you might ski past a tiny pine that looks like a miniature Christmas tree—until you remember that there are 30 more feet of tree under the snow.

To understand the weather, you have to understand the terrain. The Sierra Nevada are marked by a gentle western rise from sea level to the Sierra crest, which tops out at a whopping 14,494 feet in Sequoia National Park's Mt. Whitney, the highest point in the continental United States. On the eastern side of the crest, at the escarpment, the mountains drop sharply—as much as 5,000 feet—giving way to the Great Basin and the high-mountain deserts of Nevada and Utah.

When winter storms blow in off the Pacific, carrying vast stores of water with them, they race across the relatively flat, 100-mi-wide Central Valley. As they ascend the wall of

mountains, though, the decrease in temperature and the increase in pressure on the clouds force them to release their stores of water. Between October and April, that means snow—lots of it. Storms can get hung up on the peaks for days, dumping foot after foot of precipitation. By the time they finally cross over the range and into the Great Basin, there isn't much moisture left for the lower elevations on the eastern side. This is why, if you cross the Sierra eastward on your way to U.S. 395, you'll notice that brightly colored wildflowers and forest-green trees give way to pale-green sagebrush and brown sand as you drop out of the mountains.

The coastal cities and farmlands of the rest of the state depend heavily on the water from the Sierra snowpack. Most of the spring and summer runoff from the melting snows is caught in reservoirs in the foothills and routed to farmlands and cities throughout the state via a complex system of levees and aqueducts, which you'll no doubt see in the foothills and Central Valley, to the west of the range. But much of the water remains in the mountains, forming lakes, most notably giant Lake Tahoe to the north and Mammoth Lakes to the south. The lakes are an essential part of the ecosystem, providing water for birds, fish, and plant life.

in summer. First comes Twin Lakes, at the far end of which is Twin Falls, where water cascades 300 feet over a shelf of volcanic rock. Also popular are Lake Mary, the largest lake in the basin; Lake Mamie; and Lake George. Horseshoe Lake is the only lake in which you can swim.

The glacial-carved sawtooth spires of the Minarets, the remains of an ancient lava flow, are best viewed from the **Minaret Vista,** off Highway 203 west of Mammoth Lakes.

★ ☾ Even if you don't ski, ride the **Panorama Gondola** to see Mammoth Mountain, the aptly named dormant volcano that gives Mammoth Lakes its name. Gondolas serve skiers in winter and mountain bikers and sightseers in summer. The high-speed, eight-passenger gondolas whisk you from the chalet to the summit, where you can read about the area's volcanic history and take in top-of-the-world views. Remember, though, that the air is thin at the 11,053-foot summit; carry water, and don't overexert yourself. The boarding area is at the Main Lodge. ⊠ *Off Hwy. 203* ☎ *760/934–2571 Ext. 2400 information, Ext. 3850 gondola station* 🚠 *$16 in summer* ☉ *July 4–Oct., daily 9–4:30; Nov.–July 3, daily 8:30–4.*

The overwhelming popularity of Mammoth Mountain has generated a real-estate boom, and a huge new complex of shops, restaurants, and luxury accommodations, called the **Village at Mammoth,** has become the town's tourist center.

OFF THE BEATEN PATH

DEVILS POSTPILE NATIONAL MONUMENT – An easy 10-minute walk from the ranger station takes you to a geologic formation of smooth, vertical basalt columns sculpted by volcanic and glacial forces. A short but steep trail winds to the top of the 60-foot-high rocky cliff, where you'll find a bird's-eye view of the columns. A 2-mi hike past the Postpile leads to the monument's second scenic wonder, **Rainbow Falls,** where a branch of the San Joaquin River plunges more than 100 feet over a lava ledge. When the water hits the pool below, sunlight turns the resulting mist into a spray of color. Walk down a bit from the top of the falls for the best view.

In summer, Devils Postpile National Monument is accessible only via a shuttle bus that begins operation as soon as the road is cleared of snow—usually in June, but sometimes as late as July. The shuttle departs from the Adventure Center at the Mammoth Mountain Main Lodge gondola building approximately every 20–30 minutes, generally from 7 AM to 7 PM, with the last ride out of the valley at 7:30. The shuttle stops running at the end of September, but you can drive to the falls until the snows come again, usually around the beginning of November. Scenic picnic spots dot the bank of the San Joaquin River. ⊠ *Hwy. 203, 13 mi west of Mammoth Lakes* ☎ *760/934–2289, 760/924–5502 shuttle bus information* ⊕ *www.nps.gov/depo* 🚌 *$7* ☉ *Shuttle mid-June–mid-Sept., daily; mid-late Sept., Fri.–Sun., weather permitting.*

HOT CREEK GEOLOGIC SITE/HOT CREEK FISH HATCHERY – Forged by an ancient volcanic eruption, the Hot Creek Geologic Site is a landscape of boiling hot springs, fumaroles, and occasional geysers about 10 mi southeast of the town of Mammoth Lakes. You can soak (at your own risk) in hot springs or walk along boardwalks through the canyon to view the steaming volcanic features. Fly-fishing for trout is popular upstream from the springs. En route to the geologic site is the Hot Creek Fish Hatchery, the breeding ponds for many of the fish (typically 3–5 million annually) with which the state stocks eastern Sierra lakes and rivers. But in recent years, budget cuts have drastically reduced these numbers, and the hatchery is at minimal output; call ahead. ✉ *Hot Creek Hatchery Rd. east of U.S. 395* ☎ *760/924–5500 for geologic site, 760/ 934–2664 for hatchery* ⌦ *Free* ☉ *Site daily sunrise–sunset; hatchery June–Oct., daily 8–4, depending on snowfall.*

Where to Stay & Eat

★ **$$–$$$$** ✕ **Restaurant at Convict Lake.** Tucked in a grove of aspens, 10 minutes south of town, one of the top restaurants in the Mammoth area offers wonderful service in a rustic dining room. You can sit beside the fire under the knotty-pine cathedral ceiling and sup on such dishes as sautéed venison medallions, pan-seared local trout, and beef Wellington. This is a haven for wine aficionados, with an extensive selection of reasonably priced European and California varietals. ✉ *2 mi off U.S. 395, 4 mi south of Mammoth Lakes* ☎ *760/934–3803* ⌐ *Reservations essential* ▤ *AE, D, MC, V* ☉ *No lunch early Sept.–July 4.*

★ **$$–$$$** ✕ **Nevados.** The top choice of many locals, Nevados has a contemporary California menu that draws inspiration from Europe and Asia. Choose from imaginative preparations of seafood, duck, veal, beef, and game or the excellent three-course prix-fixe menu. The atmosphere here is convivial and welcoming—if a bit loud. ✉ *Main St. and Minaret Rd.* ☎ *760/934–4466* ⌐ *Reservations essential* ▤ *AE, MC, V* ☉ *No lunch.*

$$ ✕ **Alpenrose.** Hearty portions of classic Swiss-inspired dishes such as Wiener schnitzel, rib-eye steak au poivre, and cheese fondue are served at cozy booths beneath alpine murals. There's also a good selection of reasonably priced wines. If you're on a budget, come before 6:30 PM for the early-bird special. ✉ *343 Old Mammoth Rd.* ☎ *760/934–3077* ⌐ *Reservations essential* ▤ *AE, D, MC, V* ☉ *No lunch Mon.–Sat. in winter.*

¢–$$ ✕ **Berger's.** Don't even think about coming to this bustling restaurant unless you're hungry. Berger's is known, appropriately enough, for its burgers and sandwiches, and everything comes in mountainous portions. At lunch try the sourdough patty melt, at dinner the beef ribs. The seasoned french fries are delicious. ✉ *Minaret Rd. near Canyon Blvd.* ☎ *760/934– 6622* ▤ *MC, V* ☉ *Closed 2 wks in May and 4–6 wks in Oct.–Nov.*

¢–$ ✕ **Giovanni's Pizza.** Children love this casual restaurant. It serves standard Italian dinners, but stick to the delicious pizza. Don't come here expecting quiet conversation, though—it's a high-decibel joint. ✉ *Minaret Village Mall, Old Mammoth Rd. and Meridian St.* ☎ *760/934–7563* ▤ *AE, MC, V* ☉ *No lunch Sun.*

¢ ✕ **Schat's Bakery & Café Vermeer.** Part restaurant, part bakery, this family-run business serves everything from huge, perfectly cooked omelets to monster pancakes and terrific French toast. The pastries and breads are fresh and delicious. You can also get good sandwiches to go. Expect a wait for a table at peak times, or pick up something to go instead. ✉ *3305 Main St.* ☎ *760/934–6055 or 760/934–4203* ⌐ *Reservations not accepted* ▤ *MC, V* ☉ *No dinner.*

$$$$ ✕▥ **Double Eagle Resort and Spa.** You won't find a better spa retreat in the Eastern Sierra than the Double Eagle. Dwarfed by towering, craggy peaks, the resort is in a spectacularly beautiful spot along a creek, near June Lake, 20 minutes north of Mammoth Lakes. Accommodations are in comfortable knotty-pine two-bedroom cabins that sleep up to six, or in cabin suites with efficiency kitchens; all come fully equipped with modern amenities. If you don't want to cook (the nearest grocery is in Mammoth), the Eagles Landing Restaurant ($–$$$) serves three meals a day. Spa services and treatments are available for nonguests by reservation. ✉ *5587 Hwy. 158, Box 736, June Lake 93529* ☎ *760/648–7004 or 877/648–7004* 🖷 *760/648–7014* ⊕ *www.doubleeagleresort.com* ➯ *16 2-bedroom cabins, 16 cabin suites, 1 3-bedroom cabin* ♿ *Restaurant, café, BBQs, some kitchens, microwaves, refrigerators, cable TV, in-room VCRs, in-room data ports, indoor pool, fitness classes, health club, hair salon, 3 hot tubs, spa, steam room, boating (nearby), fishing, hiking, horseback riding (nearby), volleyball, cross-country skiing (nearby), downhill skiing (nearby), ice-skating, bar, shop, some pets allowed (fee); no a/c, no smoking* ☐ *AE, D, MC, V.*

¢–$$$$
Fodor's Choice
★

✕⛺ **Tamarack Lodge Resort.** Tucked away on the edge of the John Muir Wilderness Area, where cross-country ski trails loop through the woods, this original 1924 lodge has rustic and charming accommodations. Rooms in the main lodge can have fairly spartan furnishings, and some share a bathroom. If you prefer more privacy, opt for one of the cabins, which range from simple to luxurious; many have fireplaces, kitchens, or wood-burning stoves. In warm months, fishing, canoeing, hiking, and mountain biking are right outside. The small and romantic Lakefront Restaurant ($$–$$$) serves outstanding contemporary French-inspired dinners, with an emphasis on game. Reservations are essential. ✉ *Lake Mary Rd. off Hwy. 203* ☍ *Box 69, 93546* ☎ *760/934–2442 or 800/ 626–6684* 🖷 *760/934–2281* ⊕ *www.tamaracklodge.com* ➯ *11 rooms, 25 cabins* ♿ *Restaurant, fans, some kitchens, some kitchenettes, lake, boating, fishing, hiking, cross-country skiing, ski shop, lobby lounge; no a/c, no room TVs, no smoking* ☐ *AE, MC, V.*

$$$$
⛺ **Village at Mammoth.** This cluster of four-story timber-and-stone buildings is in the middle of the newly developed town center. The units each come with gas fireplaces, kitchens or kitchenettes, daily maid service, high-speed Internet access, DVD player, slate-tile bathroom floors, and comfortable furnishings. The buildings are connected by a ground-floor pedestrian mall, where you'll find shops, restaurants, and bars. Best of all, a gondola (winter only) whisks you right from the Village to the mountain. ✉ *100 Canyon Blvd.* ☍ *Box 3459, 93546* ☎ *760 934–1982, 800/ 626–6684* 🖷 *760/934–1494* ⊕ *www.mammothmountain.com* ➯ *277 units* ♿ *Some kitchens, some kitchenettes, cable TV, in-room broadband (fee), in-room data ports, gym, pool, 3 outdoor hot tubs, downhill skiing, ski storage, laundry facilities, free parking; no a/c, no smoking* ☐ *AE, MC, V.*

$$$–$$$$
⛺ **Juniper Springs Lodge.** One of the area's top choices for slope-side luxury, this lodging contains condominium-style units with full kitchens and ski-in, ski-out access to the mountain. Amenities include stone fireplaces, balconies, and stereos with CD players. The heated outdoor pool—surrounded by a heated deck—is open year-round. ✉ *4000 Meridian Blvd.* ☍ *Box 2129, 93546* ☎ *760/924–1102 or 800/626–6684* 🖷 *760/ 924–8152* ⊕ *www.mammothmountain.com* ➯ *10 studios, 99 1-bedrooms, 92 2-bedrooms, 5 3-bedrooms* ♿ *Restaurant, café, room serv-*

7

ice, fans, kitchens, microwaves, refrigerators, cable TV, in-room VCRs, in-room broadband, in-room data ports, 18-hole golf course, pool, exercise equipment, 3 outdoor hot tubs, mountain bikes, downhill skiing, ski shop, ski storage, bar, laundry service, concierge, meeting rooms; no a/c, no smoking ☐ *AE, MC, V.*

$$–$$$$ ▦ **Mammoth Mountain Inn.** If you want to be within walking distance of the Mammoth Mountain Main Lodge, this is the place. In winter, check your skis with the concierge, pick them up in the morning, and head directly to the lifts. In summer the proximity to the gondola means you can hike and mountain bike to your heart's delight. The accommodations, which vary in size, include standard hotel rooms and condo units; the latter have kitchenettes, and many have lofts. The inn has licensed on-site child care in winter. ⊠ *Minaret Rd., 4 mi west of Mammoth Lakes* ☐ *Box 353, 93546* ☎ *760/934–2581 or 800/626–6684* ☐ *760/934–0701* ⊕ *www.mammothmountain.com* ⌨ *124 rooms, 91 condos* ⚥ *2 restaurants, fans, some kitchenettes, some microwaves, some refrigerators, cable TV, in-room broadband (fee), some in-room data ports, Wi-Fi, hot tub, hiking, downhill skiing, ski storage, bar, video game room, shop, babysitting, playground, laundry facilities, meeting room; no a/c, no smoking* ☐ *AE, MC, V.*

$$–$$$ ▦ **Holiday Inn Mammoth Lakes.** In a town known for vintage-1970s condo units, this stands out as being the only modern, midprice hotel. Rooms and public areas are sparklingly clean, and extra amenities include voice mail, irons, microwaves, and refrigerators. In the afternoon, cookies and coffee are served in the lobby. Families enjoy the special "kids' suites," which have bunk beds and video games. There's also a year-round indoor pool. ⊠ *3236 Main St., 93546* ☎ *760/924–1234 or 866/924–1234* ☐ *760/934–3626* ⊕ *www.holidayatmammoth.com* ⌨ *71 rooms, 3 suites* ⚥ *Cafeteria, microwaves, refrigerators, cable TV, in-room data ports, Wi-Fi (fee), indoor pool, exercise equipment, hot tub, billiards, Ping-Pong, bar, laundry facilities, meeting room; no smoking* ☐ *AE, D, DC, MC, V.*

$–$$$ ▦ **Convict Lake Resort.** The lake on which this resort stands (about 10 minutes south of Mammoth Lakes) was named for an 1871 gunfight between local vigilantes and six escaped prisoners. Rustic cabins come with fully equipped kitchens (including coffeemakers and premium coffee). ⊠ *2 mi off U.S. 395* ☐ *Box 204, 93546* ☎ *760/934–3800 or 800/992–2260* ⊕ *www.convictlakeresort.com* ⌨ *29 cabins* ⚥ *Restaurant, some in-room hot tubs, kitchens, some microwaves, cable TV, lake, boating, fishing, bicycles, horseback riding, shop, Internet room, some pets allowed (fee); no a/c, no room phones* ☐ *AE, D, MC, V.*

¢–$ ▦ **Cinnamon Bear Inn Bed and Breakfast.** Though it's in a nothing-special business district off Main Street and its exterior looks more like a motel than an inn, this bed-and-breakfast has very comfortable rooms decorated in New England–colonial style. Some have four-poster beds. Rates include a delicious homemade breakfast and wine and cheese in the afternoon. ⊠ *6209 Minaret Rd.* ☐ *Box 3338, 93546* ☎ *760/934–2873 or 800/845–2873* ☐ *760/934–2873* ⊕ *www.cinnamonbearinn.com* ⌨ *22 rooms* ⚥ *Some kitchenettes, cable TV, some in-room VCRs, outdoor hot tub, ski storage, lounge; no a/c, no smoking* ☐ *AE, D, DC, MC, V* ⏣ *BP.*

⚠️ **Convict Lake Campground.** This campground, near the Convict Lake Resort, 35 mi north of Bishop, is run by the U.S. Forest Service. It's open May to October, and sites are available on a first-come, first-served basis and are extremely popular. ✉️ *2 mi off U.S. 395* ☎️ *760/924–5500* ⊕ *www.fs.fed.us/r5/inyo* 🛏️ *$15* 🏕️ *88 campsites* ⚿ *Flush toilets, dump station, drinking water, showers, fire pits, general store.*

⚠️ **Lake Mary Campground.** There are few sites as beautiful as this lakeside campground at 8,900 feet, open June to September. Accordingly, it is extremely popular. If it's full, try the adjacent Coldwater campground. You can catch trout in Lake Mary, the biggest lake in the region. A general store is nearby. ✉️ *Lake Mary Loop Dr. off Hwy. 203* ☎️ *760/924–5500* 🖨️ *760/924–5537* ⊕ *www.fs.fed.us/r5/inyo* 🛏️ *$14* 🏕️ *48 sites (tent or RV)* ⚿ *Flush toilets, drinking water, fire grates, picnic tables.*

Nightlife & the Arts

The summertime **Mammoth Lakes Jazz Jubilee** (☎️ 760/934–2478 or 800/367–6572 ⊕ www.mammothjazz.org) is hosted by the local Temple of Folly Jazz Band and takes place in 10 venues, most with dance floors. For one long weekend every summer, Mammoth Lakes holds **Bluesapalooza and Festival of Beers** (☎️ 760/934–0606 or 800/367–6572 ⊕ www.mammothconcert.com), a blues-and-beer festival—with emphasis on the beer tasting. Concerts occur throughout the year on Mammoth Mountain; contact **Mammoth Mountain Music** (☎️ 760/934–0606 ⊕ www.mammothconcert.com) for listings.

The Village at Mammoth is the site of events and has several rockin' bars and clubs. Sip Mai Tais at the tiki bar at **Lakanuki Lounge** (✉️ 6201 Minaret Rd. ☎️ 760/934–7447); Monday is karaoke and sushi night. On Saturday evenings, you can sing karaoke at **Shogun** (✉️ 452 Old Mammoth Rd. ☎️ 760/934–3970), Mammoth's only Japanese restaurant. The bar at **Whiskey Creek** (✉️ Main St. and Minaret Rd. ☎️ 760/934–2555) plays host to musicians on weekends winter and summer, and on Wednesday nights there's a DJ.

Sports & the Outdoors

For information on winter conditions around Mammoth, call the **Snow Report** (☎️ 760/934–7669 or 888/766–9778). The **U.S. Forest Service ranger station** (☎️ 760/924–5500) can provide general information year-round.

BICYCLING **Mammoth Mountain Bike Park** (✉️ Mammoth Mountain Ski Area ☎️ 760/934–0706 ⊕ www.mammothmountain.com) opens when the snow melts, usually by July, with 70-plus mi of single-track trails—from mellow to super-challenging. Chairlifts and shuttles provide trail access, and rentals are available.

DOGSLEDDING **Mammoth Dog Teams** (✉️ Kennels Hwy. 203, 4 mi east of Mammoth Lakes ☎️ 760/934–6270) operates rides through the forest on sleds pulled by teams of 10 dogs. Options range from 25-minute rides to overnight excursions; book three to seven days in advance. In summer you can tour the kennels (at 10, 1, and 3) and learn about the dogs.

FISHING Crowley Lake is the top trout-fishing spot in the area; Convict Lake, June Lake, and the lakes of the Mammoth Basin are other prime spots. One of the best trout rivers is the San Joaquin, near Devils Postpile. Hot

Creek, a designated Wild Trout Stream, is renowned for fly-fishing (catch and release only). The fishing season runs from the last Saturday in April until the end of October. **Kittredge Sports** (⊠ Main St. and Forest Trail ☎ 760/934–7566 ⊕ www.kittredgesports.com) rents rods and reels and conducts guided trips.

GOLF Because it's nestled right up against the forest, you might see deer and bears on the fairways at the 18-hole **Sierra Star Golf Course** (⊠ 2001 Sierra Star Pkwy. ☎ 760/924–2200 ⊕ www.mammothmountain.com). Greens fees run $75–$115.

HIKING Trails wind around the Lakes Basin and through pristine alpine scenery. Stop at the **U.S. Forest Service ranger station** (⊠ Hwy. 203 ☎ 760/924–5500 ⊕ www.fs.fed.us/r5/inyo), on your right just before the town of Mammoth Lakes, for a Mammoth area trail map and permits for backpacking in wilderness areas.

HORSEBACK RIDING Stables around Mammoth are typically open from June through September. There are several outfitters. **Mammoth Lakes Pack Outfit** (⊠ Lake Mary Rd., between Twin Lakes and Lake Mary ☎ 760/934–2434 ⊕ www.mammothpack.com) runs day and overnight horseback trips. **McGee Creek Pack Station** (☎ 760/935–4324 or 800/854–7407 ⊕ www.mcgeecreekpackstation.com) can set you up with horses and gear. Operated by the folks at McGee Creek, **Sierra Meadows Ranch** (⊠ Sherwin Creek Rd. off Old Mammoth Rd. ☎ 760/934–6161) conducts horseback and wagon rides from one hour to all day.

HOT-AIR BALLOONING The balloons of **Mammoth Balloon Adventures** (☎ 760/937–8787 ⊕ www.mammothballoonadventures.com) glide over the countryside in the morning from spring until fall, weather permitting.

SKIING **June Mountain Ski Area.** This low-key resort, 20 mi north of Mammoth Mountain and 20 minutes north of Mammoth Lakes, is a favorite of snowboarders, who have a half pipe all to themselves. Three freestyle terrain areas are for both skiers and boarders, and there's rarely a line for the lifts. If you want to avoid the crowds but must ski on a weekend, this is the place to go. The area is better protected from wind and storms than Mammoth Mountain. (If it starts to storm, you can use your Mammoth ticket at June.) A rental-and-repair shop, a ski school, and a sports shop are all on the premises. A lift ticket costs $50. ⊠ Off June Lake Loop (Hwy. 158), June Lake ☎ 760/648–7733 or 888/586–3686 ⊕ www.junemountain.com ☞ 35 trails on 500 acres, rated 35% beginner, 45% intermediate, 20% advanced. Longest run 2½ mi, base 7,510', summit 10,174'. Lifts: 7.

FodorsChoice ★ **Mammoth Mountain Ski Area.** If you ski only one mountain in California, make it Mammoth. One of the West's largest and best resorts, Mammoth has more than 3,500 acres of skiable terrain and a 3,100-foot vertical drop. Standing high above the tree line atop this dormant volcano, you can look west 150 mi across the state to the Coastal Range; to the east are the highest peaks of Nevada and the Great Basin beyond. Below, you'll find a 6½-mi-wide swath of groomed boulevards and canyons, as well as pockets of tree-skiing and a dozen vast bowls. Snowboarders are everywhere on the slopes; there are three outstanding freestyle terrain parks of varying technical difficulty, with jumps, rails, tabletops, and giant superpipes. Mammoth's season begins in November and often lingers until June or beyond. Lift tickets cost $62, lessons and rental equipment are available, and there's a children's ski and snowboard school. Mammoth runs four free shuttle bus routes around town and to the ski area, and the Village Gondola runs from the Village complex to Canyon Lodge. However, only overnight guests are allowed to park at the Village for more than a few hours, so if you want to ride the gondola to the mountain, take a shuttle bus to the Village. ⊠ *Minaret Rd. west of Mammoth Lakes* ☎ *760/934–2571, 800/626–6684, 760/934–0687 shuttle* ☞ *150 trails on 3,500 acres, rated 30% beginner, 40% intermediate, 30% advanced. Longest run 3 mi, base 7,953', summit 11,053'. Lifts: 27, including 9 high-speed and 2 gondolas.*

Trails at **Tamarack Cross Country Ski Center** (⊠ Lake Mary Rd. off Hwy. 203 ☎ 760/934–5293 or 760/934–2442 ⊕ www.tamaracklodge.com), adjacent to Tamarack Lodge, meander around several lakes. Rentals are available.

Mammoth Sporting Goods (⊠ 1 Sierra Center Mall, Old Mammoth Rd. ☎ 760/934–3239 ⊕ www.mammothsportinggoods.com) tunes and rents skis and sells equipment, clothing, and accessories.

SNOWMOBILING **Mammoth Snowmobile Adventures** (⊠ Mammoth Mountain Main Lodge ☎ 760/934–9645 or 800/626–6684 ⊕ www.mammothmountain.com) conducts guided tours along wooded trails.

EAST OF YOSEMITE NATIONAL PARK
FROM LEE VINING TO BRIDGEPORT

The area to the east of Yosemite National Park includes some ruggedly handsome, albeit desolate, terrain, most notably around Mono Lake. The area is best visited by car, as distances are great and public transportation is limited. U.S. 395 is the main north–south road on the eastern side of the Sierra Nevada, at the western edge of the Great Basin; drive with your lights on, even in daytime.

Lee Vining

㉗ *20 mi east of Tuolumne Meadows via Hwy. 120 to U.S. 395; 30 mi north of Mammoth Lakes on U.S. 395.*

Lee Vining is known mostly as the eastern gateway to Yosemite National Park (summer only) and the location of Mono Lake. Pick up supplies or stop for lunch here before or after a drive through the high country. In winter the town is all but deserted, but the general store remains open.

★ Eerie tufa towers—calcium carbonate formations that often resemble castle turrets—rise from impressive **Mono Lake.** Since the 1940s, the city of Los Angeles has diverted water from streams that feed the lake, lowering its water level and exposing the tufa. Court victories by environmentalists in the 1990s forced a reduction of the diversions, and the lake has since risen about 9 feet. From April through August, millions of migratory birds nest in and around Mono Lake. The best place to view the tufa is at the south end of the lake along the mile-long **South Tufa Trail.** To reach it, drive 5 mi south from Lee Vining on U.S. 395, then 5 mi east on Highway 120. There is a $3 fee. You can swim (or float) in the salty water at Navy Beach near the South Tufa Trail or take a kayak or canoe trip for close-up views of the tufa (check with rangers for boating restrictions during bird-nesting season). The **Scenic Area Visitor Center** (⌧ U.S. 395 ☎ 760/647–3044 ⊕ www.monolake.org) is open daily from June through September, 9–4:30, and the rest of the year Thursday through Monday 9–4. Rangers and naturalists lead walking tours of the tufa daily in summer and on weekends (sometimes on cross-country skis) in winter.

Where to Stay & Eat

★ **$–$$$** ✕ **Mono Inn at Mono Lake.** It's worth the long drive to get to this updated 1922 roadhouse. Impeccably decorated with Stickley furniture and contemporary crafts, the dining room has drop-dead postcard views of Mono Lake. During a full moon, the glow on the water is magical. The menu of delicious choices lists everything from dry-aged rib-eye steak and lamb shank to quail, salmon, and salads. ⌧ *U.S. 395, north of Lee Vining* ☎ *760/647–6581* ⌦ *Reservations essential* ▤ *AE, D, MC, V* ⊙ *Closed Nov.–Mar. No lunch.*

$–$$ ✕ **Tioga Gas Mart & Whoa Nelli Deli.** This culinary oasis near the eastern entrance to Yosemite has some of the best food in Mono County. FodorsChoice The succulent mahimahi tacos are delicious, as are the gourmet pizzas, ★ Angus roast-beef sandwiches, and herb-crusted pork tenderloin with berry glaze. Order at the counter and grab a seat inside or out. Oh, and while you're here, you might as well get fuel: it's hard to believe, but this place is in a gas station, perhaps the only one in the United States that serves cocktails. ⌧ *Hwy. 120 and U.S. 395* ☎ *760/647–1088* ▤ *AE, MC, V* ⊙ *Closed mid-Nov.–mid-Apr.*

¢–$ ✕ **Nicely's.** Plants and pictures of local attractions decorate this diner, which has been around since 1965. Try the blueberry pancakes and homemade sausages at breakfast. For lunch or dinner try the chicken-fried steak or the fiesta salad. There's also a kids' menu. ⌧ *U.S. 395 and 4th St.* ☎ *760/647–6477* ▤ *MC, V* ⊙ *Closed Tues. and Wed. in winter.*

¢–$ ▥ **Tioga Lodge.** Just 2½ mi north of Yosemite's eastern gateway, this 19th-century building has been by turns a store, a saloon, a tollbooth, and a boardinghouse. Now restored and expanded, it's a popular lodge that's close to ski areas and fishing spots. Rooms are simply furnished and a bit close to the road, but the views of Mono Lake can't be beat. Be sure to ask about summer boat tours. ⌧ *U.S. 395* ⌲ *Box 580, 93541* ☎ *760/647–6423 or 888/647–6423* ⊟ *760/647–6074* ⊕ *www.tiogalodge. com* ⇋ *13 rooms* ⌂ *Restaurant, boating; no a/c, no room phones, no room TVs, no smoking* ▤ *AE, D, MC, V* ⊙ *Closed Nov.–Mar.*

▌ EN
ROUTE
★
   Heading south from Lee Vining, U.S. 395 intersects the **June Lake Loop** (⌧ Hwy. **158 West**). This gorgeously scenic 17-mi drive follows an old glacial canyon past Grant, June, Gull, and other lakes before reconnecting with U.S. 395 on its way to Mammoth Lakes. The loop is especially colorful in fall.

Bodie State Historic Park

28 *23 mi northeast of Lee Vining via U.S. 395 to Hwy. 270 (last 3 mi are unpaved).*

Old shacks and shops, abandoned mine shafts, a Methodist church, the mining village of Rattlesnake Gulch, and the remains of a small Chinatown are among the sights at fascinating **Bodie Ghost Town.** The town, at an elevation of 8,200 feet, boomed from about 1878 to 1881, as gold prospectors, having worked the best of the western Sierra mines, headed to the high desert on the eastern slopes. Bodie was a mean place—the booze flowed freely, shootings were commonplace, and licentiousness reigned. Evidence of the town's wild past survives today at an excellent museum, and you can tour an old stamp mill (where ore was stamped into fine powder to extract gold and silver) and a ridge that contains many mine sites. No food, drink, or lodging is available in Bodie, and the nearest picnic area is a half mile away. Though the park stays open in winter, snow may close Highway 270. ⊠ *Museum: Main and Green Sts.* ☎ *760/647–6445* ⊕ *www.bodie.net* ⊠ *Park $3; museum free* ⊗ *Park: late May–early Sept., daily 8–7; early Sept.–late May, daily 8–4. Museum: late May–early Sept., daily 9–6; early Sept.–late May, hrs vary.*

FodorsChoice ★

Bridgeport

29 *25 mi north of Lee Vining and 55 mi north of Mammoth Lakes on U.S. 395.*

Historic Bridgeport lies within striking distance of a myriad of alpine lakes and streams and both forks of the Walker River, making it a prime spot for fishing. It is also the gateway to Bodie Ghost Town. In winter much of the town shuts for the season.

Where to Stay & Eat

$–$$$ ✕ **Bridgeport Inn.** Tables spread with white linen grace the dining room of this clapboard Victorian inn, built in 1877. The prime rib and fresh seafood are complemented by homemade soups, pastas, and a large wine list. Victorian-appointed guest rooms are available upstairs. ⊠ *205 Main St.* ☎ *760/932–7380* ⊟ *D, MC, V* ⊗ *Closed Dec.–Feb.*

★ **$–$$$** ✕ **Restaurant 1881.** Everything is made in-house at one of the eastern Sierra's few elegant haute-cuisine restaurants. Specialties include marinated chateaubriand with a black-truffle butter and cabernet glaze, rack of lamb with a pistachio crust, and fillet of local Alpers trout with a chive-leek sauce. ⊠ *362 Main St.* ☎ *760/932–1918* ⚑ *Reservations essential* ⊟ *AE, D, MC, V* ⊗ *Closed Nov.–Apr. No lunch.*

$–$$ ⬚ **Cain House.** This old home has been refurbished as a B&B in elegant country style. Afternoon wine-and-cheese service is offered daily, and all beds have down comforters. ⊠ *340 Main St., 93517* ☎ *760/932–7040 or 800/433–2246* 📠 *760/932–7419* ⊕ *www.cainhouse.com* ⇱ *7 rooms* ⚑ *Some refrigerators, cable TV, tennis court; no smoking* ⊟ *AE, D, MC, V* ⊗ *Closed Nov.–Apr.* ⦿ *BP.*

$ ⬚ **Silver Maple Inn.** Next to the Mono County Courthouse (1880), the Silver Maple is in central Bridgeport, on attractive wooded grounds with views of the nearby Sierra. Built in the 1930s, the motel provides fish-cleaning and -freezing facilities and barbecue pits in which to cook your catch. It's not fancy or modern, but it's clean. ⊠ *310 Main St., 93517* ☎ *760/932–7383* 🖷 *760/932–7419* ⊕ *www.silvermapleinn.com* 🖙 *20 rooms ⚥ Fans, some refrigerators, cable TV, some pets allowed, no-smoking rooms; no a/c* ▭ *AE, D, MC, V* ☉ *Closed Nov.–Mar.*

THE SOUTHERN SIERRA A TO Z

To research prices, get advice from other travelers, and book travel arrangements, visit www.fodors.com.

AIRPORTS & TRANSFERS

Fresno Yosemite International Airport (FYI) is the nearest airport to Sequoia and Kings Canyon national parks. Alaska, American, America West, Allegiance, Continental, Delta, Hawaiian, Northwest, Horizon, United Express, and several regional carriers fly here. *See* Air Travel *in* Smart Travel Tips for airline phone numbers. The closest major airport to Mammoth Lakes is in Reno. *See* the Lake Tahoe chapter for details.

🚩 **Fresno Yosemite International Airport** ⊠ 5175 E. Clinton Ave., Fresno ☎ 559/621–4500 or 559/498–4095 ⊕ www.flyfresno.org.

BUS TRAVEL

Greyhound serves Fresno, Merced, and Visalia from many California cities. VIA Adventures runs five daily buses from Merced to Yosemite Valley; buses also depart daily from Mariposa. The 2½-hour ride from Merced costs $20 round-trip, which includes admission to the park.

🚩 **Greyhound** ☎ 800/231–2222 ⊕ www.greyhound.com. **VIA Adventures** ☎ 209/384–1315 or 800/369–7275 ⊕ www.via-adventures.com.

CAMPING

In the national parks you can camp only in designated areas, but in the national forests you can pitch a tent anywhere you want, so long as there are no signs specifically prohibiting camping in that area. Always know and obey fire regulations; you can find out what they are in a specific area by checking with forest service rangers, either by telephone or at any of the ranger stations just inside park boundaries.

Except for Lodgepole and Dorst in Sequoia, all sites at the campgrounds near each of the major tourist centers in Sequoia and Kings Canyon parks are assigned on a first-come, first-served basis; on weekends in July and August they are often filled by Friday early afternoon. Lodgepole, Potwisha, and Azalea campsites stay open all year, but Lodgepole is not plowed, and camping is limited to snow-tenting or recreational vehicles in plowed parking lots. Other campgrounds in Sequoia and Kings Canyon are open from whenever the snow melts until late September or early October.

If you plan to camp in the backcountry in Sequoia or Kings Canyon national parks, your group must have a backcountry camping permit, which costs $15 for hikers or $30 for stock users (horseback riders, etc.). One permit covers a group of up to 15 people. Availability of permits depends upon trailhead quotas. Advance reservations are accepted by mail or fax beginning March 1 and must be made at least three weeks in advance. Without a reservation, you may still get a permit on a first-come, first-served basis starting at 1 PM the day before you plan to hike. Whether you reserve or not, permits must be picked up in person from the permit-issuing station nearest your trailhead. For more information on backcountry camping or travel with pack animals, call the Wilderness Permit Office.

Most of Yosemite's 14 campgrounds are in Yosemite Valley and along the Tioga Road. Glacier Point and Wawona have one each. Several campgrounds operate on a first-come, first-served basis year-round (some 400 of the park's sites remain open year-round), whereas some take reservations in high season; during summer, reservations are strongly recommended, if not required. It's sometimes possible to get a campsite on arrival by stopping at the campground reservations office in Yosemite Valley, but this is a risky strategy. Yosemite Campground Reservations handles all bookings for the reservable campgrounds within the park. During the last two weeks of each month, beginning on the 15th, you can reserve a site up to five months in advance. DNC Parks & Resorts at Yosemite handles reservations for the tent-cabins at Curry Village and for the camping shelters at Housekeeping Camp. If you want to overnight in Yosemite's backcountry, you'll need a wilderness permit. They're free, but it's best to reserve one in advance for $5. You can request a reservation between 24 weeks and two days ahead, but making a request doesn't guarantee a reservation. For more information, contact the Wilderness Permit Office.

RVs and trailers are permitted in most national park campgrounds, though space is scarce at some. The length limit is 40 feet for RVs and 35 feet for trailers, but the park service recommends that trailers be no longer than 22 feet. Disposal stations are available in the main camping areas.

The Sierra Nevada is home to thousands of bears, and if you plan on camping, you should take all necessary precautions to keep yourself—and the bears—safe. Bears that acquire a taste for human food can become very aggressive and destructive and often must eventually be destroyed by rangers. The national parks' campgrounds and some campgrounds outside the parks provide food-storage boxes that can keep bears from pilfering your edibles (portable canisters for backpackers can be rented in most park stores). It is imperative that you move all food, coolers, and items with a scent (including toiletries, toothpaste, chewing gum, and air fresheners) from your car (including the trunk) to the storage box at your campsite. If you don't, a bear may break into your car by literally peeling off the door or ripping open the trunk, or it may ransack your tent. The familiar tactic of hanging your food from high tree limbs is not an effective deterrent, as bears can easily scale trees. In the Southern Sierra, bear canisters are the only effective and proven method for preventing bears from getting human food. Whether hiking or camping, it's important to respect the landscape and wildlife around you. For detailed information about responsible outdoor recreation, visit the Web site of the Leave No Trace Center for Outdoor Ethics.

2 DNC Parks & Resorts at Yosemite ☎ 559/252-4848 ⊕ www.yosemitepark.com. **Inyo National Forest** ☎ 760/873-2400 ⛁ 760/873-2458 ⊕ www.r5.fs.fed.us/inyo. **Leave No Trace Center for Outdoor Ethics** ☎ 303/442-8222 or 800/332-4100 ⊕ www.lnt. org. **Lodgepole/Dorst campgrounds** ☎ 301/722-1257 or 800/365-2267 ⊕ http://reservations.nps.gov. **Sequoia campgrounds** ☎ 559/565-3341 ⊕ www.nps.gov/seki. **Sequoia National Forest** ☎ 559/784-1500 ⛁ 559/781-4744 ⊕ www.r5.fs.fed.us/sequoia. **Wilderness Permit Office, Sequoia–Kings Canyon** ☎ 559/565-3766 ⊕ www.nps. gov/seki. **Wilderness Permit Office, Yosemite** ☎ 209/372-0740 permit office, 209/372-0200 general inquiries ⊕ www.nps/gov/yose. **Yosemite Campground Reservations** ☎ 301/722-1257 or 800/436-7275 ⊕ reservations.nps.gov.

CAR RENTAL

The car-rental outlets closest to the Southern Sierra are at Fresno Yosemite International Airport, where the national chains have outlets. If you're traveling to Mammoth Lakes and the eastern Sierra in winter, the closest agencies are in Reno. *See* Car Rental *in* Smart Travel Tips for national rental-agency phone numbers.

CAR TRAVEL

From San Francisco, I–80 and I–580 are the fastest routes toward the central Sierra Nevada, but avoid driving these routes during weekday rush hours. Through the Central Valley, I–5 and Highway 99 are the fastest north–south routes, but the latter is narrower and has heavy farm-truck traffic. To get to Kings Canyon, plan on a six-hour drive. Two major routes, Highways 180 and 198, intersect with Highway 99 (Highway 180 is closed east of Grant Grove in winter). To get to Yosemite, plan on driving four to five hours. Enter the park either on Highway 140, which is the best route in inclement weather, or on Highway 120, which is the fastest route when the roads are clear. To get to Mammoth Lakes in summer and early fall (or whenever snows aren't blocking Tioga Road), you can travel via Highway 120 (to U.S. 395 south) through the Yosemite high country; the quickest route in winter is I–80 to U.S. 50 to Highway 207 (Kingsbury Grade) to U.S. 395 south; either route takes six to seven hours.

Keep your tank full, especially in winter. Distances between gas stations can be long, and there is no fuel available in Yosemite Valley, Sequoia, or Kings Canyon. If you're traveling from October through April, rain on the coast can mean heavy snow in the mountains. Carry tire chains, and know how to put them on (on I–80 and U.S. 50 you can pay a chain installer $20 to do it for you, but on other routes you'll have to do it yourself). Alternatively, you can rent a four-wheel-drive vehicle with snow tires. Always check road conditions before you leave. Traffic in national parks in summer can be heavy, and there are sometimes travel restrictions.

2 **California Road Conditions** ☎ 800/427-7623 ⊕ www.dot.ca.gov/hq/roadinfo. **Sequoia–Kings Canyon Road and Weather Information** ☎ 559/565-3341. **Yosemite Area Road and Weather Conditions** ☎ 209/372-0200.

EMERGENCIES

In an emergency dial 911.

2 Emergency Services **Mammoth Hospital** ✉ 85 Sierra Park Rd., Mammoth Lakes ☎ 760/934-3311 ⊕ www.mammothhospital.com. **Yosemite Medical Clinic** ✉ Ahwahnee Rd. north of Northside Dr. ☎ 209/372-4637.

LODGING

Most lodgings in the Southern Sierra are simple and basic. A number of agencies can help you find a room.

⏸ Reservation Services **DNC Parks & Resorts at Yosemite** ☎ 559/252-4848 ⊕ www. yosemitepark.com. **Kings Canyon Lodging** ☎ 559/335-5500 or 866/522-6966 ⊕ www. sequoia-kingscanyon.com. **Mammoth Lakes Visitors Bureau Lodging Referral** ☎ 760/ 934-2712 or 888/466-2666 ⊕ www.visitmammoth.com. **Mammoth Reservations** ☎ 760/934-5571 or 800/223-3032 ⊕ www.mammothreservations.com. **Sequoia Lodging** ☎ 559/253-2199 or 888/252-5757 ⊕ www.visitsequoia.com. **Three Rivers Reservation Center** ☎ 866/561-0410 or 559/561-0410 ⊕ www.rescentre.com.

SPORTS & THE OUTDOORS

The best way to see the Southern Sierra is on foot. For top-notch guided day-hiking or multiday treks into the national parks or the Ansel Adams Wilderness and surrounding areas, contact Southern Yosemite Mountain Guides, one of the Sierra's premier guide services. In addition to excellent interpretation, they provide all necessary equipment (including tents and bags), permits, guides, and food. On some trips, mules carry your gear, freeing you to walk unencumbered by a backpack. They also conduct fly-fishing, rock-climbing, and custom trips.

⏸ **Southern Yosemite Mountain Guides** ⌂ 621 Highland Ave., Santa Cruz 95060 ☎ 831/ 459-8735 or 800/231-4575 ⊕ www.symg.com

TOURS

San Francisco's California Parlor Car Tours serves Yosemite through one-day and overnight trips as well as some rail-bus combinations, though the latter are logistically inconvenient from San Francisco. DNC Parks & Resorts at Yosemite operates guided bus tours of the Yosemite Valley floor daily year-round, plus seasonal tours of Glacier Point and the Mariposa Grove of Big Trees. The company's Grand Tour ($55), offered between late May and early November, weather permitting, covers the park's highlights.

⏸ **California Parlor Car Tours** ✉ 1255 Post St., #1011, San Francisco 94109 ☎ 415/474-7500 or 800/227-4250 ⊕ www.calpartours.com. **DNC Parks & Resorts at Yosemite** ⌂ Box 578, Yosemite National Park 95389 ☎ 209/372-1240 (7 or fewer days in advance), 559/252-4848 (more than 7 days in advance) ⊕ www.yosemitepark.com.

VISITOR INFORMATION

⏸ **Bridgeport Chamber of Commerce** ⌂ Box 541, Bridgeport 93517 ☎ 760/932-7500 ⊕ www.bridgeportcalifornia.com. **DNC Parks & Resorts at Yosemite** ⌂ Box 578, Yosemite National Park 95389 ☎ 209/372-1000 ⊕ www.yosemitepark.com. **Lee Vining Chamber of Commerce** ⌂ Box 29, Lee Vining 93541 ☎ 760/647-6595 ⊕ www. monolake.org/chamber. **Mammoth Lakes Visitors Bureau** ✉ Along Hwy. 203 [Main St.], near Sawmill Cutoff Rd., Box 48, Mammoth Lakes 93546 ☎ 760/934-2712 or 888/ 466-2666 ⊕ www.visitmammoth.com. **Mono Lake** ⌂ Box 49, Lee Vining 93541 ☎ 760/ 647-3044 ⊕ www.monolake.org. **Sequoia-Kings Canyon National Park** ✉ Three Rivers, 93271 ☎ 559/565-3341 or 559/565-3134 ⊕ www.nps.gov/seki. **Yosemite National Park** ⌂ Information Office, Box 577, Yosemite National Park 95389 ☎ 209/372-0200 or 209/372-0264 ⊕ www.nps.gov/yose. **Yosemite Sierra Visitors Bureau** ✉ 41969 Hwy. 41, Box 1998, Oakhurst 93644 ☎ 559/683-4636 ⊕ www.yosemitethisyear.com.

The Gold Country

With Sacramento

WORD OF MOUTH

"The California Caverns were a fantastic experience! Do the rappel, even if you are mildly scared of heights. Very nice tour guide. But there are some tight squeezes, so they retain the right to reject you if you are too big."

—Lorraine

"The smell of the apple pies and pastries at Apple Hill is overwhelmingly good. Great crafts and fun for everyone. A country feel and very friendly. Fun even in the rain!"

—Michelle jacson

Updated by
Reed Parsell

A NEW ERA DAWNED FOR CALIFORNIA when James Marshall turned up a gold nugget in the tailrace of a sawmill he was constructing along the American River. Before January 24, 1848, Mexico and the United States were still wrestling for ownership of what would become the Golden State. With Marshall's discovery the United States tightened its grip on the region, and prospectors from all over the world came to seek their fortunes in the Mother Lode.

As gold fever seized the nation, California's population of 15,000 swelled to 265,000 within three years. The mostly young, mostly male adventurers who arrived in search of gold—the '49ers—became part of a culture that discarded many of the conventions of the eastern states. It was also a violent time. Yankee prospectors chased Mexican miners off their claims, and California's leaders initiated a plan to exterminate the local Native American population. Bounties were paid and private militias were hired to wipe out the Native Americans or sell them into slavery. California was now to be dominated by the Anglo.

The boom brought on by the gold rush lasted scarcely 20 years, but it changed California forever. It produced 546 mining towns, of which fewer than 250 remain. The hills of the Gold Country were alive, not only with prospecting and mining but also with business, the arts, gambling, and a fair share of crime. Opera houses went up alongside brothels, and the California state capitol, in Sacramento, was built with the gold dug out of the hills. A lot of important history was made in Sacramento, the center of commerce during this period. Pony Express riders ended their nearly 2,000-mi journeys in the city in the 1860s. The transcontinental railroad, completed in 1869, was conceived here.

By the 1960s the scars that mining had inflicted on the landscape had largely healed. To promote tourism, locals began restoring vintage structures, historians developed museums, and the state established parks and recreation areas to preserve the memory of this extraordinary episode in American history.

One of California's least expensive destinations, the gold-mining region of the Sierra Nevada foothills is not without its pleasures, natural and cultural. Today you can come to Nevada City, Auburn, Coloma, Sutter Creek, and Columbia not only to relive the past but also to explore art galleries and to stay at inns full of character. Spring brings wildflowers, and in fall the hills are colored by bright red berries and changing leaves. Because it offers a mix of indoor and outdoor activities, the Gold Country is a great place to take the kids.

Exploring the Gold Country

Visiting Old Sacramento's museums is a good way to immerse yourself in history, but the Gold Country's heart lies along Highway 49, which winds the 325-mi north–south length of the historic mining area. The highway, often a twisting, hilly, two-lane road, begs for a convertible with the top down.

About the Restaurants

American, Italian, and Mexican fare are common in the Gold Country, but chefs also prepare ambitious Continental, French, and California cuisine. Grass Valley's meat- and vegetable-stuffed *pasties,* introduced by 19th-century gold miners from Cornwall, are one of the region's more unusual treats.

About the Hotels

Full-service hotels, budget motels, small inns, and even a fine hostel can all be found in Sacramento. The main accommodations in the larger towns along Highway 49—among them Placerville, Nevada City, Auburn, and Mariposa—are chain motels and inns. Many Gold Country bed-and-breakfasts occupy former mansions, miners' cabins, and other historic buildings.

WHAT IT COSTS				
$$$$	**$$$**	**$$**	**$**	**¢**
RESTAURANTS over $30	$22–$30	$15–$21	$8–$14	under $8
HOTELS over $225	$170–$225	$120–$169	$70–$119	under $70

Restaurant prices are for a main course at dinner, excluding sales tax of 7%–8% (depending on location). Hotel prices are for two people in a standard double room in high season, excluding service charges and 7%–8% tax.

Timing

The Gold Country is most pleasant in spring, when the wildflowers are in bloom, and in fall. Summers are beautiful but hot: temperatures of 100°F are common. Sacramento winters tend to be cool with occasionally foggy and/or rainy days. Throughout the year Gold Country towns stage community and ethnic celebrations. In December many towns deck themselves out for Christmas. Sacramento is the site of the annual Jazz Jubilee over Memorial Day weekend and the California State Fair in August and early September. East of the town of Sutter Creek, flowers bloom on Daffodil Hill in March.

SACRAMENTO & VICINITY

The gateway to the Gold Country, the seat of state government (headed by Governor Arnold Schwarzenegger), and an agricultural hub, the city of Sacramento plays many important contemporary roles. Nearly 2 million people live in the metropolitan area. The continuing influx of newcomers seeking opportunity, sunshine, and lower housing costs than in coastal California has made it one of the nation's fastest-growing regions. The midtown area, just east of downtown, contains many of the city's best restaurants and quirkiest shops; downtown, pedestrians-only K Street Mall has a persistent panhandling problem. An infusion of upscale, popular restaurants, nightclubs, and breweries is nevertheless energizing the downtown scene. Ten miles west is the college town of Davis, which, like nearby Woodland, is beginning to feel more suburban than agricultural because many Sacramento workers are settling there.

GREAT ITINERARIES

Numbers in the text correspond to numbers in the margin and on the Sacramento and the Gold Country maps.

IF YOU HAVE 1 DAY Increasing traffic makes a drive from Sacramento to and along Highway 49 potentially long and frustrating. Instead, if you have only one day to spend in the area, stick to ☞ **Sacramento** ①–⑮. Begin at **Sutter's Fort** ⑭, and then walk down J Street or take a bus to the **Capitol** ⑩ for a free tour. Its huge park is pleasant for picnics. Next, head to Old Sacramento, perhaps detouring through the vibrant Downtown Plaza mall for a drink in its River City Brewing Co. Explore the **California State Railroad Museum** ①, and, time permitting, take a one-hour river cruise before dining at one of Old Sacramento's many good restaurants.

IF YOU HAVE 5 DAYS Start your trip in ☞ 📷 **Sacramento** ①–⑮, where you can visit the **California State**
Railroad Museum ① and **Sutter's Fort** ⑭ and take a riverboat cruise. On the second day, drive to **Placerville** ⑱ to see Hangtown's Gold Bug Park & Mine and continue to 📷 **Sutter Creek** ㉑. Day 3 starts with a visit to the Amador County Museum, in **Jackson** ㉒, after which you can head south on Highway 49 and northeast on Highway 4 for lunch in **Murphys** ㉔. Return to Highway 49 and continue south to Columbia State Historic Park, in 📷 **Columbia** ㉕. You can relive the 1800s by dining and spending the night at the City Hotel. If you've been itching to pan for gold, do that in the morning of Day 4. Drive back north on Highway 49 to **Coloma** ㉙ and Marshall Gold Discovery State Historic Park, and head to 📷 **Auburn** ㉚ to spend the night. On your last day, stop at Empire Mine State Historic Park in **Grass Valley** ㉛ and pay a visit to **Nevada City** ㉜.

Sacramento contains more than 2,000 acres of natural and developed parkland. Grand old evergreens, deciduous and fruit-bearing trees (many lawns and even parks are littered with oranges in springtime), and giant palms give it a shady, lush quality. Genteel Victorian edifices sit side by side with art deco and postmodern skyscrapers, though cheap-looking apartment buildings abound in midtown, and stuccoed suburbs are obliterating a lot of the greater metro area's rural charm.

Exploring Sacramento

Driving 87 mi northeast of San Francisco (I–80 to Highway 99 or I–5) not only brings you to the Golden State's seat of government, but also can take you back in time to the gold-rush days. Wooden sidewalks and horse-drawn carriages on cobblestone streets lend a 19th-century feel to Old Sacramento, a 28-acre district along the Sacramento River waterfront. The museums at the north end hold artifacts of state and national significance, and historic buildings house shops and restaurants. River cruises and train rides are fun family diversions for an hour or two. Call the **Old Sacramento Events Hotline** (☎ 916/558–3912) for information about living-history re-creations and merchant hours.

**A GOOD
TOUR**

Old Sacramento, the capitol and park surrounding it, and Sutter's Fort lie on an east–west axis that begins in the west at the Sacramento River. The walk from Old Sacramento to the state's capitol is easy, and brings you through the Downtown Plaza shopping mall and down K Street. This area becomes quite festive during the Thursday evening outdoor market. A DASH (Downtown Area Shuttle) bus and the No. 30 city bus both link Old Sacramento, the K Street Mall, the convention center, downtown, midtown, and Sutter's Fort in a loop that goes eastward on J Street and westward on L Street. The fare is 50¢ within this area, and buses run every 15 minutes weekdays, every 20 minutes Saturday, and every 30 minutes Sunday.

Park your car in the municipal garage under I–5 at 2nd Street (enter on I Street between 2nd and 3rd streets), and head to the superb **California State Railroad Museum** ❶ ▶; then browse the hardware and household items at the **Huntington, Hopkins & Co. Store** ❷. Next door are the hands-on exhibits of the **Discovery Museum History Center** ❸.

To learn more about Sacramento's role in rail history, walk a few paces south to the **Central Pacific Passenger Depot** ❹. The Central Pacific Freight Depot, next to the passenger depot, houses a public market (closed Monday) where merchants sell food and gifts. The foot of K Street (at Front Street) is a great spot for viewing the Sacramento River wharf and the restored stern-wheeler the *Delta King*. The **Old Sacramento Schoolhouse Museum** ❺, near the *Delta King,* is a popular low-tech attraction.

On 2nd Street the **Old Sacramento Visitor Information Center** ❻ is in the same block as the **California Military Museum** ❼. A must-see a few blocks south of Old Sacramento is the **Crocker Art Museum** ❽, the oldest art museum in the American West. From here walk south on Front Street to the **Towe Auto Museum** ❾. If you'd rather skip the automotive museum, walk up 3rd Street to the Capitol Mall, which leads to the **Capitol** ❿. Still going strong? Explore the **California Museum for History, Women, and the Arts** ⓫ at O and 10th streets, one block south of the capitol, and examine the facade of the handsome **Leland Stanford Mansion** ⓬, a block west of that. Or walk north to H Street and then east to the **Governor's Mansion** ⓭. Otherwise, walk back to your car via J Street.

A bit more than a mile to the east is **Sutter's Fort** ⓮, Sacramento's earliest Euro-American settlement. (Take the DASH or No. 30 city bus, or, if you feel like checking out funky shops and eateries, walk up J Street at least one way.) North of the fort is the **California State Indian Museum** ⓯.

TIMING   This tour makes for a leisurely day. Most of the attractions are open daily, except for the military, state history, and art museums, which are closed Monday, and the Huntington, Hopkins & Co. Store.

What to See

❼ **California Military Museum.** A storefront entrance leads to three floors containing more than 30,000 artifacts—uniforms, weapons, photographs, documents, medals, and flags of all kinds—that trace Californians' roles in the military throughout U.S. history. Recent exhibits have included a study of Native Americans in the U.S. Armed Forces and displays on the post–September 11 wars in Afghanistan and Iraq. ✉ *1119 2nd St.* ☎ *916/442–2883* 🎟 *$3* ☉ *Tues.–Sun. 10–4.*

PLEASURES & PASTIMES

HISTORIC HOTELS & INNS. The Gold Country abounds in well-preserved examples of gold-rush-era architecture, so why not experience the history up-close by staying at an inn or hotel that dates back to those colorful years? Plenty of old mansions have been converted to inns and B&Bs, and several hotels have been in operation since the gold rush. The very Victorian Imperial Hotel in Amador City opened in 1879, and the stone Murphys Historic Hotel & Lodge in Murphys has served guests such as Mark Twain and Black Bart since 1855. Columbia has the 1856 City Hotel and the 1857 Fallon Hotel, the latter of which was restored by the state of California. In Jamestown, the National Hotel offers an authentic 1859 experience.

SHOPPING. Shoppers visit the Gold Country in search of antiques, collectibles, fine art, quilts, toys, tools, decorative items, and furnishings. Handmade quilts and crafts can be found in Sutter Creek, Jackson, and Amador City. Auburn and Nevada City support many gift boutiques. Sacramento's commuter communities, such as Elk Grove (south), Folsom (east), and Roseville (northeast), are exploding with subdivisions, and with them inevitably come the standard suburban assortment of chain stores and strip malls.

THEATER. For weary miners in search of diversion, theater was a popular form of entertainment in the Gold Country. It still is, and you can take in a show at several venues dating from the era. The Woodland Opera House, opened in 1885, mounts musical theater productions September through July. Nevada City's Nevada Theatre, built in 1865, is the home of the Foothill Theater Company. In Columbia State Historic Park, the Historic Fallon House Theater presents dramas, comedies, and musicals.

8

NEED A BREAK? The **River City Brewing Co.** (✉ Downtown Plaza ☎ 916/447–2739) is the best of several breweries that have cropped up in the capital city. The brewery is at the west end of the K Street Mall, between the capitol and Old Sacramento.

☺ ⓫ **California Museum for History, Women, and the Arts.** California's first lady, Maria Shriver, has taken an active role in having this museum, formerly the California State History Museum, stress women's issues. Though many exhibits use modern technology, there are also scores of archival drawers that you can pull out to see the real artifacts of history and culture—from the California State Constitution to surfing magazines. Board a 1949 cross-country bus to view a video on immigration, visit a Chinese herb shop maintained by a holographic proprietor, or stand on a gubernatorial balcony overlooking a sea of cameras and banners. There's also a café. ✉ *1020 O St.* ☎ *916/653–7524* ⊕ *www.californiamuseum.org* ✆ *$5* ⊙ *Tues.–Sat. 10–5, Sun. noon–5.*

☺ ⓯ **California State Indian Museum.** Among the interesting displays at this well-organized museum is one devoted to Ishi, the last Yahi Indian to emerge from the mountains, in 1911. Ishi provided scientists with insight into the traditions and culture of this group of Native Americans. Arts-and-

crafts exhibits, a demonstration village, and an evocative 10-minute video
bring to life the multifaceted past and present of California's native peoples. ⊠ *2618 K St.* ☎ *916/324–0971* ⊕ *www.parks.ca.gov* ▣ *$2*
⊙ *Daily 10–4.*

🕭 ▶ ❶ **California State Railroad Museum.** Near what was once the terminus of
Fodor'sChoice the transcontinental and Sacramento Valley railroads (the actual termi-
★ nus was at Front and K streets), this 100,000-square-foot museum has
21 locomotives and railroad cars on display along with dozens of other
exhibits, including a massive toy-train display. You can walk through
a post office car and peer into cubbyholes and canvas mailbags, enter
a sleeping car that simulates the swaying on the roadbed and the flash-
ing lights of a passing town at night, or glimpse the inside of the first-
class dining car. Allow at least two hours to enjoy the museum. ⊠ *125
I St.* ☎ *916/445–6645* ⊕ *www.csrmf.org* ▣ *$6* ⊙ *Daily 10–5.*

★ ❿ **Capitol.** The Golden State's capitol was built in 1869. The lacy plaster-
work of the 120-foot-high rotunda has the complexity and colors of a
Fabergé egg. Underneath the gilded dome are marble floors, glittering
chandeliers, monumental staircases, reproductions of 19th-century state
offices, and legislative chambers decorated in the style of the 1890s. Guides
conduct tours of the building and the 40-acre Capitol Park, which con-

tains a rose garden, an impressive display of camellias (Sacramento's city flower), and the California Vietnam Veterans Memorial. ⊠ *Capitol Mall and 10th St.* ☎ *916/324–0333* ⊕ *www.statecapitolmuseum.com* ⚏ *Free* ☺ *Daily 9–5; tours hourly 9–4.*

Central Pacific Passenger Depot. At this reconstructed 1876 station there's rolling stock to admire, a typical waiting room, and a small restaurant. A steam-powered train departs hourly (April through September) from the freight depot, south of the passenger depot, making a 40-minute loop along the Sacramento riverfront. ⊠*930 Front St.* ☎*916/445–6645* ⚏*$3, free with same-day ticket from California State Railroad Museum; train ride $6 additional* ☺ *Depot daily 10–5. Train Apr.–Sept. weekends; Oct.–Dec., 1st weekend of month.*

Crocker Art Museum. The oldest art museum in the American West has a collection of art from Europe, Asia, and California, including *Sunday Morning in the Mines* (1872), a large canvas by Charles Christian Nahl depicting aspects of the original mining industry, and the magnificent *Great Canyon of the Sierra, Yosemite* (1871), by Thomas Hill. The museum's lobby and ballroom retain the original 19th-century woodwork, plaster moldings, and English tiles. ⊠ *216 O St.* ☎ *916/264–5423* ⊕ *www.crockerartmuseum.org* ⚏ *$6* ☺ *Tues., Wed., and Fri.–Sun. 10–5, Thurs. 10–9.*

Discovery Museum History Center. The building that holds this child-oriented museum is a reproduction of the 1854 city hall and waterworks. Interactive history, science, and technology exhibits examine the evolution of everyday life in the Sacramento area. You can pan for gold, examine a Native American thatch hut, or experience the goings-on in the former print shop of the *Sacramento Bee.* The Gold Gallery displays nuggets and veins. ⊠ *101 I St.* ☎*916/264–7057* ⚏*$5* ☺ *July and Aug., daily 10–5; Sept.–June, Tues.–Sun. 10–5.*

Governor's Mansion. This 15-room house was built in 1877 and used by the state's chief executives from the early 1900s until 1967, when Ronald Reagan vacated it in favor of a newly built home in the more upscale suburbs. Many of the Italianate mansion's interior decorations were ordered from the Huntington, Hopkins & Co. hardware store, one of whose partners, Albert Gallatin, was the original occupant. Each of the seven marble fireplaces has a petticoat mirror that ladies strolled past to see if their slips were showing. The mansion is said to have been one of the first homes in California with an indoor bathroom. ⊠ *1526 H St.* ☎ *916/323–3047* ⚏ *$2* ☺ *Daily 10–5; tours hourly, last one at 4.*

Huntington, Hopkins & Co. Store. This museum is a reproduction of the 1855 hardware store opened by Collis Huntington and Mark Hopkins, two of the Big Four businessmen who established the Central Pacific Railroad. Picks, shovels, gold pans, and other paraphernalia used by miners during the gold rush are on display, along with household hardware and appliances from the 1880s. Some items, such as blue enamelware, wooden toys, gold pans, and oil lamps, are for sale. ⊠ *113 I St.* ☎ *916/323–7234* ⚏ *Free* ☺ *Hrs vary.*

⑫ **Leland Stanford Mansion.** The home of Leland Stanford, a railroad baron, California governor, and U.S. senator, was built in 1856, with additions in 1862 and the early 1870s. Although it's been closed to the public for years, its renovated exterior is interesting to see. ⊠ *802 N St.* ☎ *916/ 324–7405.*

☾ ❺ **Old Sacramento Schoolhouse Museum.** Sacramento's first school welcomed students in August 1849 and closed permanently four months later because of muddy streets. Five years passed before another public school opened. Today it's a kid-friendly attraction that shows what one-room schoolhouses were like in the California Central Valley and foothills in the late 1800s. ⊠ *Front and L Sts.* ☎ *No phone* 🎫 *Free* ☉ *Mon.–Sat. 10–4, Sun. noon–4.*

❻ **Old Sacramento Visitor Information Center.** Obtain brochures about nearby attractions, check local restaurant menus, and get advice from the helpful staff here. ⊠ *1101 2nd St., at K St.* ☎ *916/442–7644* ⊕ *www. oldsacramento.com* ☉ *Daily 10–5.*

★ ☾ ⑭ **Sutter's Fort.** Sacramento's earliest Euro-American settlement was founded by German-born Swiss immigrant John Augustus Sutter in 1839. Audio speakers give information at each stop along a self-guided tour that includes a blacksmith's shop, bakery, prison, living quarters, and livestock areas. Costumed docents sometimes reenact fort life, demonstrating crafts, food preparation, and firearms maintenance. ⊠ *2701 L St.* ☎ *916/445–4422* ⊕ *www.parks.ca.gov* 🎫 *$4* ☉ *Daily 10–5.*

☾ ❾ **Towe Auto Museum.** With more than 150 vintage automobiles on display, and exhibits ranging from the Hall of Technology to Dreams of Speed and Dreams of Cool, this museum explores automotive history and car culture. A 1920s roadside café and garage exhibit re-creates the early days of motoring. The gift shop sells vintage-car magazines, model kits, and other car-related items. ⊠ *2200 Front St., 1 block off Broadway* ☎ *916/442–6802* ⊕ *www.toweautomuseum.org* 🎫 *$7* ☉ *Daily 10–5.*

Where to Stay & Eat

$$–$$$$ ✕ **The Firehouse.** Consistently rated by local publications as among the city's top 10 restaurants, the Firehouse has a full bar, courtyard seating (its signature attraction), and creative American cookery, such as antelope topped with a blueberry-and-walnut chutney. Visitors who can afford to treat themselves to a fine and leisurely meal can do no better in Old Sacramento. ⊠ *1112 2nd St.* ☎ *916/442–4772* 🖃 *AE, MC, V* ☉ *Closed Sun. No lunch Sat.*

★ $$–$$$ ✕ **Biba.** Owner Biba Caggiano is an authority on Italian cuisine. The capitol crowd flocks here for homemade ravioli, osso buco, grilled pork loin, and veal and rabbit specials. A pianist adds to the upscale ambience nightly. ⊠ *2801 Capitol Ave.* ☎ *916/455–2422* 🍽 *Reservations essential* 🖃 *AE, DC, MC, V* ☉ *Closed Sun. No lunch Sat.*

$$–$$$ ✕ **Rio City Café.** Contemporary and seasonal Mediterranean and Californian cuisine and huge floor-to-ceiling windows with views of an Old Sacramento wharf are the dual attractions of this bright restaurant. ⊠ *1110 Front St.* ☎ *916/442–8226* 🖃 *AE, D, DC, MC, V.*

★ **$$–$$$** ✕ **The Waterboy.** Rural French cooking and California cuisine are the culinary treasures at this popular midtown restaurant, featuring such distinct dishes as chicken potpie, veal sweetbreads, and beet salad. This is where top local restaurateurs go when they want a good meal. ✉ *2000 Capitol Ave.* ☎ *916/498–9891* ▭ *AE, D, DC, MC, V* ⊘ *Closed Mon. No lunch weekends.*

$–$$$ ✕ **Ernesto's Mexican Food.** Customers wait up to an hour for a table on Friday and Saturday evenings at this popular midtown dinner restaurant. Fresh ingredients are stressed in the wide selection of entrées, and the margaritas are especially refreshing. **Zocalo** (✉ 1801 Capitol Ave. ☎ 916/441–0303), launched in 2004 by Ernesto's ownership, is a popular launching spot for nights out on the town. ✉ *16th and S Sts.* ☎ *916/441–5850* ▭ *AE, D, DC, MC, V.*

$–$$ ✕ **Joe's Crab Shack.** This nationwide chain restaurant has a special place in Old Sacramento—hanging over the Sacramento River. A few strides south of the *Delta King,* this shabby-chic, seaside-funky restaurant has great views of a Sacramento landmark, the Tower Bridge. ✉ *1210 Front St.* ☎ *916/553–4249* ⊕ *www.joescrabshack.com* ▭ *AE, DC, MC, V.*

¢–$$ ✕ **Tapa the World.** As defined at this midtown bar and restaurant, tapas are bite-size portions of meats, seafood, chicken, and veggies shared at the table. One of Sacramento's liveliest nightspots (it's open until midnight), Tapa often presents Flamenco and Spanish classical music performers. ✉ *2125 J St.* ☎ *916/442–4353* ▭ *AE, D, DC, MC, V.*

$$$ ✕⌂ **Sterling Hotel.** This gleaming-white Victorian mansion three blocks from the capitol has rose-color guest rooms with handsome furniture, including four-poster or canopy beds. Bathrooms are tiled in Italian marble and have Jacuzzi tubs. Restaurant Chanterelle ($$) serves contemporary Continental cuisine in its candlelighted dining room and pleasant patio area. ✉ *1300 H St., 95814* ☎ *916/448–1300 or 800/365–7660* ▤ *916/448–8066* ⊕ *www.sterlinghotel.com* ⤳ *17 rooms, 2 suites* ⌂ *Restaurant, room service, in-room data ports, bar, dry cleaning, business services, meeting room, parking (fee), no-smoking rooms* ▭ *AE, D, DC, MC, V.*

★ **$$–$$$$** ⌂ **Amber House Bed & Breakfast Inn.** This B&B near the capitol encompasses two homes. The original house, the Poet's Refuge, is a craftsman-style home with five bedrooms named for famous writers. The second, an 1897 Dutch colonial–revival home named Musician's Manor, has gardens that occasionally hold weddings. Baths are tiled in Italian marble; some have skylights and two-person spa tubs. ✉ *1315 22nd St., 95816* ☎ *916/444–8085 or 800/755–6526* ▤ *916/552–6529* ⊕ *www. amberhouse.com* ⤳ *10 rooms* ⌂ *Cable TV, in-room VCRs, in-room data ports, concierge; no smoking* ▭ *AE, D, DC, MC, V* ⊙ *BP.*

★ **$–$$$$** ⌂ **Hyatt Regency Sacramento.** With a marble-and-glass lobby and luxurious rooms, this hotel across from the capitol and adjacent to the convention center is arguably Sacramento's finest. The multitiered, glass-dominated hotel has a striking Mediterranean design. The best rooms have Capitol Park views. The service and attention to detail are outstanding. Governor Schwarzenegger, whose family still resides in Southern California, camps out here several nights a week. ✉ *1209 L St., 95814* ☎ *916/443–1234 or 800/633–7313* ▤ *916/321–3799* ⊕ *www.hyatt.*

8

com 🕿 *500 rooms, 24 suites* ☼ *2 restaurants, pool, gym, hot tub, bar, dry cleaning, laundry service, concierge, business services, meeting room, car rental, parking (fee)* ▤ *AE, D, DC, MC, V.*

$$–$$$ 🏨 **Delta King.** This grand old riverboat, now permanently moored on Old Sacramento's waterfront, once transported passengers between Sacramento and San Francisco. Among many notable design elements are its main staircase, mahogany paneling, and brass fittings. The best of the 43 staterooms, all nonsmoking, are on the river side toward the back of the boat. The boat's theater stages high-quality productions. ✉ *1000 Front St., 95814* 🕿 *916/444–5464 or 800/825–5464* 🖶 *916/447–5959* ⊕ *www.deltaking.com* 🕿 *44 rooms* ☼ *Restaurant, lounge, theater, meeting room, parking (fee)* ▤ *AE, D, DC, MC, V* ⑩ *CP.*

$$ 🏨 **Holiday Inn Capitol Plaza.** Despite its lack of charm, this high-rise hotel has modern rooms—renovated in 2005—and the best location for visiting Old Sacramento and the Downtown Plaza. It's also within walking distance of the capitol. ✉ *300 J St., 95814* 🕿 *916/446–0100 or 800/465–4329* 🖶 *916/446–7371* ⊕ *www.holiday-inn.com* 🕿 *362 rooms, 4 suites* ☼ *Restaurant, minibars, cable TV, pool, gym, bar, shop, concierge floor, convention center, no-smoking rooms* ▤ *AE, DC, MC, V.*

$–$$ 🏨 **Radisson Hotel Sacramento.** Mediterranean-style two-story buildings cluster around a large artificial lake on an 18-acre landscaped site a few miles northeast of downtown. Rooms are enlivened with art deco appointments and furnishings; many have a patio or balcony. The Radisson is more resortlike than other Sacramento-area hotels. ✉ *500 Leisure La., 95815* 🕿 *916/922–2020 or 800/333–3333* 🖶 *916/649–9463* ⊕ *www.radisson.com/sacramentoca* 🕿 *307 rooms, 22 suites* ☼ *2 restaurants, room service, pool, lake, gym, outdoor hot tub, boating, bicycles, bar, convention center* ▤ *AE, D, DC, MC, V.*

¢ 🏨 **Sacramento International Hostel.** This 1885 Victorian mansion has a grand mahogany staircase, a stained-glass atrium, frescoed ceilings, and carved and tiled fireplaces. Dormitory rooms and bedrooms suitable for singles, couples, and families are available, as is a communal kitchen. ✉ *925 H St., 95814* 🕿 *916/443–1691 or 800/909–4776 Ext. 40* 🖶 *916/443–4763* ⊕ *www.norcalhostels.org* 🕿 *70 beds* ☼ *Kitchen; no room TVs* ▤ *MC, V.*

Nightlife & the Arts

Downtown Events Line (🕿 916/442–2500) has recorded information about seasonal events in the downtown area.

Nightlife

The **Blue Cue** (✉ 2730 O St. 🕿 916/442–7208), upstairs from Centro restaurant, is an eclectic billiard lounge known for its large selection of single-malt scotches. The **Fox and Goose** (✉ 1001 R St. 🕿 916/443–8825) is a casual pub with live music (including open-mike Monday). Traditional pub food (fish-and-chips, Cornish pasties) is served on weekday evenings from 5:30 to 9:30. **Harlow's** (✉ 2708 J St. 🕿 916/441–4693) draws a young crowd to its art deco bar-nightclub for live music after 9. **Streets of London Pub** (✉ 1804 J St. 🕿 916/498–1388) is popular among Anglophiles and stays open until 2 AM every night except Sunday, when it closes an hour earlier.

The Arts

Sacramento Community Center Theater (✉ 13th and L Sts. ☎ 916/264–5181) holds concerts, Broadway shows, opera, and ballet. The **California Musical Theatre** (✉ 1419 H St. ☎ 916/557–1999) presents Broadway shows at the Sacramento Community Center Theater and in the huge Music Circus tent in summer. If you want the really *big* picture, the **Esquire Theater** (✉ 1211 K St. ☎ 916/443–4629) screens IMAX movies. For art films, visit the funky **Tower Theater** (✉ 2508 Land Park Dr. ☎ 916/442–4700), a few minutes southeast of downtown. The **Crest Theatre** (✉ 1013 K St.) is another place to see art films.

Shopping

Top local artists and craftspeople exhibit their works at **Artists' Collaborative Gallery** (✉ 1007 2nd St. ☎ 916/444–3764). The **Elder Craftsman** (✉ 130 J St. ☎ 916/264–7762) specializes in items made by local senior citizens. **Gallery of the American West** (✉ 121 K St. ☎ 916/446–6662) has a large selection of Native American arts and crafts. **Arden Fair Mall** (✉ Off I–80, northeast of downtown) is Sacramento's largest shopping center. The **Downtown Plaza** and the K Street Mall that leads into it have many shops and restaurants, as well as a Thursday-night market in the summer and an outdoor ice-skating rink in winter.

Woodland

⑯ *20 mi northwest of Sacramento on I–5.*

Woodland's downtown lies frozen in a quaint and genteel past. In its heyday it was one of the wealthiest cities in California, established in 1861 by gold seekers and entrepreneurs. Once the boom was over, attention turned to the rich surrounding land, and the area became an agricultural gold mine. The legacy of the old land barons lives on in the Victorian homes that line Woodland's wide streets. Many of the houses have been restored and are surrounded by lavish gardens.

More than 300 touring companies, including John Philip Sousa's marching band, and Frank Kirk, the Acrobatic Tramp, appeared at the **Woodland Opera House,** built in 1885 (and rebuilt after it burned in 1892). Now restored, the building is the site of concerts and, September through July, a season of musical theater. Free weekly guided tours reveal old-fashioned stage technology. ✉ *Main and 2nd Sts.* ☎ *530/666–9617* ⊕ *www.wohtheatre.org* ☉ *Weekdays 10–5, weekends noon–5, tours Tues. 1–4.*

This 10-room classical revival home of settler William Byas Gibson was purchased by volunteers and restored as the **Yolo County Historical Museum.** You can see collections of furnishings and artifacts from the 1850s to 1930s. Old trees and an impressive lawn cover the 2½-acre site off Highway 113. ✉ *512 Gibson Rd.* ☎ *530/666–1045* ✎ *$2* ☉ *Mon. and Tues. 10–4, weekends noon–4.*

☾ Old trucks and farm machinery seem to rumble to life within the shed-like **Heidrick Ag History Center,** where you can see the world's largest collection of antique agricultural equipment. Also here are multimedia exhibits and a gift shop. ✉ *1962 Hays La.* ☎ *530/666–9700* ⊠ *530/*

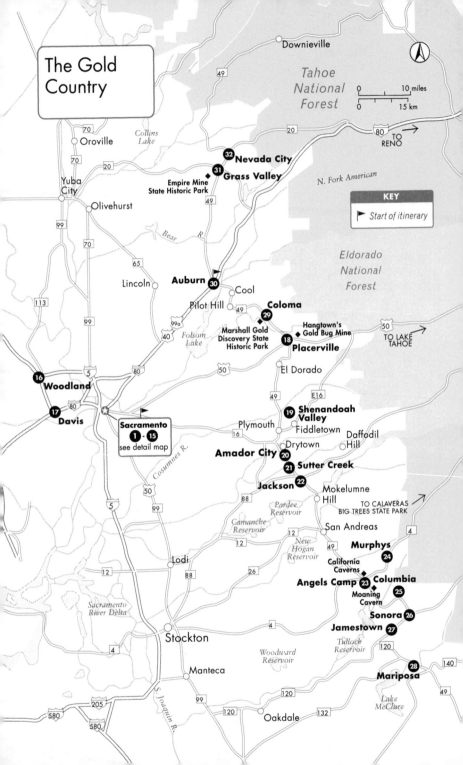

666–9712 ⊕ *www.aghistory.org* ✉ *$7* ⊙ *Weekdays 10–5, Sat. 10–6, Sun. 10–4.*

Where to Stay & Eat

$$–$$$ ✕ **Morrison's Upstairs.** The Victorian building that houses this restaurant is registered as a State Historic Landmark. Downstairs is a bar, deli, and patio. The top floor, once the attic, is full of nooks and alcoves where you can have your meal. Furnished throughout with polished wood tables that suit the style of the house, Morrison's serves burgers and sandwiches, scampi, Chinese chicken salad, pasta, prime rib, and vegetarian selections. ✉ *428½ 1st St.* ☎ *530/666–6176* ▤ *AE, D, DC, MC, V.*

$–$$ ✕ **Ludy's Main Street BBQ.** This big, casual restaurant next door to the Opera House looks like something out of the *Beverly Hillbillies.* You can tuck into huge portions of ribs, beef, chicken, or fish-and-chips, or have a half-pound burger slathered in red sauce. On the patio, water misters cool you in summer, and heaters keep you toasty in winter. There is a kids' menu. ✉ *667 Main St.* ☎ *530/666–4400* ▤ *AE, MC, V.*

Davis

⑰ *10 mi west of Sacramento on I–80.*

Though it began as—and still is—a rich agricultural area, Davis doesn't feel like a cow town. It's home to the University of California at Davis, whose students hang at the cafés and bookstores in the central business district, making the city feel a little more cosmopolitan. The city has long enjoyed a progressive, liberal reputation (it's been called "the People's Republic of Davis"), but a rash of new yuppie-stocked subdivisions reflect how Davis is becoming more of a mainstream commuter community, whether residents admit it or not. The university is a leader in viticulture education and has one of the West Coast's top veterinary programs.

The center of action in town is the **Davis Campus of the University of California,** which ranks among the top 25 research universities in the United States. You can take tours of the campus, which depart from Buehler Alumni and Visitors Center. The **Mondavi Center for the Performing Arts,** a strikingly modern glass structure off I–80, offers a busy and varied schedule of performances. ✉ *1 Shields Ave.* ☎ *530/752–8111* ⊕ *www.ucdavis.edu* ⊙ *Tours weekends at 11:30, weekdays by appointment.*

The work by northern California craftspeople displayed at the **Artery,** an artists' cooperative, includes decorative and functional ceramics, glass, wood, jewelry, fiber arts, painting, sculpture, drawing, and photography. ✉ *207 G St.* ☎ *530/758–8330* ⊕ *www.arteryart.com* ⊙ *Mon.–Thurs. and Sat. 10–6, Fri. 10–9, Sun. noon–5.*

Where to Stay & Eat

$$–$$$ ✕ **Café California.** The locals who gather at this downtown Davis eatery favor such dishes as a salad of prawns and baby greens with avocado-tarragon vinaigrette, Cajun-style prime rib with chili onion rings, and roast chicken with garlic mashed potatoes. The contemporary dining room is set with white linens. ✉ *808 2nd St.* ☎ *530/757–2766* ▦ *530/758–5236* ▤ *AE, MC, V.*

$–$$$ ✕ **Soga's.** Watercolors by local artists hang on the walls of this elegant restaurant. The California-style menu features various presentations of salmon fillet, swordfish, and veal and also offers vegetable plates. You can eat on the long, covered patio in good weather. ⊠ *217 E St.* ☎ *530/757–1733* ♠ *Reservations essential* 🖃 *AE, D, MC, V* ☉ *No lunch weekends.*

$–$$ ☷ **Aggie Inn.** This hotel, less than a block from the campus, is named for the University of California at Davis "Aggies," the school's team name. Rooms are clean and basic; convenience is what this place is about. ⊠ *245 1st St., 95616* ☎ *530/756–0352* 🖷 *530/753–5738* ⊕ *www.stayanight. com* ⇖ *25 rooms, 9 suites* ♨ *Some in-room hot tubs, some kitchenettes, outdoor hot tub, sauna, laundry service* 🖃 *AE, D, DC, MC, V* ⑩ *CP.*

$ ☷ **Hallmark Inn.** Two buildings with clean, modern rooms make up this inn, which is five blocks from the University of California campus and is next door to a restaurant. ⊠ *110 F St., 95616* ☎ *530/758–8623 or 800/753–0035* ⊕ *www.hallmarkinn.com* ⇖ *135 rooms* ♨ *Restaurant, some refrigerators, pool, free parking, some no-smoking rooms* 🖃 *AE, D, DC, MC, V.*

THE GOLD COUNTRY—SOUTH
HIGHWAY 49 FROM PLACERVILLE TO MARIPOSA

South of its junction with U.S. 50, Highway 49 traces in asphalt the famed Mother Lode. The sleepy former gold-rush towns strung along the road have for the most part been restored and made presentable to visitors with an interest in one of the most frenzied episodes of American history.

Placerville

⓲ *10 mi south of Coloma on Hwy. 49; 44 mi east of Sacramento on U.S. 50.*

It's hard to imagine now, but in 1849 about 4,000 miners staked out every gully and hillside in Placerville, turning the town into a rip-roaring camp of log cabins, tents, and clapboard houses. The area was then known as Hangtown, a graphic allusion to the nature of frontier justice. It took on the name Placerville in 1854 and became an important supply center for the miners. Mark Hopkins, Philip Armour, and John Studebaker were among the industrialists who got their starts here.

★ ♺ **Hangtown's Gold Bug Park & Mine,** owned by the City of Placerville, centers on a fully lighted mine shaft open for self-guided touring. A shaded stream runs through the park, and there are picnic facilities. ⊠ *North on Bedford Ave., 1 mi off U.S. 50* ☎ *530/642–5207* ⊕ *www.goldbugpark. org* 🖃 *$4* ☉ *Tours mid-Apr.–Oct., daily 10–4; Nov.–mid-Apr., weekends noon–4. Gift shop Mar.–Nov., daily 10–4.*

OFF THE BEATEN PATH **APPLE HILL** – Roadside stands sell fresh produce from more than 50 family farms in this area. During the fall harvest season (from September through December), members of the Apple Hill Growers Association open their orchards and vineyards for apple and berry picking, picnicking, and wine and cider tasting.

Many sell baked items and picnic food. ⊠ *About 5 mi east of Hwy. 49; take Camino exit from U.S. 50* ☎ *530/644–7692.*

Where to Stay & Eat

$$–$$$$ ✕ **Café Luna.** Tucked into the back of the Creekside Place shopping complex is a small restaurant with about 30 seats inside, plus outdoor tables overlooking a creek. The menu, which changes weekly, encompasses many cuisines, including Indian, Russian, and Thai. ⊠ *451 Main St.* ☎ *530/642–8669* ▤ *AE, D, MC, V* ☺ *Closed Sun. No dinner Mon. and Tues.*

★ **$$–$$$$** ✕ **Zachary Jacques.** It's not easy to locate (call for directions), but finding this country-French restaurant is worth the effort. Appetizers on the seasonal menu might include escargots or mushrooms prepared in several ways, roasted garlic with olive oil served on toast, or spicy lamb sausage. Standard entrées include roast rack of lamb, beef stew, and scallops and shrimp in lime butter. The attached wine bar opens at 4:30. ⊠ *1821 Pleasant Valley Rd., 3 mi east of Diamond Springs* ☎ *530/626–8045* ▤ *AE, MC, V* ☺ *Closed Mon. and Tues. No lunch.*

$–$$$ ✕ **Lil' Mama D. Carlo's Italian Kitchen.** This comfortable Italian restaurant with a pleasant staff serves large portions of homemade pasta and chicken; the vegetarian dishes are heavy on the garlic. A wine bar highlights local varieties. ⊠ *482 Main St.* ☎ *530/626–1612* ▤ *AE, MC, V* ☺ *Closed Mon. and Tues. No lunch.*

$$–$$$ ⌷ **Seasons Bed & Breakfast.** A 10-minute walk from downtown, one of Placerville's oldest homes has been transformed into a lovely and relaxing oasis. The main house, cottages, and gardens are filled with paintings and sculptures. Privacy is treasured here. A suite with a sitting room and stained-glass windows occupies the main house's top floor. One cottage has a little white picket fence around its own minigarden; another has a two-person shower. ⊠ *2934 Bedford Ave., 95667* ☎ *530/626–4420* ⊕ *www.theseasons.net* ⤷ *3 rooms, 1 suite* ⚘ *No-smoking rooms* ▤ *MC, V* ⎅ *BP.*

$ ⌷ **Best Western Placerville Inn.** This motel's serviceable rooms are decorated in the chain's trademark pastels. The pool comes in handy during hot summer months. ⊠ *6850 Green Leaf Dr., near Missouri Flats exit of U.S. 50, 95667* ☎ *530/622–9100 or 800/854–9100* 🖷 *530/622–9376* ⊕ *www.bestwestern.com* ⤷ *105 rooms* ⚘ *Cable TV, pool, free parking* ▤ *AE, D, DC, MC, V.*

Shenandoah Valley

⓳ *20 mi south of Placerville on Shenandoah Rd., east of Hwy. 49.*

The most concentrated Gold Country wine-touring area lies in the hills of the Shenandoah Valley, east of Plymouth. Robust Zinfandel is the primary grape grown here, but vineyards also produce cabernet sauvignon, sauvignon blanc, and other varietals. Most wineries are open on weekend afternoons; several have shaded picnic areas, gift shops, and galleries or museums; all have tasting rooms.

Sobon Estate (⊠ 14430 Shenandoah Rd. ☎ 209/245–6554) operates the Shenandoah Valley Museum, illustrating pioneer life and wine making in the valley. It's open daily from 9:30 to 5. At **Charles Spinetta Winery** (⊠ 12557 Steiner Rd., Plymouth ☎ 209/245–3384 ⊕ www.charlesspinettawinery.com), you can see a wildlife art gallery in addition to tasting the wine. It's open weekdays from 8 to 4 and weekends from 9 to 4:30. The gallery at **Shenandoah Vineyards** (⊠ 12300 Steiner Rd., Plymouth ☎ 209/245–4455), open daily from 9:30 to 5, displays contemporary art.

Where to Stay

$$ ⊞ **Amador Harvest Inn.** This B&B adjacent to Deaver Vineyards occupies a bucolic lakeside spot in the Shenandoah Valley. A contemporary Cape Cod–style structure has homey guest rooms with private baths. Public areas include a living room with fireplace and a music room with a view of the lake. ⊠ *12455 Steiner Rd., Plymouth 95669* ☎ *209/245–5512 or 800/217–2304* 🖷 *209/245–5250* ⊕ *www.amadorharvestinn.com* 🛏 *4 rooms* ♿ *No room TVs* ▤ *AE, MC, V* ¶◯ *BP.*

Amador City

➋⓪ *6 mi south of Plymouth on Hwy. 49.*

The history of tiny Amador City mirrors the boom-bust-boom cycle of many Gold Country towns. With an output of $42 million in gold, its Keystone Mine was one of the most productive in the Mother Lode. After all the gold was extracted, the miners cleared out, and the area suffered. Amador City now derives its wealth from tourists, who come to browse through its antiques and specialty shops, many of them on or just off Highway 49.

Where to Stay & Eat

★ $–$$ ✕⊞ **Imperial Hotel.** The whimsically decorated mock-Victorian rooms at this 1879 hotel give a modern twist to the excesses of the era. Antique furnishings include iron-and-brass beds, gingerbread flourishes, and, in one room, art deco appointments. The two front rooms, which can be noisy, have balconies. The menu at the hotel's fine restaurant ($$–$$$) changes quarterly and ranges from vegetarian to country hearty to contemporary eclectic. You can eat in the bright dining room or on the patio, but only for dinner and not on Monday or Tuesday. The hotel has a two-night minimum stay on weekends. ⊠ *Hwy. 49, 95601* ☎ *209/267–9172* 🖷 *209/267–9249* ⊕ *www.imperialamador.com* 🛏 *6 rooms* ♿ *Restaurant, bar* ▤ *AE, D, DC, MC, V* ¶◯ *BP.*

Sutter Creek

★ ➋① *2 mi south of Amador City on Hwy. 49.*

Sutter Creek is a charming conglomeration of balconied buildings, Victorian homes, and neo–New England structures. The stores along Highway 49 (called Main Street in the town proper) are worth visiting for works by the many local artists and craftspeople. Seek out the **J. Monteverde General Store** (⊠ 3 Randolph St.) , a typical turn-of-the-20th-century emporium with vintage goods on display (but not for sale), an elaborate antique scale, and a chair-encircled potbellied stove in the corner. Open only weekends 10–3, it closes in January. You can stop by the **Sutter Creek Visitor Center** (✉ 11A Randolph St. ☎ 209/267–1344 or 800/400–0305 ⊕ www.suttercreek.org), also open weekends 10–3, for information.

DAFFODIL HILL – Each spring a 4-acre hillside east of Sutter Creek erupts in a riot of yellow and gold as 300,000 daffodils burst into bloom. The garden is the work of members of the McLaughlin family, which has owned this site since 1887. Daffodil plantings began in the 1930s. The display usually takes place between mid-March and mid-April. ✉ *From Main St. (Hwy. 49) in Sutter Creek, take Shake Ridge Rd. east 13 mi* ☎ *209/296-7048* ⊕ *www. amadorcountychamber.com* ⌕ *Free* ☉ *Mid-Mar.-mid-Apr., daily 9-5.*

Where to Stay & Eat

$$ ✕ **Zinfandel's.** Black-bean chili in an edible bread tureen, and smoked mussels and bay shrimp with roasted garlic cloves are among the appetizers at this casual restaurant. On the adventurous menu are such entrées as rack of lamb marinated in red wine, garlic, and rosemary on garlic smashed potatoes with mushroom port sauce. ✉ *51 Hanford St.* ☎ *209/267–5008* ▱ *AE, D, MC, V* ☉ *Closed Mon.–Wed. No lunch.*

¢–$ ✕ **Chatterbox Café.** This classic 1940s luncheonette has only five tables and 14 counter stools. Read a vintage newspaper or examine the jazz instruments and Disney memorabilia on the shelves while you wait for your chicken-fried steak, burger, homemade pie, or hot-fudge sundae. The menu is as big as the Chatterbox is small. Beer and wine are available. ✉ *39 Main St.* ☎ *209/267–5935* ▱ *AE, D, MC, V* ☉ *No dinner Wed.–Mon.*

¢ ✕ **Back Roads Coffee House.** Airy and spacious, Back Roads is roughly in the middle of a frenzied four-block stretch of Highway 49 where traffic crawls and sidewalks bulge. Muffins, pastries, and coffee seem to be the biggest draws here, though hot, simple breakfasts are available. The lunch menu includes soups and salads. All the tables have a small stack of Trivial Pursuit cards, which should amuse baby boomers and trivia buffs. ✉ *74 Main St.* ☎ *209/267–0440* ☉ *No dinner.*

★ $$–$$$ ⊡ **Foxes Bed & Breakfast.** The rooms in this 1857 white-clapboard house are handsome, with high ceilings, antique beds, and armoires. Five have gas fireplaces. Breakfast is cooked to order and delivered on a silver service to your room or to the gazebo in the garden. ✉ *77 Main St., 95685* ☎ *209/267–5882 or 800/987–3344* ⊟ *209/267–0712* ⊕ *www.foxesinn. com* ⇄ *5 rooms, 2 suites* ⌂ *Some cable TV, some in-room VCRs; no smoking* ▱ *D, MC, V* ⦿ *BP.*

$–$$ ⊡ **Eureka Street Inn.** Original redwood paneling, wainscoting, beams, and cabinets as well as lead- and stained-glass windows lend the Eureka Street Inn—formerly the Picture Rock Inn—a certain coziness. The craftsman-style bungalow was built in 1914 as a family home. Most rooms have gas-log fireplaces, and wireless Internet is available. ✉ *55 Eureka St., 95685* ☎ *209/267–5500 or 800/399–2389* ⊕ *www.eurekastreetinn. com* ⇄ *4 rooms* ⌂ *No room TVs* ▱ *AE, D, MC, V* ⦿ *BP.*

¢–$ ⊡ **Sutter Creek Days Inn.** If you're touring the Gold Country on a budget, this hotel is a good choice. The rooms contain coffeemakers, and most

8

have queen-size beds; four rooms are wheelchair accessible. ✉ *271 Hanford St., 95685* ☎ *209/267–9177* 🖷 *209/267–5303* ⇗ *52 rooms* ☖ *Cable TV* ➦ *D, MC, V* ⁺○¹ *CP.*

Jackson

② *8 mi south of Sutter Creek on Hwy. 49.*

Jackson wasn't the Gold Country's rowdiest town, but the party lasted longer here than most anywhere else: "girls' dormitories" (brothels) and nickel slot machines flourished until the mid-1950s. Jackson also had the world's deepest and richest gold mines, the Kennedy and the Argonaut, which together produced $70 million in gold. These were deep-rock mines with tunnels extending as much as a mile underground. Most of the miners who worked the lode were of Serbian or Italian origin, and they gave the town a European character that persists to this day. Jackson has pioneer cemeteries whose headstones tell the stories of local Serbian and Italian families. The terraced cemetery on the grounds of the handsome **St. Sava Serbian Orthodox Church** (✉ 724 N. Main St.) is the most impressive of the town's burial grounds.

The heart of Jackson's historic section is the **National Hotel** (✉ 2 Water St. ☎ 209/233–0500), which operates an old-time saloon in the lobby. The hotel is especially active on weekends, when people come from miles around to participate in Saturday-night sing-alongs.

The **Amador County Museum,** built in the late 1850s as a private home, provides a colorful take on gold-rush life. Displays include a kitchen with a woodstove, the Amador County bicentennial quilt, and a classroom. A time line recounts the county's checkered past. The museum conducts hourly tours of large-scale working models of the nearby Kennedy Mine. ✉ *225 Church St.* ☎ *209/223–6386* 🖼 *Museum free; mine tours $1* ☽ *Wed.–Sun. 10–4.*

Where to Stay & Eat

¢–$ ✕ **Rosebud's Classic Café.** Art deco accents and music from the 1930s and 1940s set the mood at this homey café. Charbroiled burgers, freshly baked pies, and espresso coffees round out the lunch menu. Omelets, hotcakes, and many other items are served for breakfast. ✉ *26 Main St.* ☎ *209/223–1035* ➦ *MC, V* ☽ *No dinner.*

¢–$ 🏨 **Best Western Amador Inn.** Convenience and price are the main attractions of this two-story motel just off the highway. Many rooms have gas fireplaces. If you want an in-room refrigerator and microwave, you'll need to pay $5 extra. ✉ *200 S. Hwy. 49, 95642* ☎ *209/223–0211 or 800/543–5221* 🖷 *209/223–4836* ⊕ *www.bestwestern.com* ⇗ *118 rooms* ☖ *Restaurant, pool, laundry service* ➦ *AE, D, DC, MC, V.*

Angels Camp

③ *20 mi south of Jackson on Hwy. 49.*

Angels Camp is famed chiefly for its May jumping-frog contest, based on Mark Twain's short story "The Celebrated Jumping Frog of Calaveras County." The writer reputedly heard the story of the jumping frog from Ross Coon, proprietor of Angels Hotel, which has been in operation since 1856.

Angels Camp Museum houses gold-rush relics, including photos, rocks, petrified wood, old blacksmith and mining equipment, and a horse-drawn hearse. The carriage house out back holds 31 carriages and an impressive display of mineral specimens. ⊠ *753 S. Main St.* ☎ *209/736–2963* ✉ *$2* ☉ *Jan. and Feb., weekends 10–3; Mar.–Dec., daily 10–3.*

OFF THE BEATEN PATH ☞ **CALIFORNIA CAVERNS** – A ½-mi subterranean trail winds through large chambers and past underground streams and lakes. There aren't many steps to climb, but it's a strenuous walk with some narrow passageways and steep spots. The caverns, at a constant 53°F, contain crystalline formations not found elsewhere, and the 80-minute guided tour explains local history and geology. ⊠ *9 mi east of San Andreas on Mountain Ranch Rd., then about 3 mi on Cave City Rd., follow signs* ☎ *209/736-2708* ✉ *$12* ☉ *Daily 10-4.*

MOANING CAVERN – A 235-step spiral staircase leads into this vast cavern. More adventurous sorts can rappel into the chamber—ropes and instruction are provided. Otherwise, the only way inside is via the 45-minute tour, during which you'll see giant (and still growing) stalactites and stalagmites and an archaeological site that holds some of the oldest human remains yet found in America (an unlucky person has fallen into the cavern about once every 130 years for the last 13,000 years). ⊠ *Parrots Ferry Rd., 2 mi south of Vallecito, off Hwy. 4 east of Angels Camp* ☎ *209/736-2708* ⊕ *www.caverntours.com* ✉ *$12* ☉ *May–Oct., daily 9-6; Nov.-Apr., weekdays 10-5, weekends 9-5.*

8

Murphys

㉔ *10 mi northeast of Angels Camp on Hwy. 4.*

Murphys is a well-preserved town of white picket fences, Victorian houses, and interesting shops. Horatio Alger and Ulysses S. Grant came through here, staying at Murphys Historic Hotel & Lodge when they, along with many other 19th-century visitors, came to see the giant sequoia groves in nearby Calaveras Big Trees State Park.

The **Kautz Ironstone Winery and Caverns** is worth a visit even if you don't drink wine. Tours take you into underground tunnels cooled by a waterfall from a natural spring and include a performance on a massive automated pipe organ. The winery schedules concerts during spring and summer in its huge outdoor amphitheater, plus art shows and other events on weekends. On display is a 44-pound specimen of crystalline gold. Visit the deli for lunch. ⊠ *1894 6 Mile Rd.* ☎ *209/728–1251* ☉ *Daily 10–5.*

OFF THE BEATEN PATH **CALAVERAS BIG TREES STATE PARK** – This state park protects hundreds of the largest and rarest living things on the planet—magnificent giant sequoia redwood trees. Some are nearly 3,000 years old, 90 feet around at the base, and 250 feet tall. The park's self-guided walks range from a 200-yard trail to 1-mi and 5-mi (closed in winter) loops through the groves. There are campgrounds and picnic areas; swimming, wading, fishing, and sunbathing on the Stanislaus River are popular in summer. ✉ *Off Hwy. 4, 15 mi northeast of Murphys, 4 mi northeast of Arnold* ☎ *209/795–2334* 💲 *$6 per vehicle, day use; campsites $20* ⊙ *Park daily sunrise–sunset, day use; visitor center May–Oct., daily 10–4; Nov.–Apr., weekends 11–3.*

Where to Stay & Eat

$–$$$ ✕ **Grounds.** Light Italian entrées, grilled vegetables, chicken, seafood, and steak are the specialties at this bistro and coffee shop. Sandwiches, salads, and homemade soups are served for lunch. The crowd is friendly and the service attentive. ✉ *402 Main St.* ☎ *209/728–8663* ▤ *MC, V* ⊙ *No dinner Mon. and Tues.*

★ $$$–$$$$ ▦ **Dunbar House 1880.** The oversize rooms in this elaborate Italianate-style home have brass beds, down comforters, gas-burning stoves, and claw-foot tubs. Broad wraparound verandas encourage lounging, as do the colorful gardens and large elm trees. The Cedar Room's sunporch has a two-person whirlpool tub, and the Sequoia Room has a two-person whirlpool spa and shower. In the afternoon you are treated to trays of appetizers and wine in your room. ✉ *271 Jones St., 95247* ☎ *209/ 728–2897 or 800/692–6006* 🖷 *209/728–1451* ⊕ *www.dunbarhouse.com* 🛏 *3 rooms, 2 suites* ⚭ *Refrigerators, in-room DVDs* ▤ *AE, MC, V* ⦿*BP.*

¢–$ ▦ **Murphys Historic Hotel & Lodge.** This 1855 stone hotel, whose register has seen the signatures of Mark Twain and the bandit Black Bart, figured in Bret Harte's short story "A Night at Wingdam." Accommodations are in the hotel and a modern motel-style addition. The older rooms are furnished with antiques, many of them large and hand carved. The hotel has a convivial old-time saloon, which can be noisy into the wee hours. ✉ *457 Main St., 95247* ☎ *209/728–3444 or 800/532– 7684* 🖷 *209/728–1590* ⊕ *www.murphyshotel.com* 🛏 *29 rooms, 20 with bath* ⚭ *Restaurant, bar, meeting room* ▤ *AE, D, DC, MC, V.*

Columbia

㉕ *14 mi south of Angels Camp via Hwy. 49 to Parrots Ferry Rd.*

Columbia is the gateway for Columbia State Historic Park, which is one of the Gold Country's most visited sites.

☾ **Columbia State Historic Park,** known as the Gem of the Southern Mines, Fodor'sChoice comes as close to a gold-rush town in its heyday as any site in the Gold ★ Country. You can ride a stagecoach, pan for gold, and watch a blacksmith working at an anvil. Street musicians perform in summer. Restored or reconstructed buildings include a Wells Fargo Express office, a Masonic temple, stores, saloons, two hotels, a firehouse, churches, a school, and a newspaper office. All are staffed to simulate a working 1850s town. The park also includes the **Historic Fallon House Theater,** where a full schedule of entertainment is presented. ✉ *11175 Washington St.* ☎ *209/ 532–0150* ⊕ *www.parks.ca.gov* 💲 *Free* ⊙ *Daily 9–5.*

Where to Stay & Eat

$–$$ ✕▦ **City Hotel.** The rooms in this restored 1856 hostelry are furnished with period antiques. Two have balconies overlooking Main Street, and six rooms open onto a 2nd-floor parlor. All the accommodations have private half baths, with showers nearby; robes and slippers are provided. The restaurant ($–$$$; closed Monday), one of the Gold Country's best, serves French-accented California cuisine complemented by a large selection of the state's respected wines. The What Cheer Saloon is right out of a Western movie. Combined lodging, dinner, and theater packages are available. ⊠ *22768 Main St., 95310* ☎ *209/532–1479 or 800/ 532–1479* 🖷 *209/532–7027* ⊕ *www.cityhotel.com* ⟲ *10 rooms* ⬧ *Restaurant, bar* ⊟ *AE, D, MC, V* ⟦⊙⟧ *CP.*

¢–$$ ⊡ **Fallon Hotel.** Restored by the State of California, this 1857 hotel features rooms with antiques and private half baths. (There are separate men's and women's showers.) If you occupy one of the five balcony rooms, you can sit outside with your morning coffee and watch the town wake up. ⊠ *11175 Washington St., 95310* ☎ *209/532–1470* 🖷 *209/532–7027* ⊕ *www.cityhotel.com* ⟲ *14 rooms* ⬧ *No room TVs* ⊟ *AE, D, MC, V* ⟦⊙⟧ *CP.*

The Arts

Sierra Repertory Theater Company (☎ 209/532–4644) presents a full season of dramas, comedies, and musicals at the Historic Fallon House Theater and another venue in East Sonora.

Sonora

㉖ *4 mi south of Columbia via Parrots Ferry Rd. to Hwy. 49.*

Miners from Mexico founded Sonora and made it the biggest town in the Mother Lode. Following a period of racial and ethnic strife, the Mexican settlers moved on, and Yankees built the commercial city that is visible today. Sonora's historic downtown section sits atop the Big Bonanza Mine, one of the richest in the state. Another mine, on the site of nearby Sonora High School, yielded 990 pounds of gold in a single week in 1879. Reminders of the gold rush are everywhere in Sonora, in prim Victorian houses, typical Sierra-stone storefronts, and awning-shaded sidewalks. Reality intrudes beyond the town's historic heart, with strip malls, shopping centers, and modern motels. If the country-side surrounding Sonora seems familiar, that's because it has been the backdrop for many movies over the years. Scenes from *High Noon, For Whom the Bell Tolls, The Virginian, Back to the Future III,* and *Unforgiven* were filmed here.

The **Tuolumne County Museum and History Center** occupies a building that served as a jail until 1951. Restored to an earlier period, it houses a jail museum, vintage firearms and paraphernalia, a case with gold nuggets, a cute exhibit on soapbox derby racing in hilly Sonora, and the libraries of a historical society and a genealogical society. ⊠ *158 W. Bradford St.* ☎ *209/532–1317* ▱ *Free* ☉ *Daily 10–4.*

Where to Stay & Eat

$–$$ ╳**Banny's Cafe.** Its pleasant environment and hearty yet refined dishes make Banny's a quiet alternative to Sonora's noisier eateries. Try the grilled salmon fillet with scallion rice and ginger-wasabi-soy aioli. ⊠ *83 S. Stewart St.* ☎ *209/533–4709* ▤ *D, MC, V* ⊘ *No lunch Sun.*

¢ × **Garcia's Taqueria.** This casual, inexpensive eatery serves Mexican and Southwestern fare. Vegetarians and vegans are also well served here—a place named after and decorated in the spirit of Grateful Dead legend Jerry Garcia. ⊠ *145 S. Washington St.* ☎ *209/588–1915* ▤ *No credit cards* ⊘ *Closed Sun.*

$–$$$ ⬚ **Barretta Gardens Bed and Breakfast Inn.** This inn is perfect for a romantic getaway or a special business meeting. Its elegant Victorian rooms vary in size, but all are furnished with period pieces. The three antiques-filled parlors carry on the Victorian theme. A French bakery on the property provides the fresh pastries at breakfast. ⊠ *700 S. Barretta St., 95370* ☎ *209/532–6039 or 800/206–3333* ▤ *209/532–8257* ⊕ *www.barrettagardens.com* ◄ *5 rooms* ⬚ *Hot tub* ▤ *AE, MC, V* ⑩ *CP.*

$–$$ ⬚ **Best Western Sonora Oaks Motor Hotel.** The standard motel-issue rooms at this East Sonora establishment are clean and roomy; the larger ones have outdoor sitting areas. Suites have fireplaces, whirlpool tubs, and tranquil hillside views. Because the motel is right off Highway 108, the front rooms can be noisy. ⊠ *19551 Hess Ave., 95370* ☎ *209/533–4400 or 800/532–1944* ▤ *209/532–1964* ⊕ *www.bestwestern.com* ◄ *96 rooms, 4 suites* ⬚ *Restaurant, pool, outdoor hot tub, lounge, meeting room* ▤ *AE, D, DC, MC, V.*

Jamestown

❷ *4 mi south of Sonora on Hwy. 49.*

Compact Jamestown supplies a touristy, superficial view of gold-rush-era life. Shops in brightly colored buildings along Main Street sell antiques and gift items.

The California State Railroad Museum operates **Railtown 1897** at what were the headquarters and general shops of the Sierra Railway from 1897 to 1955. The railroad has appeared in more than 200 movies and television productions, including *Petticoat Junction, The Virginian, High Noon,* and *Unforgiven.* You can view the roundhouse, an air-operated 60-foot turntable, shop rooms, and old locomotives and coaches. Six-mile, 40-minute steam train rides through the countryside operate on weekends during part of the year. ⊠ *5th Ave. and Reservoir Rd., off Hwy. 49* ☎ *209/984–3953* ⊕ *www.csrmf. org* ▧ *Roundhouse tour $2; train ride $6* ⊘ *Daily 9:30–4:30. Train rides Apr.–Oct., weekends 11–3.*

Where to Stay & Eat

$$ ×⬚ **National Hotel.** The National has been in business since 1859, and the furnishings—brass beds, patchwork quilts, and lace curtains—are authentic but not overly embellished. The saloon, which still has its original redwood bar, is a great place to linger. The popular restaurant ($–$$$) serves big lunches: hamburgers and fries, salads, and Italian entrées. More upscale Continental cuisine is prepared for dinner (reservations essential). ⊠ *18183 Main St., 95327* ☎ *209/984–3446, 800/894–3446 in CA* ▤ *209/984–5620* ⊕ *www.national-hotel.com* ◄ *9 rooms*

⚲ *Restaurant, in-room VCRs, in-room data ports, bar* ▤ *AE, D, DC, MC, V* ⍾ *CP.*

Mariposa

28 *50 mi south of Jamestown on Hwy. 49.*

Mariposa marks the southern end of the Mother Lode. Much of the land in this area was part of a 44,000-acre land grant Colonel John C. Fremont acquired from Mexico before gold was discovered and California became a state.

At the **California State Mining and Mineral Museum,** a glittering 13-pound chunk of crystallized gold makes it clear what the rush was about. Displays include a reproduction of a typical tunnel dug by hard-rock miners, a miniature stamp mill, and a panning and sluicing exhibit. ✉ *Mariposa County Fairgrounds, Hwy. 49* ☎ *209/742–7625* 💲 *$3* ⊙ *May–Sept., daily 10–6; Oct.–Apr., Wed.–Mon. 10–4.*

Where to Stay & Eat

$–$$$ ✕ **Charles Street Dinner House.** Ever since Ed Uebner moved here from Chicago to become the owner-chef in 1980, Charles Street has been firmly established as the classiest dinner joint in town—plus, it's centrally located. The extensive menu, which won't appeal to vegetarians, includes beef, chicken, pork, lamb, duck, and lobster. ✉ *Hwy. 140 at 7th St.* ☎ *209/ 966–2366* ▤ *D, MC, V* ⊙ *Closed Mon. and Tues. No lunch.*

$ ✕ **Castillo's Mexican Food.** Tasty tacos, enchiladas, chiles rellenos (stuffed, batter-fried, mild chili peppers), and burrito combinations plus chimichangas, fajitas, steak, and seafood are served in a casual storefront. ✉ *4995 5th St.* ☎ *209/742–4413* ▤ *MC, V.*

$–$$ ⌂ **Little Valley Inn.** Pine paneling, historical photos, and old mining tools recall Mariposa's heritage at this modern B&B. A suite that sleeps five people includes a full kitchen. All rooms have private entrances, baths, and decks. The large grounds include a creek where you can pan for gold. ✉ *3483 Brooks Rd., off Hwy. 49, 95338* ☎ *209/742–6204 or 800/889–5444* 🖷 *209/742–5099* ⊕ *www.littlevalley.com* ⇔ *4 rooms, 1 suite, 1 cabin* ⚲ *Refrigerators, horseshoes; no smoking* ▤ *AE, MC, V* ⍾ *BP.*

$ ⌂ **Mariposa Lodge.** Thoroughly modern and somewhat without character, the Mariposa nevertheless is a solid option for those who want to stay within 30 mi of Yosemite National Park without spending a fortune. ✉ *5052 Hwy. 140, 95338* ☎ *209/966–3607* 🖷 *209/742–7038* ⇔ *45 rooms* ⚲ *Pool, outdoor hot tub, no-smoking rooms* ▤ *AE, MC, V.*

THE GOLD COUNTRY—NORTH

HIGHWAY 49 FROM COLOMA TO NEVADA CITY

Highway 49 north of Placerville links the towns of Coloma, Auburn, Grass Valley, and Nevada City. Most are gentrified versions of once-rowdy mining camps, vestiges of which remain in roadside museums, old mining structures, and restored homes now serving as inns.

Coloma

㉙ *8 mi northwest of Placerville on Hwy. 49.*

The California gold rush started in Coloma. "My eye was caught with the glimpse of something shining in the bottom of the ditch," James Marshall recalled. Marshall himself never found any more "color," as gold came to be called.

★ Most of Coloma lies within **Marshall Gold Discovery State Historic Park.** Though crowded with tourists in summer, Coloma hardly resembles the mob scene it was in 1849, when 2,000 prospectors staked out claims along the streambed. The town's population grew to 4,000, supporting seven hotels, three banks, and many stores and businesses. But when reserves of the precious metal dwindled, prospectors left as quickly as they had come. A working reproduction of an 1840s mill lies near the spot where James Marshall first saw gold. A trail leads to a monument marking his discovery. The museum is not as interesting as the outdoor exhibits. ⊠ *Hwy. 49* ☎ *530/622–3470* ⊕ *www.parks.ca.gov* 🖃 *$5 per vehicle, day use* ⊘ *Park daily 8 AM–sunset. Museum daily 10–3.*

Where to Stay

$–$$$$ 🛏 **Coloma Country Inn.** Four of the rooms at this B&B on 5 acres in the state historic park are inside a restored 1852 Victorian. One suite, with a kitchenette, is in the carriage house. Appointments include antique double and queen-size beds, handmade quilts, stenciled friezes, and fresh flowers. The owners can direct you to tour operators leading rafting trips on the American River. ⊠ *345 High St., 95613* ☎ *530/622–6919* 🖷 *530/622–1795* ⊕ *www.colomacountryinn.com* 🛏 *4 rooms, 1 suite* ♿ *Kitchenette* ⊟ *No credit cards* ⫧ *BP.*

Auburn

▶ **㉚** *18 mi northwest of Coloma on Hwy. 49; 34 mi northeast of Sacramento on I–80.*

Auburn is the Gold Country town most accessible to travelers on Interstate 80. An important transportation center during the gold rush, Auburn has a small Old Town district with narrow climbing streets, cobblestone lanes, wooden sidewalks, and many original buildings. Fresh produce, flowers, baked goods, and gifts are for sale at the farmers' market, held Saturday morning year-round.

Auburn's standout structure is the **Placer County Courthouse.** The classic gold-dome building houses the Placer County Museum, which documents the area's history—Native American, railroad, agricultural, and mining—from the early 1700s to 1900. ⊠ *101 Maple St.* ☎ *530/889–6500* 🖃 *Free* ⊘ *Daily 10–4.*

The **Bernhard Museum Complex,** whose centerpiece is the former Traveler's Rest Hotel, was built in 1851. A residence and adjacent winery buildings reflect family life in the late Victorian era. The carriage house contains period conveyances. ⊠ *291 Auburn–Folsom Rd.* ☎ *530/889–6500* 🖃 *Free* ⊘ *Tues.–Sun. 11–4.*

The **Gold Country Museum** surveys life in the mines. Exhibits include a walk-through mine tunnel, a gold-panning stream, and a reproduction saloon. ⊠ *1273 High St., off Auburn–Folsom Rd.* ☎ *530/889–6500* 🖅 *Free* ☉ *Tues.–Sun. 11–4.*

Where to Stay & Eat

★ **$$–$$$** ✕ **Latitudes.** Delicious multicultural cuisine is served in an 1870 Victorian. The menu (with monthly specials from diverse geographical regions) includes seafood, chicken, beef, and turkey entrées prepared with the appropriate Mexican spices, curries, cheeses, or teriyaki sauce. Vegetarians and vegans have several inventive choices, too. Sunday brunch is deservedly popular. ⊠ *130 Maple St.* ☎ *530/885–9535* ▤ *AE, D, MC, V* ☉ *Closed Mon. and Tues.*

$$–$$$ ✕ **Le Bilig French Café.** Simple and elegant cuisine is the goal of the chefs at this country-French café on the outskirts of Auburn. Escargots, coq au vin, and quiche are standard offerings; specials might include salmon in parchment paper. ⊠ *11750 Atwood Rd., off Hwy. 49 near the Bel Air Mall* ☎ *530/888–1491* ▤ *MC, V* ☉ *Closed Mon. and Tues. No lunch.*

¢–$ ✕ **Awful Annie's.** Big patio umbrellas (and outdoor heaters when necessary) allow patrons to take in the view of the Old Town from this popular spot for breakfast—one specialty is a chili omelet—or lunch. ⊠ *160 Sacramento St.* ☎ *530/888–9857* ▤ *AE, MC, V* ☉ *No dinner.*

$–$$ ▥ **Comfort Inn.** The contemporary-style rooms at this well-maintained property are softened with teal and pastel colors. Though it's close to the freeway, the motel is fairly quiet. The expanded Continental breakfast includes many choices of baked goods, cereals, fruits, and juices. ⊠ *1875 Auburn Ravine Rd., north of Forest Hill exit of I–80, 95603* ☎ *530/885–1800 or 800/626–1900* 🖷 *530/888–6424* ⇱ *77 rooms, 2 suites* ♿ *In-room data ports, pool, gym, spa, laundry facilities, meeting room, no-smoking floor* ▤ *AE, D, DC, MC, V* ☉ *CP.*

$–$$ ▥ **Holiday Inn.** On a hill above the freeway across from Old Town, this hotel has an imposing columned entrance but a welcoming lobby. Rooms are chain-standard but attractively furnished. All have work areas and coffeemakers. Those nearest the parking lot can be noisy. ⊠ *120 Grass Valley Hwy., 95603* ☎ *530/887–8787 or 800/814–8787* 🖷 *530/887–9824* ⊕ *www.6c.com* ⇱ *96 rooms, 6 suites* ♿ *Restaurant, room service, in-room data ports, pool, gym, spa, bar, business services, convention center* ▤ *AE, D, DC, MC, V.*

Grass Valley

③ *24 mi north of Auburn on Hwy. 49.*

More than half of California's total gold production was extracted from mines around Grass Valley, including the Empire Mine, which, along with the North Star Mining Museum, is among the Gold Country's most fascinating attractions. Unlike neighboring Nevada City, urban sprawl surrounds Grass Valley's historic downtown.

In the center of town, on the site of the original, stands a reproduction of the **Lola Montez House** (⊠ *248 Mill St.* ☎ *530/273–4667 or 800/655–4667*), home of the notorious dancer. Montez, who arrived in Grass

Valley in the early 1850s, was no great talent—her popularity among miners derived from her suggestive "spider dance"—but her loves, who reportedly included composer Franz Liszt, were legendary. According to one account, she arrived in California after having been "permanently retired from her job as Bavarian king Ludwig's mistress," literary muse, and political adviser. She apparently pushed too hard for democracy, which contributed to his overthrow and her banishment as a witch—or so the story goes. The memory of licentious Lola lingers in Grass Valley, as does her bathtub (on the front porch of the house). The Grass Valley/Nevada County Chamber of Commerce is headquartered here.

The landmark **Holbrooke Hotel** (⊠ 212 W. Main St. ☎ 530/273–1353 or 800/933–7077), built in 1851, was host to Lola Montez and Mark Twain as well as Ulysses S. Grant and a stream of other U.S. presidents. Its restaurant-saloon is one of the oldest operating west of the Mississippi.

★ The hard-rock gold mine at **Empire Mine State Historic Park** was one of California's richest. An estimated 5.8 million ounces were extracted from its 367 mi of underground passages between 1850 and 1956. On the 50-minute tours you can walk into a mine shaft, peer into the mine's deeper recesses, and view the owner's "cottage," which has exquisite woodwork. The visitor center has mining exhibits, and a picnic area is nearby. ⊠ *10791 E. Empire St., south of Empire St. exit of Hwy. 49* ☎ *530/273–8522* ⊕ *www.parks.ca.gov* ⊠ *$3* ☉ *May–Aug., daily 9–6; Sept.–Apr., daily 10–5. Tours May–Aug., daily on the hr 11–4; Sept.–Apr., weekends at 1 (cottage only) and 2 (mine yard only), weather permitting.*

Ⓒ Housed in the former North Star powerhouse, the **North Star Mining Museum** displays the 32-foot-high enclosed Pelton Water Wheel, said to be the largest ever built. It was used to power mining operations and was a forerunner of the modern turbines that generate hydroelectricity. Hands-on displays are geared to children. There's a picnic area nearby. ⊠ *Empire and McCourtney Sts., north of Empire St. exit of Hwy. 49* ☎ *530/273–4255* ⊠ *Donation requested* ☉ *May–mid-Oct., daily 10–5.*

Where to Stay & Eat

¢ ✕ **Cousin Jack Pasties.** Meat- and vegetable-stuffed pasties are a taste of the region's history, having come across the Atlantic with Cornish miners and their families in the mid-19th century. The flaky crusts practically melt in your mouth. A simple food stand, which sometimes closes early on dreary winter days, Jack's is nonetheless a local landmark and dear to its loyal clientele. ⊠ *Auburn and Main Sts.* ☎ *530/272–9230* ▤ *No credit cards.*

$$ 🏨 **Holiday Lodge.** This modest hotel is close to many of the town's main attractions, and its staff can help point you toward—or arrange—gold-panning excursions and historical tours of the Gold Country. ⊠ *1221 E. Main St., 95945* ☎ *530/273–4406 or 800/742–7125* 🛏 *35 rooms* ⚭ *Pool, sauna* ▤ *AE, MC, V* ⏀ *CP.*

Nevada City

32 *4 mi north of Grass Valley on Hwy. 49.*

Nevada City, once known as the Queen City of the Northern Mines, is the most appealing of the northern Mother Lode towns. The iron-shutter brick buildings that line the narrow downtown streets contain antiques shops, galleries, bookstores, boutiques, B&Bs, restaurants, and a winery. Horse-drawn carriage tours add to the romance, as do gas street-lamps. At one point in the 1850s Nevada City had a population of nearly 10,000, enough to support much cultural activity.

With its gingerbread-trim bell tower, **Firehouse No. 1** is one of the Gold Country's most photographed buildings. A museum, it houses gold-rush artifacts and a Chinese joss house (temple). Also on display are relics of the ill-fated Donner Party, a group of 19th-century travelers who, trapped in the Sierra Nevada by winter snows, were forced to cannibalize their dead to survive. ⊠ *214 Main St.* ☎ *530/265–5468* 🖾 *Donation requested* ⊗ *Apr.–Nov., daily 11–4; Dec.–Mar., Thurs.–Sun. 11:30–4.*

The redbrick **Nevada Theatre,** constructed in 1865, is California's oldest theater building in continuous use. Mark Twain, Emma Nevada, and many other notable people appeared on its stage. Housed in the theater, the **Foothill Theater Company** (☎ *530/265–8587* or *888/730–8587*) holds theatrical and musical events. Old films are screened here, too. ⊠ *401 Broad St.* ☎ *530/265–6161, 530/274–3456 for film show times.*

The **Miners Foundry,** erected in 1856, produced machines for gold mining and logging. The Pelton Water Wheel, a source of power for the mines (the wheel also jump-started the hydroelectric power industry), was invented here. A cavernous building, the foundry is the site of plays, concerts, an antiques show, weddings, receptions, and other events; call for a schedule. ⊠ *325 Spring St.* ☎ *530/265–5040* ⊗ *Weekdays 10–4.*

You can watch wine being created while you sip at the **Nevada City Winery,** where the tasting room overlooks the production area. ⊠ *Miners Foundry Garage, 321 Spring St.* ☎ *530/265–9463* or *800/203–9463* ⊕ *www.ncwinery.com* 🖾 *Free* ⊗ *Tastings daily noon–5.*

Where to Stay & Eat

$$–$$$$ ✕ **Country Rose Café.** The lengthy country-French menu at this antiques-laden restaurant includes seafood, beef, lamb, chicken, and ratatouille. If you crave seafood, try the swordfish Oscar, topped with crab, shrimp, and béarnaise sauce. In the summer there's outdoor service on the verdant patio. ⊠ *300 Commercial St.* ☎ *530/265–6248* ⊟ *AE, D, DC, MC, V.*

$$–$$$ ✕ **New Moon Cafe.** A series of small, attractively lighted rooms give diners a cozy feeling. Entrées include the colorfully named sagebrush chicken and mine shaft *coulotte*; organic flours and free-range meats are used when available. ⊠ *203 York St.* ☎ *530/265–6399* ⊟ *AE, MC, V* ⊗ *No lunch.*

$–$$$ ✕ **Cirino's.** American-Italian dishes—seafood, pasta, and veal—are served at this informal bar and grill. The restaurant's handsome bar is of gold-rush vintage. ⊠ *309 Broad St.* ☎ *530/265–2246* ⊟ *AE, D, MC, V.*

$–$$$ ✕ **Kirby's Creekside Restaurant & Bar.** This two-level restaurant-bar complex perches over the quieter side of Deer Creek. You can dine on the large outdoor deck in warm weather or sit by the fireplace on chilly days. Among the inventive Continental preparations is the pork loin stuffed with roasted peppers. ⊠ *101 Broad St.* ☎ *530/265–3445* ▭ *AE, D, MC, V.*

$$–$$$ 🏨 **Deer Creek Inn.** The main veranda of this 1860 Queen Anne Victorian overlooks a huge lawn that rolls past a rose-covered arbor to the creek below. You can play croquet on the lawn or pan for gold in the creek. All rooms have king- or queen-size beds; some rooms have two-person tubs. Wine service and a full breakfast are included. ⊠ *116 Nevada St., 95959* ☎ *530/265–0363 or 800/655–0363* 🖷 *530/265–0980* ⊕ *www.deercreekinn.com* ↩ *5 rooms* ▭ *AE, MC, V* ⦿ *BP.*

$$–$$$ 🏨 **Flume's End.** This charming inn was built in 1860 at the end of a large flume that once brought water into Nevada City's mines. Hardwood floors and antiques add an air of elegance. Two guest rooms have hot tubs, and most, including a small cottage, have creek views. ⊠ *317 S. Pine St., 95959* ☎ *530/265–9665 or 800/991–8118* ⊕ *www.flumesend. com* ↩ *6 rooms* ▭ *MC, V* ⦿ *BP.*

★ $$–$$$ 🏨 **Red Castle Historic Lodgings.** A state landmark, this 1857 Gothic-revival mansion stands on a forested hillside overlooking Nevada City. Its brick exterior is trimmed with white-icicle woodwork. A steep private pathway leads down through the terraced gardens into town. Handsome antique furnishings and Oriental rugs decorate the rooms. Red Castle features an opulent afternoon tea and morning breakfast buffet. ⊠ *109 Prospect St., 95959* ☎ *530/265–5135 or 800/761–4766* ⊕ *www.historic-lodgings.com* ↩ *4 rooms, 3 suites* ▭ *MC, V* ⦿ *BP.*

$–$$ 🏨 **Northern Queen Inn.** Most accommodations at this bright creek-side inn are typical motel units, but there are eight two-story chalets and eight rustic cottages with efficiency kitchens and gas-log fireplaces in a secluded wooded area. If you stay here, you can ride free on the hotel's narrow-gauge railroad, which offers excursions through Maidu Indian homelands and a Chinese cemetery from gold-rush days. ⊠ *400 Railroad Ave. (Sacramento St. exit off Hwy. 49), 95959* ☎ *530/265–5824 or 800/226–3090* 🖷 *530/265–3720* ⊕ *www.northernqueeninn.com* ↩ *70 rooms, 16 suites* ⚭ *Restaurant, some kitchenettes, refrigerators, pool, hot tub, convention center* ▭ *AE, D, DC, MC, V.*

THE GOLD COUNTRY A TO Z

To research prices, get advice from other travelers, and book travel arrangements, visit www.fodors.com.

AIRPORTS & TRANSFERS

Sacramento International Airport is served by Alaska, America West, American, Continental, Delta, Frontier, Horizon Air, Northwest, Southwest, and United. *See* Air Travel *in* Smart Travel Tips A to Z for airline phone numbers. A private taxi from the airport to downtown Sacramento is about $20. The cost of the Super Shuttle from the airport to downtown Sacramento is $11. Call in advance to arrange transportation from your hotel to the airport.

🚩 **Sacramento International Airport** ✉ 6900 Airport Blvd., 12 mi northwest of downtown off I-5, Sacramento ☎ 916/874-0700 ⊕ www.sacairports.org. **Super Shuttle** ☎ 800/258-3826.

BOAT TRAVEL

Sacramento's riverfront location enables you to sightsee while getting around by boat. A water taxi run by River Otter Taxi Co. serves the Old Sacramento waterfront during spring and summer, stopping at points near restaurants and other sights. Channel Star Excursions operates the *Spirit of Sacramento*, a riverboat that takes passengers on happy-hour, dinner, lunch, and champagne-brunch cruises in addition to one-hour narrated tours.

🚩 **Channel Star Excursions** ✉ 110 L St. ☎ 916/552-2933 or 800/433-0263. **River Otter Taxi Co.** ☎ 916/446-7704.

BUS TRAVEL

Getting to and from SIA can be accomplished via taxi, the Super Shuttle, or by Yolo County Public Bus 42, which operates a circular service around SIA, downtown Sacramento, West Sacramento, Davis, and Woodland. Other Gold Country destinations are best reached by private car.

Greyhound serves Sacramento, Davis, Auburn, and Placerville. It's a two-hour trip from San Francisco's Transbay Terminal, at 1st and Mission streets, to the Sacramento station, at 7th and L streets.

Sacramento Regional Transit buses and light-rail vehicles transport passengers in Sacramento. Most buses run from 6 AM to 10 PM, most trains from 5 AM to midnight. A DASH (Downtown Area Shuttle) bus and the No. 30 city bus both link Old Sacramento, midtown, and Sutter's Fort. The fare is 50¢ within this area.

🚩 **Greyhound** ☎ 800/231-2222 ⊕ www.greyhound.com. **Sacramento Regional Transit** ☎ 916/321-2877 ⊕ www.sacrt.com. **Yolo County Bus** ☎ 530/666-2837 ⊕ www.yolobus.com.

CAR RENTAL

You can rent a car from any of the major national chains at Sacramento International Airport. *See* Car Rental *in* Smart Travel Tips A to Z for national car-rental agency phone numbers.

CAR TRAVEL

Traveling by car is the most convenient way to see the Gold Country. From Sacramento, three highways fan out toward the east, all intersecting with Highway 49: I-80 heads 34 mi northeast to Auburn; U.S. 50 goes east 40 mi to Placerville; and Highway 16 angles southeast 45 mi to Plymouth. Highway 49 is an excellent two-lane road that winds and climbs through the foothills and valleys, linking the principal Gold Country towns.

Sacramento lies at the junction of I–5 and I–80, not quite 90 mi northeast of San Francisco. The 406-mi drive north on I–5 from Los Angeles takes seven to eight hours. I–80 continues northeast through the Gold Country toward Reno, about 136 mi (three hours or so) from Sacramento.

EMERGENCIES

In an emergency dial 911. Each of the following medical facilities has an emergency room open 24 hours a day.

🔲 Hospitals **Mercy Hospital of Sacramento** ✉ 4001 J St., Sacramento ☎ 916/453-4424. **Sutter General Hospital** ✉ 2801 L St., Sacramento ☎ 916/733-8900. **Sutter Memorial Hospital** ✉ 52nd and F Sts., Sacramento ☎ 916/733-1000.

LODGING

A number of organizations can supply information about Gold Country B&Bs and other accommodations.

🔲 **Amador County Innkeepers Association** ☎ 209/267-1710 or 800/726-4667. **Gold Country Inns of Tuolumne County** ☎ 209/533-1845. **Historic Bed & Breakfast Inns of Grass Valley & Nevada City** ☎ 530/477-6634 or 800/250-5808.

TOURS

Gold Prospecting Adventures, LLC, based in Jamestown, arranges gold-panning trips.

🔲 **Gold Prospecting Adventures, LLC** ☎ 209/984-4653 or 800/596-0009 ⊕ www.goldprospecting.com.

TRAIN TRAVEL

Several trains operated by Amtrak stop in Sacramento and Davis. Trains making the 2½-hour trip from Jack London Square, in Oakland, stop in Emeryville (across the bay from San Francisco), Richmond, Martinez, and Davis before reaching Sacramento; some stop in Berkeley and Suisun-Fairfield as well.

🔲 **Amtrak** ☎ 800/872-7245 ⊕ www.amtrakcalifornia.com.

VISITOR INFORMATION

🔲 **Amador County Chamber of Commerce** ✉ 125 Peek St., Jackson 95642 ☎ 209/223-0350 ⊕ www.amadorcountychamber.com. **Davis Chamber of Commerce** ✉ 130 G St., Davis 95616 ☎ 530/756-5160 ⊕ www.davischamber.com. **El Dorado County Chamber of Commerce** ✉ 542 Main St., Placerville 95667 ☎ 530/621-5885 or 800/457-6279 ⊕ www.eldoradocounty.org. **Grass Valley/Nevada County Chamber of Commerce** ✉ 248 Mill St., Grass Valley 95945 ☎ 530/273-4667 or 800/655-4667 ⊕ www.ncgold.com/chamber. **Mariposa County Visitors Bureau** ✉ 5158 Hwy. 140, Mariposa 95338 ☎ 209/966-7081 or 800/208-2434 ⊕ mariposa.yosemite.net/visitor. **Nevada City Chamber of Commerce** ✉ 132 Main St., Nevada City 95945 ☎ 530/265-2692. **Sacramento Convention and Visitors Bureau** ✉ 1303 J St., Suite 600, Sacramento 95814 ☎ 916/264-7777 ⊕ www.sacramentocvb.org. **Tuolumne County Visitors Bureau** ✉ 542 Stockton St., Sonora 95370 ☎ 209/533-4420 or 800/446-1333 ⊕ www.thegreatunfenced.com. **Woodland Chamber of Commerce** ✉ 307 1st St., Woodland 95695 ☎ 530/662-7327 or 888/843-2636 ⊕ www.woodlandchamber.org.

Lake Tahoe
With Reno, Nevada

WORD OF MOUTH

"Lake Tahoe has lots of great hikes, and water activities range from a paddle boat trip to the Emerald Bay to jet boats along the coast. There are swimming beaches, too. If you've been there skiing, it might be fun to take the ski lift and see how the scenery is different in the summer."

—Vera

Updated by
John A.
Vlahides

STUNNING COBALT-BLUE LAKE TAHOE IS THE LARGEST ALPINE LAKE IN NORTH AMERICA, famous for its clarity, deep blue water, and surrounding snowcapped peaks. Straddling the state line between California and Nevada, it lies 6,225 feet above sea level in the Sierra Nevada. The border gives this popular resort region a split personality. About half its visitors are intent on low-key sightseeing, hiking, fishing, camping, and boating. The rest head directly for the Nevada side, where bargain dining, big-name entertainment, and the lure of a jackpot draw them into the glittering casinos.

The first white explorer to gaze upon this spectacular region was Captain John C. Fremont, in 1844, guided by the famous scout Kit Carson. Not long afterward, silver was discovered in Nevada's Comstock Lode, at Virginia City. As the mines grew larger and deeper, the Tahoe Basin's forests were leveled to provide lumber for subterranean support (had the forests been left untouched, Lake Tahoe might well have become a national park). By the early 1900s wealthy Californians were building lakeside estates here, some of which still stand. Improved roads brought the less affluent in the 1920s and 1930s, when modest bungalows began to appear. The first casinos opened in the 1940s. Ski resorts inspired another development boom in the 1950s and 1960s, turning the lake into a year-round destination.

Though Lake Tahoe possesses abundant natural beauty and accessible wilderness, nearby towns are highly developed, and roads around the lake are often congested with traffic. Those who prefer solitude can escape to the many state parks, national forests, and protected tracts of wilderness that ring the 22-mi-long, 12-mi-wide lake. At a vantage point overlooking Emerald Bay, on a trail in the national forests that ring the basin, or on a sunset cruise on the lake itself, you can forget the hordes and the commercial development. You can even pretend that you're Mark Twain, who found "not fifteen other human beings throughout its wide circumference" when he visited the lake in 1861 and wrote that "the eye never tired of gazing, night or day, calm or storm."

Exploring Lake Tahoe

The typical way to explore the Lake Tahoe area is to drive the 72-mi road that follows the shore through wooded flatlands and past beaches, climbing to vistas on the rugged southwest side of the lake and passing through busy commercial developments and casinos on its northeastern and southeastern edges. Undeveloped Lake Tahoe–Nevada State Park occupies more than half of the Nevada side of Lake Tahoe, stretching along the shore from just north of Zephyr Cove to just south of the upscale community of Incline Village. The California side is more developed, particularly South Lake Tahoe, but there are no garish casino towers, and much wilderness remains immediately outside developed towns.

About the Restaurants

On weekends and in high season, expect a long wait in the more popular restaurants. During the "shoulder seasons" (April to May and September to November), some places may close temporarily or limit their hours, so call ahead. Also, check local papers for deals and discounts

GREAT ITINERARIES

It takes only one day to "see" Lake Tahoe—to drive around the lake, stretch your legs at a few overlooks, take a nature walk, and wander among the casinos at Stateline. But if you have more time, you can laze on a beach and swim, venture onto the lake or into the mountains, and sample Tahoe's finer restaurants. If you have five days, you may become so attached to Tahoe that you begin visiting real-estate agents.

Numbers in the text correspond to numbers in the margin and on the Lake Tahoe map.

IF YOU HAVE 3 DAYS On your first day stop in ⊞ **South Lake Tahoe ❶** ⌐and pick up provisions for a picnic lunch. Start in **Pope-Baldwin Recreation Area ❷** and check out Tallac Historic Site. Head west on Highway 89, stopping at the Lake Tahoe Visitor Center and the **Emerald Bay State Park ❸** lookout. Have a tailgate picnic at the lookout, or hike down to Vikingsholm, a reproduction of a Viking castle. In the late afternoon explore the trails and mansion at **Sugar Pine Point State Park ❺**; then backtrack on Highway 89 and U.S. 50 for dinner in ⊞ **Stateline ⓭** or in South Lake Tahoe. On Day 2 cruise on the *Tahoe Queen* out of South Lake Tahoe or the MS *Dixie II* out of **Zephyr Cove ⓬** and then ride the Heavenly Gondola at Heavenly Mountain Resort in South Lake Tahoe. Carry a picnic for lunch high above the lake, and (except in snow season) take a walk on one of Heavenly's nature trails. You can try your luck at the Stateline casinos before dinner. Start your third day by heading north on U.S. 50, stopping at Cave Rock and (after turning north on Highway 28) at Sand Harbor Beach. If

there's no snow on the ground, tour the Thunderbird Lodge (reservations essential) for a glimpse of life at an old-Tahoe estate just south of **Incline Village ⓫**, or else continue on to **Crystal Bay ❿**. If you have time, drive to **Tahoe City ❼** to see the Gatekeeper's Cabin Museum, or make the 45-minute drive down to ⊞ **Reno ⓮** for dinner and some nightlife.

IF YOU HAVE 5 DAYS Spend your first morning at **Pope-Baldwin Recreation Area ❷** ⌐. After a picnic lunch head to the Lake Tahoe Visitor Center and the **Emerald Bay State Park ❸** lookout. Hike to Vikingsholm or move on to **Sugar Pine Point State Park ❺**. Have dinner in ⊞ **South Lake Tahoe ❶**. On your second day take a cruise to Emerald Bay or a half-day cruise around the lake; back on land, ride the Heavenly Gondola, and possibly take a hike. Spend the late afternoon or early evening sampling the worldly pleasures of the ⊞ **Stateline ⓭** casinos. On Day 3 visit Cave Rock, and the Thunderbird Lodge (reservations essential) just south of **Incline Village ⓫**, where you can have a late lunch before heading to **Crystal Bay ❿** and playing the slots, or to nearby Kings Beach State Recreation Area, where you can spend the late afternoon on the beach. That evening, drive down to ⊞ **Reno ⓮** for dinner and entertainment. On your fourth day hang out at Sand Harbor Beach. If the high-mountain desert appeals, spend Day 5 in the Great Basin, touring Carson City and Virginia City and the vast expanse of the eastern Sierra. Alternatively, head to **D. L. Bliss State Park ❹** for a hike; then drive to **Tahoe City ❼** for lunch and a tour of the Gatekeeper's Cabin Museum.

9

during this time. Many casinos use their restaurants to attract gamblers. Marquees often tout "$8.99 prime rib dinners" or "99¢ breakfast specials." Some of these meal deals, usually found in the coffee shops and buffets, are downright mediocre, but at those prices, it's hard to complain. The finer restaurants in casinos, however, deliver pricier food, as well as reasonable service and a bit of atmosphere. Unless otherwise noted, even the most expensive area restaurants welcome customers in casual clothes—not surprising in this year-round vacation spot—but don't expect to be served in most places if you're barefoot, shirtless, or wearing a skimpy bathing suit.

About the Hotels

Quiet inns on the water, suburban-style strip motels, casino hotels, slope-side ski lodges, and house and condo rentals throughout the area constitute the lodging choices at Tahoe. The crowds come in summer and during ski season; reserve as far in advance as possible, especially for holiday periods, when prices skyrocket. Spring and fall give you a little more leeway and lower—sometimes significantly lower—rates.

	WHAT IT COSTS				
	$$$$	$$$	$$	$	¢
RESTAURANTS	over $30	$23–$30	$16–$22	$10–$15	under $10
HOTELS	over $250	$176–$250	$121–$175	$90–$120	under $90

Restaurant prices are for a main course at dinner, excluding sales tax of 7%–7¼% (depending on location). Hotel prices are for two people in a standard double room in high season, excluding service charges and 9%–12% tax.

Timing

Most Lake Tahoe accommodations, restaurants, and even a handful of parks are open year-round, but many visitor centers, mansions, state parks, and beaches are closed from November through May. During those months, multitudes of skiers and other winter-sports enthusiasts are attracted to Tahoe's downhill resorts and cross-country centers, North America's largest concentration of skiing facilities. Ski resorts try to open by Thanksgiving, if only with machine-made snow, and can operate through May or later. During the ski season, Tahoe's population swells on the weekends. If you're able to come midweek, you'll have the resorts and neighboring towns almost to yourself. Bear in mind, though, that Tahoe is a popular wedding and honeymoon destination: on Valentine's Day the chapels become veritable assembly lines.

Unless you want to ski, you'll find that Tahoe is most fun in summer, when it's cooler here than in the scorched Sierra Nevada foothills, the clean mountain air is bracingly crisp, and the surface temperature of Lake Tahoe is an invigorating 65°F–70°F (compared with 40°F–50°F in winter—brrr!). This is also the time, however, when it may seem as if every tourist at the lake—100,000 on peak weekends—is in a car on the main road circling the 72-mi shoreline (especially on Highway 89, just south of Tahoe City, and on U.S. 50 in South Lake). Weekdays are busy as well. The crowds and congestion increase as the day wears on, so the

PLEASURES & PASTIMES

CAMPING. Campgrounds abound in the Tahoe area, operated by the California and Nevada state park departments, the U.S. Forest Service, city utility districts, and private operators. Sites range from primitive and rustic to upscale and luxurious. Make reservations far ahead for summer, when sites are in high demand.

GAMBLING. Six casinos are clustered on a strip of U.S. 50 in Stateline, and five casinos operate on the north shore. And, of course, in Reno there are more than a dozen major and a dozen minor casinos. Open 24 hours a day, 365 days a year, these gambling halls have table games, race and sports books, and thousands of slot and video-poker machines. There is no charge to enter, and there is no dress code; as long as you're wearing money, you'll be welcome.

GREAT GOLF. The Tahoe area is nearly as popular with golfers as it is with skiers. More than a dozen superb courses dot the mountains around the lake, with magnificent views, thick pines, fresh, cool air, and lush fairways and greens.

HIKING. There are five national forests in the Tahoe Basin and a half dozen state parks. The main areas for hiking include the Tahoe Rim Trail, a 165-mi path along the ridgelines that now completely rings the lake; Desolation Wilderness, a vast 63,473-acre preserve of granite peaks, glacial valleys, subalpine forests, the Rubicon River, and more than 50 lakes; and the trail systems in D. L. Bliss, Emerald Bay, Sugar Pine Point, and Lake Tahoe–Nevada state parks and near Lake Tahoe Visitor Center. The Pacific Crest Trail, a high-mountain foot trail connecting Mexico to Canada, runs along the Sierra Crest just west of the lake. To the south of Lake Tahoe sits the Mokelumne Wilderness, a whopping 100,848-acre preserve, one of several undeveloped tracts that extend toward Yosemite, which is accessible via the Tahoe-Yosemite Trail, a 186-mi trek.

SKIING & SNOWBOARDING. The mountains around Lake Tahoe are bombarded by blizzards throughout most winters and sometimes in fall and spring; 10- to 12-foot bases are common. Indeed, the Sierra often has the deepest snowpack on the continent, but because of the relatively mild temperatures over the Pacific, falling snow can be very heavy and wet— it's nicknamed Sierra Cement for a reason. The upside is that you can sometimes ski and board as late as July, you probably won't get frostbite, and you'll likely get a tan. The profusion of downhill resorts guarantees an ample selection of terrains, conditions, and challenges. Snowboarding is permitted at all Tahoe ski areas. Note that the major resorts get crowded on weekends. If you're going to ski on a Saturday, arrive early and quit early. Avoid moving with the masses. Also consider visiting the ski areas with few high-speed lifts or limited lodging and real estate at their bases: Alpine Meadows, Sugar Bowl, Homewood, Mt. Rose, Sierra-at-Tahoe, Diamond Peak, and Kirkwood. Expect traffic when the resorts close; if you're driving west toward the Bay Area, make an early escape, or ski at the resorts west of the Sierra Crest: Sugar Bowl, Kirkwood, or Sierra-at-Tahoe.

9

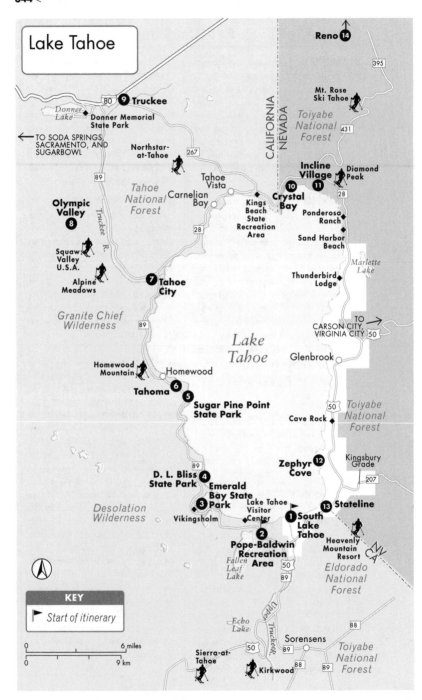

Lake Tahoe

Reno **14**

395

9 Truckee
80
Donner Lake
Donner Memorial State Park
← TO SODA SPRINGS, SACRAMENTO, AND SUGARBOWL

Northstar-at-Tahoe
267

Mt. Rose Ski Tahoe
Toiyabe National Forest
431

CALIFORNIA
NEVADA

Incline Village **11**
Diamond Peak

Tahoe National Forest

Tahoe Vista
Carnelian Bay

89

Olympic Valley 8

28

Kings Beach State Recreation Area

Crystal Bay **10**

Ponderosa Ranch

Sand Harbor Beach

Squaw Valley U.S.A.

Truckee R.

Alpine Meadows

7 Tahoe City

Marlette Lake

Thunderbird Lodge

Granite Chief Wilderness

89

Lake Tahoe

TO
CARSON CITY, VIRGINIA CITY 50

Glenbrook

Homewood Mountain
Homewood

Tahoma 6

5

Sugar Pine Point State Park

50
Toiyabe National Forest

Cave Rock

Zephyr Cove **12**

Kingsbury Grade

207

89

D. L. Bliss State Park 4

Emerald Bay State Park **3**

Vikingsholm

Lake Tahoe Visitor Center

1 South Lake Tahoe

13 Stateline

Desolation Wilderness

2

Pope-Baldwin Recreation Area

Heavenly Mountain Resort

NV
CA

Fallen Leaf Lake

50
89

Eldorado National Forest

Echo Lake

88

KEY
► *Start of itinerary*

Sorensens

Truckee R.

50
89

Toiyabe National Forest

0   6 miles
0   9 km

Sierra-at-Tahoe

Kirkwood
88   89

best strategy for avoiding the crush is to do as much as you can early in the day. The parking lots of the Lake Tahoe Visitor Center, Vikingsholm, and Gatekeeper's Cabin Museum can be jammed at any time, and the lake's beaches can be packed. September and October, when the throngs have dispersed but the weather is still pleasant, are among the most satisfying—and cheapest—months to visit Lake Tahoe.

CALIFORNIA SIDE

With the exception of Stateline, Nevada—which, aside from its casino-hotel towers, seems almost indistinguishable from South Lake Tahoe, California—the California side is more developed than the Nevada side. Here you'll find both commercial enterprises—restaurants, motels, lodges, resorts, residential subdivisions—and public-access facilities, such as historic sites, parks, campgrounds, marinas, and beaches.

South Lake Tahoe

➤ ❶ *50 mi south of Reno on U.S. 395 and U.S. 50; 198 mi northeast of San Francisco on I–80 and U.S. 50.*

The city of South Lake Tahoe's raison d'être is tourism: the casinos of adjacent Stateline, Nevada; the ski slopes at Heavenly Mountain; the beaches, docks, bike trails, and campgrounds all around the south shore; and the backcountry of Eldorado National Forest and Desolation Wilderness. The town itself, however, is disappointingly unattractive, with its mix of cheap motels, strip malls, and low-rise prefab-looking buildings that line both sides of U.S. 50. The small city's saving grace is its convenient location and bevy of services, as well as its gorgeous lake views.

Whether you ski or not, you'll appreciate the impressive view of Lake Tahoe from the **Heavenly Gondola.** Its 138 eight-passenger cars travel from the middle of town 2½ mi up the mountain in 13 minutes. When the weather's fine, you can take one of three hikes around the mountaintop and then have lunch at Adventure Peak Grill. Heavenly also offers day care for children. ⊠ *Downtown* ☎ *775/586–7000 or 800/432–8365* ⊕ *www.skiheavenly.com* 🖃 *$24* ⊙ *Hours vary; summer, daily 10–7; winter, daily 9–4.*

FodorsChoice ★

At the base of the gonodola, the **Heavenly Village** is the centerpiece of South Lake Tahoe's efforts to reinvent itself and provide a focal point for tourism. Essentially a pedestrian mall, it includes some good shopping, a cinema, an arcade for kids, and the Heavenly Village Outdoor Ice Rink.

Where to Stay & Eat

$$$–$$$$ ✕**Kalani's.** Fresh-off-the-plane seafood gets flown directly from the Honolulu fish market to Heavenly Village's sexiest (and priciest) restaurant. The sleek, industrial-chic, white-tablecloth dining room is decked out with carved bamboo, sweeping banquettes, a burnt-orange color palette, and modern-glass sculpture, which perfectly complements contemporary Pacific Rim specialties such as the succulent, melt-from-the-bone baby-back pork ribs with sesame-garlic soy sauce that are reason enough to visit the bar. There's also a good sushi menu with inventive rolls and sashimi combos. ⊠ *1001 Heavenly Village Way, #26* ☎ *530/544–6100* ⊟ *AE, D, MC, V.*

★ **$$–$$$** ✕ **Evan's.** The contemporary California menu includes such specialties as seared foie gras with curried ice cream and roast pineapple, and venison in a raspberry demi-glace. The 40-seat dining room is intimate, with tables a little close together, but the service and food are excellent and merit a special trip. ⊠ *536 Emerald Bay Rd.* ☎ *530/542–1990* ⚖ *Reservations essential* ⊟ *AE, D, DC, MC, V* ⊗ *No lunch.*

$–$$$ ✕ **Café Fiore.** This northern Italian restaurant may be the most romantic spot in town, with only seven candlelit tables. The menu lists a variety of pastas and meat dishes and several daily fish specials. Sautéed veal dishes are the house specialty. Leave room for the homemade white-chocolate ice cream. ⊠ *1169 Ski Run Blvd.* ☎ *530/541–2908* ⚖ *Reservations essential* ⊟ *AE, MC, V* ⊗ *No lunch.*

¢–$$$ ✕ **Freshies.** When you've had your fill of junk food, come here for delicious, healthful meals. Specialties include seafood and vegetarian dishes, but good grilled meats are always available, such as Hawaiian spare ribs and free-range rib-eye steaks. Though it's in a mini-mall and you may have to wait for a table, it's worth it, especially if you snag a table on the upstairs lake-view deck. ⊠ *3300 Lake Tahoe Blvd.* ☎ *530/542–3630* ⚖ *Reservations not accepted* ⊟ *D, MC, V.*

¢–$$ ✕ **Scusa!** The kitchen here turns out big plates of linguine with clam sauce, veal marsala, and chicken piccata. There's nothing fancy or esoteric about the menu, just straightforward Italian-American food. Try the exceptionally good bread pudding for dessert. ⊠ *1142 Ski Run Blvd.* ☎ *530/542–0100* ⊟ *AE, MC, V* ⊗ *No lunch.*

¢–$ ✕ **Orchid's Thai.** If you're hungry for Thai, Orchid's serves good food at reasonable prices in an attractive dining room with pumpkin-color walls. When every place in town is booked, this is a great backup. They even take reservations. ⊠ *2180 Lake Tahoe Blvd.* ☎ *530/544–5541* ⊟ *AE, D, DC, MC, V* ⊗ *No lunch Sun.*

¢ ✕ **Blue Angel Café.** A favorite of locals, who fill the half dozen wooden tables, the Blue Angel serves everything from frittatas, Benedicts, and house-made granola at breakfast to beef bourguignon, pasta carbonara, and chicken curry at lunch and dinner—and everything costs $10 or less. The cozy room make the visit feel like you're eating at a friend's house. ⊠ *1132 Ski Run Blvd.* ☎ *530/544–6544* ⊟ *DC, MC, V.*

¢ ✕ **Red Hut Café.** A vintage-1959 Tahoe diner, all chrome and red plastic, the Red Hut is a tiny place with a dozen counter stools and a dozen booths. It's a traditional breakfast spot for those in the know, who come for the huge omelets; the banana, pecan, and coconut waffles; and other tasty vittles. There's another branch in Stateline, too. ⊠ *2749 U.S. 50* ☎ *530/541–9024* ⚖ *Reservations not accepted* ⊟ *No credit cards* ⊗ *No dinner* ⊠ *227 Kingsbury Grade, Stateline, NV* ☎ *775/588–7488.*

$$$–$$$$ 🛏 **Black Bear Inn Bed and Breakfast.** South Lake Tahoe's most luxurious Fodor'sChoice inn feels like one of the great old lodges of the Adirondacks. Its living ★ room has rough-hewn beams, plank floors, cathedral ceilings, Persian rugs, and even an elk's head over the giant river-rock fireplace. Built in the 1990s with meticulous attention to detail, the five inn rooms and three cabins feature 19th-century American antiques, fine art, and fireplaces; cabins also have kitchenettes. Never intrusive, the affable innkeepers provide a sumptuous breakfast in the morning and wine and cheese in the afternoon. ⊠ *1202 Ski Run Blvd., 96150* ☎ *530/544–4451 or 877/232–7466* ⊕ *www.tahoeblackbear.com* ➮ *5 rooms, 3 cabins* ⚬ *Dining room, some in-room hot tubs, some kitchenettes, cable TV with movies, in-room VCRs, in-room data ports, Wi-Fi, outdoor hot tub, ski storage, lounge; no kids under 16, no smoking* ⊟ *AE, D, MC, V* ⦿ *BP.*

★ **$$$–$$$$** ▦ **Marriott's Grand Residence and Timber Lodge.** At the base of Heavenly Gondola, right in the center of town, stand these two giant, modern condominium properties operated by Marriott. Though both are extremely comfortable, Timber Lodge feels more like a family vacation resort; Grand Residence is geared toward luxury travelers. Units vary in size from studios to three bedrooms, and some have amenities such as stereos, fireplaces, daily maid service, and full kitchens. Ask about vacation packages. ⊠ *1001 Park Ave., 96150* ☎ *530/542–8400 or 800/627–7468* 🖷 *530/524–8410* ⊕ *www.marriott.com* ➮ *431 condos* ⚬ *Some in-room hot tubs, some kitchens, cable TV, in-room data ports, Wi-Fi, pool, gym, 2 hot tubs, ice-skating, ski shop, ski storage, laundry facilities, laundry service, concierge; no smoking* ⊟ *AE, D, DC, MC, V.*

☼ **$$–$$$$** ▦ **Embassy Suites Hotel.** All rooms are suites at this large full-service hotel just over the state line in California, where there are no casinos to disturb the quiet of the lobby. The extra-spacious accommodations are perfect for families, because every unit contains a pull-out sofa and dining table that seats four. Rates include full breakfast and evening cocktails. ⊠ *4130 Lake Tahoe Blvd., 96150* ☎ *530/544–5400 or 800/362–2779* 🖷 *530/544–4900* ⊕ *www.embassysuites.com* ➮ *400 suites* ⚬ *Restaurant, microwaves, refrigerators, cable TV with movies and video games, in-room broadband, in-room data ports, Web TV, Wi-Fi, indoor pool, exercise equipment, hot tub, sauna, ski storage, bar, lounge, laundry facilities, meeting rooms, parking (fee)* ⊟ *AE, D, DC, MC, V* ⦿ *BP.*

☼ **$$–$$$** ▦ **Lakeland Village Beach and Mountain Resort.** This 19-acre lakefront condominium complex has one- to five-bedroom semidetached town houses, and studios and suites in the lodge building. Each unit is individually owned and decorated, so there's no uniformity to the furnishings, but all are spacious and come with fireplaces and fully equipped kitchens. Some have decks overlooking the lake, but others face the highway; ask when you book. This is a great place for families and couples traveling together: the largest unit sleeps 12. ⊠ *3535 Lake Tahoe Blvd., 96150* ☎ *530/544–1685 or 800/822–5969* 🖷 *530/544–0193* ⊕ *www.lakelandvillage.com* ➮ *210 units* ⚬ *BBQs, kitchens, cable TV, in-room DVD/VCR, in-room data ports, Wi-Fi, 2 tennis courts, pool, gym, hot tubs (indoor and outdoor), sauna, beach, boating, fishing, ski shop, ski storage, dry cleaning, laundry facilities, meeting rooms* ⊟ *AE, D, MC, V.*

¢–**$$$** ▦ **Sorensen's Resort.** Escape civilization by staying in the Eldorado National Forest, 20 minutes south of town. In a log cabin at this woodsy 165-acre resort, you can lie on a hammock beneath the aspens or sit in a rocker on your own front porch. All but three of the cabins have a kitchen and wood-burning stove or fireplace. There are also three mod-

9

ern homes that sleep six. Request a room away from the road. ✉ *14255 Hwy. 88, Hope Valley 96120* ☎ *530/694–2203 or 800/423–9949* ⊕ *www.sorensensresort.com* ↪ *28 cabins, 2 rooms with shared bath, 4 houses* ⚷ *Restaurant, some fans, some kitchens, some kitchenettes, pond, sauna, boating, fishing, bicycles, croquet, hiking, cross-country skiing, ski shop, ski storage, tobogganing, library, babysitting, children's programs (ages 3–18), playground, some pets allowed; no a/c, no room phones, no room TVs, no smoking.*

★ **$$** ▦ **Inn by the Lake.** Across the road from a beach, this luxury motel has spacious, spotless rooms and suites decorated in soft autumn colors. All have balconies; some have lake views, wet bars, and kitchens. In the afternoon the staff sets out cookies and cider. ✉ *3300 Lake Tahoe Blvd., 96150* ☎ *530/542–0330 or 800/877–1466* 🖷 *530/541–6596* ⊕ *www.innbythelake.com* ↪ *87 rooms, 13 suites* ⚷ *Room service, some in-room hot tubs, some kitchens, some minibars, cable TV with movies and video games, in-room data ports, Wi-Fi, pool, sauna, bicycles, ski storage, dry cleaning, laundry facilities, meeting rooms* ▤ *AE, D, DC, MC, V* ⏀ *CP.*

$–$$ ▦ **Best Western Station House Inn.** It's a short walk to the beach, the Heavenly Gondola, or the casinos from this modern, well-kept, two-story motel off the main drag. The beds are comfortable, and the entire property is immaculate. ✉ *901 Park Ave., 96150* ☎ *530/542–1101 or 800/822–5953* 🖷 *530/542–1714* ⊕ *www.stationhouseinn.com* ↪ *100 rooms, 2 suites* ⚷ *Restaurant, cable TV, pool, outdoor hot tub, ski storage, bar, dry cleaning, Internet room* ▤ *AE, D, DC, MC, V* ⏀ *BP.*

♻ **$–$$** ▦ **Camp Richardson.** A 1920s lodge, a few dozen cabins, and a small inn make up this resort, tucked beneath giant pine trees on 80 acres of land on the southwest shore of Lake Tahoe. The rustic log cabin–style lodge has simple accommodations. The cabins (one-week minimum in summer) have lots of space, fireplaces or woodstoves, and full kitchens; some can sleep eight. The Beachside Inn has more modern amenities and sits right on the lake, but its rooms feel like those in an ordinary motel. A glass-bottom trimaran makes trips to Emerald Bay directly from the resort. Rates drop significantly in winter, making it a bargain for skiers and off-season travelers. ✉ *1900 Jameson Beach, 96150* ☎ *530/542–6550 or 800/544–1801* 🖷 *530/541–1802* ⊕ *www.camprichardson. com* ↪ *28 lodge rooms, 47 cabins, 7 inn rooms, 300 campsites* ⚷ *Restaurant, some kitchens, beach, boating, marina, waterskiing, fishing, bicycles, cross-country skiing, sleigh rides; no a/c, no phones in some rooms, no TV in some rooms, no smoking* ▤ *AE, D, MC, V.*

Nightlife

Most of the area's nightlife is concentrated in the casinos across the border in Stateline. If you want to avoid slot machines and blinking lights, you can stay in California and hear live bands play every night, right near the Heavenly Gondola, at **Mc P's Irish Pub & Grill** (✉ 4093 Lake Tahoe Blvd. ☎ 530/542–4435), which people also refer to as the Pub Tahoe.

Sports & the Outdoors

FISHING **Tahoe Sport Fishing** (✉ Ski Run Marina ☎ 530/541–5448, 800/696–7797 in CA ⊕ www.tahoesportfishing.com) is one of the largest and oldest fishing-charter services on the lake. Morning trips cost $95, afternoon trips $85. They include all necessary gear and bait, and the crew cleans and packages your catch.

GOLF   The 18-hole, par-71 **Lake Tahoe Golf Course** (⊠ U.S. 50 between Lake Tahoe Airport and Meyers ☎ 530/577–0788) has a driving range. Greens fees start at $52; a cart (mandatory Friday to Sunday) costs $22.

HIKING   The south shore is a great jumping-off point for day treks into nearby Eldorado National Forest and Desolation Wilderness. Hike a couple of miles on the **Pacific Crest Trail** (⊠ Echo Summit, about 12 mi southwest of South Lake Tahoe off U.S. 50 ☎ 916/349–2109 or 888/728–7245 ⊕ www.pcta.org). The Pacific Crest Trail leads into **Desolation Wilderness** (⊠ El Dorado National Forest Information Center ☎ 530/644–6048 ⊕ www.fs.fed.us/r5/eldorado), where you can pick up trails to gorgeous backcountry lakes and mountain peaks (bring a good map). Late May through early September, the easiest way to access Desolation Wilderness is via boat taxi ($8.50 one-way) across Echo Lake from **Echo Chalet** (⊠ Echo Lakes Rd. off U.S. 50 near Echo Summit ☎ 530/659–7207 ⊕ www.echochalet.com).

KAYAKING   **Kayak Tahoe** (⊠ Timber Cove Marina at Tahoe Paradise ☎ 530/544–2011 www.kayaktahoe.com) has long been teaching people to kayak on Lake Tahoe and the Truckee River. Lessons and excursions (Emerald Bay, Cave Rock, Zephyr Cove) are offered June through September. You can also rent a kayak and paddle solo.

ICE SKATING   If you're here in winter, practice your jumps and turns at the **Heavenly Village Outdoor Ice Rink.** You'll find the rink at the southwestern-most edge of Heavenly Village, near the Raley's supermarket parking lot. ☎ 530/541–2720 ⚏ $10, includes skate rentals ☉ Nov.–Mar., daily 10–9, weather permitting.

MOUNTAIN BIKING   With so much national forest land surrounding Lake Tahoe, you may want to try mountain biking. You can rent both road and mountain bikes and get tips on where to ride them from the friendly staff at **Tahoe Mountain Sports Ltd.** (⊠ 4008 Lake Tahoe Blvd. ☎ 530/542–4000 ⊕ www.tahoesportsltd.com).

SKIING   Straddling two states, vast **Heavenly Mountain Resort**—composed of nine
Fodor'sChoice   peaks, two valleys, and four base-lodge areas, along with the largest snow-
★   making system in the western United States—has terrain for every skier. Beginners can choose wide, well-groomed trails—accessed via the tram from the California Lodge or the gondola from downtown South Lake Tahoe—or short and gentle runs in the Enchanted Forest area. The Sky Express high-speed quad chair whisks intermediate and advanced skiers to the summit for wide cruisers or steep tree-skiing. Mott and Killebrew canyons draw experts to the Nevada side for steep chutes and thick-timber slopes. For snowboarders, there are a whopping five terrain parks. The ski school, like everything else at Heavenly, is large and offers everything from learn-to-ski packages to canyon-adventure tours. Skiing lessons are available for children age four and up; there's day care for infants older than six weeks. ⊠ Ski Run Blvd. off Hwy. 89/U.S. 50, Stateline, NV ☎ 775/586–7000 or 800/432–8365 ⊕ www.skiheavenly.

com ☞ *86 trails on 4,800 acres, rated 20% beginner, 45% intermediate, 35% expert. Longest run 5½ mi, base 6,540', summit 10,067'. Lifts: 30, including 1 aerial tram, 1 gondola, 2 high-speed 6-passenger lifts, and 5 high-speed quads.*

★ Thirty-six miles south of Lake Tahoe, **Kirkwood Ski Resort** is the hard-core skiers' and boarders' favorite south-shore mountain, known for its craggy gulp-and-go chutes, sweeping cornices, steep-aspect glade skiing, and high base elevation. But there's also fantastic terrain for newbies and intermediates down wide-open bowls, through wooded gullies, and along rolling tree-lined trails. Tricksters can show off in the Stomping Grounds terrain park on jumps, wall rides, rails, and a half pipe, all visible from the base area. The mountain gets hammered with more than 500 inches of snow annually, and often has the most in all North America. If you're into out-of-bounds skiing, check out Expedition Kirkwood, a backcountry-skills program that teaches basic safety awareness. Kirkwood is also the only Tahoe resort to offer Cat-skiing. If you're into cross-country, the resort also has 58 mi of superb groomed-track skiing, with skating lanes, instruction, and rentals. Nonskiers can snowshoe, snow-skate, ice-skate, and go dogsledding or snow-tubing. The children's ski school has programs for ages 4–12, and there's day care for children 2 to 6 years old. ⊠ *Hwy. 88, 14 mi west of Hwy. 89* ☎ *209/258–6000 downhill, 209/258–7248 cross-country, 209/258–7000 lodging information, 209/258–3000 snow phone* ☞ *65 trails on 2,300 acres, rated 15% beginner, 50% intermediate, 20% advanced, 15% expert. Longest run 2½ mi, base 7,800', summit 9,800'. Lifts: 14, 2 high speed.*

Often overlooked by skiers and boarders rushing to Heavenly or Kirkwood, **Sierra-at-Tahoe** has meticulously groomed intermediate slopes, some of the best tree-skiing in California, and gated backcountry access. Extremely popular with local snowboarders, Sierra also has two terrain parks, including a superpipe with 17-foot walls. For nonskiers there's a snow-tubing hill. Sierra has a low-key atmosphere that's great for families. ⊠ *12 mi from South Lake Tahoe off U.S. 50, near Echo Summit* ☎ *530/659–7453* ⊕ *www.sierraattahoe.com* ☞ *46 trails on 2,000 acres, rated 24% beginner, 50% intermediate, 25% advanced. Longest run 2½ mi, base 6,640', summit 8,852'. Lifts: 11, including 3 high-speed quads.*

At Sorensen's Resort, **Hope Valley Cross Country** (⊠ 14255 Hwy. 88, just east of Hwy. 89, Hope Valley ☎ 530/694–2266 ⊕ www.hopevalleyoutdoors.com) provides instruction and equipment rentals to prepare you for striding and telemarking. The outfit has 36 mi of trails through Eldorado National Forest, 6 of which are groomed.

If you don't want to pay the high cost of rental equipment at the resorts, you'll find reasonable prices and expert advice at **Tahoe Mountain Sports Ltd.** (⊠ Downhill: 4008 Lake Tahoe Blvd. ☎ 530/542–4000 ⊕ www.tahoesportsltd.com ⊠ Cross-Country and telemark: South Y Center, Hwy. 89 and U.S. 50 ☎ 530/544–2284). Downhill enthusiasts can get regular and demo-package downhill skis and snowboards, and cross-country skiers can get information on local trails.

Pope-Baldwin Recreation Area

▶ ❷ *5 mi west of South Lake Tahoe on Hwy. 89.*

To the west of downtown South Lake Tahoe, U.S. 50 and Highway 89 come together, forming an intersection nicknamed "the Y." If you head northwest on Highway 89 and follow the lakefront, commercial development gives way to national forests and state parks. One of these is Pope-Baldwin Recreation Area.

The lakeside **Tallac Historic Site** is a pleasant place to take a stroll or have a picnic. Among its attractions are **Pope House,** the magnificently restored 1894 mansion of George S. Pope, who made his money in shipping and lumber and played host to the business and cultural elite of 1920s America. There are two other estates here. One belonged to entrepreneur "Lucky" Baldwin; today it houses the **Baldwin Museum,** a collection of family memorabilia and Washoe Indian artifacts. The other, called the Valhalla, belonged to Walter Heller and is used for community events. The site hosts summertime cultural activities, including a Renaissance festival. Docents conduct tours of the Pope House in summers; call for tour times. In winter, you can cross-country ski around the site (bring your own equipment). ✉ *Hwy. 89* ☎ *530/541–5227* ⊕ *www.tahoeheritage.org* ✆ *Free; Pope House tour $5* ☼ *Grounds daily sunrise–sunset; Pope House and Baldwin Museum late May–mid-June, weekends 11–3; mid-June–early Sept., daily 10–4.*

The U.S. Forest Service operates the **Lake Tahoe Visitor Center,** on Taylor Creek. You can visit the site of a Washoe Indian settlement; walk self-guided trails through meadow, marsh, and forest; and inspect the Stream Profile Chamber, an underground underwater display with windows that afford views right into Taylor Creek (in fall you may see spawning kokanee salmon digging their nests). In summer U.S. Forest Service naturalists organize discovery walks and nighttime campfires with singing and marshmallow roasts (call ahead). ✉ *Hwy. 89, 3 mi north of junction with U.S. 50* ☎ *530/543–2674 June–Oct., 530/543–2600 year-round* ⊕ *www.fs.fed.us/r5/ltbmu* ✆ *Free* ☼ *June–late Sept., daily 8–5:30; Memorial Day–mid-June weekends 8–5:30.*

Emerald Bay State Park

❸ *4 mi west of Pope-Baldwin Recreation Area on Hwy. 89.*

Fodor'sChoice
★

Emerald Bay, a 3-mi-long and 1-mi-wide fjordlike inlet on Lake Tahoe's shore, was carved by a massive glacier millions of years ago. Famed for its jewel-like shape and colors, it surrounds Fannette, Tahoe's only island. Highway 89 curves high above the lake through Emerald Bay State Park; from the Emerald Bay lookout, the centerpiece of the park, you can survey the whole scene.

A steep 1-mi-long trail from the lookout leads down to **Vikingsholm,** a 38-room estate completed in 1929. The original owner, Lora Knight, had this precise copy of a 1,200-year-old Viking castle built out of materials native to the area. She furnished it with Scandinavian antiques and hired artisans to build period reproductions. The sod roof sprouts

9

wildflowers each spring. There are picnic tables nearby and a gray-sand beach for strolling. The hike back up is hard (especially if you're not yet acclimated to the elevation), but there are benches and stone culverts to rest on. At the 150-foot peak of Fannette Island are the remnants of a stone structure known as the Tea House, built in 1928 so that Knight's guests could have a place to enjoy afternoon refreshments after a motorboat ride. The island is off-limits from February through June to protect nesting Canada geese. The rest of the year it's open for day use. ⊠ *Hwy. 89* ☎ *530/541–3030 summer, 530/525–7277 year-round* 🖼 *Day-use parking fee $6, mansion tour $5* ☉ *Late May–mid-June, weekends call for hrs; mid-June–Sept., daily 10–4 (call for exact times).*

Sports & the Outdoors

HIKING Leave your car in the parking lot for Eagle Falls picnic area (near Vikingsholm; arrive early for a good spot), and head to **Eagle Falls,** a short but fairly steep walk-up canyon. You'll have a brilliant panorama of Emerald Bay from this spot, near the boundary of Desolation Wilderness. If you want a full-day's hike and you're in good shape, continue 5 mi, past Eagle Lake, to Upper and Middle Velma Lakes (bring a good map).

SWIMMING Hike past Eagle Falls (about 1 mi from the parking lot) to **Eagle Lake,** where you can shed your clothes (bring a suit weekends) and dive into cold, blue, alpine water.

D. L. Bliss State Park

❹ *3 mi north of Emerald Bay State Park on Hwy. 89.*

D. L. Bliss State Park takes its name from Duane LeRoy Bliss, a 19th-century lumber magnate. At one time Bliss owned nearly 75% of Tahoe's lakefront, along with local steamboats, railroads, and banks. The Bliss family donated these 1,200 acres to the state in the 1930s. The park shares 6 mi of shoreline with Emerald Bay State Park. At the north end of Bliss is Rubicon Point, which overlooks one of the lake's deepest spots. Short trails lead to an old lighthouse and Balancing Rock, which weighs 250,000 pounds and balances on a fist of granite. A 4¼-mi trail leads to Vikingsholm and provides stunning lake views. Two white-sand beaches front some of Tahoe's warmest water. ⊠ *Hwy. 89* ☎ *530/525–7277* 🖼 *Day use $6 per vehicle* ☉ *Late May–Sept., daily sunrise–sunset.*

Camping

⚠ **D. L. Bliss State Park Campground.** In one of California's most beautiful spots, quiet, wooded hills make for blissful family camping near the lake. The campground is open June to September, and reservations are accepted up to seven months in advance. It's expensive for a campground, but the location can't be beat, especially at the beach campsites. ⊠ *Off Hwy. 89, 17 mi south of Tahoe City on lake side* ☎ *916/638–5883 or 800/444–7275* ⊕ *www.reserveamerica.com* 🖼 *$25–$35* 🛏 *168 sites* ♿ *Flush toilets, drinking water, showers, bear boxes, fire pits, grills, picnic tables, public telephone, swimming (beach).*

Sugar Pine Point State Park

★ ❺ *8 mi north of D. L. Bliss State Park on Hwy. 89.*

The main attraction at Sugar Pine Point State Park is **Ehrman Mansion,** a 1903 stone-and-shingle summer home furnished in period style. In its day it was the height of modernity, with a refrigerator, an elevator, and an electric stove (tours leave hourly). Also in the park are a trapper's log cabin from the mid-19th century, a nature preserve with wildlife exhibits, a lighthouse, the start of the 10-mi-long biking trail to Tahoe City, and an extensive system of hiking and cross-country skiing trails. ⊠ *Hwy. 89* ☎ *530/525–7982 mansion (in season), 530/525–7232 year-round* 💲 *Day use $6 per vehicle, mansion tour $5* ☉ *Mansion July–Sept., daily 11–4, call ahead for June hours.*

Camping

⚠ **Sugar Pine Point State Park Campground/General Creek Campground.** This beautiful and homey campground on the mountain side of Highway 89 is one of the few public ones to remain open in winter, when it is popular with cross-country skiers. There are no hookups here, and the showers operate from late May to early September only. ⊠ *Hwy. 89, 1 mi south of Tahoma* ☎ *916/638–5883 or 800/444–7275* ⊕ *www. reserveamerica.com* 💲 *$25* 🏕 *175 sites* ⚷ *Flush toilets, drinking water, showers, bear boxes, fire pits, grills, public telephone.*

Tahoma

❻ *1 mi north of Sugar Pine Point State Park on Hwy. 89; 23 mi south of Truckee on Hwy. 89.*

The quiet west shore offers a glimpse back in time to "Old Tahoe." Tahoma exemplifies life on the lake in its early days, with rustic, lakeside vacation cottages that are far from the blinking lights of the South Shore's casinos. In 1960 Tahoma was host of the Olympic Nordic skiing competitions. Today there's little to do here except stroll by the lake and listen to the wind in the trees.

Where to Stay

★ $–$$$ 🏨 **Tahoma Meadows B&B Cottages.** Rooms in these cheerful freestanding vacation cottages are individually decorated, and some have claw-foot tubs and fireplaces. Lovingly maintained by charming on-site owners, the cottages make a great retreat for families and couples. Prices for cottages without kitchens include a delicious family-style breakfast. Down to earth and simple, this is one of Tahoe's best hideaways. ⊠ *6821 W. Lake Blvd., Box 810, 96142* ☎ *530/525–1553 or 866/525–1553* ⊕ *www.tahomameadows.com* 🛏 *15 cabins* ⚷ *Restaurant, some kitchens, cable TV, Wi-Fi, outdoor hot tub, some pets allowed (fee); no a/c, no room phones, no smoking* 🖃 *AE, D, MC, V* 🍴 *BP.*

Sports & the Outdoors

You'll feel as though you're going to ski into the lake when you schuss down the face of **Homewood Mountain Resort**—and you could if you really wanted to, because the mountain rises right off the shoreline. This

9

is the favorite area of locals on a fresh-snow day, because you can find lots of untracked powder. It's also the most protected and least windy Tahoe ski area during a storm; when every other resort's lifts are on wind hold, you can almost always count on Homewood's to be open. There aren't any high-speed chairlifts, but there are rarely any lines, and the ticket prices are some of the cheapest around. It may look small as you drive by, but most of the resort is not visible from the road. ⊠ *Hwy. 89* ☎ *530/525–2992* ⊕ *www.skihomewood.com* ☞ *56 trails on 1,260 acres, rated 15% beginner, 50% intermediate, and 35% advanced. Longest run 2 mi, base 6,230', summit 7,880'. Lifts: 4 chairlifts, 4 surface lifts.*

Tahoe City

❼ *10 mi north of Sugar Pine Point State Park on Hwy. 89; 14 mi south of Truckee on Hwy. 89.*

Tahoe City is the only lakeside town with a compact downtown area good for strolling and window-shopping. Of the larger towns ringing the lake, it has the most bona fide charm. Stores and restaurants are all within walking distance of the Outlet Gates, enormous Lake Tahoe's only outlet, where water is spilled into the Truckee River to control the surface level of the lake. Giant trout are commonly seen in the river from Fanny Bridge, so-called for the views of the backsides of sightseers leaning over the railing. Here, Highway 89 bears northwest, away from the lake, and parallels the river toward Squaw Valley, Donner Lake, and Truckee. Highway 28 continues northeast around the lake toward Kings Beach and Nevada. Expect significant traffic delays during summer afternoons on Highway 28 south of Tahoe City, particularly on weekends.

★ The **Gatekeeper's Cabin Museum** preserves a little-known part of the region's history. Between 1910 and 1968 the gatekeeper who lived on this site was responsible for monitoring the level of the lake, using a hand-turned winch system to keep the water at the correct level. That winch system is still used today. A Native American basket museum is in an adjacent wing. ⊠ *130 W. Lake Blvd.* ☎ *530/583–1762* ⊕ *www. northtahoemuseums.org* ⊠ *$3* ☉ *May–mid-June and Sept., Wed.–Sun. 11–5; mid-June–Aug., daily 11–5; Oct. weekends 11–3.*

In the middle of town, the **Watson Cabin Living Museum,** a 1909 log cabin built by Robert M. Watson and his son, is filled with some century-old furnishings and many reproductions. Docents are available to answer questions and will lead tours with advance arrangements. ⊠ *560 N. Lake Blvd.* ☎ *530/583–8717 or 530/583–1762* ⊕ *www.northtahoemuseums. org* ⊠ *$2 donation suggested* ☉ *Late May–June, weekends noon–4; July–early Sept., Wed.–Mon. noon–4.*

Where to Stay & Eat

$$–$$$$ ✕ **Christy Hill.** Sit near the fireplace in the sparsely decorated, whitewashed dining room or outside on the deck, and take in mesmerizing lake views while dining on Euro-Cal preparations of fresh seafood, filet mignon, or Australian lamb loin. The service is gracious, and desserts are especially delicious (try the pecan ice cream or fruit cobbler). Come early to see the sunset—and you'll understand why the entrée prices are so high.

There's also a less expensive café menu served at the wine bar or on the deck. ⊠ *Lakehouse Mall, 115 Grove St.* ☎ *530/583–8551* ⌔ *Reservations essential* ▤ *AE, MC, V* ⊗ *Closed Mon. No lunch.*

$$–$$$ ✕ **Jake's on the Lake.** Overlooking the water, large, handsome rooms of oak and glass are the backdrop for steaks and an extensive selection of seafood. You may forget what you eat, but you'll surely remember the views. The lounge gets packed with barhopping boaters, who pull up to the big pier outside. ⊠ *Boatworks Mall, 780 N. Lake Blvd.* ☎ *530/ 583–0188* ▤ *AE, MC, V* ⊗ *No lunch weekdays.*

★ **$$–$$$** ✕ **Wolfdale's.** Wolfdale's brought California cuisine to Lake Tahoe in 1984, and it remains one of the best restaurants anywhere around the lake. The menu changes often, but seafood is the specialty, and the imaginative entrées merge Asian and European cooking (drawing on the chef-owner's training in Japan) and trend toward light and healthful, rather than heavy and overdone. And everything from teriyaki glaze to smoked fish is made in-house. Request a window table, and book early enough to see the lake view from the elegantly sparse dining room. ⊠ *640 N. Lake Blvd.* ☎ *530/583–5700* ⌔ *Reservations essential* ▤ *MC, V* ⊗ *Closed Tues. No lunch.*

$–$$$ ✕ **Fiamma.** Join the hip, young singles at the always-bustling wine bar, or settle into one of the comfy, semiromantic booths at this modern mom-and-pop trattoria that specializes in roasted and grilled meats, home-made pastas, and pizzas from the wood-fired oven. Everything from soup stock to gelato is made from scratch. ⊠ *521 N. Lake Blvd.* ☎ *530/581– 1416* ⌔ *Reservations essential* ▤ *AE, MC, V* ⊗ *No lunch.*

★ ¢ ✕ **Fire Sign Café.** There's often a wait at the west shore's best spot for breakfast and lunch, but it's worth it. The pastries are made from scratch, the salmon is smoked in-house, the salsa is hand cut, and there's real maple syrup for the many flavors of pancakes and waffles. The eggs Benedict are delicious. ⊠ *1785 W. Lake Blvd.* ☎ *530/583–0871* ▤ *AE, MC, V* ⌔ *Reservations not accepted* ⊗ *No dinner.*

★ **$$$** ✕⌂ **Sunnyside Restaurant and Lodge.** The views are superb at this pretty little lodge, right on the lake, just 3 mi south of Tahoe City. All but four rooms have balconies and locally crafted furnishings; some have river-rock fireplaces and wet bars, and some have pull-out sofas. The lodge is great for couples, but it's not geared toward families. The inviting restaurant ($–$$$) echoes the design of old mahogany Chris Craft speedboats; it serves standard preparations of steak, seafood, and pasta (think fried zucchini, Caesar salad, and prime rib). The dockside bar gets packed with boaters and Bacchanalian revelers. Be forewarned: this is *not* a quiet place on weekends in summer. ⊠ *1850 W. Lake Blvd., Box 5969, 96145* ☎ *530/583– 7200 or 800/822–2754* ⎙ *530/583–2551* ⊕ *www.sunnysidetahoe.com* ⇆ *18 rooms, 5 suites* ⌔ *Restaurant, room service, fans, cable TV, in-room VCRs, beach, bar; no a/c, no smoking* ▤ *AE, MC, V* ⦿ *CP.*

$$$–$$$$ ⌂ **Chinquapin Resort.** A deluxe development built in the 1970s on 95 acres of forested land and a mile of lakefront lies 3 mi northeast of Tahoe City. Within are one- to four-bedroom town houses and condos with great views of the lake and the mountains. Each unit has a fireplace, a fully equipped kitchen, and a washer and dryer. Some units haven't been updated in a while; be sure to request a recently remodeled one when you book. A one-week minimum stay is required in summer and late

9

December; two- and three-night minimums apply the rest of the year. ⊠ *3600 N. Lake Blvd., 96145* ☎ *530/583–6991 or 800/732–6721* 🖷 *530/583–0937* ⊕ *www.chinquapin.com* ⇦ *172 town houses and condos* ⚤ *Kitchens, cable TV, 7 tennis courts, pool, 2 saunas, 2 beaches, dock, hiking, horseshoes; no a/c* ▤ *AE, D, MC, V.*

$$–$$$ 🛏 **Cottage Inn.** Avoid the crowds by staying just south of town in one of these tidy, circa-1938 log cottages under the towering pines on the west shore of the lake. Cute as a button, with knotty-pine paneling and a gas-flame stone fireplace, each unit typifies old-Tahoe style while embracing you with up-to-date comfort. There's also a private beach. ⊠ *1690 W. Lake Blvd., Box 66, 96145* ☎ *530/581–4073 or 800/581–4073* 🖷 *530/581–0226* ⊕ *www.thecottageinn.com* ⇦ *22 rooms* ⚤ *Some in-room hot tubs, cable TV, in-room VCRs, lake, sauna, beach; no a/c, no room phones, no kids under 12, no smoking* ▤ *MC, V* ⏛ *BP.*

$–$$ 🛏 **Tahoe City Travelodge.** As motels go, this one is very good. Its rooms are well maintained, and many are larger than average, with either double or king-size beds, big bathrooms with massage showers and hair dryers, and coffeemakers. There's also a great lake-view deck with a hot tub and a sauna. ⊠ *455 N. Lake Blvd., Box 84, 96145* ☎ *530/583–3766 or 800/578–7878* 🖷 *530/583–8045* ⊕ *www.travelodge.com* ⇦ *47 rooms* ⚤ *Microwaves, refrigerators, cable TV, some in-room VCRs, in-room data ports, pool, hot tub, sauna* ⏛ *CP* ▤ *AE, D, DC, MC, V.*

¢–$ 🛏 **Mother Nature's Inn.** Smack-dab in the middle of town, this quirky inn is Tahoe City's best bargain. It's actually a two-story motel-style layout of rooms behind a home-furnishings store. The rooms have no views and get little light, but they're surprisingly comfortable and remarkably well decorated. And you can't beat the price. ⊠ *551 North Lake Blvd. Box 7075, 96145* ☎ *530/581–4278 or 800/558–4278* 🖷 *530/581–4272* ⊕ *www.mothernaturesinn.com* ⇦ *8 rooms* ⚤ *Refrigerators, cable TV, some pets (fee); no smoking* ▤ *AE, D, MC, V.*

Sports & the Outdoors

GOLF Golfers use pull carts or caddies at the 9-hole **Tahoe City Golf Course** (⊠ Hwy. 28 ☎ 530/583–1516 ⊕ www.tcgc.com), which opened in 1917. Though rates vary by season, the maximum greens fees are $30 for 9 holes, $50 for 18; a power cart costs $16 to $24.

MOUNTAIN BIKING **Cyclepaths Mountain Bike Adventures** (⊠ 1785 W. Lake Blvd. ☎ 530/581–1171 or 800/780–2453 ⊕ www.cyclepaths.com) is a combination full-service bike shop and bike-adventure outfitter. It offers instruction in mountain biking, guided tours (from half-day to weeklong excursions), tips for self-guided bike touring, bike repairs, and books and maps on the area.

RIVER RAFTING In summer you can take a self-guided raft trip down a gentle 5-mi stretch of the Truckee River through **Truckee River Rafting** (☎ 530/583–7238 or 888/584–7238 ⊕ www.truckeeriverrafting.com). They will shuttle you back to your car at the end of your two- to four-hour trip.

SKIING The locals' favorite place to ski on the north shore, ★ **Alpine Meadows Ski Area** is also the unofficial telemarking hub of the Sierra. With 495 inches of snow annually, Alpine has some of Tahoe's most reliable conditions. It's usually one of the first areas to open in November and one

Ski-Patrol Pooches

ALL AROUND TAHOE, from bars to ski shops, you'll spot posters of dogs wearing ski-patrol vests riding a chairlift. Stars in their own right, these pooches are the search-and-rescue dogs of Alpine Meadows.

In 1982 an avalanche inundated Alpine's base lodge, destroying a building and a ski lift and killing six people. Search-and-rescue teams brought in a German shepherd named Bridget to help recover the missing from beneath the snow. Though she was unable to help save any victims, she inspired the idea for trained "staff dogs" to be on hand in case of another catastrophe.

Now an integral part of Alpine's safety preparedness, these golden retrievers and chocolate Labradors are the personal pets of ski-patrol employees. Each dog meets exacting standards of obedience and conduct and must undergo two years of rigorous training. They must be able to get on and off a ski lift, ride a snowmobile, and keep up with patrollers anywhere on the mountain, including icy cornices, craggy chutes, and steep slopes. Goldens and labs have the right temperament, the right size, and the right fur—long enough to keep them warm but short enough not to get covered in chunky snowballs that weigh them down. They're also able to smell human beings through heavy snow.

Currently there are 12 dogs on staff, including three puppies in training. You can visit them at the ski patrol hut at the top of the Summit Six, Sherwood, or Lakeview chairlift. And if you've become a fan, you can pick up the poster or patrol-puppy trading cards, with an image of a dog on the front and obscure facts and figures on the back. To obtain the free cards, call the resort at 530/583–4232 or e-mail info@skialpine.com.

9

of the last to close in May or June. Alpine isn't the place for arrogant show-offs; instead, you'll find down-to-earth alpine fetishists. The two peaks here are well suited to intermediate skiers, but for experts there's also an open boundary to the backcountry (take "High Traverse" from the summit). Snowboarders and hot-dog skiers will find a terrain park with a half pipe, superpipe, rails, and tabletops, as well as a boarder-cross course. Alpine is a great place to learn to ski, and the Tahoe Adaptive Ski School here teaches and coaches those with physical and mental disabilities. There's also an area for overnight RV parking. On Saturdays, because of the limited parking, there's more acreage per person than at other resorts. ⊠ *Off Hwy. 89, 6 mi northwest of Tahoe City and 13 mi south of I–80* ☎ *530/583–4232 or 800/441–4423, 530/581–8374 snow phone* ⊕ *www.skialpine.com* ⌖ *100 trails on 2,000 acres, rated 25% beginner, 40% intermediate, 35% advanced. Longest run 2½ mi, base 6,835', summit 8,637'. Lifts: 12, including 1 high-speed 6-passenger lift and 1 high-speed quad.*

You can rent skis, boards, and snowshoes at **Tahoe Dave's Skis and Boards** (⊠ 620 N. Lake Blvd. ☎ 530/583–0400), which has the area's best selection of downhill rental equipment. If you plan to ski or board the backcountry, you'll find everything from crampons to tranceivers at **The Backcountry** (✉ 690 N. Lake Blvd. ☎ 530/581–5861 ⊕ www.thebackcountry.net).

Olympic Valley

❽ *7 mi north of Tahoe City via Hwy. 89 to Squaw Valley Rd.; 8½ mi south of Truckee via Hwy. 89 to Squaw Valley Rd.*

Olympic Valley got its name in 1960, when Squaw Valley USA, the ski resort here, was host of the winter Olympics. Snow sports remain the primary activity, but once summer comes, you can hike into the adjacent Granite Chief Wilderness, ride horseback through alpine meadows, or lie by a swimming pool in one of the Sierra's prettiest valleys.

The centerpiece of Olympic Valley is the **Village at Squaw Valley** (☎ 530/584–1000, 530/584–6205 condo reservations, 888/805–5022 ⊕ www.thevillageatsquaw.com), a pedestrian mall at the base of several four-story ersatz-Bavarian-style stone-and-timber buildings, where you'll find restaurants, high-end condo rentals, boutiques, and cafés. The village often holds events and festivals. Make it a point to visit **Waxen Moon** (☎ 530/584–6006 ⊕ www.waxenmoon.com), a shop where you can make your own candles—a godsend for parents traveling with kids when the weather isn't cooperating. Call or stop by to make reservations, especially during high season.

You can ride the Squaw Valley Cable Car up 2,000 vertical feet to **High Camp,** which at 8,200 feet commands superb views of Lake Tahoe and the surrounding mountains. In summer you can go for a hike, sit by the pool at the High Camp Bath and Tennis Club, or have a cocktail and watch the sunset. In winter you can ski, ice-skate, or snow-tube. There's also a restaurant, lounge, and small Olympic museum. ✉ *Cable Car Bldg., Squaw Valley* ☎ *530/583–6985 cable car, 530/581–7278 restaurant reservations* ⊕ *www.squaw.com* ✉ *Cable car $19; special packages include swimming or skating* ☉ *Daily; call for hrs.*

Where to Stay & Eat

$$$–$$$$
Fodor'sChoice
★
✕ **PlumpJack Café.** The best restaurant at Olympic Valley is also the finest at Tahoe, the epitome of discreet chic and a must-visit for all serious foodies. The menu changes often, but look for tuna-tartare cones, seared Diver scallops, Sonoma rabbit three ways, or the Liberty duck breast. And rather than complicated, heavy sauces, the chef uses simple reductions to complement a dish. The result: clean, dynamic, bright flavors. The wine list is exceptional for its variety and surprisingly low prices. If not for the view of the craggy mountains through the windows lining the cushy, 60-seat dining room, you might swear you were in San Francisco. ✉ *1920 Squaw Valley Rd.* ☎ *530/583–1576 or 800/323–7666* ⚍ *Reservations essential* ☰ *AE, MC, V.*

$$$
✕ **Graham's of Squaw Valley.** Sit by a floor-to-ceiling river-rock hearth under a knotty-pine peaked ceiling in the intimate dining room in the Christy Inn Lodge. The southern European–inspired menu changes often, but expect such dishes as cassoulet, seafood paella, pheasant ragout with pasta, or a simple grilled rib eye with sautéed onions. You

can also stop in at the bar for wine and appetizers by the fire. ✉ *1650 Squaw Valley Rd.* ☎ *530/581–0454* ▤ *MC, V* �︎ *Reservations essential* 🌙 *Closed Mon. No lunch.*

★ **$$–$$$** ✕**Balboa Café.** The top choice for lunch at Squaw is also a cushy, romantic spot for dinner. Aside from having the best burger in the valley, Balboa serves a varied menu of contemporary California cuisine, including steak frites and Cobb salad at lunch, and ahi tuna tartare, Muscovy duck breast, and grilled lamb chops at dinner. ✉ *Village at Squaw Valley, 1995 Squaw Valley Rd.* ☎ *530/583–5850* 🚫 *Reservations essential* ▤ *AE, MC, V.*

$$–$$$ ✕**Mamsake.** The hip and happening spot for sushi at Squaw serves stylized presentations in an industrial-warehouse-style room. Sit at the bar and watch extreme ski movies, many of which were filmed right outside the window. Be patient: service is inconsistent. ✉ *The Village at Squaw Valley* ☎ *530/584–0110* ▤ *AE, MC, V.*

$$$–$$$$ ✕▦ **Resort at Squaw Creek.** Completely redesigned and refurbished in 2005, the rooms at this vast 650-acre resort-within-a-resort have all the amenities and services you could possibly want. The black-glass-and-concrete buildings are what you'd expect in Scottsdale, not the Sierra, but the extensive facilities make it good for large groups and families. Montagna ($$$–$$$$) serves contemporary northern Italian cuisine (dinner only). In winter the resort operates its own chairlift to the mountain. ✉ *400 Squaw Creek Rd., 96146* ☎ *530/583–6300 or 800/327–3353* 🖷 *530/581–5407* ⊕ *www.squawcreek.com* ⇆ *203 rooms, 200 suites* 🚫 *3 restaurants, coffee shop, some kitchens, minibars, cable TV with movies and video games, Wi-Fi, 18-hole golf course, 2 tennis courts, 3 pools, health club, hair salon, 4 hot tubs, sauna, spa, cross-country skiing, downhill skiing, ice-skating, ski shop, ski storage, sleigh rides, sports bar, shops, children's programs (ages 4–12), dry cleaning, laundry service, concierge, Internet room, business services, meeting rooms, free parking* ▤ *AE, D, DC, MC, V.*

9

$$$–$$$$ ▦ **PlumpJack Squaw Valley Inn.** If style and luxury are a must, make PlumpJack your first choice. The two-story, cedar-sided inn sits right next to the cable car, and has a snappy, sophisticated look and laid-back sensibility, perfect for the Bay Area cognoscenti who flock here on weekends. All rooms have sumptuous beds with down comforters, high-end bath amenities, and hooded terry robes to wear on your way to the outdoor hot tubs. The bar is a happening après-ski destination, and the namesake restaurant (*above*) superb. PlumpJack may not have the bells and whistles of big luxury hotels, but the service—personable and attentive—can't be beat. Not all rooms have tubs: if it matters, request one. ✉ *1920 Squaw Valley Rd., 96146* ☎ *530/583–1576 or 800/323–7666* 🖷 *530/ 583–1734* ⊕ *www.plumpjack.com* ⇆ *56 rooms, 5 suites* 🚫 *Restaurant, fans, some in-room hot tubs, minibars, cable TV, Wi-Fi, in-room DVD, 2 outdoor hot tubs, massage, mountain bikes, basketball, hiking, Ping-Pong, cross-country skiing, downhill skiing, ski storage, bar, shop, babysitting, concierge, meeting rooms, free parking; no a/c* ▤ *AE, D, MC, V* ❍ *BP.*

Fodor's Choice ★

$$$–$$$$ ▦ **The Village at Squaw Valley USA.** Right at the base of the slopes at the centerpoint of Olympic Valley, the Village's studios, one-, two-, or three-bedroom condominiums were built in 2000, and come complete with gas fireplaces, daily maid service, and heated slate-tiled bathroom floors. The individually owned units are uniformly decorated with granite counters, wood cabinets, and comfortable furnishings. ⊠ *1985 Squaw Valley Rd., 96146* ☎ *530/584–6205 or 888/805–5022* 🖷 *530/584–6290* ⊕ *www.thevillageatsquaw.com* 🛏 *290 suites* ⚘ *Kitchens, cable TV with movies, in-room DVD/VCR, in-room broadband, in-room data ports, exercise equipment, 2 outdoor hot tubs, billiards, downhill skiing, video game room, shops, laundry facilities, concierge, free parking; no a/c, no smoking* ═ *AE, D, DC, MC, V.*

\$\$–\$\$\$\$ 🏨 **Squaw Valley Lodge.** Ski right to the doors of this all-suites condo complex, which offers many of the amenities of a full-service hotel. The units are individually owned and styled, so there's no uniformity to the decor, but all of them come with down comforters, daily maid service, oversize soaking tubs, and well-stocked kitchens or kitchenettes. There's also an excellent fitness center with plenty of sports-conditioning equipment. The only drawback is thin walls, so request a quiet room when you book. ⊠ *201 Squaw Peak Rd., 96146* ☎ *530/583–5500 or 800/ 922–9970* 🖷 *530/583–0326* ⊕ *www.squawvalleylodge.com* 🛏 *142 units* ⚘ *Some kitchens, some kitchenettes, cable TV, in-room broadband, pool, exercise equipment, 4 indoor hot tubs, 3 outdoor hot tubs, sauna, steam room, downhill skiing, laundry facilities, concierge, Internet room, meeting rooms, free parking* ═ *AE, DC, MC, V.*

Sports & the Outdoors

GOLF The **Resort at Squaw Creek Golf Course** (⊠ 400 Squaw Creek Rd. ☎ 530/ 583–6300 ⊕ www.squawcreek.com), an 18-hole championship course, was designed by Robert Trent Jones Jr. The \$50–\$125 greens fees include the use of a cart.

HIKING The Granite Chief Wilderness and the high peaks surrounding Olympic Valley are accessible by foot, but save yourself a 2,000-foot elevation gain by riding the Squaw Valley Cable Car to **High Camp** (☎ 530/583– 6985 ⊕ www.squaw.com), where you can begin a trek to Shirley Lake and then head back down-canyon to the valley for a beautiful 4-mi, half-day hike. In late summer, there are full-moon night hikes from High Camp.

HORSEBACK RIDING You can rent a horse or a pony from **Squaw Valley Stables** (⊠ 1525 Squaw Valley Rd. ☎ 530/583–7433), which offers instruction as well as group and private rides.

ICE-SKATING You can ice-skate year-round at the **Olympic Ice Pavilion** (⊠ High Camp, Squaw Valley ☎ 530/583–6985 or 530/581–7255 ⊕ www.squaw.com). You can buy a ride up the mountain and a pass to skate for \$22, including skate rental. In summer you can pay \$5 extra to swim or sit in the hot tub after you skate. Prices drop after 5 PM.

ROCK CLIMBING Before you rappel down a granite monolith, you can hone your skills at the **Headwall Climbing Wall** (⊠ Near Village at Squaw Valley ☎ 530/ 583–7673), at the base of the cable car.

Next to the Olympic Village Lodge, on the far side of the creek, the **Squaw Valley Adventure Center** (☎ 530/583–7673) has a ropes course, a 50-foot tower, and a giant swing.

SKIING   Known for some of the toughest skiing in the Tahoe area, **Squaw Valley**
Fodor'sChoice **USA** was the centerpiece of the 1960 winter Olympics. Today it's the
★   definitive North Tahoe ski resort and among the top-three megaresorts
in California (the other two are Heavenly and Mammoth). Although
Squaw has changed significantly since the Olympics, the skiing is still
world-class and extends across vast bowls stretched between six peaks.
Experts often head directly to the untamed terrain of the infamous KT-
22 face, which has bumps, cliffs, and gulp-and-go chutes, or to the nearly
vertical Palisades, where many famous Warren Miller extreme-skiing films
have been shot. Fret not, beginners and intermediates: you have plenty
of wide-open, groomed trails at High Camp (which sits at the *top* of
the mountain) and around the more challenging Snow King Peak. Snowboarders and show-off skiers can tear up the two fantastic terrain parks,
which include a giant superpipe. Lift prices include night skiing until 9
PM. Tickets for skiers 12 and under cost only $5. ⊠ *Hwy. 89, 5 mi north-*
west of Tahoe City ☎ *530/583–6985, 800/545–4350 reservations, 530/*
583–6955 snow phone ☞ *100 trails on 4,300 acres, rated 25% begin-*
ner, 45% intermediate, 30% advanced. Longest run 3 mi, base 6,200′,
summit 9,050′. Lifts: 31, including a gondola-style funitel, a cable car,
7 high-speed chairs, and 18 fixed-grip chairs.

If you don't want to pay resort prices, you can rent and tune downhill
skis and snowboards at **Tahoe Dave's Skis and Boards** (⊠ Squaw Valley
Rd. at Hwy. 89 ☎ 530/583–5665 ⊕ www.tahoedaves.com).

Cross-country skiers will enjoy looping through the valley's giant alpine
meadow. The **Resort at Squaw Creek** (⊠ 400 Squaw Creek Rd. ☎ 530/
583–6300 ⊕ www.squawcreek.com) rents cross-country equipment
and provides trail maps.

SWIMMING   There are dramatic views from the pool deck at the **High Camp Bath and**
Tennis Club (☎ 530/581–7255 ⊕ www.squaw.com), where you can
swim laps or soak in the 25-person hot tub for $24, which includes the
cable car ride; for $3 more you can ice-skate, too, year-round. Prices
drop after 5.

TENNIS   You'll find two tennis courts at the **Resort at Squaw Creek** (⊠ 400 Squaw
Creek Rd. ☎ 530/583–6300 ⊕ www.squawcreek.com). **High Camp Bath**
and Tennis Club (☎ 530/583–6985) has six courts. Call for reservations
and information on lessons and clinics.

Truckee

9 *13 mi northwest of Kings Beach on Hwy. 267; 14 mi north of Tahoe*
City on Hwy. 89.

Old West facades line the main street of Truckee, a favorite stopover
for people traveling from the San Francisco Bay area to the north shore
of Lake Tahoe, Reno, and points east. Around 1863, the town was officially established, and by 1868, it had gone from a stagecoach station
to a major stopover for trains bound for the Pacific via the new transcontinental railroad. Freight and passenger trains still stop every day at the
depot right in the middle of town. Across from the station, you'll find
galleries, tchotchke shops, boutiques, diners, an old-fashioned five-and-

dime store, and several remarkably fine restaurants. North of the free-way, along Donner Pass Road, there are outlet stores, strip malls, and discount skiwear shops. Stop by the **information booth** (⊠ Railroad St. at Commercial Rd.) in the Amtrak depot for a walking-tour map of historic Truckee.

Donner Memorial State Park and Emigrant Trail Museum commemorates the Donner Party, a group of 89 westward-bound pioneers who were trapped in the Sierra in the winter of 1846–47 in snow 22 feet deep. The top of the stone pedestal beneath the monument marks the snow level that year. Only 47 pioneers survived, some by resorting to canni-balism, though none consumed his own kin. (For the full story, pick up a copy of *Ordeal by Hunger,* by George R. Stewart.) The museum's hourly slide show details the Donner Party's plight. Other displays and dioramas relate the history of other settlers and of railroad development through the Sierra. In the park, you can picnic, hike, camp, and go boating, fishing, and waterskiing in summer; winter brings cross-country skiing and snowshoeing on groomed trails. ⊠ *Donner Pass Rd., off I–80, 2 mi west of Truckee* ☎ *530/582–7892 museum, 800/444–7275 camping reservations* ⊕ *www.parks.ca.gov* ⊡ *Day-use parking $6* ⊙ *Museum daily 9–4.*

OFF THE BEATEN PATH

TAHOE NATIONAL FOREST – Draped along the Sierra Nevada Crest above Lake Tahoe, the national forest offers abundant outdoor recreation: picnicking and camping in summer, and in winter, snowshoeing, skiing, and sledding over some of the deepest snowpack in the West. The **Big Bend Visitor Center** occupies a state historic landmark within the forest, 10 mi west of Donner Summit. This area has been on major cross-country routes for centuries, ever since Native Americans passed through trading acorns and salt for pelts, obsidian, and other materials. Between 1844 and 1860, more than 200,000 emigrants traveled to California along the Emigrant Trail, which passed nearby; you can see rut marks left by wagon wheels scraping the famously hard granite. Later the nation's first transcontinental railroad ran through here (and still does), as do U.S. 40 (the old National Road) and its successor, I–80. Exhibits in the visitor center explore the area's transportation history. There are also occasional exhibits focusing on natural history. Take the Rainbow–Big Bend exit off I–80. ⊠ *U.S. 40, Soda Springs* ☎ *530/426–3609 or 530/265–4531* ⊕ *www.fs.fed. us/r5/tahoe/recreation* ⊡ *Free* ⊙ *Hrs vary.*

Where to Stay & Eat

★ $$–$$$$ ✕ **Moody's.** The closest thing to a supper club this side of San Francisco, Moody's serves contemporary-Cal cuisine in a sexy dining room with pumpkin-color walls, burgundy velvet banquettes, and art deco fixtures. The chef-owner's earthy, sure-handed cooking features organically grown ingredients: look for ahi tuna "four ways," house-made charcu-terie platters, pan-roasted venison, braised short ribs, and ultrafresh seafood flown in daily. In summer, dine alfresco surrounded by flowers. There's a limited afternoon menu, and Wednesday through Sunday there's live music in the borderline-raucous bar that gets packed with

Truckee's bon vivants. ⊠ *1007 Bridge St.* ☎ *530/587–8831* ⊟ *AE, D, DC, MC, V* ⌔ *Reservations essential.*

$$–$$$ ✕ **Cottonwood.** Perched above town on the site of North America's first chairlift, the Cottonwood restaurant is a veritable institution. The bar is decked out with old wooden skis, sleds, skates, and photos of Truckee's early days. In the dining area, an ambitious menu—everything from grilled New York strip steak to vegetarian risotto—is served on white linen beneath an open-truss ceiling. On weekends there's live music. ⊠ *Old Brockway Rd., off Hwy. 267, ¼ mi south of downtown* ☎ *530/587–5711* ⌔ *Reservations essential* ⊟ *AE, DC, MC, V* ⊘ *No lunch.*

$$–$$$ ✕ **Dragonfly.** Flavors are bold at this old-town restaurant, where every dish is artfully prepared and stylishly presented. The eclectic Southeast Asian–inspired menu changes twice monthly and is served in a bright, contemporary 2nd-floor dining room. In the summer, sit outside on the terrace overlooking Main Street and the train depot. Lunch is a bargain, and there are always lots of choices for vegetarians. ⊠ *10118 Donner Pass Rd.* ☎ *530/587–0557* ⊟ *D, MC, V* ⊘ *Closed Tues.*

$$–$$$ ✕ **Pianeta.** Right on the main drag of old-town Truckee, this northern Italian trattoria makes delicious pasta dishes—including homemade ravioli and lasagna Bolognese—and entrées such as double-cut marinated lamb chops with mint pesto, and jumbo-shrimp scampi. For a lighter (and less expensive) meal, sit at the bar and order from the extensive list of appetizers. The exposed stone walls may make you feel as if you're eating inside a Tuscan farmhouse. ⊠ *10069 Donner Pass Rd.* ☎ *530/587–4694* ⊟ *AE, MC, V* ⌔ *Reservations essential* ⊘ *No lunch.*

$$$–$$$$ ✕▣ **Northstar-at-Tahoe Resort.** The area's most complete destination resort is especially popular with families, thanks to its many sports activities—from golf and tennis to skiing and snowshoeing—and its concentration of restaurants, shops, recreation facilities, and accommodations (the Village Mall). Lodgings range from hotel rooms to condos to private houses, some with ski-in, ski-out access. You receive free lift tickets and on-site shuttle transportation and have complimentary access to the Swim and Racquet Club's swimming pools, outdoor hot tubs, fitness center, and teen center. True North ($–$$$; reservations essential, open winter only) serves contemporary American cooking prepared with organically grown produce and all-natural meats, well worth the drive. ⊠ *Hwy. 267, 6 mi southeast of Truckee, Box 129, 96160* ☎ *530/562–1010 or 800/466–6784* ⊞ *530/562–2215* ⊕ *www.northstarattahoe.com* ⇥ *270 units* ⌖ *6 restaurants, some kitchens, some kitchenettes, some microwaves, cable TV, in-room VCRs, 18-hole golf course, 12 tennis courts, bicycles, horseback riding, cross-country skiing, downhill skiing, ski shop, ski storage, recreation room, video game room, shops, babysitting, children's programs (ages 2–6), laundry facilities, meeting rooms; no a/c in some rooms, no smoking* ⊟ *AE, D, MC, V.*

$–$$ ▣ **River Street Inn.** This 1885 wood-and-stone inn was at times a boardinghouse and a brothel. Now completely modernized, the uncluttered, comfortable rooms are simply decorated, with attractive, country-style wooden furniture. The sumptuous beds have top-quality mattresses, down comforters, and high-thread-count sheets. Bathrooms have claw-foot tubs. The affable proprietors are there when you need them, then disappear when you want privacy. ✉ *10009 E. River St., 96161* ☎ *530/550–9290* 🖷 *530/582–2391* ⊕ *www.riverstreetinntruckee.com* 📠 *11 rooms* ☆ *Cable TV, in-room VCRs; no a/c, no room phones, no smoking* ⊟ *MC, V* ◉ *CP.*

¢–$$ 🖼 **Truckee Hotel.** Constructed in 1873, this four-story hotel is one of the town's oldest buildings. Mismatched antiques decorate the Victorian-style rooms, most of which have a too-small sink in the corner with separate hot and cold taps; several rooms, though, have private bathrooms with claw-foot tubs. All rooms are clean and more or less comfortable, if a bit small. Request a quiet room, if it matters. ✉ *10007 Bridge St., 96161* ☎ *530/587–4444 or 800/659–6921* 🖷 *916/587–1599* ⊕ *www. truckeehotel.com* 📠 *37 rooms, 29 with shared bath.* ☆ *Restaurant, bar; no a/c, no TV in some rooms, no smoking* ⊟ *AE, MC, V* ◉ *CP.*

Sports & the Outdoors

GOLF The **Coyote Moon Golf Course** (✉ 10685 Northwoods Blvd. ☎ 530/587–0886) is both challenging and beautiful, with no houses to spoil the view; fees range from $95 to $155, including cart. **Northstar** (✉ Hwy. 267 ☎ 530/562–1010) has open links–style play and tight, tree-lined fairways, including water hazards; fees range from $45 to $99, including cart. The water hazards at **Old Greenwood** (✉ 12915 Fairway Dr., off the Prosser Village Rd. exit—Exit 190—from I–80; call for specific directions ☎ 530/550–0844 ⊕ www.oldgreenwood.com), north Lake Tahoe's only Jack Nicklaus signature course, are trout streams, and you can even fish them; the $100–$170 fee includes a cart.

HORSEBACK **Northstar Stables** (✉ Hwy. 267 at Northstar Dr. ☎ 530/562–2480
RIDING ⊕ www.northstarattahoe.com) offers one- and two-hour guided trail rides ($30 and $60), private rides, and half-day and full-day excursions (for experienced riders only). Instruction is provided, ponies are available for tots, and you can even board your own horse here.

MOUNTAIN In summer you can rent a bike and ride the lifts up the mountain at **North-
BIKING star-at-Tahoe** (✉ Hwy. 267 at Northstar Dr. ☎ 530/562–2268 ⊕ www. northstarattahoe.com) for 100 mi of challenging terrain. Lift ticket and rental packages cost $64; lift ticket alone is $34.

SKIING There are several smaller resorts around Truckee, which give you access to the Sierra's slopes for half the price of the big resorts. Though you'll sacrifice vertical rise, acreage, and high-speed lifts, you can ski or ride and still have money left over for room and board. These are great places for first-timers and families with kids learning to ski.

Boreal (✉ Boreal/Castle Peak exit off I–80 ☎ 530/426–3666 ⊕ www. borealski.com) has 380 acres and 500 vertical feet of terrain visible from the freeway; there's also lift-served snow-tubing and night skiing until 9. **Donner Ski Ranch** (✉ 19320 Donner Pass Rd., Norden ☎ 530/426–3635) has 435 acres and 750 vertical feet and sits across from the more challenging Sugar Bowl (*below*). **Soda Springs** (✉ Soda Springs exit off I–80, Soda Springs ☎ 530/426–1010) has 200 acres and 652 vertical feet and lift-served snow-tubing. **Tahoe Donner** (✉ 11603 Slalom Way ☎ 530/587–9444 ⊕ www.tahoedonner.com) is just north of Truckee and covers 120 acres and 560 vertical feet; the cross-country center includes 68 mi of groomed tracks on 4,800 acres, with night skiing December to February.

Northstar-at-Tahoe may be the best all-around family ski resort at Tahoe. With two tree-lined, northeast-facing, wind-protected bowls, it's the ideal place to ski in a storm. The meticulous grooming and long cruisers make it an intermediate skier's paradise. Boarders are especially welcome, with an awesome terrain park, including a 400-foot-long superpipe, a half pipe, rails and boxes, and lots of kickers. Experts can ski the steeps and bumps off Lookout Mountain, where there's rarely a line for the high-speed quad. Northstar-at-Tahoe's cross-country center has 28 mi of groomed trails, including double-set tracks and skating lanes. The school has programs for skiers ages four and up, and day care is available for toilet-trained tots. ⊠ *Hwy. 267, 6 mi southeast of Truckee* ☎ *530/562–1010, 530/562–1330 snow phone* 🖶 *530/562–2215* ⊕ *www.skinorthstar. com* ✆ *72 trails on 2,420 acres, rated 25% beginner, 50% intermediate, 25% advanced. Longest run 2.9 mi, base 6,400′, summit 8,600′. Lifts: 17, including a gondola and 5 high-speed quads.*

Opened in 1939 by Walt Disney, **Sugar Bowl** is the oldest—and one of the best—resorts at Tahoe. Atop Donner Summit, it receives an incredible 500 inches of snowfall annually. Four peaks are connected by 1,500 acres of skiable terrain, with everything from gentle groomed corduroy to wide-open bowls to vertical rocky chutes and outstanding tree-skiing. Snowboarders can hit two terrain parks and an 18½-foot superpipe. Because it's more compact than some of the area's megaresorts, there's a certain gentility here that distinguishes Sugar Bowl from its competitors, making this a great place for families and a low-pressure, low-key place to learn to ski. There's limited lodging at the base area. This is the closest resort to San Francisco (three hours via I–80). ⊠ *Donner Pass Rd., 3 mi east of Soda Springs/Norden exit off I–80, 10 mi west of Truckee* ☎ *530/426–9000 information and lodging reservations, 530/426–1111 snow phone, 866/843–2695 lodging referral* ⊕ *www.sugarbowl. com* ✆ *84 trails on 1,500 acres, rated 17% beginner, 45% intermediate, 38% advanced. Longest run 3 mi, base 6,883′, summit 8,383′. Lifts: 12, including 4 high-speed quads.*

For the ultimate in groomed conditions, head to the nation's largest cross-country ski resort, **Royal Gorge** (⊠ Soda Springs–Norden exit off I–80, Soda Springs ☎ 530/426–3871 ⊕ www.royalgorge.com). It has 197 mi of 18-foot-wide track for all abilities, 88 trails on 9,172 acres, 2 ski schools, and 10 warming huts. Four trailside cafés, two hotels, and a hot tub and sauna are among the facilities.

You can save money by renting skis and boards at **Tahoe Dave's** (⊠ 10200 Donner Pass Rd. ☎ 530/582–0900), which has the area's best selection and also repairs and tunes equipment.

Carnelian Bay to Kings Beach

5–10 mi northeast of Tahoe City on Hwy. 28.

The small lakeside commercial districts of Carnelian Bay and Tahoe Vista service the thousand or so locals who live in the area year-round and the thousands more who have summer residences or launch their boats here. Kings Beach, the last town heading east on Highway 28 before the Nevada border, is to Crystal Bay what South Lake Tahoe is to Stateline: a bustling California village full of basic motels and rental condos, restaurants, and shops, used by the hordes of hopefuls who pass through on their way to the casinos.

The 28-acre **Kings Beach State Recreation Area,** one of the largest such areas on the lake, is open year-round. The 700-foot-long beach becomes crowded with people swimming, sunbathing, jet skiing, riding in paddleboats, spiking volleyballs, and tossing Frisbees. There's a good playground and picnic area here. ⊠ *N. Lake Blvd., Kings Beach* ☎ *530/546–7248* ⚒ *Free* ⊗ *Daily 24 hrs.*

Where Stay & Eat

★ **$$$–$$$$** ✕ **Wild Goose.** Soft leather banquettes and polished mahogany tables complement the gorgeous lake views in this casually elegant 100-seat dining room. Sliding glass doors open up to a lakeside deck beneath towering pines. Come early to see the sunset. The menu features fine European-inspired contemporary California cuisine; expect resort prices. ⊠ *7320 N. Lake Blvd., Tahoe Vista* ☎ *530/546–3640* ⚐ *Reservations essential* ▱ *AE, D, MC, V* ⊗ *Closed Mon. No lunch Oct.–May.*

$$–$$$ ✕ **Gar Woods Grill and Pier.** The view's the thing at this lakeside stalwart, where you can watch the sun shimmer on the water through the dining room's plate glass windows or from the heated outdoor deck. There are salads and sandwiches at lunch, and steaks and grilled fish at dinner, but the best meal here is Sunday brunch. At all hours in season, the bar gets packed with bacchanalian boaters who pull up to the restaurant's private pier. ⊠ *5000 N. Lake Blvd., Carnelian Bay* ☎ *530/546–3366* ▱ *AE, MC, V.*

$–$$$ ✕ **Spindleshanks.** This handsome roadhouse, decorated with floor-to-ceiling knotty pine, serves mostly classic American cooking—ribs, steaks, and seafood—as well as house-made ravioli. At peak periods, the convivial atmosphere gets loud, but after a glass of wine from the extensive list, you won't notice. In the morning the bar area becomes an espresso and breakfast café. ⊠ *6873 N. Lake Blvd.* ☎ *530/546–2191 or 530/546–8684* ⚐ *Reservations essential* ▱ *AE, MC, V* ⊗ *No lunch.*

$–$$ ✕ **Lanza's.** Lanza's serves good old-fashioned Italian-American food on red-and-white–checked tablecloths in a pine-paneled dining room. There's lasagna, manicotti, veal piccata, and eggplant Parmesan, but you can also order your own pasta-and-sauce combination. Leave room for the homemade spumoni. ⊠ *7739 N. Lake Blvd., next to Safeway, Kings Beach* ☎ *530/546–2434* ⚐ *Reservations not accepted* ▱ *MC, V* ⊗ *No lunch.*

¢ ✕ **Log Cabin Caffe.** Almost always hopping, this Kings Beach eatery specializes in hearty breakfast and lunch entrées—five kinds of eggs Benedict, Mexican and smoked-salmon scrambles, omelets, pancakes, and waffles. They also serve sandwiches and freshly baked pastries. Get here early on weekends for the popular brunch, or be prepared to wait. ⊠ *8692 N. Lake Blvd., Kings Beach* ☎ *530/546–7109* ▱ *MC, V* ⊗ *No dinner.*

★ **$$$–$$$$** ⊞ **Shore House.** Every room has a gas fireplace and featherbed at this lakefront B&B in Tahoe Vista. The lovingly tended, knotty-pine-paneled guest rooms beautifully, and simply, capture the woodsy spirit of Tahoe, but without overdoing the pinecone motif. All have private entrances and extra touches such as bathrobes, stereo CD players, and rubber duckies in the bathtubs; many have great views of the water. There's also a private beach. ⊠ *7170 N. Lake Blvd., Tahoe Vista 96148* ☎ *530/546–7270 or 800/207–5160* ⊕ *www.shorehouselaketahoe. com* ⤴ *8 rooms, 1 cottage* ⚹ *Refrigerators, Wi-Fi, outdoor hot tub, lake, beach; no a/c, no room phones, no room TVs, no smoking* ⊟ *D, MC, V* ⦿ *BP.*

¢–$$ ⊞ **Ferrari's Crown Resort.** One of the few remaining family-owned and -operated motels in Kings Beach, Ferrari's has straightforward motel rooms in a resort setting, great for families with kids. It sits right on the lake, and some rooms have awesome views. Kids love the pool; adults enjoy the hot tub. There's also kayak rental on-site. ⊠ *8200 N. Lake Blvd., Kings Beach 96143* ☎ *530/546–3388 or 800/645–2260* 🖶 *530/546–3851* ⊕ *www.tahoecrown.com* ⤴ *45 rooms* ⚹ *Some kitchenettes, some refrigerators, cable TV, some in-room broadband, pool, lake, hot tub, beach, Ping-Pong; no a/c in some rooms, no smoking* ⊟ *AE, D, MC, V.*

¢–$$ ⊞ **Rustic Cottages.** These charming clapboard cottages sit clustered beneath tall pine trees across the road from Lake Tahoe. Cozy, simple, and well cared for, they offer an inexpensive alternative to a motel. All have patios, and some have fireplaces and kitchens. If the cottages are booked, ask about the well-run sister property, Tahoe Vista Lodge and Cabins, just up the road. The service at both is terrific. ⊠ *7449 N. Lake Blvd., Box 18, Tahoe Vista 96148* ☎ *530/546–3523 or 888/ 778–7842* 🖶 *530/546–0146* ⊕ *www.rusticcottages.com* ⤴ *20 cottages* ⚹ *Some kitchens, microwaves, refrigerators, cable TV, in-room VCRs, some pets allowed (fee); no a/c, no room phones, no smoking* ⊟ *AE, D, MC, V* ⦿ *CP.*

Sports & the Outdoors

SNOWMOBILING **Snowmobiling Unlimited** (⊠ Hwy. 267, 3 mi north of Hwy. 28, Kings Beach ☎ 530/583–7192) conducts 1½-, 2-, and 3-hour guided cross-country tours, mostly along the trails in nearby Tahoe National Forest. They provide open-face helmets and mittens, but bring your own goggles or sunglasses.

WINDSURFING Learn to skitter across the blue waters of the lake with one of Tahoe's kindest instructors at **Windsurf North Tahoe** (⊠ 7276 N. Lake Blvd., Tahoe Vista ☎ 530/546–5857 or 800/294–6378 ⊕ www.tahoeholidayhouse.com).

NEVADA SIDE

You don't need a highway sign to know when you've crossed from California into Nevada: the flashing lights and elaborate marquees of casinos announce legal gambling in garish hues.

9

Crystal Bay

❿ *1 mi east of Kings Beach on Hwy. 28; 30 mi north of South Lake Tahoe via U.S. 50 to Hwy. 28.*

Right at the Nevada border, Crystal Bay has a cluster of casinos that, once you're inside, all look essentially the same, but that each have their own minor differences. The **Cal-Neva Lodge** (✉ 2 Stateline Rd. ☎ 775/832–4000 ⊕ www.calnevaresort.com) is bisected by the state line. Opened in 1927, this joint has weathered many scandals, the largest involving former owner Frank Sinatra (he lost his gaming license in the 1960s for alleged mob connections). The **Tahoe Biltmore** (✉ Hwy. 28 at Stateline Rd. ☎ 775/831–0660 ⊕ www.tahoebiltmore.com) serves its popular $2.49 breakfast special 24 hours a day and has nightly DJs or live bands with dancing. **Jim Kelley's Tahoe Nugget** (✉ Hwy. 28 at Stateline Rd. ☎ 775/831–0455) serves 101 kinds of beers. The **Crystal Bay Club** (✉ Hwy. 28 at Stateline Rd. ⊕ www.crystalbaycasino.com ☎ 775/831–0512) has a restaurant with a towering open-truss ceiling that looks like a wooden ship's hull.

Where to Stay & Eat

★ **$$–$$$** ✕ **Soule Domain.** Some of Lake Tahoe's more creative and delicious dinners are served in this 1927 pine-log cabin across from the Tahoe Biltmore. Chef-owner Charles Edward Soule IV's specialties include curried cashew chicken, lamb ravioli, rock shrimp with sea scallops, and a vegan sauté, but you'll find the chef's current passion in the always-great roster of nightly specials. In winter, request a table near the crackling fireplace. ✉ *Cove St., ½ block up Stateline Rd. from Hwy. 28* ☎ *530/546–7529* ⬦ *Reservations essential* ▭ *AE, MC, V* ⊘ *No lunch.*

$–$$ ✕ **Lake Tahoe Brewing Co.** The beer is made on-site at this microbrewery-restaurant inside a 1927 roadhouse, right on the California-Nevada border. The eclectic menu includes jambalaya, schnitzel, pot roast, and steaks that all go down easy with the homemade brews. There's live music every Friday and Saturday; in warm weather, the bands play outside, a fun scene for both locals and tourists alike. Kids are welcome. ✉ *24 Stateline Rd.* ☎ *775/831–5822* ▭ *AE, MC, V* ⬦ *Reservations not accepted.* ⊘ *No lunch weekdays Oct.–May.*

$$–$$$ ▥ **Cal-Neva Lodge.** All the rooms in this hotel-casino have views of Lake Tahoe and the mountains. The hotel also rents seven two-bedroom chalets and 12 cabins with living rooms. There is an arcade for children and cabaret entertainment for grown-ups. Though some of the public areas look a bit shabby, the rooms are generally well maintained. There are some fun peculiarities about the place such as the state line running right through the swimming pool and the secret tunnel that Frank Sinatra built so that he could steal away unnoticed to Marilyn Monroe's cabin. Tours of the latter leave Thursday, Friday, and Saturday at 7, 8, and 9 PM. ✉ *2 Stateline Rd., Box 368, 89402* ☎ *775/832–4000 or 800/225–6382* 🖷 *775/831–9007* ⊕ *www.calnevaresort.com* 🛏 *220 rooms, 20 suites, 12 cabins* ♿ *Restaurant, coffee shop, room service, cable TV with movies, in-room VCRs, Wi-Fi, tennis court, pool, gym, hot tub, massage, sauna, spa, bar, cabaret, casino, video game room, dry cleaning, concierge, airport shuttle, some pets allowed* ▭ *AE, D, DC, MC, V.*

Incline Village

⓫ *3 mi east of Crystal Bay on Hwy. 28.*

Incline Village, Nevada's only privately owned town, dates to the early 1960s, when an Oklahoma developer bought 10,000 acres north of Lake Tahoe. His idea was to sketch out a plan for a town without a central commercial district, hoping to prevent congestion and to preserve the area's natural beauty. One-acre lakeshore lots originally fetched $12,000 to $15,000; today you couldn't buy even the land for less than several million. Check out **Lakeshore Drive,** along which you'll see some of the most expensive real estate in Nevada. The drive is discreetly marked: to find it, start at the Hyatt Hotel and drive westward along the lake.

Fodor'sChoice
★
George Whittell, a San Francisco socialite who once owned 50,000 acres of property along the lake, built the **Thunderbird Lodge** in 1936. You can tour the mansion and the grounds by reservation only, and though it's pricey, it provides a rare glimpse back to a time when only the very wealthy had homes at Tahoe. You can take a bus tour from the Incline Village Visitors Bureau or South Lake Tahoe, a 45-passenger catamaran tour from the Hyatt in Incline Village, or a 1950, 21-passenger wooden cruiser from Tahoe Keys Marina in South Lake Tahoe (which includes lunch). ☒ *5000 Hwy. 28* ☎ *775/832–8750 (lodge direct number), 800/468–2463, 775/832–1606 (reservations), 775/588–1881, 888/867–6394 (Tahoe Keys boat), 775/832–1234, 800/553–3288 (Hyatt Incline Village boat), 530/544–9186 (bus shuttle from South Lake Tahoe)* ⊕ *www.thunderbirdlodge.org* ☒ *$25 bus tour, $65–$90 boat tour* ☾ *May–Oct., call for tour times.*

OFF THE
BEATEN
PATH
LAKE TAHOE–NEVADA STATE PARK – Protecting much of the lake's eastern shore from development, Lake Tahoe–Nevada State Park comprises several sections that stretch from Incline Village to Zephyr Cove. Beaches and trails provide access to a wilder side of the lake, whether you are into cross-country skiing, hiking, or just relaxing at a picnic. One of the most popular areas is **Sand Harbor Beach** (☒ Hwy. 28, 4 mi south of Incline Village ☎ 775/831-0494), so popular that it is sometimes filled to capacity by 11 AM on summer weekends. Stroll the boardwalk and read the information signs for a good lesson in the local ecology.

Where to Stay & Eat

$$–$$$ ✕**Frederick's.** Sit at one of the 15 copper-covered tables at this intimate bistro, which serves a mishmash of European and Asian cooking, mostly prepared using organic produce and free-range meats. Try the braised lamb shank, Parmesan gnocchi, or the deliciously fresh sushi rolls. Ask for a table by the fire. ☒ *907 Tahoe Blvd.* ☎ *775/832–3007* ⌚ *Reservations essential* ⊟ *AE, MC, V* ☾ *Closed Mon. and Tues. No lunch.*

★ $$ ✕**Le Bistro.** Incline Village's hidden gem, Le Bistro serves expertly prepared French-country cuisine in a relaxed, cozy, romantic dining room. The chef-owner makes everything himself, using only organically grown ingredients, and changes the menu almost daily. Try the five-course prix-fixe menu ($41), which can also be paired with wines. Service is gracious and attentive. The restaurant is hard to find; be sure to ask directions when you book. ✉ *120 Country Club Dr., #29* ☎ *775/831–0800* ♨ *Reservations essential* ☰ *AE, D, DC, MC, V* ⊙ *Closed Sun. and Mon. No lunch.*

♨ **$–$$** ✕ **Azzara's.** An Italian family restaurant with a light, inviting dining room, Azzara's serves a dozen pasta dishes and many pizzas, as well as chicken, veal, shrimp, and beef. Dinners include soup or salad, a vegetable, and olive-oil garlic bread. ✉ *Incline Center Mall, 930 Tahoe Blvd.* ☎ *775/831–0346* ☰ *MC, V* ⊙ *Closed Mon. No lunch.*

¢ ✕ **T's Rotisserie.** There's nothing fancy about T's, which looks like a snack bar, but the mesquite-grilled chicken and tri-tip steaks are delicious. ✉*901 Tahoe Blvd.* ☎ *775/831–2832* ☰ *No credit cards.*

★ **$$$–$$$$** ✕▥ **Hyatt Regency Lake Tahoe.** Once a dowdy casino hotel, the Hyatt underwent a $60 million renovation between 2001 and 2003 and is now a sophisticated full-service destination resort. On 26 acres of prime lakefront property, the resort has a range of luxurious accommodations, from tower-hotel rooms to cozy lakeside cottages. The Lone Eagle Grille ($$–$$$$) serves steaks and seafood in one of the north shore's most handsome lake-view dining rooms. There's also a state-of-the-art, 20,000-square-foot spa. Standard rates are high, but look for midweek or off-season discounts. ✉ *Lakeshore and Country Club Drs., 89450* ☎*775/831–1111 or 888/899–5019* 🖷*775/831–7508* ⊕*www.laketahoe. hyatt.com* 🛏 *432 rooms, 28 suites* ♨ *4 restaurants, café, room service, in-room safes, some kitchenettes, minibars, cable TV with movies and video games, in-room broadband, in-room data ports, Web TV, Wi-Fi, golf privileges, pool, lake, exercise equipment, hair salon, outdoor hot tub, 2 saunas, spa, beach, dock, boating, jet skiing, waterskiing, mountain bikes, volleyball, ski shop, ski storage, 3 bars, lobby lounge, casino, video game room, shop, children's programs (ages 3–12), dry cleaning, laundry service, concierge, concierge floor, Internet room, business services, meeting rooms, no-smoking floor* ☰ *AE, D, DC, MC, V.*

The Arts

Fans of the Bard ought not to miss the **Lake Tahoe Shakespeare Festival** (☎ 775/832–1616 or 800/747–4697 ⊕ www.laketahoeshakespeare. com), which is held outdoors at Sand Harbor with the lake as a backdrop, from mid-July through August.

Sports & the Outdoors

Incline Village's **recreation center** (✉ 980 Incline Way ☎ 775/832–1300) has an eight-lane swimming pool and a fitness area, basketball court, game room, and snack bar. Nonresidents pay $13.

GOLF   **Incline Championship** (✉ 955 Fairway Blvd. ☎ 775/325–8801 ⊕ www. inclinegolf.com) is an 18-hole, par-72 Robert Trent Jones course with a driving range, both completely renovated between 2002 and 2004. The greens fee of $155 includes an optional cart. **Incline Mountain** (✉ 690 Wilson Way ☎ 775/325–8801 ⊕ www.inclinegolf.com) is an executive (shorter) 18-hole course; par is 58. Greens fees start at $55, including optional cart.

MOUNTAIN   You can rent bikes and get helpful tips from **Flume Trail Bikes** (✉ Spooner
BIKING   Summit, Hwy. 28, ½ mi north of U.S. 50, Glenbrook ☎ 775/749–5349

or 775/887–8844 ⊕ www.theflumetrail.com), which also operates a bike shuttle to popular trailheads. Ask about the secluded rental cabins for overnight rides.

SKIING A fun family mood prevails at **Diamond Peak,** which has many special programs and affordable rates. Snowmaking covers 75% of the mountain, and runs are groomed nightly. The ride up the 1-mi Crystal chair rewards you with some of the best views of the lake from any ski area. Diamond Peak is less crowded than the larger areas and provides free shuttles to nearby lodging. It's a great place for beginners and intermediates, and it's appropriately priced for families. However, though there are some steep-aspect black-diamond runs, advanced skiers may find the acreage too limited. For snowboarders there's a half pipe and superpipe. **Diamond Peak Cross-Country** (⊠ Off Hwy. 431 ☎ 775/832–1177) has 22 mi of groomed track with skating lanes. The trail system rises from 7,400 feet to 9,100 feet, with endless wilderness to explore. ⊠ *1210 Ski Way, off Hwy. 28 to Country Club Dr.* ☎ *775/832–1177 or 800/468–2463 ☞ 29 trails on 655 acres, rated 18% beginner, 46% intermediate, 36% advanced. Longest run 2½ mi, base 6,700′, summit 8,540′. Lifts: 6, including 2 high-speed quads.*

Ski some of the highest slopes at Tahoe, and take in bird's-eye views of Reno and the Carson Valley at **Mt. Rose Ski Tahoe.** Though more compact than the bigger Tahoe resorts, Mt. Rose has the area's highest base elevation and consequently the driest snow. The mountain has a wide variety of terrain. The most challenging is the Chutes, 200 acres of gulp-and-go advanced-to-expert vertical, opened in the 2004–2005 season. Intermediates can choose steep groomers or mellow, wide-open boulevards. Beginners have their own corner of the mountain, with gentle, nonthreatening, wide slopes. Boarders and tricksters have three terrain parks to choose from, on opposite sides of the mountain, allowing them to follow the sun as it tracks across the resort. Because of its elevation, the mountain gets hit hard in storms; check conditions before heading up during inclement weather or on a windy day. ⊠ *Hwy. 431, 11 mi north of Incline Village* ☎ *775/849–0704 or 800/754–7673 ⊕ www.skirose.com ☞ 61 trails on 1,200 acres, rated 20% beginner, 30% intermediate, 40% advanced, 10% expert. Longest run 2½ mi, base 8,260′, summit 9,700′. Lifts: 6, including 1 high-speed 6-passenger lift.*

On the way to Mt. Rose from Incline Village, **Tahoe Meadows** (⊠ Hwy. 431) is the most popular area near the north shore for noncommercial cross-country skiing, sledding, tubing, snowshoeing, and snowmobiling.

You'll find superbly groomed tracks and fabulous views of Lake Tahoe at **Spooner Lake Cross-Country** (⊠ Spooner Summit, Hwy. 28, ½ mi north of U.S. 50, Glenbrook ☎ 775/887–8844 ski phone, 775/749–5349 reservations ⊕ www.spoonerlake.com). It has more than 50 mi of trails on more than 9,000 acres, and two rustic, secluded cabins are available for rent for overnight treks.

9

As you head south on Highway 28 toward the south shore, you can take a detour away from the lake (east) on U.S. 50 to reach two interesting towns. After about 10 mi on U.S. 50, take U.S. 395 north for 1 mi to Nevada's capital, **Carson City.** Most of its historic buildings and other attractions, including the Nevada State Museum and the Nevada Railroad Museum, are along U.S. 395, the main street through town. About a 30-minute drive up Highway 342 northeast of Carson City is the fabled mining town of **Virginia City,** one of the largest and most authentic historical mining towns in the West. It's chock-full of mansions, museums, saloons, and, of course, dozens of shops selling everything from amethysts to yucca.

Zephyr Cove

⑫ *22 mi south of Incline Village via Hwy. 28 to U.S. 50.*

The largest settlement between Incline Village and the Stateline area is Zephyr Cove, a tiny resort. It has a beach, marina, campground, picnic area, coffee shop in a log lodge, rustic cabins, and nearby riding stables.

★ Nearby **Cave Rock** (⊠ U.S. 50, 4 mi north of Zephyr Cove ☎ 775/831–0494), 75 feet of solid stone at the southern end of Lake Tahoe–Nevada State Park, is the throat of an extinct volcano. Tahoe Tessie, the lake's version of the Loch Ness monster, is reputed to live in a cavern below the impressive outcropping. For the Washoe Indians, this area is a sacred burial site. Cave Rock towers over a parking lot, a lakefront picnic ground, and a boat launch. The views are some of the best on the lake; this is a good spot to stop and take a picture.

KINGSBURY GRADE – This road, also known as Highway 207, is one of three that access Tahoe from the east. Originally a toll road used by wagon trains to get over the crest of the Sierra, it has sweeping views of the Carson Valley. Off Highway 206, which intersects Highway 207, is Genoa, the oldest settlement in Nevada. Along Main Street are a museum in Nevada's oldest courthouse, a small state park, and the state's longest-standing saloon. If you're heading to points south along the eastern Sierra, such as Mammoth Mountain or Mono Lake, Highway 267 shaves 30–60 minutes off the drive from South Lake.

Where to Stay & Eat

↻ 🏠 ⚠ **Zephyr Cove Resort.** Tucked beneath towering pines at the lake's edge stand 28 cozy, but modern, vacation cabins with peaked knotty-pine ceilings. They're not fancy, but they're immaculate and come in a variety of sizes, some perfect for families. Across U.S. 50, there's a sprawling year-round campground—one of the largest on the lake—that's geared largely toward RVers, but with drive-in and walk-in tent sites, too. The resort has horseback riding, snowmobiling facilities, and a marina with boat rentals, all of which contribute to the summer-camp atmosphere. ↻ *Restaurant, snack bar, BBQs, some kitchens, some kitchenettes, cable TV, in-room data ports, beach, laundry facilities, flush*

*toilets, full hookups, partial hookups, dump station, drinking water, show-
ers, fire pits, picnic tables, general store; no a/c ↪ 175 sites, 28 cabins
⊠ U.S. 50, 4 mi north of Stateline ☎ 775/589–4981 ⊕ www.zephyrcove.
com ⊠ $25–$48 (campsites); $139–$189 (cabins).*

Stateline

⑬ *5 mi south of Zephyr Cove on U.S. 50.*

Stateline is the archetypal Nevada border town. Its four high-rise casinos are as vertical and contained as the commercial district of South Lake
Tahoe, on the California side, is horizontal and sprawling. And Stateline is as relentlessly indoors oriented as the rest of the lake is focused
on the outdoors. This strip is where you'll find the most concentrated
action at Lake Tahoe: restaurants (including typical casino buffets),
showrooms with famous headliners and razzle-dazzle revues, tower-hotel
rooms and suites, and 24-hour casinos.

Where to Stay & Eat

★ **$$–$$$** ✕ **Mirabelle.** The French-Alsatian–born chef-owner prepares everything
on the menu himself, from puff pastry to chocolate cake to homemade
bread. Specialties include an Alsatian onion tart, escargots, and rack of
lamb. Leave room for the dessert soufflés. On Monday from April
through June, the chef holds cooking classes that culminate with a
grand repast in the casual, airy dining room. ⊠ *290 Kingsbury Grade*
☎ *775/586–1007* ⊟ *AE, MC, V* ⊙ *Closed Mon. No lunch.*

$$–$$$$ ✕▨ **Harveys Resort Hotel/Casino.** This resort, which started as a cabin
in 1944, is now Tahoe's largest. Premium rooms have custom furnish-
ings, oversize marble baths, and minibars. Although it was acquired by
Harrah's and has lost some of its cachet, Harveys remains a fine prop-
erty. The Emerald Theater is Harveys' showroom. At Cabo Wabo
($–$$), an always-hopping Baja-style cantina owned by Sammy Hagar,
sip Agave-style Tequila while munching on Mexican and shouting across
the table at your date. ⊠ *U.S. 50 at Stateline Ave., 89449* ☎ *775/588–
2411 or 800/648–3361* ⊟ *775/782–4889* ⊕ *www.harrahs.com/our
casinos/hlt* ↪ *705 rooms, 38 suites* ₺ *8 restaurants, room service,
minibars, cable TV with movies, in-room data ports, pool, health club,
hair salon, hot tub, spa, casino, showroom, concierge, meeting rooms,
car rental* ⊟ *AE, D, DC, MC, V.*

$–$$$$ ✕▨ **Harrah's Tahoe Hotel/Casino.** Luxurious guest rooms here have two
full bathrooms, each with a television and telephone. Upper-floor rooms
have views of the lake or mountains. Top-name entertainment is pre-
sented in the South Shore Room. Among the restaurants, the romantic
16th-floor Summit ($$$$) is a standout, but bring a credit card; there's
also a buffet on the 16th floor. A tunnel runs under U.S. 50 to Harveys,
which Harrah's now owns. ⊠ *U.S. 50 at Stateline Ave., 89449* ☎ *775/
588–6611 or 800/427–7247* ⊟ *775/588–6607* ⊕ *www.harrahstahoe.
com* ↪ *470 rooms, 62 suites* ₺ *7 restaurants, room service, cable TV
with movies, in-room broadband, in-room data ports, indoor pool,
health club, hair salon, hot tub, casino, showrooms, laundry service, meet-
ing rooms, car rental* ⊟ *AE, D, DC, MC, V.*

9

$–$$$ ⊞ **Caesars Tahoe.** Most of the luxury-kitsch rooms and suites at Caesars have oversize tubs, king-size beds, two telephones, and a view of Lake Tahoe or the surrounding mountains (some, however, overlook the parking lot). Famous entertainers perform in the 1,600-seat Circus Maximus. Stone Street Bar & Grill is the best sports bar in town and also has shuffleboard and occasional open-mike nights. ⊠ *55 U.S. 50, Box 5800, 89449* ☎ *775/588–3515 or 800/648–3353* ☐ *775/586–2068* ⊕ *www.caesars.com* ⤴ *328 rooms, 112 suites △ 5 restaurants, coffee shop, room service, cable TV with movies, in-room broadband, in-room data ports, Web TV, 4 tennis courts, indoor pool, health club, hair salon, hot tub, sauna, spa, casino, meeting rooms, car rental* ⊟ *AE, D, DC, MC, V.*

¢–$$$ ⊞ **Lakeside Inn and Casino.** The smallest of the Stateline casinos, the Lakeside has good promotional room rates and simple, attractive accommodations in two-story motel-style buildings away from the casino. ⊠ *U.S. 50 at Kingsbury Grade, Box 5640, 89449* ☎ *775/588–7777 or 800/624–7980* ☐ *775/588–4092* ⊕ *www.lakesideinn.com* ⤴ *115 rooms, 9 suites △ Restaurant, in-room data ports, pool, casino* ⊟ *AE, D, DC, MC, V.*

Nightlife

Each of the major casinos has its own showroom, including Harrah's **South Shore Room** (☎ 775/588–6611). They feature everything from comedy to magic acts to sexy floor shows to Broadway musicals. If you want to dance with Gen-Xers to DJ grooves and live bands, check out the scene at Caesar's **Club Nero** (⊠ 55 U.S. 50 ☎ 775/588–3515). At Harrah's, you can dance at **Altitude** (⊠ U.S. 50 at state line ☎ 775/568–6705), which has cage dancers Thursday through Sunday nights. **Harvey's Outdoor Summer Concert Series** (☎ 800/427–7247) presents outdoor concerts on weekends in summer with headliners such as the Eagles, Alabama, Sammy Hagar, Steve Winwood, and the Wallflowers.

Sports & the Outdoors

One of the south shore's best, **Nevada Beach** (⊠ Elk Point Rd., 3 mi north of Stateline via U.S. 50 ☎ 530/543–2600) has a superwide sandy beach that's great for swimming (most Tahoe beaches are rocky). There are also picnic tables, restrooms, barbecue grills, and a campground beneath towering pines. This is the best place to watch the Fourth of July or Labor Day fireworks.

On the lake, **Edgewood Tahoe** (⊠ U.S. 50 and Lake Pkwy., behind Horizon Casino ☎ 775/588–3566 or 888/881–8659 ⊕ www.edgewood-tahoe.com) is an 18-hole, par-72 course with a driving range. The $200 greens fees include a cart (though you can walk if you wish). The clubhouse has a great lake-view restaurant for lunch or dinner.

Reno

❶❹ *32 mi east of Truckee on I–80; 38 mi northeast of Incline Village via Hwy. 431 and U.S. 395.*

Established in 1859 as a trading station at a bridge over the Truckee River, Reno grew along with the silver mines of nearby Virginia City (starting in 1860), the railroad (railroad officials named the town in 1868), and gambling (legalized in 1931). Once the gaming and divorce capital of the United States, the city built itself a monument: the famous Reno Arch, a sign over the upper end of Virginia Street, proclaims it THE BIGGEST LITTLE CITY IN THE WORLD. Reno is still a gambling town, with most of the casinos crowded into five square blocks downtown. The city has lost significant business to California's Native American casinos over the past few years, which has resulted in cheaper rooms, but mediocre upkeep; there just isn't the money coming into town that there once was. But besides the casino-hotels, Reno has a number of cultural and family-friendly attractions. Temperatures year-round in this high-mountain-desert climate are warmer than at Tahoe, though it rarely gets as hot here as in Sacramento and the Central Valley, making strolling around town a pleasure. In recent years, a few excellent restaurants have shown up outside the hotels, but aside from a few notable exceptions, lodging continues to be nothing special.

Circus Circus (⊠ 500 N. Sierra St. ☎ 775/329–0711 or 800/648–5010 ⊕ www.circusreno.com), marked by a neon clown sucking a lollipop, is the best stop for families with children. A midway above the casino floor has clowns, games, fun-house mirrors, and circus acts. **Eldorado** (⊠ 345 N. Virginia St. ☎ 775/786–5700 or 800/648–5966 ⊕ www.eldoradoreno.com) is action packed, with tons of slots, good bar-top video poker, and good coffee-shop and food-court fare. **Harrah's** (⊠ 219 N. Center St. ☎ 775/786–3232 or 800/648–3773 ⊕ www.harrahs.com) occupies two city blocks, with a sprawling casino and an outdoor promenade; it also has a 29-story Hampton Inn annex. Minimums are low, and service is friendly. **Silver Legacy** (⊠ 407 N. Virginia St. ☎ 775/329–4777 or 800/687–8733 ⊕ www.silverlegacyreno.com) has a Victorian-theme casino with a 120-foot-tall mining rig that mints silver-dollar tokens. The **Downtown River Walk** (⊠ S. Virginia St. and the Truckee River ⊕ www.renoriver.org) often holds special events featuring street performers, musicians, dancers, food, art exhibits, and games. At one end, the 2,600-foot-long Truckee River white-water kayaking course runs right through downtown and has become a major attraction for water-sports enthusiasts.

On the University of Nevada campus, the sleekly designed **Fleischmann Planetarium** has films and astronomy shows. *⊠ 1600 N. Virginia St. ☎ 775/784–4811 ⊕ www.planetarium.unr.nevada.edu ⊠ Exhibits free, films and star shows $5 ⊙ Weekdays 8–8, weekends 11–8.*

★ The **Nevada Museum of Art,** the state's largest museum and only accredited art museum, has changing exhibits in a dramatic modern building. *⊠ 160 W. Liberty St. ☎ 775/329–3333 ⊕ www.nevadaart.org ⊠ $10 ⊙ Tues., Wed., and Fri.–Sun. 10–5, Thurs. 10–8.*

More than 220 antique and classic automobiles, including an Elvis Presley Cadillac, are on display at the **National Automobile Museum.** *⊠ Mill and Lake Sts. ☎ 775/333–9300 ⊕ www.automuseum.org ⊠ $8 ⊙ Mon.–Sat. 9:30–5:30, Sun. 10–4.*

9

> **OFF THE BEATEN PATH**
>
> **VICTORIAN SQUARE** – In Sparks, Reno's sister city to the east, this square is fringed by restored turn-of-the-20th-century houses and Victorian-dressed casinos and storefronts. Its bandstand is the focal point of many festivals. ⊠ *Victorian Ave. between Rock Blvd. and Pyramid Way, Sparks.*

Where to Stay & Eat

★ **$$$–$$$$** ✕ **LuLou's.** Modern art adorns the exposed brick walls of the small dining room at this innovative restaurant. Drawing influences from Europe and Asia, the chef has imported contemporary urban cooking to the Great Basin. The menu changes often, and you can expect to see anything from foie gras and duck confit to pot stickers and chicken curry. ⊠ *1470 S. Virginia St.* ☎ *775/329–9979* ⌂ *Reservations essential* ⊟ *AE, D, DC, MC, V* ⊗ *Closed Sun. and Mon. No lunch.*

$$–$$$ ✕ **Beaujolais Bistro.** Everything here is French—waiters, wine, and even the music—and the service is warm and friendly. The comfortable, airy dining room has exposed brick walls, a parquet floor, and an inviting, casual vibe. On the menu, expect modern adaptations of classics such as beef bourguignon, roast duck, coq au vin, seafood sausage, and steak frites, all lovingly prepared by the chef-owner. ⊠ *130 West St.* ☎ *775/323–2227* ⌂ *Reservations essential* ⊟ *AE, D, MC, V* ⊗ *Closed Mon. No lunch weekends.*

★ **$$–$$$** ✕ **Fourth St. Bistro.** You'll find deliciously simple, perfectly prepared cooking at this charming bistro, where the chef-owner uses organic produce and meats whenever possible. The casual white-tablecloth dining room, with its sponge-painted walls, is comfortable and inviting. ⊠ *3065 W. 4th St.* ☎ *775/323–3200* ⌂ *Reservations essential* ⊟ *AE, D, DC, MC, V* ⊗ *Closed Sun. and Mon. No lunch.*

$–$$ ✕ **EJ's Jazz Café.** The joint is always jumpin' at EJ's, where you can hear live jazz every night (except Sunday and Monday) while dining on flavorful, spicy Cajun cooking in a small, stylish dining room. ⊠ *15 S. Virginia St. (one door in from the street, along the River Walk)* ☎ *775/324–9900* ⌂ *Reservations essential* ⊟ *AE, D, MC, V.*

¢–$ ✕ **Bangkok Cuisine.** If you want to eat well in a pretty dining room but don't want to break the bank, come to this charming Thai restaurant, where delicious soups, salads, stir-fries, and curries are prepared by a Thai national. ⊠ *55 Mt. Rose St.* ☎ *775/322–0299* ⊟ *AE, D, DC, MC, V* ⊗ *Closed Sun.*

¢–$$$ ✕⌸ **Harrah's.** This is one of the nicer hotels in downtown Reno. Large guest rooms decorated in blues and mauves overlook downtown and the entire mountain-ringed valley. The dark and romantic dining room at Harrah's Steak House ($$–$$$$; reservations essential, no lunch weekends) serves excellent prime steaks and seafood that merit a special trip by meat lovers; try the Caesar salad and steak Diane, both prepared tableside by a tuxedoed waiter. ⊠ *219 N. Center St., 89501* ☎ *775/786–3232 or 800/648–3773* ⊕ *www.harrahs.com* ➬ *565 rooms* ⌂ *6 restaurants, room service, in-room safes, some in-room hot tubs, some refrigerators, cable TV with movies and video games, some in-room data ports, pool, health club, casino, video game room, dry cleaning* ⊟ *AE, D, DC, MC, V.*

$–$$ ✕🏨 **Siena Hotel Spa Casino.** Reno's most luxurious hotel has attractive rooms decorated with modern blond-wood furnishings and comfortable beds, courtesy of pillow-top mattresses and down comforters. At check-in, you won't have to navigate past miles of slot machines to find the front desk, because the casino is in a self-contained room off the elegant lobby. Lexie's ($$–$$$$; dinner and Sunday brunch only) serves steaks and fresh seafood using Tuscan-inspired recipes, served in a sleek and elegant modern dining room overlooking the river. There's also a small full-service spa. ✉ *1 S. Lake St., 89501* ☎ *775/337–6260 or 877/743–6233* 🖷 *775/321–5870* ⊕ *www.sienareno.com* ➴ *193 rooms, 21 suites ⏶ Restaurant, coffee shop, room service, minibars, refrigerators, cable TV, in-room broadband, in-room data ports, Web TV, Wi-Fi, pool, health club, spa, lounge, wine bar, casino, dry cleaning, laundry service, concierge, Internet room, business services, meeting rooms, airport shuttle* ▤ *AE, D, DC, MC, V.*

¢–$$ ✕🏨 **Eldorado.** Smack-dab in the middle of glittering downtown sits the Eldorado, an all-suites tower whose rooms overlook the mountains or the lights of the city. La Strada ($–$$; dinner only, closed Wednesday and Thursday) serves great northern Italian cooking in a romantic room; Roxy's ($$–$$$$; dinner only, reservations essential) serves wood-oven-roasted and grilled meats and seafood in an over-the-top, faux-European courtyard. Both restaurants have excellent wine lists. ✉ *345 N. Virginia St., 89501* ☎ *775/786–5700 or 800/648–5966* 🖷 *702/322–7124* ⊕ *www.eldoradoreno.com* ➴ *836 suites ⏶ 8 restaurants, room service, some in-room hot tubs, cable TV with movies, in-room data ports, Wi-Fi, pool, hot tub, casino, video game room, meeting rooms* ▤ *AE, D, DC, MC, V.*

¢–$$ 🏨 **Silver Legacy.** This two-tower megaresort centers on a 120-foot-tall mining machine that coins dollar tokens. Skywalks connect it to Circus Circus and the Eldorado. The Victorian-theme rooms have Americana furnishings and are comfortable and well kept. ✉ *407 N. Virginia St., 89501* ☎ *775/329–4777 or 800/687–8733* ⊕ *www.silverlegacy.com* ➴ *1,700 rooms ⏶ 5 restaurants, cable TV with movies and video games, pool, health club, 6 bars, casino, comedy club, video game room, shops, babysitting, concierge, Internet room, business services, meeting rooms, car rental, free parking, no-smoking rooms* ▤ *AE, D, DC, MC, V.*

Sports & the Outdoors

If you want to kayak the white-water course through downtown, call **Tahoe Whitewater Tours** (✉ 400 Island Ave. ☎ 775/787–5000 or 800/442–7237 ⊕ www.gowhitewater.com), which provides guided trips, instruction, and rentals for do-it-yourselfers. They also guide white-water rafting trips outside town.

Rent bicycles as well as kayaks from **Sierra Adventures** (✉ 254 West First St. ☎ 775/323–8928 or 866/323–8928 ⊕ www.wildsierra.com), which also guides rafting trips.

You can golf 18 holes just 4 mi outside town at **Lake Ridge Golf Course** (✉ 1218 Golf Club Dr. ☎ 800/815–6966 ⊕ www.lakeridgegolf.com), designed by Robert Trent Jones Sr. The signature 15th hole is set 140 feet above a lake; the green is on an island below. Greens fees range from $45 to $95.

LAKE TAHOE A TO Z

To research prices, get advice from other travelers, and book travel arrangements, visit www.fodors.com.

AIR TRAVEL

Reno–Tahoe International Airport, in Reno, 35 mi northeast of the closest point on the lake, is served by Alaska, Aloha, America West, American, Continental, Delta, Frontier, Northwest, Skywest, Southwest, and United airlines. *See* Air Travel *in* Smart Travel Tips for airline phone numbers.

🗾 **Reno-Tahoe International Airport** ⊠ U.S. 395, Exit 65B, Reno, NV ☎ 775/328-6400 ⊕ www.renoairport.com.

BUS TRAVEL

Greyhound stops in Sacramento, Truckee, and Reno, Nevada. Blue Go runs along U.S. 50 and through the neighborhoods of South Lake Tahoe daily from 6 AM to 12:15 AM; it also operates a 24-hour door-to-door van service to most addresses in South Lake Tahoe and Stateline for $3 per person (reservations essential). Tahoe Area Regional Transit (TART) operates buses along Lake Tahoe's northern and western shores between Tahoma and Incline Village daily from 6:30 to 6:30. They also operate five shuttles daily to Truckee. All buses cost $1.50. In summer TART buses have bike racks; in winter they have ski racks. Free shuttle buses run among the casinos, major ski resorts, and motels of South Lake Tahoe. Tahoe Casino Express runs 14 daily buses between Reno–Tahoe Airport and hotels in Stateline. Reserve online or by telephone.

🗾 **Greyhound** ☎ 800/231-2222 ⊕ www.greyhound.com. **Blue Go** ☎ 530/541-7149 ⊕ www.bluego.org. **Tahoe Area Regional Transit** (TART) ☎ 530/550-1212 or 800/736-6365 ⊕ www.laketahoetransit.com. **Tahoe Casino Express** ☎ 775/325-8944 or 866/898-2463 ⊕ www.southtahoeexpress.com.

CAR RENTAL

The major car-rental agencies—Hertz, Avis, Budget, National, Thrifty, Enterprise, and Dollar—all have counters at Reno–Tahoe International Airport. Enterprise has an outlet at the Lake Tahoe Airport (in South Lake Tahoe); Avis has one at Embassy Suites in South Lake Tahoe; Hertz has one at Harveys in Stateline; and Dollar has counters at the Reno Hilton, Reno's Circus Circus, and Caesars Tahoe. *See* Car Rental *in* Smart Travel Tips A to Z for national car-rental agency phone numbers.

CAR TRAVEL

Lake Tahoe is 198 mi northeast of San Francisco, a drive of less than four hours in good weather. Avoid the heavy traffic leaving the San Francisco area for Tahoe on Friday afternoon and returning on Sunday afternoon. The major route is I–80, which cuts through the Sierra Nevada about 14 mi north of the lake. From there Highway 89 and Highway 267 reach the west and north shores, respectively. U.S. 50 is the more direct route to the south shore, taking about two hours from Sacramento.

From Reno you can get to the north shore by heading south on U.S. 395 for 10 mi, then west on Highway 431 for 25 mi. For the south shore, head south on U.S. 395 through Carson City, and then turn west on U.S. 50 (50 mi total).

The scenic 72-mi highway around the lake is marked Highway 89 on the southwest and west shores, Highway 28 on the north and northeast shores, and U.S. 50 on the east and southeast. Sections of Highway 89 sometimes close during snowy periods in winter, usually at Emerald Bay because of avalanche danger, which makes it impossible to complete the circular drive. Interstate 80, U.S. 50, and U.S. 395 are all-weather highways, but there may be delays as snow is cleared during major storms. (Note that I–80 is a four-lane freeway; U.S. 50 is only two lanes with no center divider.) Carry tire chains from October through May, or rent a four-wheel-drive vehicle (most rental agencies do not allow tire chains to be used on their vehicles; ask when you book).

California Highway Patrol ☎ 530/577-1001 [South Lake Tahoe] ⊕ www.chp.ca.gov. **Cal-Trans Highway Information Line** ☎ 800/427-7623 ⊕ www.dot.ca.gov/hq/road-info. **Nevada Department of Transportation Road Information** ☎ 877/687-6237 ⊕ www.nevadadot.com/traveler/roads. **Nevada Highway Patrol** ☎ 775/687-5300 ⊕ http://dps.nv.gov.

EMERGENCIES
In an emergency dial 911.

Hospitals Barton Memorial Hospital ⊠ 2170 South Ave., South Lake Tahoe ☎ 530/541-3420. **St. Mary's Regional Medical Center** ⊠ 235 W. 6th St., Reno, NV ☎ 775/770-3188. **Tahoe Forest Hospital** ⊠ 10121 Pine Ave., Truckee ☎ 530/587-6011.

LODGING
The Lake Tahoe Visitors Authority provides information on south-shore lodging. The North Lake Tahoe Resort Association can give you information about accommodations on the north shore and in Truckee. Contact the Reno-Sparks Convention and Visitors Authority for lodging reservations in the Reno metropolitan area.

Lake Tahoe Visitors Authority ☎ 800/288-2463 ⊕ www.virtualtahoe.com. **North Lake Tahoe Resort Association** ☎ 800/824-6348 ⊕ www.tahoefun.org. **Reno-Sparks Convention and Visitors Authority** ☎ 775/827-7647 or 888/448-7366 ⊕ www.visitrenotahoe.com.

SPORTS & THE OUTDOORS
If you are planning to spend any time outdoors around Lake Tahoe, whether hiking, climbing, or camping, be aware that weather conditions can change quickly in the Sierra: to avoid a life-threatening case of hypothermia, always bring a pocket-size, fold-up rain poncho (available in all sporting-goods stores) to keep you dry. Wear long pants and a hat. Carry plenty of water. Because you'll likely be walking on granite, wear sturdy, closed-toe hiking boots, with soles that grip rock. If you're going into the backcountry, bring a signaling device (such as a mirror), emergency whistle, compass, map, energy bars, and water purifier. When heading out alone, tell someone where you're going and when you're coming back.

If you plan to ski, be aware of resort elevations. In the event of a winter storm, determine the snow level before you choose the resort you'll ski. Often the level can be as high as 7,000 feet, which means rain at some resorts' base areas but snow at others. For storm information, check the National Weather Service's Web page. To save money on lift tickets, look for packages offered by lodges and resorts. At some resorts it's cheaper to ski midweek; others offer family discounts. Free shuttle-bus service is available between most ski resorts and nearby lodgings. If you plan to do any backcountry skiing, check with the U.S. Forest Service for conditions. A shop called The Backcountry, with branches in Tahoe City and Truckee, operates an excellent Web site with current information about how and where to (and where not to) ski, mountain bike, and hike in the backcountry around Tahoe.

If you plan to camp in the backcountry, you'll likely need a wilderness permit, which you can pick up at the Lake Tahoe Visitor Center or at a ranger station at the entrance to any of the national forests. For reservations at campgrounds in California state parks, contact Reserve America.

The Backcountry ☎ 530/581-5861 (Tahoe City) 530/582-0909 (Truckee) ⊕ www. thebackcountry.net. **Lake Tahoe Visitor Center** ⊠ Hwy. 89 ☎ 530/543-2600 ⊕ www. fs.fed.us/r5/ltbmu. **National Weather Service** ⊕ www.wrh.noaa.gov/rev. **Reserve America** ☎ 800/444-7275 ⊕ www.reserveamerica.com. **U.S. Forest Service** ☎ 530/ 587-2158 backcountry recording.

TOURS

Several boats tour Lake Tahoe. The 500-passenger *Tahoe Queen,* a glass-bottom paddle wheeler, makes 2¼-hour sightseeing cruises year-round by reservation and three-hour dinner-dance cruises April–October from South Lake Tahoe. Fares range from $29 to $57. In winter the boat becomes the only waterborne ski shuttle in the world: $99 covers hotel transfers, a bus transfer from South Lake Tahoe or Stateline to Squaw Valley, lift ticket, and boat transportation back across the lake to South Lake. There's a full bar on board, live music, and an optional dinner for $15–$20. The *Sierra Cloud,* a large 50-passenger catamaran owned by the Hyatt Hotel, cruises the north shore area morning and afternoon, May through September. The fare is $50. The 550-passenger MS *Dixie II,* a stern-wheeler, sails year-round from Zephyr Cove to Emerald Bay on sightseeing, lunch, and dinner cruises. Fares range from $29 to $57.

Also in Zephyr Cove, the *Woodwind II,* a 50-passenger catamaran, sails on regular and champagne cruises April–October. Fares range from $28 to $36. For the same price, the *Woodwind I,* a 30-passenger trimaran, sails from Camp Richardson April–October. Woodwind Cruises also operates half-day round-the-lake cruises aboard the *Safari Rose,* a 76-foot-long wooden motor yacht; $95 includes lunch.

Lake Tahoe Balloons conducts excursions spring–fall over the lake or over the Carson Valley for $225 for hour-long flights (plan four hours total). Soar Minden offers glider rides and instruction over the lake and the Great Basin. Flights cost $95 to $210 and depart from Minden-Tahoe Airport, a municipal facility in Minden, Nevada.

Lake Tahoe Balloons ☎ 530/544-1221 or 800/872-9294 ⊕ www.laketahoeballoons. com. **MS** *Dixie II* ✉ Zephyr Cove Marina, Zephyr Cove ☎ 775/588-3508 ⊕ www. laketahoecruises.com. *Sierra Cloud* ✉ Hyatt Regency Lake Tahoe, Incline Village ☎ 775/831-1111. **Soar Minden** ☎ 775/782-7627 or 800/345-7627 ⊕ www.soarminden. com. *Tahoe Queen* ✉ Ski Run Marina, off U.S. 50, South Lake Tahoe ☎ 530/541-3364 or 800/238-2463 ⊕ www.laketahoecruises.com. **Woodwind Cruises** ✉ Zephyr Cove Resort, U.S. 50, Zephyr Cove ☎ 775/588-3000 ⊕ www.tahoeboatcrusies.com.

TRAIN TRAVEL

Amtrak's cross-country rail service makes stops in Truckee and Reno. The *California Zephyr* stops in both towns once daily eastbound (Salt Lake, Denver, and Chicago) and once daily westbound (Sacramento and Oakland), blocking traffic for 5 to 10 minutes. Amtrak also operates several buses daily between Reno and Sacramento to connect with the *Coast Starlight*, which runs south to Southern California and north to Oregon and Washington.

Amtrak ☎ 775/329-8638 or 800/872-7245 ⊕ www.amtrakcalifornia.com or www. amtrak.com.

VISITOR INFORMATION

Carson City Chamber of Commerce ✉ 1900 S. Carson St., Carson City, NV 87901 ☎ 775/882-1565 🖷 775/882-4179 ⊕ www.carsoncitychamber.com. **Lake Tahoe Visitors Authority** ✉ 1156 Ski Run Blvd., South Lake Tahoe 96150 ☎ 530/544-5050 or 800/288-2463 🖷 530/544-2386 ⊕ www.bluelaketahoe.com. **North Lake Tahoe Resort Association** ✐ Box 1757, Tahoe City 96145 ☎ 530/583-3494 or 888/434-1262 🖷 530/581-6904 ⊕ www.tahoefun.org. **Reno-Sparks Convention and Visitors Authority** ✉ 4001 S. Virginia St., Reno, NV 89502 ☎ 775/827-7600 or 800/367-7366 ⊕ www. VisitRenoTahoe.com. **U.S. Forest Service** ☎ 530/587-2158 backcountry recording ⊕ www.fs.fed.us/r5.

9

The Far North

With Lake Shasta, Mt. Shasta & Lassen Volcanic National Park

WORD OF MOUTH

"Lassen Volcanic National park is gorgeous and one of my favorite places. It is quite pretty just for scenic drives, but don't miss Bumpass Hell."

—myst

Updated by
Christine
Vovakes

THE WONDROUS LANDSCAPE of California's northeastern corner, relatively unmarred by development, congestion, and traffic, is the product of volcanic activity. At the southern end of the Cascade Range, Lassen Volcanic National Park is the best place to witness the far north's fascinating geology. Beyond the sulfur vents and bubbling mud pots, the park owes much of its beauty to 10,457-foot Mt. Lassen and 50 wilderness lakes. The most enduring image of the region, though, is Mt. Shasta, whose 14,162-foot snowcapped peak beckons outdoor adventurers of all kinds. There are many versions of Shasta to enjoy—the mountain, the lake, the river, the town, the dam, and the forest—all named after the Native Americans known as the Shatasla, or Sastise, who once inhabited the region.

Its soaring mountain peaks, wild rivers teeming with trout, and almost unlimited recreational possibilities make the far north the perfect destination for sports lovers. You won't find many hot nightspots or cultural enclaves, but you will find some of the best hiking and fishing in the state. The region offers a glimpse of old California—natural, rugged, and inspiring.

Exploring the Far North

The far north encompasses all of four vast counties—Tehama, Shasta, Siskiyou, and Trinity—as well as parts of Butte, Modoc, and Plumas counties. The area stretches from the valleys east of the Coast Range to the Nevada border and from the almond and olive orchards north of Sacramento to the Oregon border. A car is essential for touring the area unless you arrive by public transportation and plan to stay put in one town or resort.

About the Restaurants
Redding, the urban center of the far north, has the greatest selection of restaurants. In the smaller towns, cafés and simple eateries are the rule, though trendy, innovative restaurants have been popping up. Dress is always informal.

About the Hotels
Aside from the large chain hotels and motels in the Redding area, most accommodations in the far north blend rusticity, simplicity, and coziness. That's just fine with most of the folks who visit, as they spend much of their time outdoors. Wilderness resorts close in fall and reopen after the snow season ends in May.

The far north—especially the mountainous backcountry—is gaining popularity as a tourist destination. For summer holiday weekends make lodging reservations well in advance. The Web site of the **California Association of Bed & Breakfast Inns** (⊕ www.cabbi.com) lists numerous bed-and-breakfasts in the far north region.

10

	WHAT IT COSTS				
	$$$$	$$$	$$	$	¢
RESTAURANTS	over $30	$23–$30	$16–$22	$10–$15	under $10
HOTELS	over $250	$176–$250	$121–$175	$90–$120	under $90

Restaurant prices are for a main course at dinner, excluding sales tax of 7¾% (depending on location). Hotel prices are for two people in a standard double room in high season, excluding service charges and 7¼% tax.

Timing

This region attracts more tourists in summer than at any other time of year. Residents of the Sacramento Valley, which is usually dry and scorching during the dog days of summer, tend to flee to the milder climes of the mountains to the north and east. The valley around Redding is mild in winter, whereas snow falls at higher elevations. In winter Mt. Shasta is a great place for downhill and cross-country skiing—and even ice fishing at the area's many high-elevation lakes. Snow closes the roads to some of the region's most awesome sights, including much of Lassen Volcanic National Park, from October until late May. During the off-season many restaurants and museums here have limited hours, sometimes closing for extended periods.

FROM CHICO TO MT. SHASTA
ALONG I–5

The far north is bisected, south to north, by Interstate 5 (I–5), which winds through historic towns, museums, and state parks. Halfway to the Oregon border is Lake Shasta, a favorite recreation destination, and farther north stands the spectacular snowy peak of Mt. Shasta.

Chico

❶ *180 mi from San Francisco, east on I–80, north on I–505 to I–5, and east on Hwy. 32; 86 mi north of Sacramento on Hwy. 99.*

Chico (which is Spanish for "small") sits just west of Paradise in the Sacramento Valley and offers a welcome break from the monotony of I–5. The Chico campus of California State University, the scores of local artisans, and the area's agriculture (primarily almond orchards) all influence the culture here. Chico's true claim to fame, however, is the popular Sierra Nevada Brewery, which keeps locals and beer drinkers across the country happy with its distinctive microbrews.

★ The sprawling 3,670-acre **Bidwell Park** (✉ River Rd. south of Sacramento St. ☎ 530/895–4972) is a community green space straddling Big Chico Creek, where scenes from *Gone With the Wind* and the 1938 version of *Robin Hood* (starring Errol Flynn) were filmed. It provides the region with a recreational hub, and includes a golf course, swimming areas, and paved biking, hiking, and in-line skating trails. The third-largest city-run park in the country, Bidwell starts as a slender strip downtown and expands eastward toward the Sierra foothills.

GREAT ITINERARIES

Numbers in the text correspond to numbers in the margin and on the Far North map.

IF YOU HAVE 3 DAYS From I–5 north of Redding, head northeast on Highways 299 and 89 to ► **McArthur–Burney Falls Memorial State Park** ❽. To appreciate the falls, take a short stroll to the overlook or hike down for a closer view. Continue north on Highway 89. Long before you arrive in the town of ▨ **Mt. Shasta** ❼, you will spy the conical peak for which it is named. The central Mt. Shasta exit east leads out of town along Everitt Memorial Highway. Take this scenic drive, which climbs to almost 8,000 feet. The views of the mountain and the valley below are extraordinary. Stay overnight in town. On the second day head south on I–5 toward **Lake Shasta** ❺, visible on both sides of the highway. Have a look at Lake Shasta Caverns and the Shasta Dam before heading west on Highway 299 to spend the night in ▨ **Weaverville** ❹ or south on I–5 to overnight in ▨ **Redding** ❸, where you can stroll across the translucent span of the Sundial Bridge at Turtle Bay Exploration Park. The next day visit Shasta State Historic Park and Weaverville Joss House, on Highway 299.

IF YOU HAVE 5 OR 6 DAYS Get a glimpse of the far north's heritage in ► **Red Bluff** ❷ before heading north on I–5 to the town of ▨ **Mt. Shasta** ❼. On Day 2, drop by the Forest Service ranger station to check on trail conditions on the mountain and to pick up maps. Pack a picnic lunch before taking Everitt Memorial Highway up the mountain. After exploring it, head south on I–5 and spend the night in ▨ **Dunsmuir** ❻ at the Railroad Park Resort, where all the accommodations are old cabooses. On your third day take an early morning hike in nearby Castle Crags State Park. Continue south on I–5 to **Lake Shasta** ❺ and tour Shasta Dam Visitor's Center. Spend the night camping in the area or in ▨ **Redding** ❸. On your fourth morning head west on Highway 299, stopping at Shasta State Historic Park on your way to ▨ **Weaverville** ❹. Spend the night there or back in Redding. If you will be leaving the area on your fifth day but have a little time, zip north and visit Lake Shasta Caverns. If you're spending the night in Redding and it's between late May and early October, spend the next day and a half exploring **Lassen Volcanic National Park** ⑪. Highway 44 heads east from Redding into the park.

10

★ The renowned **Sierra Nevada Brewing Company,** one of the pioneers of the microbrewery movement, still has a hands-on approach to beer making. You can tour the brew house and see how the beer is produced— from the sorting of hops through fermentation and bottling. You can also visit the gift shop and enjoy a hearty lunch or dinner in the brewpub (it's closed Monday). ✉ *1075 E. 20th St.* ☎ *530/345–2739* 🖷 *530/ 893–9358* ⊕ *www.sierranevada.com* 🎫 *Free* ☉ *Tours Sun.–Fri. 2:30, Sat. noon–3 on the ½ hr.*

★ In **Bidwell Mansion State Historic Park** you can take a one-hour tour of approximately 20 of the mansion's rooms. Built between 1865 and 1868 by General John Bidwell, the founder of Chico, the 26-room home was designed by Henry W. Cleaveland, a San Francisco architect. Bidwell and his wife welcomed many distinguished guests to the distinctive pink Italianate mansion, including President Rutherford B. Hayes, naturalist John Muir, suffragist Susan B. Anthony, and General William T. Sherman. ⊠ *525 The Esplanade* ☎ *530/895–6144* 🖅 *$2* ☉ *Wed.–Fri. noon–5, weekends 10–5, last tour at 4.*

Where to Stay & Eat

$–$$ ✕ **Red Tavern.** With its warm butter-yellow walls and mellow lighting, this is one of Chico's most refined restaurants. The menu, inspired by fresh local produce, changes seasonally. If you're lucky, it might include braised duck with a tangerine glaze, asparagus, and a garlic soufflé pudding. There's a great California wine list, and also a full bar. ⊠ *1250 The Esplanade* ☎ *530/894–3463* ☲ *AE, MC, V* ☉ *Closed Sun. No lunch.*

¢–$$ ✕ **Kramore Inn.** Crepes—from ham and avocado to crab cannelloni—are this inn's specialty, along with Hungarian mushroom soup. The menu also includes salads, stir-fries, Asian dishes, and pastas. Brunch is available on Sunday from 9 to 2. ⊠ *1903 Park Ave.* ☎ *530/343–3701* ☲ *AE, D, MC, V.*

¢ ✕ **Madison Bear Garden.** This downtown favorite two blocks south of the Chico State campus is a great spot for checking out the vibrant college scene while enjoying a delicious burger and a vast selection of brews. ⊠ *316 W. 2nd St.* ☎ *530/891–1639* ☲ *MC, V.*

¢–$$ ☐ **Johnson's Country Inn.** Nestled in an almond orchard five minutes from downtown, this Victorian-style farmhouse with a wraparound veranda is a welcome change from motel row. It is full of antique furnishings and modern conveniences. ⊠ *3935 Morehead Ave., 95928* ☎ *530/345–7829 or 866/872–7780* ⊕ *www.chico.com/johnsonsinn* ⇥ *4 rooms* ♨ *Internet room, business services; no room TVs, no smoking* ☲ *MC, V* ❖❘ *BP.*

Shopping

Made in Chico (⊠ 232 Main St. ☎ 530/894–7009) sells locally made goods, including pottery, olives, almonds, and Woof and Poof creations—whimsical home decor items, such as stuffed Santas, elves, animals, and pillows. Beautiful custom-made etched, stained, and beveled glass is created at **Needham Studios** (⊠ 237 Broadway ☎ 530/345–4718). Shop and watch demonstrations of glass blowing at the **Satava Art Glass Studio** (⊠ 819 Wall St. ☎ 530/345–7985).

Red Bluff

▶ ❷ *41 mi north of Chico on Hwy 99.*

Historic Red Bluff is a gateway to Mount Lassen National Park. Established in the mid-19th century as a shipping center and named for the color of its soil, the town is filled with dozens of restored Victorians. It's a great home base for outdoor adventures in the area.

The **Kelly-Griggs House Museum,** a beautifully restored 1880s home, holds an impressive collection of antique furniture, housewares, and cloth-

PLEASURES & PASTIMES

CAMPING. In the vast expanses of the far north, pristine campgrounds make overnighting in the great outdoors a singular pleasure. There are hundreds of campgrounds here: some small and remote with few facilities; others with nearly all the conveniences of home; and still others somewhere in between.

FISHING. Cascading rivers, lakes of many shapes and sizes, and bountiful streams draw anglers to the far north. The Trinity River below the Lewiston Dam and the upper Sacramento River near Dunsmuir are excellent fly-fishing spots. Anglers say the large trout of Eagle Lake

are especially feisty quarry. Lake Shasta holds 21 types of fish, including rainbow trout and salmon.

HIKING. With so much wilderness, it's no wonder the far north has some of California's finest—and least crowded—hiking areas. In the shadow of Mt. Shasta, Castle Crags State Park has 28 mi of hiking trails, including rewarding routes at lower altitudes. Plumas National Forest, a protected area of 1.2 million acres, is laced with trails. Hikers in Lassen Volcanic National Park can explore wondrous landscapes formed by centuries of volcanic activity.

ing arranged as though a refined Victorian-era family were still in residence. A Venetian glass punch bowl sits on the dining room table; in the upstairs parlor costumed mannequins seem eerily frozen in time. *Persephone,* the painting over the fireplace, is by Sarah Brown, daughter of abolitionist John Brown, whose family settled in Red Bluff. ✉ *311 Washington St.* ☎ *530/527–1129* ✍ *Donation suggested* ⊙ *Thurs.–Sun. 1–3.*

William B. Ide Adobe State Historic Park is named for the first and only president of the short-lived California Republic of 1846. The Bear Flag Party proclaimed California a sovereign nation, separate from Mexican rule, and the republic existed for 25 days before it was taken over by the United States. The republic's flag has survived, with only minor refinements, as California's state flag. The park's main attraction is an adobe home built in the 1850s and outfitted with period furnishings. There's also a carriage shed, a blacksmith shop, and a small visitor center. Home tours are available on request. ✉ *21659 Adobe Rd.* ☎ *530/ 529–8599* ⊕ *www.ideadobe.tehama.k12.ca.us* ✍ *$4 per vehicle* ⊙ *Park and picnic facilities daily 8 AM–sunset.*

Where to Stay & Eat

$–$$ ✗ **Crystal Steak & Seafood Co.** Market-fresh seafood, garlicky scampi, and prime rib are the house specialties. Ask to be seated in the Dakota Room, an intimate booth-lined area with a hardwood floor, soft lighting, and prints of classic Old West paintings hung on the walls. ✉ *343 S. Main St.* ☎ *530/527–0880* ▭ *D, MC, V* ⊙ *No lunch weekends.*

¢ ✗ **Countryside Deli.** Heaping platters of country-fried steak and meat loaf with mashed potatoes and gravy are the draw at this deli. Its old-fash-

10

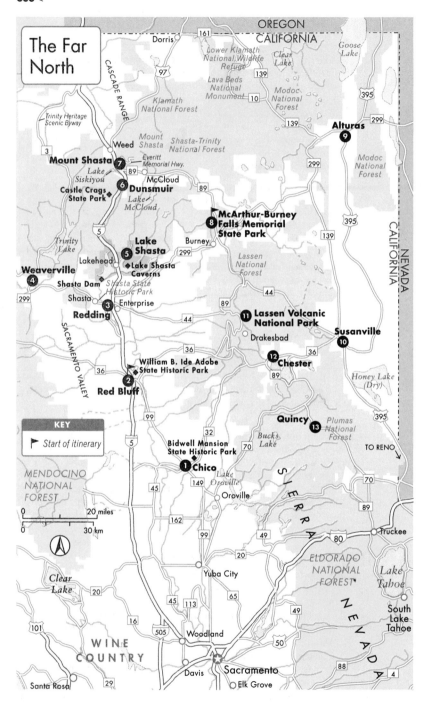

The Far North

ioned soda fountain, lined with red-topped swivel seats, is the perfect place to enjoy a hot fudge sundae or banana split. ⊠ *1007 Main St.* ☎ *530/ 529–3869* ⊟ *D, MC, V* ⊙ *Closed weekends.*

¢–$$ ⊡ **The Jeter Victorian Inn.** On sunny days, breakfast is served in the garden pavilion outside this 1881 Victorian home. The four guest rooms are elegantly decorated with antiques and period furnishings; two have private baths, and the Imperial Room has a Jacuzzi. A separate cottage is also available. ⊠ *1107 Jefferson St., 96080* ☎ *530/527–7574* ⊕ *www. jetervictorianinn.com* ⇌ *4 rooms, 2 with bath; 1 cottage* ⚫ *No room phones, no TV in some rooms, no smoking* ⊟ *MC, V* ⊙ *BP.*

¢ ⊡ **Lamplighter Lodge.** Although its name may evoke log cabins, this property is actually a motel on the town's main street. Simple rooms are equipped with mini-refrigerators and microwaves. The pool area is a great place to relax on sweltering summer days, and the Red Rock Cafe next door is open for meals and snacks. ⊠ *210 S. Main St., 96080* ☎ *530/527–1150* ⇌ *50 rooms, 2 suites* ⚫ *Microwaves, refrigerators, pool* ⊟ *AE, D, MC, V* ⊙ *CP.*

Redding

❸ *32 mi north of Red Bluff on I–5.*

As the largest city in the far north, Redding is an ideal headquarters for exploring the surrounding countryside. Curving along the Sacramento River, **Turtle Bay Exploration Park** has a museum, an arboretum with walking trails, and lots of interactive exhibits for children, including a miniature dam, a gold-panning area, and a seasonal Butterfly House where monarchs emerge from their cocoons. The main draw at the park, however, is the stunning **Sundial Bridge,** a modernist pedestrian footbridge designed by world-renowned Spanish architect Santiago Calatrava. The bridge's architecture consists of a translucent, illuminated span that stretches across the river, and—most strikingly—a soaring white 217-foot needle that casts a slender moving shadow, like a sundial's, over the water and surrounding trees. Watching the sun set over the river from this bridge is a magical experience. The bridge links to the Sacramento River Trail and the park's arboretum and botanical gardens. Children 4–16 pay about half the adult admission to the park, and there's no charge for kids under 3. Access to the bridge and arboretum is free; the fee admits you to both the museum and the botanical gardens. ⊠ *800 Auditorium Dr.* ☎ *530/243–8850* ⊕ *www.turtlebay.org* ⊠ *$11* ⊙ *Closed Mon. Sept.–May.*

FodorśChoice
★

10

Where to Stay & Eat

$–$$$ ✕ **Hatch Cover.** Dark-wood paneling and views of the adjacent Sacramento River create the illusion of dining aboard a ship, especially on the outside deck, with its views of Mt. Shasta. The menu emphasizes seafood, but you can also get steaks, chicken, pasta, and combination plates. The appetizer menu is extensive. ⊠ *202 Hemsted Dr., from Cypress Ave. exit off I–5, turn left, then right on Hemsted Dr.* ☎ *530/223– 5606* ⊟ *AE, D, MC, V* ⊙ *No lunch weekends.*

$–$$$ ✕ **Jack's Grill.** Famous for its 16-ounce steaks, this popular bar and steak house also serves shrimp and chicken. A town favorite, the place is usually jam-packed and noisy. ⊠ *1743 California St.* ☎ *530/241–9705* ▤ *AE, D, MC, V* ⊗ *Closed Sun. No lunch.*

¢–$ ✕ **Klassique Kafe.** Two sisters run this small bustling restaurant that caters to locals looking for simple but hearty breakfast and lunch fare. The hot luncheon specials served daily might include butter beans and ham with corn bread, or chicken and dumplings. ⊠ *2427 Athens Ave.* ☎ *530/244–4939* ▤ *AE, D, MC, V* ⊗ *Closed Sat. No dinner.*

★ ¢–$$ ✕▥ **The Red Lion.** Adjacent to I–5, and close to Redding's convention center and regional recreation sites, this hotel is a top choice for both business and vacation travelers. Rooms are spacious and comfortable; a large patio surrounded by landscaped grounds is a relaxing spot to enjoy an outdoor meal or snack. There are irons, ironing boards, and hair dryers in the rooms, and video games in the public areas. The hotel's restaurant, Waters Seafood Grill, is a popular place for locals. ⊠ *1830 Hilltop Dr., Hwy. 44/299 exit from I–5, 96002* ☎ *530/221–8700 or 800/733–5466* ☒ *530/221–0324* ⊕ *www.redlion.com* ⇨ *192 rooms, 2 suites* ⌂ *Restaurant, coffee shop, room service, pool, wading pool, gym, hot tub, bar, airport shuttle* ▤ *AE, D, DC, MC, V.*

$$$–$$$$ ▥ **Brigadoon Castle Bed & Breakfast.** Fifteen winding miles from I–5 is this Elizabethan-style castle, nestled atop an 86-acre estate. Guest rooms have marble baths, antique furnishings, and luxurious upholstery; in the common room are a fireplace, a satellite TV, and a wall of videos to choose from. A separate 1,250-square-foot cottage is also available. Evening snacks are included in the rates. ⊠ *9036 Zogg Mine Rd., Igo 96047* ☎ *530/396–2785 or 888/343–2836* ☒ *530/396–2784* ⊕ *www. brigadooncastle.com* ⇨ *4 rooms* ⌂ *Hot tub; no room phones, no room TVs* ▤ *AE, MC, V* ▯◎▯ *BP.*

Sports & the Outdoors

The **Fly Shop** (⊠ 4140 Churn Creek Rd. ☎ 530/222–3555) sells fishing licenses and has information about guides, conditions, and fishing packages.

▐ **EN ROUTE**   Six miles west of Redding on Highway 299, **Shasta State Historic Park** (☎ 530/243–8194 ☜ $2) stands where Shasta City thrived in the mid- to late 1800s. Its 19 acres of half-ruined brick buildings and overgrown graveyards, accessed via trails, are a reminder of the glory days of the California gold rush. The former county courthouse building, jail, and gallows have been restored to their 1860s appearance. The Courthouse Museum (Wed.–Sun. 10–5) houses a visitor center, information desk, art gallery, and interactive exhibits, including a storytelling hologram "ghost" locked in the jail. The Litsch General Store, in operation from 1850 to 1950, is now a museum, with displays of many items that were sold here.

Weaverville

❹ *46 mi west of Redding on Hwy. 299 (called Main St. in town).*

Weaverville is an enjoyable amalgam of gold-rush history and tourist kitsch. Named after John Weaver, one of three men who built the first cabin here in 1850, the town has an impressive downtown historic district. Weaverville is a popular headquarters for family vacations and biking, hiking, fishing, and gold-panning excursions.

★ Weaverville's main attraction is the **Weaverville Joss House**, a Taoist temple built in 1874 and called Won Lim Miao ("the temple of the forest beneath the clouds") by Chinese miners. The oldest continuously used Chinese temple in California, it attracts worshippers from around the world. With its golden altar, antique weaponry, and carved wooden canopies, the Joss House is a piece of California history that can best be appreciated on a guided 30-minute tour. The original temple building and many of its furnishings—some of which came from China—were lost to fire in 1873, but members of the local Chinese community soon rebuilt it. ⊠ *Oregon and Main Sts.* ☎ *530/623–5284* ✉ *Museum free; guided tour $2* ⊙ *Wed.–Sun. 10–5.*

Trinity County Courthouse (⊠ Court and Main Sts.), built in 1856 as a store, office building, and hotel, was converted to county use in 1865. The Apollo Saloon, in the basement, became the county jail. It is the oldest courthouse still in use in California.

Trinity County Historical Park houses the Jake Jackson Memorial Museum, which has a blacksmith shop, a stamp mill (where ore is crushed) from the 1890s that is still in use, and the original jail cells of the Trinity County Courthouse. ⊠ *508 Main St.* ☎ *530/623–5211* ⊙ *May–Oct., daily 10–5; Nov.–Apr., Tues. and Sat. noon–4.*

OFF THE
BEATEN
PATH

TRINITY HERITAGE SCENIC BYWAY – This road, shown on many maps as Highway 3, runs north from Weaverville for 120 mi up to its intersection with I-5, south of Yreka. The Trinity Alps and Lewiston Lake, formed by the Trinity Dam, are visible all along this beautiful, forest-lined road, which is often closed in winter. As it climbs from 2,000 feet to 6,500 feet, most of the route follows a path established by early miners and settlers.

Where to Stay & Eat

10

$–$$$ ✕ **La Grange Café.** In two brick buildings dating from the 1850s (they're among the oldest edifices in town), this eatery serves buffalo and other game meats, pasta, fresh fish, and farmers' market vegetables when they're available. There's a full premium bar, and the wine list has 135 vintages. ⊠ *226 Main St.* ☎ *530/623–5325* ▤ *AE, D, MC, V* ⊙ *Closed Sun. Nov.–Mar.*

¢ ✕ **La Casita.** A traditional selection of Mexican food is on the menu here, including quesadillas (try the version with roasted chili peppers), tostadas, enchiladas, tacos, and tamales. Many dishes are available without meat. Open from late morning through early evening, this casual spot is great for a midafternoon snack. ⊠ *254 Main St.* ☎ *530/623–5797* ▤ *MC, V.*

¢ ▦ **Red Hill Motel.** This 1940s-era property is popular with anglers, who appreciate the outdoor fish-cleaning area on the premises. The separate wooden lodgings, painted red and surrounded by pine trees, encircle a grassy knoll. One cozy cabin with full kitchen is good for families; two others have kitchenettes, and the rest have mini-refrigerators and microwaves. ⊠ *Red Hill Rd., 96093* ☎ *530/623–4331* ⊕ *www. redhillresorts.com* ⇨ *4 rooms, 6 cabins, 2 duplexes* ⟁ *Some kitchens, some microwaves, some refrigerators, cable TV* ⊟ *AE, D, MC, V.*

Sports & the Outdoors

Below the Lewiston Dam, east of Weaverville on Highway 299, is the **Fly Stretch** of the Trinity River, an excellent fly-fishing area. The **Pine Cove Boat Ramp,** on Lewiston Lake, provides fishing access for those with disabilities—decks here are built over prime trout-fishing waters. Contact the **Weaverville Ranger Station** (⊠ 210 Main St. ☎ 530/623–2121) for maps and information about hiking trails in the Trinity Alps Wilderness.

Shopping

Highland Art Center Gallery (⊠ 503 Main St. ☎ 530/623–5111) showcases painting, photography, fiber arts, ceramics, sculpture, and other handcrafted works produced by local artists and those from surrounding mountain communities.

Lake Shasta Area

12 mi north of Redding on I–5.

★ ❺ Twenty-one types of fish inhabit **Lake Shasta,** including rainbow trout and salmon. The lake region also has the largest nesting population of bald eagles in California. You can rent fishing boats, ski boats, sailboats, canoes, paddleboats, Jet Skis, and windsurfing boards at one of the many marinas and resorts along the 370-mi shoreline.

Stalagmites, stalactites, flowstone deposits, and crystals entice people of all ages to the **Lake Shasta Caverns.** To see this impressive spectacle, you must take the two-hour tour, which includes a catamaran ride across the McCloud arm of Lake Shasta and a bus ride up Grey Rock Mountain to the cavern entrance. The caverns are 58°F year-round, making them a cool retreat on a hot summer day. The most awe-inspiring of the limestone rock formations is the glistening Cathedral Room, which appears to be gilded. During peak summer months (June–August), tours depart every half hour; in April, May, and September it's every hour. A gift shop is open from 8 to 4:30. ⊠ *Shasta Caverns Rd. exit off I–5* ☎ *530/238–2341 or 800/795–2283* ⊕ *www.lakeshastacaverns. com* ⊠ *$20* ☉ *June–Aug., daily 9–4 with departures every ½ hr; Apr., May, and Sept., daily 9–3 with departures every hr; Oct.–Mar., daily 10–2 with departures every 2 hrs.*

Shasta Dam is the second-largest concrete dam in the United States (only Grand Coulee in Washington is bigger). On clear days, snowcapped Mt. Shasta glimmers on the horizon above the still waters of its namesake lake. The visitor center has computerized photographic tours of the dam construction, video presentations, fact sheets, and historical displays. Tours of the dam have resumed, with some restrictions. Call for an update. ⊠ *16349 Shasta Dam Blvd.* ☎ *530/275–4463* ⊕ *www.usbr.gov/ mp/ncao* ☉ *Visitor center weekdays 8–4:30, weekends 8–5.*

Where to Stay & Eat

$–$$$ ✕ **Tail o' the Whale.** As its name suggests, this restaurant has a nautical theme. You can enjoy a panoramic view of Lake Shasta here while you indulge in spicy Cajun pepper shrimp, charbroiled salmon, seafood fettuccine in a garlic cream sauce, and prime rib with scampi. ✉ *10300 Bridge Bay Rd., Bridge Bay exit off I–5* ☎ *530/275–3021* 🍴 *D, MC, V.*

△ **Antlers Campground.** On a level bluff above the Sacramento River arm of Lake Shasta, this campground is surrounded by oak and pine forest. Open year-round, it is adjacent to Antlers Boat Ramp, and a nearby marina resort has watercraft rentals, on-water fueling, and a small store. Some campsites are near the lakeshore, but direct access to the water is difficult. Reservations are taken for mid-May through early September only. ♨ *Flush toilets, pit toilets, drinking water, fire pits, picnic tables* ♖ *59 sites* ✉ *Antlers Rd., 1 mi east of I–5* ☎ *530/275–8113* 📠 *530/ 275–8344* ⊕ *www.reserveusa.com* ✉ *$18–$30* 🍴 *AE, D, MC, V.*

Sports & the Outdoors

FISHING **The Fishin' Hole** (✉ 3844 Shasta Dam Blvd., Shasta Lake City ☎ 530/ 275–4123) is a bait-and-tackle shop a couple of miles from the lake. It sells fishing licenses and provides information about conditions.

HOUSEBOATING Houseboats here come in all sizes except small. As a rule, rentals are outfitted with cooking utensils, dishes, and most of the equipment you'll need—all you supply are the food and the linens. When you rent a houseboat, you receive a short course in how to maneuver your launch before you set out. You can fish, swim, sunbathe on the flat roof, or sit on the deck and watch the world go by. The shoreline of Lake Shasta is beautifully ragged, with countless inlets; it's not hard to find privacy. Expect to spend a minimum of $350 a day for a craft that sleeps six. A three-day, two-night minimum is customary. Prices are often lower during the off-season (September–May). The **Shasta Cascade Wonderland Association** (✉ 1699 Hwy. 273, Anderson 96007 ☎ 530/365–7500 or 800/474–2782 ⊕ www.shastacascade.com) provides names of rental companies and prices for Lake Shasta houseboating. **Bridge Bay Resort** (✉ 10300 Bridge Bay Rd., Redding ☎ 800/752–9669) rents houseboats, Jet Skis, fishing boats, and patio boats.

10

Dunsmuir

❻ *10 mi south of Mt. Shasta on I–5.*

Castle Crags State Park surrounds the town of Dunsmuir, which was named for a 19th-century Scottish coal baron who offered to build a fountain if the town was renamed in his honor. The town's other major attraction is the Railroad Park Resort, where you can spend the night in restored railcars.

★ Named for its 6,000-foot glacier-polished crags, which tower over the Sacramento River, **Castle Crags State Park** offers fishing in Castle Creek, hiking in the backcountry, and a view of Mt. Shasta. The crags draw climbers and hikers from around the world. The 4,350-acre park has 28 mi of hiking trails, including a 2¾-mi access trail to **Castle Crags Wilder-**

ness, part of the **Shasta-Trinity National Forest.** There are excellent trails at lower altitudes, along with picnic areas, restrooms, showers, and campsites. ⊠ *15 mi south of Mt. Shasta, Castella/Castle Crags exit off I–5; follow for ¼ mi* ☎ *530/235–2684* 🖃 *$6 per vehicle, day use.*

Where to Stay

🖑 **$** 🔲 **Railroad Park Resort.** The antique cabooses here were collected over more than three decades and have been converted into cozy motel rooms in honor of Dunsmuir's railroad legacy. The resort has a vaguely *Orient Express*–style dining room and a lounge fashioned from vintage railcars. The landscaped grounds contain a huge steam engine and a restored water tower. There's also an RV park and campground. ⊠ *100 Railroad Park Rd., 96025* ☎ *530/235–4440 or 800/974–7245* 🖷 *530/ 235–4470* 🌐 *www.rrpark.com* 🛏 *23 cabooses, 4 cabins* ♨ *Restaurant, some kitchenettes, refrigerators, cable TV with movies, pool, hot tub, some pets allowed (fee)* ▭ *MC, V.*

△ **Castle Crags State Park Campground.** Craggy peaks tower above this campground surrounded by tall evergreens. It's a great base for hiking and rock climbing. The site can accommodate RVs up to 27 feet long. Six environmental sites—with pit toilets, and no parking or running water—in relatively undisturbed areas are for tents only. Reservations are essential late May–early September. ♨ *Flush toilets, pit toilets, showers, picnic tables* 🛏 *76 sites* ⊠ *15 mi south of Mt. Shasta, Castella/ Castle Crags exit off I–5* ☎ *530/235–2684* 🌐 *www.parks.ca.gov* 🖃 *$15–$20* ▭ *AE, D, MC, V.*

Mt. Shasta

❼ *34 mi north of Lake Shasta on I–5.*

The crown jewel of the 2.5-million-acre Shasta-Trinity National Forest, Mt. Shasta, a 14,162-foot-high dormant volcano, is a mecca for day hikers. It's especially enticing in spring, when fragrant Shasta lilies and other flowers adorn the rocky slopes. The paved road reaches only as far as the timberline; the final 6,000 feet are a tough climb of rubble, ice, and snow (the summit is perpetually ice packed). Only a hardy few are qualified to make the trek to the top.

The town of Mt. Shasta has real character and some fine restaurants. Lovers of the outdoors and backcountry skiers abound, and they are more than willing to offer advice on the most beautiful spots in the region, which include out-of-the-way swimming holes, dozens of high mountain lakes, and a challenging 18-hole golf course with 360 degrees of spectacular views.

Where to Stay & Eat

$–$$$ ✕ **Michael's Restaurant.** Wood paneling, candlelight, and wildlife prints by local artists create an unpretentious backdrop for favorites such as prime rib and filet mignon, and Italian specialties such as stuffed calamari, scaloppine, and linguine with pesto. ⊠ *313 N. Mt. Shasta Blvd.* ☎ *530/926–5288* ▭ *AE, MC, V* ☉ *Closed Sun. and Mon.*

★ **$–$$$** ✕ **Trinity Café.** Once a small home, this cozy restaurant has a bistro feel and a frequently changing dinner menu inspired by seasonal ingredients.

The Pacific Flyway

YOU DON'T NEED WINGS to catch the Pacific Flyway. All it takes is a car, a good map, and high-powered binoculars to follow the flight path of more than 250 bird species that migrate through far northern California and stop at wildlife refuges on their way.

Eagles and hawks make their visits in winter; more than a million waterfowl pass through in fall. Returning migrants such as pelicans, cranes, and songbirds such as the marsh wren and ruby-crowned kinglet arrive in March, just in time to herald the spring; goslings, ducklings, and other newly hatched waterfowl paddle through the wetlands in summer.

February and March are especially good viewing times, when people are scarce but wildlife thrives in the cold climate. Many birds enter their breeding season during these months, and you can hear their unusual mating calls and witness aerial ballets as vividly plumed males pursue females.

One of the most impressive Pacific Flyway stopovers is on the California-Oregon border: the 46,900-acre Lower Klamath National Wildlife Refuge, established by President Theodore Roosevelt in 1908 as the country's first waterfowl refuge. The area has the largest winter concentration of bald eagles in the lower 48 states. For $3 you can take a 10-mi auto tour through parts of the refuge, where the eagles feed from December through mid-March. (From I-5 north of Mt. Shasta, take the Highway 97 turnoff to Highway 161 and follow the signs.) Even if you're not already an avid bird-watcher, you likely will be after a visit to this special place.

The nightly specials might include a garlicky, vegetarian portobello mushroom with linguine, locally caught salmon or trout, or cabernet-braised lamb with toasted couscous. Chef-owner Bill Truby trained in Napa Valley, and brings an extensive knowledge of wine pairings to the menu. ⊠ 622 N. Mt. Shasta Blvd. ☎ 530/926–6200 ▭ AE, D MC, V ☉ Closed Sun. and Mon. No lunch.

$–$$ ✕ **Lily's.** This restaurant in a white-clapboard home, framed by a picket fence and arched trellis, serves everything from steaks and pastas to Mexican and vegetarian dishes. One of the tastiest choices is the Jalisco–marinated rib-eye steak with greens, tomatoes, and Asiago cheese. The huevos rancheros (sunny-side-up eggs on tortillas in a mildly spicy sauce) or the scrambled eggs with salsa are delicious choices for brunch. ⊠ 1013 S. Mt. Shasta Blvd. ☎ 530/926–3372 ▭ AE, D, MC, V.

¢ ✕ **Has Beans.** The aroma of fresh-roasted coffee beans wafts from this small coffee shop, a favorite gathering spot for locals. Pastries, made daily, include muffins and scones, and blackberry fruit bars in season. ⊠ 1011 S. Mt. Shasta Blvd. ☎ 530/926–3602 ▭ MC, V.

★ $–$$$ ✕ᵯ **Mount Shasta Resort.** Private chalets are nestled among tall pine trees along the shore of Lake Siskiyou, all with gas-log fireplaces and full kitchens. The resort's Highland House Restaurant, above the clubhouse of a spectacular 18-hole golf course, has uninterrupted views of Mt. Shasta.

10

Large steaks and herb-crusted calamari are menu highlights. Take the Central Mount Shasta exit west from I–5, then go south on Old Stage Road. ⊠ *1000 Siskiyou Lake Blvd., 96067* ☎ *530/926–3030 or 800/958–3363* 🖷 *530/926–0333* ⊕ *www.mountshastaresort.com* 🛏 *65 units* ⚴ *Restaurant, some kitchenettes, some microwaves, some refrigerators, 18-hole golf course, spa, sports bar, meeting room* ⊟ *AE, D, DC, MC, V.*

$ 🏠 **Best Western Tree House Motor Inn.** The clean, standard rooms at this motel less than a mile from downtown Mt. Shasta are decorated with natural-wood furnishings. Some of the nicer ones have vaulted ceilings and mountain views. ⊠ *111 Morgan Way, at I–5 and Lake St., 96067* ☎ *530/926–3101 or 800/545–7164* 🖷 *530/926–3542* ⊕ *www.bestwestern.com* 🛏 *98 rooms, 5 suites* ⚴ *Restaurant, refrigerators, indoor pool, hot tub* ⊟ *AE, D, DC, MC, V* ⦿| *CP.*

⚠ **Lake Siskiyou Camp Resort.** On the west side of Lake Siskiyou, the sites on this 250-acre resort sit beneath tall pine trees that filter the light. Group sites, evening movies, and powerboat and kayak rentals make it a great spot for families; there's also a marina, a free boat-launch ramp, and a fishing dock. ⚴ *Flush toilets, full hookups, showers, general store, swimming (lake)* 🛏 *200 tent sites, 150 RV sites* ⊠ *4239 W. A. Barr Rd., 3 mi southwest of town of Mt. Shasta* ☎ *530/926–2618 or 888/926–2618* ⊕ *www.lakesis.com* 🖳 *$18–$25* ⚴ *Reservations essential* ⊟ *D, MC, V* ☉ *Apr.–Oct.*

Sports & the Outdoors

GOLF At 6,100 yards, the **Mount Shasta Resort** golf course isn't long, but it's beautiful and challenging, with narrow, tree-lined fairways and several lakes and other waterways. Greens fees range from $35 to $50, depending on the day of the week and the season; carts rent for another $12–$18, and clubs can be rented, too. ⊠ *1000 Siskiyou Lake Blvd.* ☎ *530/926–3052* ⊕ *www.mountshastaresort.com/golfing.htm.*

HIKING The **Forest Service Ranger Station** (☎ 530/926–4511 or 530/926–9613) keeps tabs on trail conditions and gives avalanche reports.

MOUNTAIN **Fifth Season Mountaineering Shop** (⊠ 300 N. Mt. Shasta Blvd. ☎ 530/
CLIMBING 926–3606 or 530/926–5555) rents skiing and climbing equipment and operates a recorded 24-hour climber-skier report. **Shasta Mountain Guides** (☎ 530/926–3117 ⊕ www.shastaguides.com) leads hiking, climbing, and ski-touring groups to the summit of Mt. Shasta.

SKIING On the southeast flank of Mt. Shasta, **Mt. Shasta Board & Ski Park** has
☾ three lifts on 425 skiable acres. It's a great place for novices because three-quarters of the trails are for beginning or intermediate skiers. The area's vertical drop is 1,390 feet, with a top elevation of 6,600 feet. The longest of the 31 trails is 1¾ mi. A package for beginners, available through the ski school, includes a lift ticket, ski rental, and a lesson. The school also runs ski and snowboard programs for children. There's night skiing for those who want to see the moon rise as they schuss. The base lodge has a simple café, a ski shop, and a ski-snowboard rental shop. The park's Cross-Country Ski and Snowshoe Center, with 18 mi of trails, is on the same road. ⊠ *Hwy. 89 exit east from I–5, south of Mt. Shasta* ☎ *530/926–8610 or 800/754–7427* ⊕ *www.skipark.com* ☉ *Sun.–Tues. 9–4; Wed.–Sat. 9–9.*

THE BACKCOUNTRY
INCLUDING LASSEN VOLCANIC NATIONAL PARK

East of I–5, the far north's main corridor, dozens of scenic two-lane roads crisscross the wilderness, leading to dramatic mountain peaks and fascinating natural wonders. Small towns settled in the second half of the 19th century seem frozen in time, except that they are well equipped with tourist amenities.

McArthur–Burney Falls Memorial State Park

★ ☾ ┏ ❽ *Hwy. 89, 52 mi southeast of Mt. Shasta and 41 mi north of Lassen Volcanic National Park.*

Just inside the park's southern boundary, Burney Creek wells up from the ground and divides into two falls that cascade over a 129-foot cliff into a pool below. Countless ribbonlike streams pour from hidden moss-covered crevices; resident bald eagles are frequently seen soaring overhead. You can walk a self-guided nature trail that descends to the foot of the falls, which Theodore Roosevelt—according to legend—called "the eighth wonder of the world." You can also swim at Lake Britton; lounge on the beach; rent motorboats, paddleboats, and canoes; or relax at one of the campsites or picnic areas. The camp store is open from early May to the end of October. ⊠ *24898 Hwy. 89, Burney 96013* ☎ *530/335–2777* ☑ *$6 per vehicle, day use.*

Where to Stay

⚠ **McArthur–Burney Falls Memorial State Park.** Campsites here in the evergreen forests abut Burney Falls, several springs, a half dozen hiking trails, and Lake Britton. Boating and fishing are popular pursuits. Some sites can accommodate 35-foot RVs. Reservations are essential from Memorial Day to Labor Day. ⚒ *Flush toilets, dump station, showers, picnic tables, general store, swimming (lake)* ➡ *98 RV sites, 24 tent sites* ⊠ *McArthur–Burney Falls Memorial State Park, Hwy. 89* ☎ *530/335–2777* ⊕ *www.parks.ca.gov* ☑ *$15–$20* ▤ *D, MC, V.*

10

Alturas

❾ *86 mi northeast of McArthur–Burney Falls Memorial State Park on Hwy. 299.*

Alturas is the county seat and largest town in northeastern California's Modoc County. The Dorris family arrived in the area in 1874, built Dorris Bridge over the Pit River, and later opened a small wayside stop for travelers. Today the Alturas area is a land of few people but much rugged natural beauty. Travelers come to see eagles and other wildlife, the Modoc National Forest, and active geothermal areas.

Modoc County Museum exhibits—which include Native American artifacts, firearms, and a steam engine—explore the development of the area from the 15th century through World War II. ⊠ *600 S. Main St.* ☎ *530/233–6328* ☑ *Donations accepted* ☉ *May–Oct., Tues.–Sat. 10–4.*

Modoc National Forest encompasses 1.6 million acres and protects 300 species of wildlife, including Rocky Mountain elk, wild horses, mule deer, and pronghorn antelope. In spring and fall, watch for migratory waterfowl as they make their way along the Pacific Flyway above the forest. Hiking trails lead to Petroglyph Point, one of the largest panels of rock art in the United States. ⊠ *800 W. 12th St.* ☎ *530/233–5811* 🖷 *530/ 233–8709.*

Established to protect migratory waterfowl, the 6,280-acre **Modoc National Wildlife Refuge** gives refuge to Canada geese, Sand Hill cranes, mallards, teal, wigeon, pintail, white pelicans, cormorants, and snowy egrets. The refuge is open for hiking, bird-watching, and photography, but one area is set aside for hunters. Regulations vary according to season. ⊠ *1½ mi south of Alturas on Hwy. 395* ☎ *530/233–3572* 🖾 *Free* ⊙ *Daily dawn–dusk.*

OFF THE BEATEN PATH

LAVA BEDS NATIONAL MONUMENT – Thousands of years of volcanic activity created this rugged landscape, which is distinguished by cinder cones, lava flows, spatter cones, pit craters, and more than 400 underground lava tube caves. During the Modoc War (1872–73), Modoc Indians under the leadership of their chief "Captain Jack" Kientopoos took refuge in a natural lava fortress now known as Captain Jack's Stronghold. They managed to hold off U.S. Army forces, which outnumbered them 20 to 1, for five months. When exploring this area, be sure to wear hard-soled boots; other safety gear such as lights and hard hats are available for rent and sale at the Indian Well Visitor Center, at the park's south end. This is where summer activities such as guided walks, cave tours, and campfire programs depart from. ⊠ *Forest Service Rte. 10, 72 mi northwest of Alturas (Hwy. 299 west from Alturas to Hwy. 139, northwest to Forest Service Rte. 97, to Forest Service Rte. 10)* ☎ *530/667–2282* ⊕ *www.nps.gov/labe* 🖾 *$10 per vehicle; $5 on foot, bicycle, or motorcycle* ⊙ *Visitor center late May–early Sept., daily 8–5; early Sept.–late May, daily 8:30–5.*

Where to Stay & Eat

$-$$ ✕ **Brass Rail.** This authentic Basque restaurant offers hearty dinners at fixed prices that include wine, homemade bread, soup, salad, side dishes, coffee, and ice cream. Steak, lamb chops, fried chicken, shrimp, and scallops are among the best entrée selections. A full bar and lounge adjoin the dining area. ⊠ *395 Lakeview Hwy.* ☎ *530/233–2906* 🖃 *MC, V* ⊙ *Closed Mon.*

¢ 🏨 **Best Western Trailside Inn.** The only motel in town with a swimming pool, this property is just 2 mi north of Rachael Dorris Park, 3 mi south of Devils Garden, and 5 mi north of Modoc Wildlife Reserve. It's also five blocks south of the Modoc County Museum. ⊠ *343 N. Main St., 96101* ☎ *530/233–4111* 🖷 *530/233–3180* 🛏 *38 rooms* ⌂ *Some kitchenettes, some microwaves, cable TV, pool, Internet room, some pets allowed* 🖃 *AE, D, DC, MC, V.*

¢ 🏨 **Hacienda.** In the heart of farm country, this motel is marked with a large 19th-century wagon wheel out front. The spacious, spotless rooms have bright bedspreads and ample natural light from large windows. A gas station, fast-food restaurants, and a supermarket are all within five blocks. ⊠ *201 E. 12th St., 96101* ☎ *530/233–3459* ⤴ *20 rooms* ⟁ *Microwaves, refrigerators, cable TV, some pets allowed, no-smoking rooms* ▤ *D, MC, V.*

⚠ **Medicine Lake Campground.** One of several small campgrounds on the shores of Medicine Lake, this spot lies at 6,700 feet above sea level, near the western border of Modoc National Forest. Sites can accommodate vehicles up to 22 feet. The lake, 14 mi south of Lava Beds National Monument, is a popular vacation spot with fishing, boating, and waterskiing. ⟁ *Pit toilets, drinking water, fire pits, picnic tables, swimming (lake)* ⤴ *22 sites* ⊠ *Off Forest Service Rd. 44N38, Hwy. 139 to County Rd. 97 west to Forest Service Rd. 44N38, follow signs* ☎ *530/667–2246* ✉ *$7* ⟁ *Reservations not accepted* ▤ *No credit cards* ☉ *July–Oct.*

Susanville

🔟 *104 mi south of Alturas via Rte. 395; 65 mi east of Lassen Volcanic National Park via Hwy. 36.*

Susanville tells the tale of its rich history through murals painted on buildings in the historic uptown area. Established as a trading post in 1854, it is the second-oldest town in the western Great Basin. You can take a self-guided tour around the original buildings and stop for a bite at one of the restaurants now housed within them; or, if you'd rather work up a sweat, you can hit the Bizz Johnson Trail and Eagle Lake recreation areas just outside of town.

Bizz Johnson Trail follows a defunct line of the Southern Pacific Railroad for 25 mi. Known to locals as the Bizz, the trail is open for hikers, walkers, mountain bikers, and horseback riders. It follows the Susan River through a scenic landscape of canyons, bridges, and forests abundant with wildlife. ⊠ *Trailhead: 601 Richmond Rd.* ☎ *530/257–0456* ⊕ *www.ca.blm.gov/eaglelake/bizztrail.html* ✉ *Free.*

Anglers travel great distances to fish the waters of **Eagle Lake**, California's second largest, which is surrounded by high desert to the north and alpine forests to the south. The Eagle Lake trout is prized for its size and fighting ability. The lake is also popular for picnicking, hiking, boating, waterskiing and windsurfing, and bird-watching—ospreys, pelicans, western grebes, and many other waterfowl visit the lake. On land you might see mule deer, small mammals, and even pronghorn antelope. ⊠ *20 mi north of Susanville on Eagle Lake Rd.* ☎ *530/257–0456 for Eagle Lake Recreation Area, 530/825–3454 for Eagle Lake Marina* ⊕ *www.reserveusa.com.*

Where to Stay & Eat

¢–$$ ✕ **Josefina's.** Popular with the locals, Josefina's makes its own salsas and tamales. The interior's Aztec accents are a perfect accompaniment to the menu's traditional Mexican fare of *chiles rellenos* (mild, batter-fried chili peppers stuffed with cheese or a cheese-meat mixture), enchiladas, tacos, and fajitas. ⊠ *1960 Main St.* ☎ *530/257–9262* ▤ *MC, V.*

10

★ ¢ ✕ **Grand Cafe.** Walking into this downtown coffee shop, which has been owned and operated by the same family since the 1920s, is like stepping back in time. At the old-fashioned counter, the swiveling seats have hat clips on the back; the booths have their own nickel jukeboxes. Wooden refrigerators are still used here, and if the homemade chili and fruit cobblers are any indication, they work just fine. ⊠ *730 Main St.* ☎ *530/ 257–4713* ⊟ *No credit cards* ⊘ *Closed Sat. and Sun. No dinner.*

¢–$ ⊞ **Best Western Trailside Inn.** This large, modern, business-friendly motel is in the heart of Susanville but only a quick drive from the area's recreational sites. Some rooms have wet bars, and you can enjoy home-style cooking next door at the Black Bear Diner. ⊠ *2785 Main St., 96130* ☎ *530/257–4123* ⊟ *530/257–2665* ⊕ *www.bestwesterncalifornia.com* ⊅ *85 rooms* ⚹ *Some refrigerators, cable TV, in-room data ports, pool, meeting room, no-smoking rooms* ⊟ *AE, D, MC, V* ⫶⨀⫶ *CP.*

¢ ⊞ **High Country Inn.** Rooms are spacious in this two-story, colonial-style motel on the east edge of town. Complimentary Continental breakfast is provided; more extensive dining is available next door at the Apple Peddler, a 24-hour restaurant. All rooms have hair dryers and coffeepots; business suites have in-room data ports. ⊠ *3015 Riverside Dr., 96130* ☎ *530/257–3450* ⊟ *530/257–2460* ⊅ *66 rooms* ⚹ *Microwaves, refrigerators, cable TV with movies, some in-room data ports, Wi-Fi, pool, outdoor hot tub; no smoking* ⊟ *AE, D, DC, MC, V* ⫶⨀⫶ *CP.*

⚠ **Eagle Campground.** One of 11 campgrounds surrounding Eagle Lake, this site nestled among pine trees has a boat ramp. ⚹ *Flush toilets, dump station, drinking water, showers, picnic tables* ⊅ *35 tent/RV sites, 14 tent-only sites* ⊠ *County Rd. A-1, 14 mi north of Hwy. 36* ☎ *530/825– 3212* ⊕ *www.reserveusa.com* ⊠ *$18* ⚹ *Reservations essential* ⊟ *AE, D, MC, V* ⊘ *Late May–mid-Oct.*

Lassen Volcanic National Park

⓫ *45 mi east of Redding on Hwy. 44; 48 mi east of Red Bluff on Hwy. 36.*

Fodor'sChoice
★

Lassen Volcanic became a national park in 1916 because of its significance as a volcanic landscape. Several volcanoes—the largest of which is now Lassen Peak—have been active in the area for roughly 600,000 years, and have created an environment full of volcanic wonders including steam vents, mud pots, boiling pools, soaring peaks, and painted dunes. The Lassen Park Road (the continuation of Highway 89 within the park) provides access to these sights, and although it's closed to cars in winter, it's sometimes open to intrepid cross-country skiers and snowshoers. Maps and road guides are available at the Loomis Museum, and at the park headquarters, park entrance, and ranger stations. Also available is the park newspaper, *Peak Experiences,* which gives details on park attractions and facilities.

In 1914 the 10,457-foot Lassen Peak came to life, in the first of 300 eruptions to occur over the next seven years. Molten rock overflowed the crater, and the mountain emitted clouds of smoke and hailstorms of rocks and volcanic cinders. Proof of the volcanic landscape's volatility becomes evident shortly after you enter the park at the **Sulphur Works Thermal Area.** Boardwalks take you over bubbling mud and boiling springs and through sulfur-emitting steam vents. ⊠ *Lassen Park Rd., south end of park.*

The **Lassen Peak Hike** winds 2½ mi to the mountaintop. It's a tough climb—2,000 feet uphill on a steady, steep grade—but the reward is a spectacular view. At the peak you can see into the rim and view the entire park (and much farther, on a clear day). Be sure to bring sunscreen and water. ⊠ *Off Lassen Park Rd., 7 mi north of southwest entrance.*

Along **Bumpass Hell Trail,** a scenic 3-mi round-trip hike to the park's most interesting thermal-spring area, you can view boiling springs, steam vents, and mud pots up close. You'll take a gradual climb of 500 feet to the highest point before you descend 250 feet toward the hissing steam of Bumpass Hell. Near the thermal areas it's important to stay on trails and boardwalks; what appears to be firm ground may be only a thin crust over scalding mud. ⊠ *Off Lassen Park Rd., 6 mi north of southwest entrance.*

Hot Rock, a 400-ton boulder, tumbled down from the summit during an enormous volcanic surge on May 19, 1915. It was still hot to the touch when locals discovered it nearly two days later. Although cool now, it's still an impressive sight. ⊠ *Lassen Park Rd., north end of park.*

Chaos Jumbles was created 300 years ago when an avalanche from the Chaos Crags lava domes spread hundreds of thousands of rocks, many of them 2–3 feet in diameter, over a couple of square miles. ⊠ *Lassen Park Rd., north end of park. Park Headquarters* ⊠ *38050 Hwy. 36E, Mineral 96063* ☎ *530/595–4444* ⊕ *www.nps.gov/lavo* ☜ *$10 per vehicle, $5 on foot or bicycle* ☉ *Park headquarters weekdays 8–4:30.*

Where to Stay

¢ ✕⌂ **Lassen Mineral Lodge.** Rooms at this small year-round motel, nine mi from the southwest entrance to Lassen Volcanic National Park, are reserved well in advance by those who want to explore the park without the hassle of pitching a tent. A restaurant serves breakfast, lunch, and dinner seven days a week from mid-May to mid-October; the lodge is open weekends the rest of the year. You can rent cross-country skis and snowshoes at the lodge's ski shop. There's also a general store. ⊠ *Hwy. 36 E, Mineral 96063* ☎ *530/595–4422* ⊕ *www.minerallodge.com* ⟳ *20 rooms* ⚅ *Restaurant, bar; no a/c, no room phones, no room TVs* ▤ *AE, D, MC, V.*

⚐ **Manzanita Lake Campground.** The largest of Lassen Volcanic National Park's eight campgrounds is near the northern entrance. It can accommodate vehicles up to 35 feet. A trail near the campground leads east to a crater that now holds Crags Lake. Summer reservations for group campgrounds can be made up to seven months in advance. There is no running water from the end of September until snow closes the campground. ⚅ *Flush toilets, dump station, drinking water, showers, fire pits, picnic tables* ⟳ *148 tent/RV sites, no hookups, 31 tent sites* ⊠ *Off Lassen Park Rd., 2 mi east of junction of Hwys. 44 and 89* ☎ *530/595–4444* ⊕ *www.nps.gov/lavo/pphtml/camping.html* ☜ *$16* ▤ *D, MC, V* ☉ *Mid-May–late Oct., depending on snowfall.*

10

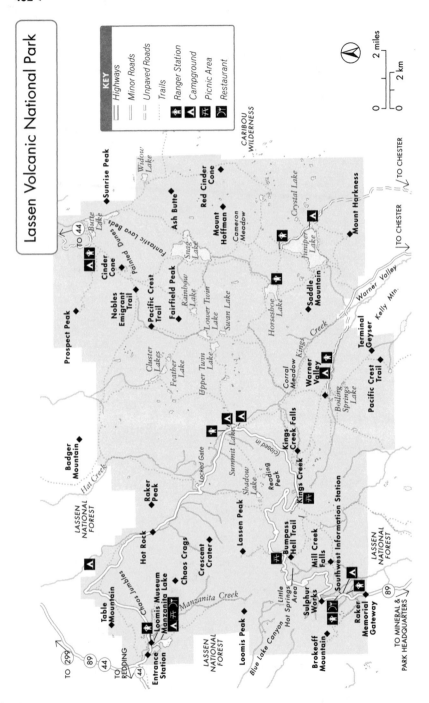

Lassen Volcanic National Park

KEY

- Highways
- Minor Roads
- Unpaved Roads
- Trails
- ⛩ Ranger Station
- ⛺ Campground
- ⛱ Picnic Area
- 🍴 Restaurant

0   2 miles
0   2 km

TO 299
TO REDDING
44
89
TO 44

Entrance Station
Table Mountain
Chaos Jumbles
Loomis Museum
Manzanita Lake
Hot Rock
Chaos Crags
Crescent Crater
Loomis Peak
Raker Peak
Lassen Peak
Manzanita Creek
Blue Lake Canyon
Little Hot Springs Valley
Bumpass Hell Trail
Sulphur Works
Mill Creek Falls
Brokeoff Mountain
Raker Memorial Gateway
Southwest Information Station
89
TO MINERAL & PARK HEADQUARTERS
LASSEN NATIONAL FOREST
LASSEN NATIONAL FOREST
LASSEN NATIONAL FOREST

Hat Creek
Badger Mountain
Prospect Peak
Cluster Lakes
Feather Lake
Upper Twin Lake
Locked Gate
Summit Lake
Shadow Lake
Reading Peak
Kings Creek (closed in)
Kings Creek Falls
Kings Creek
Corral Meadow
Warner Valley
Boiling Springs Lake
Pacific Crest Trail
Terminal Geyser
Kelly Mtn.
Warner Valley

Butte Lake
Painted Dunes
Cinder Cone
Nobles Emigrant Trail
Pacific Crest Trail
Fairfield Peak
Fantastic Lava Beds
Snag Lake
Rainbow Lake
Lower Twin Lake
Swan Lake
Horseshoe Lake
Saddle Mountain
Widow Lake
Sunrise Peak
Ash Butte
Red Cinder Cone
Mount Hoffman
Cameron Meadow
Crystal Lake
Juniper Lake
Mount Harkness
CARIBOU WILDERNESS
TO CHESTER
TO CHESTER
TO CHESTER

Chester

⓬ *36 mi west of Susanville on Hwy 36.*

The population of this small town on Lake Almanor swells from 2,500 to nearly 5,000 in summer as tourists come to visit. It serves as a gateway to Lassen Volcanic National Park.

Lake Almanor's 52 mi of shoreline lie in the shadow of Mt. Lassen, and are popular with campers, swimmers, water-skiers, and anglers. At an elevation of 4,500 feet, the lake warms to above 70°F for about eight weeks in summer. Information is available at the Chester–Lake Almanor Chamber of Commerce. ⊠ *900 W. Hwy. 36* ☎ *530/258–2426* ⊘ *Mid-May–mid-Oct.*

Lassen Scenic Byway is a 172-mi drive through the forested terrain, volcanic peaks, geothermal springs, and lava fields of Lassen National Forest and Lassen National Park. Along the way you'll pass through five rural communities where refreshments and basic services are available. Park information is available at Almanor Ranger District headquarters. ⊠ *900 W. Hwy. 36* ☎ *530/258–2141* ☜ *$10 per vehicle within Lassen National Park* ⊘ *Partially inaccessible in winter; call for road conditions.*

Where to Stay & Eat

★ $–$$ ✕ **Benassi's.** Small and nondescript from the outside but homey inside, this restaurant and full bar on the north end of town specializes in northern Italian food. Everything served is homemade, including sauces, ravioli, and tortellini. Linguine with shrimp, and roasted chicken with rosemary potatoes are favorites, along with a prime rib dinner, which is served Friday and Saturday nights only. ⊠ *159 Main St.* ☎ *530/258–2600* ⊘ *Closed Mon. Oct.–Apr. No dinner Sun.* ⊟ *MC, V.*

¢–$$ ✕ **Cynthia's.** Bordering a brook near the center of town, Cynthia's serves California home-style cuisine with a French touch. Specialties include light meat dishes, pastas, and salads, all made with fresh seasonal ingredients. Its bakery is known for rustic pizzas and artisanal breads. The bar offers wines and microbrews. Hours change frequently, so call to check. ⊠ *278 Main St.* ☎ *530/258–1966* ⊘ *No dinner Sun.–Wed. early Sept.–late May* ⊟ *MC, V.*

¢–$ ✕ **Kopper Kettle Cafe.** Locals return again and again to this tidy restaurant that serves savory home-cooked lunch and dinner, and breakfast whenever you've got a hankering for eggs with biscuits and gravy or other morning fare. A junior-senior menu, and beer and wine are available. The patio is open in summer. ⊠ *243 Main St.* ☎ *530/258–2698* ⊟ *MC, V.*

★ ¢–$$ ▥ **Bidwell House.** This 1901 ranch house sits on 2 acres of cottonwood-studded lawns and gardens, and has views of Lake Almanor and Mt. Lassen. Chairs and swings make the front porch inviting, and there are plenty of puzzles and games in the sunroom. Some rooms have wood-burning stoves, claw-foot or Jacuzzi tubs, hardwood floors, and antiques. A separate cottage, which sleeps six, has a kitchen. The inn's specialties—omelets and blueberry-walnut pancakes—are the stars of the daily

10

full breakfast. ⊠ *1 Main St., 96020* ☎ *530/258–3338* ⊕ *www.*
bidwellhouse.com ⇥ *14 rooms, 2 with shared bath* ⚭ *Cable TV; no*
a/c, no phones in some rooms, no smoking ⊟ *MC, V* ⦿ *BP.*

¢ 🛏 **Chester Manor Motel.** Within easy walking distance of restaurants and
stores, this remodeled 1950s-era one-story motel is clean and comfortable. Six of the 18 rooms are two-bedroom suites; all rooms have hair
dryers. ⊠ *306 Main St., 96020* ☎ *530/258–2441 or 888/571–4885*
🖷 *530/258–3523* ⇥ *12 rooms, 6 suites* ⚭ *Microwaves, refrigerators, cable*
TV with movies, Internet room; no a/c, no smoking ⊟ *AE, D, MC, V.*

Quincy

⑬ *67 mi southwest of Susanville via Hwys. 36 and 89.*

A center for mining and logging in the 1850s, Quincy is nestled against
the western slope of the Sierra Nevada. The county seat and largest community in Plumas County, the town is rich in historic buildings that have
been the focus of preservation and restoration efforts. The four-story
courthouse on Main Street, one of several stops on a self-guided tour,
was built in 1921 with marble posts and staircases. The arts are thriv-
ing in Quincy, too: catch one of the plays or bluegrass performances at
the Town Hall Theatre.

The main recreational attraction in central Plumas County, **Bucks Lake
Recreation Area** is 17 mi southwest of Quincy at 5,200 feet. During warm
months the lake's 17-mi shoreline, two marinas, and eight campgrounds
attract anglers and water-sports enthusiasts. Trails through the tall pines
beckon hikers and horseback riders. In winter, much of the area remains
open for snowmobiling and cross-country skiing. ⊠ *Bucks Lake Rd.*
☎ *530/283–5465 or 800/326–2247* ⊕ *www.plumascounty.org.*

Plumas County is known for its wide-open spaces, and the 1.2-million-
acre **Plumas National Forest,** with its high alpine lakes and crystal-clear
woodland streams, is a beautiful example. Hundreds of campsites are
maintained in the forest, and picnic areas and hiking trails abound. You
can enter the forest from numerous sites along Highways 70 and 89.
⊠ *159 Lawrence St.* ☎ *530/283–2050* 🖷 *530/283–7746* ⊗ *U.S. Forest Service office weekdays 8–4:30.*

The cultural, home arts, and industrial history displays at the **Plumas
County Museum** contain artifacts dating to the 1850s. Highlights include
collections of Maidu Indian basketry, pioneer weapons, and rooms depicting life in the early days of Plumas County. There's a blacksmith shop
and gold-mining cabin, equipment from the early days of logging, a restored buggy, and railroad and mining exhibits. ⊠ *500 Jackson St.*
☎ *530/283–6320* 🖷 *530/283–6081* 🖾 *$2* ⊗ *Tues.–Sat. 8–5.*

Where to Stay & Eat

¢–$$ ✕ **Moon's.** This restored 1930 building houses a restaurant that serves
such delights as honey-almond chicken, eggplant parmigiana, ravioli,
and Tuscan pasta. Sauces, salad dressings, pastas, breads, and desserts
(be sure to try the chocolate caramel fudge cake) are all made from scratch.
A verdant garden patio adds to Moon's allure. ⊠ *497 Lawrence St.*
☎ *530/283–0765* ⊟ *AE, D, MC, V* ⊗ *Closed Mon. No lunch.*

¢–$$ ✕ **Sweet Lorraine's Good Food Good Feelings.** You can choose to eat upstairs by candlelight or in the more casual downstairs bar and dining area. Sweet Lorraine's serves hearty fare such as Cajun meat loaf with roasted-garlic mashed potatoes, as well as vegetarian selections and lighter items; it also has a great assortment of microbrews and wine. Reservations are recommended. ⊠ *384 Main St.* ☎ *530/283–5300* ▤ *MC, V* ☺ *Closed Sun. No lunch Sat.*

$–$$ ▥ **Feather Bed.** The quaint romanticism of an 1893 Queen Anne Victorian plus proximity to Quincy's town center are the draws here. Furnishings are antique and the views of the Sierra Nevada spectacular. The five rooms in the main house have claw-foot tubs. Two private guest cottages have fireplaces and outside decks. Classical music plays softly in the morning, and breakfast begins with smoothies made with homegrown blackberries or raspberries. Fresh fruit or baked fruit crunch and home-baked bread or muffins accompany hot entrées. ⊠ *542 Jackson St., 95971* ☎ *530/283–0102 or 800/696–8624* ⊕ *www.featherbed-inn.com* ❧ *5 rooms, 2 cottages* ⚲ *Some cable TV, bicycles, airport shuttle* ▤ *AE, D, DC, MC, V* ⦿ *BP.*

¢ ▥ **Lariat Lodge.** Built in 1956 out of cinder blocks, this small, quiet hotel in the Plumas National Forest is 2 mi west of downtown. The hotel serves a complimentary Continental breakfast. ⊠ *2370 E. Main St., 95971* ☎ *530/283–1000 or 800/999–7199* ☒ *530/283–2154* ❧ *20 rooms* ⚲ *Some refrigerators, cable TV, pool, no-smoking rooms* ▤ *AE, D, MC, V* ⦿ *CP.*

¢ ▥ **Ranchito.** Rough-hewn beams both decorate and support the front exterior of this rustic Spanish-style motel 1½ mi east of downtown. A brook runs through the mostly wooded 2½-acre grounds. ⊠ *2020 E. Main St., 95971* ☎ *530/283–2265* ☒ *530/283–2316* ❧ *30 rooms* ⚲ *Picnic area, some kitchenettes, cable TV, no-smoking rooms; no a/c in some rooms* ▤ *AE, D, MC, V.*

THE FAR NORTH A TO Z

To research prices, get advice from other travelers, and book travel arrangements, visit www.fodors.com.

10

AIRPORTS & TRANSFERS

Chico Municipal Airport and Redding Municipal Airport are served by United Express. Horizon Air also uses the airport in Redding. *See* Air Travel *in* Smart Travel Tips A to Z for airline phone numbers. There is no shuttle service from either airport, but taxis can be ordered. The approximate cost from the airport to downtown Redding is $22–$25, and it's $14–$15 from the Chico airport to downtown.

🛈 **Chico Municipal Airport** ⊠ 140 Airpark Blvd., off Cohasset Rd. ☎ 530/345–8828. **Redding Municipal Airport** ⊠ Airport Rd. ☎ 530/224–4320. **Taxi Service, Chico** ☎ 530/893–4444 or 530/342–2929. **Taxi Service, Redding** ☎ 530/246–0577 or 530/222–1234.

BUS TRAVEL

Greyhound buses travel I–5, serving Chico, Red Bluff, and Redding. Butte County Transit serves Chico, Oroville, and elsewhere. Chico Area Transit System provides bus service within Chico. The vehicles of the Redding Area Bus Authority operate daily except Sunday within Redding, Anderson, and Shasta Lake. STAGE buses serve Siskiyou County, on weekdays only, from Yreka to Dunsmuir, stopping in Mt. Shasta and other towns, and provide service in Scott Valley, Happy Camp, Hornbrook, and the Klamath River area. Lassen Rural Bus serves the Susanville, northeast Lake Almanor, and south Lassen County areas, running weekdays except holidays. Lassen Rural Bus connects with Plumas County Transit, which serves the Quincy area, and with Modoc County Sage Stage, which serves the Alturas area.

🚍 **Butte County Transit/Chico Area Transit System** ☎ 530/342-0221 ⊕ www.bcag. org/transit.htm. **Greyhound** ☎ 800/229-9424 ⊕ www.greyhound.com. **Lassen Rural Bus** ☎ 530/252-7433. **Modoc County Sage Stage** ☎ 530/233-3883. **Plumas County Transit** ☎ 530/283-2538 ⊕ www.susanvillestuff.com/bus.html. **Redding Area Bus Authority** ☎ 530/241-2877 ⊕ www.ci.redding.ca.us. **STAGE** ☎ 530/842-8295 ⊕ www. co.siskiyou.ca.us.

CAMPING

Some campgrounds in California's far north get booked as much as a year in advance for the Fourth of July. Although that's not the norm, it's still a good idea to make summer reservations two–three months in advance. You can reserve a site at many of the region's campgrounds through ReserveAmerica and ReserveUSA.

🚍 Campground Reservations **ReserveAmerica** ☎ 800/444-7275 ⊕ www. reserveamerica.com. **ReserveUSA** ☎ 877/444-6777 ⊕ www.reserveusa.com.

CAR RENTAL

Avis and Hertz serve Redding Municipal Airport. Budget and Hertz serve Chico Municipal Airport. Enterprise has branches in Chico, Red Bluff, and Redding. *See* Car Rental *in* Smart Travel Tips A to Z for national rental agency phone numbers.

CAR TRAVEL

An automobile is virtually essential for touring the far north unless you arrive by bus, plane, or train and plan to stay put in one town or resort. I–5, an excellent four-lane divided highway, runs up the center of California through Red Bluff and Redding and continues north to Oregon. The other main roads in the area are good two-lane highways that are, with few exceptions, open year-round. Chico is east of I–5 on Highway 32. Lassen Volcanic National Park can be reached by Highway 36 from Red Bluff or (except in winter) Highway 44 from Redding. Highway 299 connects Redding and Alturas. Highway 139 leads from Susanville to Lava Beds National Monument. Highway 89 will take you from Mt. Shasta to Quincy. Highway 36 links Chester and Susanville. If you are traveling through the far north in winter, always carry snow chains in your vehicle. For information on road conditions in northern California, call the Caltrans Highway Information Network's voice-activated system. At the prompt say the route number in which you are interested, and you'll hear a recorded message about current conditions.

🚍 **Caltrans Highway Information Network** ☎ 800/427-7623.

EMERGENCIES

In an emergency dial 911.

🆘 Hospitals **Banner-Lassen Medical Center** ✉1800 Spring Ridge Dr., Susanville ☎530/252-2000. **Enloe Medical Center** ✉ 1531 Esplanade, Chico ☎ 530/891-7300. **Mercy Medical Center** ✉ 2175 Rosaline Ave., Redding ☎ 530/225-6000.

TRAIN TRAVEL

Amtrak has stations in Chico, Redding, and Dunsmuir and operates buses that connect to Greyhound service through Redding, Red Bluff, and Chico. 🚆 **Amtrak** ✉ W. 5th and Orange Sts., Chico ✉ 1620 Yuba St., Redding ✉ 5750 Sacramento Ave., Dunsmuir ☎ 800/872-7245 ⊕ www.amtrakcalifornia.com.

VISITOR INFORMATION

🆘 **Alturas Chamber of Commerce** ✉ 522 S. Main St., Alturas 96101 ☎ 530/233-4434 ⊕www.alturaschamber.org. **Chester-Lake Almanor Chamber of Commerce** ✉529 Main St., Chester 96020 ☎ 530/258-2426 or 800/350-4838 ⊕ www.chester-lakealmanor. com. **Chico Chamber of Commerce** ✉ 300 Salem St., Chico 95928 ☎ 530/891-5556 or 800/852-8570 ⊕www.chicochamber.com. **Lassen County Chamber of Commerce** ✉84 N. Lassen St., Susanville 96130 ☎ 530/257-4323 ⊕ lassencountychamber.org. **Plumas County Visitors Bureau** ✉ Hwy. 70, ½ mi west of downtown, Quincy 95971 ☎ 530/283-6345 or 800/326-2247 ⊕ www.plumascounty.org. **Quincy Chamber of Commerce** ✉464 Main St., Quincy 95971 ☎530/283-0188 ⊕www.quincychamber.com. **Red Bluff-Tehama County Chamber of Commerce** ✉100 Main St., Red Bluff 96080 ☎ 530/527-6220 or 800/655-6225 🖷 530/527-2908 ⊕www.redbluffchamberofcommerce.com. **Shasta Cascade Wonderland Association** ✉1699 Hwy. 273, Anderson 96007 ☎ 530/365-7500 or 800/474-2782 ⊕ www.shastacascade.org. **Siskiyou County Visitors Bureau** ✉ 508 Chestnut St., Mt. Shasta 96067 ☎530/926-3850 or 877/747-5496 🖷530/926-3680 ⊕www. visitsiskiyou.org.

10

INDEX

ABOUT OUR WRITERS

When not writing about California travel and outdoors, Monterey Bay and Peninsula/South Bay updater Lisa M. Hamilton can be found at the beach. Accounts of her food-related journeys have appeared in *National Geographic Traveler, Gastronomica,* and *Z Magazine.*

Constance Jones, formerly a Fodor's Senior Editor, pulled up her lifelong New York roots and relocated to California in 2004. Based in Central Coast wine country, she takes off in her very first car whenever she has time to explore another new corner of the state. Jones revised The North Coast chapter and wrote the What's Where, Quintessential California, If You Like, and Great Itineraries sections at the front of the book.

Reed Parsell, who updated the Central Valley and Gold Country chapters, is a features copy editor and travel writer for the *Sacramento Bee.*

Southern Sierra, Lake Tahoe, and Smart Travel Tips updater John A. Vlahides lives in San Francisco, spending his free time skiing the Sierra and touring California by motorcycle. A columnist, essayist, and former *Clefs d'Or* concierge, he also sings tenor with the San Francisco Symphony Chorus.

A freelance correspondent for the *Sacramento Bee,* Far North updater Christine Vovakes regularly covers area news and writes newspaper features about the region. She considers her home turf of 24 years the undiscovered gem of California.

A frequent contributor to Fodor's, Sharron Wood has been happy to call the Bay Area home for more than 13 years. She traveled all over the Wine Country to check out new hotels, restaurants, and other attractions.